THE JEWS IN THE HISTORY OF ENGLAND
1485–1850

THE JEWS
IN
THE HISTORY OF ENGLAND
1485–1850

David S. Katz

CLARENDON PRESS · OXFORD

Oxford University Press, Great Clarendon Street, Oxford OX2 6DP

Oxford New York
Athens Auckland Bangkok Bogota Bombay
Buenos Aires Calcutta Cape Town Dar es Salaam
Delhi Florence Hong Kong Istanbul Karachi
Kuala Lumpur Madras Madrid Melbourne
Mexico City Nairobi Paris Singapore
Taipei Tokyo Toronto
and associated companies in
Berlin Ibadan

Oxford is a trade mark of Oxford University Press

Published in the United States
by Oxford University Press Inc., New York

First published 1994
Paperback first published 1996

British Library Cataloguing in Publication Data
Data available

Library of Congress Cataloging in Publication Data
Katz, David S.
The Jews in the history of England, 1485–1850 / David S. Katz.
p. cm.
Includes bibliographical references.
1. Jews—Great Britain—History.
2. Great Britain—Ethnic relations.   I. Title.
DS135.E5K35 1994 941´004924—dc20 93–43220
ISBN 0–19–822912–7
ISBN 0–19–820667–4 (Pbk.)

Printed in Great Britain
on acid-free paper by
Biddles Ltd., Guildford & King's Lynn

*In Memory
of
Simon Cuttler*

PREFACE

'IT is singular that few enlightened and wealthy communities know so little of their own early history, as the Jews of Great Britain,' lamented James Picciotto in his pioneering history of Anglo-Jewry published in 1875. 'Yet few races indeed present more vicissitudes for description, or possess records offering a more interesting and extended field for investigation.'[1] Picciotto might also have discussed the fact that for many years the history of Anglo-Jewry was somewhat isolated from the mainstream of English history. This was partly due to the nature of that history itself. The Jews were never formally readmitted to England after their expulsion by Edward I in 1290, and thus there was almost no legislation which referred specifically to them, presenting an insurmountable constitutional barrier to the assumption of full civil rights. Disabilities suffered by Jews in England were almost always the result of their having fallen foul of limitations designed to exclude Roman Catholics and Nonconformists, and to ensure the Anglican character of civic and social life. Almost by definition, then, the history of the Jews in England needs to be seen through the prism of events in this country unconnected with the Jews themselves.

This approach has largely been lacking. Historians of the Jews in early modern England have mostly written from the perspective of a Judaized version of 'Whig History', that is, the writing of ends-oriented history so that emphasis is placed on 'precursors' and 'pioneers' who have in some way 'contributed' to a final event or institution, even if such men would have looked with horror at the eventual manifestation of their efforts. In the writing of English history, especially in the nineteenth century, the narrative converged on the establishment of the British parliamentary system, and the story's heroes were those whose life's work laid another stone in that great edifice. History took on an evolutionary character which developed, like man himself, into the most advanced and perfected final product.

Professor Conrad Russell once complained that a 'historian is like a man who sits down to read a detective story after beginning with the last chapter'.[2] Few historians today fail to recognize that events are not

---

[1] James Picciotto, *Sketches of Anglo-Jewish History*, ed. I. Finestein (London, 1956), p. xiii.

[2] C. Russell, 'Parliamentary History in Perspective, 1604–1629', *History*, 61 (1976), 1.

determined by an imaginary 'course of history', and that had things turned out differently they could easily have been portrayed as 'inevitable'. In the writing of Anglo-Jewish Whig History the tale came to an end with Emancipation, the grandiose term used to describe the right of a duly elected MP to take his seat in the House of Commons without having to swear a Christian oath. The history of the Jews in England was seen as the slow progress of religious toleration and the triumph of reason over medieval superstition and fear, which reached its inevitable culmination on 26 July 1858 when Lionel de Rothschild took his seat in the House of Commons and began a parliamentary career untarnished by a single speech. It is for this reason that most general works on Anglo-Jewish history effectively conclude with Emancipation.

The underlying attitude of Whig History is essentially one of optimism, of improvement and eventual arrival at the final destination. Understandably, the writing of history in this fashion flourished during the years of Britain's imperial splendour. Such a cheerful view of history has been more difficult to sustain since the Second World War, although it is still popular among some historians of English Jewry long after it had been abandoned by the Whigs themselves. But the War had another effect on the writing of Anglo-Jewish history. The rise of organized anti-Semitism and the resulting insecurity of Jewish communities everywhere led in many countries to a concerted effort on the part of Jewish intellectuals to present the case for Judaism. In Germany, on the very eve of the outbreak of war, a major Jewish publishing firm commissioned a series of books on famous Jews and their positive achievements. In England, Dr Cecil Roth wrote *The Jewish Contribution to Civilization* (1938).

Yet it is often forgotten that Roth's *History of the Jews in England* was also a product of the War. Published in 1941, his *History* never underwent any substantial alterations, and even its third and final edition was printed from the original plates with the addition of a number of new footnotes. His critics might see the work as weak in primary sources and apologist, tending to put the Jews in the best possible light and emphasizing anti-Semitism and persecution giving way to toleration and eventual emancipation. But I believe that Roth saw himself as a sort of Jewish Trevelyan, writing popular literary narrative history for an audience of educated readers who wanted to be proud of their past. Indeed, the third edition of Trevelyan's *History of England* was itself a wartime product and can justifiably be seen as contributing to the war effort.

Picciotto declared that although his book was 'written by a Jew for Jews, the author trusts that Christians, whose faith was founded by members of the Jewish race, will find in these chapters, in addition to that which is entirely new, much that may be of interest also to them'.[3] This is not quite my view, but this book does reflect an attempt to write Anglo-Jewish history in a new way—not as history written by a Jew and intended primarily for other Jews, but instead with the goal of tracing the Jewish thread throughout English life between the Tudors and the beginning of mass immigration in the mid-nineteenth century. Jews in this way become part of English religious and social history, without prejudicing the efforts of Anglo-Jewish historians to document the history of Jewish institutions and internal politics in this country. English history has very largely been framed without taking note of the Jewish presence at all, not due to any sinister motive, but simply because no book such as this one was readily to hand. In Chapter 1, for example, I discuss the Jewish element in the making of the English Reformation, showing that, in the years immediately before Henry VIII's declaration of royal supremacy, he based his entire case on Jewish law and was guided in these obscure matters by learned Italian Jews. Henry's tactics were clear to those around him in 1529 and 1530, yet English historians have been unable to see those years as he saw them himself.

But not only are Gentile historians of England guilty of the sins of omission. At the same time, a subject like the Jewish advocates of Henry VIII's divorce has been largely excluded from what was considered Jewish history, properly speaking. The actual number of Jews involved with the English king was very small, and only one of them came to London. I argue, however, that the influence of Jews in the divorce question was very great, far out of proportion to the number of Jews concerned, and thereby must fall within the purview of anyone interested in Anglo-Jewry. So too are Hebrew studies in England part of my definition of Anglo-Jewish history, whether or not actual Jews were involved at all. In Chapter 2 I discuss at length the activities of Dr Roderigo Lopez in England, especially his contacts with Spain which led to his execution in 1594 on a charge of having attempted to poison Queen Elizabeth. Lopez, the model for Shylock, had far greater influence in the long run on moulding public views and prejudices about the Jews than the worthy efforts of all the English rabbis put together, and his story is integral to understanding the role of the Jews in the history of England.

The failure to see Anglo-Jewish history through the English prism has led to a good deal of misunderstanding. In Chapter 3 I treat the subject of the readmission of the Jews into England under Cromwell's rule. Why Jews would want to settle in London is obvious; the question is why the English actively solicited their return. When viewed from the

---

[3] Picciotto, *Sketches*, p. xiv.

perspective of Cromwell and his supporters, we can see that economic matters initially played a very small part, despite the claims of most previous historians, who have made incomplete use of English non-Jewish sources. Later on, in Chapter 4, we see that the granting of a written permission for resettlement by James II in 1685 actually had very little to do with the Jews themselves, but was part of the king's campaign to obtain concessions for his fellow Roman Catholics as part of his dispute over his suspending and dispensing powers. Far from being a grand Magna Carta of Jewish liberties, the document is revealed to be almost an afterthought. This new perspective could be uncovered only by looking at the general history of the period, unhampered by Jewish historical tunnel vision.

The later chapters cover many subjects which are not usually given prominence in traditional histories of Anglo-Jewry. Eccentric figures such as Lord George Gordon, Rabbi Falk, Richard Brothers, and Joanna Southcott influenced the popular perceptions of the Jew during the era of the French Revolution more than the Talmudic reflections of erudite Jewish scholars. The prominent presence of a number of Jews in London crime helped create a prejudice and made a character like Fagin completely believable. The activities of Jewish financiers in military provisioning and on the Stock Exchange defined the image of the Jew in eighteenth- and nineteenth-century English life. More predictable subjects are not neglected in this book, such as the Jew Bill of 1753, the Reform Movement, and the emergence of Jewish institutions such as the Board of Deputies. But competent studies of these topics already exist, and reference to them is given in the notes wherever possible to avoid repetition in the text. The extensive bibliography of manuscripts and printed books reflects dozens of new sources which have not been looked at by previous historians who were unfamiliar with mainstream English history. My intention is to round out the picture by seeing the history of Anglo-Jewry as part of the religious and social history of England in general.

Apart from any questions of interpretation, it should also be self-evident that after more than half a century a new history of the Jews in England is required, especially one which fully utilizes primary printed sources and manuscripts. The title of this book reflects the new approach which I have taken. This is a study of *The Jews in the History of England*, not primarily a narrative or socio-economic study of the Jewish community here. Two works, still valuable, exist which chronicle the Sephardi and Ashkenazi synagogues.[4] This book looks at a particular

---

[4] A. M. Hyamson, *The Sephardim of England* (London, 1951); C. Roth, *The Great Synagogue London 1690–1940* (London, 1950).

minority community in England, and shows how the chief milestones of their history must be explained with reference to the English perspective rather than the exclusively Jewish one. The beginning and terminal dates of this book, 1485 and 1850, have also been consciously chosen, as non-dates in Jewish history. The book begins with the Tudors (1485) and ends with a chronological convention (1850), although the change in the law known as 'Emancipation' is briefly discussed in an epilogue, leaving me partially vulnerable to the charge of being a secret Whig Historian, but included out of consideration for those readers who will want to know what came next. In Jewish terms, this is the history of the old *yishuv*, the Jews who lived in England before the mass immigration of the nineteenth century.[5]

In many ways it is gratifying that I keep on thanking the same people. Professor Richard H. Popkin, now of UCLA, is not only a leading historian of philosophy and ideas, but a celebrated historical detective. His insight and his unrestricted willingness to share sources and ideas have opened up more avenues for me than pride allows me to reveal. Professor Hugh Trevor-Roper (Lord Dacre of Glanton) has advised me for nearly twenty years, pointed me in the right direction, and saved me from entering numerous culs-de-sac.

Others who helped in various ways include: Chimen Abramsky, Ya'ra Baron, George Bernard, Lloyd Gartner, Penny Gouk, Alon Kadish, Dana Katz, Ilana Katz, Raphael Katz, Sarah Kochav, Raphael Loewe, Stephen Macfarlane, Glyn Redworth, Kevin Sharpe, and David Wasserstein. Thanks are also due to the friendly staff at Gigi's Printing.

This book was begun under the auspices of Ivon Asquith at Oxford University Press, and brought to conclusion by Tony Morris. My sincere thanks for their efficient and courteous help.

I should especially like to thank the President and Fellows of Wolfson College, Oxford, for electing me to a Visiting Fellowship under whose benefits this book was begun, researched, and completed. I can hardly imagine finishing the book without the enjoyment of Wolfson's qualities, unique in Oxford University. So too must I thank Professor Zvi Yavetz for his invaluable help at the early stages of this project.

Most of the research was accomplished from Seat U151, the Upper Reading Room, Bodleian Library. I would also like to thank the librarians there for their cheerful help over the years.

This book is dedicated to the memory of Simon H. Cuttler, who died of cancer in 1990 at the age of 40. Simon will be well remembered by

---

[5] See now G. Alderman, *Modern British Jewry* (Oxford, 1992).

anyone who was at New College, Oxford, in the early 1970s. After finishing his D.Phil. thesis[6] Simon went on to Harvard Law School, married, and was well into a successful legal career when it was cut short.

Y'hi zichro barukh.

[6] Published as *The Law of Treason and Treason Trials in Later Medieval France* (Cambridge, 1983).

CONTENTS

ABBREVIATIONS

AHR	*American Historical Review*
AJSR	*Association for Jewish Studies Review*
BL	British Library
Bod. Lib.	Bodleian Library
Cal. SP Dom.	*Calendar of State Papers, Domestic*
Cal. SP For.	*Calendar of State Papers, Foreign*
Cal. SP Span.	*Calendar of State Papers, Spanish*
Cal. SP Ven.	*Calendar of State Papers, Venetian*
Cal. Treasury Papers	*Calendar of Treasury Papers*
Econ. HR	*Economic History Review*
EHR	*English Historical Review*
EJ	*Encyclopaedia Judaica* (Jerusalem, 1972)
Gents. Mag.	*Gentleman's Magazine*
Hist. MSS Comm.	Historical Manuscripts Commission
HUCA	*Hebrew Union College Annual*
JJ Soc.	*Jewish Journal of Sociology*
JJ Stud.	*Journal of Jewish Studies*
JQR	*Jewish Quarterly Review*
JSS	*Jewish Social Studies*
MJHSE	*Miscellanies of the Jewish Historical Society of England*
PAAJR	*Proceedings of the American Academy of Jewish Research*
PAJHS	*Publications of the American Jewish Historical Society*
PRO	Public Record Office
SP	State Papers
SPJC	Spanish and Portuguese Jews' Congregation
TJHSE	*Transactions of the Jewish Historical Society of England*

INTRODUCTION
THE NEW BEGINNINGS OF ANGLO-JEWRY

THE first evidence we have of actual Jews in Tudor England comes from a letter to Henry VII from Ferdinand and Isabella of Spain, dated from Segovia, 18 August 1494, two years after the general expulsion of the Jews from that country. The Spanish monarchs were writing on behalf of one of their subjects, a merchant named Diego de Soria, now in London. According to information which had reached them, 'certain Jews (who were among those who left our realm)' had successfully managed to impound 428,000 maravedis belonging to de Soria but deposited with another merchant named Fernand Lorenzo, on the grounds that they were owed certain debts by him. As Ferdinand and Isabella explain, they were aware of

this petition saying that the said Diego de Soria owes certain sums of money to the said Jews on certain Bills of Exchange which they should have met at the time they left our Kingdom, and because the said Jews are liable to have lost the said maravedis because they took forbidden things out of our country. And the said Diego de Soria has paid the money to us, justly in full.

The point they were making, somewhat awkwardly phrased in this letter, is that the debts owed to expelled Jews had reverted to the Spanish Crown, and since Diego de Soria had already paid that debt in Spain, it was illegal under Spanish law for the Jews in London to try to collect that money yet again outside the purview of Ferdinand and Isabella. The Spanish rulers hoped that Henry would release the money, noting that 'so just an act will give us very singular pleasure', but there is no evidence that the English took any steps whatsoever, either towards the restoration of the money or towards the expulsion of secret Jews who should not have been in London at all.[1]

Any Jewish menace which the Spanish perceived was not very high on Henry VII's list of priorities. The Spanish Jews who had come to London undoubtedly continued as they had done at home, worshipping

---

[1] Ferdinand and Isabella to Henry VII, 18 Aug. 1494, from Segovia: Archivo General de la Corona de Aragón, Registros, vol. 3573, fos. 55ᵛ–56ʳ: Eng. trans. printed in *TJHSE* 24 (1975), 215. Cf. *Cal. SP Span., 1485–1509*, no. 89 = p. 51.

according to the Roman Catholic rite and behaving outwardly in every respect like any Iberian merchant. Indeed, freshly arrived from Spain, they may not have known how to do otherwise. But the Spanish were unwilling to let the issue drop, especially now, as they were negotiating with Henry to give in marriage Catherine of Aragon, the daughter of Ferdinand and Isabella, to Prince Arthur, the heir apparent. A treaty for an Anglo-Spanish marriage was concluded on 1 October 1496, but it was not confirmed by Henry VII until 18 July 1497. The marriage by proxy between Catherine and Arthur was finally effected nearly two years later, on 19 May 1499, and was confirmed twice more before the couple were married in person on 14 November 1501.[2] The negotiations, then, were not simple, and the report which the Catholic kings received in the summer of 1498 from the chief of their mission to England reveals that the presence and possible effects of Spanish Jews in London had not been forgotten. The subprior of Santa Cruz lingered behind to talk with Henry after the official audience was over, as Ferdinand and Isabella had instructed him to do, and warned the king that there were many disaffected Spanish exiles in England and Flanders, heretics who had fled from the Inquisition, and who spoke against Spain in an attempt to stir up hatred. Henry replied that he understood the problem, and 'la mano puesta en los pechos', swore 'por la fe de su coraçón' that he would well punish 'algún judio o herege' in his territories that might be pointed out to him by Ferdinand and Isabella. The two men conversed for a long time on this subject, according to Santa Cruz, who was satisfied by the king's declaration, although nothing seems to have come of it.[3]

A study of the Jews during the reign of Henry VII would thus be very short, for apart from these two initiatives from Ferdinand and Isabella no other evidence survives. The Catholic kings quite naturally sought reliable intelligence about the fate of their forced exiles, and were evidently concerned that once abroad they might work to the detriment of Spanish interests. That was the price they were prepared to pay for racial and religious purity at home, but the marriage negotiations of their daughter, and the political alliance which went with it, gave them the opportunity to intervene in English affairs. It must have been galling to think that avowed heretics and apostates were allowed *de facto* freedom of worship in a country which was about to join the Spanish sphere of

---

[2] On Arthur's marriage and Anglo-Spanish diplomacy surrounding it, see S. B. Chrimes, *Henry VII* (London, 1972), 278–9, 283–5.

[3] Subprior of Santa Cruz to Ferdinand and Isabella, 18 July 1498: *Cal. SP Span.*, i, no. 205 = pp. 164–5. Spanish text from L. Wolf, *Notes on the Diplomatic History of the Jewish Question* (London, 1919), 126, where (rather melodramatically) he published the document under the heading 'International Anti-Semitism in 1498'.

influence. Despite the vigorous efforts of Ferdinand and Isabella, Spanish Marranos were never a problem for Henry VII, and he seems not to have been at all intrigued by the historical, commercial, or confessional implications of their discovery in London. We lack their names, and so are unable to tell how long the community thrived, if such it was. One may assume that the Jews of 1494 went on at some stage to the Spanish Netherlands, far more fertile in Marrano business opportunities. But that is only a guess and may equally be wrong, for the Marranos were quite expert at covering their tracks.

The accession of Henry VIII to the throne in 1509 was a non-event in Jewish history. For at least the first dozen years of his reign, if Jews lived in England they were very quiet. We have some evidence that in about 1521, however, Jorge Añes, or at least his wife and children, came to London. Añes was a native of Valladolid in Spain who had been baptized at the time of the expulsion and was now an agent of the Mendes brothers, who were active in the pepper trade. The firm of Francisco and Diego Mendes had headquarters in Lisbon, and had established a branch in Antwerp in 1512. Jorge Añes, or George Ames as he would be known, was the founder of a great Tudor Anglo-Jewish family, whose children and grandchildren would be very active in Elizabeth's reign. He himself was accustomed to shroud his movements in secrecy. He seems to have returned with his family to Iberia, to Portugal, where no Inquisition was established until 1540, making it much easier for a baptized Jew to conduct his affairs relatively unimpeded. After the death of Jorge Añes in about 1538, his wife Elisabeth returned to London, perhaps in 1541. The Añes/Ames family therefore have a strong claim to being the first Anglo-Jews in Tudor England, but it was certainly not a distinction that they sought to make known during the reign of Henry VIII.[4]

Thus when Marco Raphael came to London in January 1531 in order to help Henry VIII with his divorce there would have been the rudiments of a community of sorts which would have been interested in the phenomenon of a fellow convert to Christianity, presumably just as nominal, who was being fêted at the royal Court. As we shall see, there is reason to believe that a number of the musicians who played for the king were also Italian Jews. The year of Raphael's arrival in London incidentally became an important benchmark in Jewish historiography, for whatever reason, since 1531 was the date fixed as the renewal of Jewish residence in England by Samuel Usque, whose classic *Consolation for the Tribulations of Israel* provided generations of Jewish readers

---

[4] See generally L. Wolf, 'Jews in Tudor England', in his *Essays in Jewish History* (London, 1934), 73–90, esp. 75, 80, 83, 85; id., 'Jews in Elizabethan England', *TJHSE* 11 (1928), 1–91, esp. 3, 12, 18.

with an explanation for the disaster which had befallen them. When discussing 'those who have left and who are leaving Portugal since the year 5291' [1531], Usque notes that some of the exiles came to England, where they were 'despised and abused'. In the Jewish world, at least, by the 1530s it was possible to speak of a secret Jewish community in London.[5]

It is not at all clear whether Henry VIII was aware of the fact that during the years he was conducting a Jewish offensive with regard to his divorce case, a secret Jewish community had established itself in London. What we can do is to judge him by his actions, and his decision in 1532 to come to the defence of one of the most important Marrano figures in that world is very nearly inexplicable. In that year Diego Mendes was prosecuted in Antwerp for Judaism, not in itself a surprising occurrence, considering the personal risk with which Marranos conducted their business affairs. What is curious is that Henry VIII himself intervened in the case, which after all was conducted by the hated Inquisition in a foreign country, and attempted to obtain Diego's release. Whether this was because of the importance of the Mendes spice trade, or because of the help that house gave to the English in transacting loans for their Treasury, or simply with a mind to causing another minor incident in the evolving plan for an independent English church, in any case his action is extraordinary.[6]

The English connection with the Mendes family was renewed three years later in 1535, when Francisco Mendes died in Lisbon. His widow Gracia Mendes, otherwise known as Beatriz de Luna, passed through London on the way to join her brother-in-law Diego at Antwerp. She came with her daughter Reyna, and her sister-in-law, who was the widow of Dr Micas, or Miguez, formerly a physician to the King of Portugal. With this widow came her son João Micas, who as Joseph Nasi would achieve fame as the duke of Naxos and prince of the Cyclades in service to the Ottoman Empire. That these illustrious figures of the future passed through England is of some interest, especially as the Spanish Inquisition at Antwerp would be told later on that their visit was 'a stay of some duration'. A commission was appointed in Brussels in 1546 to investigate the circumstances of Gracia Mendes's flight to

---

[5] Samuel Usque, *Consolation for the Tribulations of Israel*, ed. M. A. Cohen (Philadelphia, 1977), 208. The book was written in Portuguese in about 1550. For the Jewish elements in Henry VIII's divorce, see Ch. 1, below.

[6] J. A. Goris, *Étude sur les colonies marchandes méridionales à Anvers de 1488 à 1567* (Louvain, 1925), 104; Wolf, 'Elizabethan England', 3 and n.; id., 'Tudor England', 74–6 (indicating that he had seen the original documents relating to Mendes's prosecution in 1532); A. M. Hyamson, *The Sephardim of England* (London, 1951), 4.

safety, but there is no indication that Henry VIII suffered at all for his toleration of a woman who must have been known as a Jew.[7]

More information about the community which Gracia Mendes found during her sojourn in London comes from the records of the Inquisition which sat in the Spanish Netherlands during the early 1540s. Lucien Wolf, in a paper delivered in 1929, assembled the evidence from records at Zeeland, Antwerp, and Milan, and presented a list of sixty-nine Marranos living in London during these years, including thirty-seven men, sixteen women, and sixteen children, comprising at least ten married couples. Apart from the individuals themselves, who are of considerable genealogical interest, most entrancing is the evidence of Gaspar Lopes, a cousin of Diego Mendes, who was arrested by the Milan Commission and forced to inform on his co-religionists in England. Lopes had been living in London since the mid-1530s, and was sent in 1539 to Italy as an agent of the Mendes group based in Antwerp. It was there that he was detained and compelled to make the following statement:

Further interrogated he [Gaspar Lopes] said that he knew Alves Lopes in London in whose house he, the deponent, lived for four or five days; and that he, Alves Lopes, holds a Synagogue in his house and lives in the Hebrew manner, though in secret; and that he, the deponent, saw these things and that in this Synagogue they went on one day only, the Sabbath; and that on that day there came to Alves's house other false Christians to the number of about twenty.

Not only was Lopes's house a secret synagogue, but it also served as an information centre for the Marrano community: 'and it is true that whenever any refugee false Christians come from Portugal to go to England and Flanders and thence to Turkey or elsewhere, in order to lead the lives of Hebrews, they come to the house of the said Alves, who helps them to go whither they want to go for this purpose.'[8]

According to the records of the Milan Commission cited by Wolf, once the efforts of Diego Mendes and his agents to aid fleeing Marranos came to light, the imperial authorities directed their attention to arresting some of these backsliding Jews on their way to Italy or

---

[7] Wolf, 'Tudor England', 76, presumably from the report of the commission at Brussels; Hyamson, *Sephardim*, 4; C. Roth, *The House of Nasi* (Philadelphia, 1947–8).

[8] Wolf, 'Tudor England', 76–82, with no source given, apart from a vague reference to 'the reports of the Commissions which sat in Zeeland in 1539–40 and in Antwerp in 1543–4' and 'the Depositions of two turncoat Marranos, Duarte Fernandes and Gaspar Lopes, before the Milan Commission in 1540'. Some of the names on Wolf's list can also be found in the lists of aliens drawn up for assessment for the aliens subsidy during the reign of Henry VIII: ibid. 80–1.

Salonica. In response, Diego Mendes called a meeting at his house in Antwerp, which included Antonio della Rogna, a relation of his living in London, and described as 'a tall Jew with one eye, a master of Hebrew theology'. The plan was for the Mendes agent in Milan, Gonçales Gomez, to use what influence he had with the authorities, and meanwhile to provide for the Marranos in prison. A fund of 2,000 scudi was raised, 5 per cent of which was contributed by Antonio della Rogna himself, and dispatched to Milan. Gaspar Lopes claimed at his interrogation that he had been present at the meeting, and that the real purpose of the fund was to procure the murder of the Commissioners at Milan. This last bit of testimony seems to have convinced no one, for no action was taken against Diego Mendes or his house.[9]

This, then, was the well-ordered Jewish community in London during the late 1530s and 1540s: a secret synagogue, financial support and business connections with Antwerp, and even an intelligence service, under Christopher Fernandes, who would meet the Portuguese spice ships stopping at Southampton and Plymouth to give the Marranos information about the current political and religious climate which would await them in Antwerp.[10] The testimony of Gaspar Lopes before the Inquisition was part of the change in attitude towards the Jews which would lead to their flight from England during this period. One of the first indications of change comes in a letter from Eustace Chapuys, the imperial ambassador in England, sent to Granvelle in the Spanish Netherlands at the beginning of 1542: 'The King has lately ordered the arrest and imprisonment of the New Christians that came from Portugal', he reported. 'Most likely, however well they may sing, they will not escape from their cages without leaving feathers behind.'[11] The case came before the Privy Council on 4 February 1541/2, when 'Ph. Hobbin, gentleman usher, Sir Edw. Kerne, and Dr. Peter, who, by the King's command, apprehended certain persons suspected to be Jews, presented their examinations and inventories of their goods.'[12] The following month, on 14 March, the Privy Council ordered Sir Richard Gresham, who was holding the Jews' goods, 'to deliver 300 ducats to Thos. Chamberlayne now sent to Portugal for the trial of persons suspected to be Jews'.[13]

Who were these Jews who suddenly arrested the attention of Henry VIII, who might have had more cause to look favourably on a quiet

[9] Wolf, 'Tudor England', 79, 81–3. [10] Ibid. 77.
[11] Chapuys to Granvelle, from London, 29 Jan. 1541/2: *Letters and Papers, Foreign and Domestic, of the Reign of Henry VIII, 1509–47*, xvii, no. 64.
[12] Privy Council meeting, 4 Feb. 1541/2: ibid., no. 82.
[13] Privy Council meeting, 14 Mar. 1541/2: ibid., no. 168.

mercantile community, and on its individual members, some of whose co-religionists had so recently come to his assistance in the affair of the divorce? Some of these men were certainly the Marrano merchants whose names appear in the records of the Inquisition. New evidence has come to light, however, showing that Henry employed nineteen Jewish musicians at Court, ten of whom arrived during 1539–40, so that the majority of foreign musicians working for the king were Jews. In that case, if we include probable children and add the names of the sixty-nine Jews who appear in the Inquisition records, we can surmise a Jewish community of close to 100 individuals. These Jews included Henry's viol players, and at least nine members of the royal wind band, including the five Bassano brothers who came to England in September 1531. When Chapuys remarked in 1542 that 'however well they may sing, they will not escape from their cages without leaving feathers behind', he was therefore speaking more literally than figuratively: Chapuys's birds were actually musicians. His glee at their arrest, however, was somewhat premature.[14]

The information from the Inquisition came at a bad time. Since the end of 1541 Henry VIII had been trying to repair his relations with Charles V and the Empire.[15] While Francis I was negotiating with Henry to marry the Princess Mary to his son, Henry was simultaneously plotting with the emperor for an invasion of France in 1543.[16] Indeed, Henry even lent Chapuys a ship to speed him to The Netherlands to seal the deal with the regent there.[17] Henry laid in a store of war *matériel*, but ultimately the entire plan depended on a successful conclusion to his problems with Scotland, whose king was tolerating incessant raids on the northern border. The situation with Scotland was not even temporarily stabilized until 1 July 1543, when a treaty was signed which, among other things, stipulated a marriage between Prince Edward and the infant Mary Stuart, now Queen of Scots since her accession at the age of one week the previous December. This Treaty of Greenwich was repudiated by the Scots on 11 December 1543, which led to renewed war in the spring.[18] The diplomatic union between France and Scotland made their enmity part of the same problem, and, in Henry's view during these months, the Catholic Charles V might provide a solution.

---

[14] See now the important work of Roger Prior, 'Jewish Musicians at the Tudor Court', *Musical Quarterly*, 69 (1983), 253–65.

[15] See Chapuys to Charles V, 29 Jan. 1542: *Letters and Papers*, xvii, no. 63. Generally, see J. J. Scarisbrick, *Henry VIII* (London, 1968), 434–5, 439–40.

[16] Henry VIII to Thirlby, on embassy to Charles V, July 1542: *Letters and Papers*, xvii, no. 447. Cf. Chapuys to Charles V, Apr. 1543: ibid., no. 353.

[17] Ibid., nos. 441, 447; cf. no. 595.   [18] Scarisbrick, *Henry VIII*, 435–9, 442.

Apart from the political problems involved with Anglo-imperial relations, the religious basis of a possible diplomatic union was also unsteady, and would not support the additional weight of an Inquisition-related prosecution against harmless Marrano merchants. Henry, after all, was trying to convince the Catholic emperor who had spent a good part of his life attempting to crush Lutheran heretics to support a self-avowedly schismatic English king. Any treaty document would include Henry's full style, including his awkward title of Supreme Head of the Church. Francis I was admittedly in alliance with the unchristian Turks, but Charles made more of a public show of his conscience, even when Henry noted that he had shown fewer scruples during the sack of Rome in 1527. In the end, the two leaders settled on the formula of 'Defender of the Faith, etc.', but the last thing anyone needed was an Inquisitorial prosecution in England, especially of a group which included musicians at the royal Court. The execution of Queen Catherine Howard on 13 February 1542, right in the middle of the Privy Council deliberations about the suspected Jews, put the king in a bad light, and yet another scandal at Court might have far-reaching effects.[19]

This is what apparently lay behind the seemingly bizarre exchange of letters between Chapuys and Charles's sister Mary, regent of The Netherlands and dowager queen of Hungary. Mary herself had been involved with the plans Henry made for invading France in 1543 with the help of Charles V.[20] Now she surprised Chapuys by twice writing on behalf of the Marrano prisoners, and was supported in this by another of Charles's sisters, Catherine, who with John III ruled Portugal.[21] Considering that most of the Marranos were of Portuguese origin, this must have been a weighty recommendation, something of a royal pardon. How could any English king refuse? The acts of the Privy Council, meanwhile, had brought matters rather far along. On 17 January 1542/3 the Council once again considered 'the matter betwene his Majestie and certeyne marchawntes strawngers, probably suspected to be Juis', and ordered that Dr Peter should assist the commissioners originally appointed to determine the case.[22] Some of the Jews themselves seem to have been released by that time, and the previous June all but one of the six Jewish viol players had returned to Italy. It may be that the merchants remained in prison, while the musicians close to the king and his Court were granted special privileges and allowed to

---

[19] Scarisbrick, *Henry VIII*, 440.

[20] *Letters and Papers*, xvii, nos. 441, 447; cf. no. 595.

[21] Chapuys to queen of Hungary, 10 Mar. 1542/3: *Letters and Papers*, xviii (1), no. 259.

[22] *Acts Priv. Cncl.*, i. 76 (17 Jan. 1542/3); cf. *Letters and Papers*, xviii (1), no. 52.

go free, but in any case the issue was still under discussion.[23] Only in March 1543 was the religion of the men in question finally determined to the satisfaction of the Privy Council, with the report of Dr Guent and Dr Oliver, 'who were appoynted to be Commissioners for the hiring off of certeyne Portugalles suspected off Judaisme', when 'they declared the sayde Portugalles by dew processe hadde by them on this behalff to be Christian men'.[24]

In strictly sacramental terms, the men arrested were undoubtedly Christians. But they were also Jews, and this point was either lost on the commissioners or tactfully ignored. Chapuys made his final report on the incident, now closed, to the regent, the dowager queen of Hungary, the day after the Privy Council reached its decision: 'Besides other attentions', he wrote,

this King, on the 2nd inst., sent Winchester, Westminster and Wriothesley to signify that he was content, solely for Chapuys's sake, to restore the goods of certain Portuguese (seized because of their being charged with Judaism), in whose favour she has twice written during these past months, as also have the King and Queen of Portugal. They wondered that there was no news from her to impart to their master; which Chapuys assured them was due to her great occupations, which gave her no leisure, and proposed as a remedy that the King should have an ambassador with her—a suggestion which they much liked.[25]

This letter is very revealing, for not only is Chapuys anxious to put on record the intervention of Charles's two sisters which caused him to make an abrupt volte-face on the entire issue, but he informs his superiors that Henry thought the matter significant enough to bring out some of the big guns at Court and to make some diplomatic capital out of the case. Stephen Gardiner, bishop of Winchester, was an accomplished diplomat well experienced in the German scene, and was soon to be sent on an important mission to Charles V. Sir Thomas Wriothesley, later earl of Southampton, was hardly less central to Henry's court. William Boston, the bishop of the soon-to-be-defunct see of Westminster, had been entrusted with a mission to Charles in June 1542 to finalize the plans for an Anglo-imperial invasion of France the following year.[26] These men were not ciphers, and their call on Chapuys on 2 March 1542/3, informing him that Henry VIII was releasing the Marranos as a personal favour to the imperial ambassador and his master, made the event as dramatic as it could have been.

Despite the favourable decision reached at the Privy Council in

---

[23] Prior, 'Jewish Musicians'.

[24] *Acts Priv. Cncl.*, i. 94 (9 Mar. 1542/3); cf. *Letters and Papers*, xviii (1), no. 255.

[25] Chapuys to queen of Hungary, 10 Mar. 1542/3: *Letters and Papers*, xviii (1), no. 259.   [26] Ibid. xvii, nos. 441, 447; cf. 595.

March 1543, the entire issue and the abortive inquisition seems to have wreaked a certain amount of havoc in this first, or perhaps second, Jewish community in Tudor England. The Jewish musicians, who may have caused the fuss in the first place, were not entirely lost to the Henrician Court. At least four of the viol players returned to London in November 1543, bringing with them another Jew, known alternatively as Francis of Venice or Francis Kellim, a surname not only obviously Hebrew, but actually meaning 'musical instruments'.[27] The Añes family remained in England, as did Simon Ruiz: in the depositions of Lopes and Fernandes he is described as a merchant, aged about 35, living with his wife Anna, three daughters, two sons, and his mother.[28] The will of Balthazar Alvarez, made in London in 1545, was witnessed by four other Jews.[29] In any case, the community very nearly disappeared from view, and unquestionably a number of the Jewish families completed the itinerary and evacuated to the Spanish Netherlands.

The problem with Marranos, of course, is that they are very difficult to trace: secrecy was their stock-in-trade. Their appearance in the records is a sort of historical mishap. Such an event undoubtedly occurred when in 1556 a Portuguese sailor by the name of Jurdao Vaz denounced his acquaintance Thomas Fernandes of Evora as a Jew before the Inquisition in Lisbon. The prosecution which followed revealed to the authorities that despite the disruptions among the English Marranos in 1542, not only had the Jewish community recovered and substantially replenished itself, but a further group of Marranos were living and worshipping their God in Bristol. Some of the evidence went as far back as 1545, so it is apparent that a continuous Jewish presence was maintained in England even after the persecution and imprisonment of merchants and musicians a few years before.[30]

The testimony of Jurdao Vaz was taken on 18 June 1556 in Lisbon in the Casa das Perguntas (Hall of Examination) of the Inquisition. Placing his hand on the Gospels, Vaz told the Inquisitor

That he also remembers that last year, being in Bristol, in the kingdom of England, at the house of a doctor, who had left this kingdom, whose name he cannot remember, he ate unleavened bread, on one of the Jewish festivals; and the said doctor, his wife, two nephews and two nieces—one of whom was

---

[27] Prior, 'Jewish Musicians', 258–61.

[28] Wolf, 'Tudor England', 79, 82–3, 85.

[29] Will of Balthazar Alvarez, 1545, London: Probate Office, Pynning 25: quoted ibid. 83 n.

[30] 'Autos relating to Thomas Fernandes, new Christian': Processo 9449, Lisbon Inquisition: Arquivo Nacional da Torre do Tombo: repr. and trans. *MJHSE* 2 (1935), 32–56, from the papers of Lucien Wolf, now University College London, Mocatta Library.

named Thomas Fernandes, and the other Diogo Thomas, and one of the nieces was named Beatriz Fernandes but the name of the other he does not know—and also Antonio Dias, resident of the said city of Bristol, all partook of the bread, during the whole of the ten [*sic*] days that the festival lasted; and they also kept the Sabbaths commencing on Friday evening.

Thomas Fernandes seems not to have had a chance to deny this allegation until 11 November 1557, and may indeed have spent much of the intervening time in prison. He continued to deny any Judaizing practices until his interrogation on 13 December, when he fell on his knees and told a quite different tale. Fernandes recounted that in about 1546 he had travelled to Bristol and stayed there at his uncle Henrique Nuñes's house for nearly a year. Nuñes and his wife Beatriz Fernandes began to speak with him about religious matters only towards the end of his visit, insisting 'that the law of the Jews was good, and God commanded that it must be kept, and He also commanded that the Saturdays should be observed'. His uncle and aunt also emphasized the importance of observing the Passover and of eating unleavened bread then, and of keeping the day of atonement, Yom Kippur. Fernandes confessed that henceforth he 'believed and held that the law of the Jews was good; and he observed Saturdays, doing no work on that day, and he likewise observed the fast of Kippur every year while he was in that country, with his said uncle and aunt'. Since returning to Portugal about eighteen months ago, however, Fernandes claimed, he had lived his life as an exemplary Christian and had forsworn the Jewish observances entirely.

The testimony of Thomas Fernandes is interesting as well for the minor details of Jewish life in Henrician England which it provides. His uncle apparently would receive the precise dates of the Jewish festivals from Hector Nuñez, then 'a young unmarried man living in London', later to become a celebrated figure of Elizabethan England. Simon Ruiz, one of the survivors of the early Jewish community, would also send his uncle the dates of the Passover. A number of merchants known to Fernandes seem to have made a special point of visiting Bristol during the Passover season in order to partake of the unleavened bread. A veritable Jewish ring connected Bristol and London, and the rudiments of a living community existence were maintained. As for Jurdao Vaz, his accuser, Thomas Fernandes thought he remembered him eating unleavened bread during that season, and reciting Jewish prayers on the way to a business transaction.

Thomas Fernandes's testimony before the Lisbon Inquisition also provides evidence regarding the influence and dispersion of that Marrano literary classic, Samuel Usque's *Consolation for the Tribulations of Israel*, first published in 1553. Testifying on 9 February 1558,

Fernandes recounted that about three or four years before, during a visit to Bristol, Simon Ruiz had sent down from London

a printed book of prophecies to Anrique Nuñes and his wife, confessant's uncle and aunt, the which book spoke of the troubles which the sons of Isaac suffered scattered over the kingdoms and cities where they wandered, but that they must not lose confidence nor be discouraged for Our Lord would deliver them, and send the Messiah to them, and they must live in that hope; and confessant believes that the book was sent from Italy to those ports of England, and it was entitled, 'To Beatriz de Luna, wife of Diego Mendez.' The which book was read by confessant once, and he accepted it all and was confirmed in his errors by the teaching of the said book, and by what his uncle and aunt told him. And they also read the book, and confessant on going to London returned the said book to Simao Ruiz who had sent it, and confessant supposes that he has it still; and it was written in Portuguese, and it was a quarto.

This important devotional work, dedicated to Gracia Mendes, had therefore made its way to England within a year or so of publication and, if Fernandes is to be believed, brought some measure of solace to yet another Marrano community forced to live a secret and dangerous double life.

Thomas Fernandes was convicted of his self-confessed crimes before the Lisbon Inquisition on 15 May 1558. The evidence in their view demonstrated that Fernandes, although 'a baptized Christian he, being taught by persons lost to the faith, became a Jew since the last general pardon, believing that the Law of Moses was good'. Fernandes was declared 'a heretic, apostate from our holy faith, and that he had incurred major excommunication, with all the penalties by law established in similar cases'. These included life imprisonment, with penitential habit, accompanied by religious instruction in the hope that his soul might still be saved. Fernandes's good behaviour and spiritual progress must have been exemplary, for by August, only three months later, he presented weighty testimonials to his repentance, and he was released from prison in March 1559. The following September he was even allowed to move about Portugal freely in order to conduct his business. The entire inquisition against him had cost him three years of his life, and he had named a good many names of those who no doubt would find the authorities far less conciliatory, but his freedom had been secured.

Thanks to Thomas Fernandes, we have some picture, albeit rudimentary, of the Jewish community in England between the expulsion of 1542 and the accession of Queen Elizabeth in 1558. Precious little further information, indeed, has survived at all. Fernandes gave us twenty-two names, but he did not include wives or children with any consistency, and in any case the London Jews he mentions include only those connected with his uncle's family in Bristol. One man he does mention as being a merchant in Bristol in 1554 is Diogo Alvares 'new Christian, resident of the Island of Sam Miguel, in the town of Ponta Delgada; who came frequently to the house of the doctor, uncle of the said Thomas Fernandes'.[31] It may just be that he is to be identified with 'oone Henry Alveros, Portugal, supposed to be a Jue', who was the owner of a considerable sum of money impounded in July 1545. The Privy Council ordered the money brought to him, but they were still issuing such a demand at the end of the year.[32] Early in January 1545/6 the Privy Council reported the receipt of a notarial statement from Antwerp affirming that Henry Alvaros was 'of Christes profession and no Jewe, in whiche behaulf the Emperour's Embassadour by his Secretarie made also a speciall assertion confirming the same'. Not only were his goods restored to him, but the two men who had impounded his property were ordered to testify that in delaying turning over the money to the king they had not meant 'thereby to defraude the Kinges Majeste of his interest to those goodes of Alvaro in case he had been proved a Jewe'.[33]

The end of the reign of Henry VIII saw the termination of the original connection between the Spanish and Portuguese Marranos and England. The House of Mendes, that international spice trading company which had brought the Añes family to London as early as 1521, began to break up by 1546, and, since a good number of the Jews in England were either directly agents of that firm or connected with it, the Jewish interest here was bound to decline somewhat. The persecution of the Marranos at Antwerp by Charles V in 1549–50 may also have led to a certain amount of attrition. But a number of Jews who would become much better known during Elizabeth's reign survived the death of Henry VIII on 28 January 1546/7 and, worse still, the reign of the Roman Catholic Queen Mary between 1553 and 1558. Dr Hector Nuñez, Dunstan Añes, and Simon Ruiz all remained in London, and might be said even to have prospered. In 1554 Hector Nuñes was made a fellow of the College of Physicians; in 1557 Dunstan Añes became a freeman of the Grocers' Company, although a foreigner. Dr Henrique Nuñes, that leading light of the Bristol community, fled to France in about 1555, if the testimony of Thomas Fernandes is to be believed, but he was probably disguised in England as a Calvinist rather than a Catholic and thought it rather late in the day to alter his disguise. Generally speaking, the Jews were not an issue during the interregnum between Henry and Elizabeth, and the most scandalous Jewish event of

[31] Fernandes inquisition, p. 35.
[32] *Acts Priv. Cncl.*, i. 22 (28 July 1545), 294 (14 *Dec.* 1545).
[33] Ibid. i. 305–6 (3 Jan. 1545/6), 307 (6 Jan. 1545/6).

those years may be that of May 1550, when the Mayor of London received a suit from a group of nobles and gentlemen on behalf of a certain Doctor Arnande, 'esteemed to be a Jewe, who for his naughtie lyving and develish practises was judged to ryde through the streetes in a carte'. The Privy Council ordered him banished from the realm for good measure, and his supporters were now appealing to have the entire business quashed.[34] Almost nothing else appears in the records, and it would seem that whatever the Jews of London were doing on the eve of Elizabeth's accession, they were extraordinarily discreet about it.

This, then, is the origin of the Jewish community of Tudor England whose activities during the reign of Elizabeth were so exhaustively described by Lucien Wolf in a classic article published over sixty years ago. Wolf established the genealogy of the Jewish families who were resident in England during the sixteenth century. What we shall do in the next chapters is to carry this information further and thereby see in what way these families and the Jewish issues only sometimes associated with them had an effect on the larger dimensions of policies and politics in the age of Henry VIII and the Virgin Queen.

[34] *Acts Priv. Cncl.*, iii. 28–9 (11 May 1550).

THE JEWISH ADVOCATES OF
HENRY VIII'S DIVORCE

THAT Henry VIII was unlucky in love can hardly be disputed. What exacerbated this tendency was his misfortune in timing as well. Nowhere is this more clearly seen than in the entire issue of his attempt to procure a divorce from Catherine of Aragon. His request to the pope was by no means extraordinary: other monarchs had their marriages annulled, and even in England the same service had been provided for his brother-in-law the duke of Suffolk only a short time before.[1] Henry's problem was that he delayed until after the imperial sack of Rome in 1527, after which time Pope Clement VII was a virtual prisoner of Charles V, Catherine's nephew, who vetoed the divorce without discussion: 'though the voice was Clement's, the hand was the Emperor's', as Froude put it.[2] Henry's legal strategy with the papal authorities to have his way none the less was also the victim of bad timing. For Henry based his request for an annulment on the fact that Catherine had been married to his late brother, and supported his case with reference to the Old Testament prohibitions and current Jewish practice. Unfortunately for the king, it was just at this moment that Italian Jews were reconsidering the entire issue of levirate marriage, and the result of their rabbinical rulings would leave Henry's case in ruins, with no hope other than an unequivocal declaration of royal supremacy in the English reformation.

I

King Henry VIII had several problems and more solutions with regard to the satisfactory conclusion of his Great Matter. The difficulty was that the two never seemed to coincide. By the early 1520s Henry was already looking for a way out of a marriage which was diplomatically

---

[1] Recent examples included the divorce of King Louis II of France, the confirmation by Pope Clement VII of the divorce of Henry's sister Queen Margaret of Scotland in 1527, and that of the duke of Suffolk in 1528: A. G. Dickens, *The English Reformation* (New York, 1964), 105.

[2] J. A. Froude, *The Divorce of Catherine of Aragon* (2nd edn., London, 1891), 134.

obsolete and dynastically irresponsible. Certainly by the end of 1525 a divorce was on his mind, after the half-hearted attempt to secure the succession by creating his illegitimate son duke of Richmond in June of that year, by which time in any case his heart was fixed on Anne Boleyn, who steadfastly refused to follow her sister's lead and become the king's mistress. It must have been Henry who first pointed the way to a possible annulment of his marriage, for no one else would have dared broach the matter with the king. Henry had been given a papal dispensation by Julius II to marry his late brother's widow Catherine of Aragon, and he had done so six years later on reaching the age of 18 in 1509. The dispensation was needed because the marriage was in flat contradiction to the law of God as laid down in Leviticus 18: 16: 'Thou shalt not uncover the nakedness of thy brother's wife: it *is* thy brother's nakedness.' Indeed, continued Leviticus 20: 21, 'And if a man shall take his brother's wife, it *is* an unclean thing: he hath uncovered his brother's nakedness; they shall be childless.' This was very nearly the case: Henry's marriage to Catherine had failed to produce a male heir: only the Princess Mary (b. 1516), three babies who were stillborn or died soon afterwards (two of them males), and two more (one male) who died within a few weeks of birth, apart from a number of miscarriages.[3] In 1527 Henry broached the subject of his newly found scruples with Cardinal Wolsey, the central figure in his government, who attempted to allay the king's fears, but 'cowld neuer bryng to passe to diswade hyme therfroo'.[4]

Leviticus was the solution; Deuteronomy was the problem. According to Deuteronomy 25: 5–6:

If brethren dwell together, and one of them die, and have no child, the wife of the dead shall not marry without unto a stranger: her husband's brother shall go in unto her, and take her to him to wife, and perform the duty of an husband's brother unto her.

And it shall be, *that* the first-born which she beareth shall succeed in the name of his brother *which is* dead, that his name be not put out of Israel.

Nevertheless, there may be cases, the Pentateuch tells us, when this hope is not fulfilled, and a procedure is laid down for freeing the *levir*, the brother-in-law, from his obligation. Verses 7–10 complete the commandment:

And if the man like not to take his brother's wife, then let his brother's wife go up to the gate unto the elders, and say, My husband's brother refuseth to raise

[3] Generally, see J. J. Scarisbrick, *Henry VIII* (London, 1968), chs. 6–8. Scarisbrick's views are sharpened in G. R. Elton, *Reform and Reformation* (London, 1977), ch. 5.
[4] George Cavendish, *The Life and Death of Cardinal Wolsey*, ed. R. S. Sylvester (Early English Text Society, ccxliii, 1959), 179.

up unto his brother a name in Israel, he will not perform the duty of my husband's brother.

Then the elders of his city shall call him, and speak unto him: and *if* he stand *to it*, and say, I like not to take her;

Then shall his brother's wife come unto him in the presence of the elders, and loose his shoe from off his foot, and spit in his face, and shall answer and say, So shall it be done unto that man that will not build up his brother's house.

And his name shall be called in Israel, The house of him that hath his shoe loosed.

All considered, Henry might well have had reason for believing that biblical authority leaned somewhat towards his side: the Levitical prohibition was seemingly absolute, and the Deuteronomic provision, by explicitly containing a rather detailed release clause, seemed to imply that permission to marry a brother's widow was extraordinary, designed for a particular purpose, or that at the very least it was a duty extremely unpalatable to the Children of Israel.

The biblical evidence was admittedly only one of the arrows in Henry's quiver; he would also argue that the form of dispensation granted by Pope Julius II was invalid. Furthermore, the debate over the validity of his marriage to Catherine was staged successively before three groups of arbiters: canon lawyers, theologians, and parliamentarians. So long as the Levitical argument was alive, no efforts were spared to grasp at any straw which might pull down the entire edifice of his unwanted marriage. Especially since much of the argument was conducted and researched in Italy, it was inevitable that at some stage the king of England would turn to Italian Jewry for further elucidation of the sacred text. And despite other straws in the wind, Leviticus was Henry's chosen weapon and he never abandoned it, even though it was based on the ultimately unprovable claim that Catherine had had sexual relations with his brother and had thereby consummated the sacrament of matrimony. 'Once launched,' writes Professor Scarisbrick,

the Levitical argument was an absorbing one. Its novelty, the speed with which it unrolled, its many ramifications, philological and canonical, its many side issues, like the problem of Christ's genealogy, the date of Philip the Tetrarch's death or the distinction between 'concede' and 'dispense', its appeal to scholars of many disciplines and many nations—all these made it difficult to step out of the hurly-burly.[5]

Henry believed at first that it would be necessary to exhibit only home-grown scholarship in order to prove the invalidity of the papal dispensation. The plan was that the present pope, Clement VII, hating his emperor-captor, would grant Cardinal Wolsey a decretal commission

---

[5] Scarisbrick, *Henry VIII*, 195.

capable of deciding the matter of Henry's divorce in a form unappeal-
able to Rome. Surprisingly, the commission was actually granted by the
pope, but when the document arrived in England in September 1528 it
was found to be issued jointly to Wolsey and to its bearer, Lorenzo
Campeggio, bishop of Salisbury and cardinal protector of England and
(significantly) the German Empire. The legatine court opened in
Blackfriars on 18 June 1529, but Campeggio was acting on Clement's
secret instructions to ensure its failure. Clement finally withdrew his
commission and recalled the case to Rome in response to Catherine's
formal appeal, but by the time Campeggio received Clement's ruling he
had already adjourned the court on 31 July on the flimsy excuse that it
should conform to the papal calendar and rest for the Roman summer
vacation. Campeggio by this action not only undermined the claim of the
canon lawyers to be the sole arbiters of Henry's divorce, but destroyed
Cardinal Wolsey, whose entire future was made to hang on the success
of the legatine court.[6]

During the next year the arena shifted to the universities of England
and Europe, as Henry attempted to assemble a body of evidence in
favour of the Levitical prohibition which would compel even a papal
court at Rome to rule in favour of the king's case. According to tradition,
it was a young private tutor named Thomas Cranmer who suggested this
approach in a chance meeting with court officials Stephen Gardiner and
Edward Foxe. Henry is supposed to have remarked that Cranmer had
'the sow by the right ear', and summoned the man to Court, placing him
on the road which would lead to the archbishopric of Canterbury four
years later, and eventually martyrdom at Oxford in Mary's reign. Be that
as it may, at least until August 1530, when Henry's claims became far
more assertive and well on the way to the declaration of royal supremacy
of 1534, at least until then the argument from Leviticus was at the fore,
and was the king's chief weapon for securing his release from his
unwanted marriage. Towards this end, delegations of royal researchers
swept through the universities of France and Italy rooting out
precedents, hunting through bookshops and libraries, interviewing
European scholars of all persuasions, in a desperate quest to find the
document, the 'smoking gun'—in canon law, among the writings of the
Fathers, in scriptural commentary—which would declare the supremacy
of the Levitical prohibition against levirate marriage. The hunt included
Cranmer himself, Reginald Pole (the Protestant-burning archbishop of
Canterbury under Mary), John Stokesley, the new bishop of London,
and Richard Croke, a minor-league Cambridge humanist who had

---

[6] Scarisbrick, *Henry VIII*, 209–28. Cf. G. de C. Parmiter, *The King's Great Matter: A Study of Anglo-Papal Relations 1527–1530* (London, 1967).

taught Henry Greek ten years before. As Bishop Burnet summed it up in the next century,

Crook, a learned man in the Greek tongue, was employed in Italy to procure the resolutions of divines there, in which he was so successful that, besides the great discoveries he made in searching the manuscripts of the Greek Fathers concerning their opinions in this point, he engaged several persons to write for the king's cause, and also got the Jews to give their opinions of the laws in Leviticus, that they were moral and obligatory.[7]

When Stokesley and Croke called on the Jews of Italy it was thus well in keeping with the tenor of that very academic year.

What, then, was the state of Christian research before Henry's men turned to the Jews? Once Henry had placed his faith in Leviticus, how did he justify his disavowal of Deuteronomy? There were really only five possible arguments, most of which were easily brushed aside. First, Henry might argue that levirate marriage was a ceremonial law which applied only to the Jews, and had been fulfilled and abrogated by the coming of Christ. Secondly, Henry could claim that his case was not the one specified in Deuteronomy: he had no intention of having children who would carry on his brother's name instead of his own: his goal was to produce his own heirs to the throne. Thirdly, Henry might point out that the examples of levirate marriage in the Old Testament included no evidence that the dead brother's union had been consummated, which he always maintained had been the state of relations between Arthur and Catherine. A fourth line of attack would be to interpret Deuteronomy allegorically: the dead brother might stand for the crucified Christ; the living for the preacher whose task it was to raise up Christ's seed. A last approach was linguistic, to claim that the word 'brother' in Leviticus referred to an actual sibling, while in Deuteronomy the reference was to a relative in the general sense. As can be seen, these arguments were a set piece of theological and academic debate, and there was no trouble in attracting participants to the discussion. As Professor Scarisbrick puts it, Henry 'had a chance not because his problem was a novelty but because it was a chestnut'.[8]

---

[7] Gilbert Burnet, *The History of the Reformation of the Church of England* (London, 1903), 33. Cf. G. Bedouelle, 'The Consultations of the Universities and Scholars Concerning the "Great Matter" of King Henry VIII', in *The Bible in the Sixteenth Century*, ed. D. C. Steinmetz (Durham & London, 1990), 21–36.

[8] For the state of the canon law of the Church regarding the divorce, like all others I have followed Scarisbrick, *Henry VIII*, ch. 7; cf. p. 168. See also J. Guy, 'Scripture as Authority: Problems of Interpretation in the 1530s', in A. Fox and J. Guy (eds.), *Reassessing the Henrician Age* (Oxford, 1986), 199–220, where he concludes that 'Attitudes as to the church's relationship to scripture remained ambivalent in England' until Henry's death. See also the choice words of the great J. D. Michaelis, *Commentaries on the Laws of Moses* (London, 1814), ii. 39–46.

The apparent contradiction between Leviticus and Deuteronomy was glaring even at the very beginning of Christian biblical interpretation and attracted the attention of Augustine, whose analysis was the starting-point for later exegesis. Augustine saw the problem as not only resolvable, but resolvable in more than one way. The reference in Leviticus, he wrote, was to adultery with a brother's wife while the brother was still alive; Deuteronomy permitted a brother to marry his sister-in-law after the brother's death. Alternatively, Augustine mused, Leviticus could be saying that a brother could not marry his former sister-in-law after she had been put away, say, for adultery. But most significantly Augustine argued that the examination of both texts together led to the conclusion that only when the first brother died without issue could another brother marry the sister-in-law in evasion of the Levitical provisions: the good which comes out of that marriage outweighs the bad which comes out of disobeying Leviticus.[9]

The biblical references to levirate marriage seemed to support Augustine's view, unpleasant as it was to Henry VIII. Genesis 38 tells the story of Tamar, who married Er, the son of Judah. Er 'was wicked in the sight of the LORD; and the LORD slew him.' Judah told Onan, another of his sons, to go 'in unto thy brother's wife, and marry her, and raise up seed to thy brother'. But 'Onan knew that the seed should not be his; and it came to pass, when he went in unto his brother's wife, that he spilled *it* on the ground, lest that he should give seed to his brother.' So the Lord slew Onan as well, and Tamar was forced to wait until the next son, Shelah by name, grew to marriageable age. In the end, Judah did not permit Shelah to marry her, so she disguised herself as a harlot and, enticing Judah, had twins by the father himself instead of by the reluctant and expiring sons. Judah at first wanted her burned for the deception, but eventually was brought to realize that 'She hath been more righteous than I; because that I gave her not to Shelah my son.' This was as clear a demonstration of levirate marriage and the consequences of failure to carry it out as might be wanted. For those who needed a demonstration of the Deuteronomic ceremony of legally refusing levirate marriage, this was provided in Ruth 4. Indeed, St Joseph himself was the product of a levirate marriage, for his mother married twin brothers in turn, Jacob and Heli, which accounts for the differing genealogies of Christ in Luke and Matthew: Joseph was called the son of each husband. So not only was the Pentateuchal contradiction resolvable, but sufficient additional biblical evidence could be found to make Henry's position uncomfortable.[10]

---

[9] Scarisbrick, *Henry VIII*, 168–9.
[10] Gen. 38: 6–30; Ruth 4: 1–12; Matt. 1: 16; Luke 3: 23.

It is curious that the linguistic arguments of the Hebraists hardly made themselves heard and, indeed, have been almost entirely forgotten by modern historians. In 1527, when the various options were being discussed, Henry received an offer from Richard Wakefield to 'defend your cause'. Wakefield was a Yorkshireman, trained at Cambridge and Louvain, and a close friend of John Fisher until they quarrelled over Henry's divorce. Wakefield was also very close to John Stokesley, and was praised by Richard Croke during his inaugural lecture as reader in Greek at Cambridge in 1519.[11] His attainments as a Hebraist were beyond doubt, and Erasmus himself in a letter of 1518 described Wakefield as 'exceptionally well-acquainted with Latin, Greek and Hebrew'.[12] Although Wakefield opposed the divorce at first, he was 'converted by fair promises to change his mind'.[13] Now he wrote to the king that he could defend his case by using 'the best learned and most excellent authors of the interpreters of the Hebrews', including rabbinical sources, assuring that after he had written for Henry, even his old friend Fisher would 'be ashamed to wade or meddle any further in the matter'.[14] Richard Pace had been taught Hebrew by Wakefield, supposedly within a single month, and recommended his teacher to Henry, saying that Wakefield was 'of excellent learning as well in divinity as in wonderful knowledge of many and diverse tongues'.[15]

Wakefield's argument was that the entire debate over the divorce was wrong-headed because it was based on the Latin Vulgate translations of the Old Testament rather than the original Hebrew text. According to 'learned men', Wakefield pointed out, although Leviticus 20: 21 appears in the Latin translation as prophesying that if a couple makes a levirate marriage 'they will be without children', in the original Hebrew the curse is said to be 'without sons'. Henry only had the Princess Mary, but no sons: the curse was precisely applicable to the king. Wakefield does not seem to have been correct: the Hebrew *aririm* refers only generally

---

[11] G. L. Jones, *The Discovery of Hebrew in Tudor England: A Third Language* (Manchester, 1983), 181–90; V. M. Murphy, 'The Debate over Henry VIII's First Divorce: An Analysis of the Contemporary Treatises' (Cambridge University Ph.D. thesis, 1984), 15, 111. Cf. G. Bedouelle and P. Le Gal, *Le 'Divorce' du roi Henry VIII. Études et documents* (Geneva, 1987).

[12] Erasmus, *Opus epistolarum*, ed. P. S. Allen (Oxford, 1906–58), iii. 357 (no. 855): quoted in Jones, *Discovery*, 187.

[13] According to Anthony Wood, *Athenae Oxonienses*, ed. Philip Bliss (London, 1813–20), i, col. 102.

[14] S. Knight, *The Life of Erasmus* (Cambridge, 1726), app., p. xxviii: cited in Jones, *Discovery*, 182. Cf. Murphy, 'Debate', 111.

[15] Knight, *Erasmus*, app., p. xxviii. Wakefield claimed to be able to teach all three classical languages in a three-month period, a feat confirmed by Pace in a letter to Edward Foxe: Murphy, 'Debate', 15, 20.

to barrenness. Nevertheless, it was an interesting argument and an undoubted contribution to the general debate, not the least because even a red herring might help Henry's case. Fisher, for his part, was furious with Wakefield, who left for Oxford and became a canon of Henry VIII's college, formerly Cardinal College, and later Christ Church. Fisher then wrote a treatise specifically devoted to objecting to the intervention of Hebraists in the debate over the divorce, arguing that casting doubt on the Latin Bible used for centuries would undermine the authority of the Church itself, and that in any case God would not have left his flock without guidance for so long. In the event of disagreement, translation and meaning should only be decided by the pope.[16]

Henry was therefore left with only one serious argument, slightly modified: that levirate marriage was a mere ceremonial law of the Jews, and that even when it did take place it was the result of a specific and personal dispensation given by God himself to the individual concerned, and was in any case no longer the practice of Jews, nor had it been at least since the fall of Jerusalem. Supporting Henry in the ensuing literary war were Thomas Cranmer and Edward Lee, who would be made archbishop of York in 1531. They in turn rousted up for support a poet-archbishop of the twelfth century named Hildebert of Tours, and a very minor school of Dominicans who had been writing during the past 200 years. Ranged against Henry and his champions, however, were some of the foremost theologians of his day, including Ludovico Vives, Thomas de Vio Cardinal Cajetan, and even John Fisher, Henry's own bishop of Rochester, who wrote seven books against the divorce between 1527 and his inevitable martyrdom eight years later. After Rome had spoken, Francisco de Vittoria, the Spanish Dominican, joined the list and, most devastatingly, so did Robert Bellarmine, the most considerable theologian of the early sixteenth century.[17]

Worst of all, levirate marriage had in practice actually been permitted, not only by biblical Jews but by western Christians in the very recent past and even in the present. Late medieval canonists had little cause to carry the debate beyond Innocent III of indisputable authority, who had ruled in his bull *Deus qui Ecclesiam* that levirate marriages among non-Christians were to be considered valid even without dispensation once the people involved were accepted into the Church, since such unions conformed to biblical law. Innocent's decisive pronouncement in favour

---

[16] John Fisher, 'Reverendissimis': Lambeth Palace Library, MS 2342: cited by Murphy, 'Debate', 108–11.

[17] See *The Divorce Tracts of Henry VIII*, ed. E. Surtz, and S. J., and V. Murphy (Angers, 1988).

of levirate marriage and Deuteronomy was ratified by its enshrinement in the *Corpus iuris canonici*. On that basis, a number of popes had already issued valid dispensations similar to, and much weaker than, that which Henry had received. The first dispensation for a marriage within the Levitical degrees was granted to Thomas, duke of Clarence, the brother of Henry V, at the beginning of the fifteenth century, in order that he could marry the woman who by her first marriage was actually Henry VIII's great-great-grandmother. By the end of the century, degrees as close as aunt and wife's sister were being dispensed. Pope Martin V did so with the support of the Council of Constance. More recently, Alexander VI had allowed King Emmanuel II of Portugal to marry in turn the two sisters of Catherine of Aragon herself, even though he had a son and heir by the first. The present pope, Clement VII, had allowed at least two noblemen to marry the sister of a previous wife. None of these dispensations had the backing of Deuteronomy, which seemed quite clearly to be applicable in Henry's case, even if he was the first man to receive a dispensation to marry his brother's widow.[18]

Henry was therefore in a good deal of canonical trouble. While his argument that the biblical examples had all followed on miraculous divine intervention could not be disproved, neither could it be convincingly demonstrated. The search for papal and patristic precedents was going badly and was not likely to meet with much success. Only one further course remained open to him: to show that the Jews themselves, whose knowledge of the Old Testament and its language was unmatched by any in the Christian world, had long abandoned levirate marriage and had ruled decisively against it. To consult with rabbinical authorities in Italy was the brief which Henry sent to his agents working under the very noses of the pope and his imperial captor.

II

It would appear that the initial impetus behind the appeal to Italian rabbinical authorities came from the new bishop of London, John Stokesley, sometime towards the end of November 1529. The project began with high hopes, and Henry was kept informed of its progress.[19] Initially, the tentative feelers put out by the English canonical spies among the Jews in Italy seemed to yield quite promising responses. Although Richard Croke, now in Bologna, promised Henry at the end of

[18] Murphy, 'Debate', 3–4; Scarisbrick, *Henry VIII*, 177–9. Cf. H. A. Kelly, *The Matrimonial Trials of Henry VIII* (Stanford, Calif., 1976).

[19] Richard Croke to Henry VIII, 27 Dec. 1529, from Bologna: *Letters and Papers, Foreign and Domestic, of the Reign of Henry VIII, 1509–47*, iv (3), no. 6105.

December 1529 that he would refrain from any action until the pope and the emperor left the area,[20] within a few weeks he had already made considerable progress and could not resist telling Stokesley his good news. The Jews tell him, he wrote,

that the law of Deuteronomy has never been kept since the fall of Jerusalem, and, what Stokesley was very desirous to have confirmed, that it is not intended to be kept, except where it is allowed by the Levitical law, and they do not consider it obligatory except where causes and circumstances expressly urge it, and not even then is it absolutely obligatory.

Croke said that the Jews explained that while 'it was always an alternative' to marry the brother's widow, in practice this was not done. Indeed, Croke told Stokesley with pride that he had managed to procure two letters on this point, one from a convert to Christianity, and the other from a Jewish physician. These he promised to send to Stokesley 'with a copy of the book of Francis George, by the first messenger, and also the writings of any one else whom he thinks learned enough to consult'. Meanwhile, he was trying as hard as he could to make some progress with his research, but it was difficult 'for he was only allowed to remain two hours a day in the library'.[21]

We have, then, three figures who have entered the lists for Henry VIII. The Jewish physician is most certainly Elijah Menahem Halfan, Italian rabbi, doctor, and cabbalist, the son of Abba Mari Halfan, the astronomer and grandson of Joseph Colon. This was a famous family which emigrated from Provence at the end of the fourteenth century, and Elijah Halfan was a notable exemplar of it. He himself was a fashionable physician in Venice, and had numerous contacts in the Gentile world. In 1545, long after Henry had resolved his problem in a rather more radical fashion, Elijah Halfan would write a rabbinical *responsum* arguing that it was permissible to teach Christians the Hebrew language and biblical interpretation, but not the mysteries of the cabbalah.[22] Getting Halfan to accept Henry VIII's interpretation of Leviticus was a great coup for Croke. 'Francis George' is Francesco Giorgi, the Venetian theologian, Hebraist, and Christian cabbalist. Giorgi was Croke's contact in locating Jewish scholars who might be useful to the cause,[23] and, as Croke informed Ghinucci, the bishop of Worcester, 'Mark Raphael, a learned Jew, has written most plainly on our side, and offers to defend his writings, which are in Hebrew, and

---

[20] [Croke to Henry VIII], 27 Dec. 1529: ibid., no. 6105.

[21] Croke to [Stokesley], 18 Jan. 1529/30: ibid., no. 6149.

[22] On Halfan, see C. Roth, *The Jews in the Renaissance* (Philadelphia, 1959), 142–3, 160; id. and U. C[assuto], 'Halfan, Elijah Menahem', *EJ* vii. 1187; G. Scholem, *Kabbalah* (Jerusalem, 1974), 69.   [23] Roth, *Renaissance*, 159–60.

have been translated by Father Francis.' Marco Raphael, a Venetian convert to Christianity, had been rewarded by the Council of Ten for having invented an improved variety of invisible ink, and was now in place as Giorgi's loyal link with the cloistered world of rabbinical scholarship.[24] Raphael was thus the third figure mentioned in Croke's letter.

The entrance of Francesco Giorgi on to the scene of Henry's divorce is of enormous importance. Giorgi, or Zorzi, of Venice (1466–1540) was the leading Christian cabbalist of his day, and his authority in the sixteenth century was truly impressive. The late Frances Yates devoted a very large part of her last book towards demonstrating the crucial influence of Giorgi's ideas not only during his own lifetime, but also on English writers as far afield as John Dee, Spenser (in the *Faerie Queene*), and Shakespeare (in the *Merchant of Venice*). Giorgi's most celebrated work was the cabbalistic *De harmonia mundi*, first published in 1525, and then appearing in a French translation in 1578, a move which Yates suggested may itself have been 'a gesture of "politique" toleration, preparing the way for the visit of' the duke of Alençon as suitor to Queen Elizabeth.[25] Giorgi's work made him widely known, and it was natural that he would be appealed to, primarily as a Hebrew scholar rather than as a Pichian cabbalist, in Croke's untiring efforts to find academic support for the king's view. What is perhaps surprising is that Giorgi accepted. Henry Cornelius Agrippa (1486–1535) of Cologne, another great exponent of the occult philosophy, the model for Faust, declined Chapuys's invitation to write on behalf of the emperor, despite the fact that Queen Catherine herself was said to have wished Agrippa to be her Hebraic champion.[26] For a German to refuse the emperor is almost as surprising as for an Italian to write against the pope. 'It is not quite obvious why "the King's cause" attracted the Friar of Venice', pondered Frances Yates:

---

[24] Croke to [Ghinucci], 22 Jan. 1529/30: *Letters and Papers*, iv (3), no. 6156.

[25] F. A. Yates, *The Occult Philosophy in the Elizabethan Age* (London, 1979), *passim*, esp. chs. iv, xii; pp. 61–7, 95–6, and references to Giorgi in index. Generally, see also J.-F. Maillard, 'Henry VIII et Georges de Venise: Documents sur l'affaire du divorce', *Rev. Hist. Rel.*, 181 (1972), 157–86; D. P. Walker, *Spiritual and Demonic Magic from Ficino to Campanella* (London, 1958), 112–19; F. A. Yates, *The French Academies of the Sixteenth Century* (London, 1947), 43, 88, 91–2, 126, 243–4, 254; id. *Giordano Bruno and the Hermetic Tradition* (London, 1964), 151; F. Secret, *Les Kabbalistes chrétiens de la Renaissance* (Paris, 1964), 126–40. Giorgi's *De harmonia mundi* was published first in Venice in 1525, and then in Paris in 1545. A French translation by Guy Le Fevre de la Boderie as *L'Harmonie du monde* appeared in Paris in 1578.

[26] Yates, *Occult Philosophy*, 40; *Letters and Papers*, v. 204–5; C. G. Nauert, *Agrippa and the Crisis of Renaissance Thought* (Urbana, Ill., 1965).

Was it his zeal for religious unity which made him anxious to avoid a schism? Or was it the Venetian spirit of independence, cultivating a rapprochement with England as antidote to Hapsburg domination? Nor is it at all clear (to me at any rate) why Henry VIII's English advisers thought it important to send a mission to Venice to consult Venetian Jews, and Giorgi, the Cabalist theologian, about the divorce. This is all the more strange when one remembers that Jews were not allowed in England at that time.

As we shall see, it is rather easier to understand why Henry consulted Jews than to fathom Giorgi's motives for going in on the side of the English king. At any rate, according to Frances Yates, this ensured Giorgi's fame in England, and among the likes of Spenser and Shakespeare. 'The very great influence of Giorgi's *De harmonia mundi* in Elizabethan England', she writes, 'may have some distant historical root in Giorgi's support of Henry VIII's divorce. Queen Elizabeth I might have been favourably disposed towards the philosophy of Francesco Giorgi if she knew that the Friar of Venice had supported her father's divorce, to which she owed her own existence.' This favourable disposition extended to 'Tudor reformers' in general, on the basis of Giorgi's stand on the divorce question.[27] In any case, Giorgi became and remained one of Henry's most active and loyal supporters, and continued working for his cause long after most other Italians had dropped out.

What did Marco Raphael and Elijah Halfan have to offer Henry VIII? Could they realistically provide him with a solution that had not been uncovered by eminent Christian canonists since the time of Augustine? The entire issue of levirate marriage or, to use the Hebrew term, *yeeboom* is discussed at great length in the Talmud, and is the subject of an entire tractate in which all possible contingencies are provided for. Of great concern are the rights of the widow, the *yevahmah*, and the duties of the levir, the *yahvam*, and the conditions under which he might perform the ceremony of release laid down in Deuteronomy, known as *halitzah*. The Talmud makes it quite clear that the obligation of levirate marriage is incumbent only in a case in which there are no offspring at all: not only daughters but even a deceased son would render the marriage unlawful and *halitzah* unnecessary. Furthermore, the law includes within its provisions only brothers born prior to the husband's death: if a minor, as was the case with Tamar's would-be husband Shelah, the woman must wait until he reaches the age of 13, remaining until that time in the status of an *agunah*, 'an anchored one', unable to marry anyone else. The Talmud notes that the obligation applies only to

---

[27] Yates, *Occult Philosophy*, 31–2, 96. Yates even suggests (p. 112) that 'Giorgi's *De harmonia mundi*, with its "Judaising" tendency, might have provided a bridge to conversion for the English Marrano.'

paternal brothers, and that, although the duty of levirate marriage or *halitzah* is incumbent upon the eldest surviving brother, any brother will do. The marriage or the ceremony of *halitzah* is to take place only after a three-month period of mourning, during which time the widow is designated as *shomeret yahvam*, 'awaiting the levir'.[28]

Jews did not and do not see any real contradiction between Leviticus and Deuteronomy: the former's prohibition applies to a case where the dead brother is survived by children; the latter's permission to situations where the brother dies without issue so the levir may succeed in the name of his brother. But even when the marriage is permitted, Deuteronomy makes it clear that it does not necessarily have to take place. The levir may decline to marry his sister-in-law and make use of the *halitzah* ceremony. The question discussed in post-Talmudic times, and not finally resolved until 1950, was whether levirate marriage or *halitzah* was the preferred alternative open to the surviving brother. Certainly there was a broad area of agreement that levirate marriage would not be permitted if the brother had other goals in mind than carrying on his brother's name: inheriting the dead man's property, for instance. Some communities on the periphery of Talmudic Judaism resolved the issue without much debate. The Samaritans restricted levirate marriage to a woman who had been engaged to the dead man (*kedushin*) but not actually married (*n'sooin*). The Karaites interpreted the word 'brother' in Deuteronomy as actually signifying 'relative'—this was one of Henry's rather more far-fetched arguments. But in normative Judaism, the question of priority was one that was much debated. The *tana'im* who worked on the Mishnah, the Hebraic core of the Talmud, in the first few centuries after the destruction of the Second Temple in AD 70 favoured levirate marriage as the surviving brother's first duty. Their successors, the *amora'im* who completed the series of Aramaic commentaries in the era of Augustine which, when combined with the Mishnah, would form the Talmud, were divided on the issue. The *amora'im* among the Babylonian Jews argued that the choice should be left to the levir himself, as Deuteronomy seemed to imply. The *amora'im* in Palestine, however, thought that marrying one's sister-in-law was so problematic that *halitzah* should be the preferred alternative.

Just as in the days of the Jewish 'church fathers' the problem of priority was resolved in two different ways by the two prevailing religious communities, so too in the sixteenth century two different solutions were on offer, and here is where Henry seems to have been poorly advised. The Jews who told Croke 'that the law of Deuteronomy has never been

---

[28] M. E[lon], 'Levirate Marriage and Halizah', *EJ* xi. 122–31.

kept since the fall of Jerusalem' and that 'it is not intended to be kept' were undoubtedly Ashkenazim, German or east European Jews. Ashkenazi Jews were bound by a decree, the *herem* of Rabbenu Gershom (*c.*960–1028), the great Talmudic scholar of Mainz, which prohibited polygamy. His ruling had the effect of promoting *halitzah* over levirate marriage, so as not to present a married levir with any moral dilemma. The *herem* of Rabbenu Gershom had the rule of law in most of Europe where the Ashkenazim dominated, and the priority of *halitzah* was specifically affirmed by such great scholars as Rashi, Rabbenu Tam, and, in the sixteenth century, Moses Isserles.

Unfortunately, this was only half the story. Sephardi Jews from Maimonides to Joseph Caro in Henry VIII's own time stressed the primacy of levirate marriage if at all possible. This was the rule not only among the very many Sephardi Jews in Italy, many of them refugees from persecution in Portugal and Spain, but also throughout all of the Jewish communities of North Africa from Morocco to Egypt, and on from there to Yemen, Babylonia, Persia, and the Holy Land itself. Indeed, levirate marriage was practised in Sephardi communities even in the late 1940s until the Israeli chief rabbinate in 1950 prohibited its practice among both Sephardim and Ashkenazim, and made *halitzah* obligatory, noting that most levirs do not fulfil their duty for the sole purpose of carrying on their brother's name but rather for baser motives. In the *halitzah* ceremony, the levir is still spoken to as if he has a choice in the matter, but levirate marriage was finally made a dead letter. Yet this is a development of recent years, and one may suspect that the practice still continues in some isolated Jewish communities where the writ of the chief rabbis does not run. In Henry VIII's time, levirate marriage was not only a theoretical option, but very much an accepted procedure. Had Croke realized this early on, he would never have chosen the rabbinical strategy that he did, arguing that levirate marriage had died with the fall of the Second Temple in AD 70.

Henry, of course, was told mostly what he wanted to hear. Croke reported to the king on 24 January 1529/30, if not exactly claiming progress, then not unduly pessimistic either. Ghinucci, the Italian bishop of Worcester, he wrote, 'has been treating with a learned theologian through his friends'. Croke expected something in writing any day. Although he told the king that he was limited in his activity while the pope and the emperor were still in the area, as soon as they left he would make contact with Jews in Bologna, Rome and Padua.[29] The next day, however, he had further information in his letter, to Ghinucci

[29] [Croke to Henry VIII], 24 Jan. 1529/30, from Bologna: *Letters and Papers*, iv (3), no. 6161. He wrote more or less the same thing to Stokesley three days later, also from Bologna: ibid., no. 6170.

himself. Croke reported that, while he was visiting Giorgi, a Jewish physician named Jacob Mantineus came by, on his way back from paying a call on Gregory Casale, the Italian in the service of Henry VIII whom the Jew referred to as the English ambassador. Mantineus, or Mantino as he is usually known, was not only a physician but a distinguished translator and well known in medical circles on the Bologna–Verona–Venice axis. Pope Clement VII had in fact appointed him a lecturer in medicine at Bologna only the previous year, and he was thus a well-accepted Establishment figure. It was for this reason that Clement asked Mantino to dispute on the apparent contradiction between Leviticus and Deuteronomy, which he did at Bologna, undermining Henry's case. Casale had 'asked him many questions about the affair of the king of England, and the laws of Leviticus and Deuteronomy', and about the disputation. Mantino had come to tell of these doings to Friar Francesco Giorgi, but Croke could not resist interfering in the conversation, pretending to be an opponent of the English king, and meanwhile trying to grasp Mantino's Jewish arguments against the divorce. When Mantino inquired of the priest who his guest was, Giorgi lied and said he was from Flanders, making no mention of the fact that Croke was Henry's chief biblical intelligence-gathering agent in Italy.[30]

This was not, perhaps, either clever or diplomatic: Croke would be unmasked eventually: indeed, only three days later. Croke had been paying another visit to Casale the day before, this time looking for that elusive book which would prove Henry's case, which he suspected Casale was hiding. Casale asked if Croke would dispute with a bishop then present about the divorce, which Croke refused to do, not wishing to reveal the king's arguments, or perhaps not wishing to let the other side know how very little the king's men had uncovered with which to defend their position. The following morning, Croke went round to Casale's house once again, upon which Casale immediately sent for Mantino and asked him to join them. Casale tried to goad Croke into debating with the Jew if not with the Christian. Croke refused, 'feeling indignant at being thus betrayed'. Casale claimed that Mantino was, appearances notwithstanding, a secret supporter of Henry's divorce, and had even written a paper on their side. When Croke asked Casale to allow him to have a look at these pretended papers, the Italian claimed that he did not have them at present: some he had given to his brother at

---

[30] [Croke] to Ghinucci, 25 Jan. 1529/30, from Venice: ibid., no. 6165. Cf. the text printed in *Records of the Reformation: The Divorce, 1527–33*, ed. N. Pocock (Oxford, 1870), i. 488. On Mantino generally, see D. Kaufmann, 'Jacob Mantino', *Revue des études juives*, 27 (1893), 30–60, 207–38; D. Carpi, 'On Rabbi Jacob Mantino's Stay in Padua (1531–1533)' (Hebrew), in his *Between Renaissance and Ghetto* (Tel Aviv, 1989), 85–95, esp. 87–8.

Bologna and the rest, sadly, he had lost. In any case, Casale explained, Mantino was too frightened to come out publicly on the king's side, and if any of his writings came to light he would only deny them.[31]

But Croke was on to a rather better thing, he wrote to Ghinucci, with 'the Hebrew writings of Christian Mark, a man of accurate learning in the Old Testament', which unequivocally supported Henry's case, and 'in which what Stokesley most wished is affirmed'.[32] Ghinucci was very pleased to have at last something on paper. To Henry he wrote that he sends 'also by him the judgment of a Hebrew, which he has obtained through a friend', presumably stealing Croke's thunder thereby, although this unnamed friend might equally be Giorgi, who seems to have found Marco Raphael in the first place. Indeed, Ghinucci told the king that Croke had never seen the paper, and would not be receiving it now, although he would send 'this judgment to Croke if he had time'; which, alas, he lacked and therefore he would not do so. Still, he would try to obtain other copies for Croke and Stokesley. Unfortunately, he himself did not understand the document, knowing little or no Hebrew, 'but a friend tells him' that it had the effect of affirming Leviticus at the expense of Deuteronomy.[33]

If Ghinucci hoped to take out a copyright on Marco Raphael's Hebrew *responsum*, in this he failed. On the heels of the Italian's letter to the king came Croke's, and the Englishman had the advantage of Giorgi's translation so that he had a better idea of its contents. This document, which he sent to the king 'with some writings by learned Hebrews in his favor', seemed to Croke to have

proved indisputably; viz., that the Levitical law has always been holy and intact, and never abolished nor weakened; on the other hand, the law of Deuteronomy was never in force except when the conditions therein expressed were present, and when it is allowed by the Levitical law; and that it was never observed, even by the Jews themselves, after the destruction of Jerusalem, except in matters concerning inheritance.

Croke's unimpeachable source, he wrote, was 'Raphael, who is now converted to Christ, [and who] was at one time a chief rabbi'. Apart from this very sound Jewish authority, Croke noted, few of the theologians with whom he discussed the problem disagreed with Henry's position, and the sole reason for their silence was fear of the pope. Raphael, on

---

[31] [Croke to Ghinucci], 29 [Jan.] 1529/30: *Letters and Papers*, iv (3), no. 6174; [same to same], 3 Feb. 1529/30, from Venice: ibid., no. 6194: *Records*, ed. Pocock, ii. 626–9.

[32] [Croke to Ghinucci], 29 [Jan.] 1529/30: *Letters and Papers*, iv (3), no. 6174. Cf. [same to same], 3 Feb. 1529/30: ibid., no. 6194.

[33] [Ghinucci to Henry VIII], 7 Feb. 1529/30: ibid., no. 6205. Cf. Ghinucci to ?, 28 Jan. 1529/30: ibid., no. 6173.

the other hand, 'refused to desert the cause', even when 'urged by the papal party to write against the King'. Casale, however, was rather more suspect, especially since the incident when he had urged him to discuss the debate with a bishop 'and a Jew who is hostile to the King', claiming falsely that Henry had wanted such a meeting to take place, even at the risk of revealing key arguments to his defence.[34]

Croke was understandably very pleased finally to have found a Jew who was willing to commit to writing his views in favour of the English king, in defiance of the pope and his emperor. Marco Raphael's opinion in various drafts began to be circulated in the pro-Henry camp, as Croke sent copies to Stokesley and Ghinucci for their perusal.[35] By the beginning of March Croke could write to Stokesley that he had also managed to obtain 'Hebrew writings' from the second of the 'Jewish Rabbis' who supported the divorce. The following week he informed the king himself that, in addition to the pieces by Marco Raphael, 'who is paid a salary by the Venetian government', he was enclosing 'two writings by Helias, a Hebrew, doctor in arts and medicine'. Father Giorgi's Latin translations would follow, he promised, to be sent to the king by Ghinucci. Raphael's work was important, Croke explained, because he 'proves that Deuteronomy refers to the genealogy of the Saviour'. The piece by 'Helias' shows that Deuteronomy refers 'to inheritance, and is only observed by the Hebrews under certain conditions'. 'Helias', of course, was Elijah Menahem Halfan, the Italian physician and cabbalist whom we have met before. Most interesting, Croke told his king, was that another two Jews had been taken on board: 'Those who have subscribed Helias' writings are Benedict, a German, of great weight among the Jews for his years and learning, and Calo, a doctor of arts and medicine, whose books will be sent to the King.' The identification of Benedict is still in doubt: perhaps Baruch of Benevento, the translator of the Zohar, unfortunately not a German; or possibly Baruch Bendit Axelrad of Venice, a local rabbi. Maestro Calo, Calonymus ben David, was a natural supporter since he was Halfan's own father-in-law and was himself a famous physician and translator, and very much a living example of Jewish participation in the Italian Renaissance. Things, at last, were beginning to happen. Even better, Croke promised Henry that the burden of the Jews' arguments was that

---

[34] [Croke to Henry VIII], 18 Feb. 1529/30, from Venice: ibid., no. 6229. Three days later Croke wrote to Dr Edward Foxe, from 1538 bishop of Hereford but meanwhile another royal agent in Italy, telling him the same story about Casale: ibid., no. 6235.

[35] [Croke] to Stokesley, 21 [Feb.] 1529/30: ibid., no. 6236; [Croke] to Ghinucci, 22 [Feb.] 1529/30: ibid., no. 6239; same to same, 22 Feb. 1529/30: ibid., no. 6240; [Croke to Ghinucci], 2 Mar. 1529/30: ibid., no. 6250; [Croke] to Stokesley, 2 Mar. 1529/30: ibid., no. 6251.

not only was his marriage in contravention of Levitical law, but 'that the King's marriage is impious and ought to be dissolved'. What more could Henry want?[36]

March 1530 was a good month for Richard Croke. He was convinced that the Jews of Venice had provided him with the key which would free his sovereign at no small benefit to himself. Towards the end of the month he explained his plan to Ghinucci: he 'will give a few gold pieces to Hebrews who have promised to write in proof of the following points', he revealed:

That the law in Deuteronomy refers only to inheritance, and to the case of Salphaad in the last of Numbers; that the marriage of Thamar with the sons of Judah was not consummated; that the Levitical law is of the law of nature, and always in force, being imposed on all, though Deuteronomy was imposed solely on the Jews; that Deuteronomy does not hold good where a Levitical prohibition opposes it, or except in the circumstances mentioned.

This was the task that still stood before him, Croke told his Italian partner. Croke reflected that he had spent more than Ghinucci 'would believe on scribes, librarians, and friars, but not more than necessary'.[37]

Thanks to Casale's indiscretion before Jacob Mantino, one of the pope's Jews, and no doubt as the result of the work of others as well, Henry's plan to use the Jews themselves to defeat Leviticus was circulating among the intelligence-mongers of Venice. Croke's mission was becoming even a little dangerous. He no longer dared send his letters in any ordinary fashion. When he wrote to Ghinucci about his plans for the future, he had to ask him 'to trust no Englishman with this letter', for even they might be working for the other side. 'The bearer is a converted Jew' named Marco Raphael, he explained, 'with a stipend of 200 ducats from Venice. He cannot speak Latin, but is learned in the old law and Hebrew'. Raphael 'will bring back letters', or perhaps they might be sent by Ghinucci's servant, but by no one else.[38] Writing to the king at the end of April, Croke struck a defiant and determined note: 'Attempts must be made to gain as many as possible to his Majesty's side,' he postulated, 'by help of friar Francis George, so that he may conquer by numbers as well as by justice and truth. The sayings of the

---

[36] Croke to Henry VIII, 11 Mar. 1529/30, from Venice: ibid., no. 6266. See also Kaufmann, 'Mantino', 54–5; Roth, *Renaissance*, 75–6, 160. Croke also promised to send 'some extracts made by father Francis from the Chaldaic commentaries that the Levitical prohibitions are part of the law of nature'.

[37] [Croke to Ghinucci], 26 Mar. 1530: *Letters and Papers*, iv (3), no. 6287; cf. *Records*, ed. Pocock, i. 526–7.

[38] [Croke to Ghinucci?], [26? Mar. 1530]: *Letters and Papers*, iv (3), no. 6288; [same to same?], 29 Mar. 1530: ibid., no. 6300.

Jews about Deuteronomy and Leviticus, and whatever else can be found anywhere to aid the cause, must be sent with the greatest diligence to his Majesty.' Croke was 'much indebted to friar Francis for aid in the King's cause', and was confident that with his help and translations from the Hebrew a way out of the biblical impasse would be found.[39]

<h1 style="text-align:center">III</h1>

It is curious to realize that the machinations of Croke, Ghinucci, and their Jewish allies formed virtually the only positive actions taken by Henry towards resolving his marital difficulties during the early months of 1530. As Professor Scarisbrick has observed, the 'appalling debacle of the legates' court at Blackfriars, followed by Catherine's appeal and the "advocation" of the cause to Rome, undoubtedly stupefied Henry and left royal policy in confusion for some months'.[40] But just as matters were improving for Croke and Ghinucci in Venice, the international situation was beginning to change, and in a way which would render the rabbinical pirouetting of Marco Raphael almost redundant. For early in that year in Bologna Emperor Charles V and Pope Clement VII had come to an agreement whereby the secular ruler would be crowned by the pontiff, who himself would achieve a greater measure of personal and diplomatic freedom. On 24 February 1530 Charles V won the distinction of being the last Holy Roman Emperor to be crowned by the pope, and for all practical purposes any attempts by outsiders to come between them were doomed to failure. Since the end of January, Stokesley had been trying to do exactly that, hanging around the palace at Orvieto, encumbered by Anne Boleyn's brother, who was anything but a diplomatic asset. They failed, and without the glimmer of hope that the English could drive a wedge between Charles and Clement there was almost no chance of obtaining a profitable hearing of the king's case in Rome. On 21 March 1530 Clement put the icing on the cake by issuing a bull forbidding all ecclesiastical judges and lawyers from speaking or writing on the question of Henry VIII's marriage, and suspended final judgement on the case for six months.[41]

Royal policy in the first half of 1530, then, was in a state of total confusion. The whole point of sending scholars to European archives and universities was to make the English case unassailable before the papal court. Now everyone knew that Henry would never get a fair hearing. There was little reason to continue with the fruitless search for

[39] *Letters and Papers*, iv (3), no. 6300; Croke, 'The King's Letters': ibid., no. 6353: cf. *Records*, ed. Pocock, i. 296.   [40] Scarisbrick, *Henry VIII*, 258.
[41] Ibid. 257–8.

rabbinical rulings and judicial precedents. But the task carried on none the less, driven by a momentum which was unstoppable as long as Henry was as yet unwilling to act on his still unformed notions of royal supremacy. Only a fortnight after the pope had forbidden discussion of Henry's divorce, John Casale, another member of that family still apparently loyal to Henry despite Croke's misgivings, wrote to the duke of Norfolk to inform that powerful nobleman of the situation in Venice. 'We still have many on our side,' he assured his correspondent, 'and two Jews, to one of whom Croke has already spoken, and the other is my great friend, who translated for the Pope and the bishop of Verona certain parts of the Old Testament from Hebrew into Latin.'[42] The first Jew was certainly Halfan; the second was Jacob Mantino, for Casale was as yet unaware that his 'great friend' had most sensibly come out in favour of the pope's interpretation.

Mantino was not the only Jew whose feet were turning very cold now that English intentions were out in the open. Indeed, Charles V was kept abreast of the latest developments on the Jewish front by Rodrigo Niño, one of his men in Venice: 'These English agents are doing such things that it is impossible to find appropriate terms to describe them', he informed the emperor,

they are continually looking for people who can counsel in these matters, and there is no Jew or Christian whom they do not solicit and bribe to gain their object. Yet with all this they are not over satisfied with their success. All of them have met at Bologna. To-day prothonotary Casale, the English resident ambassador at this Court, has arrived. He is the same who was in company with Ricardo, the solicitor, who went about getting the opinions of Padua and of all this territory, and with all the Jews here and at Bologna. The first thing they tell them is that the Pope and the Emperor are very glad that the affair is to be disputed, and that after that their King will grant them more favours than they can wish for.[43]

Certainly Niño was correct in observing that some of the Jews were bought. Croke was paying out money to 'two Jews, for coming home to you daily and writing'. Another Jew was given a fee 'when he subscribed'. 'Helias' Halfan received twelve crowns that we know of, and Marco Raphael six crowns, five ducats from Croke and at least £40 from Henry during the following summer.[44]

Perhaps Croke was not paying enough, or perhaps the views of the

[42] Casale to Norfolk, 5 Apr. 1530: *Letters and Papers*, iv (3), no. 6310. Cf. Kaufmann, 'Mantino', 55–6.
[43] Rodrigo Niño to Charles V, 25 May 1530, from Venice: *Cal. SP Span.* iv (1), no. 317, = p. 552.
[44] Croke's expenses, 1530: *Letters and Papers*, iv (3), nos. 6375, 6786; Payments, July 1530, 'The King's reward to Mark Raphaell': ibid., no. 6541.

emperor and his pope became more widely known, for by the spring even loyal supporters of Henry's divorce were having second thoughts. Even Marco Raphael refused to come to Ghinucci when visiting Rome, and this Italian bishop of Worcester was so shocked by this apparent treachery that he reported the matter to Croke, who in turn informed Henry VIII himself 'that Marcus Raphael, the converted Jew, who wrote so earnestly in favor of the King's cause, is in service with the Pope'.[45] This was both unkind and untrue, but when Mantino returned from Bologna three weeks later he and other Jews were full of reports of the pope's displeasure with Jewish support, such as it was, for Henry's divorce. They also told Croke that Halfan, whose 'opinion so many subscribed gladly and without stop, cannot now get one to subscribe'.[46] Mantino was hardly a neutral observer, having already come out against Henry, but it seems that he was trying to convince Croke to leave the Jews of Italy alone. Now that the cat was out of the bag, any further attempts by Jews to defy the pope and the emperor would be seen as open rebellion against established authority. Croke himself was reduced to trying to locate at least the Jews who disagreed with the king. 'Here is an Augustine friar called Felix,' he wrote from Venice, 'which was sometime a Jew, which hath written against us, and I do all that I can to get a sight of his work, to know what favourers the emperor hath in Padua and Venice.'[47] By the end of June, Croke, on his way from Padua to Venice, dropped a note to Stokesley in despair, reporting that he and Casale 'have attempted the Jews here, but they say they have such advice from Venice that they dare not write'.[48]

It was one thing to write in favour of Henry VIII; it was quite another to write actively against the divorce. One of the Jewish pronouncements which has survived came from a rabbi of Modena named Jacob Raphael ben Yehiel Haim Peglione. Rabbi Jacob's Hebrew *responsum* is a carefully reasoned argument, demonstrating that the law of Leviticus must be observed in a case where the brother has left no descendants. The verses in Deuteronomy were by no means in contradiction: they merely made clear what had been stated before.[49] Still others made their excuses. Cardinal Egidius of Viterbo, Hebraic scholar and Christian

---

[45] Ghinucci to [Croke], 21 May 1530: ibid., no. 6398; [Croke to Henry VIII], 31 May 1530: ibid., no. 6414.

[46] [Croke to Stokesley], 9 June 1530, from Venice: ibid., no. 6445.

[47] Another copy of ibid., in *Records*, ed. Pocock, ii. 638–9.

[48] [Croke to Stokesley], 19 June 1530: *Letters and Papers*, iv (3), no. 6463.

[49] Jacob Raphael Peglione of Modena: BL MS Arundel 151 fos. 190–1: repr. *Revue des études juives*, 30 (1895), 309–13. Peglione records that 'I have been asked by a distinguished priest, whose name is Messer Francisco Curtiso, concerning a point in the law of the levirate.'

cabbalist, according to Gregory Casale, 'seems desirous of pleasing the King, but cannot write for him, as the Pope has commissioned him to write on the matter, which will perhaps come before the College'. Still, the cardinal promised to keep Casale informed of what he was writing against Henry, 'from time to time'. In Egidius's view, 'there are only two people in Italy learned in Hebrew, Magister Jacob' Mantino, and 'one of those men whom the bishop of London [Stokesley] had on his side at Bologna', presumably Halfan, although perhaps not.[50] The emperor must have been pleased with this latest news, especially when he was further informed that Stokesley in Padua 'could get nothing there from the doctors and professors of the University', and that Francesco Giorgi had been forced to justify his contacts with English agents before the Venetian Senate.[51]

Probably the most important reason for this change in attitude among all parties—Jews, papists, and English agents—is that Henry's case had actually formally begun in the Rota in early June. Thomas Cranmer had arrived in the city, and with his men was trying to have the hearing delayed as long as possible so that the maximum amount of evidence could be assembled. Ghinucci dragged his feet so long that not only was nothing accomplished before the summer vacation, but the Rota was unable to deal with Henry's divorce until November. In England, meanwhile, a new approach was being developed, with well-known revolutionary consequences. On 12 June 1530 Henry forced a very substantial group of leading churchmen and nobles to sign a letter to the pope demanding that he find a solution to Henry's problem, and quickly. While conceding that it is for Clement to make the final decision, the letter insists that the bulk of scholarly opinion had come down on Henry's side and had ruled that his marriage to Catherine was invalid and had been improperly permitted by a pontifical predecessor. In other words, although Henry was still unwilling to question the basic right of the pope to rule on his case, he was already taking a far more aggressive tone. Indeed, the Levitical argument which he chose to use from the very start, by appealing to Scripture against papal authority, contained within it the germ of a full-fledged rebellion against Rome. By late August 1530 Henry was already asking his agents in Italy to lay before Clement the claim that Englishmen could not be cited out of the country to submit to a foreign, in this case papal, jurisdiction. Henry therefore demanded that the entire issue of his divorce be remanded to

---

[50] D. Gregory Casale to Goronus, from Rome, 22 June 1530: *Letters and Papers*, iv (3), no. 6499. Cf. J. O'Malley, *Gilles de Viterbe on Church and Reform* (Leiden, 1968).

[51] Rodrigo Niño to Charles V, 6 July 1530, from Venice: *Cal. SP Span.* iv (1), no. 563 = p. 869,

some combination of Church and State in England. This his agents delayed conveying to the pope until December, not only afraid of papal wrath and possible sanctions against them and their king, but also well aware that they could not really justify Henry's claim. Since September they had extended the subject of their research to cover not only the continuing and permanent validity of Leviticus, but also their new-found claim that an English king could not be cited out of his realm. Indeed, Henry expected them to go through all the registers of all the popes and to leave no document unturned. Their research, closely observed and partly restricted by the other side, came up with nothing that could be of much use, but it was the approach and the nature of the arguments which would prove crucial in the long run. As Professor Scarisbrick put it,

The late summer of 1530, then, was probably the crucial moment in the story of Henry's jurisdictional struggle with universal papalism—indeed, perhaps the crucial moment of his reign. It saw him launch the claim to a national immunity against Rome's sovereignty; it saw him announce a personal claim to imperial status which could neither acknowledge nor allow any superior on earth. It also saw the first attempt to manhandle the clerical estate within his realm.[52]

The death of Cardinal Wolsey on 29 November 1530, on his way to London to face treason charges, as much as anything symbolizes the turn which Henry had taken in his entire approach to the problem of his divorce.

IV

In the second half of 1530, then, Henry had little good news from his scholarly agents on the Continent. Even if the case were revoked to England, the issue was still seen as resting on the Levitical argument. Like it or not, the Jews still held the key to Henry's divorce. This is what Charles V was told by his agents as well: 'All his negotiations here, since his return,' it was said of Stokesley in July, 'have been conducted with the Jews'.[53] Indeed, the Jews were the only hope that Stokesley, Croke, and the Casales could hold out to an increasingly beleaguered king in London. That Jews wrote against Henry's view after the spring of 1530 is not surprising at all. What is curious is that some Jews, notably Halfan and Raphael, continued to support the king. This needs to be looked at more closely, especially in regard to Halfan, who was not only

---

[52] Scarisbrick, *Henry VIII*, 260–73, esp. 273.
[53] Rodrigo Niño to Charles V, 6 July 1530, from Venice: *Cal. SP Span.* iv (1), no. 563 = p. 869.

distinguished in his own right, but the scion of one of the most important Jewish families in Renaissance Italy. Why should Halfan have held a radically different, and far more dangerous, view of the divorce from Jacob Mantino, the other major scholar involved in the case? The simple answer is that Henry's divorce was only one manifestation of a much deeper quarrel between the two men, centring around their different attitudes to one of the most bizarre and potentially dangerous figures in sixteenth-century Jewish history: Solomon Molcho. Only by examining Molcho the Messiah can we discover how Henry was able to obtain significant Jewish support at all, in the Byzantine world of local Italian Jewish politics.

In 1524 a Jew appeared in Rome, going by the name of David Reubeni, claiming to be a native of a distant land, India or Arabia. 'My brother, the king of the Jews,' he claimed, 'has sent me here to you, my lord King, for help. And now help us that we may go to fight Sulaiman the Turk, so that we may take the Holy Land out of his power.' David Reubeni was received by our Pope Clement VII, who was intrigued by the idea of an army of Jews who might fight Suleiman the Magnificent, who only three years before had taken Belgrade, and followed up this success by conquering Rhodes as well. Clement furnished Reubeni with letters of reference to John III, king of Portugal, and, honoured by such great Gentile leaders, his status among the Jews grew as well. According to a near-contemporary report, the secret Jews of Portugal 'believed his words, saying, "He is our redeemer, for the Lord has sent him," and many gathered about him and they honored him exceedingly'. The same adulation greeted Reubeni as he returned to Italy via Spain, France, and Avignon. Reubeni presented himself as a sort of eternal mystical general; the secular authorities were more than a little worried about popular agitation in the short term. Joseph HaKohen, who discusses Reubeni at length in his sixteenth-century Hebrew history, reports that

David came also to Bologna, Ferrara, and Mantua and declared that with the consent of the Christian kings he was going to take all to the Pope about this matter and the Jews became very frightened. They would ask him: 'What shall we do with our wives now if we go to war? How about our children whom they have borne?' He would answer: 'There are many such in our land. Do not be afraid for there is no restraint to the Lord to save.'[54]

---

[54] Joseph Ha Kohen, *Emek ha-Baka*, ed. M. Letteris (Vienna, 1852), 113–17: repr. *The Jew in the Medieval World*, ed. J. R. Marcus (Philadelphia, 1938), 251–5. Joseph HaKohen (1496–1578) completed this Hebrew martyrology in about 1575, and was also the author of *A History of the Kings of France and the Ottoman Rulers*. Another contemporary report, by Abraham Farissol, is printed in both Hebrew and English by B. Halper, *Post-biblical Hebrew Literature* (Philadelphia, 1921), i. 180–4, ii. 230–4. Cf. S.

Clearly, David Reubeni did not sweep all before him.[55]

One of those greatly affected by David Reubeni was a Portuguese secret Jew named Diego Pires, said to be 'one of the secretaries of the king'. Pires returned to the faith of his fathers, had himself circumcised, and left the country for the East. He seems to have spent some time in Salonica, and eventually in Palestine, where at Safed he imbibed the cabbalistic Jewish mystical lore which would soon make that town famous throughout Europe. But Pires, now going by the name of Solomon Molcho, had come to see himself as a Messianic figure as well, and his place in Italy, close to David Reubeni, his inspiration. On the way he not only had a volume of sermons published in Salonica in 1529, but in the same year preached to Jews in Ancona and held a disputation with a Christian cleric which would have led to prosecution had not the duke of Urbino sheltered him in neighbouring Pesaro. 'Many were envious of him but they were not able to cause him any injury in Italy,' writes HaKohen, 'for he was beloved in the sight of the princes.' Molcho carried on to Rome, 'where he spoke with Clement, the Pope, who showed him favor in spite of the wishes of the theologians of the Church. The Pope gave him a permit, written and sealed in his name, allowing him to settle wherever he wanted and to declare himself a Jew.' Clement was especially interested in Molcho's prohecies that the Tiber would overflow, Portugal would be stricken with an earthquake, and numerous comets would appear in the skies. Molcho had many detractors, especially among more influential figures in both the Jewish community and the papal entourage, but when the Tiber actually overflowed on 8 October 1530 his extravagant claims acquired a new-found temporary validity. Although Reubeni was gradually being unmasked as rather less than an Arabian, Molcho 'joined himself to David and they were united at that time', at Venice in 1530.[56]

It was in Venice that Molcho made the acquaintance of our two Jewish protagonists in Henry VIII's divorce, Jacob Mantino and Elijah Halfan, and his intervention only made things worse. The claims and activities of Reubeni and Molcho in Italy had divided the Jewish community, between those who saw them as Messianic figures, or at least men with a new message which could be of benefit to all, and those who branded them as dangerous frauds. Elijah Halfan was a great supporter of Molcho: indeed, he was in charge of the Messiah's letters sent through Venice. Mantino, on the other hand, saw Molcho as a great

Simonsohn, 'David Reubeni's Second Mission in Italy' (Hebrew), *Zion*, 26 (1961), 198–207; and, generally, Roth, *Renaissance*, and id., *A History of the Marranos* (Philadelphia, 1932).

[55] See David Reubeni's diary, printed in translation by E. N. Adler, *Jewish Travellers* (London, 1930), 251–328.   [56] Ha Kohen, *Emek*, repr. Marcus.

danger to the Jews of Italy, and became almost obsessed with bringing him down. Molcho tells of how he met with both men in an attempt to bring an end to the quarrel: 'I wanted to make peace between them', Molcho wrote, but Mantino was adamantly against it. When Portugal was hit with an earthquake in January 1531, apparently proving yet another of Molcho's predictions, Mantino had even more reason for intriguing against the Messiah. Molcho fled to Rome, but Mantino followed him, and helped arrange an inquisitorial investigation which condemned the Marrano to be burnt at the stake, among other things, for backsliding. According to contemporary accounts, Molcho was saved by Clement himself, who arranged to have another man executed in his place.[57] In any case, Molcho met his end after optimistically attempting to convert Charles V to his cause. He and Reubeni met with the emperor at Regensburg in 1532, but, as HaKohen reports,

The Emperor remained firm and would not listen to him, being impatient, and even issued an order to put him and his friend Prince David and his men into prison. They remained there for a few days until the Emperor returned to Italy. Then he brought them back, shackled on wagons, to Mantua, where they were put into jail. The Emperor then spoke with his advisers, and when they found Solomon guilty and deserving death, the Emperor commanded: 'Take him out and let him be burnt.'

Molcho was executed in late 1532; Reubeni was taken to Spain, where he died, probably six years later.[58]

David Reubeni, Solomon Molcho, and the Jewish Messianic fervour of 1524–32 in Italy, Spain, Portugal, and elsewhere formed the background to the quarrel between Jacob Mantino and Elijah Halfan, which began with this issue and extended without limit. When Mantino took a stand against Henry's divorce, Halfan, as in all other things, took a stand in favour. The two men were sworn enemies, and each claimed to represent the intellectual aspirations of Venetian Jewry. This is what lay behind Halfan's extraordinary decision to write in favour of Henry VIII when all other serious Jewish commentators made it clear that it was both politically dangerous and religiously improbable to support the English king.

V

No matter where Henry's divorce would be ruled upon, in Rome or in London, the king had decided that his defence would be based upon the

---

[57] For more on Mantino, Halfan, and Molcho, see Kaufmann, 'Mantino'.
[58] Ha Kohen, *Emek*, repr. Marcus.

continuing validity of the Levitical prohibition, undeterred by the apparent exceptions raised in Deuteronomy. His entire case was founded on the premiss that, even among contemporary Jews, levirate marriage was no longer practised, the ceremony of *halitzah* taking precedence. This defence came crashing dramatically down in the autumn of 1530 as the result of an incident which Mai gleefully reported to his master Charles V: 'Your Majesty will be glad to hear that here this year, among the Roman Jews, one has been compelled to marry the widow of his brother, who has died without children, a thing which not only is not prohibited, as we maintain, but is actually enjoined by Jewish law.'[59] This untimely levirate marriage put an end to any hopes Henry might have had of basing his case on Jewish practice. Certainly, as we have seen, levirate marriage was still a going concern among the Sephardi community, yet the coincidence of such a marriage, and in Rome under the watchful eye of the pope and other opponents of Henry's divorce, makes the event more than a little suspicious. There is a reference in the writings of the Siennese rabbi and physician Isaac ben Abraham Cohen of Viterbe, who noted in 1573 that he remembered a levirate marriage which took place in his youth.[60] In that year 1573 another such marriage took place, that of Joseph ben Menahem de Foligno with Sulpicia, the widow of his brother, and sister of his own first wife Julie, a complicated arrangement which nevertheless received the approbation of all Italian rabbis.[61] So stranger things have happened than the levirate marriage which was conducted at Rome in 1530. But the perfect mistiming of the match leaves open the question of whether it was arranged by someone such as Jacob Mantino to bring to a swift conclusion any speculation about the continuing validity of Leviticus.

Henry's case in Jewish law now depended entirely on the efforts of Marco Raphael, the Venetian convert. By the autumn of 1530 even Elijah Halfan had dropped out, either because the hopelessness of the argument was now apparent, or in order to pursue his feud with Mantino in the more fertile rabbinic hunting grounds attached to the Messianic claims of Molcho and Reubeni. This new focusing of effort did not go unnoticed by the other side, which continued to place great importance on Henry's Jewish advocates, in large measure because the

---

[59] Micer Mai to Charles V, 2 Oct. 1530, from Rome: *Cal. SP Span.* iv (1), no. 446 = p. 739; cf. *Letters and Papers*, iv (3), no. 6661.

[60] Lampronti, *Pachad Yitzchak*, iii, fo. 24c (MS Halberstam, 228): Kaufmann, 'Mantino', 207 n. Roth, *Renaissance*, mistakenly gives the site of this marriage as Bologna, thus (apparently) misleading Scarisbrick, *Henry VIII*, 257, who writes of two levirate marriages in 1530, one in Rome and the other in Bologna.

[61] Lampronti, *Pachad*, iii, fo. 21 b et s: Kaufmann, 'Mantino', 207 n.

king did so himself. 'As the Nuncio was leaving the room', wrote imperial ambassador Eustace Chapuys in London to Charles V,

the king made some slight excuse for having written to Rome without first informing him thereof; but he said the fault rested with those of his Council who had sent off the courier whilst he was out hunting. Neither has the Nuncio nor have I been able to discover the nature of that despatch, nor the reason of its being sent. It may be among others, to bring over here an old Jew, now at Rome, who says he can prove incontrovertibly that the King's marriage was unlawful. Has advised Messire Mai of this, so that should the Jew be a man of such learning and parts as to inspire confidence, he (Mai) may prevail on the Pope to stop his coming [to England], at least until his arguments have been heard, so that the bishop of Rochester [John Fisher] may be prepared to refute them, *a task the Bishop desires above all things.*[62]

It was probably true that the report of the Roman levirate marriage had not yet reached Chapuys in London, but even so, it is remarkable how seriously the Jewish threat was still taken even in October 1530. Chapuys was prepared to mobilize the pope to prevent Raphael arriving in England, and was determined that John Fisher, the biggest gun among the scholarly opponents of the divorce, would himself undertake to refute the much-weakened Jewish arguments.

Chapuys, as usual, was absolutely right that Henry still had plans for Marco Raphael, according to his grand strategy, which remained based on Jewish law despite the enormous set-back he had received with the recent Roman levirate marriage. On 28 November 1530, the very day before Cardinal Wolsey's death, the emperor's agent in Rome wrote to his master informing him that

Among those who have given their opinions here in favour of the King is a converted Jew, who now goes by the name of Marco Gabriello, to whom the king of England has offered as much money as he may ask, having instructed his ambassadors to treat with him and have him sent to England. As this man's journey cannot be for a good purpose, we are afraid that with the votes the King has got already, and with Gabriello's presence in England, Parliament may be persuaded to grant that which he (the King) has so long threatened, namely, his marriage 'de facto'.

This was the problem, but Mai had a solution as well:

Considering it to be for Your Majesty's interest to prevent this man's journey to England, I have taken the precaution of writing to Scalenga at Asti, giving his *signallement* that he may be arrested if passing through that country. I have since communicated with cardinal d'Osma and Don Pedro [de la Cueva], and both are of opinion that Antonio de Leyva might also do the same, if the Jew should

[62] Eustace Chapuys to Charles V, 15 Oct. 1530, from London: *Cal. SP Span.* iv (1), no. 460 = p. 761.

happen to pass through Milan. Andrea del Burgo has likewise written to Trent, and as I have since heard that he has gone to Venice on certain private business of his own, Rodrigo Niño has been instructed to set spies upon him and have him followed to Trent, Milan, or Asti, whichever route he may take.[63]

Mai may have had Raphael's name slightly distorted, but there was no mistaking the danger which the convert Jew was perceived to be. As can be readily seen, the emperor was being advised to put into action not only imperial agents in Rome, but also very nearly every contact at their disposal. Scalenga was an Albanian captain in the service of Charles V who had been taken prisoner in 1527 but was now governor of Asti. Don Pedro de la Cueva was high commander of Alcantara, and Antonio de Leyva the commander of the imperial forces in the Milanese. Andrea del Burgo was the count of Castil Leone and served as Austrian ambassador in Venice. These men made up a considerable portion of the emperor's heavy artillery, and all was being directed at the immobilization of one convert Jew, who was thought to hold the only conceivable legal solution to Henry's problem, which otherwise was sure to go the way of Charles V and his allies. This extraordinary letter makes it clear how seriously they took the threat of a Jewish solution to their Christian conundrum.

In England, meanwhile, Henry was using praemunire proceedings as a weapon against the clergy as a whole, and moving towards a position where he himself would be 'protector and only supreme head of the English Church', limited 'as far as the law of Christ allowed'. In Italy, however, the momentum for bringing Marco Raphael to England to clinch the increasingly irrelevant Levitical argument continued unabated. By the middle of December 1530 Mai had replies from his various contacts whom he had warned to be on the look-out for the convert Jew. 'Leyva and Scalenga have written to say that they will take good care that the Jew does not pass through their territory without being arrested and searched', Mai reported to Charles V, and he was still waiting for a reply from Niño in Venice and Burgo in Trent. Yet despite the military tone of his letters, one thing was quite worrying: no one seems to have actually located Marco Raphael, who was nowhere to be found.[64]

Marco Raphael had indeed gone underground, but when he surfaced

---

[63] Micer Mai to Charles V, 28 Nov. 1530, from Rome: ibid., no. 513 = p. 825. Cf. another copy in *Letters and Papers*, iv (3), no. 6739. The same letter, misdated as 28 Nov. 1529, is included as *Cal. SP Span.* iv (1), no. 219 = p. 335; and *Letters and Papers*, iv (3), no. 6068.

[64] Micer Mai to Charles V, 13 Dec. 1530, from Rome: *Cal. SP Span.* iv (1), no. 533 = p. 842; same to High Commander, 14 Dec. 1530, from Rome: ibid., no. 535 = p. 844.

it was in London. Somehow Croke, Ghinucci, the Casales, and Henry's other agents on the Continent had succeeded in bringing to him the only man who might save the purely legalistic arrow in his quiver before more drastic measures needed to be taken. What actually occurred when Raphael came to town is told with characteristic detail by Charles V's ambassador in London, Eustace Chapuys, reporting to his ruler on 31 January 1530/1: 'The Jew, whom this king sent for, as I informed Your Majesty in a former despatch, *notwithstanding all the precautions taken by Messire Mai to prevent his passage,* arrived here in London six days ago,' he explained (that is, on 25 January).

He has already seen the King twice, and been very well received, though not so well on the first as on the second audience; most likely the graciousness of his reception will gradually decrease unless he has more agreeable news than he brought at first, for I am told that *his opinion is* that the Queen's marriage ought not to be disputed or dissolved, *but nevertheless that the King may and can very well take another wife conjointly with his first,* which opinion the King has found so extravagant and absurd that he has openly declared to the Jew himself that this will not do, and *that he must devise some other means of getting him out of the difficulty, for that he would never adopt, indeed would rather die than resort to such expedient,* as it would be an infamous and blameable act for him to have two wives at the same time.

Chapuys attempted to explain Marco Raphael's reasoning as well:

I hear that the pith of the Jew's argument is that although the King's marriage with the widow of his brother was a true and legitimate act, yet he does not style himself properly *husband* of the Queen, inasmuch as according to [Jewish] law the posterity issuing from such a union is ascribed to the first husband; and as it would be unreasonable that in order to preserve the name and race of the deceased, the survivor should be prevented from having posterity of his own and bearing his name, Law allows him to take another wife. So that the said Jew who pretends to have been baptized some time ago, would not under the cloak of charity, spread his Judaizing doctrines.

Chapuys also gave the emperor some information about the man himself:

He said to the Venetian ambassador, who reported it to me, that he had spoken to Your Imperial Majesty at Augsburgh, and had received a present from your hands, which, if it be true, is not likely to promote his credit and reputation in this country. He also pretends to have spoken to Your Majesty at Bologna.[65]

Marco Raphael's suggestion that Henry VIII take Anne Boleyn as a second wife and thereby avoid the entire question of the divorce was

---

[65] Chapuys to Charles V, 31 Jan. 1530/1, from London: ibid. iv (2), no. 619 = pp. 43–5; cf. *Letters and Papers*, v, no. 70.

sensational to say the least. The bigamy of Philip of Hesse was still eight years in the future, by which time Henry would be marrying his fourth wife. What could have possessed Marco Raphael to have made such a proposal? Was it indeed so 'extravagant and absurd' even in Jewish law, as Chapuys believed? In fact, Marco Raphael's advice was in perfect alignment with the approach to Jewish law which Henry had already unwittingly adopted. When Henry had been told that Jews no longer practised levirate marriage, as we have seen, his advisers were referring to the *herem* of Rabbenu Gershom, the eleventh-century Talmudic scholar of Mainz. Indeed, Ashkenazi Jews since those days have always taken the option of *halitzah* instead of marrying the brother's widow. This prohibition quite obviously did not apply to Sephardi Jews and, as already noted, levirate marriage continued among them until very modern times. But the *herem* only prohibited levirate marriage incidentally; its main purpose was to outlaw polygamy among Ashkenazi Jews. *Halitzah* was given priority over levirate marriage so as not to present a married brother-in-law with any insurmountable moral dilemmas. Polygamy was prohibited, but provisions for bigamy were made in certain circumstances, on condition that the second marriage was approved by at least 100 rabbis from three different districts. Such conditions might include the case of an insane first wife, or a situation in which the wife refused to accept a *get* (bill of divorcement) from her husband despite having been ordered by the courts to do so, after adultery had been proven, for example. This was clearly a possible line for Henry to follow, and was by no means as 'extravagant and absurd' as Chapuys thought. Only one problem remained: the *herem* of Rabbenu Gershom did note that a husband was prohibited from divorcing his wife against her will, which certainly complicated Henry's strategy if it were to be based on this particular aspect of Jewish law. Marco Raphael had not lost his mind, but was merely carrying Henry's argument at Jewish law to its illogical conclusion.[66]

If the reaction to Philip of Hesse's bigamy in 1539 is anything to judge by, Henry made a wise decision that day when he refused to heed Marco Raphael's advice. These were the months during which Henry's agents were working in Italy to prevent the case being heard in Rome, and trying unsuccessfully to move the venue to England or, at the very least, to some mutually agreeable alternative location. In London, Henry was trying on his new title as Supreme Head of the Church, and moving to a position where, by June 1531, he could shout at the papal nuncio that he would never consent to the pope being judge in his great affair. 'Even if

[66] Elon, 'Levirate Marriage'; B. Z. Sch[ereschewsky], 'Bigamy and Polygamy', *EJ*. In Israel during 1991 thirteen men received permission to take a second wife without divorcing the first: *HaAretz*, 22 Jan. 1992.

his holiness should do his worst by excommunicating me and so forth, I shall not mind it, for I care not a fig for all his excommunications.'[67] What Marco Raphael's task in London was is not clear. It may be that during this somewhat purposeful muddle it was thought that an additional biblical argument from a Jewish source might not be a bad thing. In any case, from the latter part of January 1531 the man was at Court, at the beginning of an English sojourn that would last at least three years.

Having had his initial interview with King Henry, Marco Raphael seems to have settled down fairly quietly in the role of a secret emergency weapon that was not likely to be of much use as the battle plan changed. Chapuys was probably better informed about Raphael's state of mind than the king himself, who during the spring of 1531 was more concerned with formulating the theoretical basis behind an independent English church. At the beginning of March Charles V was told of a new and almost imperceptibly subtle variation in Raphael's strategy. 'The Jew called hither, finding his first opinion not accepted, has forged another equally illfounded,' Chapuys wrote from London,

and says it is indeed lawful to marry a brother's widow, provided it is done with the will and intention to raise issue for the deceased brother; but without such intention the marriage is unlawful, and that God has reproved such unions by the mouth of Moses, so that issue shall not proceed of them, or shall not live long; and that it has been seen that the male children the King had of the Queen scarcely lived at all; from which he inferred that the King had not the said intention, and consequently that the marriage is unlawful.[68]

This view, too, was well established in Jewish law, but Raphael had made essentially the same point while still in Italy: he did not need to have travelled all the way to England to tell the king that. It may be that Raphael was beginning to feel that he had already outlived his usefulness to Henry, and was worried about how he might quietly return to his former life in Venice. By April 1531 he was putting out discreet feelers to the other side, implying that he was sorry: 'The Jew whom the King sent for from Italy has sent several times to me to justify himself,' Chapuys wrote to Charles V, 'saying he had done better service than is supposed, and expects at his return to kiss your Majesty's hands; of whom, in passing, you may learn some particulars.'[69] It was a little late for this last Jew on Henry's side to return to the imperial fold, but the fact that the effort was worth making already by April 1531 is a useful guide to the king's strategic timetable.

[67] *Cal. SP Span.* iv, no. 739.
[68] Chapuys to Charles V, 1 Mar. 1530/1, from London: *Letters and Papers*, v, no. 120.
[69] Same to same, 29 Apr. 1531, from London: ibid., no. 216.

Marco Raphael had clearly been reading the signs correctly. Even though Henry continued to employ agents in Italy to promote his case and to prevent its being decided upon in Rome, his gaze was directed more steadily towards events in England. At the beginning of December 1531 Francesco Giorgi, still in Henry's service, wrote to the king proclaiming himself eternally devoted to the cause. He told Henry of recent efforts to convince him to defect to the pope like everyone else, and reminded Henry of how consistently he had worked for him and of how important he had been to Croke in the early days of precedent hunting two years before. Indeed, Giorgi boasted, Croke, 'as he was ignorant of Italian affairs and customs, would have made very little progress without his assistance'. Giorgi concluded his letter by recommending 'himself and his nephew Mark Raphael to the King's notice', which has led some eager Jewish historians to claim the Italian friar as a converted Jew, but the reference is purely courteous.[70]

In London, meanwhile, Marco Raphael managed to hang on somehow. Seeing that being the king's special Jewish adviser on the divorce question was not a full-time job, in May 1532 he took out a licence to import 600 tuns of Gascon wine and Toulouse woad.[71] But, curiously, all was not lost. In October of that year Henry met with Francis I in Calais and Boulogne, in a last attempt to influence the pope. Henry, since the death of Wolsey, had lacked any real pull in the Curia, and his efforts to obtain a cardinal's hat for Gregory Casale, or Ghinucci, or even Stephen Gardiner, never really got off the ground. He hoped that a demonstration of mutual admiration and friendship with the king of France, re-enacting the pageant of the Field of Cloth of Gold years before, might put pressure on the emperor and the pope alike. The meetings with Francis were planned in great detail and were the subject of mutual anxiety lest this carefully staged expression of friendship backfire. Nothing was left to chance; everything had a purpose. Chapuys's letter to Charles V on 14 October 1532, six days before the first meeting between the two monarchs, is therefore very revealing of the role which Raphael was still expected to play. 'The King takes with him to Calais a legion of doctors and priests,' the ambassador wrote,

and among the rest three Franciscans (*courdeliers*) whom king Francis sent him some time ago from Brittany, as I informed Your Majesty by my last despatch, and likewise the Jew who came from Venice at his bidding. This last gives out that there will be [at Calais] a conference on the matter of this divorce, which

---

[70] Francis Georgius to Henry VIII, 4 Dec. 1531, from Venice: ibid., no. 567.
[71] Licence to Mark Raphael of Venice: ibid., no. 1065.

perchance at the request of this king will be discussed before the Council and cardinals of France, and then be decided by the latter.[72]

Among these French cardinals was a new one, Gabriel de Grammont, bishop of Tarbes, who three years before had suggested that Henry's marriage to Catherine might not have been valid.[73] Although nothing came of the meeting, since Francis was unwilling to fight Henry's lost cause at Rome, the fact that Raphael was brought along demonstrates that even at this eleventh hour the Jewish argument was still dominant.

VI

The meeting with the French at Calais was Raphael's swan-song. All that remains of him in the records subsequently is a series of small bills, some from Calais itself, a payment of £20 in October 1533, and, finally, some last 'Bills to be signed' in 1534.[74] With that, Raphael disappears. He may have gone back to Venice, although given his recent efforts on behalf of the English king, that might have been thought inadvisable. He may have stayed on in England, although in that case he probably would have had something to do with the teaching of Hebrew and the revival of that venerable tongue in the English universities, but no record of this survives. He may simply have died in 1534. By the time of Raphael's decline and disappearance, the Levitical argument had become a theological dinosaur, since sometime in December 1532, upon Henry's return from Calais, Anne Boleyn became pregnant. On 25 January 1533 she was secretly married to the king, and there was no time to worry about Leviticus and Deuteronomy. Anne's child had to be made legitimate at all costs. On 10 April Archbishop Thomas Cranmer opened his independent inquiry into Henry's divorce, and thirteen days later declared his marriage to Catherine of Aragon void. On 28 May 1533 Henry's marriage to Anne Boleyn was declared lawful, a little over three months before the birth of Princess Elizabeth. Marco Raphael was a witness to these great events that he had not helped to bring about, the sole survivor among the Jewish advocates of Henry VIII's divorce.

[72] Chapuys to Charles V, 14 Oct. 1532, from London: *Cal. SP Span.* iv (2), no. 1008 = p. 535. Cf. *Letters and Papers*, v, no. 1429.

[73] Generally, see Scarisbrick, *Henry VIII*, 305–9.

[74] All payments via Thomas Cromwell: *Letters and Papers*, vi, no. 299 (1533), no. 1367 (29 Oct. 1533); vii, no. 923 (1534).

2

THE JEWISH CONSPIRATORS
OF ELIZABETHAN ENGLAND

THE entire question of Jewish involvement in the numerous plots and intrigues against Queen Elizabeth I has been one of extreme sensitivity for Anglo-Jewry, to the extent that suggesting any guilt by individual Jews was tantamount to a declaration of anti-Semitism. This cautiousness is readily understandable: while the accusations of ritual murder in the days of William of Norwich and Little St Hugh of Lincoln are too fantastic to be given any credence in modern times, the notion that Jews may have been among the many Iberians who plotted against the life of the Virgin Queen is close enough to a possible picture of reality not to be so lightly dismissed. Despite their wariness about the countries of the Inquisition, the Jews of Elizabethan England did move in Spanish and Roman Catholic circles, and the opportunities for financial profit and personal gain were plentiful. One Elizabethan Jew who seems *not* to have resisted the temptation was Roderigo Lopez, the queen's personal physician, who was executed in 1594 for plotting to poison her.

I

As one might expect from a Marrano Jew, Roderigo Lopez emerges from a hazy background of suppositions and conjectures. Since the practice of physic tended to run in families, it may be that our Lopez was a relative of a certain Ferdinando Lopus, who in 1550 was convicted of 'whoredome'. According to Charles Wriothesley, Windsor Herald, Lopus was 'at the sute of themperors embassador and other of the Kinges privie counsell spared for a tyme', but was soon condemned to suffer the city's penalty for such a crime, 'rydinge in cartes with ray [striped] hoodes', and was further banished from the realm. Wriothesley adds that 'this straunger was a Jewe borne, by reporte, and should once have bene burnt in Portingale'.[1] In any case, it seems fairly certain that our Roderigo Lopez came to England about 1559, for among the

---

[1] Charles Wriothesley, *A Chronicle of England during the Reigne of the Tudors*, ed. W. D. Hamilton (Camden Soc., NS, xi, xx, 1875, 1877), ii. 36–7.

returns of the strangers in London for 1571 is a reference confirming that 'Docto^r Lopus, portingale, howsholder, Denizen came into this realme about xij yeares past, to get his lyvinge by physicke, and Lewes Lopus his brother. &c.'[2]

By that time, Lopez had become established in the medical profession in London. In 1569 he was already a member of the College of Physicians, for he was then asked to read the anatomy lecture there, a service which he declined to perform.[3] Two years later he was to be found treating Sir Francis Walsingham, soon to be appointed Secretary of State.[4] By 1571 he was involved in Burghley's household, although, initially at least, less happily. In that year one of Burghley's servants complained to the College of Physicians, and Lopez, 'a Spaniard, was obliged to return the money which he had received on undertaking to cure a swelled shin bone'.[5] In about 1567 he was appointed house physician at St Bartholomew's Hospital, presiding over a matron and twelve nursing sisters for forty shillings per annum. In 1575 the hospital admonished Lopez 'that he shall be the more paynfull in looking to the poore of the hospital'.[6] Yet, despite these set-backs, in that year the name of Lopez stands near the head of a list of the chief doctors in London,[7] a fact which may have influenced his appointment as physician in the house of the earl of Leicester.[8] By all accounts, then, Lopez was by the 1570s a man of influence and success, already an important figure in London's court life.

---

[2] J. S. Burn, 'Protestant Refugees in 1563 and 1571', *Notes and Queries*, 2nd ser. 8 (3 Dec. 1859), 448. S. L. Lee, 'The Original of Shylock', *Gents. Mag.*, 246 (1880), 188–9, suggests that Lopez was born in England, the son of Hernando/Ferdinando Lopus: cf. *Cal. SP Span.*, *1507–25*, ii, 20 Oct. 1515. John Lingard, *A History of England* (London, 1819–30), viii. 385, claims that Lopez was brought to England in 1558 as a prisoner.

[3] W. Munk, *The Roll of the Royal College of Physicians of London* (2nd edn., London, 1878), i. 64, 69.

[4] *Journal of Sir Francis Walsingham*, ed. C. T. Martin (Camden Soc., civ, Misc., vi, 1871), 12: entry for 21 Nov. 1571: 'Monsr. Lopus and Martinius came to viset me.'

[5] Hist. MSS Comm., *8th Report, App.* (1881), 227a: from the Annals of the College of Physicians.

[6] St Bartholomew's Hospital Court of Governors minute book ('The Journal'), 14 Mar. 1573, 22 Jan. 1575, 5 Nov. 1575, 3 Oct. 1578: quoted in C. Hilton, 'St Bartholomew's Hospital, London, and its Jewish Connections', *TJHSE* 30 (1989), 23–5, who also notes that the wine-tasting society at Bart's is called the Lopez Society. Cf. A. Griffith, 'Dr Roderigo Lopes', *St. Bartholomew's Hospital Journal* (Nov. 1964), 449–52; P. J. Fenn, 'Queen Elizabeth's Poisoner', *St. Bartholomew's Hospital Journal* (Feb. 1957), 49–55; F. D. Zeman, 'The Amazing Career of Doctor Rodrigo Lopez', *Bulletin of the History of Medicine*, 39 (1965), 295–308.

[7] John Stow, *The Annals of England*, ed. J. Strype (London, 1755), i. 144; *DNB*.

[8] Anon., *Leicester's Commonwealth* (London, 1584), repr. W. Oldys (ed.), *Harleian Miscellany* (London, 1808–13), iv. 576–83.

Two international developments at the turn of the decade, however, transformed Lopez's position, and provided him simultaneously with greater temptations and increased danger. The first of these was the crisis of the Portuguese succession. On 4 August 1578 King Sebastian of Portugal was killed in Africa at the battle of Alcazarquivir. Sebastian I was a young man without heirs, and in the meantime the successor to the throne was his elderly uncle Cardinal Henry, he too quite naturally without an apparent successor. There were really only four serious contenders for the Portuguese throne, all of whom were descendants of King Emmanuel, who had died in 1521, having married in succession two daughters of Ferdinand and Isabella, each of whom produced children, although the current candidates all had common grandparents in Emmanuel and Queen Maria. Perhaps the least likely to succeed were Emmanuel Philibert of Savoy and Catherine of Braganza (although her grandson would reign in the next century as John IV). The two front-runners were Don Antonio, prior of Crato, and King Philip II of Spain himself. Philip's claim rested on the fact that his mother was a daughter of King Emmanuel; Antonio's father had been a son, but, alas, the prior was illegitimate, a fact which was seen by many to be an insurmountable obstacle. Philip enjoyed the support of the regency council, since most of the Portuguese nobility were either left dead in Africa or were being ransomed for whatever was left in the national treasury. But the towns and the populace supported Don Antonio, being traditionally anti-Castilian, and on Cardinal Henry's death, the issue had to be decided by force of arms. Philip, advised once again by his father's man Cardinal Granvelle, called the duke of Alva back from his estates to take command of the army for the invasion of Portugal. Portugal's army had been decimated in Africa, and the battle of Alcantara was won for Spain. By August 1580, then, all of the Iberian peninsula was united under King Philip II of Spain, and Don Antonio had fled abroad.[9]

The second international development which influenced Lopez's position, and that of the entire Jewish community in Elizabethan England, was the changing of the Jewish guard in Constantinople, coinciding with increased diplomatic and commercial activity by the English in Turkey. In 1579 Joseph Nasi died; his mother-in-law Gracia Nasi had died ten years before. This partnership had since 1553 been a formidable power bloc in the Turkish Empire. Nasi, when he died, was duke of Naxos and count of Andros, enjoyed numerous trading privileges in Turkey and eastern Europe, and was even recognized as the lord of Tiberias in Palestine, which he attempted to revive as a commercial centre. We have already seen Gracia Nasi as having married

---

[9] J. H. Elliott, *Imperial Spain* (London, 1963), 260–7.

into the Portuguese Marrano Mendes family, which was so influential in the Jewish world in Antwerp and England during the 1540s. After her husband's death she had fled to England and then to the Low Countries, living later in Venice, then Ferrara, and now finally in Constantinople. By marrying her nephew Joseph to her only daughter she gained an ally only about fourteen years her junior. Early in 1554 he joined her in Constantinople, was circumcised, and assumed the Hebrew name of Nasi.[10]

Joseph Nasi died in 1579; his successor as the most influential Jewish agent in Constantinople was Solomon Abenaes (*c.*1520–1603), a Portuguese Marrano known originally as Alvaro Mendes. Abenaes in Portugal had been an active supporter of Don Antonio in the succession crisis of 1580, and as a result of the Spanish victory there decided to make his way to Turkey in 1585, where he changed his name and openly embraced Judaism. Abenaes was already a wealthy man, having made a fortune in Indian diamonds. The Turks created him the duke of Mytilene and allowed him to farm the customs revenues. Most importantly from our point of view, Abenaes was very active in Anglo-Turkish politics, and consistently worked against Spanish interests and in favour of bringing Don Antonio to the Portuguese throne. His most important agent in England was Dr Roderigo Lopez, a relative by marriage.[11]

Apart from these Jews, the figure in Elizabethan England to whom we have not yet alluded is Dr Hector Nuñez (1521–91). Nuñez was also a Portuguese-born Marrano who had become wealthy and successful in London after arriving there about 1550. He was made a fellow of the College of Physicians in 1554, and in the same year a fellow of the Royal College of Surgeons. In 1579, the year before the Portuguese succession crisis, Hector Nuñez was endenizened.[12]

Hector Nuñez and Roderigo Lopez, then, both Jews, were among London's leading physicians during the 1570s and 1580s, and through family and communal connections were linked both to events in Portugal and to the nerve-centre of the Ottoman Empire itself. Their contact with leading English statesmen became almost routine. In 1578 we find Lopez writing to Burghley in connection with £20 owed to a third party by a viscount's son.[13] Two years later the earl of Shrewsbury was informed that 'Doctor Lopes, now cheeff phyzycyon to my Lo. of

---

[10] C. Roth, *The House of Nasi: Doña Gracia* (Philadelphia, 1947); id., *The House of Nasi: The Duke of Naxos* (Philadelphia, 1948).

[11] Roth, *Duke of Naxos*, 133–4, 205–16, 248–9.

[12] C. Meyers, 'Dr Hector Nuñez: Elizabethan Merchant', *TJHSE* 28 (1984), 129–31.

[13] Lopez to Burghley, 18 June 1578: *Cal. SP Dom., 1547–80*, 592.

Lec", according to his information, 'is a very honest person, and zealous'.[14] When Burghley was ill he usually consulted one of the two men, most likely Nuñez. On one occasion Elizabeth's chief minister was incapacitated with a bad cough. Nuñez suggested an enema; Burghley demurred, arguing that the weather was too hot. Nuñez gave him instead a concoction made from oil of sweet almonds, sugar, and white wine, supplemented by some lozenges which Burghley particularly disliked.[15] In an age obsessed with the threat of poison, both Lopez and Nuñez enjoyed the complete trust of their powerful patients.

The doctors Lopez and Nuñez were thus very well placed to take an active part in a project which was bound to be close to the heart of any politically sensitive Portuguese Marrano: the placing of Don Antonio on the Portuguese throne. As early as the spring of 1579 Elizabeth had sent Edward Wotton to Portugal to survey the situation. Bernardino de Mendoza, the Spanish ambassador in London, had a report that Wotton was authorized to offer Antonio English military support on the day of dynastic reckoning.[16] Whether such help was really discussed is not clear, but Don Antonio's hopes were shattered along with his troops before the duke of Alva at Alcantara in August 1580. Antonio fled the country, and spent the next years shifting back and forth between France and England, hoping to link his own cause with that of one of Spain's international enemies. Initially, at least, he seems to have made a good impression in London. 'Your Lordship may hear of Don Antonio,' Burghley informed his friend the earl of Shrewsbury in August 1581,

entitling himself King of Portugal, who now lodgeth at Baynard's Castle [in London], as I think, by means of my L. of Leicester. I never as yet saw him, but some of my Lords of the Council that have spoken with him report him to be very wise, modest, slow but grave of speech. And he meaneth to try his fortune to be a king or nobody. He hath very rich jewels, having in France taken up great sums of money, wherewith he hireth ships and men both in France and England to repair to the isles of the Azores.[17]

[14] Richard Topclyffe to earl of Shrewsbury, 16 Mar. 1579/80: repr. *Illustrations of British History*, ed. E. Lodge (London, 1791), ii. 224: cf. in 2nd edn. of 1838, ii. 164.

[15] Nuñez to Burghley, 28 June 1581: BL quoted in C. Read, *Lord Burghley and Queen Elizabeth* (London, 1959), 261.

[16] Read, *Burghley and Elizabeth*, 223–4; id., *Mr. Secretary Walsingham and the Policy of Queen Elizabeth* (Oxford, 1925), ii. 26, 29. See generally M. A. S. Hume, *Treason and Plot: Struggles for Catholic Supremacy in the Last Years of Queen Elizabeth* (London, 1901), 115–51; and id., 'Conspiración del Dr. Ruy López contra Isabel de Inglaterra y supuesta complicidad de Felipe II', in his *Españoles e ingleses en el siglo XVI* (Madrid, 1903), 205–33. See now also W. T. MacCaffrey, *Elizabeth I: War and Politics, 1588–1603* (Princeton, NJ, 1992).

[17] Burghley to Shrewsbury, 8 Aug. 1581: quoted in Read, *Burghley and Elizabeth*, 261.

Walsingham was actively promoting Antonio's plan, and was trying to organize an expedition against the Azores which would be commanded by Francis Drake. The scheme was all-inclusive and self-financing: the fleet would establish a base at the Azores and wait for the Spanish treasure ships, whose cargo would repay the investors who through joint stock had set the English to sail. Walsingham hoped that Queen Elizabeth herself would subscribe, and like all the others receive a share of the booty in proportion to the amount of stock purchased. Don Antonio was to finance a quarter of the costs, and, although Drake would command the ships, they would sail under the pretender's flag, thus freeing the English of any diplomatic responsibility for the raid on the Spanish treasure fleet. Burghley, Walsingham, and Leicester were in favour of the plan, but the queen was against: she argued that all diplomatic niceties would be forgotten if Drake captured the Spanish treasure fleet, and the result would be war with Spain.[18] Burghley half-heartedly drew up a memorandum about the enterprise,[19] but had to admit to his colleague Walsingham that the queen was 'very cold in the cause of Don Antonio'.[20] Don Antonio went to try his luck in France, but for the next few years his cause in England was dead in the water.

Throughout this period the enterprise of Don Antonio was one which occupied Lopez, Nuñez, and their contacts abroad. One of these was Alvaro Mendes, not yet in Constantinople, not yet known as Solomon Abenaes. Philip II was informed in July 1581 that, of 'Don Antonio's Portuguese partisans who are going here',

There is another called Alvaro Mendez, more considerate in his talk, and they say also in what he lends. Anyway I hear he is not so rash in these matters as the other, and if he assists the count he does not do it so openly that it is known by everyone. Perhaps as a more prudent man he wishes to sail with the wind whatever offers may be made him, and in the event of not being certain to leave Don Antonio's business; thinking in such a case to keep his retreat open and not depend on others. They tell me that he is a man 'of interests,' and that for the king to get hold of him the purse is more necessary than words.[21]

Walsingham was also kept posted about Mendes/Abenaes, and was told two months later that the French king 'dined with the Portugal Alvare Mendez, accompanied by the Dukes of Lorraine and Guise and the minions'.[22] Thus, even in this first and abortive stage of Don Antonio's

---

[18] Read, *Burghley and Elizabeth*, 262; Read, *Walsingham*, ii. 51.
[19] Read, *Burghley and Elizabeth*, 262.
[20] Ibid. 263.
[21] Tassis to Philip II, 8 July 1581: *Cal. SP For. 1581–2*, 250–3.
[22] Sir Henry Cobham to Walsingham, from Paris, 19 Sept. 1581: ibid. 318.

campaign to put himself on the Portuguese throne, we find nearly all of the principal actors: Lopez, Nuñez, Burghley, Walsingham, Mendes/Abenaes, and Queen Elizabeth herself. The remark of Philip's man that 'the purse is more necessary than words' may be simply the product of his own world-view, but it was also the Spanish answer to international espionage. It was certainly a temptation that could not be brushed aside and ignored.

Walsingham's information about Mendes/Abenaes was fortuitous, for by the time the Jew arrived in Constantinople in 1585 English interests there were already well established. Until Sultan Murad III granted the English merchants their charter in 1580, England traded in the Levant under the protection of France, who claimed the right to watch over the interests of the *harbis*, the non-Muslims who inhabit those parts of the globe not yet conquered for Islam. The English had been active in the East for some time, and as early as 1553 the famous merchant traveller Anthony Jenkinson had been given a grant of privileges by Suleiman the Magnificent to trade independently throughout the Ottoman Empire. Nevertheless, only with Murad's grant of May 1580 were English rights fully secured. William Harborne, who had been sent to Turkey two years previous to this concession, was officially appointed England's first ambassador to the Sublime Porte at the end of 1582 and arrived in Constantinople on 29 March 1583. For the next five years Harborne would serve as Elizabeth's 'Orator, Messenger, Deputie, and Agent'.[23]

Lopez during the early 1580s was living in Wood Street, having let his house near St Bartholomew's Hospital so as to live in the City 'where better ayre ys'.[24] He then took a house at Mountjoy's Inn, Holborn, which had been given to him by a grateful patient. We know that he rented some property from Winchester College, where his son Anthony would study.[25] We also know something of his acquaintances at Holborn, and of his wife Sarah, with relatives at Antwerp. Later on Francis Bacon would write that 'Dr. Lopes, a physician . . . is lodged in a fair house in Holbourn, lately built by an old gentlewoman, called Mrs. Allington, hard by Grey's Inn on the fields side, where he is well

---

[23] See generally S. A. Skilliter, *William Harborne and the Trade with Turkey, 1578–1582* (London, 1977); E. Pears, 'The Spanish Armada and the Ottoman Porte', *EHR* 8 (1893), 439–66; F. L. Baumer, 'England, the Turk, and the Common Corps of Christendom', *AHR* 50 (1944–5), 26–48.

[24] 'The Journal', 9 May 1579: Hilton, 'St Bartholomew's', 25.

[25] Eight of his nine children are recorded in the parish register of St Bartholomew the Less, four of whom died in infancy or childhook: Ellyn (9 Jan.1564; d.1573), Ambrose (6 May 1565), Douglas (13 May 1573), William (24 Oct. 1577), Ann (1 Mar. 1579), John (bur. 12 Dec. 1567), Jerome (bur. 20 Apr. 1573), Ann II (christened and bur. 26 Mar. 1574), Anthony (*c.*1580): Hilton, 'St Bartholomew's', 24, 44.

entertained and used by her, for physic, as they say.' In addition to his flourishing medical practice, Lopez had also obtained a monopoly for importing aniseed and sumac. His medical contacts with the great brought him close to centres of influence and power. From almost every measurable point of view Roderigo Lopez was a success, his Portuguese Marrano Jewish origin proving to be no hindrance.[26]

Even a change in the climate of international diplomacy did not affect the influence of the two Jewish doctors, Lopez and Nuñez. Although John Hawkins was still suggesting in 1584 that a privateering war be organized under the flag of Don Antonio, by that year and the next the talk was of peace with Spain. Leicester took up his command in The Netherlands in December 1585, as part of the implementation of the Treaty of Nonsuch between the two countries, but it would have been foolish to provoke Spain in more than one theatre of war. Indeed, there were up to five different projects for making peace with Spain. One of these revolved around Walsingham, Hector Nuñez, and Antonio de Castilio, formerly the Portuguese ambassador to England and now back in Lisbon.[27]

The fact that Nuñez's efforts came to very little is perhaps beside the point. What is clear is that he was very close both to Walsingham and to Antonio de Castilio, and that the three of them were in correspondence between the autumn of 1585 and the autumn of 1586 in an attempt to reduce the tension with Spain now that England was so actively involved in the Dutch war of independence. Castilio was pleased: he referred to Nuñez in a letter to Walsingham as 'my friend Mr. Hector', who told the Portuguese that the English statesman had his 'name in your good remembrance'.[28] Nuñez wrote a rather longer memorandum to Walsingham in March 1585/6, drawing upon the information that he had received from his agent Jeronimo Pardo, who had actually gone to Portugal with Walsingham's safe conduct. By this means Nuñez believed that he had managed to convey to Philip II that Elizabeth's intentions in the Low Countries were strictly limited: 'not to possess that

---

[26] Bacon to Standen, Feb. 1592/3: Thomas Birch, *Memoirs of the Reign of Queen Elizabeth . . . From the Original Papers of . . . Anthony Bacon* (London, 1754), i. 92–3; A. Dimock, 'The Conspiracy of Dr. Lopez', *EHR* 9 (1894), 440–72; *DNB*. This was also the period of the activity in England of the Bohemian Jewish mining expert Joachim Gaunse: see I. Abrahams, 'Joachim Gaunse: A Mining Incident in the Reign of Queen Elizabeth', *TJHSE* 4 (1903), 83–101; M. B. Donald, *Elizabethan Copper: The History of the Company of Mines Royal 1568–1605* (London, 1955), 72–4, 208–15, 299, 344.

[27] Read, *Burghley and Elizabeth*, 334; id., *Walsingham*, iii. 125–8, 145–53, 174–7; L. Stone, *An Elizabethan: Sir Horatio Palavicino* (Oxford, 1956), 259.

[28] Castilio to Walsingham, 3/13 Jan. 1585/6, from Lisbon: *Cal. SP For., 1585–6*, 281. Cf. Nuñez to Walsingham, 15/25 Sept. 1585: ibid. 26.

country to her use, but only for security of her estate and the relief of the poor people there, tyrannically dealt with by the King's officers.'[29] Castilio's letter to Nuñez was somewhat less optimistic, pleased to learn that Elizabeth's efforts were all 'tending to amity and peace', but noting pointedly that if Nuñez might 'find any hope to bring this to pass with outbreach of our master's honour, I know he will yield to any good composition for the quiet of Christendom, and employ his forces in other enterprises of greater weight'.[30]

If Nuñez's chances for success seemed slim, they were made even more so by Philip's evident involvement in the Babington Plot against the life of the English queen. Walsingham left nothing to chance and wrote out for Nuñez a list of points he should make when writing to Castilio. He was to stress how difficult it would be now to talk of peace and security with Spain. As regards the United Provinces, Philip should be made to understand that they 'wyll stande greatlie upon poynt of relygio and althowght yt may seme a verye harde matter for the k. to yeld unto yet men of best judgment even such as be Catholikes' believed not only that it would be impossible to eradicate Calvinism there, but that Philip's present course would result 'that the Catholick religion should be thrust out of the whole contryes'. A far better course would be to base a compromise on the Pacification of Ghent, 'wch may be handeled in sooche sorte as the said kinge with out touche of honor or conscience may assent thereunto'.[31] Castilio declared himself ready to do service to Elizabeth, but when he received Nuñez's letter stated 'that he darse not shewe the Artickles I sente hime, Becaus it mighte have bine occasion of a newe warr'.[32] So none of this diplomatic effort came to very much, but it was Nuñez's first taste of high policy, and his involvement made it clear to both sides what a diplomatic asset the Marrano community in London could be. The question remained, however, for which side they would work.

While Dr Hector Nuñez was actively labouring with Walsingham in the cause of a Spanish peace, Dr Roderigo Lopez was quietly pursuing his medical career. In about 1586 he was appointed Queen Elizabeth's chief physician.[33] Gabriel Harvey, the poet and friend of Spenser, had some acquaintance with Lopez during this period, and made a note

[29] Nuñez to Walsingham, *c.*23 Mar. 1585/6: ibid. 472–3.

[30] Castilio to Nuñez, encl. in letter Nuñez to Walsingham, 23 Mar. 1585/6: ibid. 473–5.

[31] Walsingham's instructions to Nuñez: ibid. 84–5.

[32] Castilio to Walsingham, 25 Aug./4 Sept. 1586: ibid. 79; Nuñez to Walsingham, 30 Sept. 1586: ibid. 98–9.

[33] Lopez to [?Walsingham], [?12 July] 1589: *Cal. SP Dom., 1581–90*, 609, saying that he has served the queen for three years.

about him and some of the other famous physicians of the day. Harvey began by citing that Lopez was 'descended of Jewes', although now professing Christianity. He is, Harvey wrote, 'none of the learnedest, or expertest Physitians in ye Court: but one, that maketh as great account of himself, as the best: & by a kind of Jewish practis, hath growen to much Wealth, & sum reputation: as well with ye Queen herself, as with sum of ye greatest Lordes, & Ladyes.'[34] William Clowes, a surgeon at Bart's who had worked with Lopez, agreed that he 'showed himself to be both carefull and very skilfull not only for his counsel in dyeting, purging and bleeding, but also for his direction of Arceus apozema . . . the proofe thereof I never had until that time, but since I have used it'.[35] It was only a matter of course that Lopez would join Nuñez on a wider stage of diplomacy and intrigue.

II

The eighteen-month period before the appearance of the Spanish Armada on the English coastline was, quite naturally, one of intense diplomatic activity, often at cross purposes. Lopez and Nuñez in London, and Solomon Abenaes in Constantinople, were connected not only in family and faith, but apparently also in their mutual desire to secure an Anglo-Turkish alliance against Spain. Lopez and Nuñez, of course, were well known in London, and Abenaes was becoming more so. In March 1587 Walsingham was informed by William Harborne, the English ambassador to Turkey, that

The Admiral with much ado hath restored nine English captives which, upon the Grand Signor's commandment reiterated, he durst no longer detain, but yet for spite would not give them himself but to one Don Alvaro [Solomon Abenaes] a Portuguese, who after he had paid their charges presented them to the Ambassador [Harborne] gratis in demonstration of his affection to her Majesty's service, which he doth in all things advance without any benefit to himself whatsoever he is able by his credit in those parts, being very great in regard of his experience, wisdom and wealth. If it were thought convenient he could crave her Majesty's grateful letter to him for a mean to continue and encourage him in like endeavours.[36]

---

[34] Harvey's notes on his copy of [Georg Meier], *In Ivdaeorvm medicastrorum* (1570): BL shelfmark C.60.h.18.

[35] William Clowes, *A Proved Practice* (London, 1591), 8: cited in Hilton, 'St Bartholomew's', 44.

[36] Harborne to Walsingham, 9 Mar. 1586/7: BL MS Harl. 295, fos. 176 ff.: repr. Read, *Walsingham*, iii. 328–9.

Walsingham in his reply was enthusiastic about Abenaes's help, and wrote 'a few lines in Latin unto himself to the effect you wished, which you may accompany with all circumstances convenient'. Harborne was also instructed to inform Abenaes that Elizabeth had given Sir Francis Drake specific orders that in return for his distant efforts in Constantinople, 'all Portugals with money in their purses' which fell into English hands would be unconditionally set free, while 'he selleth the Spaniard to the Moors'. Harborne was further commanded to encourage Abenaes as far as possible, in so far as he 'might prove a good instrument to work a reconcilement underhand'.[37]

Walsingham in his letter to Harborne noted that enclosed was a packet from Don Antonio directed to Solomon Abenaes. For in this period before the launching of the Spanish Armada, Don Antonio the Portuguese pretender once again seemed to be an English asset, not the least because men like Lopez, Nuñez, and Abenaes in Constantinople did their best to create the impression that a groundswell of popular support would proclaim Don Antonio the rightful monarch immediately upon his landing in the country. The championing of a sworn enemy of Philip II and Spain by Portuguese Marranos is not in itself an interesting historical fact. What is significant is how early Roderigo Lopez began to play a double game. Indeed, after Lopez's arrest it would be claimed that he had been a Spanish pensioner since 1587.[38] On 26 March 1587 Bernardino de Mendoza, formerly Philip's ambassador in England and France, wrote a very telling letter to Don Alonso de Idiaquez, the son of Don John of Austria, and therefore himself a grandson of Charles V. According to Mendoza, his agents as early as that date 'wished to gain over Dr. Lopez' to purge Don Antonio, 'as he is in the habit of doing every fortnight', with a poisonous substance and thereby put a permanent end to the Portuguese pretender, 'but he had not ventured to speak plainly to him about it, but only by hints'. Mendoza admittedly had other plans in the hopper, such as slipping something in Don Antonio's beer: 'Two Englishmen are busy in the matter now, and they say that as Don Antonio frequently visits a countess who lives near the village where he is they will find some opportunity of giving him a mouthful.'[39] Mendoza unquestionably had a somewhat sceptical view of humanity, but he must have had some reason for thinking that one of Don Antonio's leading ostensible supporters might be drawn away with money from his cause.

---

[37] Walsingham to Harborne, 24 June 1587: Bod. Lib., MS Tanner 79, fos. 125 ff.: repr. Read, *Walsingham*, iii. 331.   [38] Birch, *Memoirs*, 151.
[39] Mendoza to Idiaquez, 26 Mar. 1587: *Cal. SP Span., 1587–1603*, 49–50.

If in March Lopez was only a potential supporter of the Spanish king, the situation rapidly became much clearer. Lopez was by now 'a great friend' of Antonio de Vega, one of the key Spanish agents in London, by whose means Philip II was informed 'that Don Antonio was in despair of the Queen's giving him help to undertake any enterprise himself, and was almost starving'.[40] The information may have been slightly exaggerated, but what is important is that by March 1587 there was a direct chain of intelligence beginning with Don Antonio and connected through Lopez to Antonio de Vega, then to Mendoza in Paris, and from him immediately to King Philip II of Spain. This was hardly the sort of connection one would have expected from a leading supporter of Portuguese independence. All that remained to be done was to provide Lopez with a financial reward to refer to him as a Spanish spy without inaccuracy.

The following month Don Antonio's position was becoming even more uncertain. According to information received in Spain, Elizabeth herself asked certain figures in the City to lend the pretender £30,000, to be guaranteed by her, and to provide him with 3,000 men. The queen's letter was read to the City men, who met with Don Antonio's representatives to discuss terms. One of the pretender's agents at the meeting was Dr Roderigo Lopez.[41] For whatever reason, probably because of the hopelessness of the cause and Elizabeth's unwillingness even in the face of plots and assassination attempts to provoke Philip more than necessary, Don Antonio did not receive all of the help that he required, although Elizabeth seems to have given him a ship. Mendoza was informed from London that Don Antonio—code name: 'my uncle'—'is on the high road to a complete breach with this lady'. It was thought that Antonio would sail to Holland and try his luck there: 'If he is well received he will stay, and if not he will dismiss his people and go to Constantinople, by way of Germany, with three or four unknown persons, unless something be done to prevent the carrying out of his design.' In Turkey, Don Antonio knew he could rely on the support of Solomon Abenaes, just as he relied on Dr Lopez in London.[42]

But by this stage Don Antonio was in worse trouble than he imagined, for the chain stretching from his door to Philip's had already been secured. On 30 April 1587 Vega gave his good news to Mendoza in Paris:

[40] Mendoza to Philip II, 28 Mar. 1587: ibid. 48.
[41] Advices from London, 20 Apr. 1587, NS: ibid. 74.
[42] Antonio de Vega to Mendoza, 30 Apr. 1587, from London: ibid. 76–8.

I have gained over Dr. Ruy Lopez, and have converted him to his Majesty's service with good promises, and he has already done wonders in trying to get him [Don Antonio] turned out of here, and to divert other matters, which will be explained at length by the afore-mentioned messenger. I do not know whether I have done right in this; pray tell me. He [Lopez] says that your lordship had already had approaches made to him through Suygo, who had offered him anything he liked to ask if he ceased to interest himself in my uncle's affairs. Pray advise His Majesty and ask his approval of what I have done, as my only aim is to serve him.

Mendoza was not surprised at all that Lopez was now irrevocably linked to Philip's plans for eliminating Don Antonio and his cause. He wrote a note on the reverse of Vega's letter as follows:

What he [Vega] says about my having sounded Dr. Lopez through Suygo is a great lie. I will write and tell him so and ask him if he is so certain about Dr. Lopez, why he [Lopez] does not have his uncle put out of the way altogether. On a mere hint that Don Guerau de Spes gave him [Lopez] he offered to purge a Portuguese who was busy about some expeditions to be sent from England to the Indies. He took the recipe to the apothecary's himself, and on his way let it fall out of his breeches pocket, in consequence of which he was kept for six months in the Tower. I will say that this other business will be well paid-for, as the said doctor knows, and it may be settled without hesitation.[43]

Martin A. S. Hume, the editor of the volume of state papers in which this document appeared, and himself the author of a book on the plots against Elizabeth, reminds us that Don Guerau de Spes was the former Spanish ambassador in London, and the Portuguese referred to in Mendoza's note was Bartolome Bayon. Although the man's murder does appear in other papers, Lopez's connection is referred to here alone, and no record exists which corroborates any term of imprisonment in the Tower. From our point of view, what is important is that by April 1587 Lopez was not only a fully fledged Spanish agent, but a man whose willingness to commit murder seemed slightly indecent even to his masters.

The defection of Roderigo Lopez to the Spanish side must have been a source of deep satisfaction for Philip, for on all other fronts concerned with the Don Antonio affair it was the Jews who worked against him, and with some success. In May 1587 Mendoza informed the king that he had 'a letter in my hands from Alvaro Mendez who went as a Jew to Constantinople and writes to Don Antonio, signing the letter Solomon' Abenaes. Mendoza also had information that Abenaes was writing to contacts in Paris, bragging that he himself had been the reason for the

---

[43] Antonio de Vega to Mendoza, 30 Apr. 1587, and the latter's notes: ibid. 76–8.

failure of a Spanish–Turkish alliance.[44] Abenaes was not a man to be moved by Spanish gold, but Philip now had Lopez, which was surely some compensation. 'I did not speak to the merchant [Lopez] respecting the matter about which you wrote,' Vega reported in reference to Don Antonio's expedition plans,

because it is necessary for me to receive first a letter which I can show him. Pending the sending of this, write to me saying that his service will be welcome, and that he shall be recompensed in accordance therewith, using fair words because he is now in a different station and reputation from formerly. He has means of knowing all that is done, and may be very useful, although I am aware he is what you say, and negligent, but if he has someone to follow him up he will always be of use.[45]

The plan to have Don Antonio lead a naval expedition to capture the Portuguese throne stayed alive in this the summer before the Armada, and even somewhat ripened. 'The Queen is caressing Don Antonio lately more than ever,' Philip was informed, 'and he is therefore quieter.' A dozen ships were being prepared, and although Leicester wrote to Lopez that those vessels would not be permitted to go in Don Antonio's service, it remained a possibility.[46] Philip was worried, but grateful at least for the fact that Lopez was in place. 'I note your reports from England', the king wrote to Mendoza. 'As they are from so good a source, and you can get them there without fail, take care that you send them often. These last have been a long while coming. Write particularly whether the talk of Don Antonio embarking with the 16 ships is going forward.'[47] Unfortunately, sometime during the summer of 1587 Lopez had a falling out with Don Antonio, apparently because the doctor had repeated to Leicester certain views expressed about the queen's favourite by the pretender. The feud lasted for nearly three months, and Lopez's Spanish masters were very concerned 'as he had better means than others of learning everything'. Vega managed to persuade Lopez to end the quarrel, and although by November Lopez was 'still very cool with him', at least the contact still existed. 'I promise you I was not at all desirous, in the interests of his Majesty's service, that he should deliberately break with him', Vega reported,

---

[44] Mendoza to Philip II, 23 May 1587, from Paris: ibid. 92. Amusingly, Mendoza also tells Philip that Abenaes 'is on very bad terms with the French ambassador [in Turkey], who treats him with contempt, as he knew him here as a professed Christian, whereas now he is a Jew'.

[45] Advices from England, from Richard Mirth [Antonio de Vega], 30 June 1587: ibid. 116.

[46] Advices from London, 13 Sept. 1587: ibid. 141–2.

[47] Philip II to Mendoza, 18/28 Sept. 1587: ibid. 142.

I am trying so far as words can do to keep him [Lopez] pledged to us, but if the resolution is to be longer delayed, I pray you to write to me saying that his Majesty will be willing to accept his services, and so relieve me personally of the responsibility of the promise made to him. Do not name him, however, but call him the merchant.[48]

By the turn of the new year 1588 Don Antonio's fate had become inevitably linked with the information which was beginning to filter in to London regarding Spanish plans for an invasion. It may be that the first such intelligence arrived in England by means of the Jewish Marrano network in which Lopez, Nuñez, and Abenaes were the key figures. At the end of February 1588 Bernardino de Mendoza, the Spanish ambassador in Paris, was sent a letter from Francisco de Valverde and Pedro de Santa Cruz in London. These two gentlemen were Spanish prisoners of war, having been captured by the English in September 1586 while on a voyage to the Canary Islands. They had been held in London on the responsibility of two Roman Catholic merchants in whose houses they lived and had just now been released. One of these Englishmen was married to a Spanish woman, no doubt as a consequence of being engaged in trade with Spain. Valverde and Santa Cruz had become quite knowledgeable about the secret Jewish community in London, and their hostess urged them to denounce two of them, Jeronimo Pardo and Bernaldo Luis, just then visiting Lisbon, perhaps themselves connected to the machinations surrounding Don Antonio and his cause. The letter which Mendoza received was extremely damning. 'However careful your friends may be to supply information,' they wrote sarcastically, 'we are sure they are not more diligent than the Portuguese Geronimo Pardo, in Lisbon, and Bernaldo Luis, in Madrid who are relatives of Dr. Nuñez, who lives here.' When Philip received the letter, he underlined this opening passage. The two Spaniards explained that 'They carefully report hither everything that passes at Madrid and Lisbon, and transmit their news by ships which they send from Spain.' Among their goods on a recent journey were 'two packets of letters in cipher, giving a full account of the warlike preparations which were being made in Spain'. Pardo himself took care of this important intelligence:

After translating them, he carried them to Secretary Walsingham, and within two months Pardo was on his way back to Lisbon. Since then he has sent three more ships . . . By this latter ship full accounts were sent of the ships, men, and stores for the Armada in Lisbon. The despatches were delivered to Dr. Hector Nuñez whilst he was at a dinner to which he had been invited. He rose in great haste, and went direct to Secretary Walsingham's house.

[48] Advice from London from Vega, 23 Nov. 1587: ibid. 167–8.

The two Spaniards provided a good deal of other detailed evidence, and closed by asserting that they had 'all the information here set down from good Catholics, and we swear on this cross + that we are writing it in all zeal for the service of God and our King'.[49]

The two Jews were arrested almost immediately, Bernaldo Luis in Spain and Jeronimo Pardo in Lisbon. As is so often the case, Spanish trial records, of the Inquisition or otherwise, provide an invaluable source for tracing the movement of Jews during the early modern period. Bernaldo Luis gave his deposition in May 1588 in Madrid. Luis told of his birth in Lisbon, and how his family, then named Freire or Freyle, went to Antwerp, where they prospered and remained until the Spanish Fury of 1576. They emigrated to London, where they lived in Tower Ward. One of his brothers, Luis testified, worked for Antonio de Vega, the chief Spanish agent in London, who indeed seems to be the man who eventually got Luis released. Luis gave a good deal of information about the Portuguese Marrano community in London, especially the supporters of Don Antonio, although he described himself as the pretender's greatest enemy. It may be that he and his brothers had offered to have him killed in 1586. Luis also denied that Nuñez, his brother-in-law, was Don Antonio's doctor, and claimed that Nuñez had refused the post of the queen's physician, preferring to be free. In 1591 Luis would be denounced, this time in London, as one of the most efficient Spanish spies in the country, and it appears that he fled England soon afterwards. So it may be that Luis turned in these last few months before the launching of the Armada, and joined Lopez as one of the conduits of information feeding into Vega, Mendoza, and Philip II himself.[50]

Once released, Pedro de Santa Cruz also added a good deal of further intelligence in his deposition, delivered in Madrid in July. Santa Cruz had only just arrived in Madrid on 23 June 1588, but hurried to pass on his information, in these last days of preparation for the Armada. He gave a full account of the Portuguese Jews living in London, whom he said were all working on behalf of English interests to the injury of Spain. The first of the names he named was Dr Hector Nuñez, the queen's physician. Interestingly, Santa Cruz notes that the Jews of

[49] Valverde and Santa Cruz to Mendoza, from London, 27 Feb. 1587/8: ibid. 219–22.

[50] Bernaldo Luis, confession in Madrid, 13 May 1588: Archivo General de Simancas, Secretaria de Estado, Legajo 839, fo. 215: repr. (in original Spanish) in *TJHSE* 11 (1928), 37–45. Cf. notice in *Cal. SP Span.*, *1587–1603*, 326 n. Cf. ibid. *1580–6*, 675–7; ibid. *1587–1603*, 23, 242–3, 299, 326, 346, 487, 601); *Cal. SP Dom.*, *1591–4*, 101. Cf. J. A. Goris, *Étude sur les colonies marchandes méridionales à Anvers de 1488 à 1567* (Louvain, 1925), 615.

England pretended to be Protestants rather than Catholics, the opposite of what they would do in the next century, a disguise which must have greatly facilitated their movement among the élite of Elizabethan England, and helped to allay suspicions of their retaining some loyalty to Philip II. 'He knows, as it is public and notorious in London,' testified Santa Cruz in Madrid, 'that by race they are all Jews, and it is notorious that in their own homes they live as such observing their Jewish rites; but publicly they attend Lutheran Churches, and listen to the sermons, and take the bread and wine in the manner and form as do the other heretics.' The Anglo-Spanish Jewish Marranos seem to have retained a sense of humour through all of this deception as well. Francisco de Valverde ran into Alvaro de Lima, apparently Nuñez's brother, on the way back from church:

when Francisco de Valverde and Juan de Valverde were coming from Mass the said Alvaro de Lima said to them: 'Where do your Worships come from?' to which they replied: 'Sir, we come from seeing God,' and the said Alvaro de Lima thereupon replied mockingly: 'It remains very much to be seen, whether your Worships have seen God.'

The so-called secret community of Marrano Jews in Elizabethan London was therefore hardly secret at all.[51]

By the time Santa Cruz's information could be digested, the international situation had changed dramatically. A few weeks after his evidence was taken, on 19/29 July 1588, the Spanish Armada was sighted off the Cornish coast. Ten days later its defeat was complete. Whatever assistance the Marrano Jews of London may have given Elizabeth's government before that historic event, their position was greatly strengthened afterwards. Not only had their information been proven correct, but their network, stretching from London to Constantinople via the Low Countries and Iberia, was demonstrated to be an effective tool of intelligence. These English Jews remained important figures in official diplomacy even after the Armada's defeat, as plans for restoring Don Antonio to the Portuguese throne enjoyed something of a renaissance in the aftermath of the summer of 1588. Howard toyed with the idea of using Don Antonio to raise Portugal after the Armada had sailed. So too had the Privy Council the previous February talked of sending Don Antonio to Portugal to disrupt the Armada's preparations. Now that the Armada had been defeated, although Elizabeth and Burghley had initially hoped that the English

---

[51] Deposition of Pedro Santa Cruz in Madrid, 4 July 1588: Archivo General de Simancas, Secretaria de Estado: Legajo 839, fo. 183: repr. *TJHSE* 11 (1928), 45–9, with partial trans. (p. 7) of above quotations. Cf. *Cal. SP Span., 1587–1603*, 326, where the place of testimony is incorrectly given as Lisbon.

navy would chase the ships as they came back to port, or even attack the Indies treasure fleet, they were soon convinced by Howard and Drake that it would not do to exaggerate the English strength, and instead they should concentrate on wiping out the survivors once they came back to Lisbon, the main base for the Spanish navy on the Atlantic. As the area was heavily defended up the Tagus, land forces would be required as well. If the populace could be persuaded to rise in favour of Don Antonio against the Spanish oppressors, then the English task would be that much easier.[52]

Once again, an important field of activity was Constantinople, where Alvaro Mendes alias Solomon Abenaes was in place working in connection with English Jews on behalf of Don Antonio. Unfortunately, a gap in the correspondence between England and Turkey between November 1587 and 15 August 1588 prevents us from seeing exactly what transpired, although this break is probably due to the fact that Harborne left Turkey on 3 August and was replaced by Sir Edward Barton, rather than to any deliberate attempt to conceal evidence. The English position, of course, was that Turkey should send its fleet against the Spanish, a classic early modern European strategy against Spain, which might be supplemented by placing Don Antonio on the Portuguese throne in the ensuing confusion. Barton had already been in Turkey during the tenure of William Harborne, so he had a good deal of experience in dealing with the Turks.[53] In the middle of August 1588, before word of the Spanish defeat had reached Constantinople, Barton sent Walsingham a detailed report on how he believed that Turkish help could be solicited in promoting the cause of Don Antonio. He discussed in detail the three schemes on offer, that of the sultan, his own, and the course recommended by 'Don Alures Mendas [a] Portingall Jewe her Mats. most affectionate servant'. The plan of Mendes/Abenaes is most interesting, not only because it was probably jointly agreed upon with the Jews in London, but also because of its intrinsic deviousness. Unlike the sultan, who proposed taking Don Antonio's son as a hostage until the father paid the Turkish costs of the expedition to put him on the throne; unlike Barton, who wanted to pay the investors with diamonds or rubies after the galleys had set sail; Abenaes had a cheaper idea. He suggested to Barton that an ordinary merchant ship be sent to the sultan bearing the rather paltry presents of four or five pieces of broadcloth, and 'without mencion of new Ambassador to kepe theise in suspence whither her Matie will continewe the league or not'. When Barton considered the plan he had to admit that

---

[52] R. B. Wernham, *After the Armada* (Oxford, 1984), 7–18.
[53] Pears, 'Spanish Armada', 443–7.

As for Don Aluaro Mendes his opinion I esteme is noe lesse pollitike then effectionnate knowinge for certaine that the Grand Signor hath great accompte of the frendeshippe league and amitie wth. her Matie. whereby if a shippe shold come hither wthout shewe of knowledge or tydinges of an Ambr. the Grand Signor would be in a great doubte of her highnes mynde I objectinge the mane fould bennefitts her Matie. hath done for him and his Empire & the infinite charges which theis 4 yeares space she hath sustayned and yett is as vppon his request and quarrell it would make him enter into the deper consideracon thereof and perhappes cause some amends of former default.[54]

Barton followed up this letter with another a fortnight later, elaborating his compromise plan, and insisting that the agent be 'some man of accompte' also 'well knowne to Don Aluaro Mendas Portingall Jewe here resident in good favour'.[55] Like Lopez and Nuñez in London, Abenaes in Constantinople was thought to be an invaluable diplomatic asset.

Barton's letters also show how out of touch he was in that distant outpost of the Turkish Empire, for even at the very end of August he still had no idea about the outcome of the Spanish Armada's invasion. As he himself notes, it was expected that a letter from London to Constantinople might take two months to arrive. There is a sad tone to his letter of 15 September 1588, complaining of

the false aduices our adversaries send hither every weeke sometimes of the overthrowe of her majestie's fleete other times of the landinge of the Spaniards power in Scotlande then of the conspiracie betweene the Spaniards and k: of Scotts then of the taking of Barwicke and 4 other Castells more within the Lande with infinite such like which goinge about the improve are not onelie credited but even laughed at, they alleadginge to stoppe my mouthe that it is my parte soe to maintaine the credit of my prince and countrie.

Barton admitted that he had only one source of solace:

were it not that Don Solomon Abyminois, Portugall Jewe, formerlie called Don Aluaro Mendas, doth maintaine and confirme my reasons against the false information of our adversaries I should hardlye have the face to visit anie of them havinge no advises of her majesties proceadings and prosperitie of my countrie but such as I heare from my enemies be forced to sue to them therefore which is a great prejudice to her majesties creditt and hinderance to my proceadings there, my enemies prevailinge with their forged fables I havinge nothinge to alleadge against them sauing the reasons my self frame upon the mercies of god, and sure hope I have of his mightie defence of his little mount Sion.

[54] Edward Barton to Walsingham, 15 Aug. 1588: *Cal. SP For., July–Dec. 1588*, 138–9: repr. Pears, 'Spanish Armada', 447–9.
[55] Barton to Walsingham, 31 Aug. 1588: *Cal. SP For., July–Dec. 1588*, 172–5: repr. Pears, 'Spanish Armada', 449–52.

No wonder the Turks laughed at him. In the future, he more practically advised Walsingham, it might be wiser 'that at the least so longe as theis warres last with the king of Spaine aduises be vsuallie sent to me . . . monthlye yea in troblesome tymes everie fortnight and oftener', with copies to the representatives of Hungary, France, Venice, and Ragusa. More particularly, Barton was grateful to Abenaes, and thought that his help should be recognized:

not forgettinge also I beseach your honnor the faithfulness and affection of the foresaid Don Aluaro whome as your Honnor by your formers made greatlie in boundes so shall sufficientlie recompence for all his travaile and industrie in her majesties affaires yf your Honnor shall againe send the like desiringe nothinge els but to be assured that his faithfull seruice is made known to her majestie and here I referre your Honnors descretion whither your Honnor shall thincke it meet perticulerlye to mencion her majestie and your Honnors gratefull receipt of the affection he performed in time of the deceased Admirall whoe havinge mortall enmitie with my predecessor sent 9 Inghlishe captives whome the Grand Signor had commanded him to sett at libtie to the foresaid Don Aluaro for a present whence he havinge well interteyned and refreshed in his howse incontinentlie sent to Mr. Harborne not without some expence vppon the Admiralls men that brought them.[56]

By standing in support of the beleaguered English ambassador to Turkey, Abenaes earned his unwavering gratitude, and simultaneously secured the far end of the Anglo-Jewish intelligence network.

News of the Armada did not arrive until the beginning of October. Giovanni Moro, the Venetian ambassador in Constantinople, wrote on 9 October 1588 to the Doge and Senate reporting the contradictory intelligence which arrived in Turkey simultaneously. 'Alvaro Mendes was the first to report that the Spanish Armada had been routed by the English,' he recounted, 'the Ragusan representatives declared the contrary, then when the English agent went to confirm the news of the Spanish defeat the Pashas merely replied, "God grant it may be so," and showed that they doubted it.'[57] Abenaes was correct, of course, having received the information most probably from his contacts in London. One would have thought that for this and his manifold other services Abenaes would be rewarded by all parties concerned. And indeed he was by English government officials. Unfortunately, it was at precisely this moment that Don Antonio, the man Abenaes had championed unswervingly during the past eight years, chose to vent his dissatisfaction

---

[56] Barton to Walsingham, 13 Sept. 1588: *Cal. SP For., July–Dec. 1588*, 199–201: repr. in full in Pears, 'Spanish Armada', 454–8.
[57] Giovanni Moro to the Doge and Senate, 9 Oct. 1588: *Cal. SP Ven., 1581–91*, 399.

with any immediate Portuguese follow-up to the defeat of the Armada
by manœuvring to have Abenaes replaced as the English Court's Jew in
the sultan's palace.

III

Don Antonio quite naturally thought that the defeat of the Armada
would give him some advantage in being restored to the Portuguese
throne. Indeed, in September 1588 Queen Elizabeth even wrote to the
sultan of Morocco, affirming that this was her intention, perhaps in an
attempt to bring the Muslim over into Don Antonio's camp. But the
pretender found it difficult to wait for any Portuguese expedition to be
organized, and laid the blame for the delay at the door of his man in
Constantinople, Solomon Abenaes. Edward Barton was astonished to
learn from Abenaes in October that he had been replaced by a certain
David Passi or Pasmo, 'of as small present creditt here wth the Grand
Signor as former little acquaintance there wth him'. Apart from anything
else, Barton affirmed, Passi was 'besides that a man more than
suspected to fauour the Spaniarde, nay publickely knowen to depend on
him'. The man was 'conversant dailie wth our mortall aduersaries and
neuer cominge into my house or presence'. Abenaes, on the other hand,
'neuer desired other than to shewe to Don Antonio the good affection
he alwaies hath and doth beare him, requiringe nothinge in lieu thereof
but the gratefull acceptance of his service and acknoweledgement of his
sincere faithfullnes in his affayres comitted to him'. Barton was writing
to Walsingham now to ascertain if he was required to consult with Passi:
'yf such thing be there agreed vppon and commanded by your honnor I
must accordinglye to my dutie doe my best'.[58] Passi was himself a
Portuguese ex-Marrano, like Abenaes, who may indeed have already
inherited the duchy of Naxos after the death of Joseph Nasi. In any case,
he was rather more of a force in the Turkish Court than Barton gave
him credit for, being involved at that time with the physician Moses
Benveniste in levying a new subsidy on all subjects. In the next century,
when Paul Rycaut wrote his history of the Turkish Empire, it would be
remembered that '*David Passy* a Jew' was one of 'the first Authors of
this new Imposition'. Rycaut claimed that when there was a general
refusal to pay the poll tax, the Sultan Murad III was glad 'to deliver the
two Perswaders thereof to the Pleasure of the *Janizaries*; who drew them
up and down the Streets at Horses Tails, and afterwards cutting off their
Heads, in scorn tossed them from hand to hand one to another, as if

[58] Barton to Walsingham, 12/25 Oct. 1588: *Cal. SP For., July–Dec. 1588*, 282.

they had been Tennise Balls'.[59] Although there may have been some reaction to Passi's plan, and indeed he may have been wounded by the janissaries, he was not killed then but lived to remain active in Turkish politics for the next few years.[60] Whether he was really a Spanish agent is not clear, but Don Antonio certainly had no reason for abandoning his loyal servant Abenaes and thereby breaking the Lopez–Nuñez–Mendes chain.

In a sense, this was the worst time for Don Antonio to drop his man in Constantinople, for finally the English seemed ready and willing to let his invasion of Portugal take place. Elizabeth herself was now very much in favour of the expedition, and invested a good deal of money in its success, working to fit it in with the campaigning season in The Netherlands. The mission was to be led by Norris and Drake, even though their view of its objectives was somewhat different from Elizabeth's. The queen wanted to burn ships, take Lisbon, and possibly invade the Azores, but most important of all was the first objective. It had taken Spain seven years to build up the Armada, and half was lost in its failure; if the rest of the fleet could be destroyed, then England would not only be secure, but her navy could begin to cull systematically the Spanish treasure fleet. The two military men, on the other hand, were more interested in setting Don Antonio on the throne, agreeing with him in February 1589 that he would pay for the army once it landed. They doubled the number of soldiers taken on board and made plans for a full-scale invasion of Portugal. Once it was learned that the survivors of the Armada had been unable to return to base at Lisbon but had been forced to put in at Spain's north-coast ports of Santander and San Sebastian, the two conceptions were even more fundamentally at odds. Elizabeth was now talking about a raid to destroy the fifty ships which had staggered home. Norris and Drake wanted to change the European map.[61]

The expedition set sail on 18 April 1589, including far more soldiers than Elizabeth had wanted, and the earl of Essex, who came as a stowaway on the *Swiftsure*. Once at sea, the entire expedition disobeyed Elizabeth's direct orders and, instead of attacking the Spanish fleet in the north, made straight for Lisbon, since the financial backers had

---

[59] Paul Rycaut, *The Turkish History*, ed. Richard Knolles (6th edn., London, 1687), i. 707–8.
[60] Passi seems to have lived in Venice before coming to Constantinople. In 1591 he unwisely sent a letter to the Chancellor of Poland including charges against the Grand Vizier Sinan Pasha. When the letter was discovered, Passi was put in chains and exiled to Rhodes. Although he returned to Constantinople after Sinan's death, he no longer took any part in public life: Roth, *Naxos*, 204–12.
[61] Generally, see Wernham, *After the Armada*, 90–100.

nothing to gain by sinking ships, only by plundering Portugal and putting an ally on the throne. Don Antonio, meanwhile, was responsible for mobilizing the genuine anti-Spanish support for him which did exist in all social classes. But Norris and Drake delayed in a pointless fortnight's stop at Corunna before meeting up with the *Swiftsure* outside Lisbon, and their forces were considerably weakened by sickness when the entire group landed at Peniche, about 45 miles from Lisbon, and marched slowly to the capital. Without artillery the English had no way of breaching the city's defences, and with about one-third of their 6,000 men out of action, and with no real sign of mass support for Don Antonio, the invaders were forced to retreat to Drake on the coast. He, meanwhile, had not fulfilled his promise to sail up the Tagus to meet them, since he was reluctant to risk the ships he would need to attack the Azores, a move which alone could recoup the expenses which had already been laid out. Instead they hung about, capturing the ships which happened to pass by, and hoping for a last-minute relief force from home, or even from Morocco. But the queen refused them point blank, and Drake and Norris were eventually forced to send their worst ships home with what prizes they had, until by the end of June 1589 all had returned to Plymouth.

Certainly one might say without risk of contradiction that the Portuguese expedition of 1589 ended in failure. The English navy had done to itself what the Spanish Armada had failed to do, and financially it had actually managed to lose money, despite the prizes with which it returned. Worse, once home, a large number of soldiers rioted at Bartholomew Fair, and terrorized the neighbouring districts. When the final accounting was made, it was found that nearly 11,000 Englishmen had died of various causes as a result of the expedition, which was more than the total number of English in The Netherlands. Drake and Norris might argue that they had scored a blow to Philip's navy, and had set off a chain reaction that led to a lack of liquid cash with which to pay Parma's army, which by mutinying saved the Dutch from an attack in August. But it seemed a rather circuitous route to that sort of limited success, and the price was far too high. Quite simply, Drake and Norris had missed a golden opportunity to destroy the remainder of the Armada and to cripple the Spanish navy beyond recovery.[62]

Certainly, the major part of the guilt should go to Drake and to Norris, who started at the wrong end of the scale and sought private gain above national service. But Don Antonio was also to blame, not only for misjudging the extent and nature of support for his claim, but also for allowing information to seep out of his poorly paid household in a period

[62] Ibid. 92–130.

when Spanish gold seemed to buy almost everyone. Antonio de Escobar, Don Antonio's agent in France; Manuel de Andrada; and Antonio de Vega all leaked important intelligence via Mendoza in Paris and thence to Philip II himself. According to the Venetian ambassador in Spain, a Portuguese noble who had been with Don Antonio in England even managed to slip away at Corunna and to relay to Philip II himself valuable information regarding the pretender's supporters in Lisbon.[63] Andrada succeeded in obtaining a summary of the agreement made by the English generals with Don Antonio as early as March 1589, and even in passing on the news that the queen herself did not know, that the fleet would go straight to Portugal and land precisely at Peniche.[64] Don Antonio must have suspected some of this, and indeed may have blamed Abenaes in part. But so many of his confidants were in illicit contact with Spain: Lopez was only one of them.

Unfortunately for Don Antonio, he seems to have missed the significance of all this information. We have already seen how he replaced Solomon Abenaes with David Passi as his agent in Constantinople. On 8 July 1589, immediately after the return of his ill-fated expedition, Don Antonio informed 'Juan Luis' alias Esteban Ferrera da Gama that 'If you write, send your letters through Dr. Ruy Lopez, the Portuguese who is in my service and that of the Queen.' This letter, naturally, quickly found its way to Philip II's desk, where he vigorously underlined this passage.[65] Indeed, Don Antonio's continuing *naïveté* is almost pathetic. The following month he is to be found writing to Antonio de Escobar, intimately confiding in him that he suspects that his letters might be going astray. His last packet to Escobar he gave to Lopez, who in turn entrusted it to Manuel Andrada, 'who now says that they captured him, and took the letter from him in a certain place. This may be true, but I confess I doubt it'. Still, Don Antonio hoped that 'Manuel Andrada will take this letter, although he is indisposed, but I know of no other person who can pass it so well.' Sadly for Don Antonio, the only person mentioned in his letter who was not a Spanish spy was himself.[66]

Lopez, then, was still a trusted agent of Don Antonio even after the Portuguese fiasco. He wrote to Walsingham on 12 July 1589, apologizing for his part in helping to convince the government to invade

---

[63] *Cal. SP Ven.* viii. 442.

[64] *Cal. SP Span.* iv. 524; Richard Hakluyt, *The Principal Navigations Voyages Traffiques & Discoveries of the English Nation* (London, 1927–8), iv. 306–54; *The Naval Tracts of Sir William Monson*, ed. M. Oppenheim (London, 1902–14), i. 205–6.

[65] Don Antonio to 'Juan Luis', 8 July 1589: *Cal. SP Span., 1587–1603*, 547.

[66] Don Antonio to Antonio de Escobar, Aug. 1589: ibid. 554.

Portugal and put Don Antonio on the throne. Lopez wrote that he was sorry that his advice had induced the queen to spend so much money to no purpose. He said he would be writing to Don Antonio, recommending him 'to take some order for himself and his Portuguese'. In the meantime, Lopez claimed financial impecunity, blaming it on the fact that his monopoly on the import of sumac and aniseed for the next thirty-one years had been denied.[67] Things had gone terribly wrong with the Portuguese adventure, and, although Lopez does not seem to have been blamed directly, especially since the crimes of Drake and Norris were so much greater in Elizabeth's eyes, he was inevitably associated with that entire unfortunate incident. Lopez may not really have been under such great financial pressure, but that is how he perceived himself. It was about this time that he began to place himself in even greater danger by beginning to plot more vigorously and more openly.

On 21 February 1589/90, Bernardino de Mendoza in Paris wrote to his master Philip II, reporting on what had become of Don Antonio now that his hopes were dashed forever. He told of the information he had received from Manuel de Andrada in London, who had been ordered by the unfortunate pretender to prepare a ship which might take him to Brazil or Constantinople. The plan actually was for Andrada to betray Don Antonio, and, once the man was aboard, to sail straight for Gravelines or Dunkirk and deliver the pretender into Spanish hands. Some of Andrada's letters went astray, however, and he was arrested. Nevertheless, another party to the conspiracy was able to conceal himself and escape. According to this second man, Don Antonio was 'so poor that Dr. Lopez had to give him some money to buy a doublet and breeches of velvet, as those he was wearing were in holes'.[68] Somehow Andrada was released: perhaps Lopez had a hand in this; perhaps it was simply that the queen herself sympathized with the vision of permanently eliminating the impecunious pretender. In any case, when Andrada himself, on his departure from London, reported on the matter directly to Mendoza, he added the information that he had persuaded a cousin of Lopez to keep Mendoza informed of any military preparations in London, and of any of Don Antonio's actions. Andrada credited Lopez with having secured his release 'by his influence with the Queen', and, as a result, Andrada noted that when he tried to bring Lopez over to the service of Spain, Lopez told him that Mendoza had already been in contact. Andrada had a plan to hide himself in Lopez's house and pass

---

[67] Lopez to Walsingham, 12 July 1589: *Cal. SP Dom., 1581–90*, 609. Cf. no. 22, p. 609.
[68] Mendoza to Philip II, 21 Feb. 1589/90, from Paris: *Cal. SP Span., 1587–1603*, 570–1.

on secret intelligence, or even to kill Don Antonio, if King Philip should command it.[69]

Andrada, at any rate, was permitted to travel to Spain. There, in Madrid, he had an interview with Philip II himself, or at least that is what he would testify to Burghley on his next visit to England. According to Andrada, the king of Spain received him sitting in a black velvet wheelchair, on account of a severe attack of gout in the legs. He had been bled four times, and was in extreme pain.[70] On the way back to England, Andrada was shipwrecked, but in his view was miraculously saved, with all of his papers, reaching Le Havre at the beginning of July. From there he wrote directly to Dr Lopez expressing his wish to serve Queen Elizabeth. All he required now was a passport for travelling to and from France which would enable him to move about in secret.[71] Five days later he sent another very similar letter to Lopez, apparently presuming that the first had not reached its destination, but now improving his requests to include an intimate interview with the queen, all carried on in secret and in disguise. If not, then he would be forced to go to the prince of Parma, as per his Spanish instructions. Ideally, he would slip into Lopez's house, report to the queen, and then ship out to the Low Countries with no one the wiser.[72] Lopez presumably passed these letters on to Lord Burghley, who endorsed the second one himself.[73] On the face of it, what happened is that Lopez had turned Andrada into a double agent during the time of his first arrest, and now he was making his first report in that capacity. Andrada, however, did not reveal the even more important secret that he was carrying, that Lopez himself was a double agent, trying to profit like everyone else in the grey world of Anglo-Spanish intelligence.

We are somewhat better placed, however, to see what drove Lopez during those months. Unknown to Burghley, a secret memorandum had already been exchanged between King Philip II and Don Christafora de Moro, the Spanish secretary of state. Moro had also met Andrada during the spy's visit to Spain, and now had a clear idea of what should be done. Moro reported to Philip that there were three things which Andrada proposed. The first was to use Dr Lopez to open peace negotiations with England: Lopez had already assured Andrada of

---

[69] Andrada to Mendoza, 5 Mar. 1590/1: *Cal. SP Dom., 1591–4*, 16.

[70] Examination of Andrada, 18 Aug. 1591: ibid. 92–3.

[71] Andrada to Lopez, 1/11 July 1591: ibid. 65.

[72] Andrada to Lopez, 6/16 July 1591: ibid. 69. There seem to have been additional letters sent from St Malo on 11 and 28 June, which have gone missing. Presumably they said the same thing as these letters of July.

[73] Translation of above letter from the Portuguese, endorsed 2 Aug. 1591 by Burghley: 'Andrada to Dr. Lopez, by the Wyder of Seville.': ibid. 69.

success. The second plan was that by 'means of the same Dr. Lopez he will undertake, if so desired, that Don Antonio shall never leave that country (England)'. The sinister hint is unmistakable. Andrada's third proposal was that if it was desired that Don Antonio's life should be spared, he might be expelled from England. Apart from these three things, Moro wrote, 'which are the main objects of his coming', Andrada also claimed to have an understanding with 'an Englishman, a brother-in-law of the said Dr. Lopes', perhaps Dunstan Añes, who 'will also attempt to do another secret service which he (Andrada) recommended to him. This understanding with the brother-in-law is unknown to Dr. Lopez'. Moro advised Philip to let Andrada carry on with the peace negotiations as a pretext for dealing with the more pressing matter of Don Antonio. Indeed, Moro's letter describes in detail what actually did occur when Andrada arrived in France: 'He may therefore go to Calais, and write from there to Dr. Lopez that his coming has been prompted by the common good, begging him to send a passport. When he receives the passport, he may proceed whithersoever Dr. Lopez may instruct him.' Andrada's story was to be that when he presented Lopez's plan for peace negotiations in Spain, the government ministers demanded letters of credence or some other sort of proof: 'This will lead them to infer that, if he had brought such credentials he would have been favourably listened to.' This ruse would enable Andrada to work through Lopez's brother-in-law and through Lopez himself, who 'gave his word to get Don Antonio expelled from England if his Majesty desired'. Lopez, Moro noted, 'should be asked to fulfil his promise in this respect, as his offer to do so has been accepted, and his good service in all things will be acknowledged'. Generally, Andrada was to be empowered and paid to spy for Spain, and to pay those who supplied him with information, including Lopez's brother-in-law. Finally, Andrada asked 'for a jewel to be given to him for the daughter of Dr. Lopez, and he attaches importance to this'. After Philip had seen the document, and approved it, Moro provided a more detailed budget, and suggested that Lopez's daughter be given 'one of the old jewels from his Majesty's caskets'. He thought it might be possible to buy off his brother-in-law in this way as well.[74]

Andrada's plan, approved by the Spanish secretary of state and the king of Spain, promoted by Dr Roderigo Lopez and members of his family, did not go entirely according to schedule. For one thing, Andrada was arrested at Rye the moment he set foot on English soil. On 2/12 August 1591 he wrote an anguished letter to Burghley begging to

[74] Memorandum concerning Andrada, Christoforo de Moro to Philip II, n.d. = 1591: repr. Hume, *Treason*, 162–4.

be interrogated by him alone or by one of his agents. He pleaded with him to keep his identity secret, and claimed to be giving out abroad that he was an agent of Philip II, sent to redeem Spanish prisoners of war held in England. He told Burghley he would explain it all when he saw him.[75] On the same day Andrada wrote to Don Antonio, begging to be forgiven for his past errors and hoping to see him soon in order to serve him. Burghley had a copy of this letter as well.[76] Burghley immediately gave instructions for Dr Lopez, 'sent by King Antonio', to journey to Rye in order to interrogate Andrada, described as a gentleman of Don Antonio, who offered to serve Elizabeth but was suspected of designs against her. Burghley ordered that Andrada was to be treated civilly at first, and then threatened 'to induce him in fear of his life to disclose the truth'. Finally, his letters and papers, Burghley commanded, were to be examined . . . by Dr Lopez.[77]

At his interrogation, conducted by Roderigo Lopez himself, and in Portuguese, Andrada gave further details of his mission, which basically was to string along the English with false hopes of a Spanish peace, while Philip prepared another attack. Andrada represented himself as a hit-man sent by Philip to murder Don Antonio, but actually acting in complete loyalty to the Portuguese pretender and the English queen his patroness, in order to serve his country, Portugal, and revenge himself for the many injustices inflicted on the persons and property of his own family and of his entire nation. It was probably at one of these meetings that Andrada passed on 'a Jewell from the King of *Spaine* to the said Doctor, with an Abrazo, as a Token of the King's Acceptance of *Lopes* Services, with Promises of great Rewards'.[78] Andrada said there was much more he could tell, but insisted on doing so in private conversation with Burghley alone. For a character reference, Andrada referred the Lord Treasurer to Dr Roderigo Lopez.[79]

IV

Lopez had therefore by the summer of 1591 become very deeply involved in the murky world of intelligence gathering and the

[75] Andrada to Burghley, 2/12 Aug. 1591, in Portuguese: *Cal. SP Dom., 1591–1594*, 82.   [76] Andrada to Don Antonio, 2/12 Aug. 1591, with trans.: ibid. 82.
[77] Instructions from Burghley to Mr Mills, 3 Aug. 1591: ibid. 82–3.
[78] *A Collection of State Papers . . . Reposited in the Library at Hatfield House*, ed. William Murdin (London, 1759), 670.
[79] Examination of Andrada, in Portuguese, 18 Aug. 1591: *Cal. SP Dom., 1591–1594*, 92–3; French trans. of above, with questions asked, endorsed as brought to Chichester by Dr Lopez: ibid. 93; Andrada to Burghley, 18 Aug. 1591: ibid. 92, 93–4.

concomitant plotting against political figures. He had given Queen Elizabeth, King Philip II, and Don Antonio of Portugal each to understand that he was primarily working for them alone, and that his chief loyalties lay with them. It may be that he intended to try his fortune in the last resort with the party that promised the greatest financial reward: a triple agent, after all, earns triple pay. But what he did not take into account were the political vicissitudes which might render his position unbearably precarious.

The first of Dr Lopez's new problems was the earl of Essex. At least after the death of Walsingham, the secret intelligence service of the earl of Essex was probably the best in England. Essex had made himself the leader of the anti-Cecil faction at Court, opposed to peace with Spain, and grounded on the earl's close personal friendship with the queen. Burghley might have continued Walsingham's contacts, but whether the reason was miserliness or inefficiency, many of his agents defected to Essex's camp. Francis Bacon's elder brother Anthony, who had formerly deciphered documents for Walsingham, now worked for Essex, as did Antonio Perez, formerly Philip II's trusted minister. A man like Andrada now had three places to which he might sell information: to Essex, to Burghley, or to Philip II. Many spies had it all ways, bringing deliberately leaked information from Philip II and delivering similar but significantly different reports to Burghley and Essex. Burghley's service relied more heavily on international merchants, which included a number of Jews, than did that of Essex. But Essex in any case was unlikely to let a potentially big fish like Lopez pass through his net unnoticed.[80]

Bishop Godfrey Goodman of Gloucester was only a child when Lopez was put on trial, but he was close enough to the events themselves for his views to have some significant weight. According to Goodman, after the death of his father-in-law Walsingham in 1590, Essex was once again restored to favour and admitted to the Court, hoping himself to inherit the mantle of chief intelligencer to the queen. Towards this end, Goodman writes, then 'did he speak to Dr. Lopez, who was a Portugal born, the Queen's physician (as at that time there were many Portugal physicians here, and we did suspect them all to be Jews, as I knew one was,) and told him that many did practise treason against the Queen'. Essex asked Lopez to be a double agent, to pretend to work for the Spanish but in reality to report directly back to him. Goodman claims that Lopez replied in these words: 'My lord, this is a very great business and a dangerous: you are now in favour, but how long you may continue we know not. You may die, and then the whole treason will be laid upon

---

[80] See generally Stone, *Sir Horatio Palavicino*, 250–3.

me.' Lopez was very wise to decline becoming involved in the schemes
laid by the earl of Essex, but according to Goodman his mistake was in
allowing the earl's offer to become more widely known. Both Essex and
Lopez himself went to the queen, who advised Lopez to stick to
medicine, but to send her any information he might receive from his
Portuguese contacts in the normal course of his business. Lopez,
according to Goodman, began only thereafter a regular intercourse of
letters:

and as soon as ever Lopez had received any intelligence, he went instantly to the
Queen and acquainted her majesty therewith; and afterwards he went to the
Earl of Essex and acquainted him: then did the Earl of Essex come to the court
and acquainted her with the same; and the Queen knowing it before, did but
laugh at the Earl of Essex; and so it fell out several times, whereby the earl saw
himself utterly disappointed, for though he had gotten an intelligencer, yet he
proved not to be his intelligencer, but he went immediately to the Queen.

Goodman thought, perhaps in understatement, that this 'bred very ill
blood between the Earl and Dr. Lopez'.[81]

Lopez's second problem involved the instability of the Jewish
connection between Don Antonio and Constantinople. The years
following the defeat of the Armada were characterized by the inexorable
decline of Don Antonio's hopes. The pretender may have suspected that
his court in exile was riddled with spies, but in any case he did make
some effort to improve his representation in Turkey, which he always
thought would come to his aid at some point in the future. There too the
situation was difficult. Edward Barton, the English ambassador,
complained that 'avarise hath stopped all their eares and I singe
continuallye to deaf men'.[82] Burghley tried to shore up English interests
there by following Barton's advice and sending Solomon Abenaes a
message of thanks in October 1590, in return for a letter that the Jew
had sent to Elizabeth via Roderigo Lopez. The Queen did 'command
me to give you thanks', Burghley wrote, 'praying you earnestly to
continue as you have done up to the present'. Elizabeth also encouraged
Abenaes to continue to serve faithfully the so-called king of Portugal,

---

[81] Godfrey Goodman, *The Court of King James the First*, ed. J. S. Brewer (London,
1839), i. 149–52. Francis Bacon also described Lopez after his trial and execution as 'of
nation a Portuguese, and suspected to be in sect secretly a Jew (though here he
conformed himself to the rites of Christian religion)': Francis Bacon, 'A True Report of
the Detestable Treason, Intended by Dr. Roderigo Lopez', in *Works*, ed. J. Spedding, *et
al.* (London, 1857–74), viii. 271–87, esp. 278. This narrative was not published until
1657.
[82] Barton to Walsingham, 3 Jan. 1588/9: *Cal. SP For., Jan–July 1589*, 12–13: printed
in Pears, 'Spanish Armada', 461–3.

Don Antonio.[83] But by that time David Passi was back in town, and soon completely usurped Abenaes as the agent of Don Antonio and his cause. By the following May, Barton seems to have gone with the tide, and wrote to Burghley adopting Don Antonio's fraudulent claim 'that the infinite riches heaped up by the said Mendes was iniustlye gotten'. Barton suggested that Burghley contact the sultan informing him of this, with the aim of confiscating Abenaes's wealth.[84]

Abenaes, however, was rather quicker than Barton, and sent a personal envoy to Queen Elizabeth to lay his case before her. His man was Salomon Cormano, who in his letter to the queen and in his conversations with government officials managed to convince the English authorities that there was nothing to Don Antonio's charges.[85] Burghley wrote to Abenaes putting him at his ease, and Elizabeth herself wrote to the sultan explaining how things stood.[86] Not only did she affirm her continued support for Abenaes, but she noted that she and many other Christian princes had invited him to live in their kingdom and enjoy the prosperity that would be his, but he chose rather to live in Constantinople, where now the schemes of the Spanish king were endangering his safety and well-being.[87] This letter apparently did the trick, and in July 1592 Abenaes wrote to Elizabeth thanking her for her timely intervention.[88]

If we look at Barton's letter to Burghley, however, we get a rather fuller picture of the complicated nature of this relationship. On 19 August 1592 Barton reported having finally received Burghley's letter of the previous April, it having been further and unnecessarily delayed by Abenaes displaying Elizabeth's to the sultan for three weeks, which 'he caried vp and doune wth him shewinge them in every tauerne and bragging of them, interpretinge them, at his pleasure to the comon people, and boastinge that by them came the confermation of my disgradinge at his suit and request'. More interesting from our point of view is the information which Abenaes gave out concerning Cormano's

---

[83] Burghley to Abenaes, 15 Oct. 1590: *Cal. SP Dom., 1581–90*, 693.

[84] Barton to Burghley, 10 May 1591: *Cal. SP For., July 1590–May 1591*, 80.

[85] Salomon Cormano to Elizabeth, in Spanish (copy), Mar. 1591/2: BL MS Lansdowne 69, fo. 70: repr. *TJHSE* 11 (1928), 64–5.

[86] Burghley? to Abenaes, 22 Mar. 1591/2, in Latin: *Cal. SP For., June 1591–Apr. 1592*, 76. Cf. pp. 503–4 (analysis), and generally Wernham, *After the Armada* for further details. Cf. T20: Barton to ?Burghley, from Constantinople, 23 Apr. 1592, fo. 169. Cf. same to same, 11 Apr. 1592, referred to in Barton's letter of 19 Aug. 1592 below.

[87] Elizabeth to sultan, in Latin (copy), Mar. 1591/2: BL MS Lansdowne 67, fo. 252: repr. *TJHSE* 11 (1928), 65–6.

[88] Abenaes to Elizabeth, in Spanish, 28 July 1592: *Cal. SP For., May 1592–June 1593*, T3.

activities while in London. According to Abenaes, Barton informed Lord Burghley, Cormano while in England

did invite and banquett your Hon^r and all the Nobilitie; that your honor ofte visited him at his house; that he and all his trayne vsed publickely the Jewes rytes in prayinge, accompayned wth divers secrett Jewes resident in London; that ofte both publickely and privately he had familiar conference with her Majestie of whom he was as royally and gratiously receaved as the Ambassadore of any Christian prince.

The whole embassy was very expensive, amounting, with banquets and gifts to English officials, to about 5,000 ducats of gold. Barton himself was still very bitter about the entire affair, and told Burghley that the main problem was whether 'ther may be any friendshipp betwene a Christian and a Jewe wch by experience I heere have of them I knowe to be a thing vnpossible'. Barton noted that what made the Abenaes affair more galling was that 'in Sinan Bassa his time I toke him out of the gallies: for wch he hath since geuen me a Jeweishe rewaurd'. In the meantime, Barton hoped that he himself would have the opportunity of defending his actions, and until then begged that Abenaes's version of events not be taken entirely at face value.[89]

The ends of the string on both sides were becoming somewhat disconnected from Lopez's point of view, then. His kinsman Abenaes, while apparently back in English favour, was at odds with Edward Barton, the English ambassador in Constantinople, and furthermore had a powerful rival for the sultan's ear in David Passi. In London, meanwhile, Essex had become a dangerous opponent, now that Lopez had refused to work for him and had embarrassed him before the queen. If what Abenaes was bruiting about Constantinople was true, then many people in London must have had some idea of the existence of a secret Jewish community there, one that conformed outwardly to Christian decorum but whose members prayed clandestinely according to the Jewish faith.

Significantly, it was just at that moment that Christopher Marlowe's *The Jew of Malta* opened in London, first performed on 26 February 1592.[90] Apart from its celebrated literary merit, the play is instructive for the information that we can glean from it of the type of picture of contemporary Jewish life which might be thought to appeal to audiences in London precisely at this time. In the very first scene of the play, Barabas the Jew lists the wealthy Jews of his age, chief among them being '*Nones* in *Portugall*'.[91] Dr Hector Nuñez, it will be remembered,

[89] Barton to Burghley, from Constantinople, 19 Aug. 1592: ibid. T1.

[90] Christopher Marlowe, *Complete Works*, ed. F. Bowers (Cambridge, 1973), i. 255.

[91] I. i. 125.

had died in March of the previous year, and we have already seen how well known he was in the capital. It is not often realized how much of a black comedy *The Jew of Malta* really is, making sport of popular stereotypes of the Jew. When a friar hears that Barabas has done something terrible, his first response is, 'What, has he crucified a child?'[92] There are references to noses: 'Oh brave, master, I worship your nose for this'; 'God-a-mercy nose; come let's begone.'[93] The Jewish diet comes in for fun: ' 'Tis a strange thing of that Jew,' Marlowe's audience heard, 'he lives upon pickled Grashoppers, and sauc'd Mushrumbs.'[94] Barabas even retained some secret belief in Christianity, as was often thought to be the case with Jews, swearing by '*Corpo di dio*'.[95] Finally, when Barabas dies, in his last breath he reverses the litany in the Book of Common Prayer, and damns 'Christians, dogges, and Turkish Infidels'.[96]

We may have some indication of a royal sense of humour regarding the Jews during the weeks that Marlowe's play was performed by Elizabeth's decision to grant Lopez, either by purchase or possibly by gift, no fewer than twenty-eight tons of papal bulls captured in an English expedition against the Spanish fleet in July 1592. These bulls, 1,458,000 in number to be precise, were papal indulgences, divided into two categories: for 'lyvinge bodyes' and for 'dead bodyes', and were to have been sold for two reals apiece. Their acquisition by Elizabeth's Jewish physician was clearly a speculative rather than a puritanical venture. As soon as he had them in his possession, Lopez and his partner planned to load them on a boat sailing for the West Indies, hoping to sell them there.[97] Philip II himself was very upset by this turn of events, and was informed by one of his agents in London that if 'they be not ransomed everything will be lost'.[98] Apart from the bulls, the ships were also carrying 112 tons of quicksilver, missals, and breviaries. Philip II was told that 'Francisco Spinola, the Genoese, a prisoner in London, who was captured on his way from New Spain, had obtained his liberation and had purchased the missals, etc.' The Spanish agent wrote to the king hoping that this was part of some devious plan, for if this was an interloping operation 'he is doing a very daring thing'. Elizabeth herself granted the bulls a Tudor equivalent of an export licence, and Spinola and Lopez bought a ship to send out the papistic

---

[92] III. vi. 49. [93] II. iii. 173; IV. i. 23. [94] IV. iv. 61–2.
[95] I. ii. 90. [96] V. v. 86.

[97] M. Oppenheim, *A History of the Administration of the Royal Navy and of Merchant Shipping in Relation to the Navy* (London, 1896), 398–400, incl. BL MS Lansdowne 70, which describes the capture of the two Spanish ships.

[98] Don Pedro de Valdes to Philip II, 19 Mar. 1592/3: *Cal. SP Span.*, *1587–1603*, 598.

documents.[99] Once the ship arrived in the New World, however, the pope's agent argued that despite their blessing from Sixtus V, they had lost their virtue by having been in the possession of unbelievers, heretics, and worse. Lopez and his agent countered that their very appearance in the New World after all these vicissitudes was a Catholic miracle, but the speculation does not seem to have been a great success.[100]

By then Lopez was already very deeply involved in Spanish espionage, at the same time that he strengthened his contacts at both the English and Turkish Courts. If Elizabeth's gift of one and a half million papal indulgences must have seemed to be a rather good joke, perhaps in the same light must be seen Lopez's trying to pass on to the queen one of the jewels that he received from Philip II. It was a gold ring, with a large ruby and a great diamond, the value of which was thought to approach 100 guineas. According to Francis Bacon, this 'jewel when Lopez had accepted, he cunningly cast with himself that if he should offer it to her Majesty, first he was assured she would not take it'. The very gift of such a valuable item, Lopez hoped, 'should lay her asleep and make her secure of him for greater matters'. Bacon claimed that when Lopez offered her the ring, 'with protestations of his fidelity', Elizabeth, 'as a princess of magnanimity, not apt to fear or suspicion, returned it to him with gracious words'.[101] The Spanish ring sent by Philip II would later become one of the most important exhibits in Lopez's trial. What made all the difference was whether Elizabeth actually knew the ring was from Philip II.

By all accounts, Lopez spent 1592 and the first half of 1593 conducting negotiations with Spanish agents for payment towards a plot against the queen. Leaving aside for the moment the question of whether or not he was acting secretly on behalf of the English, it is clear that Lopez was deeply involved in the plan. Andrada actually lived at Lopez's house,[102] and the haggling that went on did not seem to be concerned with the deed itself but rather with whether Lopez would be paid before or after the event. By now yet another old Don Antonio conspirator was involved in the negotiations: Esteban Ferrera da Gama, a down-and-out gentleman who for some reason enjoyed the confidence of Philip II, if not of Lopez, who would trust only Andrada. Later on, da

---

[99] Oppenheim, *History*, 398; Valdes to Philip II, 29 Mar. 1593: *Cal. SP Span., 1587–1603*, 598.

[100] Oppenheim, *History*, 398–9. Cf. M. J. Kohler, 'Dr. Rodrigo Lopez, Queen Elizabeth's Jewish Physician, and his Relations to America', *PAJHS* 17 (1909), 9–25.

[101] Bacon, 'True Report', 279–80. Cf. Birch, *Anthony Bacon*, i. 159, who valued the ring at £100.

[102] Richard Young, London JP, to Sir Robert Cecil, 28 Nov. 1592: Hist. MSS Comm., *Salisbury IV* (1892), 248.

Gama would claim that Lopez had sent letters to Moro in Madrid saying that he was willing to serve Philip II in every way possible, even if it meant the death of the queen. Da Gama believed that he was serious, and that the only obstacle was money: Lopez was demanding 50,000 crowns for the job, the exact sum that Don Antonio had given Lopez to be paid in Portugal. If caught, Lopez would thus be able to explain away the two payments as one. Lopez boasted of an anonymous great lord at Court who was a friend of his, and who was always close about the queen. He also said that Don Antonio would be poisoned at the first illness as well. Andrada confirmed, according to his partner da Gama, that Lopez was willing to poison Queen Elizabeth and Don Antonio both. Andrada himself left England for the Low Countries, never to return, on 24 April 1593. Thenceforth his contact with Lopez would be via da Gama and his own servant John, who would arrange to meet secretly with the doctor in the back garden of Lopez's house. By July yet another man was privy to the projected conspiracy: Manuel Luis Tinoco, a servant of Don Antonio's who was also secretly working for Philip II, perhaps because his family was still in Portugal. In any case, even Lopez must have realized by now that too many people were involved in his plot if he had any intention of keeping it a secret.[103]

V

The involvement of so many untrustworthy characters in a plot to kill Don Antonio and Queen Elizabeth was Lopez's first mistake. His second was to transform Essex's hatred into active political opposition. In the summer of 1593 Lopez took lodgings at Windsor, close to Don Antonio and to Antonio Perez, formerly a minister in the service of the king of Spain, and now in exile in England. According to Bishop Goodman, it was at one of Lopez's meetings with these men that

making merry with them, Lopez began bitterly to inveigh against the Earl of Essex, telling some secrecies, how he had cured him, and of what diseases, with some other things which did disparage his honour. But as soon as Lopez was gone, they went instantly to the Earl of Essex, and, to ingratiate themselves in his favour, did acquaint him with all the several passages.

The result was predictable:

Here the earl was so much incensed, that he resolved to be revenged on him; and now he began to possess the Queen that Lopez was a very villain, and had

[103] Confession of da Gama before the earl of Essex, Sir Thos. Wilkins and Wm. Waad, 18–19 Feb. 1593/4: *Cal. SP Dom., 1591–4*, 434; Bacon, 'True Report', 279, 282–3; *State Papers*, ed. Murdin, 671.

poisoned others, and that he suspected him for the death of his father-in-law Secretary Walsingham, and that he had other proofs against him, and so did not doubt but he played the villain on both sides, and did intend to poison the Queen; and so far prevailed with the Queen, that being then at Hampton Court, and Dr. Lopez attending there, he was arrested of high treason and carried to the Tower.[104]

This, as we shall see, is a severe telescoping of what actually happened. We have already seen that Roderigo Lopez had a long past and continuing involvement with Spanish espionage which made him far from the blameless victim of pique that Goodman would have it. Nevertheless, Goodman's testimony years after the actual event is important for the fact that he too puts his finger on that afternoon at Windsor as having been crucial for turning Essex against Lopez and thereby hastening his downfall and execution.

At the same time, Abenaes was writing to Lopez in a worried attempt to put things right in England. Abenaes was still concerned about the information emanating from Constantinople from David Passi, proclaiming his loyalty to 'King Anthony',

> And I would be gladd that the Queenes Matie (whome I am bownd to serve all my Lyfe) did know what King she hath in hir countrey, & whome she hath of me heere who day & night doe nothing ells when it falleth to purpose but extoll hir Greatnes to the heavens, and in all wherin I am heard I doe my office & part as hir trusty servaunt, ffor hir embassado^r. hath so much to doe to cleere him from matters wherin he hath medled.

'I doe well see how weary you wilbe with this longe letter', Abenaes apologized, and indeed it was a very tiresome communication. But it was addressed to 'Doctor Ruy Lopes cheeff phisician to the Queenes Matie of ingland in London', for by this means a direct connection was drawn between Elizabeth and Abenaes in Turkey, via the Council of State, which received a translation the following March. No doubt Philip II had word shortly thereafter.[105]

Everything was beginning to unravel. Da Gama was arrested in England on 18 October 1593, possibly in Lopez's own house, and handed over to Don Antonio, tainted with the definite suspicion that he had been a double agent for the Spanish Crown.[106] Da Gama, fearful for his life, thereupon took the foolhardy step of writing 'a little Ticket'

---

[104] Goodman, *Court*, i. 152–3. See also the documents in *A Spaniard in Elizabethan England: The Correspondence of Antonio Perez's Exile*, ed. G. Ungerer (London, 1974–6), esp. i. 230, 241; ii. 226, 254.

[105] 'Don Sollomon Abenn Iaex' to Roderigo Lopes, 24 Aug. 1593, recd by the Council, Mar. 1593/4: PRO, SP For., Turkey, 2: repr. *TJHSE* 11 (1928), 71–6.

[106] *Cal. SP Dom., 1591–4*, 456; Dimock, 'Lopez', 453 n.

directly to Lopez, pleading with him not to send further incriminating letters to Antwerp. Lopez compounded the error by replying, assuring da Gama that everything would be arranged towards his release. This was the first time that Lopez had actually committed himself to paper. It may be that he had not even been under suspicion before then, or, as Burghley's party would later say, 'this glymeringe and Overture brought great Light to the further Discovery of this divellishe and abominable Practyse'. But both letters were immediately intercepted, and Essex's agents had him under surveillance at least from that moment. 'Upon so narrow a point', wrote Francis Bacon after the event, 'consisted the safety of her Majesty's life, already sold by avarice to malice and ambition, but extraordinarily preserved by that watchman which never slumbereth.' Tinoco, meanwhile, was still in the Low Countries, trying to agree on terms between Lopez and Philip II.[107] He arrived at Calais at the beginning of December, and sent messages to Burghley and Queen Elizabeth proclaiming his desire to serve the English, enclosing a reference from a local English merchant.[108] But Tinoco was arrested in the middle of January upon his arrival in England, and on his person were found letters to da Gama from the Spanish ministers resident at Brussels.[109] Tinoco's claim was that all he wanted to do was 'to throw himself at Her Majesty's feet, and discover things important for her life and kingdom, which he has heard from the ministers of the King of Castile, and to reveal the intentions and secret designs of her enemies'.[110] But it was really too late for such talk: Elizabeth's ministers were more interested in obtaining information from Tinoco about the plot against the queen's life.

Tinoco's first lengthy interrogation on 15 January 1593/4 produced few surprises. 'The King of Spain has determined to murder the Queen,' he revealed, but everyone already knew that. Tinoco claimed that he had originally served Don Antonio faithfully, until July 1593, 'seeing him ungrateful, and poor of counsel and government, and in his sickness remembering nobody'. Tinoco recounted how he sought advice from da Gama, and consulted with the Spanish ministers in Brussels, who gave him the letters which had been found on his person. But in the midst of the interrogation, Tinoco let it drop that da Gama's task 'was to try and win Dr. Lopez, and endeavour to draw a letter from him,

---

[107] Bacon, 'True Report', 284–5; *State Papers*, ed. Murdin, 673.

[108] Tinoco to Burghley, 21/31 Dec. 1593, from Calais: *Cal. SP Dom., 1591–4*, 395; Tinoco to Elizabeth, 21/31 Dec. 1593, from Calais: ibid. 395; Thos. Jeffery to Burghley, 21/31 Dec. 1593, from Calais: ibid. 394–5.

[109] Count Fuentes to da Gama, 2/12 Dec. 1593, from Brussels: ibid. 390–1; Stephen de Ibarra to da Gama, 4/14 Dec. 1593, from Brussels: ibid. 391.

[110] Tinoco to Elizabeth, 21/31 Dec. 1593.

promising to do service; he was to remind Lopez that he had daughters, and they should not want marriages'. If this was his mission, da Gama was completely successful, for we have already seen that Lopez was still beyond suspicion until these letters came to light.[111]

Dr Roderigo Lopez was arrested on 21 January 1593/4. According to Francis Bacon, 'Lopez himself at his first apprehension and examination did indeed deny, and deny with deep and terrible oaths and execrations, the very conferences and treaties with Ferrera [da Gama] or Andrada about the empoisonment.'[112] Lopez was examined before Burghley, in the presence of his son Robert Cecil and the earl of Essex, the three statesmen who were now empowered by the queen to look into the entire matter. This was a strange committee of inquiry which could easily have become completely paralysed and ineffective. According to Anthony Birch, relying on the papers of Anthony Bacon, the 'matter against Lopez had been of a long time sifted out by the earl, who was opposed in his prosecution of the inquiry by the other two'. Not only were the Cecils themselves deeply involved with Lopez, but Essex and his secret service had not yet had a major intelligence success to rival their own spies. As soon as they heard the news of Lopez's arrest, Sir Robert Cecil sent a messenger down to London to brief the queen, and to have her know that 'in the poor man's house were found no kind of writings of intelligences, of which he was accused, or otherwise, that hold might be taken of him'. The three men managed to agree on putting Lopez under house arrest at Essex House under the supervision of Gilly Mericke, steward to the earl. Unfortunately, by the time Essex got to London, Elizabeth was convinced that the entire affair was baseless, and grew out of jealousy towards her personal physician. Elizabeth

took him up, calling him *rash and temerarious youth*, to enter into a matter against the poor man, which he could not prove, and whose innocence she knew well enough; but malice against him, and no other, hatch'd all this matter, which displeas'd her much, and the more, for that, she said, her honor was interested herein.

Essex was so humiliated and upset by this tongue-lashing that he retired to his quarters for two days, and refused to see anyone but Admiral Lord Howard.[113]

---

[111] Emanuel Louis [Tinoco], 'Advertisements to be made known to Her Majesty, for the safeguard of her person', 15 Jan. 1593/4: ibid. 411–14. Cf. Tinoco to Cecil, 16 Jan. 1593/4: ibid. 414–15.

[112] Bacon, 'True Report', 286. For the Lopez affair after his arrest, see also E. M. Tenison, *Elizabethan England* (Leamington Spa, 1932–51), ix. 247–67.

[113] Birch, *Memoirs*, i. 150.

Essex had cause to take heart. From his chambers, he co-ordinated the gathering of evidence which would vindicate him before the queen. On 23 January 1593/4 Tinoco gave a statement which told the story of the jewel given by Philip II to Lopez, the same stone that the doctor had attempted to give to the queen, two years before. Tinoco recounted how da Gama had promised the Spanish ministers that Lopez was willing to serve the king of Spain.[114] The Cecils were privy to this information, and were beginning to take it in, although they still refused to see Lopez as a proper conspirator. Burghley added a note to his son which he sent the same day: 'In folly I see no point of treason intended to the Queen,' he affirmed, 'but a readiness to make some gain.'[115] Essex, however, was elated that his rather sketchy information was now becoming fleshed out with further testimony. He expressed his renewed confidence in a letter to Anthony Bacon sent five days after Tinoco's latest confession. Essex described how busy he had been during the past week,

having been so tir'd with examinations, as I had scarce leisure to eat. I have discovered a most dangerous and desperate treason. The point of conspiracy was her majesty's death. The executioner should have been Dr. Lopez; the manner poison. This I have so followed, as I will make it appear as clear as the noon-day.

Indeed, the following day at noon, on 29 January 1593/4, Lopez was brought from Essex House to the Tower, and at seven in the morning next was examined before Robert Cecil and Essex himself.[116]

This was only the first of many interrogations, not only of Lopez, but of everyone who might possibly have been part of a plot to poison the queen. After the event, even the Cecils had to give grudging admiration to the fact that

a noble and steady Hand havinge gotten once one End, it was never left untill every little Fold was undon; and the whole Lengthe, Bredthe, and Depthe of the Treason laid quite and plainly open. It would make a long and unpleasant Discourse in some Respects to set downe all the Confessions, Examinations, Depositions, Declarations, Messages, Letters, Tickets, Tokens, Conferences, Plotts and Practyses taken, discovered and intercepted, being so fast a Work of Treason, as was by little and little sapped, and, like good Pioneers, every Day Ground was gotten.[117]

The first three weeks produced no further hard evidence or even provocative speculation. On 18 February 1593/4, however, a major

---

[114] Statement by Tinoco, 23 Jan. 1593/4: *Cal. SP Dom., 1591–4*, 416–17.

[115] Burghley to Robert Cecil, 23 Jan. 1593/4: Cambridge University Library, MS E e 3-56, no. 15: quoted in Read, *Burghley and Elizabeth*, 498.

[116] Birch, *Memoirs*, 152.   [117] *State Papers*, ed. Murdin, 673.

breakthrough occurred. Before Essex, Sir Thomas Wilkes and William Waad, Esteban Ferrera da Gama confessed to having been given about April last two letters from Roderigo Lopez, penned in the doctor's own house by da Gama himself, who wrote 'the letters from Lopez's lips'. They were addressed to Don Christoforo de Moro, and, although obscurely worded, their import was that Lopez would do all that Philip II desired. According to da Gama, Lopez would have poisoned the queen if required, for the doctor himself so admitted: he was merely waiting for the order from Spain, which had not yet arrived. It was only a question of money. Lopez also boasted of his friendship with 'a great Lord, always about the Queen' who might be of use in this endeavour. According to da Gama, Manuel de Andrada had told him that Lopez was willing to perform a double murder, and dispatch both the queen and Don Antonio at the same time. The queen would require a specific answer from Spain; Don Antonio would die from the first illness that befell him.[118]

Da Gama's confession was damning, if not yet fatal. Although Essex had already brought up the issue of poison in his letter to Anthony Bacon, this was the first time that this accusation against Lopez had appeared in an official document. Tinoco's confession four days later only compounded Lopez's problem. On 22 February 1593/4 Tinoco told the Council that he had just remembered some additional points, the most important of which was the fact that Andrada had told him that by order of Lopez secret intelligence was communicated to Mendoza, Philip II's ambassador in Paris. Among this information was detailed intelligence of the navy sent by the English in the Portuguese expedition, including reports of men and ammunition. On the return of the fleet, Lopez was said to have sent Andrada to Madrid, offering to poison Don Antonio, and requesting the jewel which was eventually offered to Elizabeth.[119] The following day, Tinoco amplified his confession with the additional damning nugget that, according to letters written by Andrada that he himself had been shown by Count Fuentes in Brussels, Lopez had bound himself to kill Queen Elizabeth with poison. The only problem seemed to be agreeing on the exact sum to be paid.[120]

Needless to say, da Gama and Tinoco were hardly the men of character who could produce even between them the watertight case that Essex would have preferred. Yet the details of their stories, preserved in the state papers, are extraordinarily consistent. Anthony

---

[118] Da Gama's confession, 18 Feb. 1593/4: *Cal. SP Dom., 1591–4*, 434. The original is in French.

[119] Tinoco to the Council, [22 Feb.] 1593/4: ibid. 439.

[120] Tinoco to the Council, [23 Feb.] 1593/4: ibid. 439–41.

Bacon was informed that Essex had spent the ten days between 22 February and 2 March wholly devoted to the Lopez case, in which 'he hath won the spurs and saddle also, if right be done him'.[121] Roderigo Lopez, of course, had his say as well: 'Dr Lopes hathe bene often examyned, and dyvers tymes uppon the racke', wrote Philip Gawdy of Clifford's Inn to his brother in Norfolk, anxious for news from London, 'he confesseth all thinges very franckly'.[122] Anthony Bacon, Essex's man, was informed by Waad that, although 'Great expedition was making to bring the affair before the public', nevertheless 'this could not be done so soon as the court was desirous it should, since the indictment must have many branches, and there were a great many Spanish and other foreign letters, which must be translated and abstracted'.[123] By now the case against Lopez was not only being put together by Essex, but the Cecils were fully involved, even more than their membership on the committee of inquiry required. As Lopez's activities during the previous few years became known, it correspondingly became more difficult to construct a coherent picture. We have Burghley's notes in his own handwriting. In his view, the first question to be resolved was 'How far forth the king of Spain may be avowed to have been author or privy to the conspiracy for the poisoning of the Queen's Majesty'. Chief among the 'Things to be had' were 'The Confessions of Emanuel Louys [Tinoco]. Ferera de Gama. Doctor Lopez. Signed with their hands.' Throughout, he wrote, it was essential to 'Remember to distinguish the several practices by their difference of times wherein they were done.'[124]

VI

The trial of Dr Roderigo Lopez opened at the Guildhall on 28 February 1593/4, before a special commission under the Great Seal and consisting of fifteen judges. Among them, of course, were the earl of Essex, Sir Robert Cecil, Lord Howard of Effingham, and the Lord Mayor. Other judges were Lords Buckhurst and Rich, Sir Thomas Heneage (the Vice-Chamberlain), Sir John Fortescue (Chancellor of the Exchequer), William Waad, Sir John Popham (Chief Justice of the Queen's Bench), William Daniell (a serjeant-elect), and four others. Curiously, Burghley was not among them, perhaps because of ill health.

---

[121] Birch, *Memoirs*, i. 160.
[122] Philip Gawdy to his brother Bassingborne, n.d. = 1594: Hist. MSS Comm., *7th Report*, App. (1879), 522b.   [123] Birch, *Memoirs*, i. 158–9.
[124] Burghley's notes 'To be expressed how these matters following are to be avowed': Hist. MSS Comm., *Salisbury V* (1894), 54–5.

As is apparent, the bench was not packed, and included a number of people who would have been happy to see Essex's prize catch go free and the earl humiliated once again. Attorney-General Egerton and Solicitor-General Coke were enemies of Essex. The case itself was conducted by Sir Edward Coke, and although no official account of the trial has yet been found, nor is it included in the State Trials, its conduct can be pieced together from contemporary evidence.[125]

The heads of the indictment against Lopez make his crimes quite plain. He is charged with, as early as 31 January 1590, having 'conspired the death of the Queen, and to stir up a rebellion and a war within the realm, and overthrow the commonwealth'. Four months later he was said to have 'adhered to Philip, King of Spain, and divers other aliens, the Queen's public enemies'. Lopez was said to have sent military intelligence to Philip II in August 1591, in return for which service he was sent the notorious jewel in October. At the beginning of 1593, on 20 January, Lopez was accused of having conferred with Andrada for the purpose of poisoning Queen Elizabeth, which he agreed to do on 20 February. Through Andrada, da Gama, Count Fuentes and Stephen de Ibarra, Lopez agreed on 30 September 1593 to poison the queen in return for 50,000 crowns, to be paid by Philip II. A month later he was said to have claimed that after having done the deed he would flee to Antwerp and from thence to Constantinople, where he would live.[126] Francis Bacon was present at the trial and, in his account of the conspiracy, helpfully reminded the reader that in that Turkish capital it is affirmed 'that Don Salomon, a Jew in good credit, is Lopez his near kinsman, and that he is greatly favoured by the said Don Salomon'. His connection with Abenaes, once a source of influence and power, proved therefore to be another nail in his coffin.[127]

The abstract of the evidence laid before the jury shows that Lopez's case was linked with an alleged Irish Jesuit conspiracy which came to light at about the same time, although the doctor's plot was clearly

---

[125] The other four judges were: Edward Fenner (justice of the Queen's Bench), Sir Richard Martin, Sir John Hart, and Sir William Webbe, 'and others': *Cal. SP Dom., 1591–4*, 448–9.

[126] Ibid. 445. There is a copy of this document in the state papers endorsed by Burghley, 'A report from Mr. Attorney and Solicitor General of the treasons of Dr. Lopez': ibid. Cf. BL Add. MS 21,599: drafts of bill of indictment against Lopez found among family papers by W. C. Trevelyan, Nettlecome, Somersetshire. According to the editor of the Spanish state papers, M. A. S. Hume, *The Year after the Armada* (London, 1896), 'In the Mendoza Papers in the National Archives in Paris, to which I have had access, are documents proving that he made a regular trade of poisoning—or attempting to poison, as he does not seem to have been very successful in the cases recorded.'

[127] Bacon, 'True Report', 287; Birch, *Memoirs*, i. 159–60.

prominent. The evidence was succinct and damning, and was summed up thus:

Lopez, a perjured murdering traitor, and Jewish doctor, worse than Judas himself, undertook to poison her, which was a plot more wicked, dangerous, and detestable than all the former. He was Her Majesty's sworn servant, graced and advanced with many princely favours, used in special places of credit, permitted often access to her person, and so not suspected, especially by her, who never fears her enemies nor suspects her servants. The bargain was made, and the price agreed upon, and the fact only deferred until payment of the money was assured; the letters of credit for his assurance were sent, but before they came into his hands, God most wonderfully and miraculously revealed and prevented it.

Numerous discussions between Lopez, Andrada, Tinoco, da Gama, and the Spanish ministers were detailed, all leading to the conclusion that 'Lopez undertook the poisoning for 50,000 crowns'. Here, too, the question of money was the only obstacle: 'Lopez often asked if the answer and money were come, and said he was ready to do the service.' As Francis Bacon repeated, evidence was given to prove that Lopez intended to flee the scene of the crime to Antwerp and from thence to Constantinople. In sum, the abstract concludes,

Being often charged with these treasons by his examiners, he, with blasphemous oaths and horrible execrations, denied that he ever had any speech with any person, or any understanding at all of any such matter, and yet with the same breath confessed to the contrary. All these things were plainly and fully proved, by witnesses, by intercepted letters, and by the confession of Lopez himself, to the great satisfaction of the judge, jury, and hearers.[128]

The question of Lopez's signed confession is one which was of prime importance to the judges. As Francis Bacon explained, Lopez at first denied all of the charges, but,

being afterwards confronted by Ferrera [da Gama], who constantly maintained to him all that he said, reducing him to the times and places of the said conferences, he confessed the matter; as by his confession in writing, signed with his own hand, appeareth. But then he fell to that slender evasion, as his last refuge, that he meant only to cozen the King of Spain of the money; and in that he continued at his arraignment; when notwithstanding at the first he did retract his own confession; and yet being asked whether he was drawn either by means of torture or promise of life to make the same confession, he did openly testify that no such means was used towards him.

---

[128] 'Abstract of the evidence': *Cal. SP Dom.*, *1591–4*, 445–8: seven pages in the original.

The deliberations were short: Dr Roderigo Lopez was found guilty on the first day of the trial and sentenced to death. 'Thus it may appear', Bacon noted, 'both how justly this Lopez is condemned for the highest treason that can be imagined; and how by God's marvellous goodness her Majesty hath been preserved.'[129]

Certainly, it might be argued that sixteenth-century English trials were hardly unassailable examples of modern justice. The two principal witnesses against Lopez were themselves deeply implicated. Even the accused's confession was most likely extracted at least by the threat of torture. But what is inescapable is that by the time the trial was concluded, even Essex's enemies were convinced of Lopez's guilt, and this despite the fact that the entire case provided them with a golden opportunity to bring the earl down if he had been wrong. Nowhere does this come out more clearly than in the letter which Sir Robert Cecil sent to Thomas Windebank, hours after the trial had been concluded and Lopez sentenced to death. Cecil had just returned from Guildhall, he wrote, where

The Vyllaine confessed all yᵉ day that he had indeed spoken of this matter & promised it but all forsooth to cosen ye k of Sp. but when he saw both his intent & overt Fact were apparent yᵉ vile Jew sayd that he dyd confess indead so to it that he had talk of it, but now he might tell further he did bely himself & did it only to save himself from Racking which ye Lord knoweth on my Sowle's wytness to be most untrue, & so was he told home, & the most substantial Jury that I have seene, have found him gilty in the highest degree of all Treasons, & Judgment passed against him with yᵉ applause of all yᵉ world.

Cecil's letter is no official document: it is a private communication, expressing his own views on that day, and we have the original in the state papers, endorsed by Windebank as from the 'Ultimo Februarii, being Thursday. Sir Rob. Cecil to me, by the post of London, who brought it at two o'clock after midnight, though it bare date at four of the clock afternoon'. Sir Robert Cecil, then, became convinced of Lopez's guilt, and his opinion cannot be dismissed lightly, even by modern historians.[130]

Lopez was convicted of attempted murder and high treason. The question now was what to do with him and how to present the case to the public in England and abroad. The various other conspirators continued

---

[129] Bacon, 'True Report', 277, 286–7. Cf. 'Report of the detestable treasons', *Cal. SP Dom., 1591–4*, 448–9.

[130] Sir Robert Cecil to Thomas Windebank, 4 p.m., 28 Feb. 1593/4, from the Strand: ibid. 444: text of letter repr. Dimock, 'Lopez', 466.

to confess, although they were doomed as well.[131] According to government papers, after the trial Lopez is said to have admitted to being a Marrano, and not a true Christian at all.[132] Lopez himself hardly got out of bed after his conviction, and his gaolers began to suspect that he might be trying to kill himself by the use of slow poison. Attorney-General Egerton hoped for a speedy execution, on the grounds that if Lopez should cheat the hangman and die first, it might cause great dishonour and scandal.[133] Burghley, for his part, drafted a speech for Queen Elizabeth, thanking God for her escape, but it seems that she never delivered it.[134]

In the middle of March some letters came in for Lopez sent from Constantinople. Waad read them, and reported to Robert Cecil that they contained nothing important.[135] But the Turkish connection was still essential for Elizabeth, and she was not about to let the accumulated goodwill dissolve because of Lopez's conviction. On the other hand, Solomon Abenaes in Constantinople hoped to be able to save Lopez, as Waad put it, 'being his neere kynsman and bothe Jewes', and sent Judah Serfatim, his personal messenger, to London. According to Waad in a letter to Burghley on 19 March 1593/4, Serfatim claimed that both Lopez and Abenaes were secretly working against Don Antonio the Portuguese pretender, who had lost Jewish confidence by spreading stories in Turkey that Abenaes had acquired his wealth through illegal and fraudulent means. Don Antonio was accused of 'chardginge him wth other Crymes and went about to move the Turke to confiscate his goods and to allow half of them to himselfe'. This was said to be the reason that Lopez was in contact with the king of Spain, to discredit Don Antonio and defend Abenaes. This was admittedly a rather flimsy defence of Lopez's well-documented treason, but Waad explained the case further:

But for the present the Chiefest thinge this messenger doth extreamly labor is to have the Execucon stayed of D. Lopez, as he hathe tolde yor l: and my L. Admyrall (as he saieth) for besides the dishonor as he saieth that will come to his master, he feareth yt maie be a way to his vtter ouerthrowe being already

[131] See, e.g., da Gama's confession, 8 Mar. 1593/4: *Cal. SP Dom., 1591–4*, 455; timetable of conspiracy, 10 Mar. 1593/4: ibid. 456; Tinoco to Burghley, 10 Mar. 1593/4: ibid. 456–7; Waad to Cecil, 12 Mar. 1593/4: ibid. 458; declaration of proceedings against Tinoco, da Gama, etc., 14 Mar. 1593/4: ibid. 460–1. Cf. Hist. MSS Comm., *Salisbury IV* (1892), 491.

[132] 'Memorandum respecting Lopez's treason against Her Majesty': ?9 Mar. 1593/4: *Cal. SP Dom., 1591–4*, 455–6. Cf. notes by Coke, referring to Lopez as 'a Portuguese Jew', ?Mar. 1593/4: ibid. 462.

[133] Egerton to Puckering, 14 Mar. 1593/4, from Lincoln's Inn: ibid. 460.

[134] Queen's speech, ?Mar. 1593/4: ibid. 462. Cf. Read, *Burghley and Elizabeth*, 584.

[135] Waad to Cecil, 12 Mar. 1593/4: *Cal. SP Dom., 1591–4*, 458.

sought vnder hande. I tolde him the ffact was so odious importing her Matie so highlie, and the discontentm^t of the people so greate as I assured myselfe he should finde none of yor lls: that would once make that motion, and the Execucon was in the handes of those that were Comyssioners.

Waad told Burghley that his sources revealed that on the voyage from Constantinople, Serfatim 'often did use wordes that he desyred only to fynde D. Lopez alyve, perhappes vnderstandinge of the doctors purpose to retyre to Constinople they misdoubted somethinge'.[136] Judah Serfatim himself made a separate declaration to the Privy Council, which replied with a list of twenty-five questions, in turn answered by Serfatim. The chief issue, however, was David Passi and local Turkish politics rather than Lopez.[137]

Judah Serfatim was Lopez's last chance: Abenaes's Jewish messenger was still in London on 10 April 1594, writing to Burghley, but no progress had been made towards improving Lopez's lot.[138] Even his family apparently deserted him. Lopez seems to have had a son at Winchester, and a brother in England, a merchant from Antwerp. Meeting this man at Winchester after Lopez's trial, a certain J. Harmar was surprised to discover that the brother now denied any family connection: 'notwithstanding', he reported, 'on my return home, searching out the letter which I received by this Antwerpian merchant, who is yet abiding in London, from the Doctor and finding that under his own handwriting he expressly termed him therein his brother', the real truth became clear. Harmar hurried to inform Robert Cecil of this intelligence, just to be on the safe side.[139]

Six weeks had passed since Roderigo Lopez had been condemned to death, yet the sentence had not yet been carried out. Lopez had a good deal of company in the Tower, not only da Gama and Tinoco, but a number of Jesuits who were incarcerated in connection with a different plot.[140] Lopez at least was still alive, and surprisingly it was Queen Elizabeth herself who was delaying the final scene. Bishop Goodman claims that Elizabeth had responded to Lopez's petitions with a promise that he would be freed after a short imprisonment. Meanwhile, he was safe, since prisoners in the Tower could not be executed without a

---

[136] Waad to Burghley, 19 Mar. 1593/4: repr. *TJHSE* 11 (1928), 85–6.

[137] Judah Serfatim to Privy Council, March 1593/4: BL MS Harl. 871, fos. 65–70^v: repr. *TJHSE* 11 (1928), 77–84. Cf. Serfatim's further replies, BL MS Harl. 871, fos. 71–74^v. Both documents are in French.

[138] [Serfatim] to ?Burghley, 10 Apr. 1594: *Cal. SP Dom., 1591–4*, 482.

[139] J. Harmar to Sir Robert Cecil, 4 Apr. 1594: Hist. MSS Comm., *Salisbury IV* (1892), 501.

[140] List of prisoners in the Tower, 14 Apr. 1594: *Cal. SP Dom., 1591–4*, 484.

warrant under the queen's own hand.[141] On 18 April 1594 the Lieutenant of the Tower, Sir Michael Blount, complained to Sir Robert Cecil that the day before he had received a warrant from the Attorney-General to deliver Lopez, da Gama, and Tinoco to the sheriffs of London to be executed at 9 a.m. the next day, 'but since your Honour doth signify that Her Majesty will have the executions stayed till I hear further of Her Highness' pleasure therein, I will stay the prisoners accordingly'.[142] Lord Buckhurst and Sir John Fortescue, two of the special commissioners under the Great Seal who had tried the case the previous February, were furious. They, too, on 18 April wrote to Sir Robert Cecil, describing themselves as 'perplexed, both for the general discontent of the people, who much expected this execution, as for the scandal hereby likely to ensue in the whole course of the cause'. They had taken advice with the Lord Chief Justice and the Attorney-General, and the unanimous legal opinion was that Lopez must needs be executed within the next few days before their commission expired, or else the entire legal foundation of their task would have been removed.[143] But Elizabeth was not to be moved by the pressure of legality. The following week Blount dutifully reported to Sir Thomas Heneage, the Vice-Chamberlain, and Cecil that he had received their orders of 24 April, 'wherein you declare Her Majesty's pleasure, that although I do receive any warrant to deliver Doctor Lopez to be executed, notwithstanding I shall not deliver him'. One further point, though: 'If it please your Honour that I may also understand Her Highness' pleasure for those other Portuguese, otherwise I know not what to do.' It is hard not to detect a note of sarcasm in Blount's letter.[144]

Whatever the reasons for the delay, a delay is all it was. Finally, on 7 June 1594, Lopez was carried away from the Tower and the queen's protection to Queen's Bench prison in Southwark, and then to the court of Queen's Bench at Westminster. When invited to declare why the execution of his sentence should be further delayed, 'Dr. Lopez replied, that he did appeal to the Queen's own knowledge and goodness for the acquitting of him.'[145] Furthermore, 'that he intended no Hurt against the Queen' and 'that he had no other Design in what he did, but to deceive the *Spaniard*, and wipe him of his Money'. Lopez, Tinoco, and da Gama were borne on a hurdle up the road to Tyburn. According to

---

[141] Goodman, *Court*, i. 154.
[142] Sir Michael Blount to Sir Robert Cecil, 18 Apr. 1594: Hist. MSS Comm., *Salisbury IV* (1892), 513.
[143] Lord Buckhurst and Sir John Fortescue to Robert Cecil, 18 Apr. 1594: ibid. 512.
[144] Blount to Sir Thomas Heneage and Robert Cecil, 25 Apr. 1594: ibid. 515.
[145] Goodman, *Court*, i. 154–5.

Camden, on the scaffold Lopez declared that 'he loved the Queen as well as he loved *Jesus Christ*; which coming from a man of the *Jewish* Profession moved no small Laughter in the Standers-by'.[146] Bishop Goodman's version is somewhat different:

Being brought to the place of execution, Lopez began to speak and to acquaint the people with the whole business. But there were some that stood afar off, some in one place, some in another, and they cried to him, 'Speak out, speak out'; others, that were in some nearness unto him, cried aloud, 'Hold your peace, hold your peace'; and thus was the whole time spent, and the poor man could not be heard a word, and so was turned off the ladder. This I heard from a very credible man that was then present; and the former narration I heard from a very honest man, who had it from him that did solicit Dr. Lopez' business, and was the messenger between the Queen and him.[147]

Inevitably, the three Portuguese were hanged, drawn, and quartered, the traditional penalty for traitors.[148]

VII

What needed to be done next was to communicate the government's decision regarding Lopez in such a way as to convince the public of the doctor's guilt and the complicity of the king of Spain. As early as 4 March 1593/4, less than a week after Lopez's trial and conviction, Waad was writing to Cecil enclosing an account of the conspiracy which was apparently meant to be the first draft of a published report.[149] Another draft exists, copiously corrected by Burghley, 'showing the secret practices of the King of Spain against the person of Queen Elizabeth and her estate'.[150] A good deal of effort went into this narrative: we have further versions, and further corrections by Burghley, Waad, and others.[151] On 27 October 1594 Waad was writing to Burghley yet again, with a request for advice on which incriminating letters to include in the

[146] William Camden, *The Historie of . . . Elizabeth* (London, 1630), iv. 58–9: the section on Lopez first appeared in Latin: *Annales rervm Anglicarvm et Hibernicarvm* (Leiden, 1625), 623–4. Cf. Goodman, *Court*, i. 156 n.; and E. Samuel, 'Dr Rodrigo Lopes' Last Speech from the Scaffold at Tyburn', *Jewish Historical Studies [TJHSE]*, 30 (1989), 51–3.   [147] Goodman, *Court*, i. 155.
[148] John Stow, *Chronicles* (London, 1631), 768. Cf. Philip Gawdy to brother Bassinghorne, 7 June 1594: 'This day Lopus was executed and two Portugalls more at Tyborne': Hist. MSS Comm., *7th Report, App.* (1879), 522a.
[149] Waad to Cecil, 4 Mar. 1593/4: *Cal. SP Dom., 1591–4*, 452–3, enclosing a 22 pp. account, printed in *State Papers*, ed. Murdin, 669–75. Cf. Hist. MSS Comm., *Salisbury IV* (1892), 485.
[150] 'A discourse, showing the secret practices': *Cal. SP Dom., 1591–4*, 558.
[151] Read, *Burghley and Elizabeth*, 498, citing Cecil Papers 139/41–8.

final text, and where they might be placed. 'According to your Lordship's Commandment and good Pleasure, I have used that Boldnes in the perusing this Discours', he wrote, 'which els I know would not become me. And because the whole Cours of Procedinge in that Cause is perfectly known to me, as my Memory did serve me, I have noted the same, that it may in all Points agre with the Truth.'[152] The demand for an accurate account of the Lopez case was considerable, even in Spain: on 19 November 1594 the news went out from London in Spanish that the books on Lopez's conspiracy were not yet out.[153]

A Trve Report of Sondry Horrible Conspiracies appeared in November 1594, published by Charles Yetsweirt. Those involved in the production of the final text, led by Burghley himself, elected to include the Lopez Plot with those of Yorke and Williams so as to place greater emphasis on the complicity of Philip II and the Roman Catholics.[154] Sir Edward Coke, a party to the prosecution of Lopez and therefore well placed to pass judgement on this text, made a marginal note on his copy, recording that Burghley thought best to rely principally upon the confessions of the delinquents without any interferences or arguments. This sort of book, Coke thought, was the best kind of publication.[155] Burghley worked hard to publicize this official government explanation of the Lopez Plot. As early as 28 November 1594 he was writing to Thomas Edmondes, the English envoy in Paris, enclosing a French translation of the book, which essentially accused the king of Spain of attempted murder.[156] Edmondes replied the following month:

[152] Waad to Burghley, 27 Oct. 1594: *State Papers*, ed. Murdin, 680.

[153] News from London, in Spanish, 19 Nov. 1594: *Cal. SP Dom., 1591–4*, 564.

[154] *A Trve Report of Sondry Horrible Conspiracies of Late Time Detected to Have (by Barbarous Murders) Taken away the Life of the Queen's Most Excellent Maiesty; whom Almighty God Hath Miraculously Conserved against the Treacheries of her Rebelles, & the Violences of her Most Puissant Enemies* (London: Charles Yetsweirt, Nov. 1594): Bod. Lib., 4° L 64 Art. Dimock, 'Lopez', 453 n. posits that the book was probably 'derived in substance' from BL MS Harl. 871, fos. 7–64, and 'drawn up by Coke'. Dimock's source for Coke's authorship is Bacon, *Works*, ed. Spedding, viii. 274, who suggests that the book 'appears to have been drawn up by Coke', citing in turn Coke's MS note cited below, which clearly indicates Burghley as the author chiefly responsible. Read, *Burghley and Elizabeth*, 584, also concludes that 'there can be no doubt, I think, that Burghley was the author of the official version'. Conyers Read agrees in 'Sir William Cecil and Elizabethan Public Relations', in *Elizabethan Government and Society: Essays Presented to Sir John Neale* (London, 1964), 52–3. There is another MS account by Waad, which may have contributed to the final effort, in BL Add. MS 48,029, fos. 147-184ᵛ.

[155] Sir Edward Coke, MS notes on BL copy of *Trve Report*: BL shelfmark 599 6.5.

[156] Burghley to Sir Thomas Edmondes, in Paris, 28 Nov. 1594: BL MS Stowe 166, fo. 167. Robert Cecil had already written to Edmondes on 30 Oct. 1594, asking him to explain to Henry IV the background to the Lopez Plot, stressing the involvement of

I have distributed among the best of the Court the declarations your lordship sent me of the treasons of Lopez and the rest, which have been here very welcome; but divers have since told me that they are sorry to see the same so basely (as they give it term) and weakly written of a subject which deserved a stronger and sharp expressing.[157]

The Lopez Plot was not only a political bombshell but also a good story, and it was inevitable that alternative, if basically complementary, accounts should have appeared in print, although none did so until at least sixty years after the event. The most important of these is the version offered by Francis Bacon, 'A True Report of the Detestable Treason, Intended by Dr. Roderigo Lopez', which appeared in print for the first time only in 1657. Although obviously intended for publication, its delay may have been the result of some kind of compromise between Essex, whose man Bacon was, and Burghley, who had already produced the official version. Bacon's alternative report may have been censored in the interest of unanimity. Bacon, like Burghley, summed up the plot as one in which Lopez, 'for a sum of money, promised to be paid to him by the King of Spain, did undertake to have destroyed by poison' the queen of England.[158]

Apart from Francis Bacon, we have a number of accounts which were published later, but based on contemporary evidence. Thomas Birch published in 1754 a narrative based on the papers of Anthony Bacon, the elder brother of Francis. The slant is inevitably that of the Essex party, but the earl after all was the one who first brought the conspiracy to light.[159] William Murdin published the relevant documents from the Burghley papers in 1759, which provide needed balance.[160] Bishop Godfrey Goodman of Gloucester died in 1655, but he was close enough to the events for his account to be useful. Goodman gave his chief source as Sir Henry Savile, provost of Eton, 'who was very great with the earl' of Essex, but yet 'did in truth confess unto me that he thought the earl to be a little faulty'. His discussion of the Lopez Plot was first printed in the middle of the nineteenth century, and provides yet another important source.[161] A few scattered additional manuscript

Philip II: BL MS Stowe 166, fo. 151^{r-v}; cf. fo. 177^r (11 Dec. 1594). Cf. Read, *Burghley and Elizabeth*, 584.

[157] Thomas Edmondes to [Burghley], 22 Dec. 1594: Hist. MSS Comm., *Salisbury V* (1894), 43–5.

[158] Bacon, *Works*, ed. Spedding, viii. 271–87.

[159] Birch, *Memoirs*, i. 148–60.

[160] *State Papers*, ed. Murdin, 669–75, from the papers at Hatfield House.

[161] Goodman, *Court*, i. 145–57, esp. 145. Goodman gives his other sources, apart from Savile, as the messenger between Elizabeth and Lopez when the doctor was in prison; and a courtier who was present when Essex rashly and prematurely broached the subject of a Lopez Plot to the queen.

sources survive, but none improves much on the existing evidence.[162]

In a sense, after Lopez's trial and execution, all that needed to be done was to pick up the pieces and try to see what might be salvaged after that commotion. Edward Barton, still the English agent in Constantinople, was greatly distressed by the fact that Abenaes had sent an agent to London, Judah Serfatim, 'wth lr̄es against me, in perticular has last lr̄es and seruant sent little befor the aprehension of doctor Lopes, by wch he accused me for keepting company wth spanishe spyes'.[163] Serfatim became more of a thorn in Barton's side after the Lopez affair. This in part was due to the fact that relations between England and Abenaes inevitably became somewhat strained after his kinsman was executed. In February 1595/6 Abenaes went so far as to send Serfatim on a mission to Spain to negotiate a truce between that country, Turkey, and the German Empire.[164] It transpired that Abenaes was less interested in a diplomatic volte-face than in freeing some slaves who had been captured at Patras.[165] Serfatim, in turn, cut a prominent figure at Madrid that winter, boasting that he had 'travelled much, and has been in England, where he has had dealings with Don Antonio of Portugal, and with Antonio Perez'.[166] Although Abenaes was described by the Venetian ambassador in Spain as 'an intimate frequenter of the English Embassy' in Constantinople,[167] in point of fact, relations with Barton had reached breaking-point by October 1597, immediately before the Englishman's death. Barton had been trying to convince the Turks that Serfatim was in reality a Spanish spy, and in any case of too mean a rank to be heard at all. Although Barton threatened to advise Elizabeth to make her own peace with Spain, the Turks had little time for his claims, noting that they had in the past received good service from Solomon Ashkenazi, another Jew of supposedly low rank, who had been sent to Venice in 1576 as Turkish ambassador, and successfully concluded a peace treaty.[168] Barton himself was already ill, and went to

---

[162] Bishop White Kennett's collection of biographical notes, BL MS Lansdowne 982, fo. 175^{r-v} re Lopez.

[163] Barton to Burghley, 10 Aug. 1594: PRO, SP For., Turkey, 2: repr. *TJHSE* 11 (1928), 88–9.

[164] Agustino Nani (Venetian ambassador in Spain) to the Doge and Senate, 28 Feb. 1595/6: *Cal. SP Ven., 1592–1603*, 184; cf. same to same, 7 Mar. 1595/6: ibid. 185.

[165] Same to same, 8 Apr. 1596: ibid. 189–90; same to same, 13 May 1596: ibid. 201.

[166] Same to same, 22 Mar. 1595/6: ibid. 188.

[167] Same to same, 8 Apr. 1596: ibid. 189–90.

[168] Girolamo Capello (Venetian ambassador in Constantinople) to the Doge and Senate: ibid. 290–1.

[168] Girolamo Capello (Venetian ambassador in Constantinople) to the Doge and

the island of Halki near Constantinople, where he died.[169]

It would be an undeniable understatement to say that Roderigo Lopez was executed because he fell from favour, but it was remembered even then that he had once held a position of trust and influence which put not only him but also his family in a good light. Roderigo Lopez's wife Sarah tried to draw on some residual goodwill by making a personal application to Queen Elizabeth two months after her husband's execution. Sarah Lopez begged mercy of the queen in 'consideration of her afflicted and miserable estate', being that herself 'and her poor children are innocent of her husband's crime'. She noted that she was 'the sorrowful mother of five comfortless and distressed children born in the realm (three of them being maiden children)'. Specifically, she begged to have the lease of their house, her household and other goods taken from her during her husband's first imprisonment, certain plate, the licences of sumac and aniseed belonging to Lopez, and, finally, 'a parsonage of 30*l*. a year given by the Queen to Anthony, one of her miserable children, for his maintenance at school and learning', this presumably being the child at Winchester.[170] Elizabeth did not reply until the following March, but when she did it was favourable. Lopez's wife was restored to the lease at Mountjoy's Inn which he held from Winchester College, and also the goods and chattels not exceeding £100 forfeit by the attainder. But on one point Elizabeth was adamant, if for nothing else than for symbolic purposes, for from the list of goods restored, she specifically excepted 'a jewel set with a diamond and a ruby, sent by some minister of the King of Spain to Dr. Lopez'.[171] Elizabeth seems to have relished that ring. Sir Thomas Egerton told the House of Lords in 1601, that 'I have seen her Majesty wear at her Girdle the price of her blood; I mean Jewels which have been given to her Physicians to have done that unto her, which I hope God will ever keep from her; but she hath rather worn them in Triumph than for the

---

[169] Pears, 'Spanish Armada', 465. Pears, writing in 1893, notes: 'But the unreadiness which the Turk has so often shown to arrive at any decision upon diplomatic questions until he is actually forced to do so was probably the main reason which led to Barton's failure' (ibid.).

[170] Sarah Lopes to Queen Elizabeth, [Aug. 1594]: Hist. MSS Comm., *Salisbury IV* (1892), 601, including an inventory of Lopez's goods. This letter is also mentioned in the Hist. MSS Comm., *7th Report, App.*, 196a, where among other MSS listed are: (1) Als. Baltasar Pieterson (Lopez's conspiracy); and (2) 'A Portuguese MS. in 2 parts. (History of political state of Portugal.) A Hebrew MS. in Portuguese on the same.'

[171] 'Grant to Sarah, widow of Dr. Lopez', 6 Mar. 1594/5: *Cal. SP Dom., 1595-7*, 15. As Goodman put it, 'the Queen gave them all, and would not suffer her to lose one farthing': *Court*, i. 155-6.

price, which hath not been greatly valuable.'[172] Assuming Egerton's observation to be true, it was a classic Elizabethan gesture.

Philip II was now a publicly reviled assassin in England, and no action against him could be considered entirely unjust. Essex had his way after the discovery of the Lopez Plot, and with Lord Howard of Effingham was permitted to organize the Cadiz Expedition at the beginning of July 1596. They sacked Cadiz, ravaged the Spanish coast, and captured booty. Among the prisoners, curiously, was Abraham Cohen Herrera (*c.* 1570–1635), a Jew who had already lived in Lisbon, Tuscany, Venice, and Morocco before settling in Cadiz, under licence of the Spanish Crown, on business for the sultan of Morocco. Herrera was kept a prisoner in London until released by order of the sultan. In 1600 he settled at Ragusa and there studied the Lurianic cabbala, moving on to Venice and finally Holland, where in Amsterdam he wrote his famous book *Puerta del cielo*. This celebrated work, in which Herrera tried to reconcile Jewish Lurianic cabbala with Christian Neoplatonism, was an important landmark in Jewish mysticism. That such a man should once have been the prisoner of the earl of Essex is one of the ironies of Jewish history.[173]

The Jewish community in England seems to have been hard hit by the trial and execution of one of its leading members. Dr Hector Nuñez, Lopez's medical companion, had already died in 1591. Dunstan Añes, another of their leaders, and financial agent in England of the unfortunate Don Antonio the Portuguese pretender, died in April 1594 and was buried under his pew in St Olave's Church. His daughter Sarah was Roderigo Lopez's even more unfortunate widow.[174] The only bright light seems to have been the story told by the Jewish-Dutch historian Daniel Levi de Barrios at the end of the seventeenth century. Levi de Barrios relates the account of the Portuguese Jews of Amsterdam concerning the origins of their own community, featuring the beautiful Marrano Maria Nuñes of Lisbon, who was sailing on a ship with her four relatives when the boat was seized by the English and brought to London. Levi de Barrios claims that an English duke fell in love with Maria Nuñes, who in turn was summoned into the presence of Queen Elizabeth, who wished to view the beauty herself. According to the tale, Elizabeth was favourably impressed indeed, and paraded with the Jewess through London in the royal carriage. The duke, meanwhile, failed in

---

[172] Sir Thomas Egerton (Lord Keeper), speech in House of Lords, 27 Oct. 1601: *The Journals of All the Parliaments during the Reign of Queen Elizabeth*, ed. Simonds d'Ewes (London, 1682), 599–600.
[173] For more on Herrera, see his *Puerta del cielo*, ed. K. Krabbenhoft (Madrid, 1987), and the editor's introduction.
[174] L. Wolf, 'Jews in Elizabethan England', *TJHSE* 11 (1928), 15.

his attempt to persuade Maria Nuñes to marry him, and the queen allowed the party to continue on their voyage to Amsterdam, where they threw off their disguises and lived openly as Jews. There is some evidence that this incident, or at least the capture of the ship conveying five Portuguese among whom was a young lady, took place in April 1597. Yet, even if true, Queen Elizabeth for her part would not necessarily have known of the Jewish origins of her guests.[175]

Perhaps a more lasting effect of the Lopez case was his eternalization in English literature. We have already seen how Christopher Marlowe in 1592 exploited popular images of the Jews even before Lopez was under suspicion. Much more problematic is Shakespeare's *Merchant of Venice*. Although it has been claimed that a first rough draft was put on the stage in August 1594, it is certain that at least in 1596–7 London theatre-goers had the opportunity of seeing Shylock performed. The universal meaning of this character and his play have been discussed at almost infinite length, and there is no need whatsoever to look into this matter here. Whether or not Shakespeare had intended before the Lopez Plot to develop the story which appeared in *Il pecorone* of Ser Giovanni Fiorentino, published at Milan in 1558, the trial and execution of the Jew made the entire story much more topical and certainly increased the play's attraction. It seems that Marlowe's *Jew of Malta* was revived at the time of the Lopez case by the Admiral's Men, Shakespeare's competitors, so it may be that this Jewish conspirator's most permanent contribution was not the death of an English queen but the creation of one of the most intriguing characters in English literature.[176]

That being said, Lopez himself does appear, or seems to appear, in other, rather more minor, works of literature. The anti-Puritan Thomas Nashe published in 1594 a picaresque historical narrative about *The Unfortunate Traveller*, in which a Jewish physician named Zachary buys the hero and his lover from another Jew named Zadoch in order to dissect them. The Jewish physician is also a poisoner and, like Lopez, is eventually executed.[177] Nashe returned to the same theme in the context

---

[175] Daniel Levi de Barrios, *Triumpho del govierno popular y de la antigüedad holandesa* (Amsterdam, 1683), section 'Casa de Iacob', 5; J. I. Israel, 'Manuel Lopez Pereira of Amsterdam, Antwerp and Madrid: Jew, New Christian, and Adviser to the Conde-Duque de Olivares', *Studia Rosenthaliana*, 19 (1985), 112.

[176] B. Stirling, 'Introduction', to *The Merchant of Venice*, in William Shakespeare, *The Complete Works*, ed. A. Harbage (Baltimore, 1969). Cf. S. A. Tannenbaum (ed.), *Shakespeare's The Merchant of Venice (A Concise Bibliography)* (New York, 1941), 54–69. F. Felsenstein, 'Jews and Devils: Anti-Semitic Stereotypes of Late Medieval and Renaissance England', *Journal of Literature and Theology*, 4 (1990), 15–28.

[177] Thomas Nashe, *The Vnfortvnate Traveller* (London, 1594), in *The Works*, ed. R. B. McKerrow (Oxford, 1966), ii. 205–328, esp. 303 ff.

of his dispute with Gabriel Harvey in 1596, declaring that 'I haue been big with childe of a common place of reuenge, euer since the hanging of *Lopus*'.[178] Likewise, in his faint praise of lawyers, he admitted that many were quite eloquent even when defending the guilty: 'Those that were present at the arrainmet of Lopus (to insist in no other particular) hereof I am sure will beare me record.'[179] At the turn of the century a play entitled *England's Joy* was performed at the Swan on 6 November 1602. The authorship is still disputed, but the anti-Spanish theme was helpfully made clear to the audience in a hand-out distributed to them. At one stage in the drama, they were forewarned,

the Tyrant more enraged, taketh counsell; sends forth letters, privie spies, and secret underminders; taking their othes, and giving them bagges of treasure. These signifie *Lopus*, and certaine Jesuites, who afterward, when the tyrant lookes for an answere from them, are shewed to him in a glasse with halters about their neckes, which makes him mad with fury.[180]

But it was Thomas Dekker the London playwright who was the first to provide Roderigo Lopez with full dramatic immortality, in *The Whore of Babylon*, published in 1607, thirteen years after the doctor's execution. Lopez is represented by a character called 'Ropus a Doctor of Physicke', although in the quarto he is actually given the name of 'Lupus'. Elizabeth appears as 'Titania the Fairie Queene', who relies on 'Ropus' absolutely and with perfect trust. At the critical moment, when Ropus is about to administer a poisoned draught to his queen, Fideli her counsellor intervenes. Showing her the incriminating letter, he declares:

> but heere's a theefe,
> That must haue fifty thousand crownes to steale
> Thy life: Here 'tis in blacke and white—thy life,
> Sirra thou Vrinall, *Tynoco, Gama,*
> *Andrada,* and *Ibarra,* names of Diuels,
> Or names to fetch vp Diuels: thou knowest these Scar-crowes.

(IV. ii. 113–18)

---

[178] Thomas Nashe, *Have With Yov to Saffron-Walden* (London, 1596), ibid. iii. 18.

[179] Id., *Nashes Lenten Stvffe* (London, 1599), ibid. iii. 215–16.

[180] [Nicholas Breton?], 'The Plot of the Play, Called "England's Joy." To be Playd at the Swan this 6. of Nov. 1602', W. Oldys (ed.), *Harleian Miscellany* (London, 1808–13), x. 199. Cf. S. L. Lee, 'The Topical Side of the Elizabethan Drama', *Transactions of the New Shakspere Society*, 1 (1887), 14–15; id., 'The Original of Shylock', 185–200. Lee's views are challenged by E. M. Tenison, *Error Versus Fact, a Study in Contrasts, 1880 and 1594* (Leamington Spa, 1953), an 8 pp. pamphlet printed for private circulation (which I have not seen).

Even then, the names of the conspirators were sufficiently well known to be found in a play dramatizing those tragic events. Dekker portrays the last moments of Lopez's unmasking as well:

> *Rop.* Oh mee! O mercy, mercy! I confesse.
> *Fid.* Well sayd, thou shalt be hang'd then.
> *Tita.*   Haue we for this
> Heap'd fauours on thee.   *Shee reades the letter.*
> *Fid.* Heape Halters on him: call the Guard: out polecat:
>   *Enter Guard.*
> He smels, thy conscience stincks, Doctor goe purge
> Thy soule, for 'tis diseas'd. Away with *Ropus.*
> *Omn.* Away with him: foh.
> *Rop.*   Here my tale but out.
> *Fid.* Ther's too much out already.
> *Rop.* Oh me accursed! and most miserable.   *Exit with Guard.*
>   (IV. ii. 119–28)

While Lopez's Jewish origin is not specifically mentioned in Dekker's description, the references to the doctor's smell certainly imply the *foetor judaicus*, the popular belief that Jews retained a particular odour even after baptism, an indelible racial mark.[181] Dekker returned to the subject of Anglo-Jewry in a later work which appeared in 1613. There he makes reference to 'the rest of their Iewish Tribe in the Synagogue of *Houns-ditch*'. While there is some note of an alleged Jewish community in Houndsditch later in the century, Dekker's sources are not clear, and in any case he makes no connection with Lopez's downfall.[182]

Lopez appears in prints and other literary works of the late Elizabethan and early Jacobean period, although his name never became the sort of literary catchword that eternalized the 'murderous Machiavel'.[183] Lopez appears in Christopher Marlowe's *Doctor Faustus* (1602), in Thomas Middleton's *A Game at Chesse* (1625), and in John Taylor's *Church Deliverance*, which was published in 1630 with the water-poet's other works. Beaumont and Fletcher's *Women Pleased*

---

[181] Thomas Dekker, *The Whore of Babylon* (London, 1607), in *The Dramatic Works*, ed. F. Bowers (Cambridge, 1953–61), ii. 491–592, esp. 493–6, 538, 555–7, 586. Cf. notes by Cyrus Hoy in the 1980 edn., ii. 305, 355–7.

[182] Thomas Dekker, *A Strange Horse-Race* (London, 1613), including 'The Diuels Last Will and *TESTAMENT*' from which this is taken: repr. *The Non-dramatic Works of Thomas Dekker*, ed. A. B. Grosart (New York, 1963), iii. 353.

[183] Cf., for example, *Popish Plots and Treasons, from the Beginning of the Reign of Queen Elizabeth* (London, 1569 [sic]) including one of a man wearing a Spanish ruff, said to be 'Lopas compounding to poyson the Queene': *Catalogue of Prints and Drawings in the British Museum Division I. Political and Personal Satires*, i. (London, 1870), i. 9: see plate section here. See also S. L. Lee, 'Elizabethan England and the Jews', *Transactions of the New Shakspere Society*, 2 (1888), 143–66, esp. 162.

includes a usurer named Lopez, and their *Customs of the Country* has a Jewish character in the plot. Indeed, in John Marston's *The Malcontent* (1604), when 'Mendozo', a minion to the duchess of Genoa, asks Malevole, the duke in disguise, 'Canst thou impoyson?', his reply is, 'Excellently, no Jew, Potecary, or Politian better.'[184] The unspoken reference to the Lopez Plot must have been obvious.

VIII

All 'Men, with one Consent, do fully agree,' ruled the Cecils,

that there never was so wicked, dyvellishe, and hatefull a Treason so closely, conningly and smoothly conveyed by such, as had Meanes with least Suspicion to carry it; so throughley, cleerly and wonderfully discovered; so plainly, manyfestly and evidently laid open; so authentically, fully, and demonstratively proved.[185]

The Second Treasons Act of Elizabeth defined the crime quite clearly in 1571, amplifying previous legislation. Among the actions defined as treason was when any person 'shall, within the realm or without, compass, imagine, invent, devise, or intend the death or destruction, or any bodily harm tending to death, destruction, maim or wounding of the royal person of the same our sovereign lady Queen Elizabeth'.[186] At least since 1534, the concept of treason by words had been applicable in trials: no actual action need have been committed.[187] Certainly, the activities of Dr Roderigo Lopez fell well within the boundaries set by law. Yet it is almost an act of faith that Lopez's innocence be affirmed, and that his guilt was 'unsubstantiated by genuine evidence'.[188] Even the spectre of anti-Semitism has often been brought to bear, although, as we

---

[184] John Marston, *The Malcontent* (London, 1604), in *The Plays*, ed. H. H. Wood (Edinburgh, 1934–9), i. 207 (v. iii). Cf. John Marston, *Eastward-Hoe* (London, 1605), ibid. iii. 157 (IV. ii), where the 'officer of the counter' claims to have had Jews in his gaol.

[185] *State Papers*, ed. Murdin, 673. Cf. the later, but equally vociferous, denunciation of the plot by Henry Wotton, *The State of Christendom* (London, 1657), 309.

[186] 'An Act whereby certain offences be made treasons': 13 Eliz. I, c.1: G. R. Elton, *The Tudor Constitution* (Cambridge, 1972), 73.

[187] See ibid. 59–86.

[188] e.g. H. Fisch, *The Dual Image* (London, 1971), 36; or Samuel, 'Lopes', 52: 'The Spanish state papers are intact and give no hint of a Spanish plot to use Lopes to poison the Queen'; 'There is good reason to believe that the man was unjustly condemned to death for high treason, and that Dr Rodrigo Lopes was no traitor to the Queen.' Even W. T. MacCaffrey, *Elizabeth I*, 484, writes cautiously that at 'this distance of time it is difficult to untangle the many threads of this plot or to determine the probable guilt of Lopez'.

have seen, Lopez's Jewish origin was not a key element in his prosecution. What has been consistently misunderstood by modern writers is that it is not necessary to establish that Roderigo Lopez actually plotted to poison the queen, that he procured the materials and set about working according to a secret plan. By the terms of the treason laws then current, Lopez's secret contacts with the Spanish Crown and his numerous discussions about the possibility of poisoning the queen were more than enough to hang him many times over. It may be that in some ways he acted as a double agent, and that one of the many Elizabethan court factions was kept aware of his Spanish contacts. If this was so, it was effectively hidden from the judges at Lopez's trial. A. F. Pollard once wrote that 'The nation in the sixteenth century deliberately condoned injustice, when injustice made for its peace.'[189] True as this may have been, those who would defend Lopez's innocence have yet to make their case.

[189] A. F. Pollard, *Henry VIII* (London, 1905), 437.

3

FROM READMISSION
TO REVOLUTION

THE re-establishment of a Jewish community in seventeenth-century England was not in itself a surprising historical development. The general trend in the early modern period was one of improvement in the Jewish situation in regard to their relations with political authority, particularly in places where the power of the ruler or of the pope was the most overriding. The Jews were completely dependent on the whim of the ruler, and therefore became his most loyal subjects, enjoying certain rights and privileges and *de facto* religious toleration, if not necessarily at law. The growing importance of the Jews in the economic sphere had a great influence on this process. Nevertheless, in most of these cases, the improvement in the Jewish situation was achieved behind the scenes and almost secretly, or at least in such a way that a public declaration of support for deicides was not necessary. Emperor Ferdinand I, for example, allowed many Jews to live in Vienna, but also made sure to pacify their opponents with carefully composed expressions of disgust for the chosen people. Maximilian II also preserved a certain lack of clarity concerning the Jewish question, and demonstrated prevarication and inconsistency in his declarations on the subject. Even before him, these were characteristics of official Continental attitudes towards the Jews. Despite their expulsion from Prague in 1542, for example, about 1,000 Jews continued to live in the city.[1]

In England, on the other hand, the process was entirely different. The Jewish community here grew from a secret body of Marranos which came to light only after the government in London had discussed of its own volition the question of whether it would be right and moral to allow Jews to settle and live in England, and thereby to abrogate the edict of expulsion promulgated in 1290 by King Edward I. The willingness of the English government to take the political risk of holding a public debate on the Jewish question transforms the English case to one of striking originality and makes it almost unique.[2]

[1] Generally, see J. I. Israel, *European Jewry in the Age of Mercantilism, 1550–1750* (Oxford, 1985).
[2] The first part of this chapter is a summary of my *Philo-Semitism and the Readmission of the Jews to England, 1603–1655* (Oxford, 1982). Further detailed references can be found there, and I have therefore kept the footnotes to a minimum.

I .

The origins, therefore, of the Jewish community in London are not to be found among the first Sephardi pioneers who came to England during the reign of Henry VIII, nor in the circle of Dr Roderigo Lopez. In fact, even the first established Jewish community during the English Civil War was not the principal force behind the creation of a permanent Jewish presence in London. Throughout the entire public debate about the Jews that preceded the arrival of Rabbi Menasseh ben Israel in London in September 1655, the very existence of a Jewish community in an eastern corner of London was completely unknown to the English authorities. Even when Menasseh ben Israel unmasked them against their will, the debate about the readmission of the Jews continued as if the country was completely without descendants of the Children of Israel. The only Jews of most people's acquaintance were biblical figures, literary characters, and entirely imaginary, and it may be that this lack of personal contact with such an extraordinary people facilitated their readmission.

The initiative for the return of the Jews to England came instead from the English themselves and not from the Sephardi Jews who made up the tiny Marrano community in London. Locating the origins of this unusual initiative is therefore crucial for understanding the establishment of the community, but here too nestle a number of difficulties. First, the case of the Jews was unique, not only in England but in all of Europe. Most Englishmen saw Roman Catholics, for example, as a mistaken religious group or even part of a traitorous political organization. But a Catholic who abandoned his faith and converted to Protestantism was completely purified, and promised for himself a secure and equal future limited only by his social standing. The Catholic was an Englishman who had chosen membership in the wrong club. This was not the case with the Jews. When contemporaries read the Gospel of John describing the Jews as the children of the Devil, it was not entirely clear to them whether the apostle's words were meant to be taken literally or were merely a figure of speech. It was a universally accepted fact that Jews had a peculiar smell, an odour which was not dissipated by baptism, but was instead a racial characteristic. The blood libels of William of Norwich (1144) and Little St Hugh of Lincoln (1255) achieved eternal life not only in Chaucer's *Canterbury Tales*, but also in popular ballads which presented the Jews in a negative light.[3]

[3] So also in joke books: see the section 'Of mery Iestes of the Iewes' in [Thomas Twyne?], *The Schoolemaster; or, Teacher of Table Philosophie* (London, 1576), sig. Rr: I am grateful to Sir Keith Thomas for this reference.

Secondly, as far as anyone knew, there were no Jews in England. In other words, the Jewish question was unnatural in England and did not arise from their daily presence as was true on the Continent. The Jews did not form a social and religious group whose very existence required an explanation. It is curious that in spite of the emphasis on Old Testament reading promoted by the Puritans, references to ancient Israelites did not automatically remind them of contemporary Jews. As a result, before English support of readmission could crystallize, it was necessary to awaken a certain awareness among Englishmen of the very existence of Jews in their own time, and to present them in a favourable light.

The first task before us, therefore, is to isolate the reasons which caused the Jewish question to arise in the years immediately preceding the arrival of Menasseh ben Israel in England at the end of 1655. Secondly, we must try to identify the motivation of Menasseh himself in coming to England. Thirdly, the actual process of readmission must be examined. Fourthly, we need to look at the results of these events on the establishment of the modern Jewish community in England. As we shall see, the Whitehall Conference of December 1655, which was called by Oliver Cromwell to decide on the readmission of the Jews, occurred at the meeting-point of a number of key movements and concepts which continued to exist even after the Conference ended and with no further connection to it. But at a certain point in 1655 the collective result of these ideas was to place the Jews under the spotlight and to present their case in a favourable form, even if this was a secondary product of other factors.

It is quite clear that motives of economics or trade had little to do with the readmission of the Jews to England. The claim that the economic abilities of the Jews were considerable and that their trade connections were efficient and international was usually used against them. The fear was that Jewish immigration to England would lead to the financial penetration of the country by Dutchmen, and certainly it is true that at least in the initial stages most of the Jewish immigrants to London were Sephardi Jews from Amsterdam who maintained close commercial ties with their country of origin. It was Rabbi Menasseh ben Israel himself who at the Whitehall Conference raised the question of the potential economic contribution of the Jews, and it was the English merchants who opposed the readmission on the grounds that Jews would serve as a funnel through which English wealth would be transferred to their deadly rivals, the Dutch. In order to isolate the motives behind English philo-Semitism we must therefore first look in the realm of religion.[4]

[4] See now F. E. Manuel, *The Broken Staff: Judaism Through Christian Eyes* (Cambridge, Mass., 1992).

There is no question that the precondition for the readmission of the Jews to England was the revival of Hebrew studies in the first half of the sixteenth century, as a result of the Protestant emphasis on reading the Word of God in the original languages. Christians after the Reformation were left alone with the Word, and in order to understand it without priestly intermediaries they were forced to arm themselves with the proper tools, including a basic knowledge of Hebrew. As was the case everywhere that Hebrew studies flourished, Christian interest in the Old Testament inevitably created a climate of theological opinion which attracted Jews, converted or otherwise. The pioneers of Hebrew study in the Renaissance—Pico della Mirandola, Johannes Reuchlin, and others—needed Jews in the first instance in order to gain a thorough acquaintance of the biblical text. In the next generation grammars and lexicons began to appear in Latin and eventually in vernacular languages, but the entire field was always and quite naturally connected to the presence of Jews.[5] Sixteenth- and seventeenth-century English religious life was characterized above all else by the intense emphasis placed on reading and understanding the Word of God as expressed in Scripture.[6] It was in this period that the Old Testament regained a place of honour next to the New, and the 'language of Canaan' spoken by God to the Israelites became a tool of biblical scholarship much in demand.[7]

With the end of improving Christian understanding of the original Hebrew text, Thomas Cromwell in 1535 decreed a series of injunctions at the two English universities, which were augmented at Cambridge by his commissioner Thomas Legh, soon to be the villain of the Pilgrimage of Grace. One of Legh's additions ordered the University to provide at

---

[5] Cf. S. Stein, 'Phillipus Ferdinandus Polonus: A Sixteenth-Century Hebraist in England', in I. Epstein, *et al.* (eds.), *Essays in Honour of . . . J. H. Hertz* (London, 1944), 397–412.

[6] The claim that Lady Jane Grey was a Hebraist, however, is based on a misunderstanding. Her supposed Hebrew letters to Bullinger are in fact in Latin and contain only three (beautifully executed) Hebrew words: Lady Jane Grey to Bullinger, 12 July 1551: Zurich, Zentralbibliothek, MS RP 17; same to same, 7 July 1552: MS RP 18; same to same, before June 1553: MS RP 19. These letters are printed as nos. IV–VI in *Original Letters Relative to the English Reformation*, ed. H. Robinson (Parker Soc., Cambridge, 1846/7), i. 4–7, 7–8, 9–11. On 29 May 1551 John Ab Ulmis even suggested to Conrad Pellican that he should 'honourably consecrate to her name your Latin translation of the Jewish Talmud': ibid. ii. 432. See also the three letters from Ulmis to Bullinger between Nov. 1551 and July 1552: ibid. 437, 451–2, 452–3.

[7] For some examples of Hebrew instruction in 16th-century grammar schools, see N. Carlisle, *A Concise Description of the Endowed Grammar Schools in England and Wales* (London, 1818), ii. 284, 573 n.; R. W. Elliott, *The Story of King Edward VI School Bury St Edmunds* (Bury St Edmunds, 1963), 42, 68; H. B. Wilson, *The History of Merchant-Taylor's School* (London, 1814), 37, 39; J. E. G. Montmorency, *State Intervention in English Education* (Cambridge, 1902), 75, 80, 115.

its own expense a public lecture in either Hebrew or Greek, in return for relieving it of a tax which had been levied upon it the previous year. This agreement was ratified in an act of parliament passed at the beginning of 1536 and pertaining now to both Oxford and Cambridge. The new lectureship was to be named after the king, and might now in addition to Greek and Hebrew be devoted to any of the seven liberal arts or Latin. In other words, a new teaching post was created by the king, but the Hebrew language was no longer on any probable short-list of subjects. This was changed four years later when the number of lectureships at each university was increased to five, now to be paid for by the cathedral church of Westminster. According to the new regulations, the approved subjects were deemed specifically to be divinity, civil law, medicine, Greek, and Hebrew. These were the Regius professorships. In 1546 the financial responsibility for the Hebrew, Greek, and divinity chairs was shifted to the new foundations, Christ Church at Oxford and Trinity College, Cambridge. The Regius professor of Hebrew was initially required to lecture for five hours per week, but this crushing burden was reduced to the more manageable proportions of one hour weekly from 1564.[8]

Yet the Hebrew language in the early modern period was far more than merely the language in which the Bible happened to be written. Contemporaries, and not only in England, were fascinated by the fact that God created the universe by speaking Hebrew: 'Let there be light,' he said, and suddenly all of existence came into being. Furthermore, Hebrew in their eyes was the first language, the original language, from which sprang all other modes of communication. When Adam spoke Hebrew in the Garden of Eden, every word exactly represented the thing he had in mind: Hebrew was a philosophical language, since there was no gap between word and thing, in addition to being the very first tongue used by mankind. As a result, it was reasoned, if we were able to reproduce this first language, we would be some way towards uncovering the secrets of the universe. Contemporaries were well aware of the Jewish cabbala, which itself was becoming more and more based on the study of the Hebrew language in its various permutations, and this intelligence strengthened their view that only contact with Jews could provide them with the missing parts of the puzzle. In general,

---

[8] F. D. Logan, 'The Origins of the So-Called Regius Professorships: An Aspect of the Renaissance in Oxford and Cambridge', *Studies in Church History*, 14 (1977), 277; G. L. Jones, *The Discovery of Hebrew in Tudor England: A Third Language* (Manchester, 1983), 190–201. For lists of incumbents, see *The Historical Register of the University of Oxford* (Oxford, 1900), 50–1; and *The Historical Register of the University of Cambridge*, ed. J. R. Tanner (Cambridge, 1917), 76–7. See generally I. Baroway, 'Toward Understanding Tudor-Jacobean Hebrew Studies', *JSS* 18 (1956), 3–24.

contemporaries understood 'progress' as a return to an imaginary Golden Age. The most popular image, especially in the field of science, was of Adam the philosopher in the Garden of Eden. The revival of Hebrew at all levels, from the means to understanding the Holy Scriptures to its role in the study of the cabbala, emphasized the very existence of modern Jews, and presented them in a very favourable light.[9]

As soon as Hebrew became a subject of study in the universities, and the focus of attention among philosophers, it was clear that the discussion would soon turn to the Jews themselves, although they still remained a theoretical and historical entity for a very long time. The first occasion on which contemporary Jews became the subject of interest and dispute was in connection with the controversy surrounding John Traske, an English minister who was deeply influenced by the Old Testament, until he decided to apply personally some of the command-ments meant only for the Jews, including Sabbath observance on the seventh day and Passover. Traske was convicted of various religious offences in 1618 and was eventually forced to renounce his sins publicly. But the public debate about him was the first discussion in England concerning the proper attitude a Christian should take towards the biblical commandments, and on the necessary relationship between Protestants and Jews. Traske eventually became a Baptist, but many other Judaizers followed in his footsteps, especially those who observed the Sabbath on the seventh day and according to the Jewish principles, and who were extremely influential not only in the period of the readmission of the Jews to England, but also during the Restoration and even until our own day.[10]

More important than the Judaizers in this period were the millen-arians, those who believed in the imminent Second Coming of the Messiah. According to a study of the English clergy in the first half of the seventeenth century, it appears that about 70 per cent of the ministers who published books in this period believed in this interpreta-tion, and a large proportion of them were convinced that the believer was compelled to use all of his power to bring about the return of the Messiah.[11] The place and the role of the Jews were prominent in this plan, and there were many who argued that until their conversion it would not be possible to remove all of the obstacles to the return of

[9] See D. S. Katz, 'The Language of Adam in Seventeenth-Century England', in Hugh Lloyd-Jones, Valerie Pearl, and Blair Worden (eds.), *History & Imagination: Essays in Honour of H. R. Trevor-Roper* (London, 1981), 132–45.

[10] D. S. Katz, *Sabbath and Sectarianism in Seventeenth-Century England* (Leiden, 1988).

[11] B. S. Capp, *The Fifth Monarchy Men* (London, 1972), 38.

Jesus. In order to convert the Jews it was first necessary to bring some of them to England, since, according to these millenarians, the chief reason why Jews persisted in their religion was that they had never seen the pure Protestant faith in its English interpretation. The Jews suffered from the misconception, they explained, that the entire Christian religion consisted of Roman Catholicism of the sort that they had seen in Spain, Portugal, and other places in which they lived. John Robins and Thomas Tany, two more extreme millenarians connected with the radical Fifth Monarchy Men, brought up the subject of the role the Jews would play at the End of Days and by their outlandish behaviour placed it in the centre of English public view.

An event in the Messianic mode was the spark which lit up the entire Jewish problem for the English public. In 1644 a Jew by the name of Antonio Montezinos returned to Amsterdam and claimed that he had made contact with Hebrew-speaking Jews in Ecuador, remnants of the Lost Ten Tribes. This discovery created a good deal of excitement in the entire Jewish world, and in many Christian circles as well. Among those who were entranced by Montezinos was Rabbi Menasseh ben Israel of Amsterdam, who saw his testimony as a sign of the coming of the Messiah, since according to Jewish tradition, a precondition of this cosmic event would be the scattering of the Jewish people to all corners of the globe. The discovery of Jews in South America seemed to help fulfil this prophecy. Menasseh was also well aware of philo-Semitic signs in England, and the return of Jews there would help to disperse them even to that far corner of the earth. The supposed revelation of the Lost Ten Tribes in South America therefore formed the bridge between the dormant pro-Jewish background in England and the campaign to return them there under the leadership of Rabbi Menasseh ben Israel.

In spite of what has been written about religious toleration in England and on the Continent during the early modern period, it was not possible for Menasseh ben Israel to find in England support in principle for the idea of bringing another religion into the existing religious framework. Very few people saw religious toleration as a moral value; countries which permitted more than one confession within their borders usually did so through lack of choice. When Englishmen looked around them at such places they saw only the obvious disadvantages: in France, the result of even limited religious toleration was absolutism; in Holland, dangerous democracy. It is true that at least in the period of the English Civil War, the latitudinarian argument was fashionable, that is, the claim that it is permissible to tolerate religious sects which agree on the root of the religious matter, even if disagreeing about details of ritual or observances. But in the case of the Jews this compromise could never apply. Even the Levellers, crusaders for equality from within the

English army, were ready to recognize only sects which upheld the divinity of Jesus, and in this excluded not only the Jews as potential allies, but also the Unitarians and others.

It is therefore clear that without the firm basis of philo-Semitism and support for the language and culture of the Jews which existed in England in the sixteenth century and the first half of the seventeenth, the mission of Menasseh ben Israel would have been an utter failure. In fact, even before Menasseh began to be active, the Council of State had received a request in January 1649 from two English subjects by the name of Cartwright who were then living in Amsterdam, requesting that the new revolutionary government turn to the Jewish problem in order to facilitate their readmission after 350 years. The Council responded favourably, and promised to deal with this question as soon as the trial of Charles I was concluded, and indeed he was executed shortly after that.[12] During the next seven years the Jewish question simply refused to leave the public eye, and returned again and again to the centre of discussions, almost always in a positive manner. The possible return of this mystical people itself brought with it certain fantastic developments, such as the claim that the Jews were organizing in order to purchase the Bodleian Library, or that they longed to buy St Paul's Cathedral in order to turn it into a synagogue. Nevertheless, the readmission of the Jews to England was gradually becoming more of a reality than a Messianic hope.

II

With the coming of the English delegation to Holland under the leadership of Oliver St John in 1650 in order to negotiate a trade agreement with the Dutch, contact was made with the Jews living in Amsterdam. The English visited Menasseh ben Israel at his synagogue, and the possibility of the return of the Jews to England was discussed without pause. The rabbi received a passport and permission to visit England in that year and in every year until his arrival in September 1655, after the end of the trade war between the two countries. Menasseh was already well known to the English public since the appearance in 1650 of his book *The Hope of Israel*, which in its English version was dedicated to the English Parliament. In this book, Menasseh told the story of Montezinos concerning the South American Israelites, in the hope that these claims would convince the English to discuss the

---

[12] Johanna Cartenright and Ebenezer Cartwright, *The Petition of the Jewes* (London, 1649), 1–3.

Jewish problem in the first days of the new republic, and thereby hasten the Coming of the Messiah.[13] During the next five years, that is, from 1650 to 1655, the tense period of relations between England and Holland, when further progress on the English front was impossible, Menasseh occupied himself with an effort to receive a place at the court of Christina, queen of Sweden, hoping to turn himself into a Jewish Descartes of the North. Only when this effort failed, as a result of Christina's abdication, did Menasseh turn whole-heartedly to his mission in London, the seeds of which had already been planted.[14]

Even though the Jewish question was brought up before the English Parliament in the summer and autumn of 1653, until Menasseh's son came to England in October 1654 little practical work had actually been accomplished. Samuel ben Israel arrived in England accompanied by another Jew by the name of Manuel Martinez Dormido, who saw in this voyage a means of recovering the lands that he had lost in the Portuguese invasion of Brazil. Dormido on his arrival in London submitted two petitions to Cromwell, one calling for a solution to his own personal financial problems, but another in the name of the entire Jewish people, in which he pleaded for the readmission of the Jews to England. The hopes of Dormido in submitting his petitions in themselves say something about the hints and indications which he had received, before starting his journey, about the readmission of the Jews to England.[15] Cromwell preferred not to answer these requests directly, but his actions as usual are more convincing than his public declarations. On 26 February 1655 he wrote a personal letter to the king of Portugal with a request that he help Dormido recover his property. We have no idea of what the king's response was, but the very fact that Cromwell was willing to interest himself in this matter, and to write a letter of this type on behalf of a man who not only was not an English subject but according to the perceived law of the land should not even have been present in England at all shows how convinced Cromwell was about the importance of Menasseh ben Israel's mission.[16]

---

[13] Menasseh ben Israel, *The Hope of Israel*, ed. Moses Wall (2nd edn., London, 1652). See generally Y. Kaplan, *et al.* (eds.), *Menasseh ben Israel and His World* (Leiden, 1989).

[14] D. S. Katz, 'Menasseh ben Israel's Mission to Queen Christina of Sweden', *JSS* 45 (1983–4), 57–72. Cf. S. Åkerman, *Queen Christina of Sweden and Her Circle* (Leiden, 1991).

[15] Dormido to Cromwell, 3 Nov. 1654 (autobiographical): BL MS Eger. 1049, fo. 6^{r-v}; same to same, 3 Nov. 1654 (on behalf of the Jews): BL MS Eger. 1049, fo. 7^{r-v}. Cf. Dormido to Cromwell, 4 Dec. 1655: PRO, SP 84/161, fo. 48^{r-v}.

[16] Bod. Lib., MS Rawl. A 260, fo. 57, and A 261, fo. 37^v: Eng. trans. of Latin original in Oliver Cromwell, *The Writings and Speeches*, ed. W. C. Abbot (Cambridge, Mass., 1937–47), iii. 636.

It was decided that the time had come for Menasseh himself to voyage to England to reap the benefits of the philo-Semitic movement. In May 1655 Menasseh's son reported home on having received a doctorate from Oxford University in the dual fields of medicine and philosophy. The diploma itself was forged, but Menasseh was not aware of this, and certainly believed that it had been awarded to his son as further proof of the esteem in which he and his family were held. In September 1655 Menasseh sent an open letter to the Jewish people with the aim of informing them of his mission to England, and of making them aware of the recent cosmic developments affecting their fate.[17] In the end, Menasseh made the journey to London, apparently before the Jewish New Year (Rosh Hashanah), which began on 22 September 1655. During the following month Menasseh had the opportunity of discussing the matter with Cromwell himself, as he and his mission became the talk of the town, and on 31 October Menasseh formally submitted a petition for the readmission of the Jews to England.

The original text of the petition is in French, and includes seven points for the consideration of the Council. Menasseh's first request was for the general readmission of the Jews as ordinary citizens. He also pleaded for a public synagogue and religious toleration, and the right to consecrate a cemetery. Economic rights were not neglected: Menasseh asked for the privilege of trading freely in all varieties of merchandise. He also suggested that the Jews be permitted to try their cases according to Mosaic law, with right of appeal to English civil law. The entire apparatus of readmission could be supervised by a person of quality who would receive the passports of the immigrant Jews and swear them to fidelity to England. Finally, Menasseh requested that if any anti-Jewish legislation remained in force, this might be annulled so as to leave the Jewish community in greater security. 'Lesquelles choses nous concédant', Menasseh pledged, 'nous demeurerons tousiours les très affectionnés et obligez à prier dieu pour la prospérité de uostre altesse, & de uostre illustre et très sage conseil.' The rabbi also hoped that God would give 'heureux succez à toutes les entreprises de uostre Serenissime Altesse Amen'.[18]

The Council of State received Menasseh's requests, and appointed a subcommittee to investigate the possibility of acceding to them. The committee consisted of seven of the eleven members of the Council present at the meeting of 13 November 1655, that is, President Henry

---

[17] Printed Portuguese original with autograph signature in Venetian State Archives: see plate section here.

[18] SP 18/101, fos. 275^r–276^r. Eng. trans. SP 18/101, fo. 277^{r-v}, also in Bod. Lib., MS Rawl. C 206, fo. 107^{r-v}.

Lawrence, Sir Gilbert Pickering, Sir Charles Wolseley, Lisle, Francis Rous, Major-General John Lambert, and Colonel William Sydenham.[19] The events of the next few days, however, are tainted with uncertainty. We know that the next day, on 14 November, Lisle, Wolseley, and Pickering met with Lawrence to select the men who would be invited to attend the Whitehall Conference called to advise them on the suitability of Jewish readmission.[20] By that date it was clear that whatever decision was reached, it would require the recommendation and endorsement of a broadly based body of community leaders.

There is a document preserved among the state papers which is clearly the report of the subcommittee itself, but as it is undated there is no way to determine whether the seven men offered their advice to the Council before or after the Whitehall Conference which was summoned to advise it on the Jewish readmission question.[21] It seems likely, however, that the date tentatively given in the *Calendar of State Papers*, 13 November 1655, is correct since, after the failure of the Whitehall Conference to produce the verdict that Cromwell desired, he could hardly have allowed the Council subcommittee to reach that conclusion in defiance of the advisory body which it had agreed to consult. The substance of Menasseh's petition was already known long before it was entered among the Council records, and the surviving documentation probably illustrates merely the outlines of the negotiations about the Jews during this month. Cromwell hoped for a swift conclusion of the preliminaries to Jewish readmission, which were probably arranged during the first fortnight in November, between Menasseh's initial overtures to the Council and the meeting at which the delegates to the Whitehall Conference were selected.

In any case, at some point, probably on 13 November 1655, the Council of State acknowledged the receipt of the subcommittee's report on the thesis 'That, the Jewes deservinge it, may be admitted into this nation to trade, and trafficke, and dwel amongst vs as providence shall giue occasion'. Their most significant concession was the decision that 'as to poynt of Conscience we judge lawfull for the Magistrate to admit', but only on the condition that an appended list of seven restrictions was enforced. According to the report, there were a number of weighty reasons which militated against unrestricted Jewish immigration. The motives and grounds discussed in Menasseh's book, they thought, were 'such as we conceaue to be very sinfull for this or any Christian State to

---

[19] *Cal. SP Dom., 1655–6*, 15.   [20] Ibid. 20.

[21] SP 18/101, fos. 281ʳ–283ʳ. For two views on the dating of this document, see *Menasseh ben Israel's Mission to Oliver Cromwell*, ed. L. Wolf (London, 1901), pp. xlv, liv–lv, lxxxiv; and C. Roth, *A History of the Jews in England* (3rd edn., Oxford, 1964), ch. vii.

receaue them vpon'. Public Jewish worship might influence sober Christians from their devotions, and would certainly be scandalous in any case, 'evill in it selfe'. Jewish marriage and divorce customs were contrary to English law, and Jews could not be trusted to keep their oaths, nor should Englishmen forget the injuries against them 'in life, chastity, goods or good name' before the expulsion. The final objection foreshadowed the debate in the Whitehall Conference the next month: the authors of the report pointed out that 'great prejudice is like to arise to the natiues of this Comonwealth in matter of trade, which besides other dangers here mentioned we find very comonly suggested by the inhabitants of the City of London'.[22] The merchants would elaborate on this point at the Conference.

Nevertheless, despite these very vociferous objections to the resettlement of the Jews in England, the members of the subcommittee did not entirely rule out the possibility of readmission. Instead, they offered a list of seven conditions which, if satisfied, might protect Englishmen against the economic and religious rapacity of the Jews. The first of these was that the Jews permitted to come into England should be prohibited from maintaining 'any publicke Judicatoryes, whether Civill or Ecclesiasticall', because these would give the Jews somewhat more than the status of aliens. Jews should also be prohibited from defaming Christianity, from working on Sundays, and from employing Christian servants. They should be excluded from public office, and should be restrained from taking revenge on any of their number who converted to Christianity. Jews should also be prohibited from printing anything 'which in the least opposeth the christian religion in our language'.[23] This last proviso was even more generous than it might appear at first glance, for by removing Hebrew books from the purview of the censor, Anglo-Jewry would have been spared the dangerous and degrading investigation of the Talmud so common on the Continent.

On 14 November 1655 Lisle, Wolseley, and Pickering met with Lawrence to select the delegates to the Whitehall Conference which was to advise the Council subcommittee and the Council itself as to whether these restrictions and safeguards would be sufficient to protect the nation against the likely disadvantages of Jewish immigration.[24] The list of delegates was presented and approved by the Council of State on the following day, and on 16 November 1655 each of the twenty-eight advisers was sent a letter signed by Lawrence summoning them 'to meete with a Comittee of the Councell on Tuesday the foureth of December next in ye afternoone neare the Councell Chamber in

[22] SP 18/101, fos. 281^r–283^r.　　　　　　[23] Ibid.
[24] *Cal. SP Dom., 1655–6*, 20.

Whitehall To the intent some proposalls made to his Highness in referrence to the nation of the Jewes may bee considered'.[25] Over half of those who received this letter were primarily clergymen, including such well-known figures as Thomas Goodwin, John Owen, Matthew Newcomen, Anthony Tuckney, and Henry Jessey. Walter Strickland, one of the diplomats who took part in the abortive Dutch negotiations in 1651, was called, as was his partner on that occasion, Oliver St John, although the latter declined to attend. Two other lawyers did appear, John Glynne, Lord Chief Justice of the Upper Bench, and William Steel, Chief Baron of the Exchequer. The merchants were represented by Lord Mayor Dethick, Sir Christopher Packe, the former Lord Mayor, Aldermen Riccard and Cressett, and Sheriff Thompson. William Kiffin, the merchant-parson also attended, as did Benjamin Whichcote, the provost of King's College, Cambridge, and Ralph Cudworth, the Regius professor of Hebrew there. The function of this august gathering was 'to meet with the Committee', which took part in the discussion as well.[26] Menasseh ben Israel noted the care with which this Whitehall Conference was planned: perceiving England to be 'very tender hearted, and well-wishing to our sore-afflicted Nation', he pinned his hopes on the 'Assembly at *Whitehall*, of Divines, Lawyers, and Merchants, of different perswasions, and opinions'.[27]

III

The coming of Jews to England after an interval of over three centuries was a phenomenon which was bound to take on certain improbable, even bizarre characteristics. The period of the Whitehall Conference must therefore be seen through a haze of fantasy. For example, Joseph Spence, an eighteenth-century parson, heard a tale through Dr Francis Lockier, the dean of Peterborough born thirteen years after the Whitehall Conference ended, who had it from Lord Molesworth, who was supposedly in the room when the Jews offered Lord Godolphin £500,000 for purchasing the town of Brentford along with the right to settle there with full privileges of trade. It was said that they would have paid as much as £1 million. According to Spence, the 'agent from the Jews said, that the affair was already concerted with the chiefs of their brethren abroad; that it would bring the richest of their merchants hither, and of course an addition of above twenty millions of money to

[25] SP 25/76, pp. 383/378–384/379: Council of State Order Book, entry for 15 Nov. 1655.   [26] *Cal. SP Dom., 1655–6*, 23.
[27] Menasseh, *Vindiciae Judaeorum* (n.p., 1656), 38.

circulate in the nation'. Molesworth pressed Godolphin to accept such a generous offer, but the latter wisely pointed out that the clergy and the merchants were sure to oppose: 'he gave other reasons too against it, and in fine it was dropped'.[28]

Other contemporary accounts were not nearly so shop-worn, but were no less fantastic. Henry Townshend recorded in his diary a few weeks after the Conference had ended that Menasseh and the Jews were willing to pay handsomely for the privilege of resettlement. They offered '£100,000 fine and £50,000 per annum, and also securing all persons from any Jewish Merchant breaking out of the public stock, and to bring in a Bank of £300,000 at 4 per cent'.[29] Henry Fletcher, Cromwell's seventeenth-century biographer, claimed that the Jews would have paid £200,000 for readmission and toleration.[30] Giovanni Sagredo, the Venetian ambassador to England, reported to the Doge three days after the Conference ended that

A Jew came from Antwerp and cleverly introduced himself to the Protector, having known him in that city when he was privately travelling in Flanders before he reached his present elevation. When introduced to his Highness he began not only to kiss but to press his hands and touching his whole body with the most exact care. When asked why he behaved so he replied that he had come from Antwerp solely to see if his Highness was of flesh and blood since his superhuman deeds indicated that he was more than a man and some divine composition issued from heaven.[31]

Forty years after the events themselves, the author of another Continental account would claim that it was the Jews of Asia who sent Jacob ben Azabel and David ben Eleazar of Prague and Menasseh ben Israel to Cromwell to negotiate for the return of the Jews. While waiting to see Cromwell, they were said to have made a detour to the Bodleian and Cambridge University libraries, and then to have persuaded the Protector to sell them the most valuable books and manuscripts deposited there. Cromwell agreed to the purchase in order to take revenge on the Royalists in these centres of learning. On one of their cataloguing trips to Cambridge, the Jewish delegation found time to pay a visit to Huntingdon to establish from the parish registers whether

---

[28] Joseph Spence, *Anecdotes, Observations, and Characters* (2nd edn., London, 1858), 58.

[29] Henry Townshend, *Diary*, ed. J. W. Willis (Worcestershire Hist. Soc., xxxi, 1915–20), 30.

[30] [Henry Fletcher], *The Perfect Politician* (London, 1660), 291. According to William Lilly in 1673, 'his Majesty giues the Jews 10 000 li for remitting their money hither, and to make them amends for the larg brib they gaue, etc': Lilly to Elias Ashmole, 27 Oct. 1673: Bod. Lib., MS Rawl. D 864, fos. 59–60ᵛ.

[31] *Cal. SP Ven.*, *1655–6*, 160–1.

Cromwell was of Jewish stock and, if so, whether he was of the Davidic line and therefore might be the Messiah. The writer maintained that it was the ridicule heaped on Cromwell by the news of this genealogical expedition, and a short pamphlet published about this time entitled 'Cromwell, Lion of the Tribe of Judah', that drove him to reject Jewish resettlement before his standing with the English people was damaged further.[32]

Fortunately, much more reliable accounts of the Whitehall Conference exist, even aside from the summaries printed in the news-sheets. Two complete narratives were both published anonymously, one by Henry Jessey, the Baptist Saturday-Sabbatarian, and the other by Nathaniel Crouch, who wrote numerous works under the name of Robert or Richard Burton until his death in about 1725.[33] Jessey especially emphasized the interest which the Whitehall Conference had aroused throughout England, and acknowledged that he was moved to publish an accurate account of the meeting by demand from friends in the provinces.[34]

The Whitehall Conference was opened by Cromwell himself on 4 December 1655 near the chambers of the Council of State. Menasseh's seven-point petition was read aloud, and Cromwell directed the Conference to consider whether the Jews were presenting unreasonable requests and, if not, whether it would be lawful to readmit them, and under what conditions. The terms of the debate having been set, Cromwell thereupon dismissed the Conference until 7 December, to enable the members to consider Menasseh's petition.[35] They reconvened on that day in the afternoon in a session which was, like the previous meeting, closed to outsiders. Some information inevitably leaked out, and the intelligence which appeared in the newspapers loyal to Cromwell could very well have been planted there by government officials. But, whatever the source of these reports, it is clear that the broad outlines of the proceedings at Whitehall were communicated to

[32] Raguenet, *Histoire d'Olivier Cromwel* (Utrecht, 1692), ii. 83–6. Similarly, G. Leti, *La Vie d'Olivier Cromwel* (Amsterdam, 1746), iv. 371–6: dedication dated 10 Jan. 1694; and de Larrey, *Histoire d'Angleterre* (Amsterdam, 1707–13), 341. The Jews of Prague may not have been entirely mythical if Jacob ben Azabel is the same man as 'Jacob Aszik, Hebreo d'Praga' who sent a petition to Charles II after the Restoration for permission to farm taxes among the Jews: Hist. MSS Comm., *xxii, Leeds MSS*, 38.

[33] *DNB*, s.v., 'Burton, Robert or Richard'.

[34] [Henry Jessey], *A Narrative of the late Proceeds at White-Hall* (London, 1656); [Nathaniel Crouch], 'The Proceedings of the *Jews* in *England* in the Year 1655', in *Two Journeys to Jerusalem*, ed. R. B[urton=Crouch] (London, 1719), 167–74. This book was published in several forms under different titles, including *Memorable Remarks* and *Judaeorum memorabilia*.

[35] [Crouch], 'Proceedings', 167–8; *Publick Intelligencer*, 10 (3–10 Dec. 1655), 159.

the public, and that they usually square with the more reliable accounts which emerged long after the members had been dismissed and sent home. It is therefore instructive initially to examine the reflections of the Whitehall Conference in the most contemporaneous reports before supplementing them with the later complete chronicles of Jessey and Crouch.

References to the Conference while it was in session appear in a wide variety of locations, not only in newspapers, but also in private letters and the reports of foreign ambassadors. The first account of the meeting of 7 December 1655, in which the issue of Jewish readmission was debated initially, appeared in the news-sheets: 'nothing was concluded, but there is another conference appointed to be on Wednesday next'.[36] The envoy of the grand duke of Tuscany in London, Francesco Salvetti, also reported that as yet opinion ran counter to Jewish readmission.[37] Peter Julius Coyet, the Swedish envoy, informed Charles X on that day that many 'think that they may be permitted to settle and trade, but on condition of paying a large sum annually, and of attending sermons at least once a week, in the hope that this may lead to their conversion, which is earnestly prayed for'.[38]

Among the most interesting of the private letters during these crucial days were those written by Captain Francis Willoughby, the navy commissioner at Portsmouth, to Robert Blackborne, the secretary of the Admiralty commissioners. Two days after the close of the second meeting of the Whitehall Conference Blackborne provided Willoughby with a summary of the main events there, as far as he knew them. Willoughby was very concerned by these developments, and commented that if Jews were permitted to live in England, he hoped the next issue would be 'whether a nation shall be suffered to liue amongst vs to blaspheme Christ by a law'.[39]

Cromwell was worried as well, for the Conference seemed reluctant to expedite the readmission of the Jews. After the second meeting, the Council of State agreed to pack the Conference with supporters of Jewish toleration, and the names of Hugh Peter, Peter Sterry, and John

---

[36] *Publick Intelligencer*, 10 (3–10 Dec. 1655), 160; *Mercurius politicus*, 287 (5–13 Dec. 1655), 5815–16.

[37] Salvetti's letters are preserved in the State Archives of Florence, but copies exist in BL Add. MS 27962. A transcript from the Florence MSS with a partial trans. from the Italian was repr. by C. Roth, 'New Light on the Resettlement', *TJHSE* 11 (1928), 112–42. For this reference, Francesco Salvetti to Senator Bali Gondi, 7/17 Dec. 1655, see *TJHSE* 11 (1928), 128, 137–8.

[38] Coyet to Charles X, 7 Dec. 1655, from London: *Swedish Diplomats at Cromwell's Court, 1655–1656*, ed. M. Roberts (Camden Soc., 4th ser. xxxvi, 1988), 215.

[39] SP 18/102, fo. 5ʳ: Willoughby to Blackborne, 10 Dec. 1655.

Boncle (Bunkley) were added to the list of members.[40] Boncle's role at the Conference remains hidden,[41] and no record survives of Sterry's activities there.[42] Hugh Peter, on the other hand, supported the Jewish case in print.[43] In any case, even the attendance of Cromwell and the three philo-Semites at the third meeting on 12 December 1655 proved ineffective: 'not comming to any conclusion, the conference is put off till Friday'.[44]

The obstacles in the path of Jewish readmission were becoming apparent, even to those who received only second- or third-hand reports of the Whitehall Conference and the deliberations there. Major-General Edward Whalley wrote to Thurloe from Nottingham on 12 December that

I am glad so godly and prudent a course is taken concerning the Jewes; yet cannot conceive the reason, why so great varietye of opinion should bee amongst such men, as I heare are called to consult about them. It seemes to me that there are both politique and divine reasons; which strongly make for theyre admission into a cohabitation and civill commerce with us.

Whalley did not neglect the economic factors of Jewish readmission. 'Doubtlesse to say no more,' he reminded Thurloe, 'they will bring in much wealth into this commonwealth.' But his grounds for Jewish readmission were not entirely self-serving: Whalley pointed out that it was unreasonable to pray for the conversion of the Jews while at the same time denying the means. 'Besides,' he recalled, 'when we were aliens from the covenant of promise, they prayed for us.'[45]

Whalley could not have known the details of the meeting of 12 December, but by the time Willoughby sent his next letter to Blackborne, he was already thanking him for his 'full relation' of that session. 'I know not by y^t m^r peeters came as neere as some others in his aduice,' Willoughby mused,

[40] *Cal. SP Dom., 1655–6*, 52.

[41] All of the records of the Whitehall Conference refer to Boncle as 'Bulkeley' or 'Bulkley', always of Eton College, but surely this is the same man. Boncle was headmaster at Eton from 22 Aug. 1654 to 18 Sept. 1655, and a fellow there until the Restoration. He was a Cambridge man who was admitted MA of Oxford on 22 Dec. 1652 on special letters from Cromwell, and was appointed master of Charterhouse in 1653: Anthony Wood, *Fasti Oxonienses*, ed. P. Bliss (3rd edn., London, 1815–20), ii. 174; *The Eton College Register 1441–1698*, ed. W. Sterry (Eton, 1943), xxi; Victoria County History, *Bucks.*, ii. 197.

[42] V. de Sola Pinto, *Peter Sterry* (Cambridge, 1934), 31.

[43] Hugh Peters, *A word for the Armie* (London, 1647), 11, 12.

[44] *Mercurius politicus*, 287 (5–13 Dec. 1655), 5820.

[45] *A Collection of the State Papers of John Thurloe, Esq.*, ed. Thomas Birch (London, 1742), iv. 308.

itt is a busines of noe smaule consernm^t the lord in mercy direct in itt, they are
indeed a people to whome many glorious promises are made: but they are a
people as full of blasphemy as any vnder ye sun, a selfe seeking generation, &
those psons in pticular who are ye greatest sticklers I feare minding little but
there own accomodacon: And whether they be able to proue them selues Jews is
a question to mee.[46]

Willoughby's obscure reference at the end of the letter was amplified in
his next epistle, which he wrote two days later in response to
Blackborne's report written on 15 December, the day after the fourth
and penultimate session of the Whitehall Conference. Willoughby
confessed that he found himself agreeing with Hugh Peter once again,
especially in light of the fact that 'there may be iust ground to question
whether they be Jewes'. For it seemed to him that 'some of them may
haue bin obserued to haue made but litle contience of there owne
prinsiples'.[47] Willoughby, and many of his contemporaries, were only
now coming to realize that thousands of Jews were forced to become
Marranos, and to practise their faith in total secrecy under the guise of
Roman Catholicism.

While Francis Willoughby and Robert Blackborne were exchanging
letters, the Tuscan envoy was reporting on the Conference to Italy. On
14 December 1655, the day of the penultimate meeting, Salvetti noted
that 'very few of this nation are agreed to let them make their nest in
these lands'.[48] This pessimistic assessment was reiterated by Thurloe
himself, in a letter to Henry Cromwell, with the army in Ireland:

The point of conscience hath beene only controverted yet, viz. wheither it be
lawefull to admitt the Jewes ... The divines doe very much differ in their
judgements about it, some beinge for their admittance upon fittinge cautions,
others are in expresse termes against it upon any termes whatsoever. The like
difference I finde in the counsell, and soe amongst all Christians abroad.

Thurloe noted that readmission was being 'debated with much candor
and ingenuitye, and without any heat'. Nevertheless, although the Jews
had made 'an earnest desire' to Cromwell for readmission, Thurloe was
'apt to thinke, that nothinge will be done therein'.[49]

Thurloe's assessment of the first four sessions of the Whitehall
Conference was probably the best informed of the contemporaneous
reflections of these meetings. Although not a member of the Conference
himself, Thurloe may be assumed to have been privy to the closed

---

[46] Willoughby to Blackborne, 15 Dec. 1655: SP 18/102, fo. 74^r.

[47] W. to B., 17 Dec. 1655: SP 18/102, fo. 76^r.

[48] Salvetti to Senator Bali Gondi, 14/24 Dec. 1655: repr. Roth, 'New Light', 128–9,
138. Cf. Coyet to Charles X, 14 Dec. 1655, from London: *Swedish Diplomats*, ed.
Roberts, 221.   [49] *Thurloe State Papers*, iv. 321.

sessions between 4 and 14 December 1655. It was only in the spring of 1656, when Henry Jessey published his eye-witness account, that full details of these private meetings were revealed to all. Crouch's narrative seems to have been copied directly from Jessey's, but with the important addition of the names of the speakers so that we can isolate the philo-Semites at the Whitehall Conference. Jessey neatly divided the range of opinion into three parts. 'The most' feared that if the Jews were readmitted they would seduce and cheat the English. 'The Major part' thought that the Jews might be tolerated if suitable precautions could be devised. 'Some' argued that once these safeguards were invented the English positively had a duty to readmit the Jews, not merely the opportunity to allow their immigration.[50]

The delegates in the first group, those who believed that England would suffer from Jewish readmission, were primarily merchants, although there were some divines who argued that 'though never such cautions to prevent those evils were prescribed, yet they would not be observed; and therefore they could not consent to their coming'.[51] Matthew Newcomen even argued that if the Jews were readmitted they might begin offering children to Moloch. He reminded scoffers that although such practices might seem abhorrent to sober Christians, the opinions of the Quakers and the Ranters also seemed unreasonable, yet there were many who subscribed to them.[52] Nevertheless, it was London merchants who dominated this faction at the Whitehall Conference: their argument was that Jewish readmission would enrich foreigners at the expense of Englishmen. Even some divines worried about showing mercy to the Jews at the expense of the merchants. The philo-Semites pointed out that since the Jews were primarily international traders, and did not deal in 'Husbandry, nor buying houses, nor in Manufactures', therefore:

the Jews coming and so trading might tend to the bringing lower the prizes of all sorts of commodities imported; and to the furtherence of all that have commodities vendible to be exported; and to the benefit of most of our Manufactures (where they shal live) by their buying of them. And thus, though the Merchants gains were somewhat abated, it might tend to the benefit of very many in our Nation, even in outward things, besides the hopes of their conversion; which time (it's hoped) is now at hand, even at the door.

This last somewhat incongruous point, Jessey noted parenthetically, 'was spoken of at a more private meeting'.[53]

The second faction, a majority of the delegates according to Jessey, believed that the Jews might be readmitted under suitable precautions.

---

[50] [Jessey], *Narrative*, 2–3.
[51] Ibid. 2.
[52] Ibid. 8; [Crouch], 'Proceedings', pp. 168–9.
[53] [Jessey], *Narrative*, 8–9.

This argument enjoyed the weighty backing of Justices Glynne and Steel, who revealed to the Conference that 'there is no Law against their coming'. This judgement was quite correct, in fact, since the Jews had been expelled by royal order of Edward I, rather than by Parliament, and presumably a protectoral decree could countermand the explusion. Glynne and Steel recommended that Jews be permitted in England for a trial period, under 'tearms, and agreements'. If the Jews failed to live up to expectations, they could be expelled once again with 'no just cause of exceptions'.[54] This simple declaration by two of the leading lawyers in the land was very influential in the Conference, and Jessey alluded to it several times in his narrative. The precise date on which this crucial piece of information was revealed is not known, but on 14 December 1655, the day of the penultimate session, John Evelyn recorded in his diary that 'Now were the *Jewes* admitted.'[55] The statement by Glynne and Steel is the only one which might have prompted such a conclusion.

Here again, the arguments put forward by delegates in this second faction were divine as well as politique. Jessey himself elaborated on the hope that the Jews might be converted if exposed to the pure light of the English Reformation. He argued that the English were especially likely to promote their conversion because Gentiles must provoke the Jews to jealousy and then emulation, and examples of holy life were prevalent in England.[56] Some divines had explained that although they earnestly wished for the conversion of the Jews, they worried lest their readmission serve to provide yet another sect to mislead Christians. Lawrence and Lambert therefore replied that sectarians, who 'are carried away under notion of further light, or of new discoveries of Christ, or the Gospel', were unlikely to become converts to Judaism, which denies the most fundamental points of all Christian faiths. In any case, they noted, there was so much in Judaism which was 'very ridiculous' that it was unlikely Jews could win many proselytes in England.[57] Another delegate pointed out that it was unfair to permit Turks to trade and enter England if this privilege were denied to the Jews.[58] In short, this second group would have permitted Jewish immigration, with the understanding that certain safeguards—such as prohibitions against proselytizing, cheating, blaspheming Christ and Christianity—would have to be instituted to protect native Englishmen.

The third faction at the Whitehall Conference argued that not only did the Jews deserve to be readmitted, but England had a positive duty

---

[54] [Jessey], *Narrative*, 5, 8, 9; [Crouch], 'Proceedings', 169–72.
[55] *Diary of John Evelyn*, ed. E. S. de Beer (Oxford, 1955), iii. 163.
[56] [Jessey], *Narrative*, 4.   [57] Ibid. 8; [Crouch], 'Proceedings', 168.
[58] [Jessey], *Narrative*, 8.

to readmit them, and if they failed to grasp this opportunity, the vengeance of God would be upon their heads. Justice Steel provided the Conference with a long summary of the history of the Jews in England before the expulsion of 1290. As one of the participants commented, the only conclusion that could be drawn from this sorry tale was that the Jews under English rule had '*suffered very great injuries*, and cruelties, and murders . . . as our own Chronicles shew'. This injustice was especially reprehensible because even after the Jews rejected Jesus Christ, and God rejected them, they still remained his chosen people, 'beloved for their Fathers sakes'. If God plagued Israel after Saul's death until justice had been done to the mistreated Gibeonites, how much more would England be afflicted if some kind of restitution were not made to the Jews? Readmission to England was particularly important to the Jews at this time, it was pointed out by Jessey and others at the Conference, because they were suffering in eastern Europe in the Swedish wars, which had the additional effect of interrupting the flow of alms to the Jews of Jerusalem, who in turn were being persecuted by the Turks.[59]

The millenarian aspect of Jewish readmission was especially pertinent for this most philo-Semitic faction at the Whitehall Conference. 'In our Nation', noted Joseph Caryl, 'the good people generally have more beleeved the promises touching the calling of the Jews, and the great riches and glory that shall follow to Jews, and us Gentiles.' These heavenly goals still lay before them, and in England the faithful 'have (and do stil) more often, and earnestly pray for it, then any other Nation that we have heard of'.[60] Philip Nye and Thomas Goodwin joined Caryl in putting forward this third position most vociferously before the Conference. All of the philo-Semites at the meeting agreed that once the Jews were readmitted to England, the way would be clear for them to convert to Christianity. The only technical question still unresolved was whether they would suddenly be converted together after the personal appearance of Christ on earth, or as individuals 'as of French, &c.'[61]

The published narratives, personal letters, and official accounts make it abundantly clear that Menasseh understated the point when he remarked that the members of the Whitehall Conference were 'of different perswasions, and opinions. Whereby mens judgements, and sentences were different.'[62] This assessment was written in April 1656, long after the final, and public, meeting of the Conference on 18 December 1655. Unfortunately for the advocates of Jewish readmission,

[59] Ibid. 3–7, 9; [Crouch], 'Proceedings', 169–73.
[60] [Crouch] 'Proceedings', 173; [Jessey], *Narrative*, 6–8.
[61] [Jessey], *Narrative*, 3–4, 5–6; [Crouch], 'Proceedings', 172–3.
[62] Menasseh, *Vindiciae* 38.

by the time the Conference reconvened for what was to be the last time, the tide had already turned against any formal resettlement.

One of the factors in this change was surely the dramatic about-face of one of Menasseh's chief supporters, John Dury. During the criticial period of the Whitehall Conference Dury was on the Continent, acting as Cromwell's unofficial agent in The Netherlands, Switzerland, and Germany. His absence from England obliged Samuel Hartlib, his friend and go-between, to write to him at Cassel for his views on readmission, now that toleration of the Jews had advanced beyond theorizing and had become a practical proposition.[63] Dury's reply is important because it illustrates the development in the attitude of one committed and well-informed philo-Semite, who began to waver when faced with the prospect of living Jews rather than theological abstractions. Dury argued that the admission of the Jews into a commonwealth was not only lawful, but 'expedient'. His outline of the conditions under which the Jews could be tolerated demonstrates his conviction that the prime purpose of Jewish immigration was conversion. Jews were to be compelled to listen to proselytizing sermons without debate, and were to be forbidden to discuss their religion with Christians. Dury discounted any economic factors, and sought to readmit the Jews on purely religious and conversionist grounds. The English government, in turn, was to safeguard the rights of Jews in every country, by including special clauses in contracts with nations that regularly oppressed their Jewish populations. Dury listed a number of other restrictive conditions, and minimized his earlier millenarian ideals: 'the times and seasons of their deliverance', he explained, 'are in God's hand alone, and that we are very much inclined to mistake in conjectures of that nature'.[64]

Dury wrote to England on 18 December 1655, the day of the last session of the Whitehall Conference, explaining that although Jews might be of some use in the war against Spain, restraints must be placed on their activities none the less. Dury sent the fair copy of his proposals to Thurloe, who had also requested Dury's opinion of Menasseh's controversial plan.[65] Soon after he dispatched his reply, however, Dury

[63] For more on Dury and Hartlib, see H. R. Trevor-Roper, 'Three Foreigners: The Philosophers of the Puritan Revolution', in his *Religion, the Reformation, and Social Change* (London, 1967), 237–93; G. H. Turnbull, *Hartlib, Dury and Comenius* (London, 1947); and C. Webster, *The Great Instauration* (London, 1975).

[64] John Dury, *A Case of Conscience, Whether it be Lawful to Admit Jews into a Christian Common-wealth?* (London, 1656), repr. W. Oldys (ed.), *The Harleian Miscellany* (London, 1808–13), vii. 251–6, esp. 255. The original MS of Dury's reply is now BL Add. MS 4459, fos. 164ʳ–165ᵛ, although it is not so entered in the catalogue. Fos. 166ʳ–167ᵛ are Dury's note concerning the Jews in Hesse, which he promised to send to Hartlib.   [65] Turnbull, *Hartlib*, 282.

received a copy of Menasseh's specific petition to the Council of State, and became so concerned that he amended even his moderate report in a letter to Hartlib dated 22 January 1656. England would do best 'to go warily, and by degrees' concerning the Jews, he thought, and Menasseh's request was excessive in any case. Dury noted that the Jews 'have ways beyond all other men, to undermine a state, and to insinuate into those that are in offices, and prejudicate the trade of others; and therefore, if they be not wisely restrained, they will, in short time, be oppressive; if they be such as are here in Germany'. This final judgement appeared as a postscript when the pamphlet was published in June 1656.[66]

John Dury was hardly an opponent of the Jews: even the year after his pamphlet appeared, Dury was involved with Henry Jessey in providing charity for the Jews of Jerusalem who were reduced to poverty when the Swedish navy's blockade of eastern Europe halted the flow of Jewish alms.[67] A far more dangerous enemy was William Prynne, the great polemicist, who followed the proceedings of the first four meetings of the Whitehall Conference with a less sympathetic eye. According to his own account, when the Whitehall Conference was already in session he began to collect materials hurriedly so that his book 'might come into the world in *due season*, before any *final Resolves* upon the late *Whitehall Debates*'. The first part of his *Demurrer* was already in the hands of interested delegates before the final meeting of 18 December 1655, and therefore was probably one of the most important factors in the ultimate failure of the Conference to come to any formal conclusion about the desirability of readmission. Prynne wrote afterwards that he hoped both parts of his work together would provide 'a perpetual Barr to the Antichristian Iews re-admission into England, both in this new-fangled age, & all future Generations; maugre all printed pleas, and Endeavors for their present Introduction'.[68]

The success of Prynne's work was no doubt due to the fact that it is not by any means a hysterical denunciation of the Jews and their alleged crimes. Instead, it is, as Prynne himself described the book, an 'exact *Chronological Relation*' which he had 'collected out of the best Historians and Records'.[69] His report of foreign practice with regard to the Jews made a neat summary of many of the diffuse observations scattered throughout the travel literature. This basic narrative was supplemented by a description of the obstacles to readmission to be found both in English law and in Scripture. Prynne even refused to accept that the

---

[66] Dury, *Conscience*, 256.

[67] D. S. Katz, 'Anonymous Advocates of the Readmission of the Jews to England', *Michael*, 10 (1986), 117–42.

[68] William Prynne, *A Short Demurrer to the Jewes* (2nd edn., London, 1656), ii, sig. A2.   [69] Ibid. i, title-page.

Jews might be called at the End of Days. Yet, in spite of his declared hostility to the Jews, Prynne's history remains a faithful compilation of the materials available in his day for a history of the Jews in England. His horrific account of the almost-forgotten ritual murder calumnies regarding William of Norwich in 1144 and Little St Hugh of Lincoln in 1255, added to the condemnation of imagined economic crimes before the expulsion, could not help but influence the delegates at the final meeting of the Whitehall Conference.

IV

Although it appears that Cromwell intended the meeting of 14 December to conclude the issue, another session was scheduled for 18 December 1655, and, unlike the others, this one was open to the public. One of those who pressed in among the crowd was the young Paul Rycaut, later to become well known for his activities in the East. Rycaut was very impressed by Cromwell's address to the assembled delegates, and remembered years later that he had never heard a man speak so well in his life. According to Rycaut, Cromwell first allowed the Jews to present their case, although there is no record that Menasseh ben Israel attended any of the sessions of the Whitehall Conference.[70] More likely, someone read the rabbi's proposals to the Conference members and the crowd of interested observers, since Menasseh's seven-point petition was printed in the news-sheets as part of the report of the meeting.[71] Rycaut recounted that Cromwell then asked the clergy to summarize their position, which they did in most negative terms. The Protector reminded them that the Jews would one day be called into the Church, and pointed out that it was the duty of all good Christians to work towards that end. Furthermore, given the exalted and purified state of religion in England, it would be particularly desirable to readmit the Jews so as to prevent them from falling into the hands of the idolaters on the Continent. The merchants then spoke against the Jews and argued that they would take trade from Englishmen and behave dishonestly. Cromwell seemed to agree with them and began to speak of the Jews as the most contemptible and despicable people on earth. After this diatribe he is quoted as asking the merchants, 'Can you really be afraid . . . that this mean despised people should be able to prevail in trade and credit over the merchants of England, the noblest and most esteemed merchants of the whole world!'[72]

[70] Spence, *Anecdotes*, 58–9. See below, p. 142.
[71] *Publick Intelligencer*, 12 (17–24 Dec. 1655), 191–2; *Mercurius Politicus*, 289 (20–7 Dec. 1655), 5842–3.   [72] Spence, *Anecdotes*, 58–9.

Unfortunately, despite the attractive qualities of Rycaut's narrative, it retains a somewhat fairy-tale flavour, especially in light of his inaccurate conclusion that, having silenced the critics of readmission, Cromwell 'was at liberty to grant what he desired to the Jews'.[73] In any case, although Rycaut's memory may have been faulty after decades, we may accept his account of the agenda of the final meeting, if not his conclusions.

The more reliable reports of Jessey and Crouch continue the narrative to the very end of the session, and provide the text of Cromwell's closing address. In dismissing the Whitehall Conference, Cromwell reminded the delegates that he had no interest in Jewish readmission which was not congruent with Scripture, 'and that since there was a Promise of their Conversion, means must be used to that end, which was the preaching of the Gospel, and that could not be had unless they were permitted to reside where the Gospel was preached'. He had hoped that the Conference would have come to a definite conclusion at least in regard to the theoretical value of Jewish toleration, if not to the legality of readmission, but unfortunately this was not to be. The entire question now seemed even more insoluble, Cromwell noted, but he hoped the Lord would direct him and the Council of State to the good of the nation. 'And thus', Jessey concludes, 'was the dismission of that Assembly.'[74]

Cromwell seems to have intended to allow the entire matter to cool off somewhat rather than to attempt an immediate resolution of the Jewish question in the face of strong opposition in the Whitehall Conference and among the public outside. By the end of December nothing had yet been resolved, despite the impatience and anxiety of Menasseh and other interested parties. 'No decision yet about the Jews,' Coyet informed the king of Sweden on 28 December 1655. 'The protector proceeds very cautiously: the theologians strongly oppose it, from every pulpit.'[75] On 31 December Menasseh paid a visit to the Dutch ambassador to assure him that he did not intend to bankrupt Holland of its Jewish merchants and traders, only to find a refuge for the crypto-Jews suffering at the hands of the Inquisition.[76] Cromwell had still declined to act by 11/21 January 1655/6, and Salvetti wrote that therefore 'it is not believed that he will declare it so soon as they desire, since it is a matter of great consequence, and such as to cause general

---

[73] Ibid. 59.

[74] [Crouch], 'Proceedings', 173–4; [Jessey], *Narrative*, 9.

[75] Coyet to Charles X, 28 Dec. 1655, from London: *Swedish Diplomats*, ed. Roberts, 224. Coyet also enclosed a copy of Menasseh's petition.

[76] *Thurloe State Papers*, iv. 333.

disgust in this nation'.[77] The following week brought no further revelations, but Salvetti now thought that Cromwell would 'postpone action while conniving in the meantime at religious exercise in their private houses, as they do at present' in lieu of granting the Jews permission to maintain a public synagogue.[78] This expedient solution to the request for Jewish toleration seems to have been carried out by Cromwell's government, and Salvetti confirmed this 'connivance' at private religious assemblies in two other letters in the second half of the month.[79] Salvetti's report of 8/18 February 1655/6 makes no mention of the Jews for the first time in over two months, and on 15/25 February he concluded with the note that Jewish readmission was no longer a subject of popular debate.[80]

V

The failure of the Whitehall Conference to come to any definite conclusions about the readmission of the Jews was a bitter disappointment to the English supporters of Menasseh ben Israel's mission to London. The public phase of the campaign for readmission was over: opposition from merchants and clergymen proved too strong to permit any formal invitation to the exiled Jews to return to England. Cromwell appears to have toyed with the idea of making some kind of official statement, but instead chose to let the matter rest in obscurity. The subcommittee of the Council of State declined even to submit a report of its findings. As early as the middle of January 1655/6 the fears of the Royalists had been somewhat allayed, and the unpleasant prospect of rich and influential Continental Jews in the service of the Commonwealth no longer seemed likely. 'I had almost forgot', Colonel Robert Whitley mentioned casually to Sir Edward Nicholas in a letter from Calais, 'y^t Cromwell sayes it is an vngodly thing to introduce ye Jewes; but, if he refuse y^m, it is because they refuse to purchase it at ye summe desired unlesse they may haue ye authority of a parlement for theire being there with safety.'[81] Whitley was mistaken in believing that any

---

[77] Salvetti to the Grand Duke, 11/21 Jan. 1655/6: repr. Roth, 'New Light', 131, 140–1.

[78] Salvetti to the Grand Duke, 18/28 Jan. 1655/6: repr. ibid. 131–2, 141.

[79] Salvetti to Senator Bali Gondi, 25 Jan./4 Feb. 1655/6; same to same, 1/11 Feb. 1655/6: repr. ibid. 132–3, 141.

[80] Salvetti to Senator Bali Gondi, 8/18 Feb. 1655/6; same to same, 15/25 Feb. 1655/6: see ibid. 132.

[81] *The Nicholas Papers*, ed. G. F. Warner (Camden Soc., NS xl, l, lvii; 3rd ser. xxxi; 1886–1920), iii. 255 (14/24 Jan. 1655/6).

monetary transaction was involved, for Menasseh was virtually alone at this time in trying to procure a formal readmission. The crypto-Jews of the Commonwealth were content to worship in secrecy as long as their trade was left undisturbed. In any case, the lawyers at the Conference had determined that no additional legislation was needed to readmit the Jews, and even Prynne's research did not altogether establish that the expulsion under Edward I had been ratified by Parliament.

Cromwell certainly did not believe that it would be ungodly to readmit the Jews, merely that it was untimely to do so publicly. Nevertheless, his actions spoke louder than his words. Antonio Ferdinando Carvajal, the greatest figure in the Jewish community under Cromwell, had submitted a very audacious request to the Protector on 9 November 1655, only four days after Menasseh sent his seven-point petition to Cromwell in the name of the Jewish nation. Carvajal explained that he had most of his estate in the Canary Islands, and was therefore forced to devise some means of rescuing what he could to protect himself against the new embargo and seizure of the property of English subjects. Carvajal pointed out that the Spanish ambassador had already taken notice of his endenization in England, which rendered him liable to prosecution in Spanish territory. As Carvajal explained it to the Protector, his plan was to fit out a ship with a Dutch crew and a false bill of lading to take away his goods from the Canaries. Carvajal hoped that Cromwell would 'give order to the men of warre of this commonwealth to bee ayding and assisting to the shipp in her voyadge homewards' so that he could smuggle his goods into London. Cromwell recommended this petition to the consideration of the Council on 9 November 1655, but it was formally recorded only on 18 December 1655, the very day of the last meeting of the Whitehall Conference. The entire affair was cleared up the following June.[82]

Carvajal's scheme, and Cromwell's favourable response to it, is emblematic of the attitude of the Anglo-Jewish community to the Whitehall Conference, and of the Protector's dealings with them. It is remarkable that the leading member of the secret Jewish congregation in London should promote a purely private affair before Cromwell within a matter of days after Menasseh ben Israel had arrived in London to seek the annulment of the expulsion order against the Jews. And it is no less surprising that this private petition should have been considered by the Council of State on the very day that the hopes of official readmission were dashed for ever.

Menasseh had not come to England merely in order to ratify the *de*

---

[82] SP 18/102, fos. 83ʳ–84ᵛ. On Carvajal generally, see L. Wolf, 'The First English Jew', *TJHSE* 2 (1896), 14–46.

facto toleration of the Jews which already existed, but in order to secure Cromwell's endorsement of his plan to make England a refuge for victims of the Inquisition. Menasseh was not the only one who suffered from the rejection by the delegates of Whitehall. Henry Jessey recorded that

Many Jewish Merchants had come from beyond seas to *London*, and hoped they might have enjoyed as much priviledge here, in respect of Trading, and of their Worshipping . . . here, in Synagogues, publickly, as they enjoy in *Holland* . . . But after the conference and Debate at *VVhite-Hall* was ended, they heard by some, that the greater part of the Ministers were against this: therefore they removed hence again to beyond the Seas, with much grief of heart, that they were thus disappointed of their hopes.[83]

Menasseh himself failed to realize that his mission had ended in utter failure, and had merely secured the judgement that in theory there was no legal bar to Jewish resettlement. As late as April 1656 he was still awaiting a final determination from Cromwell.[84] The secret Jews of London would soon mount a campaign for toleration on their own for entirely different reasons, but Menasseh's role would be minimal. Within three years John Sadler could lament that 'He had stayed heere so long, that he was allmost ashamed to returne to those that sent him; or to exact theyr maintenance Heere where they found so little success, after so many Hopes.'[85]

VI

The mission of Menasseh ben Israel to England cast an unwelcome spotlight on the little Jewish colony in the City, led by Antonio Ferdinando Carvajal and Antonio Rodrigues Robles, and revealed their identities publicly, even though some well-travelled Englishmen must have already suspected their true faith. But attention was not called to them unduly even after the Whitehall Conference, and they continued to receive Jewish visitors from abroad without molestation.[86] One of their number, Simon de Caceres, was even referred to casually as a Jew in an official document of 22 January 1655/6, as if his presence in

---

[83] [Jessey], *Narrative*, 10. One of these Jews was Raphael Supino of Leghorn: see Roth, 'New Light', 118–26, 137.

[84] [Jessey], *Narrative*, 10; Menasseh, *Vindiciae*, 38–9.

[85] John Sadler to Richard Cromwell, 4 Jan. 1658/9: SP 18/200, fo. 23.

[86] BL Add. MS 34015, fos. 25, 43, 46, 73: alien arrivals in London, 1656–7. These fos. include notices of individuals who were obviously Jews who had arrived in London between 14 Aug. 1656 and 13 June 1657. Repr. *TJHSE* 10 (1924), 127–8.

London was not even slightly irregular.[87] Most probably they would have continued in this fashion for much longer, had not international affairs forced them to climb on the bandwagon which Menasseh had already provided, and which lay unwanted and unused.

This personal crisis for Anglo-Jewry was sparked by the war with Spain, which rendered the goods and propery of enemy Spaniards liable for confiscation. Robles was soon denounced on 13 March 1655/6 by a scrivener named Francis Knevett, who apparently was thereby betraying the confidence of the Marrano community in London with which he had business connections. Robles at first tried to bluff his way through by claiming to be a Portuguese, but eventually he and his co-religionists were driven to confess the truth before the authorities. The Robles case forced England's secret Jews to reveal themselves formally to the English government and public, and compelled them to acquiesce in the movement on their behalf.[88]

The famous petition of England's secret Jewish community was received by Cromwell on 24 March 1655/6.[89] Little choice had been left to them but to throw themselves on the mercies of the Protector, whose sympathetic views had already been amply revealed. The list of signatories included all of the great figures of that community, except Robles himself, who submitted his own petition separately.[90] Simon (Jacob) de Caceres signed, as did Carvajal and Dormido, who had come to England with Menasseh's son and now apparently had decided to settle in London. Three other London Jews appended their signatures, but the most famous name was that at the head of the list: Menasseh ben Israel. For in March 1656 the two strands of the Jewish reaction to English philo-Semitism intertwined briefly, only to unravel again within a few short months.

'The Humble Petition of The Hebrews at Present Residing in this citty of London' included rather more modest requests than those which Menasseh had presented to the Protector four months previously. The Jewish community began by thanking Cromwell for having been pleased to grant them favours and protection 'in order that wee may with security meete priuatley in owr particular houses to owr Deuosions'. But the vicissitudes of Robles during the past fortnight had demonstrated to them that toleration on a more secure foundation was required. Now

[87] *Cal. SP Dom., 1655–6*, 128.

[88] SP 18/125, fo. 118: Spanish paper of discovery; SP 18/126, fo. 280ʳ⁻ᵛ: testimony of Philipp de la Loyhoy, 26 Mar. 1656. Many of the documents from the Robles case are repr., with many mistakes, in *TJHSE* 1 (1895), 77–86.

[89] SP 18/125, fo. 169: large photograph in *Bevis Marks Records*, i, ed. L. D. Barnett (Oxford, 1940), opp. title-page.

[90] SP 18/126, fos. 275–6: Robles to Cromwell, 24 Mar. 1655/6.

they requested that 'such Protection may be graunted vs in Writting as that wee may therwth meete at owr said priuate deuosions in owr Particular houses without feere of Molestation either to owr persons famillys or estates'. All they desired was to live peaceably under the authority of the English government. They also requested permission to establish a Jewish cemetery outside the city limits. The seven signatories closed praying for Cromwell's long life and prosperity. The Protector referred the document to the consideration of the Council of State, along with the separate petition of Antonio Robles.[91]

The Robles case, meanwhile, dragged on for almost two months. Menasseh's precise role in this investigation is unclear; his main concern presumably lay with the progress of the general petition of the Jewish community which was before the Council of State. The deliberations of the Whitehall Conference had been conducted in isolation from the realities of the Jewish presence in London, and the advantages and drawbacks of Jewish readmission had been discussed in abstraction. The failure of Robles's petition might have caused a formal re-*expulsion* of the Jews from England, for it revealed the extent of the Jewish population in London. Menasseh therefore worked feverishly to influence the outcome of the case. He may have had a hand in the writing of Henry Jessey's narrative of the Whitehall Conference, which was finished on 1 April 1656, just as Robles was confessing his Judaism before Colonel Philip Jones, one of the members of the Council subcommittee which had dealt with Dormido's petition the previous year.[92] As of that day, Jessey noted, 'no absolute *Answer* is yet returned' from Cromwell.[93] Nine days later Menasseh reiterated this statement at the conclusion of his *Vindiciae Judaeorum*, his powerful refutation of common slanders against the Jews.[94] This, his greatest work, is one of the most cogent defences of the Jewish people, and has been translated and reprinted many times during the past three centuries.

By 14 May 1656 the Admiralty commissioners had taken notice of the examinations and depositions of numerous witnesses.[95] The fact that Robles attended Mass until the outbreak of hostilities with Spain, and was not circumcised in any case, they explained, 'induceth vs to conceave he is either noe Jew or one that walkes under loose principles, and very different from others of that profession'. The commissioners therefore concluded that they 'upon examinacon doe not finde any convicting evidence to cleare vp either the Nation or Religion of the

---

[91] SP 18/125, fo. 169.
[92] SP 18/126, fo. 288: testimony of Robles, 1 Apr. 1656.
[93] [Jessey], *Narrative*, 10.   [94] Menasseh ben Israel, *Vindiciae*, 38–9.
[95] SP 18/126, fos. 277–88; SP 18/127, fo. 46^{r–v}.

peticoner'.[96] The ships, goods, and other property which had been seized from Robles were restored to him two days later.[97] The Council of State, on the other hand, chose to ignore the petition from the seven Jewish leaders.[98]

An open Anglo-Jewish community was thus a reality after the end of the Robles case. Charles and his exiled Royalists were quick to recognize the new situation, and seem to have tried to reap some advantage from the Anglo-Jewish identification with the Protectorate. Their plan was to appeal to the parent community in Amsterdam which might be more willing in consequence to curry favour with them as a form of insurance. Lieutenant-General Middleton appears to have been informed of this intention by 'some principle persons' of the Jewish congregation there, who also assured him that they had had nothing to do with Menasseh's mission, and in fact disavowed it entirely. The Dutch Jews also wished Charles a speedy Restoration. The exiled monarch therefore commissioned Middleton to promise them that if they provided him with money, arms, or ammunition, after his return to power Charles would

abate that rigour of the Lawes which is against them in our severall dominions, and . . . they shall lay a signal obligacion upon us, it will not only dispose us to be gratious to them, and to be willinge to protecte them, but be a morall assurance to them that wee shall be able to do whatsoever wee shall be willinge when we can iustly publish and declare to all men how much wee have bene beholdinge to them, and how farr they have contributed towards our restoration.[99]

There is no evidence that the Jews of Amsterdam provided Charles with anything more substantial than good wishes, although some sort of secret support might help to explain his protection of the Jews after 1660. In England, however, Fernando Mendes da Costa, 'a Jewish merchant, that hath a fine house near London, well known to his

---

[96] SP 18/127, fo. 83: report of Admiralty commissioners, 14 May 1656. The report was signed by Robert Blackborne, who reported on the Whitehall Conference to Willoughby: see above, pp. 122–4.

[97] *Cal. SP Dom., 1655–6*, 325.

[98] The claim that Cromwell replied favourably to this petition is completely unfounded: see D. S. Katz, 'English Redemption and Jewish Readmission in 1656', *JJ Stud.* 34 (1983), 73–91.

[99] Charles to Middleton, 24 Sept. 1656: BL MS Eger. 2542, fo. 240ᵛ: repr. C. H. Firth, *Scotland and the Protectorate* (Scot. Hist. Soc., xxxi, 1899), 343. Middleton was warned in a separate letter of the same date that 'if you finde ther professyons to be only generall . . . you shall requite them only with as generall expressions' (BL MS Eger. 2542, fo. 239ᵛ: repr. ibid. 342). Similarly, see BL Add. MS 4106, fo. 253: memo of first letter; and Hist. MSS Comm., lxxii, *Laing MSS*, i. 301: copy of second letter.

highness [Cromwell]', was denounced for receiving £4,000 to be used in helping to finance Royalist plots. The officer charged with investigating the case, brought forward by a woman of demonstrably disreputable character, dismissed the accusations along with 'many other stories too tedious to relate'.[100]

The great crisis of Anglo-Jewry had passed, and the secret community in London had revealed itself; everyone concerned was forced to adapt themselves to the altered circumstances. James Harrington addressed the issue directly in *Oceana*, his famous utopian work. In a barely disguised reference to Ireland, Harrington argued that her economic position might best be improved

by planting it with Jewes, allowing them their own Rites and Lawes, for that would have brought them suddainly from all parts of the World, and in sufficient numbers; and though the Jews be now altogether for Merchandize, yet in the Land of *Canaan* (since their exile from whence they have not been Landlords) they were altogether for agriculture; and there is no cause why a man should doubt, but having a fruitfull Country and good Ports too, they would be good at both.

Harrington's plan was to grant the Jews a perpetual lease to Ireland, initially for the cost of the maintenance of a provincial army during the first seven years, and afterwards for an annual revenue of £2,000,000. This might solve England's new Jewish problem, for to 'receive the Jewes after any other manner into a Commonwealth, were to maim it', because they never assimilate, and instead become parasites on the state.[101]

Yet Menasseh ben Israel seems to have failed to realize that a new era had begun for Jews in England. His single-minded dedication to obtaining a formal declaration of Jewish toleration and freedom of worship blinded him to the substantial benefits which had been achieved informally, and to the practical determination of the English government to allow the Jews to continue living in England unmolested. Menasseh thus alienated the leaders of Anglo-Jewry, who were anxious to effect a smooth transition to toleration, and they turned their backs on him. Sometime during 1656 they agreed to bring over Rabbi Moses Athias from Hamburg to lead their congregation.[102] Menasseh may have been considered for the post, but there is no evidence that his name was put

---

[100] *Thurloe State Papers*, v. 572, 578.

[101] James Harrington, *The Common-Wealth of Oceana* (London, 1656), sig. B2: repr. *The Political Works of James Harrington*, ed. J. G. A. Pocock (Cambridge, 1977), 159. See also S. B. Liljegren, *Harrington and the Jews* (Lund, 1932).

[102] J. Cassuto, 'Aus dem altesten Protokollbuch der Portugiesisch-Judischen Gemeinde in Hamburg', *Jrb. Jud.-Lit. Gft.* 6 (1909), 184.

forward at all. He seems to have been ill for some time in any case, and was forced to turn to Cromwell for assistance: 'I make my moan to your Highnesse,' he pleaded, 'as the alone succourer of my life, in this land of strangers.'[103] Cromwell, however, recognized Menasseh's services even if the Jews turned a deaf ear to him, and granted the rabbi a state pension of £100 per annum, payable quarterly, and commencing from 20 February 1656/7.[104] At least two payments of £25 each were made to Menasseh between Michaelmas 1656 and Michaelmas 1658.[105] The Jews of London, meanwhile, were at work acquiring a burial ground in the manor of Stepney, for which they paid approximately twenty times the fair rent of the tiny plot, suggesting that their formal request for a cemetery had not yet been granted at least by February 1657.[106]

By the middle of September 1657 Menasseh's hopes and patience were finally exhausted. His son Samuel having recently died, Menasseh turned to Cromwell once again for financial help to enable him to carry the body back to Holland. Menasseh offered to surrender his pension seal for £300, and to cease troubling Cromwell with his millennial dreams and pleas for aid.[107] Menasseh apparently was willing to renounce his pension for even £200 because of the intense pressure of his debts and his need to return to Holland immediately. This sum seems not to have been paid, and Menasseh was forced to return empty-handed, but he never reached Amsterdam, and died *en route* in Middelburg.[108] Samuel ben Israel was buried there, but Menasseh's body was carried to the Jewish cemetery at Ouderkerk near Amsterdam, where he was laid to rest.[109]

Menasseh's widow was left destitute and was forced to rely on charity. She sent several begging letters to Cromwell before his death in September 1658, which were entrusted to Thurloe and John Sadler, long a friend of the Jews. By the beginning of January 1658/9, she had persuaded Sadler to plead her case before Richard Cromwell. Sadler

---

[103] Menasseh to Cromwell, n.d. = prob. end of 1656: SP 18/153, fo. 253: repr. *Menasseh*, ed. Wolf, pp. lxxxvi–lxxxvii.

[104] Dept. Keeper Public Records, *5th Report*, app. ii, p. 263.

[105] Hist. MSS Comm., vii, *8th Report,App.*, pt i, pp. 94b–95a.

[106] A. S. Diamond, 'The Cemetery of the Resettlement', *TJHSE* 19 (1960), 163–90; H. S. Q. Henriques, *The Jews and the English Law* (London, [1908]), 109–12. See a fire insurance policy on the Sephardi burial ground dated 2 Jan. 1794, now SPJC, London, MS 344/63.

[107] Menasseh to Cromwell, 17 Sept. 1657: SP 18/156, fo. 173: repr. *Menasseh*, ed. Wolf, p. lxxxvii.

[108] John Sadler to Richard Cromwell, 4 Jan. 1658/9: SP 18/200, fo. 23: repr. *Menasseh*, ed. Wolf, pp. lxxxvi–lxxxviii.

[109] Middelburg burial register in *TJHSE* 7 (1915), 123–46: see p. 127; photograph of Menasseh's tombstone in L. A. Vega, *The Beth Haim of Ouderkerk* (Assen, 1975), 33.

asked the new Protector to pay the £200 'to the said Widow, & Relations of a Man so Eminent & ffamous in his owne & many other Nations; & for the honour of Christian Religio with many other Reasons'.[110] It is unknown whether Richard Cromwell honoured his father's debt.

Thus, by Cromwell's death, the Jews were firmly established in London. Some disagreement did ensue even in the last years of the Interregnum over the right of Jews to remain in England, and their value to the state, but by and large their position was secure.[111] Carvajal died and was honoured by a special knell of the bells of St Katherine Creechurch,[112] and Samuel Pepys paid his first visit to the synagogue.[113] Jews were moving openly in London now, and one in a case before the Admiralty commissioners even 'produced great testimonies under the hand of the late Lord Protector'.[114]

VII

The Jews were therefore understandably nervous when Charles was restored to his throne in 1660.[115] As early as 30 November 1660 City circles petitioned the newly returned king to reverse the policy of his usurping predecessor and expel the Jews. According to the remonstrance, the Jews had renewed the usurious practices with which they had oppressed the nation before their medieval expulsion, and flourished so profoundly during the reign of Cromwell that they tried to buy St Paul's Cathedral with an eye towards transforming it into a synagogue. The merchants demanded a revitalized Whitehall Conference, but one whose members would truly and impartially investigate the Jewish questions. In the meantime, they urged the imposition of heavy taxes on the Jews, and the expulsion of all Jews who did not have a licence to reside in this country.[116] The Jews replied through Maria

---

[110] Sadler to Richard Cromwell, 4 Jan. 1658/9: SP 18/200, fo. 23.

[111] L. Wolf, 'The Jewry of the Restoration', *TJHSE* 5 (1908), 13–18; id., 'The First Stage of Anglo-Jewish Emancipation', in *Essays in Jewish History*, ed. C. Roth (London, 1934), 115–43.

[112] Extract from churchwarden's account book repr. *MJHSE* 2 (1935), 26 n.

[113] Pepys to Edward Montagu, 3 Dec. 1659: Bod. Lib., MS Carte 73, fo. 325. Cf. W. S. Samuels, 'Carvajal and Pepys', *MJHSE* 2 (1935), 24–9; id., 'The First London Synagogue of the Resettlement', *TJHSE* 10 (1924), 1–147.

[114] *Cal. SP Dom., 1659–60*, 291.

[115] For a record of the Jews in London at that time, the so-called 'Da Costa Lists', see BL Add. MS 29,868, fos. 15, 16.

[116] Remonstrance against the Jews, addressed to Charles II, [30 Nov. 1660]: SP 29/21, fo. 257ʳ: repr. *TJHSE* 4 (1903), 188–92. Henriques, *English Law*, 124 n., 142–4, argues that this is probably the petition presented by Sir William Courtney *et al.* to the

Fernandez Carvajal, the widow of one of their most distinguished members, and on 7 December 1660 Charles II passed both petitions on to the House of Commons.[117] The documents came before them ten days later, when they were 'specially recommended to this House for their Advice therein, touching Protection for the *Jews*: Which was read', and ordered that the entire affair be taken into consideration the following morning, 18 December 1660. In the event, it seems that Parliament was content to let the matter fade away.[118]

Some merchants in London, however, still smarting from their near victory at the Whitehall Conference, continued to hound the Restored authorities with requests to expel the Jews, who were gaining an irrevocable foothold in the country. Chief among them was Thomas Violet, a goldsmith in London, who claimed to have presented a petition to the Parliament in time for the debate on the Jews. This work was printed in pamphlet form in January 1660/1, and was based on both economic and religious arguments.[119] The Lord Mayor and aldermen of London in their turn presented a petition to Charles II

y^t yor Ma^{ty} will be pleased to cause ye former Lawes made ag^t Jewes to be put in execucon, and to Recomend to y^{or} two Houses of Parliam^t to enact such new ones, for ye expulcon of all pfessed Jewes out of yor Ma^{tys} dominions & to barre ye dore after y^m wth such pvisions & penaltyes, as in yor Ma^{tys} wisedome shall be found most agreeable to ye Safety of Religion ye Hon^r of yor Ma^{ty} & ye good & welfare of yor Subjects.[120]

This petition also seems to have been ignored.

Events soon proved that the fears of the Jews were unwarranted: a

---

Privy Council, or one of the other petitions mentioned as being before the Privy Council on 30 Nov. 1660. Wolf, 'Restoration', suggests that this is the petition presented by Thomas Violet to the king in Council, but Henriques replies that this is unlikely as the document does not say that the synagogue had actually been set up, as Violet did in his published petition. Henriques also claims that there were other petitions presented against the Jews at this time, but that this was the only one thought worthwhile to preserve in the state archives.

[117] Order in Council, 7 Dec. 1660, Privy Council Registers: repr. *TJHSE* 5 (1908), 28–9.

[118] *Commons Journal*, 8: 209 (17 Dec. 1660).

[119] Thomas Violet, *A Petition against the Jewes* (London, 1661). Cf. his earlier work *The Advancement of Merchandize* (London, 1651), 13, in which he advises the Council of State to consult 'Mr *Antonio Ferdinando*' [Carvajal] regarding the trade with Spain. See also Violet to the duke of Ormonde, 17 Aug. 1660: Bod. Lib., MS Carte 31, fo. 19^r; and the pamphlet against Violet, *The Great Trappanner of England Discovered* (London, 1660).

[120] Lord Mayor and aldermen of London to Charles II, [Apr.–May] 1662: Corporation of London Record Office, *Remembrancia*, ix, fos. 19^v–21^r: repr. with many mistakes in *TJHSE* 4 (1903), 186–8.

long and fascinating description of a visit to their synagogue in 1662 by John Greenhalgh depicts them as comfortable and secure under the spiritual guidance of Rabbi Moses Israel Athias, a cousin of Carvajal's.[121] This impression is sustained by another account from Pepys written the following year.[122] Confirmation of the status of the Jews in writing, which they had requested in their petition at the height of the Robles case, was finally achieved after a further petition of 22 August 1664 signed by Dormido and two others. They protested that

> they are dayly threatned by some wth ye seizure of all their estates & are told y^t both their lives & Estates are forfeited to yor Matie by the Lawes of yor Kingdome and pticularly they are molested & disquieted by one Mr Richaut. And att ye same time they were called by ye Right Honble: ye Earle of Berksheire who told them he had reced a verball Order from yor Matie to Protect them and in case they doe not come to a Speedy agreem^t w^{t}h him he will endeavour and prosecute ye seizure of their estates.

The interest of Peter Rycaut in the Jews probably derived primarily from his brother Paul's service in Turkey, 1661–79, first as secretary to the earl of Winchelsea, English representative there, and for the last dozen years of his sojourn as consul to the Levant Company in Smyrna. This monopoly utilized the services of the local Turkish Jews, and Paul Rycaut was apprehensive of an interloping connection between Anglo-Jewry and their eastern brethren as in the days of Elizabeth. Thomas Howard, the first earl of Berkshire, the second son of the first earl of Suffolk, seems to have been merely interested in straightforward blackmail.[123]

Sir Henry Bennett (later Lord Arlington), Secretary of State, replied on behalf of the king that the Jews might 'promise themselves ye effects of ye same favour as formerly they have had so long as they demeane themselves peaceably and quietly with due obedience to his Maties Laws & without scandal to his Government'.[124] Jacob Sasportas, briefly rabbi

---

[121] Greenhalgh to Thomas Crompton, 22 Apr. 1662 (copy): BL MS Lans. 988, fos. 174^v–180: repr. *Original Letters Illustrative of English History*, ed. H. Ellis (2nd ser. iv, London, 1827), 3–21: repr. with notes in *TJHSE* 10 (1924), 49–57.

[122] Samuel Pepys, *Diary*, ed. R. Latham and W. Matthews (London, 1970), iv. 334–5: 14 Oct. 1663.

[123] Previous writers, including Katz, *Philo-Semitism*, 223, 243, have mistakenly confused Paul and Peter in the sordid affair. See now S. P. Anderson, *An English Consul in Turkey: Paul Rycaut at Smyrna, 1667–1678* (Oxford, 1989), 211. We have seen that Paul Rycaut was a witness to the Whitehall Conference: he would also be a reporter of the movements of Shabtai Sevi: ibid. 211–15.

[124] Emanuell Martinez Dormido, Elias de Lima, and Moses Baruh to Charles II, 1664: SPJC, London, MS 344/1a: photograph in *Bevis Marks Records*, i, ed. Barnett, pla. iii and cf. pp. 8–9. Cf. SP 44/18, pp. 78–9: Council Entry Book.

of the Jewish community in London until he fled back to Amsterdam during the Great Plague, reported to a correspondent in Rotterdam that

> We live at a time in which God has seen fit greatly to ameliorate the condition of his people, bringing them forth from the general condition of serfdom into freedom . . . specifically, in that we are free to practise our own true religion . . . a written statement was issued from him [Charles II], duly signed, affirming that no untoward measures had been or would be initiated against us, and that 'they should not look towards any protector other than his Majesty: during the continuance of whose lifetime they need feel no trepidation because of any sect that might oppose them, inasmuch as he himself would be their advocate and assist them with all his power'.[125]

In February 1673/4, when the Jewish community was at the 'Quarter Sessions at Guild Hall Indicted of a Ryot for meeting together for the exercise of their Religion in Dukes Place, and the Bill was found against Them by the Grand Jury', a group of Jewish merchants reminded Charles II in an urgent petition of his promise ten years before. The king immediately ordered the Attorney General to stop all proceedings against the petitioners.[126] Perhaps as a symbol of growing stability, the custom began in 1677 or 1678 of making an annual presentation to the Lord Mayor of London of a silver dish or goblet, including a large consignment of sweetmeats, altered to 50 or 60 pounds of chocolate in 1716.[127]

During the last five years of Charles's reign there were two attempts to approach the newly revealed Jewish community in a different light. William Challoner, freeman of London and Bristol, asked the Lord Mayor in 1680 for permission to debate with a dozen Jews before him, and petitioned the king with the claim that it had been revealed to him

---

[125] R. Jacob Sasportas to R. Josiah Pardo: Mocatta Library MSS, Cecil Roth Papers, AJ/151/17 (copy): English trans. by Prof. Raphael Loewe in A. Fraser, *Royal Charles* (New York, 1979), 218. Sasportas was called from Holland to replace Moses Athias, who himself would shortly perish in the Plague. The next *haham* was Joshua da Silva, who arrived from Amsterdam in 1670 and served until his death nine years later. For his successor Jacob Abendana (1681–5), see below, p. 146.

[126] Abraham de Oliveira, Jacob Franco Mendes, Abraham do Porto, and Domingo Francia to Charles II, 1673/4: SPJC, London, MS 344/1b; Charles II, Order in Council, 11 Feb. 1673/4: repr. *Bevis Marks*, i, ed. Barnett, p. 11, and pla. iv. Repr. [Philip Carteret Webb], *The Question, Whether a Jew, Born within the British Dominions, Was, before the Making the Late Act of Parliament, a Person, Capable, by Law, to Purchase and Hold Lands to him, and his Heirs, Fairly Stated and Considered* (London, 1753), 38–9.

[127] This tradition continued until 1731, when sometimes £50 or fifty guineas would be presented in lieu of a silver utensil, and finally came to an end in 1780: *Bevis Marks Records*, i, ed. Barnett, 11–12; C. Roth, 'The Lord Mayor's Salvers', *Connoisseur*, 95 (1935), 296–9.

that he would enter royal service.[128] In that same year Lord Anglesey wrote to Bennett suggesting that Sir Peter Pett be made 'the Justitiary of the Jewes' to look into the entire legal question of Jewish residence in England.[129] But these last two discussions of Jewish status seemed even then as relics from another age. More interesting, perhaps, is the involvement of Francisco de Faria, a Jew born in the New World, in the Popish Plot towards the end of 1680. Faria supplied further details for a public hungry for news, and his narrative was published by the House of Commons.[130] Even in the short run, this Jewish presence among the purveyors of raw material for the scare seems to have had little effect on the Jewish population at large.

Thus, less than a decade after Menasseh arrived in London, the Jews were granted a formal statement of toleration, and successfully weathered a number of attacks on their right to live in England. In 1664 they promulgated a formal set of forty-two regulations (*ascamoth*) for the governance of their congregation *Saar Asamaim*, the first one forbidding the foundation of any other Sephardi synagogue in London, under penalty of excommunication, without the express permission of the ruling Mahamad (the governing council). The *ascama* was revised in 1677, emphasizing that its main purpose was not only to preserve unity but to do so 'without causing scandal to the natives of this city'.[131] Although Jews would not become fully emancipated until the middle of the nineteenth century, their residence here rested on a secure foundation with the admission at the Whitehall Conference that 'there is no Law that forbids the Jews return into *England*'.[132]

---

[128] William Challoner to Charles II, July 1680: SP 29/414, fos. 73^r–74^v; Challoner to Lord Mayor, July 1680: ibid., fo. 75^{r-v}.

[129] Anglesey to [Bennett], 6 Aug. 1680: Codrington Library, All Souls College, Oxford, MS 239, fo. 423a. I am grateful to Mr J. S. G. Simmons for letting me photocopy this MS.

[130] Francisco de Faria, *The Narrative* (London, 1680); id., *The Information* (London, 1680), ordered printed by House of Commons; Narcissus Luttrell, *A Brief Historical Relation of State Affairs* (Oxford, 1857), i. 57 (25 Oct. 1680). Cf. L. M. Friedman, 'Francisco De Faria, an American Jew, and the Popish Plot', *PAJHS* 20 (1911), 115–32.

[131] *El libro de los acuerdos*, ed. L. D. Barnett (Oxford, 1931); I. Epstein, 'The Story of Ascama I of the Spanish and Portuguese Jewish Congregation of London with Special Reference to Responsa Material', in M. Ben-Horin (ed.), *Studies and Essays in Honour of Abraham A. Neuman* (Leiden, 1962), 170–214.

[132] [Jessey], *Narrative*, 9.

4

THE JEWS OF ENGLAND AND THE GLORIOUS REVOLUTION

THE commercial argument was one of the most powerful against the resettlement of the Jews in England when Cromwell put the question to the test at the Whitehall Conference of December 1655. The Protector laboured in vain to procure a formal decision, for 'the Merchants vehemently insisted upon it, That such an admission of the Jews would enrich Foreigners, and impoverish the Natives of the land.' Jews were nevertheless allowed in England on an unofficial basis from 1656, putting an end to the expulsion which had been decreed by Edward I in 1290.[1] Many of the Jews who had promoted connections with England were normally resident in Holland, so the entire issue was much more than confessional, but linked with England's traditional trade rivals. The Dutch themselves, on the other hand, had a somewhat different policy towards outsiders. 'Next to the freedom to worship God comes freedom to make one's living for all inhabitants,' wrote Pieter de la Court, a renowned political economist, in 1662:

Here (in Amsterdam) it is very necessary to attract foreigners. And although this is of disadvantage to some old residents who would like to keep the best solely for themselves and pretend that a citizen should have preferences above a stranger, the truth of the matter is that a state which is not self-sufficient must constantly draw new inhabitants to it or perish.[2]

That the Jews of England were strangers is certain; that they were foreigners was unclear by Cromwell's time; that they were aliens in the same sense as Dutchmen or Frenchmen was the crucial question at hand.

I

'The succeeding Reign of King *James* the second, being deservedly very short, affords us, likewise, but a very short Portion of *Jewish* History,'

[1] 'The Proceedings of the *Jews* in *England* in the Year 1655', in *Two Journeys to Jerusalem*, ed. R. B[urton=Nathaniel Crouch] (London, 1719), 173.
[2] Pieter de la Court, *Interest van Holland ofte Gronden van Hollands Welvaren* (Amsterdam, 1662), 38: trans. in H. I. Bloom, *The Economic Activities of the Jews of Amsterdam in the Seventeenth and Eighteenth Centuries* (Port Washington, NY, 1969 [1937]), 8–9.

ruled d'Blossiers Tovey, the eighteenth-century historian of Anglo-Jewry fifty years later.[3] The duration of James's reign is not held in doubt, but, brief though it may have been, it was characterized by two rather powerful attacks on the Jewish presence in England. As had been the case twenty-five years before, the accession of a new king on 6 February 1685 seemed to require the renewal of all private arrangements made with the Jews and others who were not strictly protected by the law. The leaders of the community presented James II with a loyal address written on parchment, and paid at least five visits to his palace in the first two months of his rule.[4] Even the written promise of protection given by Charles II was invalid, and the Jews found themselves vulnerable to pressures of various kinds. Furthermore, Rabbi Jacob Abendana, the spiritual leader of Anglo-Jewry, died at the same time as King Charles, and no replacement was found for him until well after the exile of King James.[5] The Jewish community of England was, therefore, much too valuable a prize for any adventurer who wished to take advantage of ambiguity in these unsettled times.

The first man to do so may well have been a conscientious public servant, although he certainly put himself at considerable risk, well beyond the call of duty. He was Samuel Hayne, a customs official at Falmouth, who had tried to prosecute a number of Jews who had violated certain laws, and who eventually found himself heavily in debt and imprisoned in the Fleet. Hayne's case is worth looking at in some detail, because it shows how the status of Jews in England during these years defied definition. To a customs officer, the classification of the Jews as either native religious Dissenters or foreign merchants would have important financial ramifications. Hayne's purpose, as he pleaded to the new king at the end of May 1685, was

to shew to His Majesty, that several Jews to whom His Majesty had been Graciously pleased to Grant Letters Patent of Denization, with a Clause inserted, That they should pay no more Custom than English (non obstante the Statutes,) Had Owned and Coloured the Goods of other Jews that had not such a Clause in their Patents, and of some Jews who had no Patents at all.

Hayne had been on duty in Falmouth five years before when he was called upon to examine the goods on board the *Experiment*, mostly carrying sugar from Barbados, via England, with Amsterdam the final

---

[3] D'Blossiers Tovey, *Anglia Judaica; or, The History and Antiquities of the Jews in England* (Oxford, 1738), 287.

[4] *Bevis Marks Records*, i, ed. L. D. Barnett (Oxford, 1940), 13.

[5] On Jacob Abendana, see D. S. Katz, 'The Abendana Brothers and the Christian Hebraists of Seventeenth-Century England', *Journal of Ecclesiastical History*, 40 (1989), 28–52.

destination. The goods were entered under the name of an Englishman called Henry Sutton, the master of the ship, but when pressed he signed a letter of confession dated 18 October 1680, confirming 'that the greatest quantity of the *Sugars* and Merchandizes loaden on board the said Ship, do really belong to *Jews*'. The fraud turned out to be widespread and well organized. Hayne claimed that he was offered a 100-guinea bribe, and when he refused was assailed with pseudo-legal documents of protest. Hayne ordered the ship to be unloaded, and discovered the goods to be signed with thirty-five distinct marks, indicating in his view individual owners. Hayne reckoned that the Crown was being cheated of nearly £154 in duty.[6]

The case meanwhile came to court, where the Jews were represented by a certain Mr Hutchinson, who had succeeded in garnering a good deal of support, in those times when, in Hayne's words, 'to assist the King with Money was Voted a Crime'. Hutchinson argued that many of the goods did indeed belong to Jews, but Jews who had been made denizens, such as Antonio Gomesera and Antonio Lousada, prominent members of the Sephardi community in London. Hutchinson grandly read out a patent of endenization which included the clause exempting the recipient from paying punitive duties on imported goods. Hayne pointed out that only one of the Jews was endenizened by means of a patent that included that crucial clause, and that in any case Hutchinson still left thirty-three owners unaccounted for. Hayne was eventually forced to bring the case at his own risk and charge, despite having been warned when 'my Lord *Cheyne* said, That their Purses were too Heavy for me, and that they would be too hard for me, if the commissioners did not stand by me'. Upton, one of the commissioners, actively tried to persuade Hayne to drop the case, and, when that failed, Hayne was arrested and imprisoned at the suit of Henry Sutton, the master of the ship, and spent some time in and out of gaol. Hayne says that even at this stage the Jews offered him up to 200 guineas in bribes, and that among their number was 'Mr *Levy* the Jew', perhaps the famous communal leader of that name. At the end of the day, the jury accepted the argument that all of the goods were owned by Gomesera and Lousada, the ship's affidavit notwithstanding. Hayne meanwhile was bombarded with writs from the two Jews, and remained a prisoner in the Fleet, although he was often given leave to deal with his business. Little hope lay with the law: Sir Peter Killigrew, Hayne recalled, promised that he himself would make sure he would rot in prison. The Jews informed

[6] Samuel Hayne, *An Abstract of All the Statutes Made Concerning Aliens Trading in England . . . Proving that the Jews . . . Break them All* (n.p., 1685), sig. B2ʳ (to James II, dated 29 May 1685), 15–22.

Hayne that he had better make peace, since they had already invested nearly 1,000 guineas in the case and were not about to see it lost now. Hayne settled: he received £50 and released the ship, having himself spent over £600 on the case and contracted numerous debts in gaol. At the time of writing, he had shaken off neither new writs nor old debts.[7]

Hayne had time in prison to reflect on the proper method which ought to be used in bringing Jewish commercial self-interest closer to the service of the state. His proposal to James II was simple: that the king command all Jews from the date of his accession to 'pay the *Alien* Duty, as by Law they ought to do; which will not only be many Thousands *per Annum* advance to Your Majesty in Your Customs, but also be extream grateful to all Your Majesties fair dealing *English* Merchants'. Hayne made it clear that his motivation was economic patriotism alone: 'My Endeavours (however) have not been for a total Extirpation of the *Jews*, or their Trade here, (as some have aimed) but only to oblige them to pay Your Majesties Customs, and act according to Law, that thereby the *English* Merchants might be Enabled to Sell as Cheap as themselves.' The Jews were known the world over, Hayne explained, 'for their great Wealth and they know it flows from the abundance of their Trade and Commerce', but what they were doing in England was to import goods from the West Indies and to transfer them immediately to Holland, so that 'most of their Cargoes for the *Plantations* being made up of the Growth, Product and Manufacture of those parts, and none of *English*'. Furthermore, Jews from Amsterdam, London, Barbados, New York, and Jamaica tended to club together and register the cargo under the name of the endenizened Jew from the place at which the ship was landed, thereby always avoiding paying alien duties in any place at any time. Hayne reckoned that in this way cargoes were made 20 per cent cheaper for Jews than for competing Englishmen. It may well be that many Jews would withdraw from England altogether if this anomalous situation was rectified, Hayne admitted, but even such an extreme reaction would at least have the beneficial effect of channelling more Englishmen into the gap created. They, in turn, would sell English rather than foreign manufactures, 'and so a greater Consumption would follow, and consequently an advance of His Majesties Customs'.[8]

But Hayne, after all, wrote those words from Fleet Prison. By now he knew that 'none but a person designed to dive into their Ways and Methods of *Trade*; and leaving almost all other Concerns behind his back; together with a resolution to stand his Point, come what will on't,

---

[7] Ibid. 23–33.
[8] Ibid., sig. B2^{r-v}, pp. 9–12, 37.

Poverty, Imprisonment, or (rather than fail) Life it self, is fit to attempt so Crabbed a concern, as to touch them to the quick'.[9] The entire question of the way in which Jews, both native and foreign, ought to be regarded by the customs authorities, and the problems in regulating national trade carried on by an international people, were postponed until after the Glorious Revolution, and, as we shall see, were even then not completely resolved.

Perhaps Hayne was foolish to think that a provincial customs officer could tackle the combined forces of Anglo-Jewry in such a direct manner.[10] Clearly the accession of a new king was a golden opportunity for those who saw Jewish merchants as a threat to the livelihoods of their English competitors, but a more subtle method was bound to be more effective. Such a scheme was devised at the end of October 1685 by the brothers Beaumont, Thomas and Carleton, and its progress provides an unusually striking example of how apparent issues of principle concerning the Jews were often resolved so as to serve other interests entirely. The Beaumonts took refuge in Queen Elizabeth's Act of 1581 'to retain the Queen Majesty's subjects in their due obedience', by which all recusants were obliged to pay an increased monthly fine of £20.[11] This provision was meant to be a threat to English Catholics, and was not uniformly enforced, but it served as the legal prop for the issuing of writs against forty-eight Jews on the charge of recusancy. Indeed, '38 of the principal Jews were taken off the Exchange and obliged to give bail'. The reaction of the Mahamad, the governing body of the Sephardi congregation, was swift and in accordance with past methods: it made a direct appeal to the king. The petition was signed by three leading members, Joseph Henriques, Abraham de Oliveira, and Aron Pacheco. The Jews reminded the new king of his brother's previous declaration of protection in 1664, and reaffirmed their own loyalty to king and country. Yet now they were attacked 'in your Majesties Court of Kings Bench att the suit of one Thomas Beaumont on the Exchange' as part of a plan 'sett up and managed by his Brother one Carleton, Beaumont an Attorney [of] the Said Court designing to gett great Summes of money from your Petitioners'. The Mahamad pointed out that the entire affair would be to the 'great Scandall and prejudice of their Creditt and Reputation both here and abroad', and would thereby be to the mutual

---

[9] Ibid. 9.

[10] One man, at least, who was willing to join with Hayne was Samuel Weale, the collector of the customs at Fowey in Cornwall: Samuel Weale, 'Remarks in Defence of the Exaction of Alien Duty from the Jews by the Commissioners of the Customs', *c.*1685: Bod. Lib., MS Rawlinson A 336, fos. 3 ff.

[11] 23 Eliz. I, c. 1: repr. in G. R. Elton, *The Tudor Constitution* (Cambridge, 1972), 423.

disadvantage of the king and his Jewish residents, 'their Chief dealings being in Merchandizing the major and better part of whome by Such their Said trading having Paid and Still, paying Considerable Somes of money yearly to and for your and his Late Majesties Customes'. The Jews suggested that the king was unaware of these proceedings, and thereby begged him 'to order that the Said Thomas Beaumont And Carleton Beaumont be Conveened to appeare before your Majesty' to answer for their unjustified disturbance of the religious and commercial peace of the realm.[12]

The Jews' petition was presented at court by Henry Mordaunt, the second earl of Peterborough, that rebellious noble who forty years before had led an ineffectual uprising against Parliament in the second Civil War. This essential support did not, of course, come gratis, and the Mahamad was forced to make the free gift, as it were, of 200 guineas to the earl in return for his services.[13] But it was certainly value for money: the earl of Peterborough was present in the Privy Council on 13 November 1685, when James II gave his royal Order

that his Majesties Attorney Generall, do stopp all the sayd Proceedings att Law against the Petitioners: His Majesties Intention being that they should not be troubled, upon this account, but quietly enjoy the free exercise of the Religion, whilst they behave themselves dutifully and obediently to his Government.[14]

Strangely, the king's Order does not seem to have had the desired effect immediately, and when, three weeks later, it was 'Reported that the two Beaumonts, who are prosecutors, would not surcease their suite', James II gave a further Order in Council to the Lord Chief Justice of the King's Bench, Sir Edward Herbert, 'to send for Beaumont the Atturney and examine him touching his behaviour in this affaire'. Herbert did exactly that on 9 December 1685, and summoned Carleton Beaumont to his chambers, whereupon these proceedings against the Jews were finally quashed.[15]

---

[12] SPJC, London, MS 641: also repr. in *Bevis Marks Records*, i, ed. Barnett, 13–14; newsletter to John Squire of Newcastle, 3 Nov. 1685: *Cal. SP Dom., Feb.–Dec. 1685*, 374–5.

[13] Records of the Mahamad, as reported in A. M. Hyamson, *The Sephardim of England* (London, 1951), 56–7. C. Roth, *A History of the Jews in England* (3rd edn., Oxford, 1964), 183, gives the sum as £300, for some reason.

[14] James II, Privy Council order, 13 Nov. 1685: SPJC, London, MS 344 1c: photograph in *Bevis Marks Records*, i, ed. Barnett, pl. v, facing p. 14; cf. p. 15.

[15] James II, Privy Council order, 4 Dec. 1685; note by Herbert, 9 Dec. 1685: SPJC, London, MS 344 1d; photograph in *Bevis Marks Records*, i, ed. Barnett, pl. vi, facing p. 15. When the final reckoning was made, the congregation discovered that their defence had cost them £288 8s. 6d., paid for by a special *finta* which brought in £286 14s. 0d: ibid. 15 n.

King James II thus gave the Jews of England what amounted to a Declaration of Indulgence, at the very same time when the entire issue of his suspending and dispensing powers was becoming extremely controversial, and a year and a half before he granted the same rights to all other Nonconformists. Certainly it was a strange piece of timing, even if the case in question originated neither at Court nor in the synagogue. Bishop Burnet recalled the year 1685 as one most dangerous to all non-Catholics:

This year, of which I am now writing, must ever be remembred, as the most fatal to the Protestant Religion. In February, a King of England declared himself a Papist. In June, Charles the Elector Palatine dying without issue, the Electoral dignity went to the House of Newburgh, a most bigotted Popish family. In October, the King of France recalled and vacated the Edict of Nantes. And in December, the Duke of Savoy being brought to it, not only by the persuasions, but even by the threatenings of the Court of France, recalled the Edict that his father had granted to the Vaudois. So it must be confessed, that this was a very critical year. And I have ever reckoned this the fifth great crisis of the Protestant Religion.[16]

Macaulay noted that 'Through many years the autumn of 1685 was remembered by the Nonconformists as a time of misery and terror.'[17] Not only was Judge Jeffreys hard at work in his Bloody Assizes, in the aftermath of the defeat of Monmouth's rebellion, but during the summer and autumn of that year James extended to England the practice used in Ireland of dispensing from the Test Act officers of the Roman Catholic religion. The Revocation of the Edict of Nantes by Louis XIV on 18 October 1685 seemed somehow to be part of a very sinister international plan for the eradication of Protestantism.

Let us look again at the chronology. After Monmouth's capture at the beginning of July 1685, Parliament was prorogued until 4 August, and then further adjourned until 9 November. It was during this period, when the Beaumonts were plotting against the Jews, that James filled the officers' lists with Roman Catholics, and he fully expected that he would have to defend himself and the entire issue of the use of his dispensing powers when Parliament reconvened. James opened Parliament on 9 November 1685, congratulating the nation for defeating Monmouth's rebellion, but making the point that now more than ever the nation needed a strong military, and, as regards the newly-appointed Catholic officers, warned that 'after having had the benefit of their services in

---

[16] Gilbert Burnet, *History of his Own Time* (London, 1724–30), ii. 344–5.
[17] T. B. Macaulay, *The History of England* (Everyman edn., London, 1906), i. 501. Generally, see now W. A. Speck, *Reluctant Revolutionaries: Englishmen and the Revolution of 1688* (Oxford, 1988), 51–62.

such a time of need and danger I will neither expose them to disgrace nor myself to the want of them if there should be another rebellion to make them necessary to me'. The debate on Parliament's response to James II's address opened in the House of Commons on 12 November, with the evident aim of thereby conveying to the king its displeasure with his use of the dispensing power. The following day, our day, 13 November, the House defeated by one vote a proposal that supply be voted before dealing with the question of the appointment of Catholic officers in the army. The House thereby resolved on 14 November that the commissions were illegal and in violation of the Test Act. But James had already decided to act decisively and without delay. On 20 November 1685 the king summoned both Houses and informed them without any explanation that he had decided to prorogue Parliament until 10 February 1686.[18] By this sudden decision James II lost the parliamentary grant of £700,000 which had been approved, but he had made the point that the use of his dispensing power was not a proper subject for debate.[19]

It is, therefore, against the background of the parliamentary debate on the use of the royal dispensing power in the appointment of Roman Catholic army officers that James II's extraordinary decision in favour of Jewish residence needs to be seen. Even more striking, the very day of his Order in Council, 13 November 1685, was the day on which pre-debate tension over the dispensing power reached its pitch in Parliament. In that division the Court lost a vital vote in the question of supply, which had become inextricably linked with the recent events in the army. Professor W. A. Speck has described this moment as 'a crucial loss of control'. When James issued his Order at the Privy Council, therefore, he was not only affirming the right of Jews to continue to live peaceably in his realm, but defiantly demonstrating that his dispensing and suspending powers might apply in situations unrelated to Roman Catholic officers in the army, and was an inalienable royal right which could not be altered by the parliamentary interference which was expected the next morning. His reaffirmation of that decision on 9 December, after Parliament had already been prorogued, was a decisive ratification of the principle he had expressed the previous month.

The intimate connection between the king's Order in Council regarding the Jews and the parliamentary debates over his use of the dispensing power is thus an essential element in understanding the

[18] Anchitell Grey, *Debates of the House of Commons, from the Year 1667 to the Year 1694* (London, 1763), viii. 353–69. The Parliament in fact never sat again.

[19] Ibid. 366–7. Generally on the debates in November, see R. E. Boyer, *English Declarations of Indulgence 1687 and 1688* (The Hague, 1968), 36–42; Macaulay, *History*, i. 514–28; Speck, *Revolutionaries*, 59.

policy of James II towards them. It is saddening to realize that Jewish historians who have noticed James's declaration of 1685 have failed to make this link, and have placed his decision exclusively in the realm of evolving English attitudes towards the Jews within their midst. Historians of the Glorious Revolution have also been unaware of this document and its significance. Certainly the king's actions were not related only to the political exigencies of the moment, but it is true that the Beaumont brothers and their case landed in his lap at precisely the moment when he needed them. No doubt the Beaumonts themselves reckoned that the king would relish the chance to enforce anti-Catholic legislation on non-Catholics and thereby harmlessly champion the validity of statute law. Instead, James used the opportunity to reaffirm his use of the dispensing and suspending powers, and, as far as we know, Parliament raised no objections in this instance. Their problem was with Roman Catholics, not with Jews, who had no desire to become officers in the army or ministers of state. They were strangers, albeit of a peculiar variety, whose legal status, it was acknowledged, ought best to be dealt with in another framework entirely. By means of this ambiguity, then, the Jews were permitted to enjoy their royal privileges, the last occasion on which it was necessary to have the king's protection given them in writing. The Jews were also beneficiaries of James's Declarations of Indulgence issued in 1687 and 1688, which were sufficiently vague to include them as well.[20]

The king's appreciation of the economic utility of the Jews may also have been behind the special missive he sent to his son-in-law William, prince of Orange, on 16 April 1686. On that day the mail from Harwich was robbed, and the Jews alone lost £100,000 in rough diamonds. Indeed, it was the Great Train Robbery of its day, and was remembered for many years afterwards. James II wrote a note of condolence to the Dutch ruler, a short 140-word letter, in English as usual, beginning with conventional concern over William's account of Mary's 'sore eis', and his own queen's shingles. But James's chief purpose in writing was to report that 'those that robed the Dutch maile, are both taken this day, so that I hope the Jews whose mony it was, will not be great losers'.[21]

---

[20] Declaration of Indulgence, 4 Apr. 1687, which James issued, among other reasons, 'for the increase of trade and encouragement of strangers': J. P. Kenyon, *The Stuart Constitution* (Cambridge, 1986), 389–91. The Declaration of Indulgence of Apr. 1688 was nearly identical. James's religious policy in regard to persecuted minorities has been re-examined in R. D. Gwynn, 'James II in Light of his Treatment of Huguenot Refugees in England', *EHR* 92 (1977), 820–33.

[21] James II to William, prince of Orange, 16 Apr. 1686: PRO, SP 8/3, fo. 214^{r–v}. According to *Cal. SP Dom., Jan. 1686–May 1687*, 102, it is a holograph letter. James corresponded with William in English: Speck, *Revolutionaries*, 81 n.

James's letter must have brought some comfort to the Jews of Amsterdam, although not all of the diamonds were recovered. Eight years later Anthony Wood would record the killing in Bloomsbury of a certain Captain Edward Wilson. 'A little before he dyed,' Wood wrote, 'he gave an acquaintance of his a key with 60 pieces of gold, bidding him take the latter and deliver the other to his brother with a command to burne all of the papers in his cabinet.' According to Wood, Wilson 'is supposed to be the chief person that robbed the mail from Harwich' when the Jews lost their diamonds.[22] John Evelyn, however, was not privy to such information, but noted that the 'Mysterie is, how this so young gentleman, a sober young person, & very inoffensive, & of good fame, did so live in so extraordinary Equipage; it not being discovered by any possible industry'.[23] Being a party to the Great Jewish Mail Robbery would explain Wilson's disproportionate wealth.

Jews, then, were certainly making their presence felt in trade and on the Exchange, and many others must have agreed with the Beaumont brothers that they were a competitive nuisance there. The activities of the Abendana brothers in Oxford and Cambridge provided a Jewish representation at the universities as well.[24] Unfortunately, testimonies regarding the way in which rather more ordinary Jews were seen during the reign of James II are more difficult to find. We know that the Spanish and Portuguese synagogue on Creechurch Lane must have been something of a tourist attraction, for even Henry Newcombe, the Nonconformist minister, visited it, on 26 June 1686: 'We went to the Jews' Synagogue,' he reported in his autobiography. 'I could not have belived, but that I saw it, such a strange worship, so moddish and foppish; and the people not much serious in it as it is. And I was affected to think, that many likely men of understanding should be without Christ, and live in the denial of him.'[25] Generally, though, the Jews were not a subject of popular discussion between James's declaration of 1685 and the Glorious Revolution, a position which was certainly to the liking of the Jewish communal leaders.

Some indications may perhaps be gleaned from scattered references to Jews which have survived. One of the most interesting, if somewhat

[22] Anthony Wood, *Life and Times*, ed. A. Clark (Oxford, 1891–1900), iii. 448–9: entry for 9 Apr. 1694.

[23] *The Diary of John Evelyn*, ed. E. S. de Beer (Oxford, 1955), v. 175–6: entry for 22 Apr. 1694. Cf. *DNB*, s.v. 'Edward Wilson (d. 1694)', where it is claimed that contemporaries surmised that he was either supplied by the Jews or living off the proceeds of jewels stolen from the Dutch mail.

[24] Katz, 'Abendana', *passim*.

[25] Henry Newcome, *Autobiography*, ed. R. Parkinson (Chetham Soc., xxvi–xxvii, 1852), xxvii. 262–3.

lurid, of these is a graphic account of 'a Barbarous and Bloody Murther, Committed by one *John Jones* of *Monmouthshire*, upon the Person of a *Jew* (after many pretentions of Friendship) with his own Knife in a most inhumane Manner, on the 2d of *July*, 1686'. According to the anonymous narrator, both Jew and Gentile left Newport in Wales on the same ship bound for Dover, where Jones agreed to serve as the foreigner's interpreter. That night they stayed in an inn at Canterbury, and the next morning set out for London, the Jew paying for all food and lodging. On the road from Canterbury, Jones suddenly seized the Jew and murdered him with his own knife. Jones was soon apprehended and committed to prison. In his defence, Jones said that 'the Devil put it into his mind to do the Murther not above an Hour before he Committed it', but it is by no means clear if his remark was intended as a reference to the religion of his victim. At any rate, nowhere in the surviving account of the murder is an indication that its importance was somehow lessened because the victim was a Jew. The only slight reference to the background of the murdered man himself comes at the end:

As for the Party Murthered, there were found about him Papers in *Hebrew*, which being Translated at the Request of some Gentlemen, by a Reverend Doctor of Divinity; they appeared to be Scripture Texts, taken out of *Exodus* and *Deutrinomy* [*sic*], from Verse 4, to Verse 10, and a third the 11 Chap. of *Deut.* from Verse 13 to Verse 22, and some other Papers that were likewise Translated by the same Hand. As for the Name of the *Jew* it is not yet known, he being a Stranger.

What the authorities found, of course, were the Jew's phylacteries, boxes containing biblical verses and used for morning prayer.[26]

Perhaps the last subject of Jewish interest which attracted public attention during the final months before the Glorious Revolution was the claim that in some way Jewish connections with their brethren in the Ottoman Empire were suspicious or even disloyal. This, of course, was a partially justified argument which had been used with deadly effectiveness against the Jews by both Christian and Turk at least since the fateful Battle of Mohács in 1526 which had left most of Hungary in the hands of the Muslims.[27] A short pamphlet had recently been published promoting the 'Case of Many Hundreds of Poor English-Captives, in Algier'.[28] According to one report from London, dated 7 July 1687, 'I

[26] Anon., *Strange and Wonderful News from Borton. Near the City of Canterbury* (London, 1686), broadsheet, printed on both sides: licence to be printed dated verso 16 July 1686. Cf. a similar discovery of 'mysterious' Hebrew verses in Cromwell's time: BL Add. MS 4292, ii, fos. 157–63.

[27] Generally, see R. J. W. Evans, *The Making of the Hapsburg Monarchy, 1550–1700* (Oxford, 1979).

[28] Anon., *Case of Many Hundreds of Poor English-Captives, in Algier* (n.p., 1687), 3 pp.

hear a project is forming to cause the Jews of this nation (considering they give intelligence to the Turks of Algiers of the quality of all the English captives) to redeem his Majesty's subjects at their own costs, otherwise to have no benefits of this country.'[29] Not being believed, this so-called 'project' came to naught, but the interest in the role of the Jews in the Near East may be behind the mysterious publication at about the same time of a bogus report about Shabtai Sevi, 'Now Residing at *Alkair* a City in *Ægypt*'. The broadsheet, printed at London, had supposedly been written at Cairo on 31 January 1687 and translated from Arabic into Latin by a Rabbi Ben Haddi, and was now retranslated and printed.[30] In view of the fact that Shabtai Sevi had died eleven years previously, this must be reckoned among the false Messiah's post-humous miracles.

<h1 style="text-align:center">II</h1>

The Anglo-Jewish community on the eve of the Glorious Revolution, then, was in rather a unique position. Despite residency in England, and the endenization of some of its leading figures, London's Jews were neither alien nor citizen. They were foreign in speech, dress, and manner, and must have seemed hardly touched by their place of residence at all. Small wonder that many people, especially merchants, saw the Jews as merely the English branch of a foreign company with headquarters in Amsterdam, and their very presence as a confidence trick designed to further their interests over those of the native-born. Like all half-truths, this claim had a sound basis in fact, which would become strikingly apparent by the behaviour of the Jews before, during, and after the Glorious Revolution. What saved these foreigners from decimation was the fact that their overseas base became linked with England, after which time their loyalty to the Anglo-Dutch confedera-tion could no longer be held in doubt.

Contacts between the Dutch rulers and the Jews had begun long before 1688. A Jewish community had been established in Amsterdam certainly by the middle 1590s, after the Dutch had extended their blockade of Antwerp to include other Flemish ports, driving the Jewish merchants northwards. The Dutch for their part encouraged Jewish

---

[29] Newsletter from London, 7 July 1687: Hist. MSS Comm., lxxv, *Downshire I*, i. 254.

[30] Anon., *A True and Exact Account of a Famous New Prophet now Residing at Alkair a City in Ægypt* (London, 1687), broadsheet, apparently unknown to G. Scholem, *Sabbatai Sevi* (London, 1973), but listed in C. Roth, *Magna Bibliotheca Anglo-Judaica* (London, 1937), 394.

immigration, since these newcomers brought with them commercial expertise in areas not already part of Holland's economic empire, especially those connected with the Portuguese trade, such as sugar, diamonds, and Brazil-wood. So Jewish merchants, far from competing with native Dutch tradesmen, actually helped to expand and diversify the trade arsenal of the United Provinces.[31] After the French invasion in 1672, the Jews proved themselves useful to the Dutch in yet another way. From at least 1674 the chief contractors for provisioning the Republic's land forces were the Jewish firm of Machado and Pereira. 'Vous avez sauvé l'état,' William III wrote to Antonio-Moses Alvarez Machado, and there was probably a good deal of truth in his praise. Antonio Machado and Jacob Pereira were among the most prominent army contractors in 1688 as well, as was Francisco (Abraham) Lopes Suasso, the second baron of that name. His father Antonio-Isaac had been ennobled by Charles II of Spain for services to the Spanish Netherlands, but he too fled the south in 1652 for Amsterdam. According to a well-known tradition, the second baron advanced William two million guilders to help finance the invasion of England, and refused any security whatsoever for the loan, remarking shrewdly that, 'Si vous êtes heureux, je sais que vous me les rendrez; si vous êtes malheureux, je consens de les perdre.' Jeronimo Nunes da Costa, another prominent Sephardi army contractor, for his part handled the affairs of the troops sent by the duke of Württemberg to aid in the expedition. Jewish merchants and businessmen, then, were heavily involved in the Glorious Revolution itself, and amply repaid the Stadholder for the toleration and support which he had always extended to them.[32]

The Jews of Amsterdam contributed to the invasion of England in other ways as well. Special prayers for the Glorious Revolution were offered in Dutch synagogues.[33] Some Jews even wrote Spanish poems dedicated to William III and his triumph. Manuel de Leon included a portrait of the Stadholder in the printed edition of his literary effort.[34]

[31] J. I. Israel, 'The Economic Contribution of Dutch Sephardi Jews to Holland's Golden Age, 1595–1713', *Tijdschrift voor Geschiedenis*, 96 (1983), 505–36; id., *European Jewry in the Age of Mercantilism, 1550–1750* (Oxford, 1985), 51, 61–4; Bloom, *Economic Activities*; J. H. Prins, 'Prince William of Orange and the Jews' (Hebrew), *Zion*, 15 (1950), 93–106.

[32] Israel, *European Jewry*, 127–34; D. Swetschinski, 'The Portuguese Jewish Merchants of 17th Century Amsterdam: A Social Profile' (Brandeis University Ph.D. thesis, 1979).

[33] This is clear from the three works cited in nn. 34–6.

[34] Manuel de Leon (Leao), *El duelo de los applausos, y triumpho de los triumphos, retrato de Guilielmo III* (The Hague, 1691): cited in *Biblioteca española-portugueza-judaïca*, ed. M. Kayserling (Strasburg, 1890), 57.

A rather longer work came from the pen of Joseph Penso de la Vega, among his numerous other plays and poems.[35] Poet and physician Duartes Lopes-Moseh Roseh likewise produced a stately panegyric in William's honour.[36] According to some sources, Joseph de la Penha even managed to save William from drowning about this time, for which act of valour he was awarded land in the territory of Labrador.[37]

The efforts of Dutch Jewry in the field of military supply most naturally continued in England after William landed in Torbay. Jacob Pereira dispatched his relative Isaac Pereira to look after the firm's interests there, and certainly the Anglo-Dutch Jewish military contractors were very active after James II's invasion of Ireland and the beginning of the Boyne Campaign in the spring of 1690. Isaac Pereira was assisted by Alfonso Rodriguez alias Isaac Israel de Sequeira, son of a man long associated with London Jewry. He in turn was joined by his relative, David Machado de Sequeira, and Jacob do Porto, his grandson. The contribution made by these four men to the success of the Glorious Revolution was outstanding, as we shall see by looking at each of them more closely. Particularly significant were the intertwined nature of their later careers and the results of their subsequent efforts for the establishment and strengthening of the Jewish communities in England, Ireland, and India.[38]

Isaac Pereira was the best placed of this group of Anglo-Dutch Sephardim who were actively supporting the Glorious Revolution. He seems to have forged some sort of personal relationship as well with the duke of Schomberg, the commander of the English expeditionary force to Ireland, who recommended Isaac Pereira to William III:

Je suis fort aisé d'apprendre que Votre Majesté a fait faire un traitté avec Pereyra, pour les vivres, et pour les chariots pour les porter avec l'armée qui est la chose la plus éssentielle. C'est à Pereyra à voir que ces chariots et charettes ne soient pas si pezantes comme on les fait à Londres, et d'avoir de bons chartiers qui sachent fourager.[39]

Schomberg also recounted to the king a dispute he had had with Lord Halifax on the subject of Pereira, in which Halifax said that Schomberg

---

[35] Joseph Penso de la Vega, *Retrato de la prudencia* (Amsterdam, 1690): cited in *Biblioteca*, ed. Kayserling, 87.

[36] Duarte Lopes-Moseh Rosa, *Panegýrico sobre la restauración de Inglaterra* (Amsterdam, 1690): cited in *Biblioteca*, ed. Kayserling, 95.

[37] L. M. Friedman, *Early American Jews* (Cambridge, Mass., 1934), 146–51.

[38] Isaac Pereira's agent who handled the commissariat was Francisco de Cordova: Hyamson, *Sephardim*, 68; Roth, *History*, 184.

[39] Schomberg to William III, 26 Dec. 1689, from Lisburn: quoted in T. Gimlette, *The History of the Huguenot Settlers in Ireland, and Other Literary Remains* (n.p., 1888), 273. Cf. *Cal. SP Dom., 1689–90*, 437.

desired 'favoriser ceux de ma nation; surquoy je le repliquay que je le croyais autant de sa nation que de la mienne'.[40] Pereira himself contributed £36,000 to the success of the Boyne Campaign, as part of his role as 'Commissary-General of the bread for their Majesty's Forces in Ireland'.[41] The bread itself was baked in Waringstown, County Down, in ovens built in the spring of 1690 under the direction of Pereira's twenty-eight bakers, who were shipped there from Bristol.[42] From March 1690 he had the help of his brother William, who was also taken under the wing of the duke of Schomberg.[43] In England his agent was a certain Mr Bridges, apparently a Gentile, who also had access to the Council.[44] Isaac Pereira was so successful in his task that, when the duke of Schomberg arrived in County Down, he sent back to England eighteen of Pereira's ships, each packed with beef, cheese, and beer.[45]

Indeed, there were times when everything came to a dead halt without Isaac Pereira. The earl of Danby was worried about bread for the army in February 1691, and informed Nottingham that 'the matter of the waggons stands still till Perera comes, who they tell us is dayly look't for here'.[46] Nottingham had this confirmed from another source at the same time: 'Pereyra is expected,' wrote Viscount Sidney, 'and until he has arrived that matter, I find, will be at a standstill.'[47] Pereira spoke for himself before the Council and the Committee of Ireland, and the fact of his being a Jew was not even worth commenting upon.[48]

Alfonso Rodriguez alias Isaac Israel de Sequeira was another Dutch Jew who came to England in the train of the Glorious Revolution. His father, Abraham Isaac de Sequeira had already acted on behalf of the Dutch East India Company, and it was as a result of his work that Jews

[40] *Cal. SP Dom.*, *1689–90*, 401, 452.

[41] Ibid. 453, 506. For some accounting of how much Pereira received in return, see *Cal. SP Dom.*, *1690–1*, 7, 425, 448; *1691–2*, 50, 124; *Cal. Treasury Papers*, *1556/7–1696*, 318, 381, 498; Hist. MSS Comm., xvii, *House of Lords MSS*, NS *V*, 383, 394–5, 397, 401, where payments to Machado and Pereira for bread, bread wagons, and forage for the troops in Flanders came to over £437,000.

[42] *Cal. SP Dom.*, *1689–90*, 513; *MJHSE* 1 (1925), p. xxvii; L. Hyman, *The Jews of Ireland* (London, 1972), 19, 292.

[43] *Cal. SP Dom.*, *1689–90*, 497, 509, 543, 556–7.

[44] *Cal. SP Dom.*, *1690–1*, 264, 279; Hist. MSS Comm., lxxi, *Finch III*, 446.

[45] *Cal. SP Dom.*, *1689–90*, 509; Hyman, *Ireland*, 19, 292.

[46] Thomas, 1st earl of Danby to Daniel Finch, 2nd earl of Nottingham, Secretary of State, 6 Feb. 1690/1, from London: Hist. MSS Comm., lxxi, *Finch III*, 10.

[47] Henry, Viscount Sidney, to Nottingham, 17 Feb. 1690/1: *Cal. SP Dom.*, *1690–1*, 264.

[48] General Baron van Ginkel (cr. earl of Athlone in 1692) to William Blathwait, Secretary for War, 24 Jan. 1690/1, from Dublin: ibid. 234; Blathwait to Nottingham, 6 Mar. 1690/1, from Whitehall: ibid. 297. Cf. Ginkel to Lord Coningsby, Feb.–Oct. 1691: Hist. MSS Comm., *4th Report, App.* (1874), 319, 320, 321, 324.

were first allowed to settle in Madras. His three sons all became freemen of the Company, and his youngest son Jacob was one of the founders of the principality of Madras in 1688.[49] The Pereira interests in Ireland were looked after by Isaac's relative, David Machado de Sequeira, who played a leading role in the Boyne Campaign, and helped to provide the support in money and *matériel* for the Anglo-Dutch army. Afterwards he was an important figure in the infant synagogue in Dublin.[50] Machado became most celebrated at the turn of the century for his work in disseminating the persuasive attacks on the Inquisition which had been made by Antonio Vieira, the Portuguese Jesuit mystic. Machado was in London in 1707–8, and in the latter year published an English translation of Vieira's work.[51] He even prepared a covering letter to the king of Portugal and planned to send him Vieira's book, although for some reason he changed his mind about contacting the king.[52] Afterwards he settled in Bordeaux and finally Surinam, publishing poetry and religious literature.[53]

Jacob do Porto was the last member of the group, a grandson of Abraham Israel de Sequeira, nephew of his son Alfonso-Isaac, and second son of Antonio-Abraham do Porto, sometime *gabay* and *parnas* of the Sephardi community in London. His father Abraham had himself escaped the Inquisition and was in London by 1655, for he was a witness in the Robles case, which effectively secured the readmission of the Jews to England in the spring of the following year; he seems to have been one of the richest Jews in London in his day. Like his relative Sequeira, Abraham went with his wife and eldest son to Madras in 1681 and

[49] Hyamson, *Sephardim*, 68 n.

[50] Apart from Hyman, *Ireland*, 20, see L. Wolf, 'Notes on the Early History of the Dublin Hebrew Congregation', *TJHSE* 11 (1928), 162–7.

[51] [David Machado de Sequeira], *An Account of the Cruelties Exercis'd by the Inquisition in Portugal* (London, 1708): reissued with new title-page as *The History of the Inquisition* (London, 1713). Later Spanish and Portuguese editions are often wrongly attributed to David Nieto: see I. Solomons, 'David Nieto and Some of his Contemporaries', *TJHSE* 12 (1931), 46–51, 75. On Vieira generally, see C. R. Boxer, 'Antonio Vieira S.J. and the Institution of the Brazil Company in 1649', *Hispanic American History Review*, 29 (1949), 474–97; A. J. Saraiva, 'Antonio Vieira, Menasseh ben Israel et le cinquième empire', *Studia Rosenthaliana*, 6 (1972), 27–57. Cf. C. Roth, *A History of the Marranos* (Philadelphia, 1932).

[52] *Biblioteca*, ed. Kayserling, 100.

[53] Machado settled in Bordeaux after his retirement, where he preached in the synagogue and wrote poetry. One of his funeral sermons was published in Amsterdam in 1734 (ibid. 100). In that year he also thanked the *parnassim* of the Jewish community in Amsterdam for electing him preacher and teacher in Surinam: *PAJHS* 29 (1920), 17. This was also the year that the Ashkenazim of Surinam formed their own congregation there: *PAJHS* 13 (1904), 127, 132. Cf. R. Cohen (ed.), *The Jewish Nation in Surinam* (Amsterdam, 1982).

became a freeman of the city, dying there in 1690 as his son Jacob was actively supporting the Boyne Campaign.[54] Jacob married Sarah Lobatto of the Gideon family, and had three sons and one daughter. One of his children produced Samson Gideon, the celebrated financial adviser of Walpole and the English government. Jacob seems to have stayed in Ireland for a time after the Campaign, living in Cork, but returned to London, living there as late as 1747.[55]

The role of the Jews in making both the Glorious Revolution of 1688 and the Boyne Campaign two years later successes was therefore not inconsiderable. Machado, Pereira, Sequeira, and do Porto were names heard both in Irish army camps and in the Council chamber. Yet, despite the personal union of England, Scotland, Ireland, and the United Provinces, the Dutch Jews who financed and supplied William's troops were most certainly aliens, and far removed as well from the Jewish community in London, which was now well over thirty years old.[56] The English Jews were mainly passive recipients of the Glorious Revolution and its effects. Like many Nonconformists, Anglo-Jewry must have waited anxiously to see what the new religious compromise would look like once the dust had settled. Despite the presence in England of powerful and influential Dutch Jewish army contractors and financiers, the Jews of London were hardly on anyone's mind. William's Toleration Act of 1689 made this quite clear, for it was an 'Act for exempting Their Majesties' Protestant subjects, dissenting from the Church of England, from the penalties of certain laws'. The Jews of London were many things, but they were not Protestant. To make matters worse, as opposed to James's Declarations of Indulgence, the seventeenth clause of the Toleration Act expressly excluded from its benefits 'any person that shall deny in his preaching or writing the doctrine of the blessed Trinity'. Despite the fact that this provision was

---

[54] On Abraham generally, see L. Wolf, 'The Jewry of the Restoration, 1660–1664', *TJHSE* 5 (1908), 8; Hyamson, *Sephardim*, 53, 54, 68; Hyman, *Ireland*, 20–1.

[55] L. Wolf, *Essays in Jewish History*, ed. C. Roth (London, 1934), 172–6; Hyman, *Ireland*, 20–1. Jacob do Porto was one of the four Jews of Dublin who obtained the lease of land for a cemetery in 1718; the others were David Machado de Sequeira, David Penso alias Alexander Felis (cf. Wolf, 'Note', 166–7), and Alexander Meirs (cf. cemetery deed, repr. in *TJHSE* 11 (1928), 155–7).

[56] A final, rather more mysterious, possible financial supporter of the Glorious Revolution and the Boyne Campaign was a Sephardi Jew possibly employed by Pereira, who had married a convert to Judaism. They had several sons, circumcised in London and Dublin. Their daughter married Moseh Fincey (Finzi) Mantuano, and their son was born in 1730, perhaps in Dublin, but certainly in a place where no *mohel* was yet available. On 5 Sivan 1733 Finzi was given leave by the Mahamad of the Spanish and Portuguese Congregation in London to have his son circumcised there: Hyman, *Ireland*, 21, citing the minute book of the congregation and noting that they have no record of a marriage in London of Moseh Finzi Mantuano.

directed against the rather more pressing threat of Unitarianism and Socinianism, as had often happened since the Restoration, the Jews found themselves caught in a trap set for others. The laws against recusancy were expressly re-enforced, and in any case the Test and Corporation Acts still excluded all Nonconformists from political power.

The anomalous position of the Jews during this period is nowhere more clearly demonstrated than in the potentially devastating toing and froing over the question of special Jewish taxation to support the campaign in Ireland. The Dutch Jews who supplied William's army were after all making a substantial profit, and left untouched the fabled wealth of London Sephardi Jewry. The very fact that such taxation was discussed may indicate that neither the Dutch nor the Jewish commissaries of Amsterdam saw the Sephardim of Creechurch Lane as part of the same social group which turned William's military plans into reality. In any case, the issue arose as early as 4 April 1689, when a poll tax was first discussed in the House of Commons. Not content with letting anyone fall through the net, one of the heads for discussions in the Committee of the Whole House was 'That all Merchants, Strangers, and *Jews*, shall be taxed in the said Bill'.[57] On 2 November 1689 the House of Commons resolved to give the king further funds for the reduction of Ireland, and defence against the troops of Louis XIV. Five days later the Committee of the Whole House resolved 'That, towards the raising the Supply, there be a Tax of One hundred Thousand Pounds laid upon the *Jews*'.[58] Furthermore, the poll tax was amended, so 'That every Merchant Stranger and Jew residing within this Kingdome shall pay the Summe of Ten pounds'.[59]

The point of principle aside, the amount of money which the bill for special taxation hoped to obtain from the Jews was absurdly large. The sum proposed represented about 6.25 per cent of the royal revenue in time of peace, and even now in wartime made up a considerable proportion of the whole. Most worrying, the Commons were proposing to obtain these funds from the 550–600 Jews who made up the entire Jewish community, that is, from about 0.01 per cent of the general population.[60] This was in itself a landmark, for never had the Jews been

[57] *Commons Journal*, 10: 79.   [58] Ibid.   [59] Ibid. 10: 281.

[60] During the reign of James II the annual royal revenue stood at about £1,600,000: C. D. Chandaman, 'The Financial Settlement in the Parliament of 1685', in H. Hearder and H. R. Loyn (eds.), *British Government and Administration: Studies Presented to S. B. Chrimes* (Cardiff, 1974), 144–54. According to the recent estimates of the Cambridge Group for the History of Population and Social Structure, the population of England in 1686 had fallen to 4,864,762 and did not reach five million again until 1701: E. A. Wrigley and R. Schofield, *The Population History of England, 1541–1871* (London, 1981), 207–9.

mentioned before in an act of parliament. They were placed fairly high in the scale of taxation: dukes paid £50, and earls £303, but Jews of all kinds were classed as knights and merchants not given freedom of the city. Even gentlemen with estates worth £300 paid only twenty shillings.[61]

The bill for special taxation of the Jews was presented at the House of Commons on 11 November 1689, and the response of the Sephardi community was immediate. They drew up a closely reasoned petition explaining their position, had it printed, and arranged to have it presented at the House of Commons. The document is quite extraordinary in its clarity and directness, and unusually illuminating as it attempts to define the political and legal status of a nation defined by religious criteria. The Jews begin by describing their own history in England, placing the origins of the community when, 'about the Year 1654, there came Six Jews Families into this Kingdom, which have (since King *Charles* the Second's Restauration) been increased to the Number of between Three and Fourscore Families'. Some of these, they noted, were refugees from the 'severe Persecutions of the most Horrid and Barbarous Inquisition'; several had already been endenizened and promised the same rights and liberties as native-born Englishmen. The Jews themselves reckoned that about a quarter of their number possessed 'Moderate Estates', and a further quarter 'very indifferent Estates': 'the other half consists partly of an industrious sort of People, that assist the better sort in the management of their Commerce, and partly of indigent poor people, who are maintained by the rest, and no ways chargeable to the Parishes'. The Jewish merchants, they protested, served or fined for parish offices, and paid their taxes diligently, despite their self-described moderate wealth, 'they being employed as Factors, by their Friends and Relations abroad'. Their export of wool and import of gold, silver, and foreign manufactures had greatly enriched the nation, not even considering the customs duties which they had already paid: 'one of the said Families alone hath since the Restauration paid about Two Hundred Thousand Pounds for Customs'. Likewise, the Jews had stolen away the market in diamonds from the Portuguese at Goa and removed it to the English possessions. Yet, despite all of this wealth and success, they argued, 'all the *Jews* together are not by much worth the Hundred Thousand Pounds designed to be raised upon them'.

Most interestingly, the Sephardi Jews of London approached the

---

[61] *Commons Journal*, 10: 281; and see, generally, H. S. Q. Henriques, 'Proposals for Special Taxation of the Jews after the Restoration', *TJHSE* 9 (1922), 43–4; id., *The Jews and the English Law* (Oxford, 1908), 164–7.

entire question of their alien status directly, and used it as an argument against special taxation. They noted

That the *Jews* being a Nation that cannot lay claim to any Country, do never remove from any part where they are Tollerated, and Protected; and therefore may be lookt upon to be a greater Advantage to this Kingdom then any other Forreigners, who commonly, so soon as they have got good Estates, return with them into their own Countries.

This, of course, was not precisely true: 'their own' newly adopted Dutch country had simply become politically linked with their newest place of residence. Nevertheless, they did define themselves as a landless nation rather than as a religion or even a race, a concept which must surely have worked against Jewish integration. The Sephardim were anxious to make clear what their national status exactly entailed:

And Whereas the *Jews* are informed that there is a rumour goes about, That what these are not able to pay, the *Jews* in other Parts will make up, looking upon them all to make but one Body, though at never so great a distance from each other: They humbly take leave to represent, that in Truth every one particular Man among them subsists of himself, without dependence on any other; And that they cannot expect any Assistance, or Relief from any other place whatsoever: But instead thereof, those abroad will certainly withdraw their Effects, and Correspondencies, and never be concerned any more with them; which will be the utter ruine, and Destruction of them.

So there were limits to what the English might reasonably expect in the way of financial support from a persecuted Jewish community in London.

The Jews concluded with some final points which they thought would weigh heavily in their favour. They affirmed that no Jews in London were in the retail business as shopkeepers, and that 'there are none in the whole Kingdom, but those who dwells, and Inhabits in the Cities of *London* and *Westminster*'. In other words, the merchants of London need not fear any Jewish competition. Furthermore, they denied categorically 'that the *Jews* did offer a very great Sum of Money to *Oliver Cromwel* for their Establishment in this Kingdom'; neither had they offered nor given any financial inducement to the Stuart kings for the right to remain in England. Finally, they took the opportunity to deny that they had any connection whatsoever with those holding English captives in Algiers, let alone that they had provided information about the prisoners. Only one of their number 'hath any Correspondence in those Places, and he is very willing, and desirous, to give a full account, and discharge of what he hath Acted in this Concern'. Consequently 'it cannot be supposed that the HONOURABLE HOUSE OF COMMONS will go about utterly to destroy a People that have always lived Peaceably, Quietly, and Dutifully, under the Established Government; which will certainly be their Case if this Tax proceed'.[62]

The petition of the Jews was printed and delivered to the House of Commons on 19 November 1689 before the bill was read for the first time. Their agent on this occasion was Paul Foley, member for Hereford, and later Speaker of the House.[63] The motive for Foley's advocacy of the Jewish cause is not clear, but we do know from the financial records of the Jewish community that they spent nearly £200 on defeating the bill. It would not be slanderous to suggest that some of the money found its way to Paul Foley.[64] Unfortunately, from the strictly constitutional point of view, the Jewish petition was unacceptable. Until the middle of the nineteenth century, no petition against a bill imposing a tax could be received, and if presented could not be entered into the journal of the House. The assumption was that since a tax applied equally to all parts of England, no individual or group should be permitted to treat a tax as a special burden to themselves. This was manifestly not the case here, but the procedure stood.[65] The debate on the proposal was lively, and many of the members must have seen the Jews' broadsheet, although it was not mentioned officially at any stage. 'Pray let not such Petitions be received,' pleaded Sir Thomas Lee. 'You will not receive it from others, pray begin not with the Jews.'[66]

The proposal was clearly running into a good deal of unexpected opposition. The gist of the Jews' petition, as Narcissus Luttrell understood it, was that 'they cannot pay the 4th part of the 100,000 *l.* imposed on them, and that if they have no redresse they must be forced to leave the kingdome'.[67] A newsletter of 12 November similarly reported that the 'Jews will rather remove their effects into Holland than pay the imposition which Parliament has designed to lay upon them'.[68] The threat was taken seriously; so there was very little steam left in the

---

[62] Anon., *The Case of the Jews Stated* (n.p.=London, n.d.=11 Nov. 1689); only copy in Inner Temple Library, London. I am most grateful to Mr W. W. S. Breem, librarian and keeper of manuscripts there, for supplying me with a photocopy of this broadsheet, which narrowly escaped the destruction of the library building (and 40,000 volumes) by German bombing in 1941. The pamphlet is repr. in *TJHSE* 9 (1922), 44–6. The date of the petition is confirmed by Narcissus Luttrell, *A Brief Historical Relation of State Affairs* (Oxford, 1857), i. 603. Macaulay knew of the petition's existence, but had not seen it: *History*, iii. 91 n.

[63] *Commons Journal*, 10: 290; Grey, *Debates*, ix. 437–8; William Cobbett, *The Parliamentary History of England* (London, 1806–20), v. 444.

[64] *Bevis Marks Records*, i, ed. Barnett, 21. The exact sum was £193 8s. 9d.

[65] Henriques, 'Jews', 164–5.

[66] Grey, *Debates*, ix. 437–8; Cobbett, *Parliamentary History*, v. 444.

[67] Luttrell, *Relation*, i. 603 (11 Nov. 1689).

[68] Greenwich Hospital Newsletter, 12 Nov. 1689: *Cal. SP Dom., 1689–90*, 318–19.

proposal when the bill was read for the first time on 30 December 1689. Although it was then resolved that it be committed for a second reading, the bill in fact died that day.[69] When Macaulay came to ponder the question, he took these events to prove that 'Enlightened politicians could not but perceive that special taxation, laid on a small class which happens to be rich, unpopular and defenceless, is really confiscation, and must ultimately impoverish rather than enrich the State.'[70] Be that as it may, the Jews had won their battle.[71]

Nevertheless, the principle of regarding the Sephardi Jews of London as a separated group of aliens on whom could be laid additional burdens of taxation was not abandoned, and, in fact, further efforts to obtain money from them were initiated immediately on the failure of the bill in Parliament. Indeed, the chief promoter of the special taxation for the Jews of London seems to have been the king himself, possibly advised by his Dutch Jewish army contractor Isaac Pereira. Instructions were given to the earl of Shrewsbury, William's trusted Secretary of State and one of the 'Immortal Seven', to pass the word on to the Lord Mayor of London. This he did in a letter of 10 February 1689/90:

It having been taken into Consideration that the Jews residing in London & driving so advantageous a Trade under the favour of the Government ought to be called upon at this time to shew their readines to support it; by advancing such Summs of mony on the credit of the late Acts of Parliament as they are Judged able to lend, they have been asked what they were willing to furnish towarde supplying one of their Brethren Monsieur Pereira in Part of the Contract made with him for providing bread for the Army, & they having made an offer of £12,000 which is so much below what his Majesty expected from them, that he is pleased to direct Your Lordship should send for their Elders & Principall Merchants to let them understand what obligations they have to his Majesty for the Liberty & Privildges they enjoy by his Protection & Indulgence, & how much it is their advantage as well as it is becoming them not to be wanting in all sutable retourns of affection & Gratitude for the kindness they have received & may expect & since what was demanded carrys with it so considerable a profitt to the lender by the more than ordinary Interest allowed, it was supposed they would not make a difficulty of raising among them £30,000 or if they abated of that Summe they could not propose less then £20,000 & his Majesty is willing to believe that upon second thoughts assisted by

[69] *Commons Journal*, 10: 319 (30 Dec. 1689). Cf. Greenwich Hospital Newsletter, 31 Dec. 1689: *Cal. SP Dom., 1689–90*, 374.

[70] Macaulay, *History*, iii. 91.

[71] But not completely: a separate tax on the Jews was in force in the West Indian colonies, first imposed in Barbados. In Jamaica, a lump sum on the Jews in addition to ordinary taxation began in the 1680s and continued until 1741. In Bermuda too such a system prevailed. See Henriques, 'Special Taxation', 53–4; *PAJHS* 2: 165, 5: 87–9, 18: 148–9, 177 ff., 19: 173–4.

the representation you shall make to them they will come to new resolutions & such as may be fitt for his Majesty's acceptance who relying upon Your Lordship's prudence, & zeale for his Service do's not question but you will conclude this affaire to his satisfaction.[72]

This is a letter, then, which manages to be threatening to the Jews and to the Lord Mayor of London at a stroke. Indeed, it would not be inaccurate to describe the method as blackmail. Still, £20,000 was only 20 per cent of the sum originally proposed, and it was recognized that the Jews of London were not endowed with unlimited wealth. The Jewish response seems to have been unsatisfactory, however. According to one report, it was the earl of Monmouth who conveyed the king's wishes to Michael Levy, one of the leaders of the Sephardi congregation.[73] Levy in his reply denied the ability of the Jews to pay even the reduced amount, even at 7 per cent profit, claiming that only seventeen or eighteen Jews in the entire country had any considerable estate.[74]

The special tax of £100,000 and the forced loan were two of the pressures placed upon the Jews of London after the Glorious Revolution, and seem to have been part of a deliberate policy of near persecution. The failure of the Jews to agree to special taxation also brought about a renewal of efforts to cancel exemptions they had received from the payment of alien duties, and to have them reclassified as foreign residents rather than as resident nationals of an international nation. As we have seen, the question of the customs duties and the Jews had been a vexing one for some time. The view of the English merchants was that remission of alien duties on either exports or imports 'is a Publick Damage to the Interest of Your Majesty's Kingdoms, and a Diminution of Your Revenue, and the Trade of Your *English* Merchants'. Worst of all, they saw it as 'a Means to transplant that, and the Mysteries of our Artificers into the Hands of Foreigners, to the Ruin, not only of the Trading and Working People at Home, but also of the several *English* Factories Abroad'. The language of the petitions is general, but the reference was to the Jews, who had managed to obtain

[72] Charles Taylor, 12th earl of Shrewsbury, to the Lord Mayor of London, 10 Feb. 1689/90: SP 44/97, pp. 256–7 (cf. *Cal. SP Dom.*, *1689–90*, 453). Note that, on the same day, Schomberg wrote to the king from Ireland that he was 'glad you have made a contract with Pereyra': ibid. 452.

[73] Anon., *Mr Christopher Dodworth's Proceedings against the Exportation of Silver by the Jews and Others* (London, [1690]): single sheet folio, not earlier than 7 Oct. 1690: only copy in Columbia University Library (Wing D1801A). A list of thirty-eight Jewish silver exporters is printed here, representing the majority of all merchants engaged in the trade.

[74] Ibid. For more on Mayer (Michael) Levy, the 'solicitor' of the congregation, see Hyamson, *Sephardim*, 54, 56, 64, 71.

exemption from alien duties on exports, and, it was thought, might even convince the Crown to make the same provision for imports as well. Petitions in this spirit were submitted by the Hamburg Company, the Eastland Company, and groups of internal merchants based in London.[75]

But little had been done to meet the wishes of the English merchants until this demand meshed with other pressures being brought to bear on the Sephardi community. The man promoting the case was a London customs official named Thomas Penington, who wrote to the earl of Danby, the chief minister of the Crown, on 30 January 1690, urging that the Jews should no longer be exempted from paying the alien duty.[76] The arguments brought forward by Penington and the merchants were presented to King William by one of the Lords of the Treasury, making the legal point that the exemptions granted to the Jews in their patents of denization by Charles II and James II were now void with the accession of a new monarch. Despite this undoubted fact, the king was informed that the Jews continued to enter goods in their own names, paying only the duty accruing to the merchandise of Englishmen. According to one report, William 'was so well satisfy'd with this Account, that he declar'd he wou'd not abate the *Jews* three Pence of what was legaly due to himself, which was a Moiety'. Penington was ordered to bring forward the information which he had collected, and he presented the Exchequer with claims for £58,000 in uncollected alien duty owed by Jews.[77]

Penington meanwhile managed to have twenty Jewish merchants arrested for non-payment of customs duties and charged them in the Court of Exchequer. The Jews in turn, led by Antonio Gomesera, who had fought Samuel Hayne the customs inspector at Falmouth several years before, marshalled all the economic and political influence that could be brought to bear to have this attack deflected like the rest. Exactly how this was accomplished is not clear. The English merchants claimed that only bribery would have made the Crown voluntarily remit such a substantial amount of customs duties legally owed to them. Thomas Penington himself waited for days outside the Council chamber, trying in vain to present a petition which would lay out the English merchants' case for full collection of alien duties. In the end, only the petition of the Jews was read to the Council, making the point that they, 'being made free Denizens, are by Virtue thereof discharged from paying any more Customs, than His Majesty's Natural born

[75] Cf. the petition of Jan. 1685/6, and Tovey, *Anglia Judaica*, 287–8.
[76] Thomas Penington to the earl of Danby, 30 Jan. 1689/90: Hist. MSS Comm., *11th Report, App., Part VI* (1888), 35.   [77] Tovey, *Anglia Judaica*, 288–9.

Subjects'. William, taking the entire matter into consideration, ordered the Attorney-General to quash the proceedings against the Jews, 'it being His Majesty's Pleasure, that they enjoy the full Benefit of their respective Letters Patents'.[78]

William must have had his inducements to have relented on the rather profitable question of alien duties for Jews, especially when only a fortnight before he had been pressuring the Lord Mayor of London to extract a forced loan from these very same merchants. It may be that the two attacks were connected: the Sephardi merchants could provide the king with funds directly in return for a concession on alien duties. The proposal to lay a special tax of £100,000 on the Jews had already been seen to fail. Had the Jews been willing to go along with this latest plan for financial extraction then the pleas of the English merchants might have fallen on deaf ears. The Englishmen turned to the commissioners of the customs and noted, first, that the king would thereby lose not only at least £40,000 in past customs, but at least £10,000 per annum on alien duties. Since the king would not reduce his expenses by a similar amount, 'if these Dutys were remitted to the *Jews*, they must be supply'd, altogether, by the People of *England*'. Secondly, they thought that the remission of alien duties for the Jews would provide them with an unfair competitive advantage, if they were 'let loose to over-run the Trade of the *English* Merchants, both at Home and Abroad'. They raised a few legal points, and concluded, most cleverly, by noting 'That most *English* Merchants had Estates in Land, as well as Stocks in Trade, and pay'd Taxes for them, whereas the Rich *Jews* were past finding out: and, it must needs grieve the *English* to pay any *new* Taxes if the *Jews* were illegaly exempted from Payment of any *antient* Duty.' These arguments, presented by the commissioners of the customs to the Privy Council, seem to have had some effect, for, 'notwithstanding all the *Jews* cou'd do to prevent it', William III at Hampton Court on 14 October 1690 issued an Order in Council withdrawing his previous remission, and once again levied customs duties on all English exports effected by foreign merchants.[79]

The English merchants had won, but it was a Pyrrhic victory: two months later Parliament abolished increased alien duties altogether, and presumably the back customs were not collected.[80] The notion of the

---

[78] Order in Council, 26 Feb. 1689/90, referring to petition of twenty Jewish merchants in London, incl. Antonio Gomezsera, Phineas Gomezsera, Andrew Lopez, Antonio de Costa, Joshua Bueno, Menasses Mendez, and Antonio Corea: repr. ibid. 289–92.

[79] English merchants to the commissioners of the customs, betw. Feb. and Oct. 1609, repr. ibid. 292–3; William III, Order in Council, 14 Oct. 1690: repr. ibid. 294–5.

[80] Ibid.; Henriques, 'Special Taxation', 58–65.

Jews as a special class ripe for financial exploitation was not abandoned, however, and was continued in the individual Jewish contribution mentioned in the poll tax. We have already seen how at the very beginning of the new monetary pressure on the Jews, in the amended poll tax of 1689, it was enacted that 'every Merchant Stranger and Jew residing within this Kingdome shall pay the Summe of Ten pounds'.[81] Now, in 1690, yet another loophole was filled in. Since many Jews who were not merchants lived in London, a new scale for taxing Jews was devised, whereby merchant Jews would now pay £20, double the amount laid on merchant strangers. Jewish brokers, however, would pay only £5, and every Jew aged 16 and over ten shillings. In a sense, this new provision was even more discriminatory. Merchant Jews were now paying the same amount as bishops and barons, and even ordinary Jews were assessed at ten times the rate of the rest of the population. While it was true that Roman Catholics had to pay double if they refused to take the required oaths, Jews were assessed at still greater amounts.[82] This injustice, at least, was very temporary: the poll tax of 1691 imposed no special provisions for Jews, and this reformed policy was continued until the last of the series, imposed for 1698.[83]

Four lines of attack had therefore been used against the resident Jewish population in London immediately after the Glorious Revolution: the £100,000 tax, the forced loan, the alien duties, and the special poll tax. One final and more subtle weapon against the Jews was also deployed during this period, and one which required the Sephardim not to act rather than to make themselves more prominent. This was the accusation that the Jews in London were contributing to the currency shortage by exporting precious metals. In 1689 a committee of the Commons had been appointed to investigate the entire issue, and the following year the Commons heard that enormous quantities of silver were being exported by Jews anxious to make a profit even at the expense of their native hosts. The currency shortage continued to plague the English government throughout the 1690s, and numerous

---

[81] 1 Wm. & Mar., c. 13, s. 10: *Statutes of the Realm*, ed. T. E. Tomlins, *et al.* (London, 1810–28), vi. 65. Cf. 1 Wm. & Mar., sess. 2, c. 7: ibid., vi. 152; S. Dowell, *A History of Taxation and Taxes in England* (London, 1884), ii. 48; Henriques, 'Special Taxation', 43.

[82] 2 Wm. & Mar., c. 2, s. 10: *Statutes of the Realm*, vi. 158; Henriques, 'Special Taxation', 47–8.

[83] 3 & 4 Wm. & Mar., c. 6. Cf. 4 & 5 Wm. & Mar., c. 14; 8 Wm. III, c. 6; 9 & 10 Wm. III, c. 38. See also Henriques, 'Special Taxation', 48. This, of course, did not prevent Jews from being mentioned as such in the returns: cf. that for 'Mr Jaques Consales Jew Merch.' his wife and Eight Children', assessed for £1 10s. 0d. in the 1692/3 poll tax: Corporation of London Records Office, Assessment Box, no. 35, MS 4, fo. 11 (ward of Bishopsgate Within, Corbett's Court): I am grateful to Dr Stephen Macfarlane for pointing me to this reference.

legislative attempts were made to stem the flow.[84] The Jews, for their part, by means of orders from the Mahamad, excluded themselves from the trade in gold and silver, so sensitive was this revival of the traditional accusations of sharp Jewish practice in this area. Immediately in 1689 they forbade any member of the congregation to export silver.[85] In later years they extended the prohibition to the export or import of gold, and even temporarily to the buying or selling of guineas.[86] No doubt the regulations could not be strictly enforced, but they are indicative of yet another system of defence against the forces brought to bear on the Jews during this period.

Between April 1689 and December 1690, then, the Jews already resident in London at the time of the Glorious Revolution were subjected to a number of attacks which were designed to extract as much money as possible from them. All put pressure on the Jews to demonstrate financially their loyalty to the new government. In other words, roughly during the period between Louis XIV's declaration of war against England (25 July 1689) and William's return to England (6 September 1690) after the follow-up campaign in the wake of defeating James II at the Battle of the Boyne in Ireland (1 July 1690), the Jews of London were regarded as a dormant financial asset which might be tapped in this, the Crown's hour of need. The extremely close connection which a number of Dutch Jews had with the Anglo-Dutch war effort rules out any ideological motives for William's actions. Indeed, in searching for the instigators of the king's financial strategy, one perhaps need not go any further than men like Isaac Pereira and the

---

[84] Anon., *Dodworth*.

[85] Order of the Mahamad, 6 Tebet 5450=1689: *Bevis Marks Records*, i, ed. Barnett, 22.

[86] Order of the Mahamad, 24 Tishri 5456=1695, forbidding for the next fifteen days that any Jew should buy or sell guineas or be present at the sale or purchase of guineas, under penalty of a £5 fine and exclusion from the Congregation; order of the Mahamad, 18 Adar 5456=1696, forbidding any Sephardi Jew from importing gold or silver, except for the trade with Spain, Portugal, and the Isles, and 'in view of certain petitions directed to our hurt', decreeing that no Jewish brokers or persons in the service of merchants should buy or sell for themselves or their employers guineas or gold and silver in bars. The second order was annulled and replaced on 10 Nisan 5456=1696 by another, forbidding Sephardim from exporting gold or silver in any form whether for themselves or others, under penalty of a £20 fine and exclusion, with the same penalty for those who connive to the same end; and all who had received gold or silver from abroad, from Spain, Portugal, or the Isles, which they wished to ship back, were allowed fifteen days' grace to declare it to the Mahamad, swearing that they had not already sold part of the consignment, whereupon they would receive the Mahamad's licence to ship it back: photograph of this order is pl. ix, *Bevis Marks Records*, i, ed. Barnett, facing p. 22, and see, generally, pp. 21–2. Cf. John Drummond to earl of Oxford, from Amsterdam, 18/29 May 1711: Hist. MSS Comm., *xxix, Portland IV*, 693.

Machados, who were well placed to know how much their Jewish cousins might be expected to contribute. The Sephardi Jews of London, for their part, continued to express their support for the Glorious Revolution, even to the extent of forbidding Jewish brokers to deal at all with insurance policies providing protection from the government's fall, an event which would be 'very contrary to our welfare, since we depend solely upon the toleration and benignity of Their Majesties to be able to live in this realm with modesty and temperance'.[87] The concerted attacks on the Jewish community's economic well-being passed with the consolidation of the Glorious Revolution, but demonstrated how fragile their conditions of residence still might be.

III

It is perhaps a curious fact that despite the intense interest which the new king had in the financial potential of the Jewish community, one feature of Jewish life in the era of the Glorious Revolution was an apparent reduction of popular attention towards the Jews, who were becoming yet another eccentric religious group on the London spiritual landscape.[88] John Evelyn was sensitized rather more than most in reporting on the role of the Jews in contemporary English life, yet we find him strangely silent, certainly when compared with the exciting days of the Civil War. In December 1689 Evelyn heard Dr John Hearne, the rector of St Anne's, Soho, preaching on the question of the Messiah having already come, and defending this post-millennialist theological view. Hearne told his parishioners that among other reasons for accepting this interpretation was that otherwise 'this might (if any thing) be enough to harden the Jewes, & keepe them off from believeing that Savior to be come, to which ther follows so little of those prophesies fulfilled'.[89] The following April he was in attendance at Whitehall when William Lloyd, the bishop of St Asaph and one of the famous seven who had refused to publish the deposed king's declaration two years before, brought his learning to bear on the matter in the presence of William and Mary. Lloyd

[87] Order of the Mahamad, 14 Nisan 5451=1691: no member should take up such war-risks or policies, nor solicit them in person or by an agent; under penalty of exclusion; the law was annulled on 20 Elul 5453=1693: *Bevis Marks Records*, i, ed. Barnett, 22–3.

[88] Although they still appear in popular verse, usually coupled with 'Turks': see e.g. *The Pepys Ballads*, ed. H. E. Rollins (Cambridge, Mass., 1929–32), iv. 344; v. 33, 94; vii. 271.

[89] Evelyn, *Diary*, ed. de Beer, iv. 652–3 (8 Dec. 1689).

spake relating to the calling of the Jewes, which he believed to be at hand, with other particulars relating to his long-since opinions concerning greate Revolutions to be at hand for the good of the Christian orthodox Church & destruction of the papacy: The same being the opinion of many devout Apo[ca]lyptical Divines, more than ordinarily, about this Conjuncture of the publique Affaires & Emotions in the World, & especialy Europe.

Coming in the midst of William's efforts to extract money from the Jews by means of taxes, forced loans, and alien duties, Lloyd's prophecies regarding the calling of the Jews may have struck a humorous note.[90]

Still, it may be that the constant discussion in Parliament and at Court of the Jews' financial role reawakened some interest in their potential millenarian contribution as well. Several days after hearing Lloyd, Evelyn went along on Good Friday to hear Dr Thomas Tenison, the future archbishop, preach on 'the malicious Crucifixion of the Lord Jesus'. Tenison took up the Jewish theme again, ruling that it showed the 'Jewes doing it out of spite & against their being convicted both by Prophesies, their Expectation, & his Miracles'. Though it would lead to 'the Salvation of the World', the crucifixion was 'don by the Jewes wickedly & ingratefully'. These were conventional sentiments, perhaps, but the timing of the sermon and the presence of numerous prominent Jews in London made them more relevant.[91] More importantly, Tenison was also present when Evelyn went to pay a call on William Lloyd, two months later. Also in attendance was Henry Compton, the bishop of London and son of the earl of Northampton; and Edward Stillingfleet, the Latitudinarian bishop of Worcester. The group was fired up by the apparent concurrence of Lloyd's prophecies with recent developments in Savoy, where Victor Amadeus unexpectedly gave shelter to the persecuted Vaudois against all political predictions. This step seemed to be prefigured in the Book of Revelation. Evelyn joined Bishop Lloyd afterwards

to visite Mr. Boyle & Lady Ranelagh his sister, to whom he explaind the necessity of its so falling out by the Scriptures in a very wonderfull manner, which he most skillfully & learnedly made out; with what events were immediately to follow of the French Kings ruine, The Turkes, & Calling of the Jewes to be neere at hand; but that the total Kingdom of Antichrist, would yet not be utterly destroyed til 30 years, when Christ sho[u]ld begin the Milennium, not [as] himselfe person[al]ly reigning in Earth Visibly; but that the true Religion & universal peace, should obtaine thro all the world: he shewed how Mr. Brightman, Mr. Meade, and other Interpreters of their Events, failed,

---

[90] Ibid. v. 20–1 (13 Apr. 1690). De Beer notes that this was presumably a Lenten sermon at Court, but the preacher listed for this is Dr Peter Mews, the bishop of Winchester.

[91] Ibid. v. 21 (18 Apr. 1690). Cf. v. 425 (8 Sept. 1700).

by mistaking & reckoning the yeares as the Latines & others did, to consist of the present Calculation & so many dayes to the yeare; wheras, the Apocalyps, reckons after the Persian account, as Daniel did whose Visions St. John all along explains, as meaning onely the Christian Church: &c.

These were sentiments that Boyle himself had held for many years, and recent events only seemed to confirm their validity.[92]

Robert Boyle died on 30 December 1691. His will provided for an annual stipend to be used to support a church lectureship devoted to defending Christianity 'against notorious Infidels, namely, Atheists, Theists, Pagans, Jews, and Mahometans . . . and which would be used to answer such new Objections and Difficulties, as may be started, to which good Answers have not yet been made'.[93] Boyle left the administration of the lectureship in the hands of Evelyn and Tenison, and they chose as first preacher Richard Bentley, Stillingfleet's chaplain and later to become a renowned New Testament scholar.[94] Although the Old Newtonians chosen to give Boyle's lectures did not dwell over-long on the fate of the Jews, their remarks were meant to be directed to them as well.

The interest expressed by Lloyd, Boyle, and Evelyn in the millennial fate of the Jews during the period of the Glorious Revolution was genuinely felt, but it retains nevertheless a distinct flavour reminiscent of another Revolution nearly half a century before, which so shaped their world outlook. While there may have been something of a revival in the cosmic Jewish question during the 1690s, the pattern was one of an earlier generation.[95] Even the movement of John Mason in Buckinghamshire during these years, those who believed that Christ in 1694 'would appear publicly at Pentecost & gather all the Saints Jew & Gentile, & leade them to Jerusalem, & begin the *Millenium*, & destroying & Judging the wiccked, deliver the government of the world to them &c.', has a distinctly antique patina.[96] But that these issues should appear again may show old ideas being applied to new circumstances in which once again the Jews were a topic of conversation.

---

[92] Evelyn, *Diary*, v. 25–6 (18 June 1690).

[93] Eustace Budgell, *Memoirs of the Lives and Characters of the Illustrious Family of the Boyles* (London, 1737), app., p. 25; M. C. Jacob, *The Radical Enlightenment* (London, 1981), 89–90.

[94] Evelyn, *Diary*, ed. de Beer, v. 81–3 (6 Jan. 1691/2); 88–9 (13 Feb. 1691/2).

[95] See e.g. the publication of an English trans. of F. M. van Helmont, *Seder Olam; or, The Order of Ages* (London, 1694), which predicted the conversion and restoration of the Jews to Palestine between 1742 and 1777 (pp. 53–4). Cf. id. *A Letter to a Gentleman* (London, 1690), esp. 19, 23. Generally, see A. Coudert, *The Influence of the Kabbalah in the Seventeenth Century: The Case of Francis Mercury van Helmont* (forthcoming, E. J. Brill).

[96] Evelyn, *Diary*, ed. de Beer, v. 177–8 (*c*.26 Apr. 1694); C. Hill, 'John Mason and the End of the World', in his *Puritanism and Revolution* (London, 1958).

At the same time, throughout the period when they were being milked financially, the Jews continued to be used as an extreme example when the question of religious toleration was being discussed. One anonymous writer in 1685, for example, attacked the duke of Buckingham for implying that 'a *Jew*, a *Turk*, a *Pagan*, may all according to my Lords Hypothesis be safe, so long as they believe in their own either weak or obstinate Reason'.[97] The classic statement came from John Locke, who argued that

neither Pagan nor Mahometan nor Jew should be excluded from the commonwealth because of his religion. The Gospel commands no such thing. The church, which judgeth not them that are without (1 Cor. v. 12, 13), does not desire this. The commonwealth, which receives and accepts men as men provided they are honest, peaceful, and industrious, does not require it. Will you allow a Pagan to practise his trade in your country, but forbid him to pray to God or worship him? The Jews are permitted to have dwellings and private houses; why are they denied synagogues? Is their doctrine more false, their worship more abominable, or their combination more dangerous if they meet in public rather than in their private houses? But if these things may be granted to Jews and Pagans, shall the condition of Christians in a Christian commonwealth be worse?[98]

As is readily seen, the Jews were introduced into these arguments along with Turks and pagans as a sort of extreme case used to prove the validity of the general arguments. Locke was interested in Nonconformists, not in Jews, who might nevertheless be the incidental beneficiaries of his torerationalist point of view. The entire structure of the argument must be kept in mind before attributing genuine religious toleration in the period when the concept was still largely alien.

These pleas for Jewish toleration were based on philosophical principles. Another line of argument might rest on the economic utility of the community, although, as we have seen, this claim more often than not worked against Jewish interests. In 1693 Sir Josiah Child, formerly the absolute ruler of the East India Company, reissued a pamphlet he had published twenty-five years earlier putting forth his views on trade. Child, who had many years' experience behind him, was naturally a keen observer of the Dutch economic miracle, and sought to explain it. Chief among the explanatory factors, he thought, was

Their Toleration of different Opinions in matters of Religion: by reason whereof many industrious People of other Countreys, that dissent from the

---

[97] Anon., *A Short Answer to His Grace the D. Buckingham's Paper, Concerning Religion, Toleration, and Liberty of Conscience* (London, 1685), 17.

[98] John Locke, *A Letter on Toleration*, ed. and trans. R. Klibansky and J. W. Gough (Oxford, 1968), 144–5.

Established Government of their own Churches, resort to them with their Families and Estates, and after a few years cohabitation with them, become of the same Common interest.

Far from seeing foreign residents as a danger to native-born merchants, Child looked forward to their assimilation into English society. In the later edition of his pamphlet, Child added a further reason for Dutch prosperity: 'Their giveing Liberty, or at least Connivance to all Religions, as well Jews and Roman-Catholicks, or Sectaries, gives security to all their Inhabitants at home, and expels none, nor puts a necessity upon any to Banish themselves upon that account.'[99]

The most important overseas trade of the Jewish community in late seventeenth- and eighteenth-century England was in Indian diamonds, a branch which flourished almost from readmission until the supply simply ran out towards the beginning of the nineteenth century. The discovery of diamonds in Brazil in the 1720s also signalled the change, as South America became the major source of diamonds until South Africa took her place much later on. Even after Brazilian diamonds began to appear on the scene, and despite the fact that in theory they were a Portuguese monopoly, Jews were important nevertheless, since as many as half the diamonds were smuggled, many coming to London from Amsterdam, which was their next official destination after Lisbon. Jews were to be found at all locations of the business: Portuguese Jews in Goa, Jewish businessmen in Amsterdam, and Jewish traders in London. The East India Company was not particularly concerned with the diamond trade, and allowed it to go on upon payment of a licensing fee. Among the great firms involved in the diamond trade were those of the Francos, and of Israel Levin Salomons (Yehiel Prager), whose extensive records in large measure survive. Both Ashkenazim and Sephardim were active in the diamond trade, although they paid for the jewels in different ways. The diamonds were from the start exchanged for either silver or coral, which was re-exported after arriving in London from the Mediterranean. When the demand for silver increased during the war of 1702–13 and the East India Company prohibited its export, the Sephardim moved much more strongly into the coral trade as a way of financing their diamond imports, especially as Leghorn was an important source and a number of Livornese families such as the Francos and the Montefiores controlled its operation. Since the

[99] Josiah Child, *A New Discourse of Trade* (London, 1693), 7, 14–15, 28–9, 189, repr. from his *Brief Observations Concerning Trade, and Interest of Money* (London, 1668), 5, 9, 16. An interesting case which proves Child's point is found in E. Samuel, 'Manuel Levy Duarte (1631–1714): An Amsterdam Merchant Jeweller and his Trade with London', *TJHSE* 27 (1982), 11–31.

Ashkenazim had no familial connections with Leghorn, they were forced to rely on silver once the restrictions on export were lifted in 1718. Another distinction was apparent in the place of Ashkenazim and Sephardim in the chain: the diamond importers tended to be Sephardim, who sold the uncut diamonds to Ashkenazi wholesale merchants. Many of the most famous names in Anglo-Jewish history began in the diamond trade: among the Sephardim, Franco, Salvador, and Mendes da Costa; and from the Ashkenazim, Franks, Moses, Salomons, and Goldsmid.[100]

IV

Clearly, then, what the Sephardi community needed in the trying period immediately after the Glorious Revolution was strong leadership, which is exactly what they lacked. The *haham* of the Jews between 1689 and 1700 was the unfortunate and somewhat mysterious Solomon Ayllon. The Sephardi Jews had been entirely without a spiritual leader since the death of Jacob Abendana in 1685. Four years later, Solomon Ayllon found himself in London on a mission from the Jews of Palestine collecting money throughout Europe, and when offered the post of *haham* accepted without delay. Ayllon was then about 29 years of age. He was born in Salonica of a Sephardi family, but had spent most of his life in Safed, the centre of cabbalistic studies in Palestine and arguably in the entire Jewish world. Rumour had it that he had been associated with the followers of Shabtai Sevi, the Jewish false Messiah of the 1660s, and had remained one of his secret devotees.[101] During the time when the rabbi might have been occupied with defending the Jewish community against assaults on its very existence, he was engaged unceasingly in a personal quarrel with two of his congregants, Jacob Fidanque and his son Abraham.[102] The dispute seems to have been

---

[100] See generally G. Yogev, *Diamonds and Coral: Anglo-Dutch Jews and Eighteenth-Century Trade* (Leicester, 1978), based on the Prager records, now in the Public Record Office, with a microfilm deposited in the Central Archives for the History of the Jewish People, Givat Ram, Jerusalem. See also H. Pollins, *Economic History of the Jews in England* (London, 1982), 48–50, who suggests that only with the decline of the diamond traders did the financiers come to dominate Anglo-Jewry.

[101] On Solomon Ayllon/Aelion/Haelion/Hillion see *Bevis Marks Records*, i, ed. Barnett, 27–8; Hyamson, *Sephardim*, 68–70; Kayserling, *Biblioteca*, 15 (where his dates are given as 1664–1728, with the claim that he was born in Safed, and (certainly incorrectly) that he succeeded as *haham* in 1696 and resigned in 1701. Kayserling says that Ayllon's portrait was done by J. Houbraken: *Anglo-Jewish Historical Exhibition, Catalogue* (London, 1888), 48).

[102] The quarrel between Fidanque and Ayllon apparently began much earlier: see the letter from Joseph Abendanon in London to Haham Jacob Sasportas in Amsterdam (and

extraordinarily complicated, but came to a swift resolution on 25 Nisan 5450 [1690], when Ayllon approached the members of the Mahamad and handed them an unsigned letter in Hebrew which he had received from Jacob Fidanque. The letter was insulting in the extreme, and included a devastating reference to 'las obras que hisiste en Salunique que casaste Goya de principio hasta fin' ['the deeds which you did in Salonica, when you married a Gentile woman from beginning to end']. Inquiries revealed that the letter had been written by the informant's son Abraham, who had posted it to his relative, Ishac Cohen de Lobatto in Amsterdam, requesting that he send it back to London, to Haham Ayllon. But the letter miscarried: Cohen de Lobatto refused to take part in such a disreputable scheme, and returned it. Unfortunately for Abraham Fidanque, the true author, it reached his father first, who, perhaps out of sheer innocence, delivered the letter to its intended recipient: Haham Solomon Ayllon.[103]

The Mahamad ruled that Abraham Fidanque, the author of the libellous letter, would be excommunicated until he agreed to beg pardon before the *haham* and the entire congregation, before the Ark of the Lord. But the dispute continued, and eventually the father was also put under the same ban. Indeed, the quarrel never died down, but raged throughout the entire period of Ayllon's tenure. We have a contemporary Gentile description of what conditions were like during Ayllon's term of office. The Reverend Robert Kirk went along to the synagogue on 25 January 1690 to see the Jews at prayer, 'being about 150 men, about the room, 60 boys in the middle, and 7 or 8 women in the galleries above, hardly perceived by any'. Kirk noted that the 'Jews have bad English, some Latin, but all of them Hebrew, and do not read it as their Rabbi goes before them':

When the Rabbi (who looked not like a grave learned man; for he and many Jews would have laughed and talked when they ended a paragraph) read, all did read audibly enough in Hebrew, all said Amen. They never prayed, nor discovered their heads, nor bowed the knee. The Rabbi called 6 or 7 to come to him after another and taught them, pointing with a silver pen. They had no methodical worship. They were all very black men, and indistinct in their reasonings as gipsies.[104]

formerly *haham* in London), 1676, referring to a dispute between the two in London at that time, presumably during a visit by Ayllon to the city while collecting for the Jews of Palestine: Jacob Sasportas, *Ohel Ya'akov* (Hebrew *responsa*) (Amsterdam, 1737), fos. 79 [col. D]–80 [cols. A–B]: Bod. Lib., Opp. add. fo. III. 3: *Bevis Marks Records*, i., ed. Barnett, 27 n.

[103] Records of the Mahamad: repr. *Bevis Marks Records*, i, ed. Barnett, 27–8.
[104] 'London in 1689–90', ed. D. Maclean, *Transactions of the London and Middlesex Archaeological Society* NS 7 (1933–7), 151. For the journal of an anonymous visitor to the

Eventually, in 1699, the Mahamad of the congregation was forced to appoint a committee of thirty distinguished congregants to examine all of the charges which had been laid against Ayllon. Their report was unequivocal:

We having examined the calumnies that have from time to time accumulated upon H.H.S. Ayllon, they have been found to be without any foundation; being conscious of the evident risk to our preservation, tranquillity, and precious peace, we, satisfied entirely of the exemplary virtue of H.H., promise to obey and cause to be maintained the orders and resolutions of the Mahamad and Elders, and sign.

But their efforts at clearing Haham Ayllon's name were in vain: on 7 Nisan 5460 [1700] he resigned his post. The Mahamad attempted to dissuade him, but, having failed, presented their rabbi with a fifty-guinea gift and wished him well in his new position in Amsterdam. He left his books behind, however, which had been sold to the congregation in 1691 to form the nucleus of the community's library. Ayllon's later career in Amsterdam was similarly plagued with controversy, but he remained in Holland until his death in 1728.[105]

The Fidanques, meanwhile, felt the full wrath of the community's elders. The day after Rabbi Ayllon's resignation, the Mahamad ordered that the father Jacob should be excluded from all congregational posts and various religious honours, nor should he be permitted to write marriage contracts, nor perform marriages, divorces, or any other rabbinical function such as he had done in the past. Jacob Fidanque had apparently kept pupils to whom he taught Talmud, and this exclusion must have been something of a blow. It seems to have been enforced until his death in 1701; his son Abraham died in 1708.[106]

The stewardship of Rabbi Solomon Ayllon was therefore racked by internal division, just at the moment when the Jewish community required a strong leader who could defend them against the numerous

---

synagogue in 1691, see Hist. MSS Comm., *3rd Report, App.*, 300. A Portuguese riddle composed by Solomon Judah Leao Templo for Moses Mocatta in 1691 is now at the University of Amsterdam, Bibliotheca Rosenthaliana, HS ROS. PL. B-62; where are also deposited Jacob Abendanon's two Hebrew lamentations on the death of Queen Mary Stuart, 1694: HS ROS. 585. Abendanon (not to be confused with Haham Jacob Abendana) was a teacher in the community from 1692 to 1705.

[105] *Bevis Marks Records*, i, ed. Barnett, 27–8; Hyamson, *Sephardim*, 69–70.

[106] But the Mahamad were not vindictive: they ruled that in any blessing made for Jacob Fidanque he should be designated by the title of *maskil v'navon*: 'learned and wise'. Another man dismissed at the same time, and perhaps in connection with the same dispute, was Daniel Peres, the *shochet* and *bodek*: *Bevis Marks Records*, i, ed. Barnett, 28; Hyamson, *Sephardim*, 69–70.

attacks which had been launched since William III's arrival in England. One important effect of the internal dissension within the sole English synagogue was that the Ashkenazim in about 1690 finally broke from Sephardi domination and formed their own independent community. Although numerically and culturally the Jewish community in London was still overwhelmingly Sephardi, Ashkenazi Jews had been a part of the group from the very beginning. The *shamash* (beadle) at least from 1667 was Samuel Levy, who had studied at Cracow *yeshiva* in Poland and by his own account had served as rabbi there.[107] A more prominent Ashkenazi figure of the Restoration years was Benjamin Levy the elder, who in 1667 was appointed *hazan* (cantor), and in 1671 acquired the duties of *shochet* and *bodek* (ritual slaughter and inspector) while simultaneously farming some of the community's taxes.[108] Various other Ashkenazi residents and visitors also worshipped at England's only synagogue on Creechurch Lane, but they were clearly not any more than second-class citizens in the Sephardi congregation 'Saar Asamaim'.[109]

The uncrowned king of the Ashkenazim in London during this period was another Benjamin Levy, who came to London from Hamburg in about 1669, with other members of his family. Hamburg at that time was the Ashkenazi answer to Amsterdam, the northern European capital of their interests. Levy was soon admitted a broker on the Royal Exchange, and was endenizened in March 1688/9, shortly after the Revolution. Later on, he would be found in almost every significant area of English commercial enterprise. He was the second name on the register of the newly organized East India Company in 1698, and was a very considerable shareholder. From 1688 he was a member of the Royal

[107] For Samuel Levy, see: John Greenhalgh to Thomas Crompton, 22 Apr. 1662: BL MS Lans. 988, fos. 174ᵛ–80, repr. *Original Letters Illustrative of English History*, ed. H. Ellis (2nd ser., London, 1827), iv. 3, where he describes himself as knowing Latin, and having been two years in London: 'He said he was brought up, and was a student eleven years, in the Jews College in Cracovia the chief City of Poland . . . and that himself had formerly been Priest to a Synagogue of his own nation in Poland.' He described his role in the congregation as 'Scribe and Rabbi'. Cf. *Bevis Marks Records*, i, ed. Barnett, 29; Hyamson, *Sephardim*, 20, 42 (citing the accounts for 5427 [1667]), 71, 79; C. Roth, *The Great Synagogue London 1690–1940* (London, 1950), 3. Samuel Levy died in 1701 and was buried in the Mile End (Sephardi) Cemetery: Hyamson, *Sephardim*, 20.

[108] Benjamin Levy also worked as a collector: Alderman Edward Backwell's Ledger (now Child's Bank) shows that he collected large sums from the Sephardi community: Wolf, 'The Jewry of the Restoration', *TJHSE* 5 (1908), 11, 23. The *shochet* killed the animal, and the *bodek* examined the dead animal to make sure it was free of disease and fit for consumption. Benjamin Levy in 1671 farmed the meat tax of a farthing in the pound in return for an annual payment of £20, receiving no further payment for his other functions in the community: Hyamson, *Sephardim*, 41–2.

[109] Some of these fugitive Ashkenazim are mentioned in Roth, *Great Synagogue*, 1–4; *Bevis Marks Records*, i, ed. Barnett, 29–30.

African Company. Indeed, Benjamin Levy the younger was a prominent figure not only among Jews, but in the Gentile business community as well.[110]

The very financial prominence of Benjamin Levy the younger was a communal problem in the making. On his arrival in England, Levy quite naturally began to worship in the only synagogue in the country, which was Sephardi in rite. His wealth and status led to his being awarded the dignity of *yahid*, full member of the congregation, notwithstanding his Ashkenazi background. Over the years, Benjamin Levy contributed very large sums to the congregation, and was always one of its leaders. But Benjamin Levy, his uncle Michael, and community official Samuel Levy were clearly regarded as exceptions to the rule. Ashkenazim were regarded as poor cousins, the very sort of people who would bring the congregation into disrepute. Action was first taken against them as early as 1669, when Michael Levy was empowered to complain to the Lord Mayor about the foreign poor (Ashkenazim) who were beginning to appear in unacceptable numbers at the synagogue at Creechurch Lane. In this way, the Sephardim hoped to make it plain to the authorities that they would have nothing to do with promoting the maintenance of indigent Jewish immigrants in London.

But the time for drastic steps came ten years before the Glorious Revolution, when during 1678/9 the Mahamad ruled that no 'Tudesco' ('German', i.e. Ashkenazi) should ever hold synagogue office, vote at members' meetings, receive any honour whatsoever, or even be allowed to pay the *imposta* (income tax) or make donations to charity, unless ten elders should agree to waive the prohibition. Special and permanent dispensations were immediately given to Benjamin Levy, Michael Levy, and Samuel Levy.[111] On 6 Adar 5439 [1679] a further order proclaimed that foreign Ashkenazim who came to England and begged for charity should receive five shillings and be given notice to leave the country within four days on the first available boat to Rotterdam or Amsterdam.[112] The congregational records show that this order was in fact carried out, and lists Ashkenazi Jews expelled to those two cities as well as to Hamburg.[113] Although the blanket prohibitions of 1678–9 were softened in 1682, it was clear that the Sephardim of London did not see themselves as serving the interests of the Jewish people as a

---

[110] Roth, *Great Synagogue*, 4–7.

[111] *Bevis Marks Records*, i, ed. Barnett, 30–1, where Barnett notes that it is strange that the order does not mention the elder Benjamin Levy (d. 1693); Roth, *Great Synagogue*, 7–9.

[112] *Bevis Marks Records*, i, ed. Barnett, 31; Roth, *Great Synagogue*, 8.

[113] Roth, *Great Synagogue*, 8–9.

whole, but only those who conformed to their rite and maintained a certain standard of wealth, power, and influence.[114]

This situation was intolerable, and in any case could not continue for much longer. As more Ashkenazim came to London, many of whom were poor, some place of worship would have to be found for them, on ritualistic as well as economic grounds. There is no question that groups of Ashkenazim met together informally in a prayer quorum of ten men. Perhaps they might have continued in this way for quite some time had not the Sephardi synagogue raised the question of Ashkenazi burials. On 11 January 1692/3 the Mahamad discussed the inconveniences caused by 'the many tudescos who are at present in this city and increase every day'. This was an issue that had troubled them, as we have seen, for twenty-five years. But what was different now was that they summoned to discuss the problem a body of men they referred to as the 'Mahamad of the tudescos', that is, a governing body of Ashkenazim. Certainly from that date, then, we can speak of a formally organized and separate congregation in London apart from the parent body established during Cromwell's rule.[115] This new group was presented with an ultimatum: they were told to acquire their own cemetery and to bury their dead there. The Ashkenazim were given six months to find a plot of land, after which time only those Jews who had paid, or who had been allowed to pay, the Sephardi burial tax would be given a Jewish burial.[116]

By this means, the poorer and undesirable Ashkenazim were to be kept apart from fellowship in the parent Jewish community even after death. For reasons which are not clear, but may be as simple as financial stringency, a number of years passed before a site was acquired for an Ashkenazi cemetery, although a burial society was in existence from 1695–6.[117] In the end, the responsibility fell on Benjamin Levy the younger, who although Ashkenazi was firmly entrenched in the Sephardi community, and indeed had recently buried his wife in their Mile End cemetery. Levy had his eye on a piece of ground which adjoined the Sephardi cemetery on the north side, and which belonged to a certain Captain Nathaniel Owen. Although Levy had been endenizened, he was not only a Jew but an alien, and therefore could not own land in England. He therefore made an agreement with Captain

---

[114] 16 Kislev 5443 [1682]: the Mahamad and elders ruled that voluntary offerings made by Ashkenazim should be accepted and that the presiding _parnas_ might call Ashkenazim to the reading of the Law.

[115] See 'The Membership of the Great Synagogue, London, to 1791', ed. C. Roth, _MJHSE_ 6 (1962), 175–85.

[116] Roth, _Great Synagogue_, 16–17; _Bevis Marks Records_, i, ed. Barnett, 31–2.

[117] For more on the burial society (_Hebra Kadisha_), see Roth, _Great Synagogue_, 17, 27–8.

Owen dated 2 February 1696/7 to lease the land for 1,000 years with an initial cost of £190.[118]

Unquestionably, then, at least from the beginning of 1697 it is possible to speak of a fully organized Ashkenazi community in London, possessing all of the necessary elements for communal life and death. Whether or not the Ashkenazi Jews actually met for prayer on the very site on which would be built the Great Synagogue, as has sometimes been claimed, may still be held in doubt, but the organized existence of the community was of paramount importance.[119] The Sephardi Jews, meanwhile, revised their famous monopolistic first *ascama* in 1694 by adding the clause 'That the Synagogue *Saar Asamaim* shall only serve for the Jews of our Portuguese and Spanish nation that are at present in this City and newly may come to it; and the Jews of other nations that may come shall be admitted to say prayers if it seems good to the gentlemen of the Mahamad'. Ashkenazim were not likely to be included within this group, and even the defection of numerous disgruntled Sephardim to the non-exclusivist other place did not move them.[120]

By the last decade of the seventeenth century, then, the Jews of London had consolidated the gains they had made since Cromwell's time, including in their midst an independent and considerably less affluent Ashkenazi community, and stood fast, with varying degrees of success, against both financial blackmail and threats to their security.

[118] Cemetery deed, now Jewish Museum, London MS 130 (with plan). See also Roth, *Great Synagogue*, 17–18; *Bevis Marks Records*, i, ed. Barnett, 32 and n. For some reason, both Barnett and Roth claim that the lease was for 999 years and at a peppercorn rent.

[119] The argument is Roth's, *Great Synagogue*, 14–15, 116–17. Roth relies on E. H. Lindo, *A Jewish Calendar for Sixty-Four Years* (London, 1838), who claimed that 1692 saw 'The first Germany synagogue erected in London, in Broad Court, Duke's Place, on the site of the present Great Synagogue'. Roth writes that in the 17th century Duke's Place was the term used for the entire area, but more specifically for the present Creechurch Place: the name Duke's Place was transferred to the former Shoemaker's Row (later Duke Street) in the 1920s. However, the name 'Duke's Place' was also applied to what is now Mitre Square, at the rear of the Great Synagogue site. Roth also brings to bear (pp. 116–17) a petition from Moses Hart to the Lord Mayor and aldermen in which the petitioner asserts that 'the Congregation of German Jews in London have always congregated themselves together in their Synagogue in Shoemaker Row ... and is the only Synagogue for their Worship in London' [Guildhall]. Shoemaker's Row (Duke's Place today) would be the eastern boundary of the site of the future Great Synagogue.

[120] I. Epstein, 'The Story of Ascama I of the Spanish and Portuguese Jewish Congregation of London with Special Reference to Responsa Material', in M. Ben-Horin (ed.), *Studies and Essays in Honour of Abraham A. Neuman* (Leiden, 1962), 175–7. A MS of the regulations of *Saar Asamaim* (1693–1724) is now (for some reason) at the University of Amsterdam, Bibliotheca Rosenthaliana, HS. ROS 1, purchased from the collection of Henriques de Castro in 1899.

We can obtain some idea as to their numbers from the census of 1695. In order to finance the war with France, William III levied parliamentary rates and duties on marriages, births, burials, bachelors, and widows. Each house was visited and the occupants noted, including servants and lodgers. Of the 110 London parishes (ninety-seven within the walls and thirteen without), records survive for all but seventeen. These lists have been used as the base from which to extract names which appear to belong to Jews. Some of them are of well-known communal figures; many others are those of obscure Jews; some names may or may not belong to Jews. Nevertheless, the results are illuminating.

Examination of the census lists of 1695 produces 853 Jewish names, including 598 Sephardim and 255 Ashkenazim. Of these, 681 apparent Jews lived in six parishes alone: Allhallows London Wall, St Andrew Undershaft, St Helen, St James Duke's Place, St Katherine Creechurch, and St Katherine Coleman. Two of these parishes—St James Duke's Place and St Katherine Creechurch—between them included 409 apparent Jews, nearly half of the entire community, which comprised approximately 185 families and 114 people living alone or as lodgers. Assuming that in 1695 the entire population of London within the walls was 69,581, then the total Jewish population there, 778 individuals, would comprise 1.1 per cent. Only 48 of the 110 parishes of London had any Jews at all, but clearly the important statistical proportion was the Jewish component in the six chief parishes of their residence. In St James Duke's Place they made up 264 out of 925 residents, or 28.5 per cent. In St Katherine Creechurch they included 145 of 1,623 residents, or 8.9 per cent. Looking at the six parishes together, we find 681 Jews out of a total population of 7,315 residents, or 9.3 per cent. So in St James Duke's Place parish, that is, the area bounded by Heneage Lane, Duke's Place (Bevis Marks), and today's Mitre Street, and including both the Sephardi and Ashkenazi places of worship, at least one in four residents was a Jew. This was the unofficial London ghetto of the late seventeenth century.[121]

It is clear that many of the Jews who appear on the census lists of 1695 arrived after the Glorious Revolution. We have a record of Sephardim in London made in the previous decade by Abraham Zagache, who passed through London on his way to Hamburg. Zagache was in England

---

[121] Census lists of 1695: Corporation of London Record Office. See esp. 'A List of Jews and their Households in London Extracted from the Census Lists of 1695', ed. A. P. Arnold, *MJHSE* 6 (1962), 73–5, 78–141; M. Woolf, 'Notes on the Census Lists of 1695', *MJHSE* 6 (1962), 75–7. For the estimate of London's population, see P. E. Jones & A. V. Judges, 'London Population in the Late Seventeenth Century', *EHR* 6 (1935), 45–63. Cf. I. Scouloudi, 'On alien immigration into London', *Proceedings of the Huguenot Society of London*, 16 (1937–8), 27–49.

between December 1680 and April 1684, so in any case he includes only those Jews resident in London in the last years of Charles II. According to Zagache, the entire Sephardi population included 414 individuals, that is to say, those who worshipped at the synagogue at Creechurch Lane. Benjamin Levy and his family therefore appear on his list, but the number of Ashkenazim is insignificant. Zagache's list can be cross-checked with the list of seatholders in the synagogue in 1682, and we find that most appear on both. It appears, then, that the Sephardi community of England increased from about 400 individuals in about 1680 to about 600 in 1695, or an increase of 50 per cent. We have no way of knowing how many Ashkenazim came to England after the Revolution, but the vast majority of the 255 'Tudescos' in London in 1695 must have been newcomers, or else had forgone religious attendance completely in the 1680s.[122]

The last three years of the seventeenth century were also notable for two contradictory developments in the history of Anglo-Jewry: one further regularization of their position, and one further attack on their very freedom of worship. The first event is better known. The office of broker had existed in England since medieval times: its purpose was to act as an intermediary between merchants in the wholesale trade. The number of brokers was kept down, and as late as 1674 the City of London ruled that 'broking was principally intended for the support and livelihood of decayed citizens and merchants who by great losses have been disabled to pursue their trades'.[123] This sort of activity was found to be very suitable for the Jewish businessmen of Restoration London, and as early as 1657, Solomon Dormido, a son of Samuel ben Israel's companion on that first exploratory trip to England before the readmission, was admitted a broker in the City of London. Dormido was not sworn until 1668, but the very fact that a Jew could be made a broker in a period when Jewish residence was not officially confirmed in any government document is an indication of the standing of these Sephardim in the City from the very earliest years.[124] Other Jews followed in Dormido's footsteps, not always with the proper authorization. On 30 July 1668 Joseph Flores, Emanuel da Costa, and Samuel

---

[122] Abraham Zagache, 'Memoria de la gente que ay en la nacion de Londres': Ets Haim Library, Amsterdam: repr. *Bevis Marks Records*, i, ed. Barnett, 16–20; 'Pauta Dos Lugares De Cada Su Na Snoga' (Seatholders in 5442 [1682]), in Hyamson, *Sephardim*, 423–4.

[123] Corporation of London Record Office, Rep. 79, fo. 321: I am grateful to Dr S. M. Macfarlane for having shown me how to find and use these documents. Cf. D. Abrahams, 'Jew Brokers of the City of London', *MJHSE* 3 (1937), 80–94, esp. 80–1. See also Wolf, 'First Stage', 132–5.

[124] Corporation of London Record Office, Rep. 73, fo. 213.

Sasportas were sent to Newgate 'for exercising the office of brokage without admittance or allowance of the Court of Aldermen'. Unlicensed brokers were a danger because they performed the function more cheaply, and when they failed to meet their obligations brought discredit to the profession and on the City business community itself.[125]

An inquiry was ordered during 1668: although no report was made, three years later the Court of Aldermen ruled that all candidates for the office of broker had to petition the committee which they appointed for that purpose.[126] In a sense, the Jewish brokers profited from this arrangement: on 9 February 1671 Dormido, da Costa, and Sasportas were recorded as registered brokers. Five more Jews were appointed before the year was out, another Jew in 1672, two more in 1673, and another two in 1674. Looking at the group as a whole, we find the second and third generation of Dormidos in this country, and the son of the former Haham Jacob Sasportas, who himself left England during the Great Plague.[127] An informed observer might certainly have seen that something was wrong. In 1674 the Court of Aldermen began to investigate the situation, and discovered that there were only forty-two proper Englishmen on the Royal Exchange, but thirteen aliens, Jews, and Roman Catholics.[128] Eventually, the Court of Aldermen ruled in July 1679 'that no Englishman not free of the City be admitted a broker upon the Royal Exchange', effectively a prohibition against Jews, who could not take the Christian oath required of freemen.

Curiously, this ruling had little practical effect, and Jews continued to be admitted as brokers.[129] That Jews were registered against the

---

[125] Corporation of London Record Office, Rep. 73, fo. 245.

[126] Ibid., Rep. 73, fo. 245; Rep. 76, fo. 69.

[127] Solomon Dormido's son Samuel was admitted in Mar. 1672: Corporation of London Record Office, Rep. 77, fo. 108. Samuel Sasportas was a sometime *shochet* of the community: *El libro*, ed. Barnett, 30. The congregation paid his passage to Barbados in 1665; he was dismissed from the office of broker in 1681 'for trading and merchandising to his own use': Rep. 86, fo. 234. The other Jews appointed in 1671 were Jacob Mazahod, Anthony Rodriguez de Morais, Benjamin Nunes, David da Silva, and Daniel Aboab: Rep. 76, fo. 302. Later Jews were Francis Turco and Isaac Ramos (1673): Rep. 78, fos. 290, 311; Rep. 79, fo. 293; Samuel/Francis de Caceres and Joseph Cohen d'Azevedo (1674): Rep. 79, fo. 321; Rep. 80, fo. 52. We might also include Jonas Gabay, a Jewish convert from Christianity: Rep. 77, fo. 210.

[128] Corporation of London Record Office, Rep. 79, fo. 321.

[129] e.g. Moses Barrow (Oct. 1679: Rep. 84, fo. 226); Abraham Guttieres and Abraham de Paiba (1680: Rep. 85, fo. 246); Isaac Lindo (1681: Rep. 80, fo. 234); David de Faro (Oct. 1682: Rep. 87, fo. 287); Alexander Lindo (July 1683: Rep. 88, fo. 164); Isaac Lopez (1685: Rep. 91, fo. 14); Moses Carreon, Joseph Ferdinando [son of Antonio Carvajal], Jacob Mazahod, Solomon Zuzarte (1691: Rep. 96, fo. 205). Henry Cotigno, a Jewish convert to Christianity, was admitted in 1697 and was connected with the French Church (Rep. 100, fo. 2).

protests of many City elders was shown when the Court of Aldermen in 1680 begged the Lord Mayor Elect to find a way of curbing the activities of unofficial brokers on the Royal Exchange, especially Jews. This unsatisfactory situation continued for a number of years: despite the efforts of the Court of Aldermen, the number of Jewish brokers increased, and the activity of unauthorized brokers was rife.[130] Finally, in 1697, the House of Commons began to study the means 'to restrain the Number, and ill Practice, of Brokers and Stockjobbers'.[131] A City committee decided to limit the number of English brokers to 100, and gave the Jews the right to submit twelve names, the same number allocated to all the other aliens in London put together. The Jews were not required to take up the freedom prior to authorization, and were allowed a modified oath.[132] Whether this was a recognition of the Jewish contribution to that profession or an admission that little could be done to keep them out, the committee's decision did have the effect of bringing into order a very worrying situation. Many Jews during the late seventeenth and early eighteenth centuries in any case went into the less restrictive and more lucrative handling of stocks.[133] The familiar eighteenth-century image of the rapacious Jewish stockjobber began just when they acquired the undisputed title of broker. The office of broker was abolished in 1886.[134]

The Jews in England had thus reached a new plane of legal existence. They had been transformed from a group singled out in legislation for the purpose of financial exploitation, to almost a protected species. Two final events in the last years of the seventeenth century bring this change in attitude very clearly into focus. For a long time religious authorities had been concerned about the spread of Unitarianism and had sought legislative authority for dealing harshly with its proponents. Accordingly, a bill was put forward early in 1698 'for the more effectual suppressing of Blasphemy and Profaneness', which would make offenders liable for

---

[130] A total of twenty-eight Jews were made brokers before the reform of 1697.

[131] *Commons Journal*, 11: 765 (1 Apr. 1697), 769 (6 Apr. 1697).

[132] Corporation of London Record Office, Rep. 101, fo. 206. The first twelve Jewish brokers were: Jacob Arias, David Avila, Moses Barrow, Samuel/Francis de Caceres, David de Faro, Joseph Ferdinando [Carvajal], Abraham Francke, Benjamin Levy, Elias Lindo, Benjamin Nunes, Abraham de Paiba, and Elias Paz.

[133] Indeed, in 1701 Sephardi Jews seemed to have formed more than 10% of the group which owned the minimum amount of £4,000 stock to qualify for governorship of the Bank of England, although the first Jewish director of the Bank was Alfred de Rothschild, 1868–89: J. Clapham, *The Bank of England* (Cambridge, 1944), i. 279–80; J. A. Giuseppi, 'Sephardi Jews and the Early Years of the Bank of England', *TJHSE* 19 (1960), 53–63; id., 'Early Jewish Holders of Bank of England Stock (1694–1725)' [lists], *MJHSE* 6 (1962), 143–74.

[134] See generally Abrahams, 'Jew Brokers', 83–7 and app.

three years' imprisonment. When the bill returned from the House of Lords, however, an amendment had been inserted which would render all those openly professing Judaism liable for prosecution as well. The reaction of the Commons was decisive: by a majority of 140 to 78 they rejected the amendment, and Jewish worship was allowed to continue unmolested after the implementation of the Blasphemy Act, despite the fact that the Jews openly denied Jesus Christ.[135] The second event was also a landmark of sorts: on Saturday, 18 November 1699, Luttrell reports, William III 'dined with Mr. Medina, a rich Jew, at Richmond', the first time that an English monarch had called upon a Jew in his home.[136] Seven months later, on 23 June 1700, Solomon de Medina was knighted by William III at Hampton Court, the first Jew to be so honoured, the last for a century and a half.[137] The circumstances of these singular honours were admittedly very special: Medina was part of the firm of Machado and Pereira and had been active in England since 1690. William owed the Jewish contractors a good deal of money, and Medina's honours were certainly not unconnected to this debt. But the fact remains that William's visit and Medina's knighthood symbolized for contemporaries, as they do for us, that Anglo-Jewry had arrived.[138]

V

The slings and arrows of revisionism notwithstanding, the Glorious Revolution remains of enormous importance, at least for the permanent establishment of Jewish residence in England, for it helped to resolve the question of their status in such a way that in future their presence would be an undisputed matter of fact. In an age that prized linguistic precision, the Jews were notoriously difficult to define: they simply did not fit comfortably into any of the existing categories. They were undoubtedly 'strangers', in religion, in language, in appearance, and in habits. But so were the Scots, and in any case the problem went far deeper. The Jews in England were often described as 'aliens': the Sephardim presented themselves as belonging to an international

---

[135] *Commons Journal*, 12: 168–9 (21 Mar. 1697/8); Henriques, *Law*, 167; Luttrell, *Relation*, iv. 264 (22 Mar. 1697/8), where he mistakenly gives the vote as 144 : 78; M. Watts, *The Dissenters* (Oxford, 1978), 372.

[136] Luttrell, *Relation*, iv. 583 (18 Nov. 1699).

[137] Le Neve [Peter Neve], *Pedigrees of Knights*, ed. G. W. Marshall (London, 1873), 473; W. A. Shaw, *Knights of England* (London, 1906), ii. 272. The next Jew to receive a knighthood was Moses Montefiore, in 1837: see below, p. 387. Generally, see O. K. Rabinowicz, *Sir Solomon de Medina* (London, 1974).

[138] Rabinowicz, *Sir Solomon de Medina*, 15–20.

nation. A good number had been endenizened and were thus on the road to full citizenship, but they would not get there until the middle of the nineteenth century, for the Christian oath still barred the way to emancipation, even if the notion of 'alien' must surely wear thin after two centuries. So were the Jews of England 'Dissenters'? In a strictly formalistic sense they were, since they did not take communion according to the rites of the Church of England. But so much divided Anglo-Jewry from the Presbyterians, Congregationalists, and even Unitarians who fell under this heading, that the use of the term must surely muddle rather than enlighten.

In the reign of Charles II it was clear to anyone who considered the question that the Jews would have difficulty in becoming fully assimilated Englishmen. Apart from religious and social barriers, there remained the very serious question of foreign associations, a perceived international conspiracy of Jews in England and Holland to have the best of all worlds, with attendant dangers to the commerce and security of the realm. But the Jews in England during those years were never politically organized or identified with either the Whigs or the Tories, and thus never became a political bargaining chip in the battle which attended the Glorious Revolution. If anything, they were the victims of neglect, as their special needs were forgotten in the drawing-up of new legislation. The invasion of a Dutch ruler seemed to change all that, for it subsumed the entire subject of Jewish dual loyalties in the much larger and more significant question of the role which William and his Dutch followers might play in England. At a stroke, the Glorious Revolution transformed an issue in which the Jews were worryingly conspicuous into one in which they were only a sideshow. Anglo-Jewry after 1688 fell between two thrones, and the chief problem which faced them was not a danger to their very existence, but rather the pressure of financial exploitation. Even their separate classification in various pieces of legislation was not meant to be a prelude to their general expulsion, but rather a means to a strictly monetary end. Yet none of this was intended to question the basic issue of the right to Jewish residence in England, which was never again seriously threatened. That this should have been so must be reckoned among the achievements of the Glorious Revolution.

5
ANGLO-JEWRY UNDER THE OLD REGIME, 1700–1753

THE artificiality of any periodization needs hardly to be asserted. In the case of the Jews in England, however, there is a certain irresistible logic in the year 1700 as a point of beginning. The knighting of Solomon de Medina on 23 June 1700 symbolized more than any other single event of the post-readmission period how acceptable the community itself had become. De Medina was undoubtedly a very special case, as we have seen, and the favour was not repeated until the middle of the nineteenth century, but the very fact that such an extraordinary event had occurred signalled the apparent implied declaration that the question of Jewish residence would never again be raised, nor their presence in England threatened. In the same year, the beginning of David Nieto's term of office as Sephardi chief rabbi set the tone in the Jewish community, and his presence would be dominant for the next three decades until his death in 1728. Finally, the death of William III and the accession of Queen Anne in March 1702 provides another landmark, which makes the beginning of the eighteenth century in the history of Anglo-Jewry more than a mere chronological convenience.

I

The commencement of a new century was for Anglo-Jewry nothing if not an era of adjustment. Official attitudes to the Jews still contained many of the exploitationist elements of the post-Restoration period, but there were also genuine problems of a new nature. The first, exploitationist type is very effectively illustrated by the recurrent trick of electing resident Jews to parish offices in London and then fining them when they were unable to take their positions, not only by virtue of religious inclination, but also because of the Christological oath. One Christian defender of the Jews likened his countrymen in this to the Egyptian taskmasters who compelled their forefathers to make bricks without straw.[1] An early example of this pattern, continually repeated,

---

[1] [William Arnall], *The Complaint of the Children of Israel* (7th edn., London, 1736), 29. For more on Arnall, see below, p. 238–9.

we find in the parish of St James Duke's Place, where so many of London's Jews lived. It was there on 30 May 1687 that the Lord Mayor Sir John Peake received a complaint from two parish churchwardens that it had been six weeks since Policarpis Olivaro, a merchant of the same parish, had been chosen 'Collector & Overseer of the poore' for the following year. The two disingenuous Gentiles noted

that in Execucon of the said Office the Overseer attends the pish Church every Lords day in the distribucon of bread to the poore and is to be prsent in other duties belonging to the said Church and the said Olivaro being a Jew and therefore incapeable to take upon him the said Office Upon submission of all pries to his Lopps determinacon His Lop doth Order that the said Olivaro do forthwith pay to the said Churchwardens of the said pish 5^{li} as a Fine and gratuity to the said pish.

It was also recorded that the unlucky Olivaro had previously been elected to two other parish offices, for the declining of which he had already paid a fine of £5 as well. Perhaps in sympathy to the poor man, Peake ordered that he 'upon his paym^t of the said 5^{li} shall be discharged of all Offices in the said pish', and that the churchwardens were to elect someone else to be overseer of the poor.[2]

At times even the financial motives behind the parish officials' acts are difficult to isolate. In April 1691 they elected Jacob Mendez Bellisario to the office of scavenger for St James Duke's Place. When he refused to serve, he was fined £20, and ordered to leave the parish within three months, or to pay a further fine of the same, 'which the sd Jacob Mendez pmised to pforme accordingly'.[3] Yet only seven years later Bellisario and two others were officially 'exempted as being poor Pentioners & incapable of getting their Livelyhood'.[4] Either Bellisario's economic situation had drastically deteriorated, or the parish officials had miscalculated—or, alternatively, they were using the question of parish office as a means of evicting him from their jurisdiction for some reason. Nevertheless, in a very similar case, a Jewish Doctor du Peirce was elected overseer of the poor in the parish of St Katherine Coleman, and

[2] Corporation of London Record Office, Mansion House Justice Room Charge Book, vol. i, fo. 94: I am grateful to Dr S. M. Macfarlane for this reference as well as for guidance in the use of this important source.
[3] Corporation of London Record Office, Lord Mayor's Waiting Book, 15/35: 27 Apr. 1691.
[4] Corporation of London Record Office, Charge Book, 3: 5 Aug. 1698. Cf. James Peller Malcolm, *Londinium redivivum* (London, 1803–7), ii. 73; L. Wolf, 'The First Stage of Anglo-Jewish Emancipation', in *Essays in Jewish History*, ed. C. Roth (London, 1934), 115–43; *TJHSE* 10 (1924), 48, 84–5.

had to be excused his office on account of receiving alms from the synagogue.[5]

A second, and more pressing, problem in the first years of regularization was the support of the Protestant children of Jewish residents. Under-age Jewish converts to Christianity, while comparatively rare, were by no means unknown, and were always greeted with open arms. The travails of 'Eve Cohan, Now called Elizabeth Verboon' were immortalized in a powerful work published in 1680 by Gilbert Burnet, later bishop of Salisbury.[6] Indeed, one of the chief reasons for the readmission was the necessity of exposing Jews to the true light of English Christianity, and during the recent debate over the Blasphemy Act of 1698 the point had been made that, if Jews were included in its provisions, they would leave England *en masse* and therefore never become Protestant. Converts to Christianity could not be allowed to perish economically, however, and the medieval Domus Conversorum was a dead letter. All that remained was for a test case to arise.

In May 1701 a Jewish girl aged about 18 years turned to Mr Thorold, a Church of England minister, and asked to be baptized. Thorold examined the girl, and, by his own later testimony before the House of Commons, 'being fully convinced of the Sincerity of her Conversion, did, by Direction of the Lord Archbishop of *Canterbury*, baptize her'. Even as he was doing so, 'a Person, unknown to him, but supposed to be a Jew by his Complexion, came into the Church, and, observing what was done, and being enraged thereat, swore and cursed, and wished the Church might fall, and they ... buried in the Ruins thereof'. 'Whereupon', Thorold testified, 'Endeavours were made to apprehend him; but he made his Escape.' So Mary Mendez de Breta was baptized, but even as Thorold did this, it must have been known that this incident would not be passed over in silence by the Jewish community. For Mary was the daughter of Jacob Mendez de Breta, a very wealthy Jewish merchant in London, assessed for £2,000, but known in his parish of St Andrew Undershaft as being worth three times as much. His daughter Mary had been born in Seville, but since coming to England had embraced the Protestant form of the Christianity to which she had merely conformed in her home country.[7]

Jacob Mendez de Breta viewed his daughter's apostasy with extreme discontent. A fellow Jew described him to the House of Commons as 'a

---

[5] Guildhall Library MS 1123/1/146: Vestry Minutes, St Katherine Coleman, London, 23 Apr. 1701: I am grateful to Dr S. M. Macfarlane for this reference.

[6] [Gilbert Burnet], *The Conversion & Persecutions of Eve Cohan* (London, 1680). See also Anon., *The Amorous Convert* (London, 1679); and Eve Cohan to Sir Francis North, n.d. [=1680]: *Cal. SP Dom., 1680–1*, 120.

[7] *Commons Journal*, 13: 798–800 (16 Mar. 1701/2).

very cholerick and troublesome Person', an appraisal which seems to have been perfectly justified.[8] His relations with his own Jewish community were not always without difficulty, and in the same year of his daughter's conversion he was fined (along with Solomon de Medina) for refusing to serve as a *parnas*, one of the community's leaders. Their motivation was almost certainly not opposition to community policy but rather a sense that their efforts could be more profitably applied elsewhere.[9] For all intents and purposes, then, Jacob Mendez de Breta was a wealthy and powerful member of the Sephardi congregation who had felt treachery at home. His daughter did not put any blame on him at all, but rather testified that 'soon after her Father came into *England*, he sent for her from *Spain*, and always owned her for his Child; and that he kept her in very decent Habit, provided plentifully for her, sent her to the Dancing School, and allowed her an Education suitable to his Degree and Quality'. Her father, on the other hand, immediately disowned her and disavowed any financial responsibility. Mary, 'being afraid of her Father's Anger', as she said, applied to Sir Thomas Abney, the Lord Mayor of London, for protection. He, in turn, ordered the churchwardens of St Andrew Undershaft to provide for her, so that, the Commons were informed, 'she has been ever since very decently maintained at the Charge of the said Parish'.[10]

Therein lay the problem: although the parish officials of St Andrew Undershaft were pleased that Mary Mendez de Breta had seen the light and in this presaged the conversion of her entire people, they were unhappy about having to shoulder the burden of all Christendom by themselves. The parish therefore on 16 June 1701 had her father bound over at £200 to the sessions at the Guildhall, accompanied by four other Jews who were also bound over at either £20 or £100.[11] Jacob Mendez de Breta's argument at the Guildhall was ingenious: in the presence of the parish officials he claimed that the 'said Mary was not his Daughter' at all. The parish, however, brought a number of witnesses who testified that she had always been supported by her father in a manner suitable to 'A Jew of great Substance', and he was ordered to compensate the parish to the sum of £12 for past expenses, and to contribute twenty shillings each week for his daughter's future maintenance.[12] Mendez de Breta, in turn, had recourse to the court of King's Bench, which set aside the

---

[8] Ibid. 13: 798–800.

[9] A. M. Hyamson, *The Sephardim of England* (London, 1951), 87–8.

[10] *Commons Journal*, 13: 798–800.

[11] City of London Record Office, Charge Book 4; Waiting Book 16: 16 June 1701.

[12] Ibid., SMB 71. For a similar paternity case see that of Abraham Henriques, ibid., Lord Mayor's Waiting Book 16 (n.p.): 30 Dec. 1700.

grant of maintenance irrespective of the religious issues involved, on the grounds that it was made without proper jurisdiction.[13] The parish of St Andrew Undershaft was back to square one, burdened by a worthy but costly convert with no legal basis to their claim for compensation.

The solution agreed upon by the parish officials was to create just such a basis for future legal action. On 18 February 1701/2 they petitioned the House of Commons along with five nearby parishes,

setting forth, That most of the Jews in *London* live in the said Parishes; and, though they enjoy the Protection of the Government, and the free Exercise of their Religion, and grow rich, yet they bear such a Hatred to our Natural Religion, that, in case any of their Children embrace the same, they utterly disown them, and treat them with great Cruelty.

A particular instance of this general Jewish phenomenon, they thought, was the recent case of Jacob Mendez de Breta, 'a rich Jew in *St. Andrew's Undershaft*', their very own parish, who had disowned his daughter upon her conversion, forcing the parish to maintain her. In brief, their aim in petitioning the Commons at this time was 'That a Bill may be brought in to oblige *Jacob Mendes de Breta* in particular, and the Jews in general, to maintain, and provide for, their Protestant Children.' The petition was received, and referred to a committee consisting of thirty-five members who met during the following month to consider the implications of such a proposal.[14]

Sir Robert Clayton reported to the House on 16 March, representing the committee of which he was a part. He reviewed the facts of the case, noting that Jacob Mendez de Breta had always owned the girl Mary for his child, and so she was registered in the parish books. Witnesses had been called and their testimony cited, not only from the minister who baptized her, but from others acquainted with the case and with the family. One witness reported that Mary's father had even gone to the extent of having his daughter arrested on a false charge of having stolen some cloth from him. Another warned the committee that her father might be plotting to kidnap her and send her abroad. Jacob's explanation was difficult to swallow. He denied that Mary was his daughter at all, claiming 'That the said *Mary*, with Two or Three more Children, were laid at his Door; and that he took them in, and maintained them, purely out of Charity.' The girl became his servant, he said, and never sat with him at table. If she was registered for purposes of the poll tax as his daughter, it was without his knowledge. To support this unlikely claim,

---

[13] *Inhab. St. Andrew Undershaft* v. *de Breta*, Lord Raymond's Reports, i. 699: H. S. Q. Henriques, *The Jews and the English Law* (Oxford, 1908), 167–9.
[14] *Commons Journal*, 13: 748 (18 Feb. 1701–2).

Jacob Mendez de Breta brought forward three witnesses, who had little effect on the members of the committee, which resolved to accept Mary's claim, and to bring in a bill compelling Jews to support their children converted to any version of Protestantism. Sir Robert Clayton, Sir Thomas Powis, and Sir Rowland Gwyn were ordered to prepare such a bill for presentation to the House of Commons.[15]

Sir Thomas Powis presented the bill to the Commons on 20 March 1701/2: it passed its first reading on 9 April and its second on the 17th.[16] By that time, however, the Jews of London had organized a formal protest. At the end of March the Mahamad and the elders appointed their own subcommittee to formulate a Jewish response, consisting of Jacob Gonzales, John Mendes da Costa, Jacob Salvador, and Moses Francia, with a brief 'to attend to the business of the Nation which is before Parliament'.[17] When the bill was read the second time, this committee of Sephardi Jews petitioned the House, asking to be heard, as 'so much of the Bill as concerns them, and does not concern the said *Jacob Mendez de Breta* in particular'.[18] All that could be obtained was a proposal for a minor change in the wording, but when this was put to the House, it divided 30 : 54 against, the very paucity of participants giving some indication of the amendment's lack of importance.[19] The bill passed its third reading on 12 May 1702, and Sir Rowland Gwyn brought it to the Lords, where it was passed four days later.[20]

'An Act to Oblige the Jews to Maintain and Provide for their Protestant Children' took effect on 24 June 1702. Despite all of the efforts of the Sephardi community, and their outlay of over £255 in expenses, the bill was passed with hardly any serious opposition. The community records refer to Mary as the bastard child of Jacob Mendez de Breta, but this was not the verdict of Parliament. The act, passed in the first few months of Queen Anne's reign, ruled that

If any Jewish Parent, in order to the Compelling his or her Protestant Child to Change his or her Religion, shall Refuse to Allow such Child a fitting Maintenance, suitable to the Degree and Ability of such Parent, and to the Age and Education of such Child, then (upon Complaint thereof made to the Lord High Chancellor of England, or Lord Keeper of the Great Seal, or Commissioners for the Great Seal for the time being) it shall and may be Lawful for the said Lord Chancellor, Lord Keeper, or Commissioners, to make

---

[15] Ibid. 13: 798–800 (16 Mar. 1701–2).
[16] Ibid. 13: 813, 839 (20 Mar. and 9 Apr. 1702).
[17] Hyamson, *Sephardim*, 124.
[18] *Commons Journal*, 13: 848 (17 Apr. 1702).
[19] Ibid. 13: 886 (8 May 1702).
[20] Ibid. 13: 889, 895 (12 and 16 May 1702); *Lords Journal*, 17: 125, 126, 128, 131, 148 (12, 13, 15, 16, 25 May 1702).

such Order therein, for the Maintenance of such Protestant Child, as he or they shall think fit.[21]

While certainly an unwelcome law from the Jewish point of view, and of uncertain effect, from the English perspective it removed yet another obstacle to conversion, and would remain important even in the nineteenth century. The unequivocally negative reaction of the Jews to the children of apostates, on the other hand, would lead to the claim in 1732 that they had murdered a woman and her new-born child because the father had been a Christian. King's Bench declared the rumours unfounded, but suspicions seem not to have been entirely put to rest.[22]

Nevertheless, by the time that Parliament had passed this awkward act, the Jewish community in England, or the dominant Sephardi branch at least, had been immeasurably strengthened by the acquisition of a new leader, Rabbi David Nieto. As we have seen, his predecessor, Solomon Ayllon, resigned his post in 1700 in less than friendly circumstances, with a whiff of Sabbatian heresy about him, and went to Amsterdam to serve there as *haham*.[23] 'After him,' Nieto recalled, 'I received a call from London from the city of my habitation, Leghorn, where I was Dayan and Preacher of the Congregation and Physician, and came here at the end of Elul 5461 [1701]; and the city of my birth is Venice.'[24] Nieto arrived in London at the age of 48, and remained until his death at the beginning of 1728. He was determined on his arrival to get off on the right foot. His first publication was a quarto pamphlet in Spanish, which appeared in December 1701, and consisted of a prayer by the congregation offered up to God to help King William III with his government of the country.[25] As far as anyone could tell, Nieto's term of office seemed to promise a period of dignified tranquillity.[26]

---

[21] 'An Act to Oblige the Jews . . .' [1 Anne, *c.*24]: University of London, Mocatta Library, Mocatta Cupboard. For *Vincent* v. *Fernandez*, a case of 1718 brought under this statute, see N. Bentwich, 'Anglo-Jewish Causes Célèbres', *TJHSE* 15 (1976), 95–6. The Act was repealed in 1846: James Picciotto, *Sketches of Anglo-Jewish History* (new edn., London, 1956), 453.

[22] Henriques, *English Law*, 9–10; *Bevis Marks Records*, i, ed. L. D. Barnett (Oxford, 1940), 35. The pamphlet itself was written by a certain Osborne, and led to a number of Jewish immigrants in Broad Street being attacked.

[23] See above, p. 177–9.

[24] David Nieto to Christian Theophilus Unger (pastor in Herrenlaurschutz), 27 Tamuz 5479 [1719], from London: repr. *TJHSE* 12 (1931), 39–44.

[25] [David Nieto], *Devota, y humilde suplicación* [London, 1701]: BL 4033 h. 31 (7).

[26] Johann Schult, a Swedish Christian Hebraist, visited London and Oxford during Nov. 1702–Jan. 1703 to study Hebrew MSS and had many discussions with Nieto: see his Latin diary in the University of Lund library; and a photocopy and microfilm at University College, London, Mocatta Library, AJ/96 and AJ/151/13/3.

This hope was dashed on 20 November 1703, when David Nieto preached his weekly sermon on the portion of the week, *parashat v'yashave*. His subject was Divine Providence, and some of those present saw in the rabbi's exposition distinct traces of Spinoza's pantheism. Indeed, Nieto was accused of having argued that God and Nature were one. One of the congregants, Joshua Zarfati, went so far as to refuse to enter the house in which a wedding was being celebrated soon afterwards, on the grounds that the rabbi, a self-declared heretic, was inside. Zarfati explained his position to another of the guests, who immediately reported these views to the Mahamad. In strictly legalistic terms, Zarfati had violated an *ascama* of 1699, promulgated during the tenure of the unfortunate Rabbi Ayllon, that anyone who should speak critically of present or past *hahamim* would be liable to a fine of £5. Likewise, any who were privy to information about others were obligated to report it to the Mahamad. Zarfati was called before the board, but steadfastly refused to reconsider his position, choosing instead to withdraw from the congregation voluntarily.[27]

Zarfati's parting shot, however, was to issue a challenge to the Mahamad to leave off legalities and to deal with the heart of the matter. Zarfati offered to forfeit £100 if he could not prove his allegation of Nieto's pantheism, the decision to be rendered by any Jewish congregation. Zarfati put his case in writing, but the Mahamad submitted it to Nieto, with whom Zarfati declined to meet. He was subsequently and formally excluded from the synagogue building itself, Zarfati protesting that he was not permitted to enjoy the house of worship to the building of which he himself had contributed. The entire issue of Nieto's alleged championing of Spinoza was therefore left unresolved, and Zarfati was forced to take his case to the public, which he did in a work published in the Spanish language, and therefore easily accessible to non-Jews as well.[28] Nieto put his side into writing as well, also in Spanish, in a book entitled *De la Divina Providencia*. As *haham*, Nieto perhaps felt it unseemly that he should have to reply at all, even

[27] Generally, see I. Solomons, 'David Nieto and Some of his Contemporaries', *TJHSE* 12 (1931), 1–101, esp. 10; Hyamson, *Sephardim*, 90–1. On 22 July 1705 the Mahamad made yet another alteration in their monopolistic *Ascama* I whereby anyone withholding information about a rogue Sephardi congregation would suffer the same penalty of *herem* (excommunication) as an actual participant in illicit prayers. It would appear that Zarfati was not the only defector from *Saar Asamaim*. The *Ascama* I was reaffirmed in similar circumstances in 1738: I. Epstein, 'The Story of Ascama I of the Spanish and Portuguese Jewish Congregation of London', in M. Ben-Horin (ed.), *Studies and Essays in Honour of Abraham A. Neuman* (Leiden, 1962), 176–7, 181.

[28] *Relación del caso de Jehosuah Zarfatti*: Solomons, 'Nieto', 10–11; Hyamson, *Sephardim*, 91.

though this work became one of his most famous writings.[29] In his letter to the pastor Unger, he noted years later that

In this book I have not inscribed my name openly on account of the squabbles of a minority of the Yehidim of the Holy Congregation with me; but if your Highness will look at the letters that the typesetters use to index the printed matter he will find under A vel B, from leaf 1 to leaf 53, Sr H.H.R. David Netto Rab del K.K. de Londres.[30]

This book, Nieto and his many supporters hoped, would put an end to a painful and unnecessary communal quarrel.

Zarfati believed that right was on his side, and was unwilling to give in for the privilege of returning to his seat in the synagogue. In this he was not alone, and the Mahamad took the slightly unorthodox step of obtaining a legal opinion from the Attorney-General, Sir Edward Northey, regarding the entire question of *en bloc* excommunication. They wanted to know, if Zarfati should bring his case to the Gentile authorities, 'if there is any statute against Excommunication or any particular Court (and wich) where this matter proprely shall bee Litigated'. Furthermore, they asked Northey if they were obligated to bury such an excommunicate in their communal cemetery, even if they had already received the fee for the future provision of a grave site. Sir Edward Northey replied on 12 June 1705, supporting the Mahamad, although his convoluted phrasing must have left some of the community in the dark. 'I am doubtfull', he ruled,

that the pronouncing excommunicating being an act of ecclesiasticall Jurisdiction, the Synagogue of the Jewes are not allowable by the Lawes of England to exercise the pronouncing of same, & for assuming the exercise of ye power in England, may be psecuted by indictment or Information, & may be prohibited from pronouncing ye like by writ of phibition to be granted by the Queens courts of law.

Furthermore, he was of the opinion that the Mahamad could indeed exclude an excommunicate even from the grave site that he had already purchased.[31] The Mahamad had the opportunity for putting his opinion into practice on the death of Joseph Cohen d'Azevedo, one of Zarfati's supporters: he was interred in the neighbouring Ashkenazi cemetery, as close as possible to the wall that separated it from the Sephardi plots.[32]

The entire issue, therefore, would have to be resolved by the Jews

---

[29] [David Nieto], *De la Divina Providencia* (London, 1704): BL shelfmarks 4033 b. 41 and 4033 h. 31 (1). A second edn. was published at London in 1716: BL 702 d. 24.

[30] Nieto to Unger, see n. 24 above. Actually, the printers' letters spell 'S^r HH David Neto Rab del KK de Londres Ylul Anno 5464'.

[31] Enquiry of the Mahamad to Attorney-General Edward Northey, and his reply, 12 June 1705: SPJC, London, MS 163.   [32] Hyamson, *Sephardim*, 93.

themselves. Perhaps yielding to the pressure of Zarfati's supporters, or Nieto's enemies, the Mahamad turned to the rabbinical court in Amsterdam for a ruling. The fact that the chairman of this body was their own former *haham* Solomon Ayllon must have been a factor in their decision. At the same time, a number of Zarfati's followers themselves wrote a letter to the court in Amsterdam stating their position.[33] Whether for reasons of tact or policy, the rabbis of Amsterdam declined to rule in the question of Nieto, and thereby offended their Sephardi brethren in London even further. The English Jews resolved that they would never again make the mistake of referring to their colleagues in Amsterdam for advice.[34] But Zarfati's group insisted on the question being determined, and pressured the Mahamad to turn to another authority outside of England. The *haham* of Hamburg would be almost as unimpeachable as that of Amsterdam, but the post was vacant. Instead they chose to put their collective trust in the renowned Ashkenazi rabbi of Altona, Rabbi Zvi Ashkenazi. Reb Aberle of the Ashkenazi community in London served as middleman, and in a letter of 28 September 1704 the famous rabbi agreed to officiate, requesting supporting documents.[35]

Rabbi Zvi Ashkenazi deliberated nearly a year, and in a letter sent to London on 7 August 1705, and co-signed by two other rabbinical judges at Altona, exonerated David Nieto of all charges and the taint of Spinozan heresy. Indeed, in concluding his decision, Rabbi Zvi Ashkenazi went out of his way to heap praise on the *haham* of London:

We must thank H.H.R. David Nieto, whom God preserve, for the sermon he preached to warn the people not to allow themselves to be led away by the opinion of philosophers who treat on Nature, because great injury arises therefrom, and he enlightens the eyes with the true belief, which is that everything comes from the providence of God. I say, may God fortify his

---

[33] Thirteen London Jews to the *parnassim* and *gabbai* of the Sephardi community in Amsterdam, 7 Heshvan 5465 [1704], from London: Bibliotheca Rosenthaliana, Amsterdam: repr. in English trans. from the Spanish in *TJHSE* 12 (1931), 12–13; same to same, 17 Tevet 5465 [1704]: *TJHSE* 12 (1931), 13–14.

[34] Solomons, 'Nieto', 12–15; Hyamson, *Sephardim*, 93–4; M. Gaster, *History of the Ancient Synagogue of the Spanish and Portuguese Jews* (London, 1901), 106–7.

[35] Gaster, *Ancient Synagogue*; D. Kaufmann, 'Rabbi Zevi Ashkenazi and his Family in London', *TJHSE* 3 (1899), 102–25. These documents were subsequently printed as quarto pamphlets: *Decisión del doctíssimo, y excelentíssimo Señor H.H. . . . Zevi Asquenazi* (London, 1705), although curiously by two different printers: James Dover on Tower Hill (cf. Solomons, 'Nieto', 16 n., 66, noting that this edn. is unknown to bibliographers), and Tho. Ilive (?Hive) of Aldergate Street (BL 4033 h 31 (3), catalogued under 'Tsebi, ben Jacob Ashenazi'). A later edn. appeared as well, printed at London in 1712: BL 702 d. 24; and two 1705 edns. in Hebrew (Solomons, 'Nieto', 67). Cf. Epstein, 'Ascama I', 178–82.

strength and valour, and all, who after having seen these words, shall think hardly of him, in my opinion, incur sin.

A more conclusive defeat for Nieto's enemies could hardly have been imagined, and his place at the head of the Jewish community remained unassailable.[36]

Nieto was later involved in another theological controversy which also concerned Zvi Ashkenazi. Nehemiah Hiyya Hayon (*c.*1655–*c.*1730), a notorious Sabbatian fellow-traveller, made the claim that there was a distinction between the First Cause and the *Ein-Sof* (the Infinite Being), a duality highly objectionable to normative Judaism. Hayon spent much of his early life in Palestine and the East, but travelled throughout Europe, and in 1713 arrived in Amsterdam, possibly because of rumours about the Sabbatian leanings of Rabbi Solomon Ayllon of the Sephardi congregation there. Zvi Ashkenazi, now the rabbi of the Ashkenazim in Amsterdam, bitterly opposed Hayon and everything he stood for, and among the many who wrote against him was Rabbi David Nieto, who had succeeded Ayllon in the post at London. In the end, everyone lost: Zvi Ashkenazi was forced to leave Amsterdam, and Hayon became an outcast, finally wandering to North Africa, where he died about 1730.[37] Nieto's tract, a Platonic-style dialogue called *Esh Dath*, was published in Hebrew with a parallel Spanish edition at London in 1715.[38] In the preface to the Spanish edition, although not in the Hebrew, Nieto notes the existence of a manuscript supplement to his work, in which he further elaborates the points which he made for publication.[39] It is quite clear that for Nieto the problem was more than theological: he was concerned that out of respect for the previous *haham*, some members of his flock might be willing to give Hayon a hearing, which might in turn

---

[36] Quoted in Solomons, 'Nieto', 17. The case is discussed in the *responsa* of Zvi Ashkenazi, part i, printed at Amsterdam in 1712, no. 18 = p. 23. Curiously, this page has been torn out of the copy in the Bod. Lib., Opp. fº 932. An English trans. by Leon Roth was pub. in the *Chronicon Spinozanum*, i (1921), 278–82. Cf. Moses de Medina in defence of David Nieto: *He'etaik ha-iggeret she-katav* (London, *c.*1705): Bod. Lib., Opp. 4º 792 (10).

[37] On Hayon, see the article by Gershom Scholem in the *EJ* vii. 1499–1503.

[38] David Nieto, *Esh Dath* (Hebrew) (London, 1715); id., *Es Dat o Fuego legal* (London, 1715).

[39] Three copies of Nieto's MS exist, in each case bound up between the Hebrew and Spanish printed texts of the bilingual edition: (1) Mocatta Library, University College, London, shelfmark Mocatta Cupboard W220 NIE; (2) Bod. Lib., Oxford, shelfmark Opp. add. 8º II. 63; (3) Columbia Univ., New York, shelfmark B893.1/N51. Professor Raphael Loewe, 'The Spanish Supplement to Nieto's "*Esh Dath*" ', *PAAJR* 48 (1981), 267–96, suggests that the London copy, which is the best, may be the work of Joseph ibn Danon. Loewe prints the Spanish text (pp. 284–92), followed by a translation into English (pp. 292–6).

split his group into rival camps around the issues of Shabtai Sevi and cabbala. Fortunately, as with the Zarfati case, here too Nieto's views prevailed and peace was maintained.[40]

Nieto also had the opportunity of officiating at the opening of a grand new synagogue for the community which had recently been completed, almost for him. The community of Sephardi Jews had long outgrown its original site on Creechurch Lane, and although the withdrawal of the Ashkenazim into their own synagogue did something to ease the pressure of space, it was only a matter of time before a new building would have to be erected. A suitable site having been found nearby, an agreement was made with a Quaker builder named Joseph Avis on 12 February 1699. The new synagogue was to cost £2,650, payable in instalments. The land belonged to the Pointz family, who signed a lease which ran originally for sixty-one years, with an option to extend it for a further thirty-eight years, rent being set at £120 per annum. Eventually, the least was converted into freehold. The foundation stone was laid in August 1700, and the building continued steadily (Saturdays and Jewish holidays excepted, apart from ordinary building practice) until the new synagogue could be opened for worship in September 1701). The cost of the building overran estimates, but the builder seems to have refused additional payment, a surprising decision made understandable, perhaps, only by his Quaker sentiments. It was widely believed that Princess Anne herself presented an oak beam which was used in the construction, but this seems to be a legend based on her visit to the congregation a number of years before. At any rate, the Sephardim of London were now provided with a very impressive building indeed, and the social and psychological effects of this stately house of God can hardly be over-emphasized.[41]

A grandiose new synagogue and a famous foreign rabbi: these were the palpable symbols of the firm establishment of a Jewish (or at least a Sephardi Jewish) community in London. Perhaps this self-assertion, even lack of discretion, may be held partially responsible for the flurry of anti-Jewish activity that we have already discussed: the act for supporting convert children and the various cases of unwanted parish offices all fall within the years 1700–01, when the Jews were building themselves a personal monument in the heart of London. Sir Solomon de Medina, the Jewish knight, was himself a living symbol of how far at

---

[40] See generally Solomons, 'Nieto'; J. J. Petuchowski, *The Theology of Haham David Nieto* (New York, 1954); M. B. Amzalak, *David Nieto* (Lisbon, 1923).

[41] Picciotto, *Sketches*, 52–3; Hyamson, *Sephardim*, 74–8; Corporation of London Record Office, Rep. 104, pp. 341 (28 May 1700), 349 (4 June 1700), 399 (27 June 1700). Cf. John Stow, *A Survey of the Cities of London and Westminster* (London, 1720), i. 81–2, and map of Aldgate Ward opp. p. 54.

least one Jew had risen, even if in 1702 he left England for Holland, where he remained until his death in 1730. The Sephardi community, in turn, was unhappy about Jews who spoiled their image and self-image as substantial and almost aristocratic English Nonconformists. Many Jews were shipped back to Holland, or found themselves thrown on the secular authorities. Such a man was 'Jacob Jessaroone an idle vagrant Jew who refuseth to Worke or goe to Rotterdam the place of his aboad haveing lately reced xvi^s of the Jewes Synnagogue to defray his charge & yett returned againe to this City' at the end of 1691. He was committed to Bridewell. The Lord Mayor's Waiting Book at the turn of the century contains many references to Jews or suspected Jews who were issued passes to return to Holland.[42] Similarly, the Mahamad wrote to Amsterdam, asking them to stop sending *shlichim* (emissaries) from Palestine, because they were already overburdened with caring for Sephardi poor fleeing from Spain and Portugal. They wrote directly to Jerusalem with the same demand, in an attempt to reduce outside requests for assistance.[43]

Converts to Christianity were also a problem, particularly in these first years when Anglo-Jewry was trying to establish itself as an accepted and fixed part of the religious landscape in England. Since the decline of the Domus Conversorum, its charity for the relief of converted Jews had been administered by the Master of the Rolls. From January 1717 the two lucky apostates were Joseph Jonah and Henry Contigno. The latter petitioned the Treasury unsuccessfully on 4 February 1716/17 for back pay, on the grounds that he had converted to Christianity in 1686.[44] Many of these converts published short narratives of how they discovered the truth of Christianity. John Alexander published such a pamphlet in 1689, as did Theodore John, who was baptized a Lutheran on 31 October 1692.[45] Sometimes we can trace the more extensive connections which lead up to a conversion. Such was the case with John

---

[42] Corporation of London Record Office, Lord Mayor's Waiting Book 15, fo. 54^v (9 Nov. 1691), and *passim*, esp. fo. 52 (18 Sept. 1691): I am grateful to Dr S. Macfarlane for these references.

[43] R. D. Barnett, 'The Correspondence of the Mahamad of the Spanish and Portuguese Congregation of London during the Seventeenth and Eighteenth Centuries', *TJHSE* 20 (1964), 1–50, esp. 4. Barnett made English summaries of much of the material from the Mahamad before 1800, which is kept in loose-leaf notebooks shelved with the original minute books at the SPJC, London.

[44] Petition of Henry Contigno, 4 Feb. 1716/17: Treasury, In-Letters, Treasury Board Papers (T.1) 206, No. 18: cited in *Anglo-Jewish Historical Exhibition Catalogue* (London, 1888), p. 36. Contigno and Jonah replaced Peter Samuel and John Meza as Master of the Rolls converts.

[45] John Alexander, *God's Covenant Displayed* (London, 1689); Theodore John, *An Account of the Conversion* (London, 1693).

Xeres of Sophia, who had been converted through contact with English merchants who put him in touch with Peter Allix in London.[46] Allix tried to convince the Jews that the Second Coming would be very different from the First, and that they would be unwise to wait until their temporal condition had been altered to resemble what it had been before the fall of the Second Temple.[47] Charles-Marie de Veil (1630–85), a Jew from Metz, became successively an Augustinian canon, a Huguenot, an Anglican clergyman, and a Baptist minister. 'Dieu veuille qu'il ne fasse pas, comme le soleil, le tour du zodiaque', commented Pierre Bayle on de Veil's death in 1685.[48] Some Jewish converts to Christianity found employment as purveyors of Hebraic wisdom to English scholars, as did Philip Levi, who served as Hebrew lecturer at Magdalen College, Oxford, from 1706 until his death in 1709. Levi also published a Hebrew grammar, which he used in his classes at Oxford.[49] 'Aaron, an old Jew', followed him at Magdalen between 1726 and 1734.[50] Salomon Israel taught Hebrew calligraphy at Oxford in 1745, converted successively to Catholicism and then Protestantism under the name of Ignatius Dumay, and then returned to Oxford, working for and then attacking Dr Benjamin Kennicott for his biblical scholarship.[51] A Venetian Jew named David Aboab converted to Christianity and tried to interest the learned public in a Hebrew–English dictionary that he was preparing for the press.[52] Indeed, the demand for conversionist literature during these years was so great that it was thought worthwhile to translate foreign examples of this genre, as was done with the

[46] John Xeres, *An Address to the Jews* (London, 1710). Xeres replaced Contigno in 1730 as Master of the Rolls convert.

[47] Peter Allix, *A Confutation of the Hope of the Jews* (London, 1707), pp. iv–v.

[48] W. T. Whitley, 'Charles-Marie de Veil', *Baptist Quarterly*, 5 (1930–1), 74–85, 118–29, 177–89; *Nouvelles de la république des lettres*, 11, 1029. Cf. C. M. du Veil [*sic*], *A Commentary on the Acts of the Apostles*, ed. F. A. Cox (Hanserd Knollys Soc., London, 1851; 1st pub. 1685), esp. biog. introd.

[49] Bursars' Acts, Magdalen College, Oxford, for 1706–9: *A Register of the Members of St. Mary Magdalen College, Oxford*, ed. W. D. Macray (London, 1894–1915), iv. 54–5; Philip Levi, *A Compendium of Hebrew Grammar* (Oxford, 1705). Cf. Humphrey Wanley to Dr Arthur Charlett, 1 Aug. 1705, about Levi; and same to same about Isaac Bernard, a Jewish possible replacement for Levi, 15 Jan. 1710/11: Bod. Lib., MS Ballard 13, fos. 116^r–117^v, 121^r.

[50] *Register*, ed. Macray, v. 9; Thomas Hearne, *Remarks and Collections*, ed. H. E. Salter, xi (Oxford, 1921), 245–6. For some additional details, see U. Dann, 'Jews in 18th-Century Oxford: Further Observations', *Oxoniensia*, 54 (1989) [1991], 345–53; C. Roth, 'Jews in Oxford after 1290', *Oxoniensia*, 15 (1950), 63–80.

[51] C. Roth, 'Salomon Israel, Writing Master in Oxford, 1745—*alias* Ignatius Dumay', *Oxoniensia*, 28 (1963), 74–8.

[52] David Aboab, *The Mercy and Truth* (London, 1748), esp. 46.

narrative of Daniel ben Alexander, 'Baptised unto *Christ*, in the Reformed Church of *Rouen*'.[53]

Anthony d'Almanza, now a Christian merchant, but formerly a Jew named Aron, learned the hard way that leaving the fold might have commercial as well as religious consequences. Almanza, originally from the Low Countries, lent some £2,000 to a certain Francis Davila, apparently a Jew, who later declined to pay his debt. Instead, he combined with his friends to have Almanza repeatedly arrested as if the debt were the other way around. Almanza's wife was also served with warrants and his 10-year-old servant was sent to Bridewell. Prostitutes were brought over from Paris to testify falsely against him. In court, Almanza tried to have it both ways: when asked to swear, 'the Attorney obliged him to beware how he took his Oath: to which he answer'd before several Persons, That he did it like a *Jew* as he was, tho' several Persons in the Company knew him to be a *Papist*'. In the end, Almanza 'found himself deprived of all help, not finding a Person to whom he might make himself understood, because he spoke no *English*'. Almanza eventually gave in, and went away with some promises, but probably no money.[54] Almanza's story was mirrored almost exactly by the trials in Exeter of 'Joseph Ottolenghe, A Poor Convert Jew' eventually delivered in 1735 'out of Southgate Prison; Into which he was cast by a Jew, after his Conversion to Christianity'.[55] Their fate was apparently not uncommon, and three London merchants in 1719 advertised in the press that they were organizing a Christian support group for baptized Jews who were reduced to penury by their courageous conversion to Protestantism.[56]

II

Despite these various vicissitudes, the Sephardi community of early eighteenth-century London remained united. The Ashkenazim, on the other hand, exhibited the centrifugal tendencies so common to Jewish

[53] Daniel Tnangam Alexander, *A Call to the Jews* (London, n.d.); Daniel ben Alexander, *A Declaration of the Christian Faith* (2nd edn., London, 1703). Cf. *Proposals for Establishing a Charitable Fund* (London, 1706), sigs. A4^{r–v}.

[54] Aron de Almanza, *A Declaration of the Conversion* (London, 1703); [id.], *The Case of Anthony d'Almanza* (London, 1704).

[55] Lewis Stephens, *The Excellencies of the Kindness* (Exeter, [1735]). Stephens, archdeacon of Chester and a canon of Exeter Cathedral, also complains 'that That which might greatly have encouraged' the conversion of Jews to Christianity 'is quite taken away: (I mean the *House of Converts*)': p. 27 n.

[56] *Weekly Journal; or, British Gazetteer* (7 Nov. 1719), 1440.

congregations everywhere. The origins of the split are almost comic, but the results were long felt and indeed were almost permanent. When David Nieto was fighting his battle against the accusation of Spinozism, the rabbi of the Ashkenazi community was Jehuda Loeb ben Ephraim Anschel of Hamburg, whose staff consisted of five teachers and two scribes.[57] His misfortune was to be disliked by the most dominant lay figure in the community, Abraham of Hamburg, known as Reb Aberle. Like others in the congregation, Reb Aberle was a dealer in precious stones, among other things, and his success gave him the confidence to intervene in all aspects of community affairs.[58] Reb Aberle was almost certainly behind the humiliating incident in 1705 when it was discovered that the rabbi's prayer shawl was defective, lacking one of the obligatory fringes. In theory, this important piece of devotional equipment should have been checked before use, and Rabbi Jehuda must have done so. Sabotage was not ruled out, but the effect was the same, and the validity of the rabbi's prayers was called into doubt. Rabbi Jehuda resigned in humiliation: as a contemporary described subsequent events, 'he turned away and left, and the Lord (blessed be He) came to his aid, and he was immediately accepted upon arrival as rabbi in Rotterdam'.[59] From Reb Aberle's point of view, the way was now clear towards the consolidation of his power.

It was towards this end that Reb Aberle joined forces with two new figures who made their appearance at this time in Ashkenazi Jewish London, the Hart brothers. They were the sons of Naphtali Hertz of Hamburg, a prosperous Jewish resident of that city, and between them covered the world of commerce and scholarship. The older son was named Uri Feibush/Phoebus or Aaron Hart; the younger was called Moses Bressler or Moses Hart. Uri Phoebus/Aaron described himself as a rabbi and the head of a *yeshiva;* his brother Moses made his way to London in about 1697 and established a family bridgehead there.[60] By the time of the incident of the defective prayer shawl, Moses Hart was,

[57] Jochanan Holleschau, *Ma'aseh Rav* (Hebrew) (Amsterdam, 1707), fo. 9c. For an interesting window into the daily life of the Ashkenazi Jews at that time, see the nine Yiddish letters in BL MS Harl. 7013, fos. 91ᵛ–101ᵛ, repr. in the original by J. Maitlis, 'London Yiddish Letters of the Early Eighteenth Century', *JJ Stud.* 6 (1955), 153–65, 237–52.

[58] See Kaufmann, 'Zevi Ashkenazi', 104–5; C. Roth, *The Great Synagogue London 1690–1940* (London, 1950), 29–30. Cf. Uri Phoebus Hamburger [Aaron Hart], *Urim v'Tumim* (Hebrew) (London, 1707), 16d; Holleschau, *Ma'aseh*, 2.

[59] Holleschau, *Ma'aseh*, 176.

[60] Hart, *Urim*, 3; Kaufmann, 'Zevi Ashkenazi', 105–6. The Hart brothers seem to have been the nephews of Benjamin Levy, who had founded the congregation in 1690. For a document testifying to the transfer on 22 May 1712 of a £1,000 Treasury loan by Moses Hart, signed by Walpole, see Jewish Museum, London, MS 8A.

with Reb Aberle, a leading member of the Ashkenazi community, and had already brought over his brother Aaron the rabbi to serve as the spiritual leader to replace the disgraced Rabbi Jehuda. The connection between Aaron Hart's new position and the defective prayer shawl of the previous incumbent was made even more apparent by the fact that to take the post the new rabbi had to break an oath that he had made to Jehuda Loeb not to replace him for the next three years, even if selected. Rabbi Aaron Hart may have had his reasons, for he remained in the post for over half a century, until 1756, spanning the entire period between Queen Anne and the Jew Bill.[61]

There were now definitely two parties within the Ashkenazi community, those who accepted the suzerainty of Reb Aberle and his rabbi Aaron Hart, and those who felt that the previous incumbent had been unfairly treated. These first years of Aaron Hart's tenure were also those of Nieto's troubles over the alleged sympathy for Spinoza, with which, as we have seen, Reb Aberle himself got involved, serving as the intermediary between the Sephardi community and Rabbi Zvi Ashkenazi in Altona. Relations within the Ashkenazi congregation became so tense that Reb Aberle used the opportunity of a dispute with one of the worshippers to have the rabbinical court pass a resolution forbidding outside places of worship, under pain of excommunication. In this way, Aberle hoped to keep the Ashkenazim united. Unfortunately, as we shall see, this very rule was to prove the cause of their disintegration.[62]

On 27 August 1706 Rabbi Aaron Hart privately, almost clandestinely, divorced Ascher Ensel Cohen/Katz from his wife, freeing him to leave England and his numerous creditors behind. In order to ensure secrecy, a scribe from the Sephardi community was used. Despite all of these precautions, news of the divorce leaked out, and among those in the community most offended by these under-the-counter dealings was Marcus (Mordecai) Hamburger Moses.[63] Originally from Hamburg, and indeed the son of one of the founders of the community there, Marcus Moses had married a daughter of Glückel of Hameln, the famous Jewish lady diarist of early modern Germany. The route from Hamburg to London was a well-travelled one on the Jewish itinerary, and Marcus Moses in the first years of the eighteenth century took his wife and his trade in precious stones to London.[64] Once there, he immediately encountered difficulties in his relations with Reb Aberle,

[61] Holleschau, *Ma'aseh*, fo. 6a; Kaufmann, 'Zevi Ashkenazi', 106; Roth, *Great Synagogue*, 33–4.

[62] Holleschau, *Ma'aseh*, fo. 6a; Kaufmann, 'Zevi Ashkenazi', 107.

[63] Kaufmann, 'Zevi Ashkenazi', 109–10.

[64] Roth, *Great Synagogue*, 35–6.

the uncrowned lay king of the community. Perhaps thinking that London was as pluralistic as Hamburg, Marcus Moses and two others toyed with the idea of opening a Beth Midrash, a study house in which prayers would quite naturally be conducted at the appropriate times during the day. They thought they might convert the house of Abraham Nathan, one of the group, to serve this purpose. Reb Aberle thought otherwise, and with Moses Hart saw Rabbi Aaron's dignity as being injured by the presence of an alternative Ashkenazi house of worship, however informal. Moses Hart enlisted the co-operation of Abraham Mendez of the Sephardi congregation, itself worried about break-away movements, and the two took the step of appealing on 20 March 1704/5 to the English authorities to suppress what they described to the Court of the Lord Mayor and Aldermen as 'a new Synagogue in Saint Mary Aix'.[65] The court no doubt thought that two existing synagogues so close together were quite enough for a Christian city, and ruled two days later that 'they will not permitt nor suffer the said Place to be converted or turned into a Synagogue for the Exercise of the said Jewish Religion or for a Schoole or Colledge for yᵉ Education and Instruction of any Persons in the Jewish Law or Religion'. Those who disregarded the ruling of the aldermanic court, they noted, 'will Answere the same at their Peril'.[66]

Marcus Moses therefore had his reasons for objecting to a very questionable divorce proclaimed in the name of the community, and this he did in as public a fashion as possible. Yet Marcus Moses surely knew that since the twelfth century the 'Excommunication of Rabbenu Tam' had stood as the statutory albeit apparently theoretical punishment for any Jew who questioned the decision in a divorce case, a harsh and irrevocable penalty meant to ward off an even more divisive series of claims and counter-claims in such an instance. Indeed, the ex-communication is said to hold valid until 'the High Priest stands dressed in the Urim and Tumim' at the coming of the Messiah, and its effects stay with the victim even after his death.[67] Rabbi Aaron Hart knew that his moral and legal ground was very shaky, and offered to have the case decided by a special court consisting of himself, Haham David Nieto, and another Sephardi official. Johanan Holleschau, one of the Ashkenazi community's teachers, and tutor to Marcus Moses's children,

---

[65] 'Jews new Synagogue', 20 Mar. 1704/5: Corporation of London Record Office, Rep. 109, pp. 199–200.
[66] 'Jews not to pceed in building a new Synagouge', 22 Mar. 1704/5: ibid. 215–16.
[67] G. W. Busse, 'The Herem of Rabenu Tam in Queen Anne's London', *TJHSE* 21 (1968), 138–47. Busse claims that no other case is known apart from this one in which the *herem* of Rabbenu Tam was actually imposed. In 1765 threats were made at Cleves (Kleve) to apply it in a local case there, but this was not actually done.

however, sided with his employer, and collected supporting documents which were sent to a Moses brother in Hamburg. Reb Aberle, meanwhile, was in Hamburg on business, and on his return made sure that no attempts at conciliation would continue: the 'Excommunication of Rabbenu Tam' would be put into practice. Marcus Moses was formally excluded from the community, and, worst of all, no Ashkenazi Jew was allowed to have business dealings with him or even to speak to him. Within a short time Marcus Moses was very nearly ruined, and his offer to retract his previous statements and pay a fine of £500 was rejected by Reb Aberle.[68]

For European Jewry, however, the backwater rabbinical court of London was hardly supreme. Marcus Moses had a brother in Hamburg, as we have already seen, and it was he who laid the entire issue before that rabbi who had already mediated in the case of David Nieto: Zvi Ashkenazi. This great authority examined the relevant documents, and swifty concluded that absolute and total excommunication was far too severe a penalty for the offence committed, especially when considering the circumstances involved. Zvi Ashkenazi sent his letter in the middle of September 1706, arguing that the 'Excommunication of Rabbenu Tam' did not apply here. Other rabbis were also consulted, and the prevailing opinion went against eternal excommunication. Reb Aberle and his man Rabbi Aaron Hart refused to give in to more learned authority, however, and even caused a resolution to be passed denying Marcus Moses a burial site when the time should come. Marcus Moses now had little alternative, especially since the Sephardi congregation had just passed a resolution forbidding Ashkenazim even from entering the synagogue, let alone becoming full members of the community, and thereby shattering the fragile balance in the little world of Anglo-Jewry. His only choice now was to go ahead with what he had attempted to do several years earlier, and to open his own synagogue in his own house. The rabbi, of course, was Johanan Holleschau, and this was the congregation which would become known as the Hambro [Hamburg] Synagogue. Moses also acquired a piece of land at Hoxton to serve as a cemetery: he knew that he at least would one day be in need of such an institution.[69]

---

[68] Kaufmann, 'Zevi Ashkenazi', 108–13; Roth, *Great Synagogue*, 38–40.

[69] Kaufmann, 'Zevi Ashkenazi', 113–14; Roth, *Great Synagogue*, 41–3. The original minute book of the Hambro Synagogue is now lost; what survives from the earliest period relates from 1726 onwards: Jewish Museum, London, MS 647. The congregation moved from Marcus Moses's house to its new home in Magpie Alley, Church Row (or Passage), Fenchurch Street, in 1725, where they remained until 1892, when the building was closed. The synagogue archives were transferred to the cellars of the Central Synagogue, where they were badly affected by damp. In 1894 the then Chief

One interesting by-product of this epic dispute between Reb Aberle and Marcus Moses was the inauguration of Hebrew printing in London. Rabbi Aaron Hart, no doubt at the instigation of his patron, published a book at London in 1707 entitled *Urim v'Tumim*, a pointed reference to the vestments worn by the High Priest of the Jews in ancient times, in which he argued the justice of the case for the excommunication. This was the first book to be printed in Hebrew in London, or, as was proclaimed on the title-page, 'published in London under the great kingdom of our gracious and successful lady the Queen'. The book itself is badly produced and poorly written, but forms a significant land-mark.[70] Johanan Holleschau's reply, *Ma'aseh Rav*, published at the Athias press at Amsterdam the same year, was a production of an entirely different order. The title itself is clever, a Hebrew pun which could mean either 'a great event' or 'a rabbi's story'.[71] Holleschau's book became quite well known, and was translated into German for the benefit of a wider audience. Its supporting depositions in Yiddish even give a linguistic insight into community life. Holleschau's patriotic declaration is also almost moving:

I have no fear; for we, or brethren of the House of Israel, live in the kingdom of England, under rulers and princes and lords who deal with us with kindness and mercy. They may indeed be reckoned as the Pious Ones of the Nations of the world. If a man give them a houseful of gold and silver they would do no injustice or wrongdoing, but act only as is written in their lawbooks.

It is almost ironic that this statement should come in the context of such a petty communal row.[72]

Marcus Moses had won the battle which led to the opening of a

---

Rabbi Hermann Adler allowed Professor David Kaufmann of Budapest to borrow some of these records for his article on Zvi Ashkenazi cited above, and they were not returned after Kaufmann's premature death. Among the missing documents were not only the first minute book, but also the pages that referred to Lord George Gordon's famous donation of £100 on being called to read the Law, which were exhibited at the Anglo-Jewish Historical Exhibition in 1887 (item no. 601). Cf. *Archives of the United Synagogue: Report and Catalogue*, ed. C. Roth (London, 1930), 15.

[70] Hart, *Urim*: the Bod. Lib.'s copy is listed under the name of 'Uri (Phoebus) Hamburger': Opp. 4° 462 [St. 7330].

[71] Holleschau, *Ma'aseh*: the Bod. Lib.'s copy is listed under the name of 'Johanan b. Isaac, of Hollischau'. Cowley suggests that the first edn. of this work might have been printed in London: shelfmarks Opp. 4° 613 and Opp. add. 4° II 234 (1). A second edn. appeared in 1707 at Amsterdam, entitled *Tshuvat HaGeonim*, combining the story at London with rabbinical opinions on the pronunciation of Hebrew: Bod. Lib., Opp. 4° 612.

[72] Holleschau, *Ma'aseh* also includes many complaints about the standard of religious life in contemporary Jewish London.

second Ashkenazi synagogue in London, but his business was very nearly ruined, and he went out to the West Indies in 1714 to try to recoup his losses.[73] His later history continued to be intertwined with English communal affairs. After seven years in the Caribbean he returned to England in 1721 a wealthy man.[74] In his absence the Hambro Synagogue continued to flourish, apart from anything else because the Ashkenazi leaders of the parent congregation were adamant about keeping the secessionists out. In 1725 the latter further institutionalized their separation by building a new synagogue in Magpie Alley, Fenchurch Street, funded not only by Marcus Moses but by another wealthy Jew connected with the Hambro, Benjamin Isaac, originally of Bohemia, and also known as Wolf Prager or Zeev Wolf. Unable to let old quarrels die out, the parent Ashkenazim immediately tried the same tactic of turning to the secular authorities to prevent the building of an edifice which would make eventual surrender even more unlikely than it already was.[75] The Sephardim of Bevis Marks backed the Ashkenazi religious establishment, and lent their solicitor to fight the case. He was Philip Carteret Webb (1700–70), who acted for the Jews over the course of many years, from the very beginning of his career, until it came to an unfortunate end through his association in the John Wilkes affair. From the point of view of the parent Sephardi and Ashkenazi communities in London, P. C. Webb was their ambassador to the Gentile world.[76]

Philip Carteret Webb advised the two original congregations to lay petitions before the Lord Mayor and Court of Aldermen. Webb noted in his casebook that 'The German Jews in London ever since they have

[73] Moses Marcus, *The Principal Motives and Circumstances that Induced Moses Marcus to Leave the Jewish, and Embrace the Christian Faith* (London, 1724), xvii: Moses Marcus was the apostate son of Marcus Moses: here he says he was born in 1701 and was 13 years old when his father left for the Indies.

[74] Ibid., p. xx. Roth, *Great Synagogue*, 114 and n., claims that he returned to England after a ten-year absence; that he brought back from the Indies a 'superb diamond whose equal had never before been seen in Europe'; that in 1711 he offered for sale in Paris on behalf of Governor Pitt the famous Pitt diamond, subsequently owned by the duc d'Orléans and subject of many legends. Roth vaguely cites as evidence 'the Hebrew sources', although it is by no means clear to what he refers.

[75] Roth, *Great Synagogue*, 114–16.

[76] See generally A. S. Diamond, 'Problems of the London Sephardi Community, 1720–1733: Philip Carteret Webb's Notebooks', *TJHSE* 21 (1968), 39–63, describing BL MSS Lansdowne 629 and 630: Webb's notebooks, 1720–33, including about thirty Jewish cases. For P. C. Webb and Wilkes, see G. Rudé, *Wilkes and Liberty* (Oxford, 1965), 23, 28–9, 31–3, 36. Wilkes lost his post at the Treasury in July 1765, unjustly in his view. Webb was then Treasury Solicitor, and Wilkes charged him with perjury and the bribery of a witness. Webb had to defend himself in the House of Commons even in the year before his death.

been in England assembled themselves for th[r] Relions Worship in a Synagogue in Shoomaker Rowe London wch as is apprehended y[e] Civil Governm[t] of the City alotted them at their first comeing over it being built on Lands belonging to the City.'[77] Moses Hart in his petition noted that the Ashkenazi Jews had already paid £300 for a lease on land adjoining the synagogue, and agreed to pay out a further £400 for enlarging the structure, yet the actual cost came to over £2,000, which was invested on the assumption that there would be only one Ashkenazi synagogue in London. Now, however, Marcus Moses and his associates

with an Intent to divide & weaken the s[d] synagogue have withdrawn themselves from y[e] same in contempt of the Order of this Hono[ble] Court & . . . are now actually Erecting & Building a Synagogue in Maypiy Alley which should it go on wou'd in a short time manifestly tend to the Impoverishing of the s[d] Congregacon wch for some years past hath found it very difficult to Maintaine & render it unable to support them for the future & thereby bring a great & inevitable charge on the Parishes where they live.[78]

The prohibition of 1705 was therefore shown to be not forgotten despite the twenty-year lapse in which the Hambro Synagogue had been allowed to continue to operate. Supporting Moses Hart were the parishioners of St Katherine Coleman, led by their minister and churchwardens. In their view, the building of a new synagogue 'will if continued be a very great disturbance to y[e] Pishoners who Inhabit near the said Synagogue by bringing numbers of Jews into the Alley wch is a Thoroughfare not exceeding three foot in Width will in a great Measure block up the passage'. This second petition was said to be signed by the rector and fifty parishioners.[79]

The Court of Aldermen heard the two petitions and, being informed that Marcus Moses was at the door, let him testify as well, before concluding that 'they will not pmit or suffer the s[d] Building complained of to be converted or turned into a Synagoge for the Exercise of the s[d] Jewish Religion as they will answer y[e] same, at their peril'.[80] Marcus Moses was undeterred by this decision, as he had been over twenty years before, and went ahead with plans for the grand opening. Webb noted in his casebook that 'Marcus Moses is fitting up & in a few days will begin to Exercise their Religion publickly in this New Synagogue & M[r] Moses

---

[77] BL MS Lansdowne 629, fo. 16[r].

[78] Ibid., fos. 17[r-v], dated 8 June 1725. Cf. the version from the Guildhall Archives printed in Roth, *Great Synagogue*, 116–17.

[79] BL MS Lansdowne 629, fo. 16[v]. Cf. the version from Guildhall archives printed in Roth, *Great Synagogue*, 118–19, with a total of forty-seven signatures noted.

[80] BL MS Lansdowne 629, fo. 17[v]. Cf. Roth, *Great Synagogue*, 118–19, from Guildhall archives.

puts the Court of Aldermen & Parish at Defyance'.[81] These were the facts that Webb put to a number of his legal colleagues in an attempt to enforce the court's decisions. The results of his survey were hardly what he expected. Serjeant Thomas Pengelly was asked whether there was a 'Method for ye Pishoners to put a Stop to the Exercise of the Jewish Worship in this new Synagogue', and replied that the complaining Christians had no interest in the land upon which the new house of worship was being built, so that until the Jews became an actual public nuisance there was nothing they could do.[82] Sir Clement Wearg, the Solicitor-General, in his opinion added that he did not believe that it was possible to indict someone for defying an order of the Lord Mayor and aldermen, although he thought that the Jews might be prosecuted under the Conventicle Act.[83] Sir Philip Yorke, the Attorney-General, also thought the court's decision unenforceable and advised Webb to wait until the Jews caused a genuine disturbance in the parish.[84]

Marcus Moses himself was not idle: although he must have known that the unfavourable decision of the Lord Mayor and aldermen was unenforceable, he took the trouble of making a written offer to the parish officials of St Katherine Coleman to pay them £100 down and £20 for twenty years if they dropped their opposition to the new Hambro Synagogue.[85] Having accepted this generous provision, the major prop in the Jewish prosecution collapsed. Undeterred, P. C. Webb turned to J. Lingard, Common Serjeant, in a last-ditch attempt to stop the Ashkenazi secessionist movement, now that the entire issue of public nuisance had become a dead letter. Lingard replied that a prosecution under the Conventicle Act was always a possible line of attack, even if the parishioners of St Katherine Coleman declined to come to Webb's aid. Nevertheless, Lingard sagely added, although this might be done,

But it ought to be well considered by the Jews of other Synagogues how far it will be prudent in them to stir up a Matter of this Nature, and whe^r or no they themselves are not liable to the same Inconveniencys & whether such a prosecution may not provoke Marcus Moses to set up a prosecution ag^t other Synagogues, wch as far as I can see are but in the same Circumstances with this.[86]

Marcus Moses and the congregants of the Hambro Synagogue thereby won the day and secured their independence as the first Ashkenazi

---

[81] BL MS Lansdowne 629, fo. 17^v.
[82] Ibid., fos. 17^v–18^r, dated 5 Oct. 1725.
[83] Ibid., fo. 18^r–v, dated 5 Oct. 1725.
[84] Ibid., fo. 18^v, dated 18 Oct. 1725.
[85] Webb to Lingard: ibid., fos. 18^v–19^r.
[86] Ibid., fo. 19^r.

community not under control of the congregation on Shoemaker's Row, which would soon become known as the Great Synagogue.[87]

Marcus Moses and his associates had broken the monopoly of Ashkenazi worship in England, and it was not until 1750 that the Great Synagogue rescinded the excommunication of the worshippers at the Hambro. Indeed, when Hart Lyon was appointed rabbi of the Great Synagogue in 1758, the members of the Hambro recognized his authority and contributed to his salary. It might be said that, at that moment, the chief rabbinate of England came into being, which even today represents the Ashkenazim alone. The following year the Hambro Synagogue agreed to contribute one-third of the cost of maintaining Ashkenazi poor in London.[88] This, in a sense, was the signal for the next split in Ashkenazi Jewry, once the principle had been established. At the end of May 1761 the *Lloyd's Evening Post* noted that yet another synagogue had been established in Bricklayers' Hall.[89] This group, led by a silversmith named Moses Jacobs, acquired a burial ground in Ducking Pond Lane (Brady Street), and thereby founded the 'New Synagogue', the third of Ashkenazi Anglo-Jewry.[90]

The career of Marcus Moses and his family, however, was not quite over even after the formal establishment of the Hambro Synagogue on its new site. Marcus Moses emigrated to India in 1731, and died there four years later.[91] His son, confusingly called Moses Marcus, carried on the family tradition of maximizing trouble. Even before the court case over the new building in Magpie Alley, Moses Marcus had already converted to Christianity on New Year's Day 1722/3. This son had been the beneficiary of a Jewish education in Hamburg, sent there by his parents to acquire the knowledge which could not be obtained effectively in London. There he became a rabbi, but also met some German Protestant divines, who convinced him on his return to London to convert to Christianity. Having done so, Moses Marcus caused his father further dishonour by publishing a pamphlet about it, dedicated to the archbishop of Canterbury.[92] Curiously, he simultaneously sent his parents a letter from Amsterdam, dated 2 May 1724, in which he disavowed his actions. 'Ever Honoured Father & Mother', he wrote,

[87] The Hambro Synagogue remained on the same site until 1892, when it moved to Adler St., Commercial Road, staying there until 1936, when it rejoined the Great Synagogue from which it had seceded over two centuries before.

[88] Roth, *Great Synagogue*, 120.

[89] *Lloyd's Evening Post*, 29 May–1 June 1761: Bod. Lib., N 2287 c. 9.

[90] In 1837 they moved to Great St Helen's, and in 1915 to Stamford Hill. See below, p. 274.

[91] Roth, *Great Synagogue*, 119.

[92] Marcus, *Principal Motives*. On Bod. Lib., Mason AA 419, is a MS notation opp. the title-page: 'Moses Marcus taught me Hebrew. J. Sarum.'

I hope you will pardon ye folly I committed I never had Committed it if several people had not perswaded me to it telling me by turning Christian I could oblige you to give me a Sum of Money but as I was born a Jew so I will Die a Jew I go here to Sinagogue & Live as a Jew ought to do so I hope God Allmighty will pardon my Sins likewise I beg pardon of you.[93]

The parliamentary provision that parents must support their Protestant children thus proved to be a temptation for at least this impecunious offspring.

Moses Marcus enjoyed some notoriety in later years as one of that group of Jewish converts to Christianity who made a living peddling Jewish knowledge. In 1729 he issued an English translation of Carpzov's *Critica sacra Veteris Testamenti*, which had appeared in Leipzig only the previous year. Moses Marcus claimed to have heard the professor lecture there, 'more than once'. He saw this as his contribution to the challenge issued by Isaac Vossius, Richard Simon, William Whiston, and others about the biblical text. 'But I must further own,' he confessed,

that I had a particular Ambition to vindicate the *Jews*, my own Brethren and Countreymen, from so heavy and heinous a Charge, as that of maliciously and sacrilegiously corrupting and depraving the *sacret Text*. A hideous Crime, such, as I am confident, they could never have thought of without Horror and Detestation, having been *ever* most religiously scrupulous in regard to the *sacret Text*, and not at all less conscientious, in that respect, than even the most pious *Christians*. Their Infidelity, and Opposition to *Christ Jesus* my Saviour, (owing to the unconquerable Prejudices of Education) I heartily condemn.

Carpzov's book was printed with the notes of Moses Marcus, who described himself as 'A Converted *Jew*, and Teacher of the *Oriental Languages*'.[94]

Moses Marcus followed this first entry into theological polemics with another book two years later about circumcision. Apparently he was still nominally a Christian in spirit, if a Jew in flesh.[95] At one point he was put into prison for debt, and sent a begging letter to Sir Hans Sloane offering his linguistic services in return for his release.[96] He also produced 'A Scheme whereby any Person of the meanest Capacity may

[93] BL MS Lansdowne 988, fo. 374: repr. C. Roth, *Anglo-Jewish Letters* (London, 1938), 97–8.

[94] Moses Marcus, *A Defence of the Hebrew Bible, in Answer to . . . Whiston* (London, 1729), pp. iv–v, ix–x.

[95] Moses Marcus, *An Answer to the Letter to Dr Walerstand in Relation to the Point of Circumcision* (London, 1731).

[96] Moses Marcus to Sir Hans Sloane, 16 Aug. 1737: BL MS Sloane 4055, fos. 162–163^v.

in a very short time perfect himself in the Hebrew Language without the assistance of a Master'. Indeed, he claimed, many gentlemen had experienced to their entire satisfaction the virtues of his plan, which (alas) was never published.[97]

III

As has been seen, the period between the Toleration Act and the Jew Bill of 1753 was for the Jews in England one characterized by both fissure and consolidation. The single, unified synagogue of Cromwell's day divided first in about 1690 between Sephardim and Ashkenazim, and the Ashkenazim split apart in 1705, and would yet again in 1760-1. On the other hand, despite these communal disputes, and despite their turning to secular authorities to resolve their quarrels under the spotlight of tolerant Gentiles, there was little doubt during the first half of the eighteenth century that the Jewish community in England had very nearly as much right to be there as any other Nonconformist confession: more, perhaps, for they were explicitly loyal and apolitical. The Jews in early eighteenth-century English politics would provide material for a very short chapter indeed, but a number of instances did occur, and, as always with regard to the Jews, there was a certain synecdochic effect.

The most prominent exception to this general rule of Anglo-Jewish loyalty was the affair of Francis Francia, who was arrested on 19 September 1715 on the charge of attempting to overthrow the government by supporting the cause of the Old Pretender, the soi-disant James III, whose rebellion had begun a fortnight before in Scotland, 'The Fifteen'.[98] Francia was well known to be a sympathizer of the Stuart cause, having in May 1702 appeared as a witness in the prosecution of a man who had expressed some doubts about the legitimacy of Queen Anne.[99] Most importantly, from our point of view, Francis Francia was, in the words of one report,

of Jewish extraction, descended from the tribe that hold themselves to be that of Benjamin, and was born about 45 years since in the city of Bourdeaux in France, a place eminent for its produce and vent of most excellent wine and brandies, by trading in which with the English and other nations his father got great wealth.

[97] BL Add. MS 4377, fos. 34–5.
[98] The only secondary work on him is M. Lipton, 'Francis Francia—the Jacobite Jew', *TJHSE* 11 (1928), 190–205. Cf. Z. Szajkowski, 'French 17th–18th Century Sources for Anglo-Jewish History', *JJ Stud.* 12 (1961), 59–66.
[99] *Cal. SP Dom., 1702–3*, 59, 66.

According to the same unofficial document, Francia had been baptized in France, and was therefore shunned by the Jews in London, leaving him to conduct his business with English Gentiles. Nevertheless, when the day of his interrogation finally came, Francia declined to swear on the New Testament, producing out of his pocket instead a Jewish *siddur* of prayers.[100] In any case, there was never any doubt that he was a Jew, and his actions reflected to some extent on the community as a whole and would have a lasting effect. Even ten years later, the Jews were thought to be conducting a secret correspondence with the Pretender.[101]

The case against Francia was grounded on the interception of letters addressed to him from France, on the basis of private intelligence, in which connections with supporters of the Old Pretender there were made clear. When Francia's house was searched, further incriminating documents were discovered, especially copies of letters that he himself had sent abroad. Francia did everything in his power to have the trial delayed, quibbling over the careless errors in the indictment, and challenging as many jurors as possible. Once the trial was finally under way, Francia and his lawyers called to testify the accused's brother Simon Francia, his uncle Jacques Gonsales, and two others from Bordeaux, presumably Jews. Gonsales, like the accused, declined to swear on the New Testament, taking his oath instead on the Hebrew Bible, which had been permitted in English courts of law since the late 1660s. Francia argued that the copies of the treasonable letters were not in his handwriting, and that he could not be held responsible for receiving such writings. The Lord Chief Baron Bury, summing up the evidence, put the case very neatly:

Now if you believe those letters were wrote to him and by him, and that they contain correspondence of a treasonable nature, inciting or encouraging any persons to levy war against the King, or anything which shows he was privy and assenting to it, then he is guilty of High Treason. If you don't believe those letters were his, or that they don't amount to such a correspondence, then you must acquit him.

Within half an hour, Francia was acquitted.[102]

Such a verdict was enough to raise an eyebrow even in the eighteenth century. 'It must frankly be owned', wrote a contemporary, 'that some of

---

[100] Anon., *Case of Mr. Francis Francia, the Reputed Jew* (London, 1716): 12 pp. fol.

[101] Dr William Stratford to Edward Harley, 1 Jan. 1725–6: Hist. MSS Comm., *xxix*, *Portland VII*, 412–13. Cf. his further remarks about questionable Jewish stock trading: ibid. 415–18.

[102] *Case of . . . Francia, passim.* The official account of the case was published as *Tryal of Francis Francia* (London, 1717): 68 pp. fol.: Bod. Lib., L.Eng.B.75.c(2).

the best lawyers were of opinion that there was not sufficient legal proof of Francia's having written the treasonable letters found in his copybook and upon which the accusation was chiefly grounded.'[103] Nevertheless, there was a considerable amount of circumstantial evidence, and later on, at the beginning of the nineteenth century, proof was finally obtained that Francis Francia had been working for the Jacobite cause for quite some time, even after his arrest and acquittal.[104] As Father Graeme, one of the Old Pretender's supporters, wrote to the Jacobite duke of Mar at the end of 1717, 'the Jew is really a very honest fellow and a man of mettle'.[105] This was an assessment which would change over time, when it was discovered in the spring 'that he spreads about the town every word of news he gets from the other side, and tells a thousand lies to boot. I saw a letter', Graeme informed Mar in March 1718, 'he had from Lord Sunderland inviting him to go over to England and assuring him his fortune should be made, provided he performed what he had promised.'[106] This information may indeed make Francia a double agent of the English government, as has sometimes been alleged in a loyal attempt to spare a Jew from the taint of treason, but it is more likely that, like Roderigo Lopez in the sixteenth century, Francia was playing both sides with the strictly monetary aim of maximizing profits. Unlike Lopez, he seems to have succeeded.[107]

IV

Perhaps less successful at manipulating the secular authorities were some of the Jewish army contractors. We have already seen how Sir Solomon de Medina became the trusted agent of William III, and looked at the crucial role of Isaac Pereira in Ireland during the era of the Glorious Revolution.[108] The man who hoped to succeed them in all

[103] Abel Boyer, *Political State of Great-Britain* (London, 1717), 44–85: 'VI. An Historical account of the remarkable tryal of Francia, the Jew, for High Treason.'

[104] Hist. MSS Comm., lvi, *Stuart II*, 227: a letter of 11 June 1716 is the earliest document relating to Francia, in the Jacobite letters and papers obtained by the prince regent in 1804 from Italy.

[105] Graeme to Mar, 20 Oct. 1717: ibid., *Stuart V*, 148.

[106] Graeme to Mar, Mar. 1718: ibid., *Stuart VI*, 143, 211.

[107] Cf. ibid., *Stuart III*, 87, 525; *Stuart IV*, 428, 454, 490, 496, 499, 503, 510, 516, 519; *Stuart V*, 13, 38, 45, 71, 84, 95, 96, 148, 209, 229, 271, 287, 313, 414, 494; *Stuart VI*, 77, 128, 143, 211, 478–80, 552; *Stuart VII*, 12, 102, 225, 289, 348, 382, 394–5.

[108] For a clear picture of Solomon de Medina's part in the English war effort, see John Churchill, 1st duke of Marlborough, *The Letters and Dispatches*, ed. G. Murray (London, 1845), covering the period 1702–12, esp. i. 532–3, 580; ii. 196–7, 440; iii. 77–8, 322, 694; iv. 353, 359, 567–8, 692, 707; v. 170, 171, 255–6, 274, 484. See also

meanings of the word was Joseph Cortizos (1656–1742), originally from Antwerp, and probably connected with the firm of Machado and Pereira as well.[109] Cortizos became in 1705 the chief supplier of the allied forces fighting in the Spanish War of Succession on behalf of the Austrian Archduke Charles in order to secure the throne for him rather than for the French candidate Philip V, duke of Anjou, the grandson of Louis XIV.[110] In this capacity he was sent to Morocco to acquire draught animals and entered into correspondence with the sultan there.[111] On 15 May 1706 a contract was made between Cortizos and the earl of Peterborough, the allied commander of the military and the naval forces, for the provision of supplies for both the English and the Portuguese fighting men. But Peterborough was removed from his command nine months later, and, at least from April 1707, Joseph Cortizos was petitioning to have the money owed him for his work in the allied war effort.[112] In 1711 he left Barcelona and settled in London, where for the next thirty years he laboured ceaselessly to obtain the £100,000 (and that figure not including interest) which was his due. In the end, he seems to have received only half of this amount, but lost all of it in unsuccessful business deals as a result of bad luck and poor judgement of character.[113]

Joseph Cortizos, like Sir Solomon de Medina himself, had hoped to make substantial profits from supplying the allied armies in the War of the Spanish Succession. Both men were financially devastated by the ill faith of the allied governments: de Medina ended up nearly bankrupt, and Cortizos died in utter poverty.[114] Harley had been accused at the beginning of the war of ruining the English in order to enrich Jews and other foreigners, but this was clearly not the case at the end of the

Narcissus Luttrell, *A Brief Historical Relation of State Affairs* (Oxford, 1857), iv. 583; vi. 718–19; John Francis, *Chronicles and Characters of the Stock Exchange* (London, 1849), 30; and generally O. K. Rabinowicz, *Sir Solomon de Medina* (London, 1974).

[109] Generally, see C. Rubens, 'Joseph Cortissos and the War of the Spanish Succession', *TJHSE* 24 (1975), 114–33; and J. I. Israel, *European Jewry in the Age of Mercantilism, 1550–1750* (Oxford, 1985), 130–2.

[110] Carlos III appoints Cortizos, 25 July 1705 and 11 Sept. 1705: repr. Rubens, 'Cortissos', 122–3, from the Cortissos Papers, Mocatta Library, University College, London, AJ/144 (50 items). These papers were transferred to the Mocatta Library from the Jewish Museum, to which the papers had been presented in 1935 by the firm of public notaries De Pinna and Venn. They had guarded the documents since the 18th century as part of the claims made by Cortizos and his descendants against the British government: Rubens, 'Cortissos', 115.

[111] Carlos III to the sultan of Morocco, 28 June 1704: repr. Rubens, 'Cortissos', 122.

[112] Ibid. 123–4.

[113] Ibid. 126. Cf. Chancery Proceedings, *Cortissos* v. *Mead* (1722–31), and *Cortissos* v. *Mendes* (1724–35): ibid. 128–30.

[114] See Rabinowicz, *Medina*.

day.[115] Nevertheless, Jews were very prominent in supplying the allied armies against Louis XIV, not only in England and Holland, but even more dominantly in Germany, through Samuel Oppenheimer of Heidelberg, the *Oberskriegsfaktor* of the Empire, with his son Emmanuel Oppenheimer, and his associates Moses Gomperz and Samson Wertheimer, and others.[116] The association of Jews and generals invited comment and criticism, and the fact that de Medina had bribed Marlborough in order to secure the bread contracts was exploited by the general's enemies and helped bring him down in 1711–12.[117] But the military men knew the Jews could get the job done, as is very well brought out by Daniel Defoe, who included the following long remarks in his fictional memoirs of Captain Carleton:

The Jews, in whatever part of the world, are a people industrious in the increasing of Mammon; and, being accustomed to the universal methods of gain, are always esteemed best qualified for any undertaking where that bears a probability of being a perquisite. Providing bread and other requisites for an army was ever allowed to carry along with it a profit answerable; and Spain was not the first country where that people had engaged in such an undertaking. Besides, on any likely appearance of great advantage it is in the nature as well as practice of that race strenuously to assist one another, and that with the utmost confidence and prodigious alacrity.

After these general ruminations, 'Captain Carleton' continues to give the reader the benefit of his service with the allied armies in Spain:

One of that number, both competent and willing enough to carry on all undertakings of that kind, fortunately came at that juncture to solicit the Earl of Peterborough to be employed as *proveditor* to the army and troops, which were, or should be, sent into Spain.

It will easily be admitted that the Earl, under his present exigencies, did not decline to listen. And a very considerable sum being offered by way of advance, the method common in like cases was pursued, and the sum proposed accepted; by which means the Earl of Peterborough found himself put into the happy capacity of proceeding upon his first concerted project. The name of the Jew who signed the contract was Curtisos; and he and his friends with great punctuality advanced the expected sum of one hundred pounds sterling or very near it; which was immediately ordered into the hands of the paymaster of the forces. For, though the Earl took money of the Jews, it was not for his own but public use. According to agreement, bills were drawn for the value from

---

[115] Hist. MSS Comm., *xxix, Portland VIII*, 96.

[116] Israel, *European Jewry*, 123–37. Cf. Lt.-Col. Charles Russell to his wife, from Rhynbach, 28 Mar. 1743: Hist. MSS Comm., *lii, Astley*, 229; Egmont Diary, 8 Aug. 1739 and 1 Mar. 1743/4: Hist. MSS Comm., *lxiii, Egmont Diary*, iii. 79, 290.

[117] Rabinowicz, *Medina*, 61–74.

Lisbon, upon the Lord Godolphin (then Lord Treasurer), all which were on that occasion punctually complied with.

In short, 'Captain Carleton' concludes, the 'Earl of Peterborough having thus fortunately found means to supply himself with money, and by that with some horse', was able to conduct his campaign without delay.[118] But Peterborough himself would later remark that Cortizos 'dealt better with other people than they did with him', leaving the Jew without redress from the English authorities.[119] Joseph Cortizos, for his part, had himself painted on his arrival in England, poker-faced, holding his famous petition lightly in his hand. On his death in 1742, thirty years later, that scene looked particularly pathetic.[120]

The Jewish involvement in the War of the Spanish Succession was crucial, and almost entirely ranged on the side of England and her allies against Louis XIV. Once again afterwards in the period before the Jew Bill Anglo-Jewry was involved in international affairs, this time in an attempt to prevent the expulsion of their brethren from Prague in 1744. This was the culmination of the anti-Jewish policies of the Empress Maria Theresa, who found it difficult to stomach Jews within her territories. The legal basis for her policies of persecution was the Familiants Law of 1726, which limited Bohemian Jewry to 8,541 families. The regulation had the desired effect, as Bohemian Jewry became progressively weaker and smaller, until it could no longer defend itself against persistent attack.[121] The Jews of Prague called on their brethren all over Europe to come to their aid, and sent a copy of Maria Theresa's edict to the Ashkenazi Jews of London, 'together with several Letters that have been transmitted to them Requesting them to Commiserate their distress'd condition & Interceed with his Brittanick Majesty on their behalf'. The Ashkenazi Jews immediately sprang into action. Representing the Great Synagogue, Moses Hart and Aaron Franks sent a petition to King George II.[122] Moses Hart is well known to us, but Aaron Franks was equally important in his day. He was born in 1685, the son of Abraham Franks, one of the two Ashkenazim among

---

[118] [Daniel Defoe], *Memoirs of Captain Carleton*, ed. C. H. Hartmann (London, 1929; 1st pub. 1728; 2nd edn., 1741; 3rd edn., 1743; 4th edn., ed. Sir Walter Scott, 1808–9), 73–4.

[119] Rubens, 'Cortissos', 127.

[120] Portrait printed here in plate section.

[121] Israel, *European Jewry*, 239, and generally J. Krengel, 'Die englische Intervention zu Gunsten der böhmischen Juden im Jahre 1744', *Monatsschrift für Geschichte und Wissenschaft des Judenthums*, 44 (1900), 259–81; and A. Newman, 'The Expulsion of the Jews from Prague in 1745 and British Foreign Policy', *TJHSE* 22 (1970), 30–41.

[122] Moses Hart and Aaron Franks to George II, n.d. [=1744]: BL Add. MS 23,819, fo. 63[r].

the Jewish brokers appointed in 1697. His uncle, Benjamin Franks, had served with the infamous Captain William Kidd, and later gave evidence that helped bring his renegade employer to the gallows, which may be one reason why Benjamin Franks emigrated to New York. As we shall see, Aaron Franks mingled with English high society, entertaining Horace Walpole and others at his house at Isleworth. In old age he would marry the daughter of Moses Hart, just as his brother Isaac had married another of the daughters, in the presence of King George I, after having won £20,000 in the lottery of 1719.[123] In short, Moses Hart and Aaron Franks had a strong claim to represent the oldest Ashkenazi community when they appealed to George II.[124]

Moses Hart and Aaron Franks explained to the English king that their brethren in Bohemia had been expelled without any reason given at all, leading them to suspect that they had been falsely accused of some crime. If some individual Jews were guilty of crimes they should be brought to justice, but it was wrong to expel the entire community, which Hart and Franks numbered at about 50,000 families. Closing, the two Jews begged George II to intercede with Maria Theresa on their behalf, asking her to revoke the edict and to establish a commission of inquiry in order to discriminate between the guilty and the innocent.[125] The Jews' appeal had some effect on the king, who received Hart and Franks in audience. More practically, George II had William Stanhope, earl of Harrington, in his capacity as Secretary of State instruct the English ambassador at Vienna, Sir Thomas Robinson, to deal with the matter. Harrington set the number of Jews in Bohemia at 60,000 families, and reported that upon application of the 'principal Merchants of the Jewish Nation established here', and 'His Majesty finding that the States General have already interposed Their Good Offices in Their Behalf', it was the king's pleasure that he join with the Dutch envoy in trying to prevent the expulsion from taking place. He was to point out to the Viennese court that not only would other nations be against a policy of collective punishment, but Maria Theresa in her capacity as queen of Hungary would lose a good deal of revenue from the expulsion of so many taxpayers. Harrington enclosed copies of the petition of the

[123] *Original Weekly Journal*, 7 Nov. 1719, p. 1581 (Isaac Franks: marriage and lottery); A. Bateman to Abigail Harley, 27 Sept. 1720, reporting wedding of previous day, 'where all the nobility and gentry were invited': Hist. MSS Comm., *xxix, Portland V*, 602. C. Roth, *The Rise of Provincial Jewry* (London, 1950), 16, claims that it was Moses Hart who won the lottery in 1720. Cf. H. F. Finberg, 'Jewish Residents in Eighteenth-Century Twickenham', *TJHSE* 16 (1952), 129–35.

[124] Moses Hart also had a grand house on the Thames between Twickenham and Isleworth: Finberg, 'Twickenham', 129.

[125] Hart and Franks to George II, [1744].

English Jews, and further information that Hart and Franks had obtained from Bohemia. 'I am to add to what is above,' he concluded,

> that, as His Majesty does extremely commiserate the terrible Circumstances of Distress to which so many poor & innocent Families must be reduced, if this Edict takes Place, He is most earnestly desirous of procuring the Repeal of it by His Royal Intercession, in such Manner that the Guilty only may be brought to Punishment; for obtaining which, you are to exert yourself with all possible Zeal & Diligence.[126]

Sir Thomas Robinson's reply from Vienna on 27 March 1745 shows how involved the English government was in trying to stop Maria Theresa from expelling her Jews. Robinson was at a loss in trying to determine the empress's motives: 'My Lord,' he wrote to Harrington in a secret report written partly in cipher,

> there is no accounting for this singular affair, but by imputing it to some rash vow, or at least to some very early insurmountable prejudice in the course of her education. Her aversion to the sight of a Jew was too great to be concealed, when at Pressburg she could not pass from the town to her palace, but through the very street that was thronged by that people, & the first order she gave upon her arrival in Prague the year before last, was that no Jew should presume to enter into the precinct of the palace during her residence there, but as to the supposition of some rash vow, that obstacle might be removed, one would think, by a papal absolution, the Pope having by his Nuntio been as solicitous for the repeal of the edict, as the Elector of Mentz, or the King of Poland, or any other catholic Prince whatever.

So just as Jews throughout Europe were appealing to their governments to intervene, the English king was not alone in trying to reverse the expulsion of the Jews from Bohemia, supported even by the most Catholic pope. Not that Robinson met with much success: 'Bad arguments & despairing gestures were all we had in return', he reported. When Robinson's pleas reached Maria Theresa through Count Ulfeld, his man at the Viennese Court, she was 'bien ulcérée', and 'the Queen gave him too disagreeable a parting that he should remember it all his whole life, for what she has said upon the particular affair of the Jews in question, had drawn the repetition of many old reproaches'. Robinson closed in the hope that George II would recognize that his envoy had done his duty, even if success was not immediately forthcoming.[127]

The English intervention in the case of Bohemian Jewry was not only

---

[126] Harrington to Robinson, from Whitehall, 28 Dec. 1744/8 Jan. 1745: BL Add. MS 23,819, fo. 61^{r-v}.

[127] Robinson to Harrington, 27 Mar. 1745, from Vienna: PRO SP 80/168: repr. Newman, 'Expulsion', 38–41.

extraordinary in itself, but also effective. In 1748 Maria Theresa was obliged to moderate the expulsion order, and many of the Jews who had left returned to Prague and the community survived to reap the benefits of the Edict of Toleration issued by her son Joseph II. Bohemian Jewry had nevertheless suffered a severe blow, delivered ironically by the successor to Rudolf II, who in the previous century had conducted cabbalistic discussions with the rabbi of Prague.[128] While it is true that the empress's action aroused a storm of protest across Europe, perhaps sparked by Jews but delivered by Gentile governments, it is instructive that the leaders of Anglo-Jewry were able to convince the English authorities to act on their behalf even before it was known that other countries were protesting the expulsion as well.[129] Likewise, the Sephardi and Ashkenazi congregations in London clubbed together on this issue, leaving all communal rivalry aside, to create a fund for refugee relief, capped by a joint administrative committee.[130] In a sense, this body would later be seen as part of the ancestry of the Board of Deputies which was created in 1760.

V

The Jewish support of the allied cause in the War of the Spanish Succession; the English support of the Jewish cause in having Maria Theresa rescind her arbitrary edict of expulsion for Bohemian Jewry: these were mighty issues which give some indication of Jewish involvement in high policy during the first half of the eighteenth century. As far as the general public was concerned, however, the event which most attracted their attention to the Jewish question during these years was more likely to be the highly embarrassing court case against Kitty da Costa Villareal for breach of promise, brought forward by her disappointed cousin in 1732. Kitty, or Catherine, also known by her Jewish name of Rachel, was the granddaughter of Alvaro da Costa, born in Lisbon and one of the pioneers of Anglo-Jewry.[131] The eighteenth-century Jewish community in England was extraordinarily intermarried, and almost everyone was ultimately related to everyone else, but among

---

[128] See Israel, *European Jewry*, 39–41, 239.

[129] For an instructive parallel, see H. Z. (J. W.) Hirschberg, 'Jews and Jewish Affairs in the Relations between Great Britain and Morocco in the 18th Century', in H. J. Zimmels, *et al.* (eds.), *Essays Presented to Chief Rabbi Israel Brodie* (London, 1967), 153–81.

[130] Newman, 'Expulsion', 30.

[131] Alvaro da Costa seems to have been the first Jew to be naturalized in England: *Commons Journal*, 24 Oct. 1667; 'A List of Jewish Persons Endenizened and Naturalised 1609–1799', ed. W. S. Samuel, *et al.*, *TJHSE* 7 (1970), 115.

Kitty's closer and more famous relatives was her uncle by marriage Antonio (Isaac), first baron Lopes Suasso, the influential financier whose services to Charles II of Spain were so great that this practising Jew was actually made a baron of the Spanish Netherlands. At the age of 18 she was married to a man over twenty years her senior, John/Joseph/ Isaac da Costa Villareal. The marriage was in itself an honourable one, but was to set off a chain reaction whose effects were felt in Anglo-Jewry until well into the nineteenth century.[132]

Kitty's future husband, Joseph da Costa Villareal, had arrived in England in 1726, already a wealthy man. According to a newspaper account dated 26 August 1726:

We are informed that Mr. John Da Costa Villareal, one of the rich Jews who, being threatened by the Inquisition, made his escape lately from Lisbon with his family, consisting of about seventeen persons, and his effects, during a great conflagration in the city, hath, since his arrival here, given the sum of £2,000 to be distributed among the poor Jews in the city and suburbs of London. He was Proveditor to the King of Portugal's armies, and acquitted himself in that and all other stations with good Reputation; and has brought over with him to the value of £300,000 and upwards.[133]

A few months after his arrival in England he made a will in his own hand in the Portuguese language, giving thanks for 'those goods which the same God has been pleased to give me which were gott by my care and Industry In pursuit of which I was continually employed maintaining my selfe and my house'. The sum total of his possessions was substantially less than the figure quoted in the press, but it came nevertheless to nearly £90,000, of which over two-thirds was given to the synagogues of the Sephardi diaspora and their charities, with £32,500 going to Bevis Marks alone. These were certainly substantial bequests, but possibly not inconsistent with the wishes of an aging bachelor.[134]

---

[132] See generally M. J. Landa, 'Kitty Villareal, the Da Costas and Samson Gideon', *TJHSE* 13 (1936), 271–91. Landa also published a novel about Kitty Villareal in 1934. Her genealogy, and that of 18th-century Anglo-Jewry in general, can be pieced together by a reader with a good deal of patience from the family tree compiled by the celebrated naturalist and embezzler Emanuel Mendes da Costa, FRS (expelled), whose mother was Kitty's father's sister: BL Add. MS 29,867, fos. 19ᵛ–28ʳ, printed in rationalized form in the *Gents. Mag.* 82 (pt. 1) (1812), 21–4. Cf. the 'Jewish Pedigrees' in the Collyer-Ferguson collection, Mocatta Library, University College, London.

[133] *Daily Journal* (26 Aug. 1726): repr. Landa, 'Kitty Villareal', 272–3. Cf. Luttrell, *Relation*, vi. 622. Joseph/John's father was also known as John, but he was not a rich man. The father died in 1737, both his sons having predeceased him.

[134] The English trans. of Villareal's will comes from the notebooks of P. C. Webb, solicitor to the Jews. Specifically, the synagogues to which money was left were those of Amsterdam, Leghorn, Genoa, Bordeaux, Bayonne, Rome, and Jerusalem: BL MS Lansdowne 630, fos. 27ʳ–31ʳ.

On 24 May 1727 the situation was changed substantially when Joseph/John da Costa Villareal married Catherine/Kitty/Rachel da Costa. They had two children, Sarah (b. 1728) and Abraham (b. 1729), and in order to provide for their financial security their father made a codicil to his will on 16 April 1730 appointing his wife and children his sole heirs. This was fortunate timing, since Joseph Villareal had little time left, and died eight months later, on 27 December 1730, aged 42. Clearing away his papers, a third document was found, also in Portuguese, making a number of small gifts to various people and charities. Unfortunately, it seems to have been only the draft of another codicil, undated, blotted, unsigned, and indeed only partly legible. Joseph Villareal in his draft codicil of 1730 made some vague reference to the possibility of further changes and conditions, and many thought that this document was the result of deep and thoughtful ruminations. The Sephardi congregation of Bevis Marks hoped that this surfeit of documentation might somehow put back the clock to the original will of 1726 which granted them £32,500 in benefactions. They turned to their solicitor P. C. Webb, who, it should be said, went about the case with complete scrupulousness, and sought the advice of five of his legal colleagues before coming to the view himself that only the properly signed document of 1730 was valid. Indeed, it was the only one admitted to probate, and the effect of his decision was that Kitty da Costa Villareal was left a very rich widow indeed.[135]

Only three weeks after her husband's death, Kitty Villareal became engaged to Philip/Jacob Mendes da Costa, two years her senior, and her first cousin, his mother being her father's sister. This branch of the family was not in itself objectionable: Philip's brother Emanuel would one day be secretary of the Royal Society and an international authority on fossils, even if his end would be disgrace.[136] There had been some talk of a family agreement when the two fiancés were mere children, forgotten during Kitty's first marriage, and now conveniently remembered. But, more importantly, Philip was soon seen as an undesirable adventurer interested in the young widow's fortune alone, and her family kidnapped her to her father Joseph da Costa's country estate at Coppeed Hall, Totteridge, where she was kept under close guard.[137] Kitty's father also prevailed upon her to assign to him the

---

[135] BL MS Lansdowne 630, fos. 31ʳ–37ʳ.

[136] On Emanuel Mendes da Costa, see D. S. Katz, 'The Chinese Jews and the Problem of Biblical Authority in Eighteenth- and Nineteenth-Century England', *EHR* 105 (1990), 893–919.

[137] Jacob [Philip] Mendes da Costa, *Proceedings at Large in the Arches Court of Canterbury, between Mr. Jacob Mendes da Costa and Mrs. Catherine da Costa Villa Real, Both of the Jewish Religion, and Cousin Germans. Relating to a Marriage Contract* (n.p.=London,

guardianship of her two children, and to agree that if they should die before coming of age, he would have half of their inheritance, estimated at £27,000 apiece.[138] Philip was unable to see her, let alone marry her, and, after the year of mourning for Kitty's first husband had passed, he turned to the Court of the Arches, the court of the archbishop of Canterbury, which entertained pleas of first instance. Legally, this was perfectly proper, as the ecclesiastical courts dealt with matrimonial offences, but it is ironic that on the first occasion in which a Jew turned to a higher court in England, this was the branch of the judicial system chosen.

The case took a very long time to grind through the legal system. Kitty had papers served on her on 11 January 1732, but the sworn affidavits, in place of oral evidence, were not delivered until the spring of the following year. In the end, on 25 June 1733, Dr Bettesworth ruled in the case, deciding against Philip Mendes da Costa and in favour of Kitty, or at least of her wealthy father.[139] Interestingly, the solicitor brought into the deliberation Alvaro/Jacob Israel Suasso, the brother of the second baron, an important figure in Sephardi Jewry in his own right, and first cousin to both parties.[140] Philip, however, was unwilling to see Kitty's fortune slip entirely out of his grasp, especially as it was now estimated to be closer to £200,000, twice its original valuation. He turned now to the King's Bench, but, despite numerous legal opinions and feverish activity, without hearing witnesses Lord Chief Justice Hardwicke on 27 February 1734 at Westminster Hall upheld the previous verdict at the Court of Arches. Philip Mendes da Costa was left to pay the £180 in costs.[141] A contemporary 'Grotesque Pantomine' portrayed a Jew named Mordecai, 'with Horns upon his Head', suitor to Kitty, in the company of a Harlequin.[142]

1734): this book, over 400 pp. in length, covers the case in great detail. Landa, 'Kitty Villareal', 275–6, says that there is an ed. of 1734 under the name of 'Philalethes', and that Roth found one of 1735. C. Roth, *Magna Bibliotheca Anglo-Judaica* (London, 1937), 249, says that the other edn. (J. Jacobs and L. Wolf, *Bibliotheca Anglo-Judaica* (London, 1888), no. 621) is apparently non-existent and has been deleted from the BL catalogue. But no. 622 in Jacobs and Wolf = *The Famous Jew Case between J. M. da Costa and Mrs. C. da Costa Villa Real* (1735), 8°.

[138] Clement Tudway Swanston, *Reports of Cases Argued and Determined in the High Court of Chancery, during the Time of Lord Chancellor Eldon* (London, 1821–7), ii. 533, 535: agreement dated 3 May 1734. For a contemporary engraving of Joseph da Costa's estate, see Hyamson, *Sephardim*, opp. p. 96.

[139] Mendes da Costa, *Proceedings*; Landa, 'Kitty Villareal', 274–6.

[140] Alvaro Suasso was also elected a fellow of the Royal Society in 1735: Hyamson, *Sephardim*, 110.   [141] Legal opinions now BL MS Lansdowne 588.

[142] Theophilus Cibber, *The Harlot's Progress* (London, 1733), 10–11: performed at the Theatre Royal in Drury Lane.

By 1734, then, Kitty Villareal's situation had much improved. Still only 25 years old, she was now not only an extremely wealthy and unmarried woman, but untroubled by legal action designed to make her share the wealth with others. It was in this capacity that Kitty met William Mellish, ex-Eton and Cambridge. 'The family of Mellish were originally merchants, trading to Portugal, by which they amassed immense wealth', wrote the author of a nineteenth-century history of Nottinghamshire. 'The father of the above gentleman, Edward Mellish, Esq., it was who first purchased the estate at Blyth, which his son embellished with many choice and magnificent works.'[143] William Mellish was married on 27 February 1735 to 'Mrs *Villa Real*, Widow, Daughter to Mr *Da Costa*, a rich Jew Merchant of this City, with a Fortune of 35,000 l.', and the bride was baptized at St George's, Bloomsbury.[144] While not the first intermarriage since the readmission of the Jews, this Jewish invasion of the English landed gentry seems to have passed without noticeable comment. The bride's wealth was no doubt a significant attraction, although from the Jewish side we find rather more demonstrable objections.

Indeed, Kitty's wealthy father Joseph da Costa fought her in the Chancery Court in 1738 when she tried to recover her two children, who were still living with their grandfather at Coppeed Hall. Kitty was not permitted to visit them alone without a certain Frenchwoman being present. She asked the court to allow the children to live with her and Mr Mellish, or at least to sanction unchaperoned visits and liberty for the children to visit her. By that time she had two boys from her marriage to William Mellish: Charles (b. 1737) and Joseph (b. 1735). Kitty's father retained the Attorney-General, Sir John Welles, and Nicholas Fazakerly, MP. Lord Hardwicke once again found her in his court, this time in his role as Lord Chancellor, and once again ruled in her favour. Kitty recovered her Jewish children unconditionally, and had them baptized forthwith.[145]

---

[143] Thomas Bailey, *Annals of Nottinghamshire* (London, 1852–5), iii. 1189. A painting of Kitty Villareal and her two children by J. Ellys done during this period (1732) was in 1936 still at Hodsock Priory where the last of the Mellishes then lived: Landa, 'Kitty Villareal', 289.   [144] *Gents. Mag.* 5 (1735), 107; Landa, 'Kitty Villareal', 277–9.

[145] *Villareal* v. *Mellish*, in Chancery, 17 Mar. 1737: repr. Swanston, *Reports*, ii. 533–9: Swanston says that he prints the report from a MS in his possession, which agrees nearly verbatim with a note among Lord Colchester's MSS, and notes a further, but very imperfect, report in 2 Atk. 14, under the title of *Mellish* v. *Da Costa*. Swanston prints the document in connection with the Bedford Charity Case of 1819, in which it was ruled that Jews in Bedford were ineligible to have benefit from it: ibid. ii. 470–532, and cf. below, p. 363–5. The court also noted that Kitty and her new husband ratified the custody agreement in Mar. 1735, immediately after their marriage, without any protest having been made: ibid. ii. 535. Cf. *Daily Advertiser*, 12 Apr. 1738.

What is perhaps most striking about the argumentation in Kitty Villareal's custody case is how straightforward the discussion actually was. No one denied that as 'to what may concern the religion of the infants . . . that should be the choice of every person'. The supposed spiritual advantages of a Christian upbringing were not put forward, although the court did discuss the social and economic results of the children being a different religion from the newly converted mother. Lord Chancellor Hardwicke summed up the case nicely:

Much has been said on the point of religion; holds the true state of the question to be, whether this court shall not take the infants out of the hands of a person who has no right of guardianship, and put them into the hands of the person who has the right, and is of the religion of this country? Do not by any means intend, but declare the contrary, to take the children of Jews from their parents, any farther than as required by the act of parliament.

Hardwicke thereupon ordered 'the children to be delivered forthwith to the mother'.[146]

All of these difficulties in the past, and equipped with a Christian wife, two children of his own, and two Christian stepchildren, William Mellish was free to fulfil the duties of his standing and present himself for election to Parliament in 1741. His wife's vast fortune was no doubt of some aid in this achievement, and certainly she would have been pleased to have her own social standing thus ensured. Curiously, a strange legend grew up about Mellish's election to Parliament. According to the story, Mellish 'in early life married a lady of the Jewish persuasion, of very large expectations, but which possessions, by a whimsical clause in the will of her father, her husband could not claim until chosen a member of parliament'. This, of course, is utter nonsense, as Kitty's fortune came from her late husband, not from her wealthy, but now estranged, father. 'Accordingly,' the tale continues, 'Mr. Mellish, at the first opportunity, offered himself as a candidate for the borough of East Retford.' The plan was for Mellish to take two horses of different colours with him to Retford on polling day, and to send a particular one back with a messenger so that his anxious wife could know the outcome as soon as the man was in sight. As readers of classical literature must already have guessed, a horse of a different colour was dispatched, with disastrous results: 'At this intelligence the poor lady, whose feelings were before wrought up to the most painful pitch of anxiety, fell into strong hysterical fits, from which she could never be perfectly recovered; so that within the course of two or three days, nature became entirely exhausted, and she sank in death.'[147] In fact, Kitty Villareal died in

---

[146] Swanston, *Reports*, ii. 535.

[147] Bailey, *Annals*, iii. 1189–90. Cf. John S. Piercy, *The History of Retford* (Retford, 1828), 74–5 n.; Cornelius Brown, *A History of Nottinghamshire* (London, 1891), 174–5.

1747, six years after her husband began to sit for East Retford.[148]

The later history of Kitty Villareal's family is itself interesting, adding more 'firsts' to those already accumulated. Sarah/Elizabeth Villareal, baptized in 1738 at the age of 10, in 1747 married the heir of the first Viscount Galway, who himself succeeded to the title in 1751 as the second viscount of that name. By this means, Elizabeth Villareal became the first Jew to marry into the peerage.[149] Kitty's Jewish son William (formerly Abraham) Villareal was somewhat less successful in infiltrating English high society. He had achieved some standing: in 1757 he was selected to be High Sheriff of Nottinghamshire, although he wrote to the duke of Newcastle asking to be excused.[150] Less than a year later William Villareal was quick off the mark when he heard that Brigadier Lord Howe, MP for Nottingham, had been killed fighting the French in America in July 1758, offering himself as a candidate for the now vacant seat.[151] Newcastle put him off immediately, making the excuse that the next member really depended on the wishes of Lord Howe's mother, who in the event planted her younger son Colonel Howe in his brother's place.[152] Privately, Newcastle wrote to Job Charlton, MP for Newark, expressing his disgust that Villareal should think of standing for the great town of Nottingham at all.[153] In hindsight, considering the fact that William Howe would command the British forces at Bunker Hill, perhaps neither man was entirely suitable for high public office.[154]

VI

If historical thinking is always teleological, the history of the Jews in England in the first half of the eighteenth century takes on a tragic,

[148] The documents published in Hyamson, *Sephardim*, 119–20 n. relate to Kitty's sister-in-law Rachel, the wife (and niece!) of her late husband's brother Jacob and not to herself (also known as Rachel among the Jews).

[149] Kitty Villareal is thus the ancestor of the marquis of Crewe as well, whose second wife was a descendant of N. M. Rothschild. Cf. N. Perry, 'La Chute d'une famille séfardie, les Mendes da Costa de Londres', *Dix-huitième siècle*, 13 (1981), 11–25.

[150] William Villareal to Newcastle, 19 Nov. 1757: BL Add. MS 32,876, fo. 35: repr. *TJHSE* 13 (1936), 284.

[151] Villareal to Newcastle, 25 Aug. 1758: BL Add. MS 32,883, fo. 98: repr. *TJHSE* 13 (1936), 284.

[152] Newcastle to Villareal, 29 Aug. 1758: BL Add. MS 32,883, fo. 170: repr. *TJHSE* 13 (1936), 285.

[153] Newcastle to Job Charlton, 28 Aug. 1758: BL Add. MS 32,883, fos. 141–3: repr. *TJHSE* 13 (1936), 285. Another candidate who presented himself, whom Newcastle also mentions with disgust, was Sir Robert Clifton, who had been imprisoned for debt and was involved in a scandal with Lady Lamb.

[154] Cf. BL Add. MS 32,883, fo. 308.

almost a doomed character in light of the dénouement of the Jew Bill controversy of 1753. The ground gained in the courts, the increase in social acceptability, and the very regularity of the Jewish presence in London pales before the later crisis, which seems to show how illusory that social progress had been. If the Jewish military contractors, the aid to Bohemian Jewry, and the case of Kitty Villareal were the most public demonstrations of English actions and attitudes towards the Jews, other rather more long-term trends can be traced as well, which ultimately would have an even greater effect.

For one thing, descriptions of the Jews and their worship in the first part of the eighteenth century no longer portray them in quite so eccentric a fashion as had been the case previously. Nevertheless, it was often almost as difficult for English visitors to comprehend what they were seeing as it had been for the first guests in the years following the readmission. John Grindley the Shropshire farmer was by his own testimony 'permitted many Times into the Jews Synagogue which is clean and decent', but what he reported was far from encouraging:

what I have seen with these Eyes I can say, the Man of the most honourable and holy Employment, as I did believe, because he held up the Law to all the rest, and turned him round about with the Law as I took it to be in his two Hands, when that very Man came in, he sat him down on his A—se with his Hat on his Head without ever kneeling down, and he had not sate above 10 Minutes I am sure, but he did call to another Man that did sit 4 or 5 Yards off to bring him a Pinch of Snuff, and I saw the other bring it to him and he took it, there is no Doubt but he had an attentive Thought upon his Creator, there came in some about 8 a Clock in the Morning or quickly after, and some about 9 a Clock, and some about 10, and some near 11, some would stay about 5 Minutes, some 15, and some about half an Hour, some 2, and some near 3 Hours, some would sing, and some would pray, and a great many at the same Time did talk about their Business, but every one with his Hat on his Head, both coming in, and all along, and going out, to express their Zeal to the Service of God indeed.

Grindley gives no indication if his visit was to the Sephardi congregation at Bevis Marks, or to one of the Ashkenazi synagogues, but his interest in the Jews was more than transitory. It appears as well that his sarcasm was well repaid. According to Grindley, on 11 November 1721 he gave fifty books of some kind to the Jews, probably conversionist literature, and when he returned to the synagogue some days later, although some Jews did ask him for more books, others broke into singing, 'there is the Farmer that gave us the Books', and made him look rather ridiculous.[155]

---

[155] John Grindley, *The Jews Generosity Explain'd* (London, n.d. [1722]), esp. 3, 31–2. Cf. his earlier book *The Farmers Advice, to the Unbelieving Jews* (Shrewsbury, n.d. [?1720]), where he describes himself as of Ellesmere, Shropshire.

Foreign visitors also made it their business to see the Jews at prayer in Hanoverian London. César de Saussure, a widely travelled diplomat and the scion of a Huguenot family at Lausanne, came to London in the spring of 1729 and paid a call at the Great Synagogue of the Ashkenazi Jews. Saussure thought that the chief reason for the toleration and open worship which the Jews enjoyed in England was their commercial contribution. 'They are not forced to bear a distinctive mark,' he notes, 'as is the case in many countries; if you see Jews wearing beards you will know that they are Rabbis, or new-comers to this country.' Saussure tells the amusing story of meeting a young Englishwoman at the synagogue, who had also come to observe the Jews in their natural setting. A circumcision was to take place that day, and Saussure convinced the woman that it was the godfather who was to undergo this holy operation. Although she rose to leave, 'her curiosity got the better of her modesty', and it was not until the infant was brought in that she realized that she had been the victim of a foreigner's joke.[156]

Don Manoel Gonzales, a Portuguese merchant of New Christian descent on both sides, made an even more extensive Jewish tour of London when he visited in 1730. He seems to have seen both Bevis Marks and the Great Synagogue, and was struck by the fact that women sat separately from men, and that the Jewish house of worship faced east, as was customary among Christians. He also provided his readers with a detailed description of the Jewish section on the Royal Exchange, noting the Jewish station at the inner south-eastern corner, sandwiched in between the Spanish, French, and Portuguese merchants: 'those who have business with them, assemble distinctly; so that any merchant or commander of a vessel is readily found, if it be known to what country he trades'. When Gonzales went to Cambridge, he also took an interest in his supposed ancestors, and suggested that the round church in the formerly Jewish district might have been their synagogue.[157]

Similarly, Jews in early Hanoverian England sometimes turned to the English language and described their own community. The first to do so was Abraham Mears, who converted to Christianity to the consternation of his distinguished Ashkenazi family. He published his book, over 300 pages in length, under the pseudonym of 'Gamaliel ben Pedahzur, Gent.', but it was not long before his true identity was known. Although

---

[156] César de Saussure, *A Foreign View of England in the Reigns of George I. & George II: The Letters of Monsieur César de Saussure to his Family*, trans. and ed. Madame van Muyden (London, 1902), 317, 328–30. The exact date of his visit was 29 Apr. 1729.

[157] Don Manoel Gonzales, *The Voyage*, in *Travels*, ed. John Pinkerton (London, 1808–14), ii. 1, 49, 53, 124. Cf. William Maitland, *The History of London* (London, 1739), 420 for another near-contemporary description.

Mears's aim was to discredit his parent community by revealing superstitious practices and general foolishness, his motives do not necessary invalidate his entire testimony. For example, he claims that among the Jews in London there are some women 'that pretend to cure all Distempers, which they believe to proceed from an evil Eye, by the Sympathy of Fumigation'. The usual procedure was for the patient to present a piece of his clothing, which the woman would hold over a certain smoking substance; when returned to its owner, it would almost always guarantee a complete cure. The price varied with the item of clothing: a child's cap, one shilling; a man's pair of trousers, half a crown, with Sephardim paying more than Ashkenazim 'because the Smoakers are *Germans*'. While perhaps not a practice to boast about, the description Mears gives is entirely consistent with numerous other methods of practical medicine, and there is no reason to dismiss it out of hand. Most significant, of course, was the fact that Mears printed in over 150 pages the entire Jewish prayer-book, followed by the *haftoroth* and the grace after meals in an additional forty pages. This was the first time that this central core of the Jewish daily worship had been made available to the Christian reading public, and to the less knowledgeable Jews themselves, who, Mears wrote, 'may not be less obliged to me for explaining the Meanings of, and citing the Quotations for theirs; to instruct the Illiterate of their Nation, in what they are ignorant of at present'. Indeed, it seems hardly likely that before Mears's book appeared, the vast majority of Anglo-Jewish women had any idea of the meanings of the Hebrew prayers.[158]

Mears made his criticism known to the general public in the English language. Dr Meyer Schomberg confided his remarks to a thirty-eight-page Hebrew manuscript which was, if anything, even more devastating, if more discreet. Schomberg was born in Fetzburg, Germany in about 1690, trained as a physician, and was admitted to the Royal College of Physicians in 1722. His success was legendary, and he soon became one of the most widely demanded doctors in London.[159] Whether because of envy, or more substantive reasons, Schomberg fell out with his co-religionists at the Great Synagogue, who objected to the fact that he carried a sword and travelled on the Sabbath to call on his patients. Moreover, he worked mostly outside the community, claiming that the

---

[158] 'Gamaliel Ben Pedahzur, Gent.' [Abraham Mears], *The Book of Religion, Ceremonies, and Prayers; of the Jews* (London, 1738), esp. pp. iv, 77–8, 96–251, 252–91. The introduction appeared anonymously in 1753, under the title *Jewish Ritual: or, The Religious Customs and Ceremonies of the Jews* (London, 1753). The identity of Mears was known at least to John Clemens, a correspondent to the *Gents. Mag.* 28 (1758), 468. See also C. Roth, 'Gamaliel Ben Pedahzur and his Prayer Book', *MJHSE* 2 (1935), 1–8.
[159] *DNB*.

Jews would not pay his rates. In any case, the central section of Schomberg's manuscript is a demonstration of the myriad ways in which the Jews of London broke the Ten Commandments, especially the Sabbath, ate unclean food, and married Gentile women.[160] Schomberg's particular gripe was against Jacob de Castro Sarmento, who was elected to the Royal Society over Schomberg's protests.[161] Schomberg's rejection of his community led to his own family's abandoning the faith, and all but one of his sons left Judaism and converted to Christianity, becoming, respectively, a physician, a dramatic writer, a lieutenant-colonel in the army, and commander of the naval detachment with Wolfe at Quebec (subsequently knighted).[162] Nevertheless, the apostasy of the Schomberg family does not negate his criticisms, which fit in well with other contemporary reports about the conduct of Anglo-Jewry from Rabbi Sasportas onwards.

The accounts of Mears and Schomberg were critical in the extreme, and each had his reasons for placing the Jews in such a negative light. A far more positive and, in many ways, comprehensive account was published in May 1752 in a London periodical. The interest in the Jews began the previous month with a large engraving of the Jewish synagogue at Bevis Marks, and was followed in May with an account of the 'present State of the Jewish Nation and their *Worship*, as now practised in England by the Portuguese and Spanish Jews'. According to the editor, the text was written by a Jew 'from among the chief of that people', and in fact the account does not belie that advertisement. One of the interesting facts presented here is the author's estimate of the Sephardi population of mid-eighteenth-century London as 'about 600 families, containing about 2000 people'. The Gentile reading public was informed that the salary of the *haham* was about £200, apart from a free house, fuel, and candles, and any additional fees that he might obtain at weddings, which 'in rich families are very considerable'. Preaching, of course, was still in Spanish. In light of contemporary disputes about placement in church services, readers must have been gratified to note that the same applied to the Jews:

---

[160] Meyer Schomberg, 'Emunat Omen': Jewish Theological Seminary, New York City, MS Adler 2245: photograph of entire MS repr. E. R. Samuel, 'Dr. Meyer Schomberg's Attack on the Jews of London, 1746', *TJHSE* 20 (1964), 83–111 (101–11 being the reproduction). Chief Rabbi N. M. Adler exhibited the MS at the Anglo-Jewish Exhibition of 1887 (no. 783), but it is unknown how the Adler family acquired the document.

[161] See now R. Barnett, 'Dr Jacob de Castro Sarmento and Sephardim in Medical Practice in 18th-Century London', *TJHSE* 27 (1982), 84–114.

[162] *DNB*; Roth, *Great Synagogue*, 83–5; [Ralph Schomberg], *The Modern Quacks Detected* (London, 1752), esp. 19–20.

In the synagogue each male person has his place assign'd him, according to his rank; the single gentlemen are generally placed in the middle of the synagogue; the poor, charity children, &c. are plac'd behind the pillars; the *parnassim* or elders are placed in an alcove behind the pillars on the left-hand side going into the synagogue . . . The women are seated in the galleries above, and are quite separate from the men in the place of worship. An example worthy imitation.

The anonymous Jewish author went on to describe the cemetery, concluding funereally that the 'excommunicated are buried by 'emselves'. His discussion of Jewish holidays is also interesting, and worthy of a man self-described as an acquaintance of 'the celebrated Dr. *Pococke*', the son of a more famous father.[163]

Such accounts, rather favourable than not, could not but produce more direct advocates of the Jews. Certainly the most famous of these was John Toland, in his anonymous analysis of the reasons for naturalizing the Jews in Great Britain and Ireland, 'Containing also, A Defence of the *Jews* against All vulgar Prejudices in all Countries'. In many ways this is a curious work, published at the end of 1714, probably in November. Apart from anything else, only two copies survive, which may or may not indicate a smaller than average circulation.[164] Toland's motives in writing the work are in themselves unclear. He had been in favour of the measure passed in 1709 which provided for the naturalization of foreign Protestants, and, although this was repealed the following year, Toland was in a sense strengthening his case by

---

[163] 'The Present State of the Jewish Nation', *New Universal Magazine; or, Gentleman and Lady's Polite Instructor* (May 1752), 338–42. Cf. Apr. 1752, 296 and esp. 295: foldout engraving of 'The Jewish Synagogue'.

[164] [John Toland], *Reasons for Naturalizing the Jews in Great Britain and Ireland, On the Same Foot with All Other Nations* (London, 1714). It must have been published between 18 Oct. 1714 and 1 Dec. 1714, because a reply appeared at that time: Anon., *Confutation of the Reasons for Naturalizing the Jews* (London, 1715). Cf. *Monthly Catalogue*, 1/8 (1714), 53. The two copies are at the Jewish Theological Seminary, New York City; and Trinity College, Dublin. A repr. can be found in *Pamphlets Relating to the Jews in England in the Seventeenth and Eighteenth Centuries*, ed. P. Radin (San Francisco, California State Library, Sutro Branch, 1939): occ. paper, Eng. ser. no. 3. Generally, see G. Carabelli, *Tolandiana* (Florence, 1975), 188–9. S. Ettinger, 'Jews and Judaism as Seen by the English Deists of the 18th Century' (Hebrew), *Zion*, 29 (1964), 182–207, argues that, apart from Toland, the Deists' conception of Jews and Judaism was so negative that we ought to see them as the link between ancient and classical anti-Judaism and modern anti-Semitism. See also M. Wiener, 'John Toland and Judaism', *HUCA* 16 (1941), 215–42, and I. E. Barzilay, 'John Toland's Borrowings from Simone Luzzatto', *JSS* 31 (1969), 75–81, who argues that many of the ideas in Toland's work appeared in Luzzatto's Italian book published in 1638. See also the recent book by F. E. Manuel, *The Broken Staff: Judaism through Christian Eyes* (Cambridge, Mass., 1992); and his earlier study, 'Israel and the Enlightenment', *Daedalus* (1982), 33–52, repr. in his *The Changing of the Gods* (London, 1983), 105–34.

exploiting the extreme example of the Jews. Nevertheless, Toland's quite detailed defence of the Jews and his use of Simone Luzzatto's *Discorso circa il stato de gl'Hebrei*, a Jewish apologetic work published at Venice in 1638, raises his own interest to a quite different order. Indeed, according to Toland himself, he planned 'in convenient time [to] publish the translation'. So it appears that Toland's interest in the Jews was genuine and not designed solely to fuel some other Deistic argument, nor to attack indirectly the validity of Christian revelation.[165]

Toland opens his plea with an address to the bishops and archbishops of Great Britain, noting that 'as by your Learning you further know how considerable a part of the *British* inhabitants are the undoubted offspring of the *Jews* (to which the old *Irish* can lay no claim)', and praying that 'as you are the advocates of the *Jews* at the Throne of Heaven, so you will be their friends and protectors in the *Brittish* Parliament'. Toland then proceeded to attack the question from every possible angle, religious, economic, and social alike. Toland noted that Jews would never become embroiled in disputes between Protestant churches, being indifferent to such questions; that 'their having no Country of their own, to which they might retire, after having got Estates here', they would not drain England of her wealth; and that they would serve as brokers, bringing further trade and commerce to England. Toland explained that it was force of law and circumstance that prompted the Jews to turn to money-lending and other financial expedients: with freedom and security, he wrote, 'I doubt not, but they'll insensibly betake themselves to Building, Farming, and all sorts of Improvement like other people.' They might even become soldiers, as they were in ancient times, although Toland mused that, if they joined the navy, there 'must indeed be an intermixture of other seamen, by reason of their *Sabbath*'. Toland rejected completely the notion of racial characteristics adhering to the Jews, especially the claim that Jews emitted a certain smell that even baptism could not wash away.[166]

Toland also provided a short history of the Jews in England, dwelling on their misfortunes under the Norman kings, and reminding his readers that, after they had been readmitted during Cromwell's reign, under King Charles II 'they were conniv'd at and tolerated, but not authoriz'd by Charter or Act of Parliament: nor are they on any other terms than permission to this day, tho they have deserv'd much better by

---

[165] Nevertheless, like the other Deists, Toland's views about the Jewish religion were as critical as his views about Christianity, and, like most Christians, he saw the Talmud as a collection of nonsense. Toland also published a translation of La Crequinière, *Agreement of the Customs of the East-Indians, with those of the Jews* (London, 1705).

[166] Toland, *Reasons*, sig. A4^v; pp. 10–17, 19.

their obedience and affection to the Government, towards the support of which, their purses have been always open'. In Toland's eyes, the banishment of the Jews from England in 1290 was no less heinous than the expulsion of the Jews from Spain: 'they were both equally against the common good'.[167] Toland even advances a theory that a 'great number of 'em fled to *Scotland,* which is the reason so many in that part of the Island, have such a remarkable Aversion to pork and black-puddings to this day, not to insist on some other resemblances easily observable'. So pleased were the Jews to be readmitted into England, Toland claims, that they 'made extraordinary rejoicings every where, observing it as a sort of new Æra, keeping ever since an annual feast in commemoration of such a blessing'.[168] 'In a word,' Toland stated, 'they ought to be so naturaliz'd in *Great Britain* and *Ireland,* as, like the *Quakers,* to be incapacitated in nothing, but where they incapacitate themselves.'[169]

Toland's motives may still be a subject for debate, but the specific arguments which he advances nevertheless give the impression that he has thought about the problem beyond any immediate polemical advantage. More typical, perhaps, were the millenarian advocates of the Jewish cause in the half-century before the Jew Bill. Some of the arguments were based on the traditional mystical views about the Jews, their language, and their culture. This is the case of the anonymous interpreter of the 'Celestial Hebrew Alphabet', according to which the stars in the heavens formed Hebrew letters rather than traditional constellations. Indeed, he explained, 'these Planets, which by reason of their Wanderings, cannot be here set down, do daily, by their various Motions, create New, and Different Letters'.[170] On a more sophisticated plane, many people continued to champion ideas which had been heard a century earlier. Isaac Newton, for example, made a note to himself that he observed 'that the restauration of the Jewish nation so much spoken of by the old Prophets respects not the few Jews who were converted in the Apostles days, but the dispersed nation of the unbelieving Jews to be converted in the end when the fulness of the Gentiles shal enter'. This was the reason that he objected to 'the humour which has long reigned

[167] Toland, *Reasons* 28–38. Toland especially admired 'Our second Josephus, the reverend Mons. Banage' (p. 27).

[168] Ibid. 37–8. On this, Toland notes that he has 'a very handsom Poem that was penn'd on this subject by *Barrios*', called 'Epistle to *Kahal-Kados* (that is, the Holy Church) at *London*.'   [169] Ibid. 45.

[170] *The First Table of the Celestiall Constellations, Expressed by Hebrew Characters* (n.p., n.d.). The copy in the Bod. Lib. (Heb. c. 6 [fos. 52–3]) was acquired in 1913, having been found in the copy of Moses Edrehi, *An Historical Account of the Ten Tribes* (London, 1836), which had been owned by one Elizabeth Clarke. It seems to be a work of the early 18th century.

among the Christians of boasting our selves against the Jews, and insulting over them for their not believing, [which] is reprehended by the Apostle for high-mindedness and self-conceit, and much more is our using them despightfully, Pharisaicall and impious'.[171]

Such millenarian sentiments continued throughout this period, expressed by people much less distinguished than Isaac Newton. One anonymous correspondent to the *Gentleman's Magazine* in 1745 predicted that the world would come to an end within the next ten years, and proposed to make over all of his possessions to the Jews at the end of 1749, 'provided only their nation would promise to receive me and mine at that time to dwell in *Israel*, as *Rahab* did, if then the dangerous and painful part of their long expected glorious restoration shall be visibly over'.[172] An even more vociferous champion of the Jews was Robert Clayton, the Irish bishop. Clayton had been introduced at Court by Dr Samuel Clarke, and soon took on his patron's opinions as to Arianism and other heretical views. Indeed, it was only Clayton's death in 1758 that saved him from prosecution.[173] Clayton believed that the end was only relatively nigh, and would occur in about the year 2000. Indeed, he argued that the Jewish prominence in the precious metals trade was a fulfilment of the prophecy of Isaiah about the ships of Tarshish coming 'to bring thy sons from far, their silver and their gold with them'.[174] Clayton looked forward to 'the Coming of the *Messiah* in his State of Exaltation and Glory; when the Jews are to be restored to their own Land; and the *Messiah* shall make a triumphant and a personal Appearance on Mount *Zion*; at which Time the Jews and Gentiles shall be united into one People under *Messiah*, the *Shepherd* and King'.[175] Clayton reckoned the Semites as 10 per cent of mankind, a figure which in itself reflected part of the divine miracle.[176]

---

[171] Jewish National Library, Jerusalem, Israel: MS Yahuda 9.2, fo. 158^r: quoted in F. E. Manuel, *The Religion of Isaac Newton* (Oxford, 1974), 67. Newton was also very interested in the dimensions of the Temple. For the famous maker of the Temple model, see A. L. Shane, 'Rabbi Jacob Judah Leon (Templo) of Amsterdam (1603–1675) and his Connections with England', *TJHSE* 25 (1977), 120–36.

[172] N.R., in *Miscellaneous Correspondence ... Sent to the Author of the Gentleman's Magazine*, 5 (1745), 220. I am grateful to David Harley for this reference. For an opposing view, see R.O., *Reasons why Jews, Turks, Infidels, and Hereticks Cannot be Saved* (Douai, 1720).

[173] J. P. Ferguson, *An Eighteenth Century Heretic: Dr. Samuel Clarke* (Kineton, 1976), 157; Thomas Wilson, *The Diaries*, ed. C. L. S. Linnell (London, 1964), 35–6.

[174] Robert Clayton, *A Dissertation on Prophecy* (London, 1749), esp. 80–1, 111–12, 152–64, including the narrative of Samuel Brett on the Jewish Council in Hungary.

[175] Robert Clayton, *An Enquiry into the Time of the Coming of the Messiah* (London, 1751), 4–5.

[176] Robert Clayton, *A Vindication of the Histories of the Old and New Testament, in Answer to ... Bollingbroke* (Dublin, 1752), 200; cf. 120–1, 174–5. See also id., *An*

It was probably inevitable that some of this positive interest in the Jews and their fate would be translated into more practical action in attempting to secure for them rights and privileges similar to those enjoyed by other non-Anglicans. Here, too, the counsel for the Sephardi community, Philip Carteret Webb, was apparently the first in the field, soliciting opinions on whether an English-born Jew or one endenizened could own land. The first opinion was received in February 1719 from Sir Robert Raymond, Attorney-General and later Chief Justice. A dozen further views were acquired in February 1723/4, and, with only minor qualifications, the overwhelming judgement was that there was no legal bar to Jews owning land.[177] In the view of Dr William Stratford, canon of Christ Church, Oxford, the import of this decision was that 'the Jews have carried it against Jesus Christ'.[178] In 1723 Jews were exempted from including the words 'on the true faith of a Christian' in the Oath of Abjuration required of all landowners since the previous year, this privilege being the first time that Jews had been described in legislation as English subjects.[179] The occasion for this outburst of activity is not difficult to fathom. In 1724 the Sephardi Jews of London purchased an area of 2.5 acres for use as an extension to their cemetery. The plot was bought by Joseph da Costa and Gabriel Lopes for £450, presumably on the basis of the lawyers' decision.[180] Webb had cause to refer to these deliberations once again thirty years later, when he published a short book on the subject of the Jews owning land, in the context of the debates over the Jew Bill of 1753.[181]

The question of the right of Jews to own land was thus brought to public attention as a result of the practical need to acquire another plot of land to serve as an extension to the existing cemetery, not because of any overwhelming need to clarify this point at law. *The Complaint of the Children of Israel, Representing their Grievances under the Penal Laws*, then,

Impartial Enquiry into the Time of the Coming of the Messiah (London, 1751), esp. 5, 8, 121–2. Cf. [Samuel Collet], *A Treatise of the Future Restoration of the Jews* (London, 1747), esp. 24.

[177] Twelve lawyers' opinions: SPJC London, MS 344, fos. 57a–f; P. C. Webb's notebooks for cases 1720–33: BL MS Lansdowne 629, p. 36.

[178] William Stratford to Edward Harley, 19 Mar. 1723/4: Hist. MSS Comm., *xxix, Portland VII*, 377.   [179] 10 Geo. I, c. 4: Picciotto, *Sketches*, 61.

[180] Hyamson, *Sephardim*, 320.

[181] [Philip Carteret Webb], *The Question, Whether a Jew, Born within the British Dominions, Was, before the Making the Late Act of Parliament, a Person, Capable, by Law, to Purchase and Hold Lands to him, and his Heirs, Fairly Stated and Considered* (London, 1753).

although ostensibly written by 'Solomon Abrabanel, of the House of David', was unlikely to have been written by a Jew. In fact, the author was William Arnall, a political writer in the pay of Sir Robert Walpole. Arnall's point was that it was unfair that dissenting Jews should suffer greater discrimination than dissenting Protestant sectarians:

though from the *rigid* Institutions of our Religion we every one of us must suffer *certain Mutilations of the Flesh*, yet ought not from any Consideration, either Human or Divine, to suffer such a *Civil Circumcision* as to be cut out of all Employments, even in our native Country, under a Government whose authority we have obeyed, and whose Establishment we have supported with such irreproachable Fidelity, and such disinterested Zeal.

Arnall/Abrabanel pointed out that, unlike the Protestant Dissenters, the Jews never caused the English injury: 'We never turned you out of your *Churches*; we never set up *Chapter Lands* to Sale; nor pulled down your *Hierarchy*.' On the contrary, 'it is *to us* that you owe your *Mitres* and your *Revenues*, your Privileges and Pre-eminencies', since they ultimately derive from Jewish institutions. Times have changed since the days of Cromwell, when Jews were suffered admittance as foreigners: 'we their Children are *natural-born Subjects* of *Britain*: so that what Incapacity or Disability may remain upon us, is entirely to be laid to the Charge of Religion'.[182]

There is no doubt that many Jews in England saw their situation exactly as Arnall described it: civil disabilities on the basis of religious confession alone were meant to have disappeared in the settlement after the Glorious Revolution. The excitement of the Jew Bill controversy in 1753 demonstrated that the answers were not nearly so simple as Arnall believed.

[182] 'Solomon Abrabanel' [William Arnall], *The Complaint of the Children of Israel*, esp. 6, 11, 35. At least the second edn. also dates from 1736.

6

JEW BILL AND GEORGE III

HORACE WALPOLE, one of the keenest observers of the eighteenth-century political and social scene, put the entire story of the outcry in 1753 over the Jew Bill in the most succinct fashion:

The English parliament, which opened on the 15th of November, was employed till the end of the year in an affair, which showed how much the age, enlightened as it is called, was still enslaved to the grossest and most vulgar prejudices. The year before an act had passed for naturalizing Jews. It had passed almost without observation, Sir John Barnard and Lord Egmont having merely given a languid opposition to it, in order to reingratiate themselves with the mobs of London and Westminster. The bishops had honestly concurred in removing such absurd distinctions, as stigmatized and shackled a body of the most loyal, commercial, and wealthy subjects of the kingdom. A new general election was approaching; some obscure men, who perhaps wanted the necessary sums for purchasing seats, or the topics of party to raise clamour, had fastened on this Jew Bill; and in a few months the whole nation found itself inflamed with a Christian zeal, which was thought happily extinguished with the ashes of Queen Anne and Sacheverel.[1]

Certainly from the quantitative point of view, more was published about the Jews, their religion, their character, and their behaviour in 1753 than any year before or possibly since. Yet there is the danger of taking the bare statements for and against the Jews too literally, and regarding them as in some way expressing the deep-seated feelings of a nation. The debate over the Jew Bill was never about the retrospective wisdom of readmission, nor about the theoretical desirability of expulsion or even restriction of immigration. After the Jew Bill had been repealed and the parliamentary elections of 1754 decided, the entire case was very nearly forgotten, and had no effect whatsoever on the status of Jews in this country.

I

The root of the problem lay in the very method by which Jews had been allowed to return to England. Cromwell's decision in 1656 to turn a

---

[1] Horace Walpole, *Memoires of the Last Ten Years of the Reign of George the Second* (London, 1822), i. 310–11.

blind eye to Jewish residence and immigration, having failed to obtain a clear decision at the Whitehall Conference, meant that no special laws or privileges were ever enacted with regard to the legal position of the Jews in England. The so-called Jewish disabilities, therefore, were held in common with other Nonconformist groups and were never individually directed at the Jews alone. Although both the Blasphemy Act of 1698 and the Marriage Act, passed in the same year as the Jew Bill, did make special provisions for the Jews, their basic legal position was held in common with other non-Anglicans. Jews, like them, were not permitted to hold municipal office, nor could they be 'employed in any office or trust, civil or military'. They were of course also barred from taking a degree in the two universities, and could not vote nor be elected to parliament, because of the oaths required. Jews might have been able to acquire the freedom of the City of London, that is, the right to engage in retail trade, but since the oath had to be taken on the New Testament, this too was kept from them, although they were permitted to be wholesale traders, and we have already seen that twelve Jews at a time could obtain licences as commodity brokers.[2]

But those who particularly suffered from a double burden were those English Jews who had the misfortune of having been born abroad. Classified as aliens, they were not permitted to own land, and the more secure forms of tenure were denied to them as well. The publication of a forgotten statute of 1271 forbidding the Jews from owning land, which appeared in d'Blossiers Tovey's history of Anglo-Jewry in 1738, may have increased Jewish fears.[3] In theory, they could not own or be partner in the ownership of a British ship, and in any case the Restoration Navigation Act excluded them from the colonial trade. Those who did engage in foreign trade were required to pay irksome alien duties which could be extraordinarily high.[4]

[2] See H. S. Q. Henriques, *The Jews and the English Law* (Oxford, 1908), 154–7, 170–1, 198–201, 230–41, for the question of Jewish legal rights. See also R. A. Routledge, 'The Legal Status of the Jews in England 1190–1790', *Journal of Legal History*, 3 (1982), 91–124. Cf. V. D. Lipman, 'Sephardi and Other Jewish Immigrants in England in the Eighteenth Century', in A. Newman (ed.), *Migration and Settlement* (London, 1971), 37–62, incl. lists of names.

[3] D'Blossiers Tovey, *Anglia Judaica; or, The History and Antiquities of the Jews in England* (Oxford, 1738). Robert Liberles, 'The Jews and their Bill: Jewish Motivations in the Controversy of 1753', *Jewish History*, ii (1987), 29–36, argues that the resolution of the land ownership question lay behind the Jewish support for the bill. Cf. id., 'From *Toleration* to *Verbesserung*: German and English Debates on the Jews in the Eighteenth Century', *Central European History*, 22 (1989), 3–32.

[4] Cf. W. Samuel, 'Anglo-Jewish Ships' Names', *MJHSE* 3 (1937); M. Woolf, 'Eighteenth-Century London Jewish Shipowners', *TJHSE* 24 (1975), 198–204. The most prominent Jewish shipowners at the time of the Jew Bill were Aaron Franks, Francis Salvador, and Jacob Mendes da Costa, among others.

The obvious solution for a Jewish trader would be to acquire the same rights and privileges as any Englishman enjoyed. The most straight-forward way would have been to lobby for the passage of a private naturalization act in which he would be the beneficiary, but a clause in the statute of 1609 which established this option excluded all but Anglicans from applying it. Another alternative was to emigrate to the American colonies, for an act of 1740 provided for the naturalization of Quakers and Jews who resided there for seven years. This Plantation Act (13 Geo. II, c. 7) was the means by which 189 Jews obtained British nationality, but all but thirty-eight were residents of Jamaica, and only a handful of the rest, if any, probably made their way back to London as naturalized Englishmen.[5] For foreign-born Jews who had no intention of emigrating to the New World, the only other alternative was to be made 'free denizens' by the purchase of royal letters patent, and indeed about 150 Jews were made denizens between the Restoration and the end of the century. Denization opened the colonial trade to those who acquired it, but it was not retroactive, and children born before the acquisition of that status remained aliens and therefore could not inherit real property. Worst of all, denization did not provide for exemption from alien duties. Even the Crown thought that this was not entirely fair, but when Charles II and James II ceased to demand alien duties from endenizened Jews, the native English merchants protested, and in the end William III issued an Order in Council in 1690 restoring the obligation of denizens to pay the full fees.[6]

In brief, naturalization was the distant and impossible goal of the prosperous, and therefore inevitably Sephardi, foreign-born Jewish merchant in England. Only by this means could he compete on equal terms with his brother traders; only by naturalization could he enjoy full rights of property: but, as long as the sacramental test was in force, short of conversion to Anglicanism it could never be obtained. The simplest solution to this conundrum was to pass a general act of parliament which would allow Jews to be excused from taking the Anglican sacrament, a requirement which in any case had always been directed mainly against Catholics. Put another way, what was required was to extend the privileges of the Plantation Act to the mother country, so that rich Jews who could afford it would be able to arrange for the passage of a personal naturalization act in parliament. This was the Jew Bill of 1753.

[5] For one such Jew who went out to Barbados in 1753 and returned to London two years later, but not naturalized, see C. Roth, 'The Remarkable Career of Haham Abraham Gabay Yzidro', *TJHSE* 24 (1975), 211–13.

[6] See C. Robbins, 'A Note on General Naturalization under the Later Stuarts and a Speech in the House of Commons on the Subject in 1664', *Journal of Modern History*, 34 (1962), 168–77.

The idea for change originated as a result of the failure of such a bill in the Irish Parliament, in which defeat was initially secured by a narrow margin and on the second trial only due to the intervention of the primate of Ireland, who scotched the bill just before it was due to receive the royal assent.[7] Admittedly, the Irish case in some ways resembled the situation in the plantations, but the feeling that change was in the air prompted the Spanish and Portuguese community in London to appoint a standing committee to lobby for such a bill in England.[8] At the same time, they were encouraged by the course of debate over Robert Nugent's 'General Naturalization Bill' introduced in 1747 and 1751, by means of which foreign Protestants could be naturalized without the expense of a private act. In the course of defeating his bill, it was argued that, in failing to provide a clause enabling Jewish naturalization as well, Nugent was driving away a handful of rich Jews in favour of a swarm of indigent Protestants. Even earlier precedents were cited, especially the failed proposal of 1693–4, which would have naturalized foreign Protestants, and that of 1709, the Whig act which allowed naturalization without a private act for foreigners who swore the required oaths and took communion in a Protestant church. This last law stayed on the books until the elections of the following year, when the Tories came into power and repealed it, but by then nearly 10,000 German Protestants, mostly poor, had immigrated into England and were permitted to remain.[9] It was against this background that John Toland pressed for the naturalization of the Jews, who were thought to be more of an economic asset than their indigent Protestant fellow immigrants.[10] With all of this support for easier naturalization of certain rich Jews which appeared to be under the surface, all that seemed to be needed was to take an initiative.

This was the task of Joseph Salvador alias Joseph Jessurun Rodrigues, one of the most prominent Jews of his day. Among the Newcastle papers is a memorandum described as 'Mr. Salvadore's Paper Concerning the

[7] L. Hyman, *The Jews of Ireland* (London, 1972), ch. viii.

[8] R. D. Barnett made English summaries of much of the Mahamad records before 1800, kept in black loose-leaf notebooks shelved with the minute books themselves at the SPJC, London.

[9] On the Jew Bill generally, see the useful book by T. W. Perry, *Public Opinion, Propaganda, and Politics in Eighteenth-Century England: A Study of the Jew Bill of 1753* (Cambridge, Mass., 1962). Cf. A. M. Hyamson, 'The Jew Bill of 1753', *TJHSE* 6 (1912), 156–88, incl. a bibliography of pamphlet literature; and N. Perry, 'Anglo-Jewry, the Law, Religious Conviction, and Self-Interest (1655–1753)', *Journal of European Studies*, 14 (1984), 1–23.

[10] [John Toland], *Reasons for Naturalizing the Jews in Great Britain and Ireland* (London, 1714): see above, pp. 234–6.

Jews', dated from London, 14 January [1753]. Salvadore's proposal, as he stated it simply, was that

It is Desired that it be enacted, that any Person professing the Jewish religion whom it may in future be thought proper to Naturalize, shall in Lieu of taking the Holy Sacrament take the oaths of Supremacy & Allegiance, or such other oaths as may be thought proper, on or before the Second Reading of the bill for Naturalizing him in either of the Houses of Parliament.

Salvador followed with a list of seven reasons justifying his proposal. The present law, he argued, completely excluded Jews, while in other countries Jews were able to be naturalized, and therefore rich Jews tended to gravitate abroad rather than to England. If the law were changed, it would only open the possibility for certain rich Jews to be naturalized while others could still be denied this exceptional privilege, despite the fact that it would be unconstitutional to forbid even poor Jews the right to enter England at all. Indeed, Salvador wrote, 'the Rich among them have by Experience been found to be true Friends to the Government in all its Parts, and if further encouraged will be more closely connected with it, as they have no Connection or Tie with any other Government or State whatsoever', and Salvador had no need to add that this had been most recently demonstrated, of course, in the loyalty shown by the Jews during the rebellion of 1745. Jews who go to the plantations are able to be naturalized, he concluded, and it was not just that those who protect them at home in England should be denied the same rights.[11]

Whig supporters of the embryonic Jew Bill were easily to be found in Parliament. Robert Nugent, author of the failed general naturalization bill, was in favour, as was Lord Halifax, the President of the Board of Trade.[12] Most importantly, it had the backing of the so-called 'Triumvirs' who ran the English government at that time: Henry Pelham, the duke of Newcastle his brother, and the earl of Hardwicke, the Lord Chancellor. Apart from the commercial advantages of the Jew Bill, they no doubt recognized that the exemplary behaviour of the Jewish community in 1745 made them among the country's most loyal subjects. Nevertheless, they were reluctant to introduce the bill themselves, and delegated this responsibility to a third party, Lord Halifax, who presented the text probably written by Thomas Sewell, a lawyer who specialized in the problems of Nonconformists. Accordingly,

---

[11] Salvador to the duke of Newcastle, 14 Jan. 1753: BL Add. MS 33053, fo. 56^{r-v}: repr. *Anglo-Jewish Letters*, ed. C. Roth (London, 1938), 129–30.
[12] Claud Nugent, *Memoir of Robert, Earl Nugent* (London, 1898), 42–7, 62–4.

on 3 April 1753 the Jew Bill was read for the first time in the House of Lords.[13]

The Jew Bill itself was fairly innocuous, and made more so in its final form after certain changes and amendments had been introduced in the House of Lords. The framers began by pointing out that according to the rules determined by the Jacobean act of naturalization, all its beneficiaries were required to receive the Anglican sacrament within one month 'before the Bill for such Naturalization be exhibited'. They then went on to describe the Plantation Act of 1740 which exempted those Jews who have lived seven years or more in any of the American colonies without having been absent for more than two months during that time. The purpose of the present bill was 'That Persons professing the *Jewish* Religion may, upon Application for that Purpose, be naturalized by Parliament, without receiving the Sacrament of the Lord's Supper', provided that they had resided in Great Britain or Ireland for at least three years, without having been abroad more than three months at any one time during this period. The candidate was also required to produce two witnesses testifying to his Judaism. Converts to Judaism were also eligible to enjoy the provisions of the Jew Bill, providing that they had professed that religion for at least three years. Finally, a clause was inserted prohibiting 'every Person professing the *Jewish* Religion' from exercising ecclesiastical patronage of any kind, a change which actually circumscribed the legal rights of all Jews, including those born in England.[14]

The Jew Bill was introduced in the House of Lords on 3 April 1753, and, after being sent to committee, which 'made several Amendments thereunto', it achieved its final passage without a division thirteen days later.[15] In the House of Commons itself, where the bill was first read on 17 April 1753, although some lively discussion did take place, no further amendments or changes were made, and the proposal passed on 22 May 1753. The general public seems to have been unaware of or uninterested in the progress of the proposed law. Only between the second and the third readings, that is, about 21 May 1753, did some outside influence begin to filter through, in the form of four petitions presented to the Commons, two in favour of the Jew Bill and two

---

[13] Generally, see Perry, *Jew Bill*, 17–22. L. B. Namier, *The Structure of Politics at the Accession of George III* (London, 1957), 371 suggests that Sewell actually wrote the text.

[14] 26 Geo. II, c. 26: *An Act to Permit Persons Professing the Jewish Religion to be Naturalized by Parliament; and for Other Purposes therein Mentioned* [London, 1 June 1753].

[15] *Lords Journal*, 28: 73, 80, 84, 88, 90, 91, 93 (3, 6, 10, 11, 12, 13, 16 Apr. 1753).

against.[16] Even the extreme Tory *London Evening Post* did not mention the Jew Bill until 10 May, with a mild letter from 'A Briton' protesting that any 'poor beggarly Foreigner' could profess himself a Jew and thereby take advantage of its provisions. By the time of its passage, apart from printing one of the petitions before the Commons, the paper had hardly mounted any sort of organized campaign against the measure.[17]

Royal assent was to be forthcoming within two weeks, so, technically speaking, the Jew Bill was not yet law, although it was unlikely that it would or could be opposed by George II, whose agreement transformed the Jew Bill into 26 George II, c. 26. By that time the public clamour had begun to mount, and would continue unabated until the Jew Bill was repealed in December and rumble on past this date until the parliamentary elections of May 1754.

Even with the benefit of hindsight, it is difficult to know what to make of this great public outcry. Unquestionably, it was primarily a Tory stick with which to beat the Whigs in a period notable for the lack of such clear distinctions of principle. Certainly the entire issue of the Jew Bill has provided those who look for a continuity of anti-Jewish prejudice in Europe with a battery of quotations with which to justify their case. But the storm passed over mid-eighteenth-century England like a dark cloud and left little trace behind nor any lasting effect on Anglo-Jewish relations. The forms the issues took are themselves almost as interesting as the views expressed therein.

The Tory *London Evening Post*, for example, made a point of bringing up the Jew Bill in every number of the paper once it became law. Some of the information may be based on fact, such as the report of the Wiltshire MP who went back to his country seat with a train of six attendants, all wearing labels in their hats proclaiming 'no Jews, no Naturalization Bill, old England and Christianity for ever'. The election slogan in Somerset was said to be 'No Judaism; Christianity for ever', while in Lancashire it was 'No Jews; Christianity and the Constitution'.[18] On the other hand, the advertisement of 'Moses Ben Amri, Surgeon' that he 'Circumcises In the Safest, Easiest, and most Expeditious Manner' is certainly apocryphal, as is the London pub supposedly named the 'Talmud and Crown'.[19] Some of the old fables

[16] *Commons Journal*, 26: 770, 775, 803, 808–9, 823, 824, 827, 828–9 (16–17 Apr. 1753; 3, 7, 15, 16, 21, 22 May 1753); *Parliamentary History of England*, ed. William Cobbett (London, 1806–20), xiv. 1363–1432. When taken over by the printer T. C. Hansard in 1812 [=vol. xiii], the title was changed to *The Parliamentary History*.

[17] *London Evening Post*, 3985 (10–12 May 1753), 1; 3978 (12–15 May), 1; 3979 (17–19 May), 1; 3980 (19–22 May), 4; 3981 (22–4 May), 1. See esp. G. A. Cranfield, 'The "London Evening-Post" and the Jew Bill of 1753', *History Journal*, 8 (1965), 16–30.

[18] *London Evening Post*, 3988 (7–9 June 1753), 1; 4005 (17–19 July 1753), 4.

[19] Ibid. 3986 (2–5 June 1753), 1; 4042 (6–9 Oct. 1753), 1.

from readmission days were even resurrected, such as the claim that the Jews had offered £200,000 to Oliver Cromwell. A certain 'Manasseh-Ben-Israel' is introduced, promising the electors of Great Britain that the Jews will never cause Englishmen to be circumcised against their will.[20] Contemporary Jews, such as Moses Hart, Joseph Salvador, and Aaron Franks, were presented as both lobbying for the Jew Bill before passage, and swanning around their betters as if they were already English citizens.[21] Even Philip Carteret Webb, the Jewish solicitor on this occasion, was not spared the indignity of public criticism, and it was reported that he had himself been circumcised and converted to Judaism, changing his name to Rabbi Achitophel Kor in order to please his clients.[22] Current stereotypes of the Jews as fences, criminals, and underhanded businessmen were also reinforced by the supposed presentation of news.[23] While the medieval Jewish blood libel was not expressly repeated, the paper did report the story of a curate in Northumberland who was called to christen a child, but circumcised him instead, causing the infant's death.[24] Even Jewish loyalty in the rebellion of Forty-five was impugned: the *London Evening Post* published a detailed list of the Jewish subscriptions in that year, which came according to their calculations to only £514 12s., or about 2.7 per cent of the total sum contributed.[25] As had also been the case in the seventeenth century, a good deal of foreign news about the activities of Jews abroad was repeated. But even the *London Evening Post* was careful to make its point clear, for example, in this letter from a (probably) imaginary reader who called himself 'Old England':

But to every *Freeholder* of the Land I humbly and earnestly give this Advice, as of the last Consequence to himself, and the whole Nation, that he would not give his Vote to any Candidate for a Seat in the Senate, though he was his Landlord, or the most popular Man in the County, 'till he had made him a most solemn Promise, to use all his Endeavours to have the supposed Law repeal'd, as soon as possible; and then we shall have nothing to fear from the next Election.[26]

Indeed, as the end of the year approached the *London Evening Post* printed many parliamentary instructions against the Jew Bill in various

---

[20] Ibid. 3992 (16–19 June 1753), 1; 3998 (30 June–3 July 1753), 1.
[21] Ibid. 4001 (7–10 July 1753), 1; 4002 (10–12 July 1753), 1; 4006 (19–21 July 1753), 1; 4009 (26–8 July 1753), 1; 4046 (16–18 Oct. 1753), 1.
[22] Ibid. 4014 (7–9 Aug. 1753), 1; 4018 (16–18 Aug. 1753). 'Kor' is 'web' in Hebrew.
[23] Ibid. 4001 (7–10 July 1753), 1; 4013 (4–7 Aug. 1753), 1; 4021 (23–5 Aug. 1753), 4.
[24] Ibid. 4030 (8–11 Sept. 1753), 1.   [25] Ibid. 4018 (16–18 Aug. 1753), 1.
[26] Ibid. 3985 (31 May–2 June 1753), 1.

counties. Clearly then, more than anything else, the Jew Bill was an election gimmick used by the Tories to cast further aspersions on the loyalty of the Whigs.

Perhaps a somewhat more balanced picture can be gleaned from the *London Magazine*, which while opposing the Jew Bill was nevertheless somewhat more moderate. In common with other contemporary periodicals of this sort, the *London Magazine* mostly published material that had appeared elsewhere. Apart from publishing a detailed description of the Jew Bill itself, they also reprinted parliamentary debates, evading the prohibition under the transparent device of calling it a 'Journal of the Proceedings and Debates in the Political Club', conducted by such men as 'A. Nonius' and 'Jul. Drusus Publicola'. The *London Magazine* also had its share of satirical pieces about the Jews, such as the 'News for One Hundred Years hence in the Hebrew Journal', reprinted from the *Craftsman*, which gave a full picture of an England in the grip of the Jews, building a new Temple, launching a ship called *Benjamin Salvadore*, and whipping Christians for speaking disrespectfully about the Mishnah.[27] By printing lists of books and pamphlets published each month, the *London Magazine* also provides a more detailed picture of ephemeral publications that have not survived. The more famous *Gentleman's Magazine*, however, supported the Jew Bill, although they also printed a good deal of material against the measure.

Interestingly, not all of the Jews in London were in favour of the Jew Bill, nor did they applaud its approval. The most famous contemporary case was that of Samson Gideon, who was English-born and therefore would not personally profit from the Act in any case. Nevertheless, his social-climbing and his prominent public profile caused his name to be taken in vain as a supporter and even a chief mover of the bill, and his portrayal in pamphlets and satirical prints was more than he could bear. When the Spanish and Portuguese Synagogue implied that he should be numbered among the supporters of the Jew Bill, his ire was so increased that he wrote formally on 5 September 1753 to the Mahamad, the governing council, protesting that

Your assuming a power of representing me in point of political or Civil Interest, as I understand you have done in a late Instance, is certainly as little consistent with prudence, as with the Law of Nature, or of the Land, and the more so, as you knew the matter solicited for, to be directly contrary to my declared Sentiments, and my dislike to all Innovations. But to prevent all future, as well as to rectify all past mistakes, Take notice, that I for my Self do in the most

---

[27] *London Magazine* (July 1753), 302. Cf. Arthur Murphy, *The Works* (London, 1786), v. 286–92, reprinted from *Gray's-Inn Journal* of June and July 1753.

solemn manner disavow all power that you may at any time have assumed, in civil or secular Affairs, and more especially that, which you, without any Colour, have taken upon your Selves, to represent the Jews in general, and to request things in their names.

In order to make the point more vivid, Samson Gideon proclaimed in the same letter his complete and total resignation from the synagogue and virtually from the Jewish community.[28]

The public clamour was greatest outside Parliament and was strongly felt even without the newspapers and magazines. Horace Walpole, no doubt with a good deal of exaggeration, reported on his own adventures in a letter to Richard Bentley, the famous classicist:

You will be diverted with my distresses at Worcester. I set out boldly to walk down the High Street to the cathedral: I found it much more peopled than I intended, and, when I was quite embarked, discovered myself up to the ears in a contested election. A new candidate had arrived the night before, and turned all their heads. Nothing comforted me, but that the opposition is to Mr. T[racy, MP for Worcester and Walpole's enemy]; and I purchased my passage very willingly with crying, 'No T—! No Jews!' However, the inn where I lay was Jerusalem itself, the very headquarters, where T— the Pharisee was expected; and I had scarce got into my room, before the victorious mob of his enemy, who had routed his advanced guard, broke open the gates of our inn, and almost murdered the ostler—and then carried him off to prison for being murdered.[29]

Certainly, many others, like Walpole, perceived that the entire issue was political in nature and more than slightly comical and absurd. One observer, writing in the *Craftsman* in the midst of the controversy, protested that

If ever what has been premised carried with it any colour of truth, it is certainly at this juncture, when the act of parliament in favour of the *Jews* engrosses so much of our conversation, and is artfully made use of by the male-contents to create uneasiness in the minds of his majesty's subjects, to render the ministry odious to the people, and to inflame a spirit of opposition to the administration, even at a time when every salutary law is promoted, that can have any manner of tendency to encrease the honour and wealth of our nation.[30]

---

[28] Gideon to the Spanish and Portuguese Congregation: SPJC, London, MS 344/ 24: photograph in *Bevis Marks Records*, i, ed. L. D. Barnett (Oxford, 1940), pl. xiv; letter repr. in *Anglo-Jewish Letters*, ed. Roth, 131–2; and partially repr. in A. M. Hyamson, *The Sephardim of England* (London, 1951), 131–2.

[29] Walpole to Bentley, Sept. 1753: Horace Walpole, *Correspondence*, ed. W. S. Lewis, *et al.* (London, 1937–83), xxxv. 150. In the same letter Walpole includes a first report of Hutchinsonianism, p. 156.

[30] *A Collection of the Best Pieces in Prose and Verse, against the Naturalization of the Jews* (London, 1753), 51.

A number of pamphleteers, even those against the Jew Bill, did not hesitate to bring forward the actual provisions of the measure. Among the supporters of the Jew Bill, the mild character of the law was one of the strongest arguments in their arsenal. 'Philo-Patriae', the mysterious and vociferous champion of the Bill, summed up the law as being 'to settle a Method, whereby any one of their foreign Brethren, who shall reside here three Years, and can prove his Utility to this Country, may, if the Legislature think proper, enjoy the same Liberties and Immunities as those born here now enjoy'. He estimated that there were about 8,000 Jews present in England out of a total population of eight million inhabitants, hardly a major threat.[31] Similar points were made by Josiah Tucker, a clergyman from Bristol whose chief political interest was campaigning against monopolies. Tucker reviewed the entire legal question of the situation of the Jews before and after the Jew Bill was passed into law, and concluded that the entire clamour was nothing more than 'Words of Course, invented purely for the Sake of inflaming the unthinking Populace against the next general Election'.[32] Indeed, he pointed out,

As to the Bill itself, it only empowers *rich* Foreigners to *purchase Lands*, and to carry on a free and *extensive* Commerce, by importing all Sorts of Merchandise and *Raw Materials*, allowed by Law to be imported, for the Employment of our own People, and then Exporting the Surplus of the Produce, Labour, and Manufactures of our own Country, upon *cheaper* and *better* Terms than is done at present. This is all the Hurt, that such a Bill *can* do; for this is the Meaning of that odious word *Naturalization*.[33]

Unlike the debate over readmission in the previous century, the discussion about the Jew Bill was hardly linked at all to religious concerns. It was true, as William Romaine the cantankerous London divine pointed out, that in Cromwell's time it was argued that allowing the immigration of Jews would facilitate their conversion to true Protestant Christianity. 'But hitherto no such good Effect has been produced,' he declared. 'We have had Experience of them near One

---

[31] Philo-Patriae, *Considerations on the Bill to Permit Persons Professing the Jewish Religion to be Naturalized by Parliament* (London, 1753): dated 15 July 1753 on p. 60. See esp. p. 3. Cf. id., *Further Considerations on the Act to Permit Persons Professing the Jewish Religion, to be Naturalized by Parliament* (London, 1753). See E. R. Samuel, 'The Jews in English Foreign Trade: A Consideration of the "Philo Patriae" Pamphlets of 1753', in J. M. Shaftesley (ed.), *Remember the Days: Essays on Anglo-Jewish History Presented to Cecil Roth* (London, 1966), 123–43.

[32] Josiah Tucker, *A Second Letter to a Friend Concerning Naturalizations* (London, 1753): dated 13 Nov. 1753 on p. 44: see esp. pp. 3, 18–20.

[33] Josiah Tucker, *A Letter to a Friend Concerning Naturalization* (London, 1753), 6. See also Anon., *Remarks on the Reverend Mr. Tucker's Letter* (London, 1753).

Hundred Years, and how many Converts have been made in all that Time? So few, that for our own Honour we had better conceal their Number.' Even if there was a divine plan for the conversion of the Jews before the Second Coming, Romaine despaired, 'I have lived much among them, and know them well, and I solemnly declare, that I never met with one *Jew*, who had any Inclination to be converted.'[34]

Some of the quasi-religious points made were undoubtedly facetious. One anonymous pamphleteer warned that the Jew Bill laid England at the mercy of the Wandering Jew: 'Now if this strange old Vagrant should chance to be tired of his present pedling way of Life, and choose to take Advantage of this Act (which by the by it will be impossible to prevent, as he is not personally known to any one Man now living) what alas! may not be apprehended from a Man in his extraordinary circumstances?' The same author also suggested that this 'Act will be very pernicious to the inland Trade of these Kingdoms. It must sensibly lessen the Consumption of *Brawn, Hams, Bacon, Black-puddings*, &c, &c.'[35] Yet, despite all this, many observers were probably sincere in agreeing with one anonymous pamphleteer that the 'very Circumstance of several Hundred Jews being naturalized by Act of Parliament in so short a space of Time as 13 Years, is the greatest Shock that this, or any other, *free* Nation, ever sustained in Time of profound Peace and Tranquility'.[36]

Very many pamphlets were published against the Jew Bill, and it would be too tedious to try to summarize them all.[37] The same themes appeared with tireless variation, relieved only by the numerous satirical prints which gave some imaginary colour to the debate.[38] The Jew Bill had become a political code without connection to the original merits or disadvantages of its terms. Some supporters of the Bill, admittedly, made a valiant effort to try to disengage the subject from the maelstrom of protest. P. C. Webb, who had been hired by the Jews to support their case, published a work designed to show that, even before the Jew Bill was passed, Jews had the right to own land, and that therefore this

---

[34] [William Romaine], *An Answer to a Pamphlet, Entitled, Considerations on the Bill* (2nd edn., London, 1753), 22, 24.

[35] Anon., *Seasonable Remarks on the Act Lately Pass'd in Favour of the Jews* (London, 1753), 14–15, 19.

[36] Anon., *A Reply to the Famous Jew Question* (London, [1754]), 78.

[37] Apart from the pamphlets cited in the notes here, others which deserve an honourable mention at least for wit include: 'Timothy Telltruth', *A Proposal Humbly Offered to the Legislature of this Kingdom* (London, 1753); [George Coningesby], *The Jewish Naturalization Considered* (n.p., 1753).

[38] See esp. Israel Solomons, 'Satirical and Political Prints on the Jews Naturalisation Bill, 1753', *TJHSE* 6 (1912), 205–33.

supposedly new privilege was not in fact novel.[39] Apart from Webb, the Jew Bill was defended by Thomas Birch and, more importantly, by Josiah Tucker.[40] Some supporters of the Jew Bill revived the millenarian arguments which had been so influential at the time of their readmission in the previous century.[41] Others tried to cover their tracks. Dr John Thomas, the bishop of Lincoln, excused himself by saying, 'I did not oppose the Bill, because I was then extremely Deaf and in no Condition to oppose nor did I choose to be Singular, but I was in my Heart against it.'[42] But it was a lost cause, and the government soon realized that it would do well to prepare the ground for a strategic retreat. Other less unpopular measures had been quickly withdrawn in the face of public protest, such as the Excise Bill and the Quarantine Act of 1721, and the lessons of the Sacheverell Case, where the government persisted and was voted out at the next election, were before its eyes.

The government's plan was to defuse the Opposition by itself introducing a bill of its own for repeal, on the very first day of the new session. The repealing bill would be introduced in the House of Lords, where the rules of procedure allowed bills to be read and debated on the first day of the session without prior notice being given. At the last minute Bishop Secker suggested that the clause forbidding Jews to present to livings be left on the books, so that it could be argued that the position of the Jews after the repeal of the Jew Bill would actually be worse off than it had been before 1753. The final session of Parliament

[39] [Philip Carteret Webb], *The Question, Whether a Jew, Born within the British Dominions, Was, before the Making the late Act of Parliament, a Person, Capable, by Law, to Purchase and Hold Lands to him, and his Heirs, Fairly Stated and Considered* (London, 1753). Webb was paid £542 12s. 10d. 'in relation to the applications to Parliament concerning Naturalization', between the years 1742–1753. Of this sum, £290 12s. 10d. comprised Webb's own fees, which did not include other work he did for the Spanish and Portuguese Congregation unrelated to the Jew Bill, and for which he received additional and separate payment: SPJC, London, MS 344/25a–b.

[40] Other notable defences of the Jew Bill came from Peter Peckard, *The Popular Clamour against the Jews Indefensible* (London, 1753); T. Winstanley, *A Sermon Preached . . . on Occasion of the Clamours against the Act for Naturalizing the Jews* (London, 1753); and the anonymous pamphleteers who wrote *An Earnest and Serious Address to the Freeholders* (London, 1753); *An Apology for the Naturalization of the Jews* (London, 1753); *An Address to the Friends of Great-Britain* (London, 1753); and *The Impartial Observer* (London, 1753). Curiously, the introduction to 'Gamaliel Ben Penahzur, Gent.' [=Abraham Mears], *The Book of Religion, Ceremonies, and Prayers; of the Jews* (London, 1738), originally a somewhat anti-Jewish work, was reissued anonymously now under the title *The Jewish Ritual* (London, 1753), and put the Jews in a rather favourable light.

[41] See e.g. Anon., *An Earnest Persuasive and Exhortation to the Jews* (London, 1753); Anon., *The Full and Final Restoration of the Jews and Israelites, Evidently Set Forth to be Nigh at Hand* (London, 1753).

[42] Thomas to Edward Weston, 29 Dec. 1753: Hist. MSS Comm., x, *Eglington & c.* (1885), 448.

opened on 15 November 1753, and although the king's speech made no reference to the clamour that had gripped the political nation throughout the summer, the duke of Newcastle immediately rose after the vote of thanks and moved the first reading of the repealing bill which he held in his hand. This new measure was rushed through the House of Lords in three days, 20–22 November, and arrived in the commons on the following morning. The Commons measure received its final reading on 28 November, and, overcoming the proposal by the Tory member Lord Harley that the Jewish naturalization provision of the Plantation Act of 1740 be overturned as well, the repeal of the Jew Bill received the royal assent in its original form on 20 December 1753.[43] When the general election was held the following April and early May, the Jew Bill had been nearly forgotten, especially as it was the government that had seized the initiative by putting the repeal bill forward and then waiting five months before calling the nation to the polls.[44] Horace Walpole, in a letter to his friend Richard Bentley, claimed that

The great cry against [Robert] Nugent at Bristol was for having voted for the Jew Bill: one old woman said, 'What, must we be represented by a Jew and an Irishman?' He replied, with great quickness, 'My good dame, if you will step aside with me into a corner, I will show you that I am *not* a Jew, and that *I am* an Irishman.

But Walpole was no doubt engaging in his habitual tendency for exaggeration when he implied that this situation was at all common.[45]

The historian of the Jew Bill summarized his research by saying that

when we examine the controversy of 1753 closely, we see that at bottom it was not, as it first appears, a singular and isolated outburst of anti-Semitic passion as such, but rather a renewal—albeit a somewhat artificial one, aimed at an approaching election—of a long-standing dispute over immigration and naturalization policy.[46]

By December 1753 Walpole would already be writing to a correspondent that 'I tell you nothing of Jew-Bills and Jew-Motions, for I dare to say you have long been as weary of the words as I am.'[47]

---

[43] Perry, *Public Opinion*, chs. 8–9.

[44] See esp. R. J. Robson, *The Oxfordshire Election of 1754: A Study in the Interplay of City, County and University Politics* (London, 1949).

[45] Walpole to Bentley, 9 July 1754: *Correspondence*, xxxv. 178. In this same letter, Walpole told an amusing story of Samson Gideon's son learning the Christian catechism with a minimum of understanding (see pp. 269–70 below).

[46] Perry, *Public Opinion*, 178.

[47] Walpole to George Montagu, 6 Dec. 1753: *Correspondence*, ix. 156–8.

II

In a letter of 1761 George Montagu wrote to his friend Horace Walpole that ' 'Tis strange how much I love to read of the court of Lewis the XIV, I, who am so indifferent to my own that I have at hand; I know more of the Fronde than the Jew Bill.'[48] Montagu was not alone, for one of the most curious results of the debate over the Jew Bill was that it had almost no lasting effects. Public attitudes towards the Jews did not appear to change, either for the better or for the worse. Indeed, little reference to the unfortunate events of 1753 appears at all in subsequent discussions, which may indicate that this storm in a teacup dissipated extraordinarily quickly. Even the negative images of the English Jew, which became so pronounced in the second half of the eighteenth century, owe their origins to other sources.

One point on which both Christians and Jews were unanimous was the low quality of Anglo-Jewish life during the period between the Jew Bill and the French Revolution. Edward Goldney, for example, was anti-Deist, but not anti-Jewish, yet his report on a visit to the rabbi of the Great Synagogue Aaron Hart (who died in 1756) was hardly flattering. Goldney even recommended to Archbishop of Canterbury Thomas Secker 'a Sociableness with the Wealthy *Jews* in and about this great Metropolis, that Your Lordship, acquainting Them that their Entertainment should be Provided for Them in every Respect, after their own Manner'. Goldney was confident that Secker's 'Excellent Nervous Way of Reasoning with Them' would have the desired effect, and that he 'would soon Convert Them to be Real Christians, and thereby cause the poorer Sort of *Jews* to become Christians also'. It is interesting that Goldney asks Secker to invite the rich Jews in order to persuade the poorer Jews to convert, but, none the less, his approach was one of courteousness and respect. It was in this spirit that Goldney followed the advice of Jews who counselled him 'to wait on Mr. Aaron Hart (who was then living) an eminent and very aged High-Priest, who as they said, his life and conversation was unblemished'. Goldney arrived armed with a letter of recommendation from some of his Jewish acquaintances, informing the rabbi 'that I had frequently conversed with many persons who called themselves Jews, and that I had really discovered a great deal of ignorance in them relating to the Messiah'. Rabbi Hart's first response was diplomatic: 'We English Jews, are not fond of gaining proselytes, as for his part, his father, grandfather, and great-grandfather are Jews; and that if it had been his fortune to have been born and bred a

---

[48] George Montagu to Horace Walpole, 11 Jan. 1761: ibid. ix. 333.

Mahometan, or in the principles of any other religion, he should have continued as such.' Goldney was intensely disappointed by this 'poor, low, mean answer from a gentleman of his years, (who was upwards of eighty) and high station in the Jewish church'. Rabbi Hart soon tired of being harangued on the subject of the Messiah, and without a word took down a book from the shelf and showed it to Goldney, who judged it to be 'a burlesque on the resurrection of Christ from the dead; most ridiculous, scandalous, impious, dogmatical'. Hart would not permit Goldney to see the title-page of the book, but the Christian soon discovered that it was William Whiston on miracles. Goldney therefore pitied the 'High-priest himself, as well as their laity, having no better arguments to have recourse to, than those of their education, and the tradition of their fathers to justify or vindicate their belief'. Despite the fact that we have only Goldney's account of the interview, the incident described is instructive in that it portrays a Jewish leadership unwilling to become involved in an intellectual battle that they were bound to lose, and a desire to continue their policy of theological self-effacement.[49]

Certainly there was social contact between wealthy Jews, mostly Sephardim, and the English landed class. Horace Walpole provides an outstanding example of this phenomenon. On one occasion in 1763 he wrote to his friend George Montagu that 'I have given my assembly, to show my gallery; and it was glorious; but happening to pitch upon the Feast of Tabernacles, none of my Jews could come, though Mrs Clive proposed to them to change their religion. So I am forced to exhibit once more.' Walpole was thus on such terms with his Jewish acquaintances as to stage the entire event once again, and indeed claimed that he was going to invite fourteen Jews to his next soirée.[50] These Jews were probably his neighbours Moses Franks, Abraham Prado and his wife, and Jael Mendez alias Mrs Hampden Pye, who married two Christians successively, the second an officer in the Foot Guards and the brother of the Poet Laureate, and who wrote and published indifferent poetry and what Walpole described as 'a most inaccurate, superficial, blundering account of Twickenham and other places'.[51] On another occasion a

---

[49] Edward Goldney, *Epistles to Deists and Jews* (London, 1759), pp. v, viii, 6–13, 165–76. The preface is dated 24 May 1759 (p. viii). Cf. id., *A Friendly Epistle to the Deists* (London, 1760), 5–7.

[50] Walpole to Montagu, 3 Oct. 1763: *Correspondence*, x. 106–7.

[51] Walpole to Revd. William Cole, 25 Apr. 1775: ibid. i. 366–9. Abraham Prado (d. 1782) lived on Twickenham Common. Moses Franks (1719–89) lived in Teddington nearby, and was married to his first cousin Phila, painted by Joshua Reynolds in 1766. Jael Mendez's first husband was John Neil Campbell of Bedfordshire: the book to which Walpole refers is her *The Peep into the Gardens at Twickenham*: cf. *London Chronicle*, 23–5 Feb. 1762 and 21–3 Oct. 1766; *Gents. Mag.* 32 (Feb. 1762), 93; 36 (Oct. 1766), 494.

number of years later, Walpole wrote to a friend at Cambridge describing 'a most brilliant fête that I gave' at which he 'had three Jews of Abraham's standing, and seven Sarahs who still talk of the second temple'.[52] Indeed, in 1774 Walpole's neighbour Abraham Prado provided him with a moment of salon glory by giving him a present of 'a bunch of grapes as big—as big—as that the two spies carried on a pole to Joshua'. Walpole recounted to Lady Ossory that in 'good truth this bunch weighted three and a half, *cote rotie* measure; and was sent to me by my neighbour Prado of the tribe of Issachar, who is descended from one of the aforesaid spies, but a good deal richer than his ancestor'. Walpole put Prado's present to good use: 'Well, Madam,' he recalled,

I carried it to the Marchioness, but gave it to the matre d'hotel, with injunctions to conceal it till the dessert. At the end of dinner, Lady Blanchford said, she had heard of three immense bunches of grapes at Mr Prado's at a dinner he had made for Mr Ellis. I said, those things are always exaggerated. She cried, oh! but Mrs Ellis told it, and it weighed I don't know how many pounds, and the Duke of Argyle had been to see the hothouse, and she wondered as it was so near I would not go and see it. 'Not I, indeed,' said I; 'I dare to say there is no curiosity in it.' Just then entered the gigantic bunch. Everybody screamed. 'There,' said I, 'I will be shot if Mr Prado has such a bunch as yours.'[53]

Unquestionably, such incidents do not give the impression of anything approaching social equality, but there is no doubt that the very notion of Jews mixing with the great and the good was not an impossible concept, and that such meetings did occur.

Foreigners who visited England were not sure what to make of this mixture of social intercourse and exclusion. Carl Philip Moritz came to see England in 1782 and published his impressions in German the following year. 'In Kensington, where we pulled up,' he wrote,

a Jew wanted to join us; but there was no room inside and he didn't want to ride on the outside. This caused my travelling companions to demur. They couldn't understand why a Jew should be ashamed of travelling on the outside; anyway, as they said, he was nothing but a Jew! I have noticed that here in England this anti-Semitic prejudice is far stronger than it is among us Germans.

On another occasion, in Dunstable, 'One started on about the Jews in the Old Testament and maintained that the present race of Jews sprang

---

See generally M. Brown, 'Anglo-Jewish Country Houses from the Resettlement to 1800', *TJHSE* 28 (1984), 20–38; R. Daiches-Dubin, 'Eighteenth-Century Anglo-Jewry in and around Richmond, Surrey', *TJHSE* 18 (1958), 143–69; H. F. Finberg, 'Jewish Residents in Eighteenth-Century Twickenham', *TJHSE* 16 (1952), 129–35.

[52] Walpole to William Mason, 11 Oct. 1778: *Correspondence*, xxviii. 445, 447.

[53] Walpole to Lady Ossory, 14 Sept. 1774: ibid. xxxii. 207.

from them. Said the other, "They are eternally damned," as cold-blooded and certain of himself as if he already saw them burning.' Moritz was told that 'there is a Jew living here from whom the clergy order sermons to be written for money'. Interestingly, when the German edition was published in English thirteen years later, the phrase 'is a Jew' was altered to 'are a few'.[54]

French observers also echoed the rather positive public image that some of the Jewish community enjoyed in late eighteenth-century England. Grosely's work on London included a chapter on the Jews, where he contrasted the elegant English Sephardi community with the Jews that he had seen on the Continent. 'The psalmody of the English synagogue surprized me, by the sweetness as well as the agreeable simplicity of its modulation. My astonishment was caused by a comparison of this symphony with the vociferation of the German synagogues, and even with the church music which I had heard in England.' Grosely was used to a different sort of Jew, Ashkenazim who would wail in the synagogues, accompanied by 'the handkerchiefs with which they muffle themselves up whilst at their devotions', led by 'the cries of the rabbies'. Grosely briefly surveyed Anglo-Jewish history, lighting on Toland and mentioning the Jew Bill, and summed up his observations on the Jews of England thus:

Since their being restored in England by Cromwell, the Jews dispersed through the different classes of commerce, share public offices with the other merchants, amongst whom they distinguish themselves by sentiments and punctuality in their dealings, from which those of their perswasion think themselves dispensed in countries where the name of a Jew is a mark of ignominy and reproach. Their wealth makes part of the capital of a nation, and they contribute to its splendor. Thus they can excite envy only upon the same account as the English merchants; besides, envy is a passion which owes its birth to idleness; persons whose minds are entirely engrossed by their own affairs, busy themselves but very little with those of other people. The Jews at last, warned by the events in which they had been sufferers, left to the natives the whole profit of the finances, which in England is not always to be depended upon.[55]

François Lacombe, another French visitor to England, put the matter even more succinctly: 'Il faut espérer', he concluded, 'que la nation Anglaise, plus éclairée qu'aucune nation de la terre, fera époque en

---

[54] Carl Philip Moritz, *Journeys of a German in England in 1782*, ed. and trans. R. Nettel (London, 1965), 105, 181, 187. The first German edn. appeared in 1783, and the second two years later, from which this English trans. was done, instead of repr. the English trans. of 1795.

[55] Grosley, *A Tour to London* (London, 1772), i. 363–9. Cf. id., *Londres* (Lausanne, 1770), ii. 221–30.

naturalisant cette industrieuse peuplade, & la rappellera dans ses royaumes. C'est le seul moyen d'enrichir & de peupler un si beau pays, que l'impôt du *Timbre* a déjà appauvri.'[56]

The rather negative view of the Ashkenazi Jewish community was confirmed by their own new rabbi, Hirschel Lewin, more usually known by his Anglicized appellation of Hart Lyon. The death of his predecessor, the venerable Aaron Hart, in the spring of 1756 prompted the community to turn to the son of the Ashkenazi rabbi in Amsterdam, recently dead. The fact that Hart Lyon's mother was a daughter of Rabbi Zvi Ashkenazi, who had been consulted during the congregation's infancy at the beginning of the eighteenth century, was an added mark in his favour. Hart Lyon served the Ashkenazi Jews of London between 1756 and 1764, that is, during the entire period of the Seven Years War, and his testimony is therefore worth considering at length.[57]

Soon after his arrival, at an intercession service ordered by the king in June 1757, Lyon delivered one of his first diatribes against his own congregation. Speaking in Yiddish, quoting Aristotle, and praising the treatment of the Jews by the English government, Lyon said that he came to

warn you against the small sins you have fallen victims to. The shaving of the beard, a non-Jewish custom, strictly and repeatedly forbidden in our Torah . . . but you regard them as minor matters, not realizing that they are the pillars on which Judaism stands. You direct a non-Jewish servant to light the fire, to make fresh tea or coffee on Sabbath. Do not forget the punishment for this sin is that fire breaks out in your houses.

On other occasions, Lyon condemned his Jews for collecting their mail at the Post Office on Sabbath morning, and asking passing Gentiles to open letters for them: 'Although this is not forbidden,' he ruled, 'I have heard that it is a scandal in the eyes of Gentiles.' Indeed, he cried,

Day by day, we can see with our own eyes the decay of our people. We sin and act against the law of God; all our endeavours are to associate with the Gentiles and to be like them. That is the chief source of all our failings. See, the women wear wigs and the young ones go even further and wear décolleté dresses open two spans low in front and back. Their whole aim is, not to appear like daughters of Israel. On the one side we claim with pride that we are as good as any of our neighbours. We see that they live happily, that their commerce dominates the world, and we want to be like them, dress as they dress, talk as they talk, and want to make everybody forget that we are Jews . . . See where these thoughts lead you to, and how we live here. We dress on non-Jewish

---

[56] [François Lacombe], *Observations sur Londres et ses environs* (Paris, 1777), 43–4.

[57] Generally on Hart Lyon, see C. Roth, *The Great Synagogue London 1690–1940* (London, 1950), 108–23.

holidays better than on our own festivals; the Christmas pudding which the Christians prepare in memory of the Apostles is more favoured than the Mazzoth. Even the children call the non-Jewish feasts 'Holy' days and do not seem to know that our holy day is the Sabbath. Soon they will come to regard the 'Habdalah' service [on Saturday night] . . . as a sign for the beginning of the Sabbath.

In short, Rabbi Hart Lyon declared, it 'were better if you would read at least secular books instead of playing cards'. He was disgusted with the fact that 'instead of gathering in the houses of learning, people go to operas, plays, concerts, and clubs'.[58]

Under such circumstances, it was no wonder that Hart Lyon was not long for England. He opened negotiations with the community in Halberstadt in 1763, and left London the following year. He remained in Halberstadt for about seven years, was translated to Mannheim, and finally to Berlin, where he died in 1800, having served there for about eight years, making the acquaintance of Moses Mendelssohn and other leading lights of the *Haskalah* (Enlightenment). Summing up his life's work, Rabbi Hart Lyon was said to have remarked that in London he had money but no Jews; in Mannheim, Jews but no money; but in Berlin he had no money and no Jews either.[59] Even taking into account a certain amount of clerical exaggeration, it is clear that the Jews in England were somewhat of a disappointment to a learned Continental clergyman.

III

If foreign Gentiles favourably compared the Jews of England with those they had seen in Germany, foreign Jews usually saw things the other way round, and preferred piety and learning amidst persecution to freedom at any price. The native English Gentile population lacked any basis of comparison, and by the second half of the eighteenth century the Jews had become so indelible a part of the landscape that their image of the Jew could be independently formed. Unfortunately, what attracted their attention most of all was the apparent link between the Jews and crime, for, more often than not, the average London fence might be a Jew.

'The Jews are the most notorious receivers of stolen plate, and

---

[58] Jewish Theological Seminary, New York City, MS Adler 1248, 84 fos., including most of Hart Lyon's sermons in London. I have not seen this, but relied on the trans. in C. Duschinsky, 'The Rabbinate of the Great Synagogue, London, from 1786–1842', *JQR* 9 (1918–19), 103–37, 371–408; 10 (1919–20), 445–527; 11 (1920–1), 21–81, 201–36, 345–87: here 9: 109–23. This long article was printed in book form as well (London, 1921) and repr. 1971.   [59] Ibid. 9: 130–7.

consequently the greatest encouragers of housebreakers in this kingdom,' wrote William Jackson, whose *Newgate Calendar* in six volumes provided late eighteenth-century England with an encyclopaedia of evil. Jackson's tomes are filled with casual references to Jewish fences throughout the entire period under his purview, beginning about 1700: '. . . which they sold to the Jews on the following day', '. . . the whole of which they disposed of to the Jews', '. . . and sold them to their old acquaintance, the Jews', and so on. Certainly it was known that any pickpocket or housebreaker could find an easy and ready market for his booty in Duke's Place.[60]

A typical transaction was one which took place at the beginning of 1771. Two Gentiles, Luke Cannon and John Siday, having committed a burglary, brought their loot to Moses Levi, 'a dealer in old cloaths'. Levi purchased the items from the two men, consisting of 'some valuable cloaths, and 650 ounces of plate, paying for it upwards of one hundred and seventy pounds in cash and a note'. Levi in turn passed the hot gold on to a certain Joseph Jacobs, who like his father Lazarus was a fence. The entire gang was eventually discovered, tried, and convicted. The two Gentiles were executed on 27 February 1771; the lives of the two Jews, 'though they made very artful defences', also hung in the balance. At the end of the day, Moses was transported for fourteen years, and Joseph was entirely acquitted.[61]

Another characteristically Jewish crime was what was called 'queer bail' or even 'Jew-Bail'. According to another observer, 'Hounds-ditch and Duke's Place furnish the King's-Bench and Old-Bailey with Jewish geniuses ready for all cases.' The con went like this:

A Jew was lately examined, in order to *justify bail* in the King's-Bench. The Counsel demanded, 'what street he live in, and what shop he kept?' He replied, 'Houndsditch; but he kept no shop.' 'How was his property vested?' 'In monies.' 'Where is it vested?' 'I have it about me.' He then pulled out a small pocket-book, which handing to one of the Judges, he said, 'If your Lordship will take the *throubles*, (for I don't want to *throuble* your Lordship or the Court) to open dat book, you'll find I have properties enough.'—His Lordship opened the pocket-book, and finding in it Bank-bills to the amount of three or four thousand pounds, ordered the Bail to be taken. Moses at his going out of Court, meets another Brother-Jew, to whom he returns the pocket-book, and so the Bail is justified; and is what is called *Jew-Bail*.[62]

---

[60] William Jackson, *The New and Complete Newgate Calendar* (London, [1795]), ii. 147, 147 n., 148, 149. Cf. ii. 388, 391; iii. 96, 163, 167, 168, 169; iv. 81, 133. For a chapbook dramatization of Jewish avarice, see *The Northern Lord; or, The Cruel Jew's Garland* (Hull, [c. 1785]).   [61] Jackson, *Newgate*, v. 15.

[62] G. Parker, *A View of Society and Manners in High and Low Life* (London, 1781), ii. 21–3.

Another common swindle with which Jews were rightly or wrongly associated was even more complex, as William Jackson explains:

one of them hires a house, and appears as a merchant of great credit and importance; while his accomplices get credit of any one who is weak enough to trust them, and give bills on the supposed merchant. These bills are generally received without suspicion; for previous enquiry having been made respecting the character and circumstances of the merchant, no doubt of either remains; and these impostors proceed for a long time, undetected.

According to Jackson, among 'the number of these atrocious offenders, the Jews have been principally concerned; and it is not unfrequently that a Jew merchant is the acceptor of the false bills; but the acceptor is never to be found when the day of payment arrives'.[63]

Jews were not traditionally associated with violent crimes, although some prominent exceptions show that such a connection was not unthinkable. One famous case took place in October 1747, when Hosea Youell and Jacob Lopez were tried for the murder of a certain Captain Johns in Devonshire Square. Johns had been robbed of his watch and money by the two Jews, but when he cried for help Youell deliberately returned and mortally stabbed his victim, who managed to identify his assailant before expiring. Lopez was acquitted of the murder charge, but Youell was sentenced to hang:

After conviction the prisoner said that he was only eighteen years of age, and born of Jewish parents, who lived in Creed-lane, Leadenhall-street. He was so illiterate that he could neither read Hebrew nor English. The ordinary of Newgate representing to him the advantages of the Gospel over the Mosaic dispensation, he said that, as he was born and bred a Jew, he would die such. He was attended by a person of his own persuasion.

Hosea Youell was hanged at Tyburn on 16 November 1747.[64]

Another Jewish murder which was somewhat less straightforward began on Wednesday, 16 January 1793, when an elderly and apparently wealthy Jew named Aaron Fernandes de Silva was murdered along with his housekeeper by a gang of five or six men, who then stripped the house. The chief suspect was his nephew, a certain Mr Mendez who lived near Moorfields, but he produced a bevy of respectable witnesses who swore to his alibi. The jury was forced to deliver a verdict of 'wilful murder by persons unknown'. Later on further evidence was found that tied Mendez to his uncle's murder, but before he could be apprehended he managed to swallow nearly half a pint of arsenic and thereby cheated the gallows. William Jackson, the chronicler of Newgate, mused that 'the extraordinary end of this man seems a corroboration of the guilt laid to

---

[63] Jackson, *Newgate*, iii. 998.   [64] Ibid. iii. 149–51.

his charge, as doubtless, the man capable of *murdering himself*, is capable of murdering his uncle!'[65]

But unquestionably the most notorious Jewish crime of eighteenth-century England was the Chelsea Murders of 1771, an armed robbery that went very wrong. The leader of the gang of eight Jews was a physician named Levi Weil, who had studied at the University of Leiden, and now, with his brother, brought over a group of Dutch Jews to assist him in crime. They began with a number of successful housebreakings, and intended to carry on with their well-tried methods at the home of Mrs Elizabeth Hutchins in Chelsea. The robbers forced their way into the house on the evening of 11 June 1771, overpowered the maidservants and Mrs Hutchins, and then upstairs murdered one of the manservants in his bed, while another servant who lay with him at the time made his escape through the window, pursued by bullets. The gang left the house soon afterwards, carting away a considerable quantity of plunder, and at least sixty-four guineas in cash.

The identity of the perpetrators remained unknown for a number of months, until Daniel Isaacs, one of the gang who had been brought over from Holland, was compelled by economic misfortune to turn to Naphtaly Hart Myers, an officer of the Ashkenazi Great Synagogue, requesting charity. Myers refused to aid a man who after all was not strictly speaking one of his parishioners, but after the authorities had offered a reward for the apprehension of the Chelsea Murderers, Isaacs returned to Myers and confessed his guilt, hoping to be granted immunity (and the reward) in return for information. Myers took the thief to Sir John Fielding, the Bow Street magistrate, and his testimony led to the arrest of six of the seven remaining criminals.[66]

The trial was held at the Old Bailey on 6 December 1771. All of the accused 'kept to the same story, declaring they never were at Chelsea, and that they were totally innocent', speaking in Yiddish, employing the services of Naphtaly Hart Myers as their interpreter. Dr Levi Weil went one step further, and produced a woman to swear 'that the Doctor was with her the night the robbery was committed; that he came to her at Bethnal-green, about nine at night, remarkably chearful; that he told her

---

[65] Jackson, *Newgate*, iv. 154–7.

[66] For the Chelsea Murders, see esp. ibid. v. 17–25 and *London Chronicle*, 2335 (28–30 Nov. 1771), 527; 2337 (3–5 Dec. 1771), 544; 2338 (5–7 Dec. 1771), 551–2; 2339 (7–10 Dec. 1771), 557–9; 2340 (10–12 Dec. 1771), 568. Other sources include *Gents. Mag.* 11 (1771), 518, 521, 566; Andrew Knapp and William Baldwin, *The New Newgate Calendar* (London, 1826), iii. 282; R. Leslie-Melville, *The Life and Work of Sir John Fielding* (London, 1934), 261–4. An important primary source is PRO, SP 37/8. See also T. Endelman, *The Jews of Georgian England 1714–1830* (Philadelphia, 1979), 198–202.

it was his birth-day'. As one newspaper account laconically reported, 'Her evidence had no weight either with the Court or Jury', which took exactly twenty minutes to come to a verdict of 'guilty' regarding the Weil brothers and two of the four others on trial.[67]

On the following day, a Saturday, the convicted men were 'anathematized in the synagogue', and on Monday, 9 December 1771, they were taken from Newgate Prison to Tyburn, where they were hanged. They were comforted by a rabbi at the prison, who gave each of them a Hebrew book, but he 'declined attending them to the place of death, nor even prayed with them at the time of his visit'. The six Jews were by then the talk of the town, and the subject of numerous references in the popular press: 'They were attended to the place of execution by immense crowds of people, who were anxious to witness the exit of wretches whose crimes had been so much the object of public notice.' At Tyburn, having 'prayed together, and sung an hymn in the Hebrew language, they were launched into eternity'.[68]

Even after death, the Chelsea Murderers were public spectacles. As was customary, their corpses were delivered to Surgeons' Hall to serve the needs of medical students. Only a few days later a lecture was given at the Royal Academy on the anatomy of painting, 'exemplified by a real subject, one of the Jews executed on Monday being brought to the Academy for that purpose', namely the mortal remains of Dr Levi Weil. Meanwhile, at Surgeons' Hall, it was necessary to call for the service of two sheriffs, 'in order to disperse the mob assembled to see the bodies of the Jews, but their endeavours were fruitless; the concourse of people was so great, that the Gentlemen of the Faculty, whose business it was to attend, were obliged to be dragged in at the Hall windows'.[69]

The extraordinarily overt Jewishness of the Chelsea Murderers, and perhaps even the enforced presence of a synagogue official at the trial as translator from the Yiddish, was bound to have some spillover on to the Jewish community as a whole. According to one observer, 'A Jew could scarcely pass the streets but he was upbraided with the words, "Hutchins" and "Chelsea", and many of them were pulled by the beards; while those, who ought to have taken the insulters into custody, stood calmly by, and triumphed in the insult.'[70] Just before the trial began at the Old Bailey, a London newspaper reported that 'Within these few days a great number of Jews have left the kingdom.'[71] Horace Walpole noted that even gamblers were affected by the public reaction

[67] *London Chronicle*, 2339 (7–10 Dec. 1771), 557–8.
[68] Ibid.; Jackson, *Newgate*, 22.
[69] *London Chronicle*, 2340 (7–10 Dec. 1771), 568.
[70] Jackson, *Newgate*, v. 23.
[71] *London Chronicle*, 2337 (3–5 Dec. 1771), 544.

to the Chelsea Murders, now without a means to finance their habit, since 'it is not so easy *to borrow a Jew*', he complained in a letter of 14 December 1771, 'now so many are hanged or run away'.[72]

Francis Place likewise painted a very vivid picture of the public mood against the Jews in the aftermath of the Chelsea Murders:

Every Jew was in public opinion implicated, and the prejudice, ill will and brutal conduct this brought upon the Jews, even after they had been detected and punished for it, did not cease for many years. 'Go to Chelsea' was a common exclamation when a Jew was seen in the streets and was often the signal of assault. I have seen many Jews hooted, hunted, cuffed, pulled by the beard, spit upon, and so barbarously assaulted in the streets, without any protection from the passers-by or the police, as seems when compared with present times, almost impossible to have existed at any time. Dogs could not be used in the streets in the manner many Jews were treated.

Interestingly, Place suggests that the appearance of Jewish boxers such as Daniel Mendoza in the following decade helped to change all this, for he 'set up a school to teach the art of boxing as a science, the art soon spread among the young Jews and they became generally expert at it. The consequence was in a very few years seen and felt too. It was no longer safe to insult a Jew unless he was an old man and alone.' Nevertheless, Place notes, 'even if the Jews were unable to defend themselves, the few who would [now] be disposed to insult them merely because they are Jews, would be in danger of chastisement from the passers-by and of punishment from the police'.[73] This demonstrably was not yet the case in the early 1770s.

Even William Jackson, who was hardly a friend to the Jews, thought that public reaction to the Chelsea Murders had gone too far: 'a whole body of people were insulted for the crimes of a few individuals,' he noted;

There is something wantonly cruel in affronting the whole body of a people, because a few individuals of that people have rendered themselves obnoxious by the atrocity of their guilt. As well might we affront an Englishman, because an Englishman may have suffered the sentence of the law, as a Jew, because that fatal sentence may have followed the crimes of some of his profession.

Yet, from his point of view, the Chelsea Murders were an untypical Jewish crime in a sea of serious violations of the law, and some action would have to be taken. First, Jackson thought, the Jewish fences should be put out of business. 'If we had a law to make the receiving of stolen-

---

[72] Walpole to the countess of Upper Ossory, 14 Dec. 1771: *Correspondence*, xxxii. 68.
[73] BL Add. MS 27287, fos. 145–6: quoted in M. D. George, *London Life in the Eighteenth Century* (New York, 1964), 132.

goods a capital offence', he argued, 'the property of honest house-keepers would be more secure than at present.' Secondly, the Jews might be specially taxed in order to return to society what they had illegally taken from it: 'In ancient times Jews have been expelled the kingdom; and in other instances, such taxes have been laid on them as were almost equal to an expulsion. It is pity this practice does not yet prevail, as these people are the most flagrant encouragers of thieves, by the reception of stolen goods.'[74]

Richard King, another observer of London low life, was similarly in two minds about what to do with regard to the problem of Jewish involvement in crime. 'I would not be mistaken,' he explained, 'I do not mean to arraign the whole people; wandering, dispersed as they are, they need not be oppressed; but facts are strong against many of them, and Jew swindlers and Jew bail are notorious in this metropolis.' The rights of English Gentile victims needed also to be taken into consideration:

The many notorious depredations and outrages committed by Jews, are very alarming in a Christian country such as Great Britain is, remarkable for laws and liberty; and it is to be lamented that no effectual means can be found to stop the growing evil, which, of late years, has overspread the country. The many horrid and shocking murders and burglaries they have committed, and escaped, call for the interference of the legislative power, and the maturest wisdom, in adjusting a code of laws particularly to affect this numerous race of unbelievers, who look upon it as a virtue to destroy, cheat, and gull the christian world.

King's plan was identical to that of Jackson, a special tax on the Jews. This, he thought, 'would become of great utility to the state in general, as it might be applied towards discharging the national debt, which they, from time to time, have considerably helped to increase, by hoarding up their vast riches'.[75]

Such views were known to the leaders of Anglo-Jewry, and, even before the Chelsea Murders, steps were taken to try to reduce the incidence of Jewish crime. Sir John Fielding, who would be the leading light at the trial of the Chelsea Murderers, had written to Naphtaly Hart Myers and Napthaly Franks of the Ashkenazi Great Synagogue as early as 25 May 1766, thanking them 'for the Assistance they have already given to the civil Power, to detect the Receivers of stolen Goods, in Duke's Place & Houndsditch; & also for their laudable Declarations to continue their Assistance, 'till the Evil itself is suppressed'.[76] In their

[74] Jackson, *Newgate*, ii. 147 n.; iii. 998 n.; v. 23.
[75] Richard King, *The Frauds of London Detected* (London, [1770]), 110–15; id., *The Complete Modern London Spy* (London, 1781), 49, 52–3, 81.
[76] Sir John Fielding to Napthaly Hart Myers and Napthaly Franks, 25 May 1766 (copy): BL Add. MS 5832, fos. 227ᵛ–228ʳ.

reply the following day, the two synagogue leaders reiterated their resolve 'to detect those few infamous Receivers of stolen Goods', confident that 'we shall receive the Applause of every Jew'.[77] These were admirable sentiments, and the letters were reprinted in the press in order to publicize the determination of the Jewish leaders even further. William Cole the Cambridge antiquary was one of those who remained sceptical: 'Notwithstanding these fair Beginnings of detaching those few infamous Receivers of stolen Goods', he confided to his commonplace book,

as the Presidents eccho from the civil Expression of 'a few Persons only', of Sir John Feilding, yet it is not probable that a People, ragged, wretched, poor & miserable, Thieves by Education, as well as Necessity, who come into this Kingdom by Shoals, & have nothing to subsist on but their Wits, & the Charity of the Synagogue, which we may very charitably suppose, had rather they would supply themselves any other way, than solely out of their Pockets, as it must be very burthensome to them, the Rich being so few, & the Poor so exceedingly numerous: I say, it is most probable, that such a Race, who are every where the same, I mean Brokers, from the highest to the lowest, would always continue to be the Pawn-Brokers; that is, the Receivers of stolen Goods, or Extortioners & Usurers, wherever they happen to be settled.[78]

Another result of the Chelsea Murders was that the entire issue of Jewish immigration came to be examined more closely. Sir John Fielding became aware of the fact that the packet boats from Holland included many Jews among their passengers, including such men as those recruited by the infamous Dr Levi Weil. Fielding was informed by the synagogue elders that this recent immigration was 'partly on account of the late disturbance in Poland, partly to share charities distributed in this kingdom from their chest at the Synagogue'. It appeared that Jews embarking from Holland 'there plead poverty and get passes by our agent there, by which means they get their passage free'. The elders of the Great Synagogue themselves were anxious to restrict immigration, not only because it brought them into conflict with the English authorities, but because the immigrant destitute put an unacceptable burden on their finances.[79] It was finally decided that Jews coming to England would have to prove that they were travelling on legitimate business and would not become a burden on the state. Furthermore, in December 1771 it was ordered that Jews could not board the packet

[77] N. Franks and N. H. Myers to Fielding, 26 May 1766 (copy): BL Add. MS 5832, fo. 228[r].

[78] Revd. William Cole, commonplace book: BL Add. MS 5832, fo. 228[r].

[79] Sir John Fielding to the earl of Suffolk: SP Dom. Geo. III, parcel 8: quoted in George, *London Life*, 128.

boats unless they paid the full fare. This regulation was finally put into effect on 10 October 1774, when it was decided that 'Jews are in no instance to be admitted on board without paying the full Passage Money of 12/6 each.'[80]

IV

Despite this apparent predominance of Jews in crime out of proportion to their numbers, in many circles the Jewish question was ineradicably connected with the personalities of a number of key figures in the community. First among these in mid-eighteenth-century England was Samson Gideon (1699–1762), one of the most famous financiers of his day.[81] Although he was a scion of the famous Abudiente family from Portugal, Gideon's father had been born in Germany and came to England from Barbados as a wealthy and well-connected Sephardi West Indian merchant.[82] Samson Gideon dabbled in his father's trade, but his heart lay in the business of stockjobbing, trading in shares in the three main joint stock companies, the Bank of England, the East India Company, and the South Sea Company. Gideon also dealt in lottery tickets and government securities, and was an outstanding *habitué* of Change Alley and the coffee-houses where such transactions were conducted. The South Sea Bubble of 1720 built his fortune, and nine years later he was given one of the twelve brokerage licences reserved for Jews among the total number of 100. Gideon's phenomenal financial success was all the more remarkable in light of the extreme precariousness of his trade. Stockjobbers disregarded the prohibition against their appearing personally on Change Alley or to job in stock themselves, and, after a new bill passed in Parliament in 1734, they also ignored the injunction against dealing in futures, which were the mainstay of their business. Dealings in stocks continued unabated, but with the difference that no debts were recoverable at law. This anomaly was not rectified until the early 1770s, after Gideon was dead.[83]

---

[80] Advertisement and cover letter regarding full payment by Jews, 9 Sept. and 10 Oct. 1774: Jewish Museum, London, MS 85.

[81] Generally, see John Eardley Wilmot, 'A Memoir of the Life of Samson Gideon', in J. Nichols, *Illustrations of the Literary History of the Eighteenth Century* (London, 1817–58), vi. 277–84; John Francis, *Chronicles and Characters of the Stock Exchange* (London, 1849), 88–91; L. S. Sutherland, 'Samson Gideon: Eighteenth Century Jewish Financier', *TJHSE* 17 (1953), 79–90; id., 'Samson Gideon and the Reduction of Interest, 1749–50', *Econ. HR* 16 (1946), 15–29; Hyamson, *Sephardim*, 128–33.

[82] Gideon to Newcastle, c.1757: BL Add. MS 33055, fo. 219; *Bevis Marks Records*, i, ed. Barnett, 42–4. [83] Sutherland, 'Financier', 80–1.

But it was Gideon's steadfast loyalty to the English government which brought him not only a handsome profit, but also very nearly a peerage. Straightforward taxation was already in the eighteenth century a very inefficient and inelastic method of raising money, especially during periods of crisis. New systems had to be developed, the most prominent of which was the 'Closed Subscription', an exclusive loan with separately negotiated conditions offered by a single individual on behalf of a list of subscribers. In 1742, for the first time, Gideon was able to have his list of Jewish subscribers accepted by the government. Several years later, during the Jacobite rebellion in 1745 of the Young Pretender, Gideon put together a package of well over a million pounds for Pelham's government, an act of courage which soon yielded a very substantial profit for him and his subscribers as well. Despite public outcry after the fact, Pelham stood by the terms of the loan, although he now produced open subscriptions which allowed others to cash in on a system which only now was proving to be relatively secure.[84]

Gideon's financial activities and economic services to the British government were both numerous and celebrated. By 1750 his capital stood at £180,000, he had already been granted a coat of arms, and had purchased a country estate in Kent, Belvedere House. He also owned lands in Lincolnshire and Buckinghamshire, and probably elsewhere as well.[85] As we have already seen, Gideon opposed the Jew Bill of 1753, 'solicited in folly and want of knowledge', and withdrew from the synagogue at Bevis Marks when it was implied that he supported their cause.[86] Gideon was very active in financing the Seven Years War, and hoped that he would be rewarded with the social position appropriate to a great landed gentleman.[87] His daughter married Viscount Gage in 1757, and the following year he himself approached the duke of Devonshire with the proposal that he be given a baronetcy in recognition of long service to the Crown.[88] He included in his letter a list of such services, and a record of Jews who had been granted peerages in other

---

[84] Sutherland, 'Financier', 82–3.　　　　　　　　　　　　　　[85] Ibid. 84–5.

[86] Wilmot, 'Gideon', 283. A contemporary caricature of 1753 portrayed a scene 100 years hence, when a statue of an ennobled Gideon would stand in front of St Paul's, in place of that of Queen Anne: repr. Hyamson, *Sephardim*, opp. p. 129. In any case, Gideon would himself derive no benefit from the Jew Bill, being native born. Gideon's name was connected with the Jew Bill in [Romaine], *An Answer to a Pamphlet*, 33.

[87] Other Jews who carried on the Anglo-Jewish tradition of financing and supplying the English war effort during this period were Abraham Prado (see below, p. 255) and the brothers of the famous and eventually notorious Emanuel Mendes da Costa, David and Jacob. David Mendes da Costa left a war diary of 1758: BL MS Eger. 2227: a typed transcript is now at University College, London, Mocatta Library, AJ/151/13/1.

[88] Sutherland, 'Financier', 86–7.

countries, especially Antonio Lopes Suasso, and others. Among the points to his credit, Gideon noted that

Samson the Son of Rowland Gideon (a West India merchant & a free & Levery Man of London) was Boorn in England married an English Protestant. his Sons, & Daughters, were all Babtiz'd by the Sub Dean of St Pauls, few days after their birth. were Strictly Educated & so many of them that are Living Continu to Profess Christianity.[89]

Gideon may well have deserved a baronetcy, but he had two very blatant black marks against him: his Jewishness, and the fact that he was in reality a stockjobber rather than a landed gentleman. The duke of Devonshire's reply must not have come as a complete surprise:

the King seemed extremely well disposed, Spoke very handsomely of you, and Said he shoud have no Objection himself to Oblige you, but as you was not bred up in the religion of the Country he was afraid it woud make a noise & that in a time of Confusion & Publick Distress as the present is he was afraid they would make an Ill use of it, and therefore desired That I woud Inform you in the Civilest manner that it was not Convenient for him to Comply with y^r request.[90]

Gideon was not entirely defeated, however, and understood that 'in a time of confusion and public distress' extraordinary measures might have to be taken, but this would be true for both sides. Several months later, in December 1759, the duke of Newcastle was once again treating with Gideon for the following year's loan, but this time it was made clear that the rewards would need to be somewhat more than financial. 'One word at this Crisis will do, which if Neglected, may not be Ever recovered,' Gideon wrote, 'his Father has it at heart, and dreads being Disapointed, be the Object of his desire great or Small.' He now pressed for his son to be made a baronet, and forwarded a copy of his baptismal certificate.[91] Some indication that Gideon did not take the conversion of his son to Christianity entirely seriously comes in a letter of Horace Walpole to his friend, the celebrated classicist Richard Bentley in 1754. I must 'tell you a story of Gideon', he wrote,

He breeds his children Christians: he had a mind to know what proficience his son had made in his new religion; 'so,' says he, 'I began, and asked him, who made him? He said, "God." I then asked him, who redeemed him? He replied very readily, "Christ." Well, then I was at the end of my interrogatories, and did not know what other question to put to him—I said, "Who—who—" I did not

---

[89] See n. 82 above.

[90] Devonshire to Gideon, 13 June 1758: BL Add. MS 32886, fo. 243^{r-v}.

[91] Gideon to Devonshire, 9 Dec. 1758, enclosing baptismal certificate: BL Add. MS 32886, fo. 241; Gideon to Newcastle, 21 Jan. 1759: Add. MS 32887, fos. 274–6; J. West to Newcastle, 18 Apr. 1759: Add. MS 32890, fos. 162–3.

know what to say—at last I said, "Who gave you that hat?" "The Holy Ghost," said the boy.'—Did you ever hear a better catechism?[92]

In May 1759 young Sampson, son of Samson Gideon, was created baronet: Gideon wrote to his 13-year-old son at Eton, reminding him that it 'is the lowest hereditary honor, but the first step'. Thirty years later he would be raised to the peerage as Lord Eardley.[93]

From his own point of view, Gideon had now reached the summit of his ambition, and the will he drew up two years before his death in October 1762 gives some indication of how he wished to be remembered. Careful provision was made for his heirs, but should none remain alive, his estate was to go to the duke of Devonshire, the man who had helped him reach his desired goal. Among his legacies, the most interesting one was to the Bevis Marks synagogue, £1,000, along with a request that he be buried with full rites at the Jewish cemetery in Mile End. Should that last request be refused, he hoped to be buried at the Christian cemetery at Spalding, and left money in that event to be used for their charitable purposes.[94] During the deliberation on Gideon's request, a venerable member of the congregation revealed that Gideon had secretly contributed an annual sum to the community since his resignation in 1753 more than equal to the amount required for membership.[95]

Gideon was replaced, in many senses, by another Sephardi Jewish financier, Joseph Salvador (1716–86). Salvador himself was born in England, but his family had emigrated from The Netherlands in the late seventeenth century. From about 1757, Salvador was becoming increasingly prominent in government finance, having the field to himself after Samson Gideon's death. Like Gideon, Salvador craved public recognition and social status, his route being a fellowship in the Royal Society from March 1759. Salvador was very much involved with Clive and the East India Company, although he was not a director, as is sometimes claimed. Salvador was quite clearly in decline by the mid-

[92] Walpole to Bentley, 9 July 1754: *Correspondence*, xxxv. 177–80.
[93] Samson Gideon to Sampson Gideon, May [1759]: quoted in Sutherland, 'Financier', 88–9, orig. letter apparently in private hands. The title died with Lord Eardley, but through a daughter Gideon blood descended to Robert Erskine Childers, the Irish writer and patriot: Hyamson, *Sephardim*, 130. For the royal grant creating Sampson Gideon Lord Eardley, see the document on display on the rear staircase, Broughton Castle, Banbury.
[94] Samson Gideon's will, 1760: described in Sutherland, 'Financier', 89.
[95] James Picciotto, *Sketches of Anglo-Jewish History* (new edn., London, 1956; 1st pub. 1875), 59. 'Simpson de Rehuel Abudiente' is still recalled as a benefactor of the congregation in the service at the close of the Day of Atonement: Hyamson, *Sephardim*, 133.

1750s, having suffered financial loss in the great Lisbon earthquake of 1755, and the credit crisis of the Seven Years War, which so benefited Samson Gideon.[96]

More exciting, perhaps, was his involvement with the figures of high society, such as Kitty Fisher, the renowned courtesan painted by Reynolds, whose widower he sued for recovery of money lent.[97] He was also involved with Mrs Caroline Rudd—'Consort of Rudd, and choice of Salvadore!'—another treasured woman of the same profession, whose name was linked with a famous forgery case in the late 1770s, for which two men were hanged.[98] Salvador even had a bastard son by the countess of Moriencourt, the Belgian woman whose acquaintance, the secretary to the French ambassador in London, involved Salvador in a plot to speculate on a war between England and Spain over the Falkland Islands, a plan which caused severe financial loss for all involved.[99] As a public demonstration of his status, Salvador built himself a grand London residence at White Hart Court, Bishopsgate, and would retire to the country to his landed estate at Tooting. By 1784 Salvador was ruined, and was forced to retreat to South Carolina, where he had purchased 100,000 acres of land thirty years before as a hedge on his speculative investments. Salvador died there two years later, but not before writing a fascinating account of life in the colony to Emanuel Mendes da Costa, his contact in the Royal Society, now disgraced.[100]

Salvador, like Gideon before him, craved contact with the greatest figures of English court society. Unlike Gideon, he lived much closer to the edge, and eventually paid the price of profligacy. In his heyday he was much in demand. Haim David Azulai, who travelled through Europe collecting money for the poor of Hebron, described a meeting

---

[96] See generally M. Woolf, 'Joseph Salvador, 1716–1786', *TJHSE* 21 (1968), 104–37; Finberg, 'Twickenham'.

[97] In 1770, three years after Kitty's death, Salvador brought action against her widower John Norris, MP for Rye, for recovery of the money. Norris claimed that the money was a gift, and read out in court a letter proving this. Woolf, 'Salvador', 110–11.

[98] *Gents. Mag.* 45 (1775), 443; Woolf, 'Salvador', 111. Cf. *Gents. Mag.* 79 (1809), 581. Mrs Rudd was the accomplice of Robert and Daniel Perreau, who, having lost £1,300 speculating on a war with Spain, planned the famous forgery for which they were hanged at Tyburn in 1776: cf. H. Bleackley, *Some Distinguished Victims of the Scaffold* (London, 1905), 48; id., *Trial of Henry Fauntleroy* (London, 1924), 174. Cf. Daniel Perreau's narrative, repr. Woolf, 'Salvador', app. B.

[99] Woolf, 'Salvador', 111. Salvador even followed Barthelemy Tort (the secretary to the Comte de Guines, the French ambassador to London) to France in a futile attempt to recover his money: *Annual Register* (1775), 128; *Mémoire pour le comte de Guines* (Paris, 1775); *Mémoire contre le comte de Guines* (Paris, 1775).

[100] Woolf, 'Salvador', 110, 112–13; Picciotto, *Sketches*, 153–6; Salvador to E. M. da Costa, 22 Jan. 1785: BL Add. MS 28542, fos. 90–2: repr. Woolf, 'Salvador', app. C. Cf. C. Reznikoff and U. Z. Engelman, *The Jews of Charleston* (Philadelphia, 1950).

with Salvador in 1755. Azulai went to see the leaders of the Sephardi community, and was told that

We do not know what you can do, but if you are wise, behold Señor Joseph Salvador, who is one of the Parnassim, is going to the waters; he is very clever and whatever he says is done immediately and, when Joseph returns home, if you find favour in his eyes, he will not rest until he has completed the matter well. So when Señor Joseph Salvador came, I went to him and saw him eye to eye and I spoke as to my mission in a humble and insinuating manner.

Salvador was of great help to Azulai, who was surprised by how much trouble the great man was willing to take over the matter.[101] Count Frederick Kielmansegge, coming to England in 1761, also heard that among the Jews to be seen at Court was 'a very rich Portuguese Jew, Salvadore, who is to be met everywhere in society, at Munchhausen's, the foreign ministers', and elsewhere. As they do not wear beards, they cannot be distinguished at all from other people'.[102] This, of course, is exactly what pained the leaders of the Jewish community, who saw how easily their wealthiest Jews were assimilating into the higher ranks of English society.

V

Joseph Salvador was also a leading figure in the creation of the representative body of Anglo-Jewry which in retrospect appears as the act which led to the invention of the Board of Deputies. George III came to the throne on 25 October 1760, and the Sephardi Jews of Bevis Marks, ever anxious to demonstrate their loyalty to the Crown, organized seven representatives to deliver the community's respects, led by Joseph Salvador. On 19 November the financier was empowered to take the steps necessary to procure an audience, and this he did with the help of his benefactor, the duke of Devonshire.[103] The 'Community of

---

[101] Haim David Azulai, 'Ma'agal Tov', autograph diary: Jewish Theological Seminary, New York City, partially trans. E. N. Adler, *Jewish Travellers* (London, 1930), 345–68, esp. 348–9. For more on 'Hida' and his descendants, see R. D. Barnett, 'Isaac Leonini Azulay', *TJHSE* 19 (1960), 81–96.

[102] Frederick Kielmansegge, *Diary of a Journey to England in the Years 1761–1762* (London, 1902), 169–70. The count crossed over from Holland with 'some rich Portuguese Jews from Amsterdam, one of whom, named Cappadocci, was a real epicure' (p. 13).

[103] The Board of Deputies of British Jews, first minute book: Jewish Museum, London, fos. 1ʳ–2ʳ. I am grateful to Mr David Massel, then Executive Director of the Board, for his permission to photocopy this important document, and to Mr Edgar Samuel, the Director of the Jewish Museum, for having the work done. See the photograph of the minutes of the first meeting of the committee appointed by Bevis Marks to convey their congratulations to George III on his accession, 19 Nov. 1760: *Bevis Marks Records*, i, ed. Barnett, pl. xvi. On the founding of the Board of Deputies

Portuguese Jews' explained in a letter to Devonshire on 21 November 1760 that 'being so small a Body, have not had the Honour to address, but have been permitted to testify their Duty to the Sovereign on his Accession to the Throne'.[104] The address of the Jews was presented by Devonshire and Newcastle, and was graciously received by the new king.[105]

The Sephardi Jews of Bevis Marks acted throughout as if they represented the entire Jewish population of England, and certainly they had history on their side. The Ashkenazim, however, were no longer willing to leave such matters entirely in the hands of their Spanish and Portuguese co-religionists, who still regarded the 'Tudescos' with a generous measure of contempt. Aaron Franks, a member of one of the most prominent Ashkenazi families, made a formal application to the Mahamad, and it was finally agreed that in future the two parts of the community would deal in tandem with the Christian government outside.[106] Accordingly, on 11 December 1760 Joseph Salvador of Bevis Marks, Aaron Franks of the Great Synagogue, and Henry Isaacs of the Hambro had the honour to kiss hands with the new queen, and likewise with the duke of York and the Princess Augusta. Indeed, the entire affair passed over with a maximum of cordiality and respect.[107] Three days later, on 14 December 1760, the representatives of the Sephardi community passed a resolution 'that whenever any public Affair should offer that may Interest the two Nations, We will on our parts communicate to the Committee of the Dutch Jews Synagogues what we think proper should be done, & that we desire the same Gentlemen may do the same & make a Minute thereof'.[108] Although, with hindsight, 14 December takes on a new significance as the date of the founding of the Board of Deputies of British Jews, the institution which today formally represents Anglo-Jewry, even in 1760 it must have appeared as the beginning of a new era of co-operation between the two parts of the small Jewish community in England. When the representatives of the Board, led by Joseph Salvador, called on the royal chamberlains in November 1761 to congratulate the king and queen on their marriage, the new body was further established on a firm footing, although, in the

generally, see Picciotto, *Sketches*, 107–14; Hyamson, *Sephardim*, 134–9; Roth, *Great Synagogue*, 112–14.

[104] Portuguese Jews to Devonshire, 21 Nov. 1760: Board of Deputies Minute Book.
[105] William Toby, royal chamberlain, to the Sephardi community, 24 Nov. 1760: ibid. [106] Board of Deputies Minute Book, entry for 7 Dec. 1760.
[107] Ibid., entry for 11 Dec. 1760. See also the report of deputies to Sephardi Mahamad, 3 Apr. 1761: SPJC, London, MS 344 (31).
[108] Board of Deputies Minute Book, entry for 14 Dec. 1760. Cf. minutes of Bevis Marks committee of elders, 14 Dec. 1760: *Bevis Marks Records*, i, ed. Barnett, pl. xvii.

early years, meetings were not held on a regular basis and the Ashkenazi deputies were not always invited.[109]

Yet, while the Jewish community was representing itself to the outside world as a diverse but unified body, within the situation was far less harmonious. At the same time that the joint representation of Anglo-Jewry was being organized, about sixty-five Ashkenazi Jews formed another breakaway synagogue which, as had been the case with their predecessors the Hambro congregants, angered the leaders of the parent congregation in Duke's Place. The new group met at Bricklayers' Hall in Leadenhall Street, the original occupants having fallen on hard times and been forced to vacate the premises. Although they recognized Rabbi Hart Lyon as their ultimate spiritual leader, they asked his approval for the appointment of Rabbi Lipman Speyer of Halberstadt as their own rabbi. Despite the fury of the Great Synagogue, the secessionists were determined to establish themselves, and acquired a burial ground on what would become Brady Street, then Ducking Pond Lane. In June 1762 the cornerstone of their new building in Leadenhall Street was laid, and 'The Society of Bricklayers' Hall' became known as the New Synagogue, the third Ashkenazi congregation in eighteenth-century London.[110]

It was also about this time, no later than 1761, that a group of Jews living outside of the London city limits began to meet at the home of Wolf Liepman in Great Pulteney Street, having formed the 'Hebra Kaddisha shel Gemilluth Hassadim, Westminster'. Within four or five years they had moved to a rented room in Denmark Court, Strand, migrating to another adjoining site, and finally settling in Sans Souci, Thomas Dibdin's theatre nearby. The Westminster, or Western, Synagogue remained here until 1826, when they moved to Haymarket,

---

[109] Report by representatives of the Board of Deputies on their mission, 20 Nov. 1761: SPJC, London, MS 344a; duke of Manchester to Salvador, conveying queen's thanks, 23 Nov. 1761: ibid., MS 344b; Lord Boston to Salvador, conveying thanks of dowager princess, 20 Nov. 1761: ibid., MS 344c. See generally for the later history of the Board, the short book by A. Newman, *The Board of Deputies of British Jews 1760–1985* (London, 1987): a list of Board presidents is printed on p. 52. Cf. *A Report on the Records of the Board of Deputies of British Jews 1839–1966*, ed. R. A. Routledge (Hist. MSS Comm., 1976).

[110] Picciotto, *Sketches*, 131–2; Roth, *Great Synagogue*, 120–2. The New Synagogue moved in 1837 from Leadenhall Street, facing Cree Church, to Great St Helen's, and in 1915 to Stamford Hill, where it remains today. The burial register of the New Synagogue, in two volumes, c.1777–83 and 1786–c.95, is now University College of London, Mocatta Library, AJ/266/1–2. A collection of sermons delivered at the New Synagogue, 1794–1806, is now at University of Leeds Library, Roth MS 730. For three smaller prayer groups, see C. Roth, 'The Lesser London Synagogues of the Eighteenth Century', *MJHSE* 3 (1937), 1–7.

and in the process acquired in 1815 their own cemetery, becoming thereby a completely independent community. Indeed, they even managed to provoke a sub-secession in 1810 over the question of seat rentals during Yom Kippur, pursued by a group that soon settled down in Maiden Lane as a separate congregation. The parent group even went so far as to take one of the seceders to the Gentile courts in order to recover back rentals for a seat no longer used.[111] The Maiden Lane congregation remained apart for a century until rejoining the Western Synagogue, which eventually included men like Rabbi Tobias Goodman, perhaps the first English rabbi who regularly preached in English, and Solomon Bennett, whose quarrels with the chief rabbi would become famous.[112]

Soon after these defections, the angry departure in the spring of 1764 of Rabbi Hart Lyon left the Ashkenazi Great Synagogue without a spiritual leader. It was said that when Hart Lyon was asked why he was leaving, he replied that it was because that question was the first religious enquiry he had ever received here.[113] The post went the following February to Rabbi David Tevele Schiff, who had been *dayan* in Frankfurt. Aaron Goldschmidt, one of the community leaders of the Duke's Place congregation, would even years later assert that 'we have, thank God—as is known far and wide—done well in selecting him, may God prolong his days!' According to Goldschmidt, 'in those days everything was done through me, because I had received a recommendation from our late uncle R. Johanan and, thank God, I succeeded,

[111] Generally, see A. Barnett, *The Western Synagogue through Two Centuries (1761–1961)* (London, 1961); and M. Levy, *The Western Synagogue* (London, 1897). Thomas Dibdin would become well known for his sympathetic portrayal of Jews: see below, pp. 345–6. For the court case, see '*Israel and Others* v. *Simmons*', 6 May 1818: *Reports of Cases, ed. Thomas Starkie* (London, 1820), ii. 356–60. The Maiden Lane Synagogue reunited with the Western Synagogue in 1907, which built a new building in Alfred Place, Tottenham Court Road, in 1915, destroyed in a German air attack in 1941. They were not relocated permanently until 1957, at Crawford Place, Marylebone. Although many of their archives were lost in the bombing, since the War they have acquired the first regulations of the Hebra Kaddisha drawn up in Hebrew and Yiddish by Philip Abraham in 1767, which had previously been in the Gaster Collection. These are written in a curious mixture of Yiddish, Hebrew, and English: e.g. 'Hot der parnas-president mah korin b'la'az castin vote v'al piv yefsok ha-din' (my transliteration of Hebrew characters): Levy, *Western Synagogue*, 5. Cf. *Records of the Western Synagogue 1761–1932*, ed. C. Roth (London, 1932).

[112] See Tobias Goodman, *A Sermon, on the Universally Regretted Death of the Most Illustrious Princess Charlotte* (London, 1817), which may be the first sermon in English to be preached in a synagogue. See his other works, *Behinoth Olam* (London, 1806); and *Faith of Israel* (London, 1834) in English. For Solomon Bennett, see below, pp. 328–9.

[113] Quoted, without source, by Roth, *Great Synagogue*, 121.

as it is known here in the whole community that practically I alone was instrumental in carrying through his election'.[114] The only other possible candidate for the post was Rabbi Israel Meshullam Zalman (or Solomon), the son of the famous rabbi Jacob Emden, himself the son of Rabbi Zvi Ashkenazi, who had advised the community and visited London in 1714. It was indeed a very small world, for the defeated candidate was also the first cousin of the departing rabbi, and the implied insult was ultimately too great to bear, so Israel Meshullam Solomon was eventually appointed rabbi of the breakaway Hambro Synagogue, which until then had contented itself with the combined stewardship of the rabbi of Duke's Place.[115]

This was for all concerned except Rabbi Solomon an unfortunate arrangement. That he had some support outside London as well is indicated by the fact that when the synagogue in Portsmouth split in two in 1765–6, one of the factions rebelled against the authority of the Great Synagogue and pledged their allegiance to Meshullam Solomon and the Hambro.[116] Meshullam Solomon fell foul of a doubtful decision regarding a divorce decree given in Amsterdam, and then had divorce problems of his own.[117] Despite his distinguished parentage, ultimately, in 1780, he was forced to go, dying in Hamburg fourteen years later. Rabbi David Tevele Schiff described the scene to his brother Rabbi Meir in Frankfurt:

As regards the Rabbi of the Hamburger [congregation], all is at an end. From hour to hour he begged the community to allow him to remain; nevertheless they insist upon what they decided, to give him £50 yearly for life. He is leaving next week, and your astonishment still holds good, why I should have to do everything without being paid for it, apart from presents on Purim and Rosh-Hashana from those who were in the habit of remembering me on those occasions (I have no income from the Hambro Synagogue). As to weddings, it is

[114] Aaron Goldschmidt to Rabbi Jacob Kik (his sister's son) in Hamburg, 21 Adar 5536 [1776]: Jewish Theological Seminary, New York City, MS Adler 4095: trans. Duschinsky, 'Rabbinate', xi. 206–7.

[115] Duschinsky, 'Rabbinate', x. 445–6. N. Cohen, 'Non-religious Factors in the Emergence of the Chief Rabbinate', *TJHSE* 21 (1968), 304, suggests that 'it is possible that Meshullam Zalman has been accorded an unfair obloquy as a sort of Anglo-Jewish anti-pope', and warns that we should not be anachronistic about the status of the Chief Rabbi.

[116] The two factions came to an agreement in 1771 and reunited in 1789 after Solomon left England: C. Roth, 'The Portsmouth Community and its Historical Background', *TJHSE* 13 (1936), 157–87; id., *The Rise of Provincial Jewry* (London, 1950), 94–5.

[117] See C. Duschinsky, 'Jacob Kimchi and Shalom Buzaglo', *TJHSE* 7 (1915), 272–90; H. Loewe, 'Solomon ben Joseph Buzaglo', *TJHSE* 16 (1952), 35–45; and C. Roth, 'The Amazing Clan of Buzaglo', *TJHSE* 23 (1971), 11–21.

now usual with them, in accordance with an order from their Board of Management, that the parents of the bridal couple have the choice, and can take either me or their Hazan. As the Hazanim—wrongly—flatter their congregants, I did not, during the whole of last year, perform more than one wedding ceremony.

Now that Rabbi Schiff was the only Ashkenazi show in town, one might have thought that his situation would have improved, but he was unalterably pessimistic:

others of the respected men [of the Hambro Synagogue] think that in time the right to perform wedding ceremonies will fall exclusively to me, but at present it is still far from that. It may be that in time some newcomers will also send me presents at the periods mentioned [namely Purim and Rosh Hashanah], but a separate salary from that congregation is not to be expected. It might be that my community will ask the Hamburger congregation for a contribution towards the salary they give me, namely the £200 a year, and according to my opinion they will be able to tear out of them £50, but of that not one penny will go into my pocket, but even with that I am satisfied because, as I have already written you, the salary of £200 I have from the congregation is insecure, and at every meeting of the Kahal they spoke of reducing the salary of the Rav and of other officials of the congregation, on account of the increase in the expenses and reduction of the income.

Like his predecessor, Rabbi Schiff was intensely dissatisfied with his position, and generally with the community of English Jews that he found in London. 'In short,' he lamented to his brother in Frankfurt, 'were I to write you many sheets full, you would still not understand the way of this town. You imagine London is a Kehilla [community]. No! Far from it!'[118]

Rabbi Schiff's correspondence is fascinating not only for the information about the Jewish community contained therein, and for his diverting prose style—which even occasionally includes an English word written in Hebrew characters, despite the fact that he never learned English—but also because we can sometimes see the events of the Gentile world outside reflected in his writings. In a letter to his brother about a certain young man who hoped to come to London, Schiff advises that if he 'has already left, do not frighten his family', but, if he is still in Frankfurt, warn him

that since a few days it is spoken of again that Parliament will put pressure [on Jewish travellers?] like last year, and he has the choice whether he will come

---

[118] Rabbi David Tevele Schiff to Rabbi Meir, *dayan* in Frankfurt, 1 Iyar 5540 [1780]: MS Adler 4095, trans. Duschinsky, 'Rabbinate', xi. 207–14. A blank page with a watermark date of 1798, used for writing *ketubboth* (marriage contracts), is preserved in University College, London, Mocatta Library, De Sola Pamph. (9), last item.

here or not. In any case, if he does make up his mind to come, he should see to it that in the passport he obtains from the government authorities there, should be said more than is usually said in a health-pass [certificate], and, if possible, should be added that he is a Schutz-Jude from there who travels thither as a merchant to buy goods. Please do not fail to let him have this message in full if he is still there, but if he has already left, your silence will be better than words, and God may bless his journey.[119]

The general tone of Rabbi Tevele Schiff's letters to his brother is pessimistic, yet this did not prevent Rabbi Meir from asking for money throughout the winter of 1782. 'I have to repeat what I have already said,' Schiff wrote to his brother in exasperation,

Leave off with this! It is impossible for me to help you, I have enough to do to keep myself. My income at present has diminished so far, that with difficulty only can I make both ends meet, and it is getting less every day. Were it not for the little [income] I receive in interest from Government Loan I could not exist, as the expenses increase on account of the war, the taxes are great and heavy, and for other causes. My salary of £200 is not being paid me punctually, and every moment I have to expect that it will be reduced. It is not, as you seem to think, that I am not on good terms with them, on the contrary, I have many of the leaders as my friends, who appreciate me and are anxious for my welfare. The gist of the matter is, and I am surprised at you, how do you imagine to be able to understand a place which neither you nor your forefathers knew. As little as anybody in another land understands this war, the ways of the Parliament and the powers of the king here—even what the papers will write there now about peace with America—as little will any one understand the ways of the Kehilla and anything about my income and expenditure.[120]

Rabbi David Tevele Schiff was thus far from happy in his post, and he made determined efforts to find a position on the Continent, in Rotterdam or in Würzberg, but to no avail. He died in England in December 1791 and was buried at Mile End.[121]

The Sephardim of Bevis Marks were also troubled in their internal affairs during the second half of the eighteenth century. Their *haham*, Moses Gomes de Mesquita, died in 1751, and was replaced on a temporary basis by his unsuccessful predecessor Isaac Nieto, the learned son of a more learned father. Perhaps Nieto had hoped to be restored to his former leadership, but competing with him was a young man from Holland named Moses Cohen d'Azevedo, who had married the daughter of the recently deceased *haham*. Nieto resigned from the rabbinical court the moment Cohen d'Azevedo was appointed to it, and was livid when his rival was officially given the post of *haham* in 1761 on

[119] Duschinsky, 'Rabbinate', 212–13.
[120] Schiff to Meir, 22 Adar 5542 [1782]: repr. ibid. 221–8.
[121] Ibid. x. 482–3.

turning 40 years old.[122] Nieto poured out a stream of complaints and objections during this entire period, even arguing that the meat which was approved for the consumption of Sephardi Jews was not in fact properly kosher.[123] Happily, Isaac Nieto was now freed for the scholarly work that suited him best, and until his death in 1773 was hard at work on numerous literary projects, the crown of which was the translation of the prayer-book into Spanish, the first volume of which he had published as long ago as 1740. All of Nieto's works were published in London, and with the imprimatur of the Sephardi Mahamad, which did not let their exasperation with the rejected rabbi colour their appreciation of his scholarly efforts.[124]

Isaac Nieto's prayer-book was one of the outstanding literary

[122] Benjamin Mendes da Costa to the rabbinical court of Amsterdam, stating that he intends to nominate Cohen d'Azevedo as *haham*, 28 Heshvan 5521 [1761]: SPJC, London, MS 344 (53h); Isaac Nieto, memo in objection of disciple [Cohen d'Azevedo] being preferred when his master is in the town, n.d. [?1761]: ibid., MS 344 (53h); questionnaire in Hebrew submitted by the London Mahamad to rabbinical court in Amsterdam concerning the authority of Isaac Nieto, with Portuguese summary, n.d. [?1761]: ibid., MS 344 (53i–j); Mahamad to Amsterdam acknowledging letter and saying that they would be referring the questions of their own rabbinical court, the office of *haham* being vacant, asking for a prompt reply, 10 Kislev 5521 [1761]: ibid., MS 344 (53k); 20 Kislev 5521 [1761], Amsterdam to Mahamad: ibid., MS 344 (53l); Amsterdam rabbinical court to London Mahamad endorsing unanimous decision against Isaac Nieto, with Hebrew copy, n.d. [1761]: ibid., MS 344 (53m–o); Hyamson, *Sephardim*, 182–4.

[123] See e.g. Isaac Nieto to the Mahamad, 13 May 1757, asserting that of the 3,000 oxen killed in the previous twelve months by Rabbi Haim Albahaly, only 100 were kosher; and declaring that all cattle killed by Ashkenazim are *treif*: SPJC, London, MS 344 (53g); Isaac Nieto to Joseph Salvador, 28 Oct. 1760, thanking him for sympathy expressed on death of his daughter Esther, and criticizing Cohen d'Azevedo: ibid., MS 344 (53f); and letter of Joseph Salvador to the Mahamad, 24 Apr. 1761, objecting that his view that most of the oxen killed are *treif* was omitted from the minutes: ibid., MS 344 (35). The entire issue was discussed at length in Jacob Kimchi, *Shaylah Tshuvah* (Hebrew) (Altona, 1760), and in Duschinsky, 'Kimchi'. Kimchi, who had come from Constantinople of a distinguished family, supported Nieto's objections, and went so far as to lay the entire case before the famous Rabbi Jonathan Eybeschutz in the form of his pamphlet of 1760. Eybeschutz, the rabbi of Altona, Hamburg, and Wandsbeck, is well known *inter alia* for his fierce dispute with the son of Haham Zvi Ashkenazi, Rabbi Jacob Emden ('Yavetz'), whom Eybeschutz accused of being a secret follower of Shabtai Sevi. Eybeschutz was already quite old when Kimchi's pamphlet reached him, and never replied before his death in 1764. Emden, on the other hand, was more personally involved in the case, since his son Israel Meshullam Solomon was rabbi of the Hambro Synagogue and wrote to his father in 1766 asking him to resolve the matter, as many Jews in London were still refusing to eat meat ruled kosher by Sephardi ritual slaughterers. Emden ruled against Nieto, declaring the meat kosher, and branding Kimchi as *oto ha-m'fatpate* ('that gossiper'): Duschinsky, 'Kimchi', 281–4.

[124] Isaac Nieto, *Sermon . . . y problemático diálogo* (London, 1703); id., *Sermao funebre* (London, 1728); id., *Orden de las oraciones* (London, 1740–71).

productions of the Jews of England during the later eighteenth century, but by no means the only one. Indeed, his perennial rival, Moses Cohen d'Azevedo, made sure to publish an English translation of the sermon he delivered on an official fast day called for 13 December 1776 to wish the forces of George III speedy success in putting down the American Revolution. Cohen d'Azevedo called for 'Divine Assistance in behalf of His Majesty's Arms, that he may obtain victory and success over those American Provinces, that have withdrawn their Allegiance and raised a Rebellion against their lawful Prince and the Constitution of this Kingdom'. The American colonists were 'deluded fellow subjects', while the Jews of England were bound to remain steadfast to George III, 'not only as loyal subjects and true Israelites (whose character has always been, in every place of their dispersion, that of true and faithful subjects to their Sovereigns) but likewise as being conformant to what our Holy Law enjoins us'.[125]

Moses Cohen d'Azevedo also gave his imprimatur (*haskamah*) to a vocabulary of Hebrew words put out in 1773 by Jacob Rodrigues Moreira, with translations into Spanish and English, the latter task being performed by the author's son. The *haham* gave Rodrigues Moreira a ten-year copyright on his production, as well as his approval. The work is a milestone in its way, for in its preface the author took pains to explain the development of the Hebrew language over time, and to emphasize the necessity of having to 'fabricate Names, and devise Words, for such Phrases as are not to be found in the Holy Bible'. For this, the author went to the rabbinical writings, and noted the neologisms carefully in the text of his work.[126]

Rodrigues Moreira's dictionary was published by Alexander Alexander, who with his son Levi dominated the Jewish printing trade in London until the early nineteenth century. The elder Alexander published a translation into English of the prayer-book, noting that, despite the religious and cultural importance of the Hebrew language, 'being imperfectly understood by many, by some not at all, it has been thought necessary to translate our prayers into the language of the country wherein it hath pleased the Divine Providence to appoint our lot'. The following year, in 1771, he produced a similar prayer-book for the High Holy Days, also printed for the benefit of subscribers.[127]

---

[125] Moses Cohen d'Azevedo, *The Form of Prayer . . . 13th December, 1776* (London, 1777).

[126] Jacob Rodrigues Moreira, *Kehilath Jahacob: Being a Vocabulary of Words in the Hebrew Language* (London, 5533 [1773]).

[127] A. Alexander and B. Meyers, *Tephilloth* (London, 5530 [1770]); Alexander Alexander, *The Evening and Morning Service of the Beginning of the Year* (London, 5331 [1771]). Further edns. of these prayer-books followed in later years.

VI

David Tevele Schiff and Moses Cohen d'Azevedo, then, were the leaders of the two branches of Anglo-Jewry during the later eighteenth century. When Schiff died in December 1791 he was not replaced until Solomon Hirschell arrived in 1802. When Cohen d'Azevedo died in 1784 there was an even longer hiatus: Haham Raphael Meldola did not take over until 1806. As Schiff's letters make clear, the attractions of being a rabbi in London were minimal, especially when compared with the myriad opportunities abroad. In spite of their tendency to denigrate their posts and the communities they served, it was during this period that new imperial concepts were applied in Anglo-Jewry. At some stage during the late eighteenth century, both the terms 'Great Synagogue' and 'Chief Rabbi' were applied to the Duke's Place Synagogue and to the rabbi therein. On 29 August 1766 the newly enlarged and restored synagogue was opened there, and the phrase was used for the first time in a publication connected with the ceremony.[128] In a sense, it was natural that its rabbi be considered chief, at least among the Ashkenazi Jews, a counterpart to the *haham* of the Sephardim. Rabbi David Tevele Schiff was after all a commanding figure, and the tiny new provincial Ashkenazi communities referred their disputes to him, although, in the case of Portsmouth, not without a considerable wrangle. For it was also during the period before the uproar over the Jew Bill that London Jewry began to expand outside the confines of the metropolis. Although scattered references to individual Jews in the provinces appear throughout the late seventeenth and early eighteenth centuries, it seems that there were no organized communities outside London until after 1740. D'Blossiers Tovey, one of Anglo-Jewry's first historians, asserted in 1738 that there were no Jewish permanent settlements outside of London. Yet, by the time Jews became a public issue in 1753, there were already synagogues in Bristol, King's Lynn, Liverpool, Plymouth, Portsmouth, Birmingham, Falmouth, Ipswich, Norwich, and Penzance. While a problem of definition does exist as to when a community can truly be said to be organized, it is clear that Jewish worship was beginning to be found outside of the capital during the early part of the eighteenth century.[129] Rabbi Schiff came to be seen as the chief rabbi of

[128] *Prayer Used at the Opening of the Great Synagogue* ([London], 1766).
[129] See Roth, *Great Synagogue*, 128–30; and generally id., *Rise of Provincial Jewry*, consisting of articles which had appeared ten years earlier in *Jewish Monthly*. See esp. his table of provincial Jewish communities, pp. 110–11, compiled from several possible sources. For other studies of the beginnings of Jewish communities outside London, see A. Levy, 'The Origins of Scottish Jewry', *TJHSE* 19 (1960), 129–62; G. D. Guttentag,

all Anglo-Jewry: certainly after the departure of Meshullam Solomon in
1780 there was no one else.

The opening of the Great Synagogue in its newest incarnation was
itself a grand affair, not only for Anglo-Jewry, but for all of London. A
contemporary publication described it well:

This afternoon the ceremony of the dedication of the new-built synagogue in
Duke's Place, was performed with the greatest pomp and solemnity, in which
the chief and other eminent Rabbies belonging to the Portuguese Jewish nation
assisted; when the prayer for their Majesties and the Royal family, which was
always read in their liturgy in Hebrew, was at this time pronounced by the chief
Rabbi in English, and followed by Handel's coronation anthem, performed by a
numerous band of the most eminent musicians. The procession and other
ceremonies on that occasion in the synagogue, were accompanied with several
anthems, chorusses &c. by the same performers.[130]

According to John Entick, in his survey of London published the same
year, this 'synagogue is just now enlarged with an addition of building in
brick, that makes it as large again as it was before; and has approached
so near to the church of *St James's Duke's Place*, that the congregations
may be heard from each other'. This building, he wrote, 'is the
synagogue of the *Dutch Jews*, as they are commonly called, with whom
the *Jews* from all the northern regions communicate'. Apart from them,
of course, were the Jews of Bevis Marks, in 'an handsome, large, and
commodious brick building'.[131] The leaderless Ashkenazi community
made use of the interregnum at the end of the eighteenth century to set

---

'The Beginnings of the Newcastle Jewish Community', *TJHSE* 25 (1977), 1–24; L.
Olsover, *The Jewish Communities of North-East England, 1775–1980* (Gateshead, 1980);
Hyman, *The Jews of Ireland*; M. A. Shepherd, 'Cheltenham Jews in the Nineteenth
Century', *JJ Soc.* 21 (1979), 125–33; A. Newman, *Leicester Hebrew Congregation: A
Centenary Record 1874-5634–1974-5734* (Leicester, 1974); id. (ed.), *Provincial Jewry in
Victorian Britain* (London, 1975); L. P. Gartner, 'Urban History and the Pattern of
Provincial Jewish Settlement in Victorian England', *JJ Soc.* 23 (1981), 37–56; B.
Williams, *The Making of Manchester Jewry, 1740–1875* (Manchester, 1976); B. Susser,
'Social Acclimatization of Jews in Eighteenth and Nineteenth Century Devon', in R.
Burt (ed.), *Industry and Society in the South-West* (Exeter, 1971); D. M. Lewis, *The Jews of
Oxford* (Oxford, 1992); D. Cohn-Sherbok, *The Jews of Canterbury 1760–1931*
(Canterbury, 1984) [based on 4 vols. of records in the Mocatta Library]. See also the
pinkas of the Jewish community of Penzance, Cornwall (1807–29), Yiddish and English,
82 fos., now at the University of Leeds, Roth MS 202; minute books of same, 1843–64,
1864–92 (in English, 43 fos. and 36 fos.): Roth MSS 203–4; revised registers of same,
1844: Roth MS 205. These documents were apparently given to Roth on 4 Nov. 1932
by George Joseph.

[130] *Annual Register* (1766), 131: entry for 31 Aug. 1766.
[131] John Entick, *A New and Accurate History and Survey of London* (London, 1766), iii.
357–8.

their house in order by promulgating *takkanoth*, written constitutions for the various synagogues and their charities. Thus new rules were issued and standing ones revised during these years by the Great Synagogue (1791), the Hambro (1795), and the Western Synagogue at Denmark Court (1799), documents written in a similar pattern in the Yiddish language with a Hebrew introduction and the occasional English phrase.[132] Bevis Marks, the Great Synagogue, the Hambro, and the New Synagogue, all in a triangle of Jewry near Aldgate, formed the centre of Anglo-Jewry in the second half of the eighteenth century, ruled very lightly and intermittently by a chief rabbi and a *haham*.

[132] S. Stein, 'Some Ashkenazi Charities in London at the End of the Eighteenth and the Beginning of the Nineteenth Centuries', *TJHSE* 20 (1964), 63–81, esp. 63.

7
AGAINST THE BACKDROP
OF REVOLUTION, 1789–1812

THE French Revolution was far more than an event in temporal history, and its almost supernatural implications were felt at the time and have been discussed extensively in modern historiography. The far-reaching changes affected the lives of the Jews in France, not only by means of emancipation, but also through a recognition that the end of the Old Regime was in many ways parallel to the last days of the Old Dispensation. In France itself, the abbé Grégoire was preparing his *Essai sur la régénération physique, morale et politique des juifs*, which was published at Metz in 1789.[1] At the same time Grégoire sent a sociological questionnaire to a colleague in England, specifically requesting detailed information about the Jews there. No record of a reply to Grégoire has survived, but it is possible to supply the lack ourselves.[2]

I

Despite the change in status of the Jews in France, and while certainly many of their co-religionists must have hoped that a similar improvement in circumstances might be forthcoming in England, the loyalty of the Jews here was unquestionable. Some of this policy is apparent in the address the Jews of the Sephardi congregation at Bevis Marks delivered on the occasion of the recovery of George III in the winter of 1789. The letter was given personally to Lord Sydney, who passed it on to the king on 31 March 1789. 'When the Allmighty was pleased to afflict these Kingdoms with your Majesty's Late indisposition,' they explained,

we were early & persevering in joining the rest of your Majesty's faithfull Subjects with Supplications to the Omnipotent for Mercy. To the God of Israel our prayers were directed, He has been graciously pleased to answer us propitiously. And the recovery of your Majesty's invaluable health has restored

---

[1] On Grégoire generally, see R. F. Necheles, *The Abbé Grégoire 1787–1831* (Westport, Conn., 1971).

[2] I intend to publish the full text of this interesting and important document in the near future.

happiness to your People. As much impressed by our Religious Principles as By the full sense of the many benefits we enjoy under the protection of Your Majesty's Government, the equity of the Laws, & the Liberal spirit of the British Nation, Our duty and inclination unite in devoting our Prayers to the Almighty disposer of events, for the Long continuation of your Majesty's health & Government, & the Glory & increasing felicity of Your Kingdoms.

The address was signed by all of the leading members of the community.[3]

Once the French Revolution had begun in earnest, however, the loyalty of the Jews in England again came into question. The new Aliens Act of 1793 was but a symbol of the general feeling that revolution was a foreign import and as such its purveyors ought to be strictly watched. Anglo-Jewry in response sought to protest its loyalty by means of numerous special sermons dedicated to king and country. One such occasion was the rededication of the Great Synagogue, which had recently been enlarged and redecorated, thanks to the financial contribution of Judith Levy, the daughter of Moses Hart.[4] This magnificent building, destroyed by German bombing in the Second World War, reminiscent of the Bevis Marks synagogue or the one in Amsterdam, was in itself no doubt an object of attention, and no doubt many Jews thought that the timing was bad for such an edifice to be put in front of Gentile eyes at this critical moment in the nation's history. David Tevele Schiff, the rabbi of the Great Synagogue, composed a fulsome poem in praise of the king, which was translated into English by David Levi, the famous Jewish controversialist:

> As in this country, where GEORGE the Third sways the sceptre,
> Whose sole ambition, is to promote his subjects happiness; governing
> them with kindness and equity:
> *And* whose amiable Queen CHARLOTTE, excels the most eminent women in
> virtue;
> May they enjoy a long *and happy* life, with GEORGE Prince of Wales, and all
> the Royal family.

A further prayer for the royal family followed.[5]

---

[3] SPJC, London, MS 344 (46): also repr. *London Gazette*, 13081 (28–31 Mar. 1789), 178.

[4] Judith Hart Levy (1705–1803) married Elias, the son of Benjamin Levy, the important figure in the early days of the Great Synagogue. According to James Picciotto, *Sketches of Anglo-Jewish History* (rev. edn., London, 1956), 90–1, she lived in great splendour on £6,000 a year and moved in noble circles. The 'Queen of Richmond Green' died without leaving a will at her house in Albemarle Street and was buried at Mile End.

[5] David Solomon Shiff, *A Song and Praise . . . at the Dedication of the Great Jews Synagogue* (London, 1790), 4–5, 18–19.

After the renewal of the war with France in May 1803, Jews were allowed to enlist along with the myriads of other volunteers who offered their services to fight against Napoleon. According to one contemporary report,

The 7th Regiment mustered at ten o'clock, at their parade ground, and proceeded to Aldgate Church. The sermon preached to them on the occasion was delivered by the Rev. Mr. HART. As many Gentlemen belonging to this Corps are Jews, when the Oath of Allegiance was administered to the Corps, they retired to the Vestry to receive it, according to the forms of their religion.[6]

Another Jewish volunteer went to the trouble of obtaining a document testifying to his military service. 'I do hereby certify', wrote Lieutenant Colonel H. C. Coombe on 24 October 1803, 'that the Bearer Alexander Cohen (of a swarthy complexion and five feet five inches high) is enrolled and serves in the Tenth Regiment of Loyal London Volunteers and that he has taken the oath of allegiance to the King.'[7] These sentiments were echoed in a sermon given by J. Luria at Bevis Marks on 19 October 1803, on the occasion of a general fast in order to ensure 'success to his Majesty's arms, &c'.[8] In addition, a sermon by Rabbi Solomon Hirschell, newly appointed to the Great Synagogue, celebrating the victory at Trafalgar, was translated into English by Joshua van Oven, one of the leading Jews in London.[9]

War brings death and injury to some, but prosperity to others. One of the most celebrated winners was Nathan Mayer Rothschild (1777–1836), who had settled in Manchester in 1797 in order to represent the family's interests and those of Landgrave William IX of Hesse-Kassel. Nathan's father Mayer Amschel Rothschild (1744–1812) had put the family on the path to fortune by supplying the landgrave with the rare coins which he collected, a business which expanded to include other antiques and contemporary currency changing. Nathan moved to London in 1803, abandoning the trade in cotton which he had conducted in Manchester, and moving over to activity on the Stock Exchange. His marriage in 1806 to Hannah, the daughter of Levi Barent Cohen and sister of Moses Montefiore's wife, placed him in a superb dynastic position to complement his growing financial stature.

---

[6] 1803: Collyer Ferguson Collection of ephemera: Mocatta Library, University College, London.

[7] Certificate pasted on the back of a portrait of a soldier: Jewish Museum, London, MS 190.

[8] J. Luria, *A Penitential Sermon* (London, 1803), title-page; pp. vii, 16–17.

[9] *Voice of Jacob* (1841–6) 2: 68; C. Duschinsky, 'The Rabbinate of the Great Synagogue, London, from 1786–1842', *JQR* NS 9 (1918–19), 103–37, 371–408; 10 (1919–20), 445–527; 11 (1920–1), 21–81, 201–36, 345–87.

Nathan was deeply involved in financing Wellington's army in Spain, and later would extend this work to include supporting England's European allies during the Napoleonic wars, and in participating in the economic recovery after the Congress of Vienna.[10]

Benjamin and Abraham Goldsmid, two Ashkenazi merchant bankers in London, also made a fortune from the revolutionary wars. Each married well, Abraham to a wealthy woman of Amsterdam, and Benjamin to the daughter of Yehiel Prager, a fabulously wealthy Jewish East Indian merchant. Benjamin had mighty social ambitions and, after living for a time at Stamford Hill, built a large mansion on a 60-acre site at Roehampton in 1792 at which he entertained on a lavish scale, even including the prince of Wales among his guests, and on a Sabbath too. His celebration on the occasion of Nelson's victory at the Battle of the Nile in 1798 was reputed to be the most extraordinary fête within living or written memory. Abraham began with a country seat at Morden, but soon purchased Merton Place, the home of Lady Hamilton, Nelson's celebrated mistress, and one of his frequent house guests.[11] According to John Francis, an observer of the Stock Exchange, the newspapers

bore an almost daily testimony to their munificence ... the grandeur of an entertainment to royalty was recorded ... Entertainments to princes and ambassadors reviving the glory of the Arabian nights, were frequent; and galleries, with works of art worthy the magnificence of a Medici, graced their homes. They were awhile Fortune's chief and most especial favorites.[12]

[10] The literature on the Rothschild family is prodigious, especially on Mayer Amschel Rothschild, the founder of the Frankfurt-based dynasty, and his five sons, each of whom ran the operation in a different city: Amschel (1773–1855) at Frankfurt; Solomon (1774–1855) at Berlin and later Vienna; Nathan Mayer at London; Karl (1788–1855) at Naples; and Jacob/James (1792–1868) at Paris. Lionel Nathan de Rothschild (1808–79), Nathan Mayer's eldest son, was the first Jewish MP, and his own eldest son Nathaniel (Natty) Mayer de Rothschild (1840–1915) was created a baron of the United Kingdom in 1885, and was thus the first Jewish peer. Generally, see F. Morton, *The Rothschilds* (London, 1961), with its extensive family tree. For contemporary views of N. M. Rothschild, see e.g. [C. M. Westmacott], *The English Spy* (new edn., London, 1907 [1826]), ii. 123–8; John Francis, *Chronicles and Characters of the Stock Exchange* (London, 1849), 296–311.

[11] On the Goldsmids generally see Levy Alexander [and Henry Lemoine], *Memoirs of the Life and Commercial Concerns of the Late Benj. Goldsmid* (London, 1808); P. H. Emden, 'The Brothers Goldsmid and the Financing of the Napoleonic Wars', *TJHSE* 14 (1935–9), 225–46; *Universal Magazine*, 9 (Jan.–June 1808), 453; *The Times*, 29 Sept 1810; Francis, *Chronicles and Characters*, 160–7.

[12] Francis, *Chronicles and Characters*, 60: quoted in T. M. Endelman, *The Jews of Georgian England 1714–1830* (Philadelphia, 1979), 253. For another view of the Goldsmids, see Thomas Grenville to William Wyndham, Lord Grenville, 17 Oct. 1810: Hist. MSS Comm., *xxx*, *Fortescue X*, 56.

Both brothers came to tragic ends. Benjamin hanged himself from a silk cord in 1808; his brother Abraham committed suicide by shooting himself in the throat two years later. Yet the Goldsmid family remained crucially important in the history of nineteenth-century Anglo-Jewry, as we shall see.

Before his death Abraham Goldsmid was instrumental in orchestrating an event which lived for a very long time in the memory of the Ashkenazi Jewish community in London. On 30 March 1809 Abraham informed the *parnassim* of the Great Synagogue that the royal dukes of Cambridge and Cumberland, the sons of George III, had expressed their wish to visit the Jews at prayer in a fortnight's time, and asked rhetorically if this might be possible.[13] There were precedents for visits of members of the royal family to Jewish synagogues in London. During the stewardship of Jacob Abendana, Princess Anne had come to call in 1681 at Bevis Marks.[14] Furthermore, the king's brother the duke of Gloucester had visited the Great Synagogue as recently as 10 April 1801. But the present occasion was meant to be the grandest, and a special order of service was compiled to mark it. On the day, 14 April 1809, the dukes were accompanied by another brother, the duke of Sussex, whose attachment to the Jews and their culture would be permanent. As they entered, they were greeted by the words, sung in Hebrew and English,

> Open wide the gates for the princely train,
>   The Heav'n-bless'd offspring of our King,
> Whilst our voices raise the emphatic strain,
>   And God's service devout we sing.

Pious prayers for the king, his queen, and the entire royal family followed.[15]

A contemporary news-sheet summed up the event in a particularly vivid fashion:

Yesterday, at half past six o'clock, the Dukes of Cumberland, Sussex and Cambridge attended the Great Synagogue in Duke's Place to witness the Hebrew form of worship. The preparation made to receive the princes evidenced the loyalty of the Jewish people, and the spectacle was magnificent

---

[13] Abraham Goldsmid to the *parnassim*, 30 Mar. 1809: letter printed in C. Roth, *The Great Synagogue London 1690–1940* (London, 1950), 205, without reference, but presumably from the synagogue archives, which Roth catalogued.

[14] See above, p. 146.

[15] See esp. *Order of Service to be Performed at the Great Synagogue, Duke's Place, on the Occasion of the Presence of their Royal Highnesses the Dukes of Cumberland, Sussex, & Cambridge on Friday, April 14. A.M. 5569* (London [1809]); and generally I. Abrahams, 'Hebrew Loyalty under the First Four Georges', *TJHSE* 9 (1922), 103–30, esp. for Christian productions. See below, p. 373.

and most solemn. The Synagogue was most suitably decorated on the occasion. The seats on each side were raised and the pulpit in the centre was adorned by crimson and gold. A space between the pulpit and the ark was appropriated to the Royal Dukes and the Nobility, who stood on a rich platform with four beautiful Egyptian chairs and stands for their books, flowers, etc. The Synagogue was brilliantly illuminated by chandeliers. The High Priest, Rabbi Hirschell, in his sacerdotal habit displayed unusual magnificence: he was dressed in a robe of white satin of considerable value and ordered expressly for him by Abraham Goldsmid, Esq. The Royal Dukes arrived in the carriage of Mr. Goldsmid, and their own carriages followed with several ladies of distinction. The singing was excellent and the Royal Dukes appeared much gratified by the Choruses. When the Ark was opened to take out the Five Books of Moses the Princes were conducted by Mr. Goldsmid to view the interior, at which they expressed great satisfaction, the structure being grand and beautiful. The galleries were crowded with beautiful Jewesses who attracted much the attention of the Royal Party. After the service, the Royal Dukes drove to the mansion of Mr. A. Goldsmid, where a sumptuous entertainment was provided, which was followed by a grand concert.[16]

This indeed must have been one of the greatest official occasions for Anglo-Jewry during the tense and worrying period between the French Revolution and the final defeat of Napoleon.

At the Great Synagogue, David Tevele Schiff was the rabbi at the outbreak of the French Revolution, remaining in his post until his death on 17 December 1791. Afterwards the Ashkenazi Jews there used the services of Moses Myers, the rabbi of the New Synagogue, until the appointment in 1802 of Rabbi Solomon Hirschell. The Hambro Synagogue was entirely without a rabbi, Israel Meshullam Solomon having left England under a cloud in 1780. Moses Cohen d'Azevedo was the *haham* of the Sephardi Jews from 1761 until his death in 1784, and no replacement was found until Raphael Meldola arrived in 1806. The impression one gets is of an overwhelming lack of leadership during a critical period.

We can get a rather full if somewhat uncomplimentary picture of Anglo-Jewry during the era of the French Revolution from an interesting and anonymous work claiming to be 'a peep into the synagogue'. 'Scarcely one in five hundred, understands the Hebrew language, beyond the translation of the Pentateuch,' claimed the author, who was even more scandalized by what he saw as the commercialization of religion among English Jews. They would discuss business in the synagogue, he wrote: 'you even turn your Synagogue into an Exchange; and communicate to each other, the news of the day, the fluctuation of Markets, the advancement or fall of Stocks'. But the author's chief

---

[16] Quoted in Roth, *Great Synagogue*, 206–7, without reference.

objection was reserved for the lack of decorum in the awarding of ritual honours:

the Holy Sanctuary is transmuted into a Sale-Room, and the whole audience busily employed at an Auction! A *Christian* or *Musselman* would be puzzled in this place to conjecture what kind of articles are exposed to sale, but in order to obviate that difficulty, I will endeavour to explain what I mean. In the Synagogue there is a Clerk, called a *Shamos*, who mounts the pulpit, as an Auctioner does his Rostrum, and then exclaims aloud, 'One penny for opening the door of the Ark!' Another bids more, a third more still, and sometimes the contention is so strong (for ambition is the spur that goads it on) that six, seven, or eight guineas is given for the superstitious privilege; and when it is obtained, it is of no utility to the purchaser, except giving him an opportunity of shewing his superior ostentation over his competitors; by being the highest bidder for the insignificant prize.

The procedure our author describes is not in itself significantly different from that which continues in some synagogues today, albeit with a considerably increased sensitivity to public decency, and this alone is an indication of the reliability of this testimony.

Other practices incensed the author hardly less. He particularly objected to 'the ceremony of *swadling*, or folding a cloth round the Pentateuch, or five Books of *Moses*, as a nurse would round an Infant'. The displaying of the scrolls of the law also seemed to him a ceremony that 'savours more of *parade* than sincerity'. He had a particular aversion to the Yiddish language, which he saw as 'a kind of *Gibberish*, or fulsome compound of Hebrew, German and Dutch, which none but the *German Jews* are capable of understanding'. He thought that it was this linguistic isolation which contributed to the suppression of Jewish women, who had little opportunity to learn another language which might enable them to communicate with the non-Jewish world. Yiddish, he postulated, was 'a Language not recognized by any Nation under the Sun'. His solution towards integrating Jews into English society was to alter 'the mode of doing religious duty in the Synagogue':

I do not mean to change the fundamental principles of the Jewish profession; but to have the service performed in the tongue, or language of that country it is performed in: such as German in Germany, or English in England &c. The Hearers will then know what the Priest is saying, and will be able to join him in his devotion. It will render unnecessary the stupid method of learning that mungrel jargan used among the Jews, which prevents them from ever speaking well, the language of any Country, and it will not only prevent that evil; but it will give them a fair opportunity, of acquiring a correct knowledge of the language of that nation in which they are born; and finally do away with that prejudice, which their own singularity has drawn against them.

This pamphlet, no doubt written by a Jew or a convert from Judaism, is striking in its knowledge of the Jewish situation in late eighteenth-century England, but also for its constructive criticism. In large measure, the proposals he suggested would be adopted in the next century by the Reform Movement.[17]

Fortunately, this report can be supplemented by the testimony of a number of Gentiles, some English and some visiting from abroad, who made it their business to seek out the Jewish community in England. Johann Wilhelm von Archenholz, formerly a captain in the service of the king of Prussia, made a visit to London on the eve of the French Revolution and noted the great difference between the Ashkenazi and Sephardi communities. 'The Jews are allowed in England, as well as in Holland, the free exercise of their religion', he wrote,

their numbers and their riches are therefore continually augmented. One is astonished at the prodigious difference between the Portuguese and German Jews established in that island. Dress, language, manners, cleanliness, are all in favour of the former, who indeed can scarce be distinguished from Christians. This extends even to their prejudices and their publick worship: the features peculiar to the whole race are the only peculiarity that they have common.

Archenholz recalled the efforts of Toland and the promoters of the Jew Bill to improve the situation of the Jews in England, but noted that these endeavours were doomed to failure because of the Ashkenazi Jews, 'a class of men who may be looked upon as the very refuse of human nature'. Indeed, he wrote,

All the children of Israel, who are obliged to quit Holland and Germany, take refuge in England, where they live by roguery; if they themselves do not steal, they at least help to conceal and to dispose of the plunder. They are therefore so much hated in England, that the honesty of their Portuguese brethren cannot weaken the unfavourable impression which such a band of robbers has occasioned.

Archenholz himself was the victim of an Ashkenazi Jewish thief in the streets of London, and caused such a public commotion that passers-by informed him that in England no outrage could justify such an

---

[17] Anon., *A Peep into the Synagogue; or, A Letter to the Jews* (London, n.d.). Some of this author's criticisms were echoed by the converted Jew Hyam Isaacs, *Ceremonies, Customs, Rites, and Traditions of the Jews* (London, n.d. [?*c.*1830]), esp. 253–4. Cf. his *A Solemn and Affectionate Address to Both Jews & Christians* (London, n.d. [?*c.*1820]). For another 18th-century convert's view, see John Payne, *Paradise Restored: Being a Visitation of Love, to the Jews* (n.p., n.d.).

undignified response, and that the Jew would be within his rights to prosecute, which he fortuitously declined to do.[18]

Isaac d'Israeli, whose status as Gentile was equivocal to say the least, sought a deeper explanation for the condition of Anglo-Jewry. 'The state of the modern Jews', he pondered,

is not less severe than that of the ancient. They groaned in ages of persecution, and in ages of toleration they are degraded. In England it is doubtful whether the Jews be citizens; they are merely tolerated inhabitants; even this express is too gentle. Since their last banishment, they attempted to return under Oliver; but the fanatics could not agree. Charles, gained by bribes, and indifferent on religious professions, connived at their admission; but the parliament of England has never abrogated their decree of expulsion. This British land, which when the slave touches he becomes free, retains the child of Jacob in abject degradation. The Jew cannot purchase the house which he inhabits, and is not permitted to elevate himself among his horde by professions which might ennoble his genius and dignify his people.[19]

D'Israeli might not be entirely accurate about the legal status of the Jews at the turn of the eighteenth century, but there is no question that the humiliation which he reviles existed, and that, to a great extent, this was a consequence of the public image of the Jew which had some basis in fact.

The situation described by the anonymous, and probably Jewish, author of *A Peep into the Synagogue*, and supported by d'Israeli, was also echoed by John Corry in his satirical view of turn-of-the-century London. 'A very distant class of the inhabitants of London consists of Jews', he wrote, and suggested that they might number about 20,000: 'though a few of them are respectable characters, the majority are notorious sharpers. Their adherence to the Mosaic law prevents them from mixing with the rest of their fellow-citizens; hence they absolutely subsist on the industry of others, and become public nuisances'. Corry rehearsed the principal arguments relating to the prevalence of Jews in the trade in stolen goods and counterfeit money, but concluded with a positive suggestion:

Were the magistracy of London to suppress this iniquitous traffic, and oblige the Jews to follow some handicraft art, they might contribute to the benefit,

---

[18] Johann Wilhelm von Archenholz, *A Picture of England* (Dublin, 1791), 113–14, 162–3, 211: trans. from the French, originally published in Leipzig in 1787 under the title *England und Italien*. For W. Hamilton Reid's criticism of this work, see *Gents. Mag.* 8 (1810), part ii, 111. For a view from the other side, see Elizabeth Sarah Villa Real Gooch, *The Life of Mrs. Gooch. Written by herself* (London, 1792), iii. 74–5. Some interesting begging letters are deposited in the Jewish Museum, London, MS 98.

[19] [Isaac d'Israeli], *Vaurien* (London, 1797), ii. 239–40. Cf. ii. 214–15, 220, 221–2 n., 230 n., 235–6 n., 243, 247 n.

instead of plundering society. Why should they not be reclaimed? Even the worse Jew has, in common with the rest of the human race, an inborn principle of rectitude, which requires only to be cherished and called into action for the regulation of his conduct. Seminaries instituted for the education of Jews, and places appropriated for their instruction in some mechanical art, would promote their happiness; they would soon learn to venerate their reformers, and if they did not actually relinquish their superstition and become Christians, they would no longer glory in the arts of deception, by which they now impose on the rest of the community.[20]

Corry was especially fascinated by Jewish quack doctors, such as the notorious Drs Brodum and Solomon.[21]

These were also the views expressed by William Austin, an American in London at the beginning of the nineteenth century. He argued that it was absurd to try to convert the Jews and teach them on Sunday the Christian duties of charity, sympathy, community, and equality when on Monday the same Jew would find himself politically excluded and socially ostracized. This was the reason, he thought, that the Jews in England were compelled to prey on the public: 'Eligible to no office, incapable of holding land, or even of possessing a house, with the additional hardship of being despised; they are a sort of Indian Parias, and are absolutely proscribed from the social compact, and reduced to a state worse, than that of simple nature.' The Jew therefore had 'a moral right to contervail, by every means in his power'. This situation was made even worse, Austin suspected, by Shakespeare's Shylock, who 'has prejudiced thousands of christians, who never saw a Jew, against the whole tribe of Israel'. Austin therefore thought that the granting of political rights might be a solution to wean Jews away from parasitic trades, and if 'the Jews were more disposed to agriculture', he mused, 'they might find in the United States a resting place, and notwithstanding their religion, they might flourish as well there, as at Jerusalem'.[22] Austin's American countryman Benjamin Silliman, sent to Europe by Yale University in 1805 to buy books and chemical apparatus, came across Jews in London, in Rotterdam, and in Amsterdam, and also was not entirely negative about what he saw. 'This dispersed and despised people exhibit a living proof of the truth of prophecy,' he concluded, 'and are a striking monument of the wrath of God; they are every where mingled with the nations, and yet remain separate.'[23] Henry

[20] [John Corry], *A Satirical View of London at the Commencement of the Nineteenth Century* (London, 1801), 47–9.

[21] Id., *The Detector of Quackery* (2nd edn., London, 1802), 3, 13–33, 42 n., 50.

[22] William Austin, *Letters from London* (Boston, 1804), 43, 55–7, 67–71.

[23] Benjamin Silliman, *A Journal of Travels in England, Holland and Scotland* (New York, 1810), i. 215, 333; ii. 143, 179–80.

Meister, a Swiss who had lived before the Revolution in Paris, changed his views about the Jews when he saw a Jewish girl in London request to be imprisoned with her father, 'who was to suffer for coining, during the short time he had to live'. This was not the sort of behaviour he had been led to expect from Jews.[24]

James Peller Malcolm probably knew of Shylock when he visited the Jewish quarter of London at the beginning of the nineteenth century in order to view the architecture and so complete his new survey of London, but what he saw was stronger than any preconceptions about the Jews. On arriving at Duke's Place, he wrote,

We are now immersed in filth; and whether we turn to the left or the right, proceed or return, is a matter of indifference. Jews and their dwellings surround us; and dirty men, women, and children, pass and repass in great numbers. As *Unbelievers* let them pass; with Religion and the conscience I never did and never will intermeddle; but with the *dirt* of a nation or tribes I have a right to make implacable war.

Malcolm goes on to describe the scene with which one is presented in the Jewish district of London:

Why should Jews choose to distinguish their residence by characteristic filth? I allude to the lower classes of those people. When a Jew accumulates riches, he is not to be distinguished in his house or his person from the rest of the community, and his liberality keeps pace with his gains. Those of antient families are Christians in every thing but their faith. On the contrary, the dealer in cast-off apparel and other articles is uniformly, and almost invariably, an upright bundle of rags, from which a head, hair, beard, and hands emerge, calculated to impress the beholder with abhorrence. He appears to sleep in this habit; and he issues from his nest at day-break, wandering in pursuit of his business, till, exhausted by fatigue, he returns to his family, who bask the day at least in comparative idleness.

Malcolm's conclusion was that 'the genius of the Syrians discovers itself in the bulk of the Jews as in the whole nation of the Turks and Orientalists', but it cannot be said that his description of the area around Duke's Place and Creechurch Lane varies in any significant degree from other accounts. Malcolm records that not only were the buildings in decay, so that 'the repairs resemble the patches on a beggar's garment', but that even the paving stones had sunk into the ground to such a degree and with such irregularity that the pedestrian's 'walk *per force* resembles the effect of intoxication'. On the other hand, he was very positive about the beauty of the Great Synagogue, and thought that

---

[24] Henry Meister, *Letters Written During a Residence in England* (London, 1799), 62–3.

the ark of the law was 'particularly magnificent'. He was also impressed by the New Synagogue, also an Ashkenazi congregation.[25]

Rather more influential were the articles written by Henry Lemoine in the *Gentleman's Magazine* at the beginning of the nineteenth century. Lemoine was a friend of David Levi, whose epic controversy with Joseph Priestley, as we shall see, was one of the more colourful aspects of revolutionary Anglo-Jewry. Lemoine helped Levi obtain the books he required for the debate, and his own work on the Jews was meant to present them in a favourable light. He began by noting that 'loyalty and sobriety are the most interesting criterions in their character in every country throughout their dispersion'. Lemoine provided a thumbnail history of the Jews in England, culminating in the readmission under Cromwell, when 'he let them settle, and privileged a part of London near Aldgate for their residence'. That being said, he pointed out, 'it is evident that a Jew born here is not, therefore, a natural-born subject; for our Laws have always considered his infidelity as an absolute disqualification'. As for conversion, he thought, the members of the London Society were misguided in thinking that the Jews could ever be transformed into Christians, 'for they will be found too tenacious of their principles to give way to any argument in favour of Christianity, where pecuniary interest is not the principle'.[26]

Lemoine's article provoked a minor controversy in the pages of the *Gentleman's Magazine*. One member of the London Society wrote to the editor defending their efforts to convert the Jews, noting pointedly that the granting of citizenship to the Jews was one of the brighter acts of the French Revolution, 'but how much nobler the effort to raise them to present and everlasting happiness!' At the same time a man describing himself as 'An Unconverted Jew and Englishman' wrote in, protesting the entire tone of Lemoine's contribution.[27]

In terms of actual existence in England, then, this revolutionary period was a fallow one for Anglo-Jewry. As is so often the case, the most important and far-reaching developments occurred outside the confines of the Jewish community itself, or even in the impressions Gentiles had of this community. The role of the Jew was greater than its parts.

---

[25] James Peller Malcolm, *Londinium redivivum; or, An Ancient History and Modern Description of London* (London, 1803–7), iii. 321–3; iv. 1–3.

[26] Henry Lemoine, 'On the Present State of the *Jews*', *Gents. Mag.* 80 (1810), i. 15–18, 514–16. Lemoine also worked on a life of Abraham Goldsmid with Levi Alexander. Cf. his obituaries in the *Gents. Mag.* 82 (1812), i. 493, 673–4, where the authorship of the life of Goldsmid is claimed.

[27] H.B. of Penzance, in letter dated 6 July 1810: ibid. ii. 27–8.

II

Nowhere is this principle more evident than in the storm of controversy which raged between Joseph Priestley (1733–1804) and David Levi (1740–99). 'Though by no means a match, as a controversialist, with Dr. Joseph Priestley,' summed up the *Gentleman's Magazine* years later, 'David Levi, by the assistance of Lemoine, in procuring him books, cut a figure by no means disreputable. This was just before the breaking out of the French war, at which time Lemoine was in the habit of taking suppers with Levi and other literary men in an humble sphere.'[28] Priestley hardly needs any introduction: Unitarian minister, political thinker, educationalist, and scientist, whose discoveries ranged from oxygen to soda water. Between the years 1779 and 1791 he lived as a minister in Birmingham, until a mob commemorated the second anniversary of the fall of the Bastille by burning down his house, destroying both his library and his laboratory and driving him to the United States.[29] David Levi, on the other hand, was a London-born failed shoemaker and sometime hat-dresser who devoted himself to the dual task of studying the Jewish tradition and defending it against Gentile calumnies.[30] As one observer put it, Levi was 'the only Jewish writer ever known to vindicate the faith of his ancestors in this country'.[31] He made his publishing début in 1783 with a massive if, in Levi's phrase, 'succinct account, of the rites, and ceremonies, of the Jews'. Levi meant his work to be utilized by both Christians and Jews, for although Jewish religious practices 'are all set forth in Hebrew, yet, as it hath pleased Divine Providence, to appoint our Lot in a Country, where the Hebrew is not used as a common Language', it was insufficient to rely on existing texts. A third of Levi's book was devoted

---

[28] H.B. of Penzance, 82 (1812), i (supplement), 673–4.

[29] The literature on Joseph Priestley is quite overwhelming, even specifically regarding his religious views. Generally, see F. W. Gibbs, *Joseph Priestley* (London, 1965); C. Robbins, 'Honest Heretic: Joseph Priestley in America', *Proceedings of the American Philosophical Society*, 106 (1962), 60–76, which covers his theology. Specifically on Priestley and the Jews, see C. Garrett, *Respectable Folly: Millenarians and the French Revolution in France and England* (Baltimore, 1975), ch. 6; J. Fruchtman, Jr., *The Apocalyptic Politics of Richard Price and Joseph Priestley: A Study in Late Eighteenth-Century Republican Millenarianism* (Philadelphia, 1983); J. van den Berg, 'Priestley, the Jews and the Millennium', in D. S. Katz and J. I. Israel (eds.), *Sceptics, Millenarians, and Jews* (Leiden, 1990), 256–74.

[30] For David Levi, see Anon., 'Mr. David Levi, the Learned Jew', *European Magazine*, 35 (1799), 291–4; *DNB*. Cf. C. Roth, 'The Haskalah in England', in H. J. Zimmels et al. (eds.), *Essays Presented to Chief Rabbi Israel Brodie* (London, 1967), 365–76.

[31] *Gents. Mag.* 82 (1812), i (supplement), 673.

to summarizing the Mishnah, or oral law, a subject which had fascinated English Protestants since the seventeenth century.[32] Levi followed up this initial success with a quite extraordinary and very large three-volume work on the Hebrew language, consisting of a Hebrew grammar, a Hebrew–English dictionary comprising all of the vocabulary of the Old Testament, and an English–Hebrew phrase book. One of the purposes of this work, Levi suggested, would be to retard the growth of Deism, the principal cause of whose increase, he thought, was the failure to understand the deeper meanings of the Old Testament.[33]

Levi's ire was raised by the letters to the Jews which Priestley published in 1786 and 1787, 'inviting them to an amicable discussion'. Priestley brought forth numerous arguments and pieces of evidence regarding the true nature of the Messiah, and concluded that if one compared the 'historical evidence of the two religions', it would be manifest that they 'are perfectly consistent with, nay, they imply each other, and must stand or fall together'.[34] Priestley was pleased with the result, and even hoped to get it translated into Hebrew, through the help of a Jew at Birmingham who had agreed to do the work. He thought that as this was the first time that a Unitarian had appealed to the Jews to convert, 'there is some little chance of being attended to by some of them'. Three months later, he was less hopeful, and wrote that 'I do not expect to make any converts soon: their prejudices against Christianity are deep-rooted.' Nevertheless, his work had been 'much noticed by that people in this country', and there was some reason to suspect that his efforts had not been entirely in vain.[35]

Levi's reply to this appeal for negotiation occasioned a sharp response from Priestley, who published a second part of his letters to the Jews, dated from Birmingham, 1 July 1787. In his pamphlet Priestley wrote that he was glad that at least one Jew had answered his call, although he confessed that he 'should have been more happy if he had been better acquainted with profane literature' and had therefore been a more

---

[32] David Levi, *A Succinct Account, of the Rites, and Ceremonies, of the Jews* (London, n.d.=1783), esp. 5–6. See also D. S. Katz, 'The Abendana Brothers and the Christian Hebraists of Seventeenth-Century England', *Journal of Ecclesiastical History*, 40 (1989), 28–52.

[33] David Levi, *Lingua sacra: In Three Parts* (London, 1785–7).

[34] Joseph Priestley, *Letters to the Jews* (London, 1786): repr. as part i (Birmingham, 1786); and then again, (2nd edn., Birmingham, 1787), printed with part ii, which is the edn. that appears in the *Theological and Miscellaneous Works*, ed. J. T. Rutt (London, 1817–31), xx. 227–50. This edn. was repr. at New York in 1794, when Priestley was living in the United States.

[35] Priestley to Revd. T. Lindsey, 14 July 1786: *Life and Correspondence*, ed. J. T. Rutt (London, 1831–2), i. 395; P. to Revd. J. Toulmin, 6 Oct. 1786: ibid. i. 396.

worthy adversary.[36] In private correspondence Priestley revealed his deeper disappointment with the contest. Before receiving Levi's letters, Priestley was convinced that no English Jew at all would reply, although he had been informed that he would have an answer from Vienna.[37] Indeed, at first, Priestley had thought that Levi's letters were 'below my expectation, so much so, that I hardly think it will be worth while to reply to them'.[38] A few days later, however, he conceded that, on 'second thoughts, I am of opinion, that it will be right to take the opportunity of Mr. Levi's Answer, poor as it is, to address the Jews once more. It will tend to keep up their attention, and may bring forth something of more value'.[39]

One supposed Jew who added his name to the lists against Priestley was the imaginary Solomon de A.R. The author's main argument was with Unitarianism, and with the effrontery of Priestley in offering the Jews a 'mungrel religion' based on a selective reading of the Scriptures. On what authority, he asked, did Priestley declare some parts of the New Testament to be false and introduced by heathens? In brief, he complained,

There is a degree of candor and benevolence (real or affected you best know) running through your Letters, which could not avoid being extremely pleasing, were it not for that air of superciliousness and superiority, with which the whole is contaminated. The persons to whom you address yourself, appear in your Letters to be little better than contemptible children, or idiots, incapable of attending to solid manly arguments, and therefore to be amused with gewgaws and trifles.

Solomon's solution was for Priestley to offer himself to the Turks, and if that failed, to circumcise himself.[40] One of Priestley's admirers wrote to a colleague that this counterfeit work was 'full only of passion and low, unanswerable scurrility', but the *Gentleman's Magazine* in its review was pleased to recommend that this 'smart retort on the Doctor, by some waggish Oxonian, in the guise of a Jew, is the best and shrewdest detection of his sophisms, contradictions, and inconsistencies, that has yet appeared'.[41]

[36] Joseph Priestley, *Letters to the Jews, Part II: Occasioned by Mr. David Levi's Reply to the Former Letters* (Birmingham, 1787): repr. *Works*.
[37] Priestley to Revd. C. Rotheram, 23 Oct. 1786: *Correspondence*, ed. Rutt, i. 397.
[38] Priestley to Lindsey, 11 June 1787: ibid. i. 409–10.
[39] Same to same, 17 June 1787: ibid. i. 410.
[40] Solomon de A. R., *The Reply of the Jews to the Letters Addressed to them by Doctor Joseph Priestley* (Oxford, 1787). Cecil Roth, *Magna Bibliotheca Anglo-Judaica* (London, 1937), 260, suggests that this pamphlet was written by George Horne, the Hutchinsonian, but equally it could have been written by Henry Lemoine himself.
[41] Lindsey to Revd. Joseph Bretland, 7 July 1787: *Correspondence*, ed. Rutt, i. 410 n.; *Gents. Mag.* 57 (1787), 620.

Priestley, meanwhile, was convinced that his letters were beginning to have some effect. 'I hear of no converts among the Jews', he wrote to the Revd. Newcome Cappe at York,

but a learned Jew of Koningsberg is translating my Letters into Hebrew, and we shall print them here. He has sent me the numbers for three years of a periodical work, designed to promote literature among the Jews. It is in Hebrew, with a small part of it in High Dutch, consequently it is of little use to me. I find by my correspondence with him that my Letters have gained universal attention. They are translated into German; but many Jews, he says, in Poland, &c., understand neither English nor German.[42]

Certainly, Priestley's letters attracted a good deal of attention, and specific replies came from Anselm Bayly, John Hadley Swain, Philip David Krauter, Richard Beere, James Bicheno, and Jacob Barnet, a converted Jew.[43] David Levi himself returned to the fight, having meanwhile met Priestley personally, answering some of the issues raised by the above Gentiles, and facing squarely the criticism that his endeavours had evoked in the quiescent Jewish community itself, referring to

the consternation into which the greatest part of our nation were thrown on the appearance of my reply to your first letter; at the same time highly blaming my temerity, in thus entering into a contest that might cost them dear; for having long felt the iron hand of persecution, for the most frivolous and groundless accusations, they consequently dreaded the most distant attempt at what might by malevolent persons be construed as an attack upon the established religion, as this hath allways been studiously avoided by us.

Levi managed to convince the Jews of London that there was no danger of a Christian backlash as a result of his attacking Joseph Priestley, who advocated a sort of church, Levi wrote, that was neither Jewish nor Christian.[44] Priestley, for his part, determined that 'David Levi is unworthy of any notice', neither he nor 'his puffs in the papers'.[45]

---

[42] Priestley to Cappe, 23 Jan. 1788: *Correspondence*, ii. 8.

[43] 'Antisocinus' [Anselm Bayly], *Remarks on David Levi's Letters to Dr. Priestley* (London, 1787); R.W., *Letter to the Jews* (London, 1787); John Hadley Swain, *Objections of Mr. David Levi* (London, 1787); Philip David Krauter, *New Succinct and Candid Examination of Mr. David Levi's Objections* (London, 1787); Richard Beere, *Epistle to the Chief Priests* (London, n.d.); James Bicheno, *A Friendly Address to the Jews* (London, n.d.); Jacob Barnet, *Remarks upon Dr. Priestley's Letters* (London, 1792); Thomas Witherby, *An Attempt to Remove Prejudices Concerning the Jewish Nation* (London, 1804), esp. 80–2; *Gents. Mag.* 57 (1787), 497–8.

[44] David Levi, *Letters to Dr. Priestley . . . Part. II* (London, 1789), dated 14 Oct. 1788, p. 6.

[45] Priestley to Lindsey, 3 Apr. 1789; Priestley to Bretland, 7 May 1789: *Correspondence*, ii. 21, 23.

Presumably this was also his view about Solomon de A.R., who returned with a second answer, taunting the Unitarian Priestley once again with the possibility of entering the covenant of Abraham, reminding him that 'Judaism, without circumcision, is like the excise without a stamp.'[46]

David Levi, meanwhile, continued his crusade against misunderstanding the Jewish position, and addressed a series of letters to Thomas Paine, whose book on the age of reason caused a storm of protests among believers.[47] Levi also produced a five-volume edition of the Pentateuch, with an English translation on each facing page.[48] Priestley too continued to publish on Jewish questions and on related issues such as prophecy and the millennium.[49] Even in 1810 William 'Talib' Cuninghame, one of the leading figures in the London Society for Promoting Christianity amongst the Jews, published a refutation of David Levi, claiming that, when he wrote his work, 'he did not know that David Levi was no longer in life'.[50]

III

The debate between Priestley and Levi was conducted on the theoretical level, and although the events of the French Revolution may have influenced their positions, they remained intellectual rather than practical. Others were less willing to leave the Jewish question to the inscrutable workings of Providence. Certainly any contemporary remembering the personalities whose activities illuminated the life of English Jews during the late eighteenth and early nineteenth centuries would strike upon two individuals, one Jewish and the other nearly so. The first of these was Samuel Jacob Falk, also known as Doctor Falk or even Doctor Falckon, but most popularly as the Baal Shem of London, the greatest Anglo-Jewish cabbalist of his day. Falk seems to have been born in Poland although his father was described as 'Raphael, the Sefardi', and he apparently spent some time in Fürth, which enjoyed his charity throughout his life. Falk came to London about 1742, and lived

---

[46] Solomon de A. R., *A Second Letter to Dr. Joseph Priestley* (Oxford, 1790), esp. 53.

[47] David Levi, *A Defence of the Old Testament . . . Addressed to Thomas Paine* (London, 1797).

[48] David Levi, *The Holy Bible* (London, 1822).

[49] See e.g. Joseph Priestley, *Notes on All the Books of Scripture* (Northumberland, 1804), repr. *Works*, ed. Rutt, xii. 306–8, 341–3; xiv. 503.

[50] 'Talib' [William Cuninghame], *Remarks upon David Levi's Dissertations* (London, 1810). The controversy was also remembered by S. H. Jackson, *The Jew* (New York, 1824), 55, who thought that the 'philosophical, the learned, the wise, the potent Doctor Priestly, has been silenced, together with all the clergy of England, by David Levy'.

in Wellclose Square until his death forty years later. The Baal Shem was as famous among the Gentiles as he was well known among the Jews. Archenholz, writing at that time, included in his description of England a report that

There is a person of this nation called Cain Chenul Falk, but better known by the name of Doctor Falcon, who for thirty years has been famous for his cabalistical discoveries. He lives in a large house; is attended by a small number of domesticks; is engaged in no manner of business; and gives away a great deal of money to the poor. When he goes out, which indeed is but seldom, he is always clothed in a long robe, which agrees very well with his flowing beard, and noble figure. He is in the 70th year of his age. I shall not here recount the wonderful and incredible stories told of this old man. It is most probable that he is a very great chymist; and that he has, in that occult science made some extraordinary discoveries, which he does not choose to communicate.[51]

In France it was said that Falk had given a ring to the duke of Orléans which would ensure that he would succeed to the throne: 'cette bague, que Philippe-Égalité portait encore au moment de monter à l'échafaud, aurait été remise par lui à une Juive, Juliette Goudchaux, qui la fit passer au duc de Chartres. Louis-Philippe garda ce bijou jusqu'à mort, et le transmit au moment d'expirer au comte de Paris.'[52]

The Baal Shem of London was received very equivocally by the Jews themselves, however, although he seems to have been friendly with Rabbi David Tevele Schiff, whom Falk referred to as the 'rabbi of London and the entire country'.[53] At the same time Falk managed to secure the enduring enmity of Rabbi Jacob Emden, the son of Rabbi Zvi Ashkenazi. Emden was the scourge of cabbalists, Sabbatians, and mystics of all kinds, and vowed to a follower of the Baal Shem of London that 'Were I not already entangled in a controversy with the Eybschutzer I would send forth my denunciation against you', a reference to his epic quarrel with Rabbi Jonathan Eybeschutz, whom Emden accused of being a closet Sabbatian.[54] Haim David Azulai

---

[51] Archenholz, *Picture*, 111. Generally on Falk, see H. Adler [Chief Rabbi of England], 'The Baal Shem of London', *TJHSE* 5 (1908), 148–73, also reproducing a portrait of the Baal Shem. See also M. Oron, *Mysticism and Magic in Eighteenth-Century London* (Hebrew) (forthcoming); and M. K. Schuchard, 'Yeats and the "Unknown Superiors": Swedenborg, Falk, and Cagliostro', in *Secret Texts*, ed. M. Roberts and H. Ormsby-Lennon (forthcoming).

[52] Edouard Drumont, *La France juive* (Paris, 1887), i. 281 and n.

[53] Falk's commonplace book: Jewish Museum, London: United Synagogue Beth HaMidrash Library, London, as summarized in Adler, 'Baal Shem', 149, 166–73. The book consists of 59 octavo pages, and had previously been in the possession of Solomon Hirschell, Chief Rabbi of England after Schiff. It now seems to be missing.

[54] Jacob Emden, *Gath Drucha* (Hebrew): trans. Adler, 'Baal Shem', 160–1. According to Solomon Schechter, 'The "Baalshem"—Dr. Falk', *Jewish Chronicle*, 9

('Hida'), the fund-raiser for Hebron, also had to deal with questions about Falk when he was in Paris at the end of 1777. He was asked by the marquise de Croix about the famous Baal Shem of London, and received a louis for Hebron in return for his information. Azulai answered as best he could, but noted privately with disgust 'how many Christians have been led away by the man called *Baal-Shem* who, in his pride and presumption, has revealed the practices of the Kabbalah and the adjurations to so many nobles and ladies out of vanity. I have been plied with many questions about him, which I have answered'.[55]

The stories told of his supernatural deeds were the talk of the town. According to one account, it was Falk's custom to make clandestine visits to Epping Forest in his carriage. On one of these occasions a wheel came loose from the vehicle on the Whitechapel Road, but followed the carriage all the way to the forest. When Falk ran short of coal, he was said to have performed a magical feat involving three shirts and a ram's horn.[56] Falk was also able to keep candles burning miraculously, and to transport objects from one place to another. Sometimes these items would include his own valuables which he had been forced to pawn, despite his general wealth, but not before he had paid the premium. The story also circulated that he had saved the Great Synagogue from a fire raging in the neighbourhood by writing four Hebrew letters on the pillars of the door.[57]

Perhaps the most famous tale of Rabbi Falk concerns his connection with the death of Aaron Goldsmid, one of the Baal Shem's executors appointed in his will. According to Levi Alexander, the publisher and biographer of Benjamin Goldsmid, Aaron's more famous relative, Falk

left a packet of papers carefully sealed, in the care of the first gentleman [Aaron Goldsmid], to be securely treasured up, but never opened, nor looked into on the strictest injunction, as such an attempt to discover their contents would be peremptorily attended with fatal consequences to the person who opened it; but on the contrary, if carefully preserved, himself and family would be highly prosperous in all their undertakings.

Mar. 1888, 15–16, Falk was connected with the movement of Shabtai Sevi, but there does not seem to be any evidence for this.

[55] Diary of Haim David Azulai: repr. E. N. Adler, *Jewish Travellers* (London, 1930), 359–60.

[56] Isaacs, *Ceremonies, Customs, Rites, and Traditions of the Jews*, 355–6.

[57] Alexander, *Memoirs of the Life of Benjamin Goldsmid*, 46–50: cited in Adler, 'Baal Shem', 162–4. See also a letter by Susman Shesnowzi to his son in Poland, concerning Falk, repr. in Emden, *Gat*, 69b and trans. in ibid. 158–60.

The warning seems to have gone unheeded, for

Curiosity, the most impulsive power over the human mind, acted over Mr. Goldsmid's resolution to keep this secret depot inviolably closed, till at last he yielded to the silly desire of investigating the contents of one packet; when, astonishing to relate, his death ensued the same day, and threw the family into the greatest consternation. When the fatal paper was found, it was covered with Cabalistical figures and Hieroglyphics.[58]

Some of Falk's unusual abilities can be corroborated with reference to his remarkable commonplace book, which still survives. He does make frequent reference there to a 'forest meeting room', where he placed a chest full of gold in the custody of a rabbi named Tobias and his two rabbinical sons, Simeon and Abraham. He also includes lists of objects that he had received as pledges, and which he sold when not redeemed. When he purchased lottery tickets he included a special prayer for their success. Personal notes, recipes, and details of business transactions compete with lists of books and cabbalistical *aides-mémoires*.[59]

The Baal Shem of London died on 17 April 1782, and until recently payments to the United Federation of Ashkenazi synagogues in London were still being made according to the investments stipulated in his will.[60] Falk's death was felt not only among his followers in London, but abroad as well. General Charles Rainsford, employed on the Continent to secure foreign troops to fight for the British against the American rebels, was a Freemason, and was eager for any news he could obtain about the Baal Shem. In October 1782 he wrote to a friend in Paris, reporting that all was upset by the unexpected death of Dr. Falk. Rainsford had just returned from North Africa, and he wrote, 'Croyez moi que j'ai trouvé des Nouvelles de cet Juif, parmi les Juifs d'Algiers et on m'a conté des Histoires singulières de lui, jusqu'à lui attribuer le Succès contre les Espagnols—violà!'[61] Nevertheless, whatever Falk's origins and the scope of his activities, supernatural or otherwise, he was unquestionably one of the best-known figures of the Jewish religious world in the late eighteenth century.[62]

The second individual whose activities focused attention on late eighteenth-century Anglo-Jewry was the eccentric Lord George

---

[58] Adler, 'Baal Shem', 158–60.   [59] See n. 53 above.

[60] Adler, 'Baal Shem', 157, 168–9 (inscription on Falk's tombstone at Mile End), 170–2 (Falk's will, dated 14 Apr. 1782), 173.

[61] Gen. Charles Rainsford correspondence: BL Add. MS 23669, fos. 85–86ᵛ. See also G. P. G. Hills, 'Notes on Some Contemporary References to Dr. Falk, the Baal Shem of London, in the Rainsford MSS. at the British Museum', *TJHSE* 8 (1918), 122–8.

[62] Another contemporary description of a cabbalist which almost certainly refers to Falk appears in *Gents. Mag.* 32 (1762), 418–20.

Gordon (1751–1793). Gordon was a younger son of the third duke of that name, was sent to Parliament in 1774, and five years later became the president of the United Protestant League. His name will forever be associated with the Gordon Riots against Roman Catholics which he sparked in June 1780, and which broadened their scope to lash out against the rich, Newgate gaol, and the Bank of England. The rioters caused ten times as much damage during that single week as occurred in Paris throughout the French Revolution, and paid the price of 290 deaths during the disturbances and twenty-five executions afterwards. Lord George Gordon was tried for high treason at the beginning of the following year, and pleaded insanity. Although the jury refused to accept this explanation of his conduct, he was acquitted nevertheless.[63]

When and why Lord George Gordon converted to Judaism is still a subject of some dispute. Dr Robert Watson, who wrote Gordon's biography only two years after his death, contended that he 'had long entertained doubts concerning the truths of Christianity, and observed "that its professors were both at variance with revelation and reason; whilst the Jews literally adhered to the laws of Moses" '.[64] Charles Dickens concluded his novel about the Gordon Riots, *Barnaby Rudge*, with an epilogue containing the claim that Gordon converted to Judaism in August 1788, but this is impossible, since he was already a Jew when arrested the previous year.[65] We have the evidence of a Hebrew letter written by the Prussian Jew who acted as Gordon's tutor in matters Jewish, a certain Meyer Joseph, also known as Michael Josephs. According to him,

Lord George Gordon submitted, at an advanced age, to the operation of circumcision. The rite of the covenant of Abraham was administered to him in the town of Birmingham. The name of the individual who performed the operation was Rabbi Jacob Birmingham. When Lord G. Gordon, recovered from the effects of the circumcision seal, he came to London; (and being already pretty well tutored in Jewish rites and customs, and was also able to read Hebrew with some degree of fluency,) he attended the Hamburgh Synagogue,

[63] On Gordon and the Gordon Riots, see P. Colson, *The Strange History of Lord George Gordon* (London, 1937); C. Hibbert, *King Mob* (London, 1959); J. de Castro, *The Gordon Riots* (London, 1926); R. Porter, *English Society in the Eighteenth Century* (Penguin edn., Harmondsworth, 1982), 116. See the written opinion of Lord Kenyon (24 Jan. 1782) that the Sephardi synagogue should not be assessed for raising monies against the inhabitants of the City of London on account of the Gordon Riots, nor to be distrained in case of non-payment: SPJC, London, MS 344/56a.

[64] Robert Watson, *The Life of Lord George Gordon: With a Philosophical Review of his Political Conduct* (London, 1795), 77.

[65] Charles Dickens, *Barnaby Rudge* (London, 1841), 'Chapter the Last'.

where he was called up to the reading of the law; and was honoured with Me Shebayrach. He presented that synagogue with 100 *l.*[66]

Since we also know that Gordon was sent a respectful letter from the Protestant Association on 7 August 1786 and that he was already a Jew when arrested in December 1787, it would seem that his conversion occurred sometime between those two dates, probably in the latter part of 1787 when he was living in Birmingham, hiding out disguised as a Jew in order to evade arrest on a rather tedious charge of libel.[67] It may be that Gordon also applied to Rabbi David Tevele Schiff of the Great Synagogue, either for conversion or for membership, but the correspondence connected with this application has disappeared.[68]

In retrospect, one can see certain signs of continuing interest on behalf of the Jews expressed by Gordon in the years before his conversion. Gordon protested on 14 March 1782 to Emperor Joseph II against the poor treatment suffered by Jews in Germany, and on 10 August 1785 he sent a discourteous letter to the emperor, blaming his current political misfortunes on his tendency towards anti-Semitism.

[66] Meyer Joseph to ?, n.d., repr. Moses Margoliouth, *The History of the Jews in Great Britain* (London, 1851), ii. 122–4. 'Rabbi Jacob Birmingham', the *mohel* who circumcised Gordon, may be surnamed Tettenborn, residing at Norwich: R. D. Barnett, 'The Correspondence of the Mahamad of the Spanish and Portuguese Congregation of London during the Seventeenth and Eighteenth Centuries', *TJHSE* 20 (1964), 10 n. For more on Joseph, see I. Solomons, 'Lord George Gordon's Conversion to Judaism', *TJHSE* 7 (1915), 238 n. The old minute book of the Hambro Synagogue, exhibited at the Anglo-Jewish Historical Exhibition of 1887, contained an entry relating to Gordon. Unfortunately, the document has since disappeared: it may be in Budapest, if it was lent to Professor David Kaufmann for the preparation of his article on Zvi Ashkenazi, published in the *TJHSE* 3 (1899). Cf. Anglo-Jewish Historical Exhibition, Catalogue (London, 1888), 19 [no. 601]; and *Archives of the United Synagogue*, ed. C. Roth (London, 1930), 15. According to L. Hyman, *The Jews of Ireland* (London, 1972), 321, Gordon was taught his Hebrew by Rabbi Zalman Ansell of the London *beth din*.

[67] Letter from the Protestant Association cited in M. E. Wemyss, *Temple Bar*, 79 (1887), 367; Solomons, 'Gordon', 238. See also I. A. Shapiro (ed.), *Birmingham Jewry, 1749–1914* (Manchester, 1980). Gordon's conversion may have been arranged by 'Rabbi' Phillips of Birmingham: Hyman, *Ireland*, 53, 100. For more on the beginnings of the Jewish community at Birmingham, see Roth, *Provincial Jewry*, 32–3; Z. Josephs (ed.), *Birmingham Jewry 1749–1914* (Birmingham, 1980); id. (ed.), *Birmingham Jewry, ii: More Aspects 1740–1930* (Birmingham, 1984).

[68] It is unlikely that any London rabbi would consent to convert so prominent a man as Lord George Gordon, in light of the communal ban on proselytization made in 1751: see Roth, *Great Synagogue*, 89–93. According to ibid. 141, the correspondence between Gordon and Schiff was read by Chief Rabbi N. M. Adler (Schiff's great-nephew), so it must still have been in existence this century. NB, however, that id., 'Lord George Gordon's Conversion to Judaism', in his *Essays and Portraits in Anglo-Jewish History* (Philadelphia, 1962), 183–210, is entirely derivative of Solomon's earlier article of the same name.

Gordon also noted that in late 1783 he himself sent letters to the Jews of England in their various congregations, 'requesting those rulers to submit my best intended endeavours to the consideration of Judah and the tribes of Israel, whithersoever dispersed over the whole world'. Gordon said he never disguised his sentiments, notwithstanding the fact that the imperial officials at the English Court 'loaded me continually with reproaches, insults, and injuries, because I loved the Jews'.[69]

Gordon's letter to the Jews bears further scrutiny. It is addressed to Elias Lindo, a *parnas* of the Bevis Marks synagogue, and Nathan Solomon, the lay head of the Ashkenazi New Synagogue, later involved with the Goldsmid brothers. The style is disturbingly apocalyptic, flavoured with Hebrew phrases such as 'Shemah Israel!' and 'Shemah Koli!' Gordon's aim was to advise the Jews of England to side with the Protestants and to oppose the Catholics irrevocably, not only in England, but in America as well: 'Believe me, Israel! I am your friend,' he wrote. Indeed, the

tribes of Israel will soon be driven out of this pleasant land, like chaff before the wind, if they set themselves against God, and his People, to serve Idolators. There is no time to be lost. The Protestants in Europe, as well as in America, will insist with vigour on your shewing themselves on their side, against the Jesuits.

Gordon went to the trouble of having his open letter printed in the form of a broadsheet, which presumably was distributed in the Jewish districts of London.[70] He also appealed to the Jews in other papers that he wrote and distributed in England and Holland, begging them to cease lending the money which fuelled the contemporary European wars.[71]

Lord George Gordon's conversion to Judaism may therefore have been more than a convenient ploy, more perhaps than a clear demonstration of his insanity. His contemporary biographer Watson himself was not clear about Gordon's motives, but did not dismiss the possibility that 'perhaps he expected to have led back the Israelites to their *fathers' land*', and noted that Gordon frequently quoted such prophecies. Watson also considered the notion that 'he chose rather to be considered as the *leader* of the *Jews*, than the humble *disciple* of *Jesus*'. In any case, Gordon's conversion to Judaism was immediately detrimental, for, as Watson explained, it 'was no sooner universally believed that he had embraced Judaism, than the Courts of Versailles and

---

[69] Gordon to Joseph II, 10 Aug. 1785, from Welbeck Street, London: repr. Solomons, 'Gordon', 229–30, noting that 'I cannot trace the magazine from which this cutting is taken.'

[70] George Gordon, *Copy of a Letter* (London, 26 Aug. 1783), broadsheet: BL 1880. C.1. (150): repr. Solomons, 'Gordon', 235–7.   [71] Watson, *Gordon*, 75.

London determined to prosecute him', in a trial that took place in June and July 1787.[72]

Lord George Gordon's offence, so trivial in comparison with the outrages committed in his name seven years earlier, was in having libelled in the press the good name of Marie Antoinette, whose reputation had already sunk low over the notorious case of the diamond necklace, a million-livres fraud which relied on public knowledge of her indecent passion for jewels.[73] Gordon was also accused of having produced a pamphlet on prison reform which was a libel on the judges and the administration of the laws of England. Gordon may already have been a Jew by this time—Watson thought so—but after being pronounced guilty he took advantage of the judge's failure to set bail by fleeing to Holland. The Dutch were unhappy at the presence of this sudden visitor, so popular with the revolutionary elements, and promptly shipped him back under guard to Harwich, where he arrived on 22 July 1787.[74]

Gordon was back in England, but still free, since the Dutch did not see their brief as extending to extradition. 'He retired *incog.* to Birmingham,' Watson recounts, 'and he resided at the house of a Jew, disguised by a long beard and a broad shaded hat, after the Polish fashion.' He was circumcised, and took the name of Israel Bar Abraham George Gordon. In this fashion he lived in Birmingham for four months, until he was betrayed, perhaps by his landlord, and apprehended by an officer of Bow Street on 7 December 1787.[75] Gordon declined to travel on the Sabbath, so the party left that night or early the next day, arriving too late in London to be received by the marshal of the King's Bench prison, which forced him to lodge at the Grand Hotel, Covent Garden. Gordon's return was a London sensation, and the first of the two major topics of discussion that winter was the gap between the convert's style of life now while in town, and the fact that while he resided in Birmingham, he 'lodged in one of the dirtiest houses in Dudley street, where the Jews chiefly inhabit'.[76] The other was the length of Gordon's beard, computed by the reporter for the *London Chronicle* at 4 inches.[77] Horace Walpole also recounted an elegant dinner at which the 'conversation soon fell on Lord George Gordon's

[72] Ibid. 79–80.

[73] For a full account of this wonderful affair (1784–6), see J. O. Fuller, *The Comte de Saint-Germain: Last Scion of the House of Rakoczy* (London, 1988), 304–7.

[74] Watson, *Gordon*, 80–3; Hibbert, *King Mob*, 178–9. The said libellous pamphlet on the judges was his *The Prisoners Petition* (London, 1786).

[75] Watson, *Gordon*, 82–3.

[76] *Gents. Mag.* 57 (1787), 531–3, 545, 634–5, 1120–1. Cf. extracts from the newspapers of mid-Dec. 1787 repr. Solomons, 'Gordon', 243–7.

[77] *London Chronicle*, 4855 (8–11 Dec. 1787), 558.

Mosaic beard—on which one of the company said, it was lucky when *converts* wore distinguishing marks by which they might be reconnoitred'.[78]

Gordon was sentenced on 28 January 1788 in the court of King's Bench to five years in Newgate, fined £500, and notified that on his release he would be required to find sureties for his good behaviour to the amount of £10,000 and two further persons who would ensure it on the basis of £2,500 each, for the following fourteen years. 'His Lordship made a very grotesque figure', a newspaper reported from the courtroom, 'he was wrapped up in a great coat, his hair lank as usual, his beard about three inches long, extending under his chin and throat, from ear to ear, and differing from the colour of his hair.'[79] Gordon began serving his sentence with the rest of the felons in the unspeakable conditions of Newgate gaol, but the efforts of his friends and his brother the duke of Gordon prevailed, and he was eventually given his own room. Meyer Joseph, who was in contact with Gordon at that time, described the scene:

Whilst in prison, he was very regular in his Jewish observances; every morning he was seen with his phylacteries between his eyes, and opposite to his heart. Every Saturday he had a public service in his room, by the aid of ten Polish Jews. He looked like a patriarch with his beautiful long beard. His Saturday's bread was baked according to the manner of the Jews, his wine was Jewish, his meat was Jewish, and he was the best Jew in the congregation of Israel. On his prison wall were to be seen, first the ten commandments, in the Hebrew language, then the bag of the Talith, or fringed garment, and of the phylacteries.[80]

Gordon established a sort of prison salon, accommodating visitors 'frequently so numerous as to prevent their sitting down', entertained by 'the Duke of York's band, and other persons about the Court, whom it is not safe to name. They came sometimes in their uniform, and sometimes in disguise', and might meet there the duke of York himself,

[78] Horace Walpole to Lady Ossory, 15 Dec. 1787: *Correspondence*, ed. W. S. Lewis, *et al.* (London, 1937–83), xxxiii. 587–8. Walpole thought Lord George Gordon's conversion to be a very amusing subject: see also his letters to Hannah More (4 Nov. 1789): ibid. xxxi. 332; and to Mary Berry (26 Feb. 1791): ibid. xi. 210.

[79] Walpole to Sir William Hamilton, English envoy at Naples, 17 Jan. 1788: ibid. xxxv. 436–7; Watson, *Gordon*, 83. See also the *London Chronicle*, 4857 (13–15 Dec. 1787), 569; 4858 (15–18 Dec. 1787), 579; 4877 (26–9 Jan. 1788), 103. Cf. T. B. Howell, *State Trials* (London, 1809–28), xxi. 485–687; xxii. 235–6; and *Whole Proceedings on the Trials of . . . Lord George Gordon* (London, 1787).

[80] Meyer Joseph to ?, n.d., repr. Margoliouth, *History*, ii. 122–4. One member of Gordon's prison *minyan* was Moses Hyams of Vilna, according to family history: Hyman, *Ireland*, 55–6, citing a MS deposited in the American Jewish Archives in Cincinnati.

who took to conversing with Gordon's two handmaids, one of whom was Jewish. Everyone was welcome in his cell, apart from Jews who had shaved their beards and went about with their heads uncovered, Gordon's objection to which was embodied in his published correspondence on the subject. Gordon usually had at least half a dozen people to dinner in his rooms, and was attended fortnightly by a bagpiper, 'and he had often a large concert of music, and parties of dancing'. On the rare occasions when he had no company, Gordon himself would play his violin for the edification of the other felons.[81]

Although imprisoned, Lord George Gordon remained politically active, and was greatly heartened by the events of 14 July 1789, 'a preliminary step to the overthrow of that imperious woman, to whose intrigues, in part, he had fallen a victim'. Gordon wrote to the National Assembly of France on 23 July, asking for their intervention with the English courts, presenting himself in some sense as a precursor of the French Revolutionaries. Gordon received a reply dated 24 February 1790 from the celebrated abbé Grégoire, who regretted having to deny Gordon's request since 'as you are a foreigner, and detained in the prisons of England, it would be improper to deliberate upon the subject'. Gordon responded to Grégoire's letter immediately upon receipt, pointing out that he had been imprisoned as the result of an appeal from the agents of the French monarchy, so he did not understand why he could not be freed by means of an appeal from the French revolutionary government: 'Has the army of your Monarch become withered in the department of *foreign affairs*, in the very moment of regeneration?' he asked. Although great interest was shown in his case in France, and Grégoire and Gordon continued to exchange letters, no official action was taken.[82]

Lord George Gordon remained in prison until his death four years later, occupying himself with the events of the French Revolution and the fight against slavery. He became a sort of standing joke, and numerous satirical prints and ballads paid tribute to the originality of his

---

[81] Watson, *Gordon*, 107–9; *A Letter from Angel Lyon, to . . . Lord George Gordon, on Wearing Beards: With Lord George Gordon's Answer* ([London, June 1789)]: very rare; repr. Solomons, 'Gordon', 251–5.

[82] Gordon to National Assembly of France, 23 July 1789; Grégoire to Gordon, 24 Feb. 1790, annexing opinion of the Committee of Reports; Gordon to Grégoire and National Assembly, Mar. 1790; Grégoire to Gordon, 4 July 1791; Gordon to Grégoire, 23 Aug. 1791, answering the latter's request for the English view of the French Revolution: all repr. Watson, *Gordon*, 91–7, 112–24. See also Gordon's letter to W. Smith about the Polish Revolution (London, 2 Aug. 1791), published in pamphlet form (BL 8093 bb. 16), part. repr. Solomons, 'Gordon', 247; and Lord George Gordon, *Memorial* ([London, 1789?]).

decision to convert to Judaism.[83] He was also a magnet for bizarre characters, most notably a young woman who claimed to have conceived immaculately by the power of the Holy Ghost. It was the angel Gabriel who assured her that the end of the world was at hand, and that the child she was about to bring forth was to announce these changes to the rest of mankind. Gabriel also commanded her to seek the advice of Lord George Gordon, who with his companions 'smiled at her miraculous conception'. There was a limit even to their credulity.[84]

Gordon's prison sentence expired on 28 January 1793, and he duly appeared in the court of King's Bench, covering his head in Jewish fashion, but giving up his original idea of sporting a red night-cap, choosing instead a tricoloured handkerchief, bound in the form of a turban. Having failed to supply the financial sureties required for his release, Gordon was returned to Newgate. Watson claims that attempts by others to stand bail for Gordon were frustrated by the government and the Court. Certainly Edmund Burke was pleased to have Gordon remain in gaol. 'We have Lord George Gordon fast in Newgate', he gloated,

and neither his being a public proselyte to Judaism, nor his having, in his zeal against Catholic priests and all sorts of ecclesiastics, raised a mob (excuse the term, it is still in use here) which pulled down all our prisons, have preserved to him a liberty of which he did not render himself worthy by a virtuous use of it. We have rebuilt Newgate and tenanted the mansion. We have prisons almost as strong as the Bastille for those who dare to libel the queens of France. In this spiritual retreat, let the noble libeller remain. Let him there meditate on his Talmud until he learns a conduct more becoming his birth and parts, and not so disgraceful to the ancient religion to which he has become a proselyte; or until some persons from your side of the water, to please your new Hebrew brethren, shall ransom him.[85]

In October 1793, Gordon caught a dose of gaol fever, apparently typhus, and took to his death-bed. According to Watson, a 'few hours before his death, he repeatedly exclaimed, "O, Duke! Duke!" and, after singing *Ça ira*, he bade the world an eternal adieu, on the 1st of November, 1793'.[86] The Jews of London, understandably nervous about having

---

[83] See the list of engraved portraits and caricatures of Gordon in Solomons, 'Gordon', 265–71 and some of the ballads, 257–60. Solomons's extensive collection of Gordonalia is now deposited in the Jewish Theological Seminary, New York City: *TJHSE* 12 (1931), 1.

[84] Watson, *Gordon*, 127–8. Cf. the 'Letter sent to him by a certain Great Lady', repr. in *The Christian Turned Jew* (n.p., n.d.) (BL 4418, fo. 17 (12)): copy destroyed by German bombing.

[85] Edmund Burke, *Reflections on the Revolution in France* (London, 1790), vi. 1.

[86] Watson, *Gordon*, 130–3, 135–7.

such a man eternally among them, refused him burial, and his remains, it was solemnly reported, 'were interred on the 9th with the utmost privacy, in a vault in St. James's burying-ground, on the Hamptstead road'.[87]

At the end of the day, it was not clear which of Lord George Gordon's offences was the most objectionable: his role in the riots which bear his name, his conversion to Judaism, or his unqualified championship of the French Revolution, like many of his more apocalyptically inclined fellow religious radicals. The anonymous obituary writer for the *Gentleman's Magazine* thought that although Gordon had many good qualities and his suffering was genuine, his incarceration was imperative: 'Those, however, in whose memory the riots of 1780 are yet fresh, when they consider the present state of political speculation, and weigh the character, genius, and talents of Lord George, must in candour admit, that such a person could not well be at large without some degree of hazard to the good order of society.'[88] Indeed, as Watson wrote, 'Lord George Gordon, whether we reflect on the eccentricity of his character, or on the vicissitudes of fortune which he experienced, was undoubtedly one of the most extraordinary persons of the age.'[89]

IV

Falk and Gordon were exceptional figures in their eccentricity, but it might certainly be said that their behaviour was not especially deviant in relation to the times in which they lived. Other writers promoted the wisdom of the Jews, either as millenarians, or as Christian Hebraists. Joseph Eyre, for example, published a work on prophecy in 1771 praising Joseph Mede and Isaac Newton as eminent scholars of prophecy. Eyre's point was that the 'great happiness' described in the Old Testament referred not to Christians at all, but only 'to the conversion and restoration of the *literal Israel*, the *Jews* and ten tribes, in the latter times, and to that reign of Christ when the church shall be *triumphant*'.[90] Richard Clarke, a curate of Hackney, saw the prophecies as proving that the Jews would be converted by a vision or a voice from Heaven, and that 'Earthquakes, Storms, and Inundations, since the Year 1755, particularly' indicated that this day was drawing near.[91] E. W.

---

[87] Gordon's obituary, *Gents. Mag.* 63 (1793), 1056–7.   [88] Ibid.
[89] Watson, *Gordon*, 134.
[90] Joseph Eyre, *Observations upon the Prophecies Relating to the Restoration of the Jews* (London, 1771), pp. vii–viii, xvi.
[91] Richard Clarke, *Signs of Times* (London, 1773), pp. iv–v, vii.

Whitaker, the Canterbury cleric, was more circumspect in his dissertation on the prophecies relating to the final restoration of the Jews, and noted that the 'figurative language of prophecy, and its emblematical descriptions, are equally calculated to mark with precision the several events when they come to pass, and to keep men till then so far in the dark'.[92] With the coming of the French Revolution, such prophecies seemed more than possible.

Both the Baal Shem of London and Lord George Gordon worked, so to speak, from within the Jewish community. Others whose activities gave English Gentiles a new perspective on the Jews within their midst acted according to an entirely different programme. Most famous among these divine co-workers was Richard Brothers (1757–1824), a former naval officer who had a heavenly vision in 1792 naming him Prince of the Hebrews, nephew of the Almighty. Brothers was arrested in 1795 for treasonable practices, and was examined before the Privy Council. He was committed to an insane asylum, where he spent the next eleven years. On his release in 1806 Brothers lived at the home of one of his followers, and from 1815 with John Finlayson, a Scottish lawyer who had been convinced of the prince's mission in 1797.

Brothers had a great influence in England during these troubled years, and the extreme reaction of the government shows how potentially dangerous he was thought to be. His actual views were similar to those of other millenarian thinkers. He awaited the imminent onset of the millennium, at one stage pinpointed at 19 November 1795, at which time Brothers would lead the Jews back to the Holy Land and there begin the rebuilding of Jerusalem. Brothers's Jews were not only the 'visible Hebrews' with whom one might come into contact, but also the 'invisible Hebrews', the descendants of the Lost Ten Tribes, a number of whom were living in England as he spoke. Brothers saw himself as a descendant of King David through Jesus's brother James, and knew that representatives of various tribes were included among his followers.

One of Brothers's devotees was Nathaniel Brassey Halhed, a member of Parliament for Lymington and an expert on Indian philology. Halhed became fascinated with Brothers and his understanding of the times, and insisted that the subject be discussed in Parliament during the spring of 1795. What interested Halhed was Brothers's interpretation of prophecy, and his claim that it was the divine will that peace be made with France. In many respects, Brothers's views were not as radical as they appear on first sight, and certainly his star declined when the millennium failed to materialize in November 1795. In a sense,

---

[92] E. W. Whitaker, *A Dissertation on the Prophecies Relating to the Final Restoration of the Jews* (Canterbury, 1784), 85.

Brothers's was an anti-war movement with divine support, but from our point of view his utility was that he kept the question of the millennial role of the Jews before the public eye, and gave them a part to play in the divine scheme.[93]

Joanna Southcott (1750–1814) was in some ways the successor of Richard Brothers, not only because of the ideas she promoted, but also because many of the Almighty Nephew's disappointed followers eventually went over to her banner, such as Thomas Philip Foley, a Worcestershire rector.[94] Southcott was born a farmer's daughter in Devon, and after domestic service joined the Methodists. The divine inspiration came upon her in 1792, and over the next twenty-two years she wrote sixty-five pamphlets and left behind her many unpublished manuscripts. It has been estimated that about one-quarter of her writings were autobiographical and in reference to contemporary events, while the rest consisted of communications from the Holy Spirit and interpretations of Scripture. Southcott would seal up her prophecies with the intention that they be opened after they had been fulfilled in order to testify to their veracity. She also 'sealed' her followers by giving them a piece of paper, a sort of membership card in the new sect which was gradually being formed, despite her declared intention of remaining (like the first Methodists) under the umbrella of the Established Church. She herself was the 'woman clothed with the sun' of Revelation, destined to deliver the Messiah by virgin birth. Signs of pregnancy did indeed appear in 1814, but with their diminishing came her death on 27 December. To the surprise of her followers, she was not resurrected on the fourth day and was instead laid to rest in St John's Wood cemetery, across the way from the grave of Richard Brothers.[95]

Southcott's work was continued after her death by a number of loyal disciples and leaders of offshoot movements. Thomas Philip Foley was one of these, as was George Turner, a Leeds merchant. Interestingly, the Jewish elements in her theology became more practically prominent after her death in the subsidiary movements. Mary 'Joanna' Boon, an illiterate shoemaker's wife, ordered her followers to observe the Mosaic law, including the Jewish Sabbath on Saturday.[96] Better known was the

[93] The literature on Richard Brothers is enormous, although the Jewish element in his theology has not been discussed sufficiently. Meanwhile, see J. F. C. Harrison, *The Second Coming: Popular Millenarianism 1780–1850* (London, 1979), ch. 4.

[94] See esp. Foley to Richard Brothers, 25 Dec. 1801, declaring his allegiance: University Library, Leeds, Roth MS 251.

[95] Generally on Southcott, see Harrison, *Second Coming*, ch. 5; J. K. Hopkins, *A Woman to Deliver Her People: Joanna Southcott and English Millenarianism in an Era of Revolution* (Austin, Tex., 1982).

[96] For Mary 'Joanna' Boon, see *Gents. Mag.* 95 (1825), i. 460; John Field, 'Stone Mason', *Zion's Recorder and Truth's Advocate*, 1 (1825); Harrison, *Second Coming*, 137.

group around John Wroe (1782–1863), who joined the movement only after the death of its founder. Wroe had visions in which he was commanded to become a Jew, and although the synagogues at Liverpool and London refused to comply with the divine request, he was not deterred and tried to take over the entire Southcottian movement and shift it to a more Jewish direction. He travelled through Europe in the early 1820s, visiting synagogues and promoting his case. Wroe's plan was different from that of Richard Brothers in that instead of hoping to lead the Jews back to the Holy Land, he ordered Christians to observe the Mosaic law. Although his sect was strongest in the Bradford area, he made missionary tours to America and to Australia, where the so-called 'Christian Israelites' became fairly well established.[97]

V

Richard Brothers and Joanna Southcott captured the limelight of radical millenarian enthusiast support for the divine role of the Jews as they perceived it. Nevertheless, it should not be forgotten that beneath, or above, this noisy excitement, the expression of millennial interest in the Jewish fate continued unabated as it had done since the earliest days of the Reformation, unaffected and even embarrassed by the outlandish activities of Brothers and Southcott. Jews were still regarded as privy to divine secrets. Samuel Bernard, a Jewish banker who died on the eve of the French Revolution, leaving behind an enormous fortune, was said to have 'had a favourite black cock, which was regarded by many as uncanny, and as unpleasantly connected with the amassing of his fortune'. The bird supposedly died a day or two before its master.[98] Other views were more conventionally millenarian. E. W. Whitaker, for example, a rector of Canterbury, wrote a number of works dedicated to understanding the prophecies connected with the Jewish destiny, taking note of the fact that the new discoveries of Jewish communities 'scattered over the extensive regions of Arabia, Persia, Tartary, northern

---

[97] On John Wroe, see his works: *The Vision of an Angel* (Bradford, 1820); *The Word of God* (Wakefield, 1834); *Divine Communications and Prophecies* (Wakefield, 1834); *The Laws and Commands of God* (Wakefield, 1835); *An Abridgement of John Wroe's Life and Travels* (4th edn., Gravesend, 1851); *Communications Given to John Wroe* (4th edn., Gravesend, 1852); *A Guide to the People Surnamed Israelites* (Gravesend, 1852). There is now even a novel about him: J. Rogers, *Mr Wroe's Virgins* (London, 1991), which was made into a television film.

[98] William Henderson, *Notes on the Folk Lore of the Northern Counties of England*, ed. S. Baring-Gould (London, 1866), 115–16 n. I am grateful to David Harley for this reference.

India, and China' gave proof to the remarkable nature of the Jewish providence.[99] Thomas Taylor also discussed the gathering in of the Jews, praising them, among other things, for not being associated with the slave-trade, and noting that

the term, North country, cannot refer to Babylon, for that is not north, but south-east from Jerusalem; and it is still more remarkable, that I suppose more Jews dwell in Holland, Germany, Poland, and the Russian empire, and in some of its neighbouring states, than in all the world besides; and from thence they shall be gathered.[100]

William Cooper, a young minister in Whitechapel, claimed that his preaching was frequently graced with the presence of Jews, and he resolved to dedicate his work to them. 'Gentile sinners,' he told his congregation, 'you are this day highly honoured with the presence of a noble nation. Behold the ancient Israel of God; and, conscious of your own inferiority, reverence them as your superiors.' Cooper was also careful to warn his Jewish hearers against Richard Brothers, whose words were 'the whimsies of such a madman'. Indeed, he claimed, the 'prophecies of this enthusiast are not fulfilled, nor ever will be'.[101] Richard Beere, the author of a number of tracts relating to the restoration of the Jews, wrote to William Pitt defending the millenarian interpretation, noting that 'what I have written, is not an Utopian or visionary scheme, or the effects of a fruitful imagination; but founded on Revelation, Historical facts, & sound argument with the most accurate calculations—I trust it will be found deserving of an attentive consideration'.[102] Interestingly, Emanuel Swedenborg (1688–1772) seems to have been somewhat unfavourably disposed towards Jews, an attitude which may have been intensified when two Jews stole his gold watch from under his pillow while he was in a trance in London. When asked to return the watch the Jews replied, 'Do you not know that in

---

[99] E. W. Whitaker, *The Manual of Prophecy* (Egham, 1808), esp. pp. iii, 150–2; id., *A General and Connected View of the Prophecies Relating to the Times of the Gentiles* (Egham, 1795). See also D. S. Katz, 'The Chinese Jews and the Problem of Biblical Authority in Eighteenth- and Nineteenth-Century England', *EHR* 105 (1990), 893–919.

[100] Thomas Taylor, *Ten Sermons on the Millennium* (Hull, 1789), esp. 149, 156, 158.

[101] William Cooper, *The Promised Seed: A Sermon, Preached to God's Ancient Israel, the Jews, at Sion-Chapel, Whitechapel, on Sunday Afternoon, August 28, 1796* (3rd edn., London, 1796), esp. 3, 9, 13, 35–6, 37; id., *Christ the True Messiah* (2nd edn., London, [1796]), esp. pp. iii–iv, 5, 28. Cooper made approving reference to 'Zeres, the Jew' in both sermons.

[102] Richard Beere to William Pitt, 10 Nov. 1790: Mocatta Library, University College, London, Mocatta Cupboard, Mocatta 3304. Cf. Richard Beere, *Epistle to the Chief Priests and Elders of the Jews . . . Answer to Mr. David Levi* (London, [1789?]); id., *Dissertation on the 13th and 14th Verses of the 8th Chapter of Daniel* (London, [1790]).

your ecstasy you seized the watch yourself, that you went out into the street and threw it into the gutter?' Swedenborg, however, refused to prosecute.[103]

VI

However, it was of course the continued public perception of a disproportionate Jewish involvement in crime that helped form attitudes to the Jewish population of London during the revolutionary period. Curiously enough, at least one Jewish crime had a link with France, that being the famous and notorious robbery in 1791 of jewels from Madame du Barry, the mistress of Louis XIV. The thieves were identified as four Jews named John Baptiste Levit, Simon Josephs, Jacob Moses, and Moses Abrahams, who fled to London after committing the robbery on the night of 10–11 January 1791. The quantity of jewellery was prodigious indeed, including gold chains, diamonds, and coins, and crowned by 'pictures of Louis XIV and XV, richly mounted, etc., etc.' Madame du Barry stayed in a hotel on Jermyn Street, the Jews were committed to Newgate, and the lady prosecuted an action of trover at the Guildhall in July. There being no doubt that they were her property, she recovered them in March 1791, and was 'magnificently entertained' by the Lord Mayor at the Mansion House. Horace Walpole, as usual, saw the amusing side of the entire incident, and informed a friend in Italy that 'though London is apt to produce Wilkeses, and George Gordons, and Mrs Rudds and Horne Tookes and other phenomena wet and dry, the present season has been very unprolific, and we are forced to import French news, as we used to do fashions and *opéras comiques*'. Walpole explained that he wanted 'the King to send her four *Jews* to the National Assembly, and tell them it is the change of *la monnaie* of Lord George Gordon, the Israelite'. Madame du Barry died in 1793; the jewels remained in England and were ordered sold by the Lord Chancellor, bringing in a profit of £30,000.[104]

Patrick Colquhoun the police magistrate returned in 1796 to the ever

[103] C. O. Sigstedt, *The Swedenborg Epic* (New York, 1952), 190; A. G. Duker, 'Swedenborg's Attitude towards the Jews', *Judaism*, 5 (1956), 272–6. But now see the work of M. K. Schuchard, 'Swedenborg, Jacobitism, and Freemasonry', in E. J. Brock, *et al.* (eds.), *Swedenborg and His Influence* (London, 1988), pp. 359–79; and id., 'Yeats'. Dr Schuchard argues that Swedenborg deliberately de-Judaized his work in order to protect himself.

[104] Walpole to Mary Berry in Florence, 26 Feb. 1791: *Correspondence*, xi. 205–11. Madame du Barry was born Jeanne Bécu (1743–93) and married in 1768 Guillaume, comte du Barry.

popular subject of Jewish crime in his famous treatise on the metropolitan police. Colquhoun paid careful attention to what he called a 'Class of Cheats of the society of Jews, who are to be found in every street, lane, and alley, in and near the Metropolis, under the pretence of purchasing old clothes, and metals of different sorts'. Their real purpose in life, he revealed, was to serve as fences and 'temptations to the servants to pilfer and steal small articles, not likely to be missed, which these Jews purchase at about one third of the real value'. Colquhoun reckoned that there must be about 2,000 such Jews among the 20,000 Jews that he estimated to be living in London at that time, to which must be added the 5,000–6,000 Jews who resided in the provinces. These criminal Jews were educated 'in idleness from their earliest infancy' and topped up their fencing with dealing in base money, fraud, and perjury. 'The mischiefs which must result from the increase of this depraved race', he urged, 'arising from the natural course of population, are so obvious, that a remedy cannot be too soon applied.' Despite these strong words, Colquhoun was not entirely damning of the Jewish people as a whole, even in London. 'It is also much to be wished', he wrote,

that the leading and respectable persons of the Jewish religion would consider it as incumbent on them to adopt some means of employing, in useful and productive labour, the numerous youths of that persuasion, who are at present rearing up in idleness, profligacy, and crimes. If the superstitious observance of institutions, with regard to meat not killed by Jews, and to the Jewish sabbath, shall exclude these youths from being bound to useful employments and mixing with the mass of the people, by becoming servants or apprentices; surely it is proper some care should be taken that they shall not become public nuisances; an evil that must inevitably arise from a perseverance, in the system which now prevails, in the education and habits of this numerous class of people; and which is directly hostile to the interests of the State, and to the preservation of morals.

In brief, Colquhoun laid at the door of the Jews and their leaders the sad fact that London had suffered of late a great increase in petty crime.[105]

Colquhoun's book appeared in several editions before the Jews thought it possible to reply convincingly. Their representative was Joshua van Oven, surgeon and community leader, who produced a plan in 1802 which was meant to address some of the very solutions which Colquhoun had proposed. Van Oven admitted that the 'Jewish nation in England is now a body of some magnitude', and that, even if it might be argued that Christian workhouses and hospitals were open to all, 'the peculiarity of their religious rites and diet' effectively excluded them,

[105] [Patrick Colquhoun], *A Treatise on the Police of the Metropolis* (3rd edn., London, 1796), pp. vii, 40–1, 113–14, 125, 158–61, 176, 374.

and forced the Jews to provide for their own poor. This they had managed to do, he claimed, until the middle of the eighteenth century, when even the rich supporters of the community were overwhelmed by the size of the philanthropic task before them. The Ashkenazi Jews were the hardest hit and had no means of acquiring a secure financial basis for poor relief, since the 'funds in all these synagogues are raised by the rent every person pays for his seat in that which he frequents, together with the offerings made on festivals and particular occasions; and as they have no direct means of enforcing payment, a great deal of this income is very uncertain'.

Van Oven pleaded that 'the Jews are a good and industrious people, notwithstanding a contrary imputation, resulting from the combination of adventitious circumstances'. That being said, any plan for ameliorating the condition of the Jewish poor must be arranged 'without the smallest infringement of their ceremonial law'. Therefore, van Oven concluded

The most feasible means by which this great work could be effected, appears to be the establishing a House of Industry, which should take in the helpless poor and children, and have an attached hospital for sick; the whole arranged on a strict Judaic plan with respect to prayers, education and diet; and which at the same time should comprehend a method of assisting the out-poor with occasional relief.

It was quite obvious to all, however, that the capital necessary to float such a grand operation would never be donated voluntarily by the Jews, and it was unreasonable to expect the English Parliament to finance it. Van Oven's idea was to petition Parliament for the Jews to receive at least part of the money that their householders contributed in the form of taxes, funds which would be administered by a 'Board for the Management of the Concerns of all the Jewish Poor in the Metropolis'. This group of worthy Jews would supervise the care of the poor and of a House of Industry, and thereby help to eliminate the pernicious problem of Jewish crime.[106]

Van Oven put his idea to Patrick Colquhoun in the hope of receiving his blessing, which indeed was forthcoming in March 1801. Summing up, Colquhoun wrote:

There appears to me to be no error in the principle of the plan which has been laid before me, nor is there any thing in the laws or constitution of the country that can be opposed to its completion, more especially since, if well administered, it promises to be productive of the greatest benefits, not only to the Jewish people, but to society at large.

---

[106] Joshua van Oven, *Letters on the Present State of the Jewish Poor in the Metropolis with Propositions for Ameliorating their Condition* (London, 1802), esp. 6–9, 16–19.

Colquhoun's letter was published along with the outline of the plan for a new system of Jewish philanthropy, and included van Oven's expression of thanks for the support which had been given to his idea from the very man who had been instrumental in publicizing the role of the Jews in metropolitan crime.[107]

The agreement between van Oven and Colquhoun might have been expected to yield immediate benefits, especially as the Jew claimed that he had found expressions of support from 'some gentlemen of respectability among the Jewish Nation'.[108] Yet not all Jews were of the same mind as these two outspoken foes of crime. One of the most vocal opponents of van Oven and Colquhoun was Levi Alexander, the obstreperous adversary of the Jewish Establishment during that period. Alexander was incensed by the notion that a Jew would ever voluntarily relinquish his sovereignty to the Gentile authorities. Furthermore, Alexander hounded Colquhoun for his stereotyped view of the state of the Jews in England, allegedly devoted to Talmudic and biblical studies to the exclusion of all other pleasures, and desiring to aid their brethren in distress. Indeed, he told van Oven, this

position I cannot credit, as I never knew an English Israelite who could understand his prayers without an English translation besides yourself, and a few others. As for their charity, it is never secret, they never seek out the modest deserving and obscure poor, they like the pomp and stare of a printed subscription, where their names blazoned in the front of a newspaper tells the world so much good has been done; very unlike the noble spirit that employs a secretary to distribute what the ebullitions of the heart designs for worthy objects.

Even assuming that the plan could be organized, the two men greatly over-estimated the size of the Jewish wealthy class, so that the bulk of the cost would fall on the middling. 'You observe the rich were few,' wrote Alexander, 'they are few still, and if you look about you, I cannot think you can nominate twenty-five in the Great Synagogue, twenty in the Fenchurch Street, and not four in the New Synagogue, and among these some have not more than five or six thousand pounds capital.' As for the suggestion that Jews earn their livings at trades learned in Houses of Industry, Alexander provided a list of Jews who had attempted just that, but had discovered that the prejudices of Gentile London were too great to be overcome and to afford them a decent living. Indeed, one might argue that 'the separate state we seem doomed by Heaven for ever to live in, and which our Prophecies have declared

---

[107] Ibid. 25–30.   [108] Ibid. 28.

thousands of years ago can never be overcome by any newfangled scheme however specious it may appear'.[109]

Nevertheless, van Oven's revolutionary plan went forward, with the backing of Abraham Goldsmid, one of the leaders of the community, who tried to promote the idea among his influential friends, Jewish and Gentile. But the Jewish community was divided. The older Ashkenazi congregations worried that they would be ineradicably associated with the indigent poor. The Sephardim were still managing to take care of their own, and saw no reason to contribute to the upkeep of recent 'Tudesco' immigrants. Despite these misgivings, Goldsmid's backing was sufficient to have the scheme actually laid before Parliament on 25 February 1802 by George Tierney, MP. This, however, was as far as the proposal advanced, and it was killed even before it could be incorporated into an actual bill. Not only were the Sephardim determined to disassociate themselves from the measure, thereby cutting off the chief source of potential financial support, but those in Parliament who considered van Oven's plan rightly recognized that in a more general sense, its import was to allow the Jews in England to erect a sort of state within a state, administering a system based on a broad range of powers.[110]

That being said, at least in the courts the power of the Jews to manage their own affairs was upheld. This is quite clear from two famous cases of marriage without the consent of the parents which came before the ecclesiastical consistory court of London in the last decade of the eighteenth century. The first case was brought by the guardian of Esther Lindo in 1795 against her husband, Aaron Mendes Belisario, before Sir William Scott (later Lord Stowell), who declared immediately that 'I am to apply the peculiar principles of the Jewish law, which I conceive is the obligation imposed upon me.' The question, Scott noted, 'which is perfectly new, and which may affect the rights of a great body of *British* subjects', could only be decided on the basis of Jewish law. The judge took advice from Jewish witnesses and authorities on Jewish law and came to the conclusion that the marriage was not valid. 'It is possible there may be an error in the determination', he admitted,

I am sensible of the extreme difficulty which is to be encountered upon a subject so far out of the reach of the ordinary studies of this profession. But it is my comfort that, if there is error, it is not mine. It lies with those who have given

---

[109] L[evi] Alexander, *Answer to Mr. Joshua van Oven's Letters on the Present State of the Jewish Poor in London* (London, 1802), 4–5, 22–7, 38–41. Cf. Philo-Judaeis, *A Letter to Abraham Goldsmid . . . on Mr. Joshua van Oven's Letters* (London, 1802).

[110] *Parliamentary Register.* 17 (1802), 63–4. See also Endelman, *Jews of Georgian England*, 231–6.

this information—who are bound to give it conscientiously, and I am bound conscientiously to receive it. If I was to determine the question of marriage on principles different from the established authorities amongst the Jews, as now certified, I should be unhinging every institution; and taking upon myself the responsibility, as Ecclesiastical Judge, in opposition to those who possess a more natural right to determine on questions of this kind.[111]

In 1798, Sir William Scott was called upon to judge a very similar case in *Goldsmid* v. *Bromer*. Once again, Scott's initial premisses were unequivocal:

The Jews, though *British* subjects, have the enjoyment of their own laws in religious ceremonies; and the marriage act acknowledges this privilege, by excepting them out of its provisions: To deny them the benefit of their own law, upon such subjects, would be to deny to a distinct body of people, the full benefit of the toleration, to which they have long been held to be entitled. This being a question of Jewish law then, the Court must be content to learn that law, as well as it can, from the professors of it.

The enraged father's case hinged on the fact that when the 16-year-old Maria Goldsmid took the ring at the Shakespeare Tavern in Covent Garden as the traditional marriage words were spoken, the witnesses present were non-observant Jews and therefore ineligible for this honour. A man testified in court that one of the witnesses to the marriage was seen 'eating part of a round of beef with sauce, appearing to be melted butter'. Furthermore, as the judge noted, it was 'stated that he had profaned the Sabbath, by riding in coaches, and snuffing lighted candles, stirring the fire, and eating forbidden meats;—acts trifling to us, perhaps, who have no law applying to them, but not so according to the rites and ordinances of the Jewish religion'. Once again, Sir William Scott ruled that the marriage was invalid, to the joy of the girl's father.[112]

In many respects, the judicial decisions of Sir William Scott were quite extraordinary, not only for their general conclusions, but more surprisingly because of the degree of understanding for the Jewish situation that they demonstrate. The eighteenth clause of Lord

[111] *Reports of Cases Argued and Determined in the Consistory Court of London*, ed. John Haggard (London, 1822), i. 216–61. Among the documents brought forward as evidence was the Cartwright petition of 1649: i. 507–8. Belisario appealed to the Court of Arches, which in 1796 upheld the verdict of the lower court: Picciotto, *Sketches*, 104. Cf. the list of 'Equity Proceedings in the Court of Chancery (1750–1800)', ed. G. Dworkin, *MJHSE* 6 (1962), 195–8.

[112] *Reports of Cases*, ed. Haggard, i. 324–36. The case was tried in Dec. 1798. For a similar use of the Jewish law in a marriage case, see ibid. ii. 385.

Hardwicke's Marriage Act of 1753 exempted Jews from the provision that all unions be performed by an Anglican priest under banns or licence in order to have full protection under the law.[113] These cases carried this privilege one step further by emphasizing that Jewish marriages had to be tried entirely within the confines of Jewish law. One needs to remember that any gains made by Jews anywhere in Europe were always compared with the changes in their status which had occurred under Napoleon in France. By the turn of the century many Jews reflected on the fact that their lot in England might be seen as only marginally more disadvantaged than that of their co-religionists in France. 'Will any one dare tell me that in England we have not more liberty?', asked L. Cohen of Exeter, 'Can it then be said with any degree of propriety, that we are not so happy here as the Jews are in France?' Even if marginal gains might be recorded for the Jews of Paris, Cohen reminded his readers that Anglo-Jewry should take into account 'the stability of the *English* Government', certainly as compared to the situation in France. Furthermore, by regarding the French Jews as ordinary citizens, Napoleon actually damaged the future prospects of the community, by placing them 'in a direct road of degeneracy by their intermarriages'. Indeed, Cohen summarized, it 'is true in the British Empire, our lot has fallen in "pleasant places" '.[114]

[113] See I. Finestein, 'An Aspect of the Jews and English Marriage Law During the Emancipation: The Prohibited Degrees', *JJ Soc.* 7 (1965), 3–21; H. S. Q. Henriques, *Jewish Marriages and the English Law* (London, 1909).

[114] L. Cohen [of Exeter], *Sacred Truths, Addressed to the Children of Israel, Residing in the British Empire* (Exeter, [?1807]), 3–5, 19, 22–8. For more on the early Jewish community of Exeter, see C. Roth, *The Rise of Provincial Jewry* (London, 1950), 59–61.

8

UNEMANCIPATED NINETEENTH-CENTURY ANGLO-JEWRY

THE history of Anglo-Jewry has always been more teleological than most. James Picciotto, writing in 1875, prided himself on being 'the first Israelite who has given a full and connected account of the vicissitudes passed through by the Jews of Great Britain, from the days of the Saxon kings until the middle of the present century'. When he finished this task, some 400 pages later, he summed up his people's history by proclaiming that 'Social prejudices against Israelites are fast vanishing, and the Jews have rendered themselves completely worthy of their improved position, and kept full pace with their Gentile neighbours in the onward march of progress.'[1] The pinnacle of this slow but ever-upward rise inevitably occurs in Anglo-Jewish historiography on 26 July 1858, when Lionel Nathan de Rothschild takes his seat in the House of Commons as the first practising Jew to sit as a member of Parliament. The fact that he never spoke in the House is not considered to be pertinent, nor the fact that even contemporaries were aware that many if not most Jews were unmoved by the spectacle of a Rothschild taking his place among other rich men in the legislature. Looking again at the history of nineteenth-century Anglo-Jewry without the artificial border of 1858 restores the perspective of contemporary events to something like the way they seemed to those who took part in them.

I

Certainly from the point of view of the English Jews themselves, one of the most dominating figures in that world was the so-called Chief Rabbi of Ashkenazi Jewry, Solomon Hirschell. By an ironic twist of fate Hirschell was actually born in London, in 1761, for his father Hart Lyon (also known as Hirschel Lewin) was rabbi of the Great Synagogue until he left in a huff three years later. Hart Lyon's son, Solomon Hirschell, received a rabbinical post at Prenzlau in Prussia in about 1792 and

---

[1] James Picciotto, *Sketches of Anglo-Jewish History* (new edn., London, 1956: 1st pub. 1875), pp. xiv, 409.

served there until 1801, when he was offered the position of rabbi of the Great Synagogue, London. The post indeed had been advertised, and, of the three candidates, Solomon Hirschell was the clear favourite.[2] Hirschell's election was noticed even by the Gentile press. The *Gentleman's Magazine* reported that

The Congregation of German Jews in London have elected, after a vacancy of 10 years, a High Priest of their nation, with a salary of 4000l. a year. The choice has fallen on the Rev. Dr. Soloman Hart, a son of a former High Priest. He is a native of England, but went with his father to the Continent, where he afterwards settled. On his arrival, he was met at Rumford by the Elders, Rabbis, and many other respectable Jews. The Venerable Chief seemed much affected by the favourable reception he experienced. As he is a zealous promoter of good morals, it is hoped his example and influence will have a powerful effect in suppressing the vice and immorality among the Jews, which often exposes them to hatred and contempt.[3]

A portrait of Rabbi Hirschell by Frederick Barlin survives, which perhaps does not do justice to the impression he made in person. According to the writer of his obituary in 1842,

The personal appearance of R. Solomon was at all times commanding, and highly characteristic; his stature was above the common height, he had an exceedingly high forehead, and a searching eye; and his countenance was both benignant and intellectual. His appearance abroad, in the Polish costume to which he restricted himself, commanded the reverence of the rudest hind that walked the streets; and there were few but touched their hats, and made way for 'the High Priest of the Jews', as he was familiarly, but erroneously, termed.

Hirschell's 'countenance', noted the anonymous author of the obituary, 'was too peculiar to be mistakeable'.[4]

   The election of Solomon Hirschell to the rabbinate of the Great Synagogue was not in itself surprising, not only given his father's association with the community and his own native birth, but also due to the fact that his brother Saul had returned to London before him, where he died soon after, on 16 November 1794. Saul had been rabbi of Frankfurt an der Oder and amused himself by writing pseudonymous works, including forged *responsa*, designed to facilitate certain reforms in Jewish law and practice. When discovered, Saul Berlin (as he was known) was forced to flee abroad, and thereupon came to London,

---

[2] On Hirschell generally see the work of the amateur historian H. A. Simons, *Forty Years a Chief Rabbi: The Life and Times of Solomon Hirschell* (London, 1980); and Hirschell's obituary in *Voice of Jacob*, 2 (1842–3), 57–61.

[3] *Gents. Mag.* 71 (1802), 967: entry for Sunday, 12 Sept. 1802.

[4] *Voice of Jacob*, 2 (1842), 59.

although he did not live long enough to see his brother installed in state. Meyer Joseph, who would become one of the pillars of the Ashkenazi community, recalled half a century later that

It was in the year 1794 when this exceptional man died here, and I think I have a right to publish this article as I was the only friend he had here. He was on a long journey, the object of which I do not remember any more, and intended also to stay in London for some time. I visited him daily, we remained often together for hours at a time, and, although I am now [in 1844] 83 years old, the impression he made upon me, his eloquence and his whole personality remain unforgettable to me. A few months after his arrival he fell ill with cramp and it was I who closed his dying eyes. On his death the London community paid him respect. He was buried with great honours on the 25th of Heshvan, 1794. On arranging the things he left behind him I found this will, which I then copied for myself.

Saul Berlin's will revealed him to have become repentant about his earlier activities, and it is very possible that he himself played a role in securing his brother's appointment as rabbi of the Great Synagogue.[5]

James Picciotto, the Victorian historian of Anglo-Jewry, thought that Solomon Hirschell was somewhat of a disappointment and rather unequal to the task of guiding his flock through the changes as he 'represented the spirit of a bygone age'.[6] Certainly he was not himself a scholar of the first rank, and left behind him not a single published work. Nevertheless, the rabbinical court records of Hirschell's day show him to have been active in the communal side of the affairs of Ashkenazi Anglo-Jewry. Two volumes of these minutes of the Beth Din survive, the first covering 1805–35, and the second bringing the records up to 1855. Most of the proceedings were divorce cases, about fifteen each year, but there are a surprisingly high number of conversions to Judaism, mostly of women who were about to marry Jews, or who had children by them. Despite the fact that these conversions were in direct contravention of the Blasphemy Act of 1698, the courts seem to have turned a blind eye to this regularization of family practice. One reason for this was undoubtedly that the conversions themselves were not performed in England. Proselytes had to go to Holland or elsewhere on the Continent, and the London Beth Din merely confirmed what had been executed abroad, 'because there is no permission in this country to convert anyone', as the records stated in 1833. There were occasions,

[5] On Saul Berlin, see C. Duschinsky, 'The Rabbinate of the Great Synagogue, London, from 1786–1842', *JQR* NS 9 (1918–19), 103–37, 371–408; 10 (1919–20), 445–527; 11 (1920–1), 21–81, 201–36, 345–87, esp. 9: 376–89, and Saul Berlin's will repr. 9: 406–8, with a transcription of his tombstone. His two scandalous books were 'Obadiah b. Baruch', *Mitzpeh Yekutiel* (Berlin, 1789), and *Besamim Rosh* (Berlin, 1793).
[6] Picciotto, *Sketches*, 300–1.

however, when the proselyte was asked to undergo a ritual bath on arrival, when the authority of the converting Beth Din was held in doubt, as was the case, for example, with New York. Although most of these proselytes went to Rotterdam, others preferred Amsterdam or The Hague, but there is even a case of a woman who had her conversion done in Paris, in preparation for marrying 'one of the brothers called Rothschilds'. Witnesses were recorded, sometimes rather unofficially, as happened when the rabbinical court called 'the woman Nissel the daughter of the late Joseph that everyone called "Jew boy" ', with the English letters of the nickname standing out from the lofty Hebrew preface.[7]

Solomon Hirschell was also famous for being a great correspondent. Indeed, he received so many letters from Poland that in 1827 he asked the Post Office to allow him not to pay postage on letters delivered, especially as many were destined for poor members of his flock in London, a request to which the authorities seem to have agreed. His own letters show a wide circle of friends and acquaintances. After dinner in the Goldsmid house in 1840, we find him writing to the philo-Semitic duke of Sussex, apologizing for having left without saying goodbye. Other letters include references to the Damascus blood libel of 1840, a refusal to take part in a debate with a Christian clergyman, a request to a parishioner to bring up her children in the Jewish faith, replies to missionaries, and communications with Moses Montefiore, A. M. Rothschild, Solomon Heine, and others. Most of the correspondence, apart from these pearls, consists of letters to provincial congregations.[8]

Despite the oft-repeated claims of universal regard and reverence, not everyone was satisfied with Solomon Hirschell's performance even during his tenure. His most vocal dispute was with Levi Alexander, son of the famous Jewish printer Alexander Alexander, and like his father of the same profession. Levi Alexander had for twenty-five years been producing cheap Yiddish almanacs, and in 1807 conceived the idea of publishing a new *machzor*, a festival prayer-book, based on the earlier

---

[7] Minutes of the London Beth Din, 1805–35: University Library, Leeds, MS 267: 65 fos.; ibid. 1833–55: Jewish Theological Seminary, New York, MS Adler 2257: 65 fos. The Leeds MS is from the Roth collection; the New York records from that of E. N. Adler. How these MSS came into private hands is not clear. Generally, see Duschinsky, 'Rabbinate', 10: 484–93.

[8] Solomon Hirschell's correspondence is at the now Jewish Theological Seminary, New York, MS Adler 4160, 269 fos. [with about 50 blank] in large 4°, mostly English letters, 1826–40: see Duschinsky, 'Rabbinate', 10: 494–513. Unlike the Ashkenazim, the Sephardim always allowed their communal leaders to keep their own papers, the result being that few have survived.

and now-scarce production of the celebrated printer and controversialist David Levi, but with the mistakes corrected. According to Alexander's own account, as soon as his prospectus was published, three Jews, including a certain Isaac Levi who was probably a relative of the original author, immediately assailed Alexander and his plan, denouncing any change as for the worse. It now appeared that they had for some time planned to reissue David Levi's prayer-book, and feared that Alexander would spoil their market. The Levi faction managed to enlist the support of Rabbi Solomon Hirschell himself, for some reason, whom they persuaded 'publicly to declare in the shop of Mr. Isaac Levi, Grocer, Duke's Place, that the odds were two to one in favor of their work'. Alexander, however, was pleased to discover that when they finally put out the new edition of the Levi prayer-book, even more numerous errors were to be found, to the point 'that six whole passages were absolutely omitted in their Evening Service for the first night of the new year'. Alexander was unable to perceive the possibility that the rabbi of the Great Synagogue would knowingly endorse a defective prayer-book, so on 13 March 1808 he wrote to him for an explanation. Receiving no reply, Alexander wrote again on 3 and 14 April 1808, and published his letters on the wrappers of his own new prayer-book. In the end, Alexander could only conclude, and that publicly, that

you are one of that class of society, who are distinguishable only by the consequence of their situation, which obdurates their minds to every thing contrary but to their interest. Liberality from you, Reverend Sir, was what at this period of our difference, I had to expect, when I have only found obstinacy, pride, and mystery of reference ... for my own satisfaction I shall enquire of foreign [*rabbanim*] what their opinion of your conduct in this matter may amount to ... remembering that we are brothers in the same community.[9]

Levi's parting words here are more than a conventional signature. It should be remembered that this dispute with the man regarded as the Chief Rabbi of the Jews, rightly or wrongly, was conducted in full view of Gentile society, and in the English language. As Alexander's prayer-book began to appear in its instalments, new vituperations were printed

[9] A. [i.e. Levi] Alexander, *The Form of Prayers, for the Day of Atonement* (London, 1807), pp. i–x. Cf. his *Alexander's Hebrew Ritual, and Doctrinal Explanation of the Whole Ceremonial Law* (London, 1819), a 309 pp. survey of Jewish practices dedicated by permission to the duke of Kent. The rival prayer-book (1807) was published by E. Justin, a Gentile printer, with an engraved portrait of Solomon Hirschell as the frontispiece, executed by Frederick Barlin. Interestingly, of the 807 volumes subscribed, 725 went to London, but the eighty-two provincial subscribers were distributed as follows: Portsmouth (37), Liverpool (19), Greenwich (9), Portsea (8), Sheerness (4), and one each to Bath, Sheffield, Deptford, Bedford, and Bristol: N. Cohen, 'Non-religious Factors in the Emergence of the Chief Rabbinate', *TJHSE* 21 (1968), 306.

on the wrappers of the book, combined with doggerel, jingles, and various criticisms of Rabbi Hirschell and 'the faulty hodge-podge Edition, published in opposition to this grand work'.[10]

Rabbi Hirschell also became hopelessly embroiled in a controversy over a new Jewish compendium of the faith that appeared in Hebrew and then in an English translation produced by Joshua van Oven and approved by both Hirschell and his Sephardi counterpart, Haham Raphael Meldola.[11] The book itself was written by Salom Ben Jacob Cohen, a Polish Hebraist who came to London in 1813. His attempt to found a new Hebrew school failed, and he returned to the Continent, where he published the original Hebrew version, entitled *The Elements of Faith*.[12] Cohen's work provoked a furious response from Solomon Bennett, a cantankerous Russian Jew who had achieved rather impressive artistic success in Denmark and Berlin as an engraver. Bennett's grievance against Rabbi Hirschell seems to be that he was (by his own account) fined and imprisoned for having plagiarized the prayer-book portrait of the rabbi, which he reproduced in Levi Alexander's epic work against the felling of the trees in the old burial ground.[13] In any case, Solomon Bennett now published a violent pamphlet in Hebrew in which he not only criticized Cohen's catechism and Rabbi Hirschell's endorsement of it, but the entire Anglo-Jewish community as well.[14] Bennett's diatribe was answered by Mayer Cohen Rintel, a local ritual slaughterer.[15] In his counter-reply, Bennett pointed out that as Rintel could not speak English, it was highly likely that the true author of the work was Rabbi Hirschell himself, a fact which did not add to his personal honour.[16]

Solomon Bennett was admittedly something of an eccentric individual

---

[10] Alexander's wrappers are, understandably, extremely rare: five of them can be found in the Mocatta Library, University College, London, Mocatta Cupboard RP 6 Ale (Myers Collection).

[11] Generally, on the cordial relations between Hirschell and Meldola, see R. D. Barnett, 'Haham Meldola and Hazan de Sola', *TJHSE* 21 (1968), 1–38; and cf. id., 'More Letters of Hazan de Sola', *TJHSE* 24 (1975), 173–82.

[12] S. I. Cohen, *Elements of Faith, for the Use of Jewish Youth of Both Sexes* (London, 1815).

[13] L. Alexander, *The Axe Laid to the Root; or, Ignorance and Superstition Evident in the Character of the Rev. Solomon Hirschell, Major Rabbi* (London, 1808). Most of this 27 pp. pamphlet is repr. in Simons, *Forty Years*, 123–52. The original portrait was by Frederick Barlin: see n. 9 above.

[14] Yomtob [Solomon] Bennett, *Tenneh Bikkurim* (Hebrew) (London, [1817?]).

[15] Meir HaCohen [Rintel], *Minkhat Kanaoth* (Hebrew) (London, 1817). A collection of letters to Salom Cohen concerning the attacks by Solomon Bennett on his book was published by Meir Hahn, *Shot Lashon* (Hebrew) (Altona, 1817).

[16] Solomon Bennett, *The Present Reign of the Synagogue of Duke's Place* (London, n.d.): not seen; very rare. Hirschell's English was actually very rudimentary.

in early nineteenth-century Anglo-Jewry.[17] Not only did he arrive in London in November 1800 after three years at the Danish Academy of Arts and with a certificate from the Royal Academy of Painting, Sculpture and Architecture of Denmark for his profession as engraver, but he also boasted a patent from the Berlin Academy for engraving a life-size portrait of Frederick the Great.[18] He was a member of the Western Synagogue and may have engraved their seal.[19] He had at least one daughter but certainly six sons, five of whom became shorthand writers: one of these was named Isaac Newton Bennett. In later life he seems to have made up with Rabbi Hirschell, who was one of the patrons of Bennett's study of Ezekiel's temple, which was published in 1824. Bennett was also a biblical scholar, and was friendly with noblemen, including the duke of Sussex, and bishops, among them Thomas Burgess, the Hebraist bishop of Salisbury.[20] His dissatisfaction with Anglo-Jewry was proverbial. English Jews, he affirmed, 'though their feeling for their antiquity and geneology [is ?], yet possess very little tendency towards their sacred records, the Hebrew Doctrines in general, or for any branch of literature; nor do they comprehend to make a proper use of the "beneficial, just, and impartial laws of the government under which they exist!" '[21]

Despite the fact that many of these disputes were carried out in English, to some extent these were internal polemics and could always be presented as not meant for public consumption. Dissatisfaction with the state of early nineteenth-century Anglo-Jewry passed out of the confines of the small world of Jewish London, however, and, when this happened, undoubtedly caused no small amount of consternation. First among the groups of external critics were the converted Jews, such as

---

[17] Generally on him see Arthur Barnett, 'Solomon Bennett, 1761–1838: Artist, Hebraist and Controversialist', *TJHSE* 17 (1953), 91–111. Bennett's unpleasant qualities earned him Picciotto's description of his work as 'neither a learned nor a well-written production', but this is unduly harsh: Picciotto, *Sketches*, 234. See also Bennett to David Meldola, 6 Mar. 1817: SPJC MSS: repr. *TJHSE* 21 (1968), 15–18, where it appears that Bennett's grievance with Hirschell went back to their mutual days in Berlin.

[18] Jews' College, London, MS 116: six diplomas and certificates of Solomon Bennett.

[19] Arthur Barnett, *The Western Synagogue through Two Centuries (1761–1961)* (London, 1961), 51–5, with a portrait of Bennett opp. p. 51.

[20] Solomon Bennett, *The Temple of Ezekiel* (London, 1824): cf. MS copy in Jews' College, London, MS 4. See also Bennett's *Discourse on Sacrifices* (London, 1815); id., *Theological and Critical Treatise on the . . . Holy Language* (London, 1835); id., *Specimen of a New Version of the Hebrew Bible* (London, 1836). Bennett was also involved in a translation of the Old Testament published in 1841.

[21] Solomon Bennett, *The Constancy of Israel . . . Reply to . . . Lord Crawford* (London, 1812; 1st pub. 1809), esp. 220–8.

Hyam Isaacs, a former glass-cutter who turned to Christianity after being injured in an industrial accident which left him almost blind. Isaacs claimed to have lectured 4,000 times in 1,200 different places, proclaiming the truth of Christianity as seen by a converted Jew. Isaacs was full of praise for the reformed Jews, or, as Rabbi Hirschell referred to them in scorn, 'British Jews'. Isaacs was particularly appalled by the poor state of learning among Jews in England:

not one in five among British-born Jews, although very fluent in the Hebrew, can understand the meaning or interpretation of their prayers, which might be in a great measure dispensed with, as far as they are concerned. This may be a matter of surprise to some; for it is a very general idea that all Jews are capable of conversing in Hebrew. Such is not the case; for although they can follow or chant the various prayers, they do not understand their significance, but repeat them from long habit, as repetition from infancy perfects them in these prayers.

Generally, however, despite Isaacs's many criticisms of the Jews and their religion, he praised their attitude to charity, and noted that 'indeed, it can be stated, without fear of contradiction, that as a body they evince more generosity than any section of worshipping Christians in the whole world'.[22]

A more subtle critic of his Jewish contemporaries was Isaac d'Israeli (1766–1848), who certainly had more cause. He was the son of Benjamin d'Israeli (1730–1816), a Jewish merchant from Ferrara, who arrived in England at the age of 18 and set up as an importer of straw bonnets. He eventually branched out into finance and became a successful stockbroker. His son Isaac grew up with little contact with or interest in organized Jewish worship. Nevertheless, he paid his *finta*, his synagogue tax of £10 per annum and contributed to Jewish charities. In 1813 he was unexpectedly elected to the communal office of *parnas*, which he declined, pleading ignorance and puzzlement that he should have been given such an honour: 'I am willing to contribute, so far as my limited means permit, to your annual subscriptions,' he explained, 'but assuredly without interference in your interior concerns.' The Mahamad refused to climb down, and in an exchange of letters with d'Israeli argued that he had the same rights and obligations as any other member of the congregation, including communal office, and when d'Israeli refused to heed a summons he was informed that declining the office would cost him a fine of £40. D'Israeli's reply made his position clear:

A person who has lived out of the sphere of your observation, of retired habits of life, who can never unite in your public worship, because as now conducted it

[22] Hyam Isaacs, *The Awakening of the Jews from their Slumbers* (London, 1842), pp. iii–iv, 3–4, 133.

disturbs instead of exciting religious emotions, a circumstance of general acknowledgement, who has only tolerated some part of our ritual, willing to concede all he can in those matters which he holds to be indifferent; such a man, with but a moderate portion of honour and understanding, never can accept the solemn functions of an elder of your congregation, and involve his life and distract his business pursuits not in temporary but permanent duties always repulsive to his feelings.

D'Israeli called on the Mahamad to withdraw his name from appointees to communal office. 'If you will not retain a zealous friend,' he wrote, 'and one who has long had you in his thoughts, my last resource is to desire my name to be withdrawn from your society.'[23]

The entire d'Israeli case was very problematic. By 1814 he was already a well-known writer, and since the publication of his book, *The Curiosities of Literature*, which began to appear in 1791, being a celebrated collection of anecdotes and character sketches, his fame had continued to mount. Despite his Jewish background, he was a central part of the London literary scene, and praised by fellow writers such as Scott, Byron, and Southey. He was financially secure and well connected in the Jewish world, having married in his mid-thirties Maria Basevi of the family of Jewish merchants from Verona who settled in England in 1762. His father-in-law was president of the Jewish Board of Deputies from 1801.[24] Apart from Isaac d'Israeli's seemingly unassailable position within both the Jewish and Gentile communities in early nineteenth-century England, the entire issue was really quite avoidable, and got as far as it did only as a result of two or three votes, Haham Raphael Meldola advising compromise. D'Israeli for his part was willing to pay the *finta*: it was the fine for non-service which stuck in his throat.[25]

At any rate, the matter remained dormant for a time, until March 1817, when it surfaced again. From Isaac d'Israeli's point of view, one crucial component had been altered: his father Benjamin had died the previous year, leaving him an extraordinary fortune of £35,000, and, as his mother hated Judaism, there was little reason not to see the thing through. Ignoring summonses to meetings of the Mahamad, Isaac

---

[23] Isaac d'Israeli to the Mahamad, 3 Dec. 1813: printed in Picciotto, *Sketches*, 289–90: see generally 287–93; Albert M. Hyamson, *The Sephardim of England* (London, 1951), 242–6; T. M. Endelman, *Radical Assimilation in English Jewish History, 1656–1945* (Bloomington, Ind., 1990), 28-30; J. Ogden, 'Isaac d'Israeli and Judaism', *HUCA* 37 (1966), 211–22; id., *Isaac d'Israeli* (Oxford, 1969); L. Wolf, 'The Disraeli Family', *TJHSE* 5 (1902–5), 202–18.
[24] Robert Blake, *Disraeli* (New York, 1967), ch. 1.
[25] Picciotto, *Sketches*, 291–3.

d'Israeli resigned from the congregation, followed by his wife's Basevi family. Two months later his mother would ask the Mahamad to put a new tombstone on her husband's grave, but her son was done with them, although the community itself did not deign to reply to the letter of resignation. In 1821, however, Isaac d'Israeli found that he needed their co-operation after all, when he applied for birth certificates for himself and his family. After some unpleasant negotiation, a compromise was struck through the good offices of his brother-in-law Ephraim Lindo, who was married to Miriam d'Israeli's sister Sarah Basevi. At first the Mahamad stuck by its original demand for £100 2s., including the fine, but Lindo bargained them down to £40 17s., the fine being cancelled. The resignation of Isaac D'Israeli and his family was thus accepted, signalling the end of their formal connection with the synagogue.[26]

No doubt one reason for the Sephardi community's willingness to be rid of the d'Israelis was that meanwhile they had crossed over to the other side. While Isaac declined to join any other religious group, he was persuaded by a family friend, Sharon Turner, the historian of Anglo-Saxon England, at least to have the children baptized. This was done, at the Church of St Andrew's, Holborn, but one at a time, for some reason. In the end he seems to have been somewhat less reluctant than is sometimes claimed. His friend Robert Southey, describing the scene thirteen years later, wrote that Isaac d'Israeli, having 'slipt out of the synagogue, but thinking it necessary that his children should belong to some community . . . got Sharon Turner to take them some years ago to St. Andrew's, in Holborn, and there the present Bishop of Barbadoes christened them'.[27] His son Benjamin, five months short of his thirteenth birthday, was baptized on 31 July 1817, and was taken out of the Gentile boarding school at which he was excused prayers and received private Hebrew lessons and transferred to another, where he would make a fresh Anglican start. By this symbolic act of baptism Benjamin Disraeli was able to be elected to Parliament in 1837 rather than after Emancipation in 1858, and thereby to begin the ascent up the greasy pole which would take him to the Prime Minister's office in 1875. There is no doubt that without having been baptized he would not have had enough time to become the leader of his party, and for his fortunate

---

[26] Blake, *Disraeli*, 11; Picciotto, *Sketches*, 291–3; Hyamson, *Sephardim*, 245–6. Ephraim Lindo was also elected a *parnas* in 1825, but he paid the fine at first, resigning and then converting only four years later: Hyamson, *Sephardim*, 246.

[27] Southey to C. W. W. Wynn, MP, Whitsunday 1830: *Selections from the Letters of Robert Southey*, ed. J. W. Warter (London, 1856), iv. 177. Southey also informs his correspondent that 'The Society for converting the Jews has *wasted* more money than any other society in this country, which is saying a great deal' (p. 178).

exclusion he had only to thank the short-sighted *parnassim* of the Sephardi community in London.[28]

Despite the self-exclusion of Isaac d'Israeli from organized Judaism, his fascination with his people's history and culture did not wane, any more than did that of his son Benjamin, who, in the words of his biographer Lord Blake, 'later became intensely interested in it himself to the point of being something of a bore on the subject'.[29] Isaac's chief work on the Jews was a book he published anonymously in 1833 on *The Genius of Judaism*, part of the growing literature which would advocate the emancipation of Anglo-Jewry. The work itself is not uncritical of the Jews, especially those imprisoned in their past. But the emphasis is on the beneficial effects of assimilation. 'After a few generations the Hebrews assimilate with the character, and are actuated by the feelings, of the nation where they become natives', he wrote. 'What a distinct people are the Jews of London, of Paris, and of Amsterdam, from the Jews of Morocco, of Damascus, and the Volga!' Summarizing his view, d'Israeli wrote:

Whatever political boon Christians may concede to their ancient brothers, it is quite evident that the social reform of the English Jews must mainly depend upon themselves. It would be an act of political justice that the name of Briton, which now must be attached to the Hebrew born in the dominions of Great Britain, should no longer be held in disregard; and it would be an act of political wisdom to remove all those civil disabilities and privations which hitherto have aggrieved and degraded so considerable a portion of our fellow-subjects. It is not less evident that there are certain privileges which a Christian government can never concede to a Jewish subject.

D'Israeli called on 'the Jews to begin to educate their youth as the youth of Europe, and not of Palestine; let their Talmud be removed to an elevated shelf, to be consulted as a curiosity of antiquity, and not as a manual of education'. In general, he thought, Jews should attempt to become part of the country in which they live: 'The civil and political fusion of the Jewish with their fellow-citizens, must commence by rejecting every anti-social principle; let them only separate to hasten to the Church and to the Synagogue.'[30]

[28] Hyamson, *Sephardim*, 245–6; Blake, *Disraeli*, 11. For more on Benjamin Disraeli's Judaism, see also I. Berlin, 'Benjamin Disraeli, Karl Marx and the Search for Identity', in his *Against the Current* (London, 1980), 252–86; A. Gilam, 'Disraeli in Jewish Historiography', *Midstream* (Mar. 1980); id., 'Benjamin Disraeli and Jewish Identity', *Wiener Library Bulletin*, 32–3 (1980), 2–8; B. Jaffee, 'A Reassessment of Benjamin Disraeli's Jewish Aspects', *TJHSE* 27 (1982), 115–23; T. M. Endelman, 'Disraeli's Jewishness Reconsidered', *Modern Judaism*, 5 (1985), 109–23.

[29] Blake, *Disraeli*, 49.

[30] [Isaac d'Israeli], *The Genius of Judaism* (London, 1833), esp. 199–201, 238–57, 265–6.

This, then, was an unabashed call for the Jews to reject their self-isolation, although not necessarily their religion, for the sake of advancement and accommodation. Certainly the success of Benjamin Disraeli indicated what could be done by religious conversion. David Ricardo, the great economist, also turned his back on Judaism and his father's respected standing at Bevis Marks by marrying a Christian woman and abandoning his family.[31] John 'Jew' King alias Jacob Rey married the countess of Lanesborough without giving up his religion, yet walking the border with Christianity in his career as a money-lender and political activist.[32] There was a myth circulating 100 years later that Isaac d'Israeli, now old and blind, came in from the country to attend the inauguration of the Reform West London Synagogue of British Jews in 1842.[33] While this is probably wishful thinking alone, certainly the Reform Movement went some way towards achieving the ideals expressed by Isaac d'Israeli. Had it existed in 1817, it is likely that the entire family would have stayed within the fold.

Indeed, immediately after the d'Israeli family quarrel steps were taken to try to modernize the worship in English synagogues. In 1821 a committee of seven men chaired by Isaac L. Goldsmid was appointed by the Ashkenazi Great Synagogue to propose a plan for training young men for the ministry, and warned that immediate changes would have to be made. In their final report, these distinguished gentleman affirmed that 'they are convinced that the small attendance in the Synagogue is, in some measure, to be ascribed to the present mode of reading the service; that it has led, and, if unchanged, will lead, to alterations which they most sincerely deprecate, and which may be fatal to the dearest interests of the Jewish nation'.[34] Likewise, in 1836 a group of Sephardi worshippers laid a list of proposed changes before the elders of the Bevis Marks parent congregation, but here opposition to change was more determined. On 13 December 1836 a counter-memorial was signed by over 150 Jews connected with the synagogue, and in the end only a few cosmetic changes were made. The demand for modernization refused to die, and often abusive discussions were a main feature of life at Bevis Marks throughout the later 1830s.[35]

Eventually, the tense and antagonistic situation in both of the first Jewish congregations, Ashkenazi and Sephardi, became intolerable, and the modernists decided to secede. Their decision was no doubt partly motivated by the existence of a similar movement in Germany, a demand

[31] A. Heertje, 'On David Ricardo (1772–1823)', *TJHSE* 24 (1975), 73–81.
[32] T. M. Endelman, 'The Checkered Career of "Jew" King: A Study in Anglo-Jewish Social History', *AJSR* 7–8 (1982–3), 69–100.
[33] According to Cecil Roth, *Benjamin Disraeli* (New York, 1952), 19, citing a vague 'oral tradition'.   [34] Picciotto, *Sketches*, 362.   [35] Ibid. 363–5.

for change which gained considerably with the appointment of the progressive Rabbi Abraham Geiger to the post of rabbi of Breslau in 1839. Geiger was a scholar as well as a clergyman, and his works demonstrated a critical and scientific approach to Jewish sources. But the connections between the German reform movement and the English demand for a modern synagogue closer to their own homes should not be overemphasized or read backwards from later developments.[36]

On 15 April 1840 a meeting was held of twenty-four leading community figures, and together they founded the West London Synagogue of British Jews. No doubt one reason for creating a new congregation was that many of the better-off members of the Anglo-Jewish community lived in the West End, far away from the old synagogues, and certainly not within walking distance, which made Sabbath attendance awkward if not impossible. But the ideological reasons were more significant, and they looked for a dignified worship which would be congruent to their social status. Their joint declaration was perhaps deliberately ambiguous:

We, the undersigned, regarding public worship as highly conducive to the interests of religion, consider it a matter of deep regret that it is not more frequently attended by members of our religious persuasion. We are perfectly sure that this circumstance is not owing to any want of general conviction of the fundamental truths of our religion, but we ascribe it to the distance of the existing Synagogues from the place of our residence, to the length and imperfections of the order of service, to the inconvenient hours at which it is appointed, and to the absence of religious instruction in our Synagogue. To these evils we think that a remedy may be applied by the establishment of a Synagogue at the western part of the metropolis, where a revised service may be performed at hours more suited to our habits, and in a manner more calculated to inspire feelings of devotion, where religious instruction may be afforded by competent persons, and where to effect these purposes, Jews generally may form a United Congregation under the denomination of British Jews.[37]

This revised form of worship they began immediately in temporary quarters at the Bedford Hotel in Southampton Row.

It is instructive to look for a moment at the twenty-four (later twenty-five) men who were the founding fathers of what would evolve to be the Reform Movement in England. Nineteen were Sephardim, and of this group nine were members of the Mocatta family, three were Montefiores, and three further rebels were Henriques. Joseph d'Aguilar Samuda, a

---

[36] Generally, see R. Liberles, 'The Origins of the Jewish Reform Movement in England', *AJSR* 1 (1976), 121–50, although his argument makes too strong a connection with the struggle for emancipation; and D. Philipson, *The Reform Movement in Judaism* (New York, 1907), ch. 5.   [37] Picciotto, *Sketches*, 367.

prominent member of the community, signed with the rebels, but later got cold feet. The six Ashkenazim were Aaron Asher Goldsmid, Francis H. Goldsmid, Frederick D. Goldsmid, Albert Cohen, Montague Levyssohn, and Solomon Lazarus.[38] These, then, were by all accounts leading figures from leading families, and their hiring of David Woolf Marks (1811–1909), soon to become professor of Hebrew at University College, London, capped a very distinguished rebellion indeed, what Marks described as 'a strenuous movement' led 'by some of the better educated of the laity to stamp with a higher character the Anglo-Jewish Synagogue, which had long seemed a merely servile copy of the Middle Ages'.[39]

As bad luck would have it, the venerable congregations were at that moment without effective leadership. The Sephardim were without a *haham* at all, Raphael Meldola having died in 1828.[40] His son David filled in to some extent, but he was merely head of the rabbinical court and lacked comprehensive authority. Rabbi Solomon Hirschell was by now very old, and quite simply was not up to the challenge.[41] The result was panic and over-reaction.

The initiative in the official Anglo-Jewish response to the Reform Movement therefore fell on the enormously influential layman Moses Montefiore (1784–1885), who was president of the Board of Deputies almost without interruption from 1835 to 1874.[42] Although born in

[38] C. Roth, *The Great Synagogue London 1690–1940* (London, 1950), 254.

[39] D. W. Marks and Albert Löwy, *Memoir of Sir Francis Henry Goldsmid* (2nd edn., London, 1882), 50–1.

[40] Meldola asked to be buried next to Haham David Nieto. His funeral was a great local event: cf. *Sunday Herald*, 8 June 1828, quoted in M. Gaster, *History of the Ancient Synagogue of the Spanish and Portuguese Jews* (London, 1901), 162–4.

[41] For a backstairs view of the Great Synagogue during these years, see its adjustments of disputes book, 1835–58: University College, London, Mocatta Library, Mocatta Cupboard, BA 27 GRE. See also the lectures in English given at the Hambro Synagogue in 1840 by I. M. Myers: University College, London, Mocatta Library, Mocatta Cupboard MS. RN 20 MYE.

[42] The literature on Moses Montefiore mushroomed as the year of the centenary of his death and bicentenary of his birth approached. See V. D. Lipman (ed.), *Sir Moses Montefiore: A Symposium* 1 (Oxford, 1982); S. and V. D. Lipman (eds.), *The Century of Moses Montefiore* (Oxford, 1985). Montefiore kept a diary throughout his life, but almost his entire archive was senselessly destroyed in the 1890s, including the diaries and correspondence, by Sir Joseph Sebag-Montefiore (1822–1903), his heir and president of the Board of Deputies from 1895 until his death. A few diaries survived the conflagration, including one which covers Montefiore's mission to Alexandria in order to solve the 'Damascus Affair' (see below). This diary is printed by R. D. Barnett as 'A Diary that Survived: Damascus 1840' in Lipman and Lipman, *Century*, 149–70. For the rest, we need to rely on the edited and printed edition: *Diaries of Sir Moses and Lady Montefiore*, ed. L. Loewe (London, 1890), and in a facsimile edition published at London in 1983 with a foreword by Professor Raphael Loewe.

Leghorn, he was of Anglo-Jewish parents, and by the time of the Reform crisis had long moved out of the wholesale grocer and tea business to becoming one of the twelve 'Jew brokers' of the City of London. His marriage to Judith Cohen made him a brother-in-law of Nathan Mayer Rothschild, but Montefiore retired from active business in 1824 at the age of 40 and devoted the rest of his extraordinarily long life to philanthropic and specifically Jewish interests. He was especially admired for his work in Palestine, and the Jewish quarter of Yemin Moshe outside the walls of Jerusalem was built on his initiative and named after him. His first visit to Palestine in 1827 also changed his attitude to orthodox Judaism, and from that time until the end of his life he remained observant. In the early years he would make the long trek from his house at Grosvenor Gate, Park Lane, to Bevis Marks, a journey which sometimes required his leaving at 6.00 a.m. in order to arrive in time for the beginning of prayers. He purchased East Cliff Lodge in Ramsgate in 1831, and two years later dedicated a synagogue there, which made his weekends less arduous. Montefiore was not only extremely rich and well-connected but also physically impressive, about 6 foot 3 inches in height, elegant and well dressed, certainly compared with N. M. Rothschild, who was not especially attracted to English high society, despite his financial standing. Montefiore's election to a fellowship in the Royal Society on 23 February 1837 was thus more of an indication of his position in London life than recognition of any especial contribution to science. Montefiore was elected to be one of the two sheriffs of London in 1837, and was knighted by Queen Victoria in the same year, being the first Jew since Sir Solomon de Medina in 1700 to be so honoured. Characteristically, just as de Medina's knighthood was not entirely designed to honour the man and even less so the Jew, so too was Montefiore's knighthood almost an accident, Queen Victoria's intention having been to bestow the honour on the men who happened to be the city sheriffs on her first state visit to London after acceding to the throne. Be that as it may, Montefiore's baronetcy in 1846 would more than compensate him for the backhanded status given him in the previous decade.[43]

Montefiore came to the question of the Reform Movement in England immediately after his greatest victory against those who would have persecuted the Jews. On 5 February 1840 a certain Father Thomas, the superior of a Capuchin monastery in Damascus, disappeared, along with his servant Ibrahim. As they had been seen close to the time in the Jewish quarter of the city, the local Jews were soon

[43] For Montefiore's early life, see S. L. Lipman, 'The Making of a Victorian Gentleman', in Lipman and Lipman, *Century*, 3–22.

accused of having kidnapped and killed the men with the intention of using their blood for the preparation of Passover matzoth. Several Jews were arrested and confessed under torture, and some of these men died. A cry for help reached the West in the form of a letter from the Jewish community of Constantinople to Rothschild, dated 27 March 1840. This letter, along with other documentation, was passed on to Montefiore, who had already acquired the reputation of being an expert in Middle Eastern affairs. Montefiore laid the entire matter before the Board of Deputies and a group of others at an emergency meeting held at his home on Park Lane on 21 April 1840. A further meeting held at the New Synagogue the following month determined that Sir Moses Montefiore was the man most suited to represent the British Jews in a mission of protest to the Mehemet Ali, the ruler of Egypt who had conquered Damascus in 1831. Montefiore thereupon went to Alexandria, accompanied by Adolphe Crémieux, and managed to convince Mehemet Ali to release the imprisoned Jews unconditionally. Eventually, as a result of this mission, the Sultan Abdul Mejid (then 17 years old) issued a firman on 6 November 1840, affirming that 'One can conclude, then, that the violence to which the Jews have been subjected, results from calumny and no more.' It was on the wave of this great triumph that Sir Moses Montefiore returned to London to face the brewing crisis over the Reform Movement in Anglo-Jewry.[44]

Sir Moses Montefiore's extremely negative view of the contemplated changes in the form and place of Jewish worship therefore carried a very great deal of weight. According to his associate Dr Louis Loewe,

He entertained the most liberal principles in matters of religion; although himself a staunch supporter of the time-honoured usages of his religion, he did not interfere with the opinions or acts of those who differed from him unless compelled to do so by actual duty. But when, as President of the Board of Deputies, or of any other institution, he had to give his opinion on religious matters, he invariably referred to the Spiritual Head of the community for guidance; he regarded a word from him as decisive, and obeyed its injunctions at whatever cost to himself.

There was never any doubt in his mind as to the spirit which should prevail in their deliberations on the intended reform in the community; and he maintained that the religious tenets of Israel, as revealed in the Code of Sinai, would invariably stand the test of reason.

[44] Generally, see T. Parfitt, ' "The Year of the Pride of Israel": Montefiore and the Damascus Blood Libel of 1840', in Lipman and Lipman, *Century*, 131–48; id., *The Jews in Palestine, 1800–1882* (London, 1987), 131–5; id., 'Sir Moses Montefiore and Palestine', in Lipman (ed.), *Montefiore*, 31–42; U. R. Q. Henriques, 'Who Killed Father Thomas?', in Lipman (ed.), *Montefiore*, 50–75.

Loewe is careful to present Montefiore as a man of moderation, but he too admits that things got out of hand. 'Some of his colleagues at the Board, however', he writes,

did not acknowledge the authority of the Ecclesiastical Chief of the community, and relying entirely on their own judgment, would not accept the dictates of the ancient teachers by whose decisions and interpretations of the sacred text Hebrew communities had been guided for thousands of years. The result was that the debates at their meetings became very heated, and bore evidence of the fervour displayed in a cause they had so deeply at heart, thus foreshadowing a struggle which threatened to extend beyond the confines of the Board.[45]

From the Sephardi point of view, they at least had some legal justification on their side. Their very first resolution back in 1664, reaffirmed many times, was the famous *Ascama I*, which asserted even then that 'we in unanimity and harmony forbid that there be any other Congregation in this city of London, its districts, and environs, for reading prayers with Minyan [quorum]'. The first English Jews did take into account the possibility of expansion, and ruled that this *ascama* held 'unless in future times to come through circumstances that may happen it may be needful to divide ourselves as may be found fitting, whereof the disposition remains reserved for the Mahamad which shall be in office at the time, being united and harmonious and under a government as we are at present'. The example they gave was Amsterdam, where the congregations divided by mutual consent. This obviously was not the case in London in 1840.[46]

The formation of the new congregation was rightly recognized as a serious threat. On 16 May 1841 the wardens of Bevis Marks described the situation to the elders in almost apocalyptic terms:

Several valued and influential members of our congregation have associated themselves with members of other communities in this city, for the purpose of establishing a Synagogue westward. This is already an infraction of the fundamental law of the congregation, which has been our bond of union since our admission into this country, now nearly two centuries since; still it admitted of excuse and palliation in the acknowledged inconvenience experienced by those respected friends and their families from the distance to our Synagogue and the want of accommodation near them. But it is to be apprehended that their contemplated establishment is to be on principles opposed to the received religious institutions and ordinances of our nation, that it is not to be subject to ecclesiastical discipline in religious matters, and that its promoters are engaged in alterations and abridgements of our established ritual to form a new order of

---

[45] Montefiore, *Diaries*, ed. Loewe, i. 301–2.
[46] *El libro de los acuerdos*, ed. L. D. Barnett (Oxford, 1931), 3.

prayers and service unsanctioned by any competent or regularly-constituted authority. Then their proceedings thus assume a character of so serious a nature as to call for the united interposition of the Jewish nation.[47]

The rebels of the West London Synagogue, for their part, addressed an uncompromising letter to the elders of the parent body on 24 August 1841, in which they spelled out once again and in great detail the reforms they were seeking, and stressed that they had no wish to make a demonstrative insurrection against Bevis Marks. On the contrary, they hoped to work in tandem with their brethren, especially in the field of charity.[48] These conciliatory words fell on deaf ears, and the elders of Bevis Marks issued a declaration threatening with excommunication any member who joined with the West London congregation or who used their revised liturgy.[49]

Not to be outdone, the Great Synagogue of Ashkenazi Jews followed suit in condemning the new congregation. On 9 September 1841 a meeting was held at Rabbi Hirschell's house, presided over by Moses Montefiore and attended by leaders of the London synagogues and other Jewish worthies, when a 'Caution' was read and approved in these terms:

Information having reached me, from which it appears that certain persons calling themselves British Jews, publicly and in their published book of prayers, reject the Oral Law, I deem it my duty to declare, that according to the laws and statutes held sacred by the whole House of Israel, any person or persons declaring that he and they reject and do not believe in the authority of the Oral Law, cannot be permitted to have any communion with us Israelites in any religious rite or sacred act.[50]

While not exactly a *herem*, an excommunication, it was fairly close. In any case, all care was taken to bring the rebels back into the fold, and this 'caution' was not officially read in the synagogues until Saturday, 22 January 1842, probably as a clear response to a letter of conciliation sent to Bevis Marks from the new congregation nine days before. Even then, the Western Synagogue refused to have any part of it and declined to have the 'caution' read to the congregants.[51]

There was little to be done now except firmly to close the door behind

---

[47] Picciotto, *Sketches*, 368.   [48] Ibid. 369–71.

[49] Ibid. 371–2. For a contemporary view of the entire proceedings, see the *responsa* of Abraham Belais (1773–1853), *Pri Etz Haim* (Hebrew) (Livorno, 1846). Belais was a teacher in the Sephardi community who arrived in London just as the crisis broke. See translations of excerpts from his work in I. Epstein, 'The Story of Ascama I of the Spanish and Portuguese Jewish Congregation of London', in M. Ben-Horin (ed.), *Studies and Essays in Honour of Abraham A. Neuman* (Leiden, 1962), 182–90.

[50] Piciotto, *Sketches*, 373–4.   [51] Ibid. 374–6; Hyamson, *Sephardim* 287–90.

them. On 27 January 1842 the West London Synagogue was consecrated at its new site on Burton Street off Euston Road in what had once been a Dissenting chapel. Professor Marks, as he now was, presided, using his new revised prayer-book, and pronouncing the Hebrew in the Sephardi fashion. It would be another month before the synagogue was properly open for prayer at Burton Street, but it had already become an accepted feature of the West End. The founding wardens were two Sephardim—Abraham Mocatta and J. B. Montefiore— and an Ashkenazi, Francis Goldsmid. Daniel Mocatta was the chairman of the founders. Within five years even the parent congregations had accepted defeat, and on 28 February 1847 the excommunication on the rebels was cancelled by the elders of Bevis Marks. That being said, all rancour did not entirely cease.[52] On the death in 1848 of Benjamin Elkin, one of the early members of the West London Synagogue, the Great Synagogue made such trouble over whether he could be buried at his wife's side that Sir Isaac Lyon Goldsmid, an ex-warden, resigned and transferred to the West London Synagogue the legacy of £3,000 that he was going to leave to his first congregation.[53]

All of this activity in England, of course, went on against the background of the growing reform movement in Germany, where in the middle 1840s a number of important rabbinical conferences of modernist rabbis set the tone of change. In time, the West London Synagogue would evolve with the entire English Reform Movement to being rather more conservative in theology and practice than their initially uncompromising attitude might have suggested. In 1901 'Liberal Judaism' would appear on the scene, a movement which was somewhat more radical, and with the formation the following year of the 'Union of Liberal and Progressive Synagogues' the English landscape began to assume a familiar form.[54]

Rabbi Hirschell's death in 1842 might have provided an opportunity for compromise, but his successor Nathan Marcus Adler (1803–90), chief rabbi from 1845, was dead set against change. Adler was born in

---

[52] Hyamson, *Sephardim*, 290–3; Picciotto, *Sketches*, 376–9; Marks and Löwy, *Memoir of Sir Francis Henry Goldsmid*, 50–3.

[53] Roth, *Great Synagogue*, 254. Dissatisfaction with the pace of social, political, and religious change also led Goldsmid in 1838 to refuse to serve on the Board of Deputies, headed intermittently by the ultra-conservative Moses Montefiore from 1835 to 1874: L. P. Gartner, 'Emancipation, Social Change and Communal Reconstruction in Anglo-Jewry, 1789–1881', *PAAJR* 54 (1987), 73–116, esp. 90–1.

[54] S. Sharot, 'Reform and Liberal Judaism in London, 1840–1940', *JSS* 41 (1979), 211–28. See also T. M. Endelman, 'The Englishness of Jewish Modernity in England', in J. Katz (ed.), *Towards Modernity: The European Jewish Model* (New Brunswick, 1987), 225–46.

Hanover and educated at university, and was a great-nephew of Rabbi David Tevele Schiff. Adler was the first chief rabbi to be formally elected by the Anglo-Jewish Ashkenazi community through a representative body on behalf of nineteen cities in Great Britain and Ireland. Even if the three oldest synagogues in London effectively had an automatic majority, the symbolic effect of national participation made Adler a genuine British Chief Rabbi, overcoming the attempt by Manchester's Solomon Schiller-Szinessy (1820–90) to set himself up as a northern equivalent. Adler promulgated soon afterwards a code of practice for Victorian orthodox synagogues, which made them stately reflections of their Anglican counterparts.[55] The Sephardim, meanwhile, at least repealed their *Ascama I* on 8 January 1843, and revoked the *herem* against its previous offenders in 1849.[56]

Eventually, the very expansion of Anglo-Jewry would dictate change. Even the Great Synagogue was forced to yield to demographic realities and open a branch in the West End in 1855, the Central Synagogue, led by the celebrated Aaron Levy Green (1821–83).[57] This was only the first step to the decay of the Great Synagogue, which would soon find the tail wagging the dog. To their credit, the leaders of Victorian Anglo-Jewry saw this change coming, and began to take steps to keep the Jews of England under one administrative roof. In 1834 the three original Ashkenazi synagogues—the Great, the Hambro, and the New—made a formal agreement not to poach each other's members. The foundation of the Board of Guardians for the Relief of the Jewish Poor in 1859 co-ordinated the charities which were designed to help the poor help themselves to becoming pale copies of West End London Jews.[58] In

---

[55] N. M. Adler, *Laws and Regulations for All the Synagogues K.K. Ashkenazim in the British Empire* (London, 1847); H. D. Schmidt, 'Chief Rabbi Nathan Marcus Adler (1803–1890): Jewish Educator from Germany', *Leo Baeck Inst. Year Book*, 18 (1962), 289–311; M. Goulston, 'The Status of the Anglo-Jewish Rabbinate, 1840–1914', *JJS* 10 (1968), 55–82; R. Lehmann-Goldschmidt, 'Nathan Marcus Adler: A Bibliography', in *Studies in Judaica, Karaitica and Islamica Presented to Leon Nemoy* (Ramat-Gan, 1982), 208–61; R. Loewe, 'Solomon Marcus Schiller-Szinessy, 1820–1890: First Reader in Talmudic and Rabbinic Literature at Cambridge', *TJHSE* 21 (1968), 148–89; V. D. Lipman, 'Synagogal Organization in Anglo-Jewry', *JJS* 1 (1959), 80–93; Cohen, 'Non-religious Factors', *TJHSE* 21 (1968), 304–13; S. Singer, 'The Anglo-Jewish Ministry in Early Victorian London', *Modern Judaism*, 5 (1985), 279–99, based on his Yeshiva University Ph.D. thesis (1981), 'Orthodox Judaism in Early Victorian London, 1840–1858'.

[56] Epstein, 'Ascama I', 190–214, based in part on the *responsa* of Mordecai Samuel Ghirundi of Padua (1779–1852), Jews' College, London, MS Montefiore 164.

[57] A. M. Jacob, 'Aaron Levy Green, 1821–1883', *TJHSE* 25 (1977), 87–106.

[58] This organization is now known as the Jewish Welfare Board: V. D. Lipman, *A Century of Social Service: 1859–1959: The Jewish Board of Guardians* (London, 1959). See also his *Social History of the Jews in England 1850–1950* (London, 1954).

1866, after Emancipation, negotiations began to make a binding union of the middle-class Ashkenazi congregations in London, including their respective trust funds and charitable organizations. An act of Parliament was required in order to put this on a firm footing, which was duly passed in 1870 as the United Synagogue Act, which gave the new body almost draconian powers, under the rule of the Chief Rabbi.[59] The provincial communities, especially Manchester, initially had some misgivings about continuing domination from London, but their inclusion on the Board of Deputies helped assuage some of this unhappiness.[60] The shabby synagogues and prayer-rooms of working-class London Jewry were left to their own devices.

II

Jewish criticism of the conduct and character of Anglo-Jewry was most important in so far as it influenced the general English conception of the Jew, with all of the attendant social and political consequences. Far more significant is to trace the changes in attitude to the Jews in England as they were expressed by Gentile commentators, a shift which would ultimately manifest itself in support for the growing movement towards emancipation. This alteration was probably first apparent in the image of the Jew in late eighteenth- and early nineteenth-century literature.

The stage Jew was a figure of fun or horror, a Shylock preying on the goodwill and weaknesses of Christians. This was the Jew who was recognizable to the public, the Jew whom they expected to see portrayed in the theatre and in published literature. One of the first authors to break this mould was Richard Cumberland, who showed the Jews in a rather different light. Cumberland's maternal grandfather was Richard Bentley, and, whether for that reason or another, his interest in the Jews grew with time. His first stage Jew was a negative figure, Napthali the broker, who appeared in *The Fashionable Lover* (1772), unfortunately to be revived at Drury Lane in 1818 after his death and subsequent to his reputation as a defender of the Hebrews. In 1785, in an essay in his own publication the *Observer*, Cumberland wrote on the Jewish question

---

[59] A. Newman, *The United Synagogue 1870–1970* (London, 1976). Cf. *Archives of the United Synagogue*, ed. C. Roth (London, 1930). The first president was Sir Anthony de Rothschild (1810–76), son of N. M. Rothschild. The Anglo-Jewish Association was founded the following year (1871) to provide aid to Jews abroad.

[60] B. Williams, *The Making of Manchester Jewry, 1740–1875* (Manchester, 1976), 219–31.

using as a foil an imaginary Jew whom he called Abraham Abrahams, supposedly complaining of his own treatment when he went to the theatre and of the usual portrayal of the Jew as a usurer and a rogue.[61] Cumberland rectified this deficiency in his celebrated play appropriately entitled *The Jew*, which was performed at Drury Lane in 1794. The work itself is a rather crude story of a kind-hearted Jewish stockbroker named Sheva, but it was played many times by companies throughout England, and was revived at Drury Lane in 1815, 1818, and 1821. It was printed soon after production, ran through seven editions in seven years, and was translated into a number of languages. The character of Sheva became a byword, and broadsheets with doggerel verse were sold in the streets of London.[62]

Public reaction to this change of direction was curious. James Boaden, a veteran observer of the late eighteenth-century theatrical scene, was very positive: 'One of the first and best novelties produced in the new [Drury Lane] theatre', he wrote,

was the comedy of the Jew, written by Cumberland. That ancient people had been rather scurvily treated by either the political or literary world. Their wealth, a distinction which they owe to themselves, subjects them to hatred for its use, and to pillage on every indecent pretext. Even Shakespeare, who has made his Shylock triumphant in his logic, and affecting in his misery, seems to enjoy his defeat by a quibble, and his conversion by a halter. But this ill-used people, on the 8th of May [1794], had the satisfaction to see their benevolent feelings admitted by a great nation, and Sheva pronounced at least as natural a character as Shylock.

As Boaden testifies, 'The *Jew* became popular all over these islands' and was 'clearly the best of Mr. Cumberland's latter pieces'.[63]

Paradoxically, the Jewish reaction to Cumberland's somewhat vulgar play was rather equivocal. Indeed, Cumberland himself had cause to complain about the Jewish lack of response, and in his memoirs he gave vent to these feelings: 'The public prints gave the Jews credit for their sensibility in acknowledging my well-intended services;' he wrote,

my friends gave me joy of honorary presents, and some even accused me of ingratitude for not making my thanks for their munificence. I will speak plainly on this point. I do most heartily wish they had flattered me with some token, however small, of which I could have said, this is a tribute to my philanthropy,

---

[61] *Observer*, 38 (1785): repr. *The British Essayists*, ed. James Ferguson (London, 1819), xxxviii. 252–3. Generally on Richard Cumberland, see L. Zangwill, 'Richard Cumberland Centenary Memorial Paper', *TJHSE* 7 (1915), 147–79; L. I. Newman, *Richard Cumberland* (New York, 1919).

[62] For an example of such verse, see Zangwill, 'Cumberland', 177–9.

[63] James Boaden, *Memoirs of the Life of John Philip Kemble, Esq.* (Philadelphia, 1825), 326, 328–9.

and delivered it to my children as my benevolent father did to me his badge of favour from the citizens of Dublin; but not a word from the lips, not a line did I ever receive from the pen of any Jew, though I have found myself in company with many of their nation; and in this perhaps the gentlemen are quite right, whilst I had formed expectations that were quite wrong; for if I have said of them only what they deserve, why should I be thanked; and if more, much more, than they deserve, can they do a wiser thing than hold their tongue?[64]

Sir Walter Scott, himself the author of a more famous literary work which put the Jews in a favourable light, had a convincing explanation for Jewish indifference to Cumberland's 'philanthropy'. In his view, 'the people in question felt a portrait in which they were made ludicrous as well as interesting, to be something between an affront and a compliment. Few of the better class of the Jewish persuasion would, we believe, be disposed to admit either Abraham or Sheva as fitting representatives of their tribe'.[65] This was Scott's opinion in 1824, after Cumberland had died, and with the benefit of the perspective of time. Cumberland himself was undismayed, and went on to write another play, *The Jew of Mogadore*, in 1808, which included the admirable Nadab the Jew.

While not exactly constituting a vogue, Cumberland's novel figure of the positive, warm-hearted Jew helped make such a construction acceptable to public taste. One of the first to change tack was Thomas Dibdin, whose play *The Jew and the Doctor*, performed at Covent Garden in 1798, extolled the virtues of Abednego, the aforementioned Jew who brings up from infancy a Christian girl named Emily and gives her £5,000 so that she can marry her lover. Dibdin himself recounts how he was approached by a leading actor, who

lamented he could not get the character of a comic Jew to perform in town: he wanted one quite as benevolent, but more farcical, than Mr. Cumberland's Sheva, in which part he had made a most successful beginning of his since long and still more successful career. I told him I thought it was a style of character I should like to attempt writing . . . I therefore agreed to try the experiment, and on that day se'nnight presented Dowton with the farce of 'the Jew and the Doctor'.

This, then, was even less of a great literary work than Cumberland's, and written with much less conviction. Cumberland himself came to the play to see if it was essentially a plagiarism. Dibdin, for his part, followed up this first commercial venture with another play on *The School for*

---

[64] Quoted in Picciotto, *Sketches*, 230–1: Picciotto adds that 'Richard Cumberland speaks with all the courtesy and dignity of a true gentleman; which increases our chagrin at his being constrained to give vent to such utterances.'
[65] Quoted Zangwill, 'Cumberland', 168.

Prejudice, performed in 1801, also at Covent Garden, in which Ephraim finds £10,000 in the lining of an old coat and returns the money to its owner. This play even enjoyed a revival in 1825, when it was converted into a three-act opera and renamed *The Lawyer, The Jew and the Yorkshireman*.[66]

Dibdin's downfall came in December 1802 when he produced his latest play, *Family Quarrels*. It was suggested to him that he include a song for three ladies of easy virtue, a standard theme, but with the additional twist of making them Jewish. 'Heaven knows that I', pleaded Dibdin, 'who had written and even played Abednego in "the Jew and the Doctor", and Ephraim in the "School for Prejudice", with no trifling applause from the critics of Whitechapel, Duke's-place, and Russell-court, never entertained . . . "the minutest atom of an idea" that the harmless joke, as harmlessly suggested, could be taken as the most distant intention of giving offence.' Nevertheless, before the first performance the song was already circulating in London in the form of a cheap booklet, which led to a large number of Jews buying tickets with the express purpose of disrupting the evening. In the event, the Jews succeeded in shouting down the play. The following evening the most offensive passages were omitted from the text, and although this performance did not pass entirely without interruption, the show was allowed to go on. Dibdin, for his part, was not disappointed, for the comedy was a great commercial success.[67]

The Jews of London thus demonstrated that they were not to be publicly ridiculed and that they would use very nearly violent means to defend their rights. The press found the incident rather bizarre. 'The natives of Yorkshire had as good right to remonstrate against the liberties taken with them through the medium of the character (performed by Emery) named Mushroom', wrote a critic in the *Oracle*: 'If this degree of affected delicacy be justifiable, we ought soon to expect remonstrances from Scotland, Ireland, and every part of England against jokes passed on them by poets of all ages.'[68] Anglo-Jewry thought their position was rather less secure than that of the Scottish or the Irish, yet the form of their protest shows that they were confident enough to break the law in their own defence.

Not all contact with the Gentile literary world needed to be confrontational. A much more positive relationship was that between the

---

[66] Thomas Dibdin, *The Reminiscences* (London, 1827), i. 209–13, 218; ii. 318.

[67] Ibid. i. 337–49 (where contemporary press reviews are also reprinted); Boaden, *Kemble*, 445–6. See, for comparison, M. Baer, *Theatre and Disorder in Late Georgian London* (Oxford, 1992), about the Old Price riots of 1809, in which Jews were involved, according to Thomas Tegg, *The Rise, Progress, and Termination of the O.P. War* (London, 1810), 47–9, 55.   [68] Dibdin, *Reminiscences*, i. 347.

celebrated Lord Byron (1788–1824) and Isaac Nathan (1792–1864), a cantor's son from Canterbury who became one of the best-known composers of his time. Nathan had been sent as a child to Cambridge with the intention that he prepare for entering the university, despite the fact that he would eventually be unable to take his degree. Nathan was determined to study music, however, and was apprenticed to Domenico Corri, a singing master and music publisher in London. In 1812 Nathan married one of his pupils, a 17-year-old Gentile girl named Elizabeth Rosetta Worthington, who three months later had already converted to Judaism and was married in a London synagogue. She died in childbirth twelve years later, and shortly thereafter her five surviving children were baptized into the Church of England, with the extravagant Lady Caroline Lamb serving as godmother.[69]

Nathan, unlike his towering contemporary John Braham, never really made the difficult transition from singing in the synagogue to performing successfully on the London stage. Nevertheless, he did achieve for himself a respectable slot in musical history, publishing a book on vocal technique, and serving as George IV's music librarian and vocal coach to Princess Charlotte of Wales. He also composed and performed for Lady Caroline Lamb, whose affair with Lord Byron in 1812 was a matter of some notoriety. It was probably by this means that Nathan had the idea of collecting Jewish melodies and then finding a great literary figure to write lyrics to them. Nathan's first choice was Sir Walter Scott, who declined, but in 1814 he wrote to Byron, who eventually agreed to collaborate. Nathan claimed that these melodies dated back many centuries, some indeed before the destruction of the Second Temple, and no doubt this romantic pedigree had some attraction for the young lord. Byron thereupon sent a number of poems to Nathan and agreed that his name could be used. Meanwhile, John Braham, the famous Jewish singer, promised to perform the songs at the Drury Lane theatre. A collaboration was thereby begun between Byron and Nathan, which blossomed until Nathan had obtained a total of twenty-nine poems from Byron's pen.[70] Byron's publisher John Murray

---

[69] For Nathan's life and much of the background to his partnership with Byron, see I. Braham, I. Nathan, and Lord Byron, *A Selection of Hebrew Melodies Ancient and Modern*, ed. F. Burwick and P. Douglass (Tuscaloosa, Ala., 1988), 3–41. See also O. S. Phillips, *Isaac Nathan: Friend of Byron* (London, 1940); C. MacKerras, *The Hebrew Melodist: A Life of Isaac Nathan* (Sydney, 1963); C. H. Bertie, *Isaac Nathan: Australia's First Composer* (Sydney, 1922); E. R. Dibdin, 'Isaac Nathan', *Music and Letters*, 22 (1941), 75–80; E. Wood, 'Isaac Nathan', in S. Sadie (ed.), *The New Grove Dictionary of Music and Musicians* (London, 1980) and *DNB*.

[70] Braham, Nathan, and Byron, *Hebrew Melodies*, ed. Burwick and Douglass, 3–41. Cf. I. Nathan, *Musurgia vocalis* (London, 1823).

was keen to be the first to unveil these new works to the anxious public
in the complete works which were being published, but Nathan was
quicker and produced his first edition of twelve songs in April 1815, a
full month before Murray's larger version, which included two dozen
poems.[71] Ultimately, of course, it was the musicless Hebrew melodies
which eclipsed Nathan's compositions, but it is nevertheless extraordinary that such a fruitful partnership should have evolved, a fact
which did not go unnoticed by the reviewers of the work, some of whom
thought that Byron's role here did not increase his dignity. In any case,
Byron's early attraction to Jews and their music would soon prove to be
far from his worst peccadillo. Later on, Byron's views towards the Jews
would shift somewhat when he discovered that they quite naturally
thought it prudent to be well disposed towards the Turkish rulers of
Palestine and thus were unsympathetic to Greek independence. This
new attitude he expressed in 1823 in a poem entitled *The Age of Bronze*.
Nathan for his part, after a series of financial failures, emigrated to
Australia in 1840, and was killed twenty-four years later stepping off a
tram into the street in Sydney.[72]

Lord Byron's other associate in this matter, John Braham (1774–
1856), was himself one of the most celebrated singers of his day.
Braham, like Nathan, began as a cantor, and his performances in Duke's
Place led to a début at Covent Garden in 1787 aged about 13. He found
the patronage of Abraham Goldsmid, which enabled him to develop his
talents to their full extent. His success was consistent, and from 1805 he
was mainly attached to Drury Lane, although he appeared endlessly up
and down the country and featured in almost every important concert
between about 1815 and 1840, and did not retire officially until 1852. In
1816 he married Fanny Bolton, the 17-year-old daughter of a dancing
academy master, and his six children were all brought up in the Church
of England. His daughter Frances married Earl Waldegrave, and herself

---

[71] Nathan's first edition of Apr. 1815 included twelve songs; Murray's of May 1815 a
total of twenty-four: in Apr. 1816 Nathan reissued the first number bound with the
second number, including all of the first twenty-four songs. Nathan's edition of 1828–9
was published in four numbers and included twenty-eight songs, the four new ones
being in the final number. A further song was included in Isaac Nathan, *Fugitive Pieces
and Reminiscences of Lord Byron* (London, 1829), which on pp. 147–96 also discusses his
performances for Lady Caroline Lamb. *Hebrew Melodies* was published in a Hebrew
translation by J. L. Gordon in 1884, and in a Yiddish version by Nathan Horowitz in
1926. For modern editions see *Byron's Hebrew Melodies*, ed. T. L. Ashton (Austin, Tex.,
1972) for the textual variants; and *Lord Byron: The Complete Poetical Works*, ed. J. J.
McGann (Oxford, 1980–6), iii. 249–72; 465–72.

[72] For critical assessments, see J. Slater, 'Byron's Hebrew Melodies', *Studies in
Philology*, 49 (1952), 75–94. Oddly enough, F. H. Goldsmid, the first Jewish barrister,
was killed in a similar fashion: see below, p. 388 n.

became a celebrated hostess of Victorian society, living at Horace Walpole's Strawberry Hill. An illegitimate son by his long-time partner, the soprano Nancy Storace, actually took orders and ended up as a minor canon of Canterbury and the chaplain to the Hebraist duke of Sussex.[73] To say that Braham was completely accepted by the English would be an exaggeration, partly exacerbated by the singer's tendency to astonish his audience with vocal dexterity which was regarded by many critics as simply pandering to vulgar tastes. Leigh Hunt, one of Byron's friends, expressed in a more extreme form a view which was widely held. Braham 'had wonderful execution as well as force,' he postulated,

and his voice could also be very sweet, though it was too apt to betray something of that nasal tone which has been observed in Jews, and which is, perhaps, quite as much, or more, a habit in which they have been brought up, than a consequence of organization. The same thing has been noticed in Americans; and it might not be difficult to trace it to moral, and even to monied causes; those, to-wit, that induce people to retreat inwardly upon themselves; into a sense of their shrewdness and resources; and to clap their finger in self-congratulation upon the organ through which it pleases them occasionally to intimate as much to a bystander, not choosing to trust it wholly to the mouth.

Still, when Braham was singing Handel, he was not to be compared, 'and you might have fancied yourself in the presence of one of the sons of Aaron, calling out to the host of the people from some platform occupied by their prophets'. King George IV, hearing Braham sing in a private performance, was barely dissuaded from knighting him on the spot.[74]

Yet it was in the written word that the more positive public image of the Jew was most apparent. Perhaps the earliest nineteenth-century manifestation of this was in *Harrington* (1817) by Maria Edgeworth (1768–1849), the Irish writer of historical and regional novels. Some of her earlier books had Jewish characters who were presented in a negative fashion, such as the Jewish wife of Sir Kit, the new master of *Castle Rackrent* (1800), the 'damned rascal' Mordecai in *The Absentee* (1811), or the three Jewish criminals in *Moral Tales* (1801). Edgeworth's usurer in *Belinda* (1801) was also a typical stereotyped character.

---

[73] Picciotto, *Sketches*, 222–4; M. Sands, 'John Braham, Singer', *TJHSE* 20 (1964), 203–14. Endelman, *Radical Assimilation*, 46–7. See also O. W. Hewett, *Strawberry Fair: A Biography of Frances, Countess Waldegrave, 1821–1879* (London, 1956).
[74] James Henry Leigh Hunt, *The Autobiography* (London, 1850), i. 231–3. Cf. a similar view in [John Feltham], *The Picture of London, for 1818* (19th edn., London, 1818), 278–9. See also J. M. Levien, *The Singing of John Braham* (London, 1944), and R. Crichton, 'John Braham', *New Grove Dictionary*.

According to her father, it was 'an extremely well-written letter, which Miss Edgeworth received from America, from a Jewish lady, complaining of the illiberality with which the Jewish nation had been treated in some of Miss Edgeworth's works' that inspired her to write a sort of apology to the Jews, in the form of her novel *Harrington* (1817). The attitude of the eponymous hero towards the Jews develops throughout the novel, until he finds himself in love with a Miss Bernice Montenero, the daughter of a Jewish gentleman merchant. Even Maria Edgeworth thought that it would be unrealistic and perhaps indecent to allow her Harrington to marry a Sephardi Jewess, so, as luck would have it, the girl turns out to be the child of a Christian mother and to have been baptized. Nevertheless, the novel was path-breaking in that it not only provided such positive characters as Bernice Montenero herself and her father, but respectable Jewish businessmen, a professor, and even an honest and kind-hearted old-clothes man.[75]

But of course it was *Ivanhoe* (1819) that really made Jews respectable in English literature. Sir Walter Scott's (1771–1832) story of Wilfred of Ivanhoe the noble Saxon, and his ultimately successful attempt to overcome political opposition to his love for Rowena, his father's ward, was a model historical novel: exciting, adventurous, and inaccurate. After many escapades, Ivanhoe and Rowena are united, to the disappointment of Rebecca, daughter of Isaac of York, the two Jews who saved his life, who now leave England in dejection. The character of Rebecca seems to have been based on a real person, Rebecca Gratz (1781–1869) of Philadelphia, the daughter of a family of local merchants and community leaders who herself was very active in social welfare. Scott apparently heard of her from his friend Washington Irving.[76] In any case, many readers then and now thought it odd that Ivanhoe should spurn the resourceful Rebecca in favour of Rowena, who although a descendent of Alfred the Great was much less attractive. Scott himself, in the introduction to a later edition, explained his reasons:

The character of the fair Jewess found so much favor in the eyes of some fair readers, that the writer was censured because, when arranging the fates of the characters of the drama, he had not assigned the hand of Wilfred to Rebecca rather than the less interesting Rowena. But, not to mention that the prejudice of the age rendered such a union almost impossible, the author may, in passing,

---

[75] Maria Edgeworth, *Harrington*, in *Tales and Novels: The Longford Edition*, ix (London, 1893), p. iii. The name of the Jewish lady was Miss Rachel Mordecai: M. S. Butler, *Maria Edgeworth* (Oxford, 1972), 238.

[76] See Rebecca Gratz, *Letters*, ed. D. Philipson (New York, 1929); and R. G. Osterweis, *Rebecca Gratz: A Study in Charm* (New York, 1935).

observe that he thinks a character of highly virtuous and lofty stamp is degraded rather than exalted by an attempt to reward virtue with temporal prosperity.[77]

Be that as it may, Scott had time to repent of excessive sympathy for the Jews in his novel *The Surgeon's Daughter* (1827). Here he presented the character of Richard Middlemas, a half-Jewish violent and treacherous man who meets his end being crushed by an elephant in India. Nevertheless, it was *Ivanhoe* that captured the popular imagination, and spawned a swarm of imitators who introduced Jews into historical novels set in distant and more romantic times.[78]

These were only some of the nineteenth-century literary works in which Jews appeared, and their influence must have been significant in the half-century before Emancipation.[79] Jews also appeared in Thackeray,[80] and in poems by Wordsworth[81] and Browning.[82] Apart from works written by Gentiles, there were numerous books written by English Jews, especially women,[83] the most notable of whom were Celia and Marian Moss,[84] Grace Aguilar,[85] and Charlotte Montefiore.[86] There were also 'conversionist' novels, which gave an accurate picture of Jewish life at the same time as delivering a message advocating their conversion, most notably the works published under the name of Amelia Bristow.[87] The point is that there were alternative Jews on public display

[77] Quoted in M. F. Modder, *The Jew in the Literature of England* (Philadelphia, 1939), 143. For other general works, see H. Michelson, *The Jew in Early English Literature* (Amsterdam, 1926); E. N. Calisch, *The Jew in English Literature, as Author and as Subject* (Richmond, 1909); and E. Rosenberg, *From Shylock to Svengali: Jewish Stereotypes in English Fiction* (London, 1960).

[78] Such as Horace Smith, *Zillah, a Tale of the Holy City* (2nd edn., London, 1828); Charlotte Anley, *Miriam* (London, 1829), set in Westmorland; Spindler, *The Jew* (London, 1832), set in 15th-century Germany. See also the chap-book set in Germany, *The Wonderful Discovery of the Murder of a Jew* (Dublin, 1823).

[79] For a list of 19th-century fiction of Jewish interest, see Modder, *Literature*, 412–26.

[80] See now S. S. Prawer, *Israel at Vanity Fair: Jews and Judaism in the Writings of W. M. Thackeray* (Leiden, 1991).

[81] Such as 'The Jewish Family' (1828).

[82] Such as 'Holy Cross Day' (1855); 'Rabbi Ben Ezra' (1864); and 'Jochanan Hakkadosh' (1883).

[83] Generally, for books written by English Jews see L. G. Zatlin, *The Nineteenth-Century Anglo-Jewish Novel* (Boston, 1981).

[84] *The Romance of Jewish History* (1840); and *Tales of Jewish History* (1843).

[85] *Records of Israel* (1844); *The Vale of Cedars; or, The Martyr* (1850); and *Home Scenes and Heart Studies* (1853). See also B. Z. L. Abrahams, 'Grace Aguilar', *TJHSE* 16 (1952), 137–48. [86] *Caleb Asher* (1845).

[87] *Sophia de Lissau* (2nd edn., London, 1828); *Emma de Lissau* (London, 1828); and *The Orphans of Lissau* (London, 1830). Robert Southey thought the first of these novels 'worth reading, because it is in the main (I have been assured) true': Southey, *Letters*, ed. Warter, iv. 178.

to Shylock or even Fagin, who made his appearance in 1838 in *Oliver Twist*.[88] The alteration of the figure of the Jew who was thought to be recognizable to public audiences was an important factor in preparing the English public for the greater rigours of Jewish Emancipation.

III

Sir Walter Scott's Jews were literary personalities, perhaps very different from the sort one was likely to meet in the streets of nineteenth-century London. Most Englishmen had little opportunity to form a first-hand impression of living Jews, and, apart from literary works which did not purport to paint a totally accurate picture, were forced to rely on contemporary accounts of the Jew and his history. Descriptions of the Great Synagogue were very popular, especially because the Jewish old-clothes men were usually Ashkenazi. Robert Southey, writing under the pseudonym of 'Don Manuel Alvarez Espriella', utilized the literary device of printing 'letters from England' written by a foreigner to his compatriots abroad. Southey has his character visit a synagogue and the Jewish quarter of London, and whether or not his views reflect his maker's, the effect was generally unpleasant. Southey makes mention of the Wandering Jew, Cromwell, Menasseh ben Israel, the Jew Bill, George Gordon, Mary de Breta the child convert, and Napoleon, and works his way up to a description of London Jewry:

A race of Hebrew lads who infest you in the streets with oranges and red slippers, or tempt school-boys to dip in a bag for gingerbread nuts, are the great agents in uttering base silver; when it is worn too bare to circulate any longer they buy it up at a low price, whiten the brass again, and again send it abroad. You meet Jew pedlars every where, travelling with boxes of haberdashery at their backs, cuckoo clocks, sealing wax, quills, weather glasses, green spectacles, clumsy figures in plaister of Paris, which you see over the chimney of an alehouse parlour in the country, or miserable prints of the king and queen, the four seasons, the cardinal virtues, the last naval victory, the prodigal son, and such like subjects, even the Nativity and the Crucifixion; but when they meet with a likely chapman, they produce others of the most obscene and mischievous kind. Any thing for money, in contempt of their own law as well as the law of the country;—the pork-butchers are commonly Jews. All these low classes have a shibboleth of their own, as remarkable as their physiognomy; and in some parts of the city they are so numerous, that when I strayed into their precincts one day, and saw so many Hebrew inscriptions in the shop windows,

[88] See L. Lane, 'Dickens' Archetypal Jew', *Proceedings of the Modern Languages Association*, 73 (1958), 94–100; H. Stone, 'Dickens and the Jews', *Victorian Studies*, 2 (1958–9).

and so many long beards in the streets, I began to fancy that I had discovered the ten tribes.

Southey concludes with a description of Jewish stockbrokers in a coffee house dealing with some bad news, crying, 'My Gott! de stokes!' In brief, he writes, 'England has been called the hell of horses, the purgatory of servants, and the paradise of women: it may be added that it is the heaven of the Jews—alas, they have no other heaven to expect!'[89]

Joseph Ballard, an American merchant from Boston who visited England in 1815 and recorded his experiences, encountered Jews the moment he stepped off the boat in Liverpool. 'The next day we were much pestered by Jews who wished to purchase our gold,' he recounted. 'It was extremely amusing to hear these fellows talk of their American connections. They all positively declared that they did all the trade that was done in their line with America. They also asked many curious questions—"Were Charlestown, S.C., Baltimore and Norfolk near Boston!" &c. &c.' On 4 July in London he encountered a parade of American soldiers led by a Jew playing on a hand organ. Four days later he decided to visit the famous, or infamous, Duke's Place himself to see the Great Synagogue:

It being the Jewish Sabbath I was induced to visit the Synagogue near Duke Street, the residence exclusively of these Shylocks. The church is a neat edifice. It is lighted with seven chandeliers, the pulpit, or desk, where the priests stand being in the centre: at the end is the altar or holy of holies, toward which they turn their faces and bow while repeating their prayers. The men sit with their hats on. The women are in a screened gallery, apart from the men! The service was chanted in Hebrew, the congregation joining in at times in 'din most horrible'. I came away disgusted with the little reverence they seemed to pay to that Being who pronounced them His chosen people![90]

Rather a more favourable view of the Jews and their habits was given great prominence by that indefatigable Victorian editor and promoter Leigh Hunt (1784–1859), friend and protector of Byron, Keats, Shelley, and a host of others. A great supporter of Hebrew language and literature, in theory at least, Hunt recalled in his autobiography that 'I used to go with some of my companions to the synagogue in Duke's Place; where I took pleasure in witnessing the semi-catholic pomp of their service, and in hearing their fine singing; not without something of a constant astonishment at their wearing their hats.' Indeed, he wrote,

These visits to the synagogue did me, I conceive, a great deal of good. They served to universalize my notions of religion, and to keep them unbigoted. It

[89] [Robert Southey], 'Don Manuel Alvarez Espriella', *Letters from England* (London, 1807), repr. ed. J. Simmons (London, 1951), 338, 392–8.
[90] Joseph Ballard, *England in 1815* (Boston, 1913), 10, 107, 126, 128–9.

never became necessary to remind me that Jesus was himself a Jew. I have also retained through life a respectful notion of the Jews as a body . . . I never forgot the Jews' synagogue, their music, their tabernacle, and the courtesy with which strangers were allowed to see it. I had the pleasure, before I left school, of becoming acquainted with some members of their community, who were extremely liberal towards other opinions, and who, nevertheless, entertained a sense of the Supreme Being far more reverential than I had observed in any Christian, my mother excepted.

These were views he formed early in life, and to which he remained faithful.[91]

Apart from London and the ports, Jews were beginning to be found in the fashionable watering-holes, and this too did not escape comment. John, the son of Walter Spencer-Stanhope, MP, wrote from Bath in August 1819 to his family on holiday in France. 'What a multitude of people we have here,' he complained,

Jews, Haberdashers, and money-lenders without number, a sort of Marine Cheapside, Mr Solomons, Mrs Levis, and all the Miss Abrahams; in short, Hook Noses, Mosaical Whiskers and the whole tribe of Benjamin occupy every shop, every donkey-cart, and every seat in Box, Pit, and Gallery. I am very tired of them, and shall probably take flight at the end of the week to Worthing.[92]

Charles Cochrane, in his pseudonymous journal of a tour by a Spaniard through Great Britain and Ireland, also reports the prominent presence of Jews in Bath. He was shaken to see there, he noted, that so many ugly Jews had such pretty wives.[93]

As efforts for the political emancipation of Anglo-Jewry began to pick up pace, rather more serious attempts at summing up the Jewish experience began to appear. One of the first of the nineteenth-century efforts was John Allen's description of what he called 'Modern Judaism'. 'A firm believer in Christianity himself,' he assured his readers, 'the Author cannot but contemplate Modern Judaism as an awful delusion.'

---

[91] Hunt, *Autobiography*, i. 172–5.

[92] *The Letter-Bag of Lady Elizabeth Spencer-Stanhope*, ed. A. M. W. Stirling (London, 1913), i. 342: letter dated 7 Aug. 1819. As early as 1761 Dr Isaac Schomberg noted that 'we have a good many of [*Benai Israel*] at Bath': BL Add. MS 28542, fo. 163: J. Nichols, *Illustrations of the Literary History of the Eighteenth Century* (London, 1817–58), iv. 768; Roth, *Provincial Jewry*, 27. Jews also became established at Brighton in the late 18th century, attracted even before the town became fashionable: see Roth, *Provincial Jewry*, 34–40. Cf. 'The Plymouth Aliens List 1798 and 1803', ed. V. D. Lipman, *MJHSE* 6 (1962), 187–94. Canterbury, while not exactly fashionable, also attracted a significant community: 'At present, the habitations of the Jews, who are very numerous in this city and its suburbs': E. Hasted, *History of Canterbury* (Canterbury, 1799), 40; D. Cohn-Sherbok, *The Jews of Canterbury 1760–1931* (Canterbury, 1984), 13.

[93] [Charles Cochrane] 'Juan de Vega', *Journal of a Tour* (London, 1830), i. 370–87; ii. 30.

That being said, Allen showed a surprising amount of knowledge, some of it gleaned from the writings of Menasseh ben Israel, of such arcane subjects as the River Sambatyon, Karaites, and even the Jewish pseudo-gospel, *Toldoth Yeshu*.[94] Allen also published a translation into English of William Outram's seventeenth-century dissertation on sacrifices, and therefore approached the problem of the Jews from the standpoint of a Christian Hebraist.[95] The publisher John Murray, in his 'Family Library' series, published three little volumes in 1829 described as *The History of the Jews*, the first edition of Henry Hart Milman's as-yet-anonymous classic. 'The Jews, without reference to their religious belief, are among the most remarkable people in the annals of mankind', began Milman.

Scattered from that period over the face of the earth—hated, scorned, and oppressed, they subsist, a numerous and often a thriving people; and in all the changes of manners and opinions retain their ancient institutions, their national character, and their indelible hope of restoration to grandeur and happiness in their native land.

The history itself contained a good deal of information, ranging from the Jews of China to Shabtai Sevi, Jacob Frank, and the Jews of Great Britain. The author retailed some of the usual stories about the Jews, including the claim that they had attempted to buy St Paul's Cathedral and the Bodleian Library in Cromwell's time, and the account of the 'great Meeting of Jewish Rabbins in the plain of Ageda, about thirty miles from Buda, in Hungary' in 1655. Yet it was on the whole a favourable view of the Jews, and a book which could be put into the hands of every interested Englishman.[96]

The book by John Elijah Blunt, barrister of Lincoln's Inn, was more obviously a pro-emancipation tract. Blunt thought it unjust that the Jews laboured under certain disabilities 'which, except in their case, is confined to the traitor, the felon, or the outlaw'. The most obvious problem which confronted the historian of Anglo-Jewry, he thought, was the status of the Jews with regard to owning property, and here we should be aware of the 'present daily discoveries that are made of ancient documents and records'. In Blunt's view,

[94] John Allen, *Modern Judaism; or, A Brief Account of the Opinions, Traditions, Rites, and Ceremonies, of the Jews in Modern Times* (London, 1816), esp. pp. v–vi, 6–7.

[95] William Outram, *Two Dissertations on Sacrifices*, trans. John Allen (2nd edn., London, 1828; 1st pub. 1677).

[96] [Henry Hart Milman], *The History of the Jews* (London, 1829) [vols. v, vi, and ix of 'The Family Library' published by John Murray], i. 3–4; iii. 163–6, 377–9, 380–1, 381–9, 390–1, 400, 411–13, 416. Further editions followed.

Under the existing state of the law, the Jews have no direct interest in supporting the general welfare. They are prevented from acquiring the only species of property which can give them any permanent interest in the country, or by which they may hope to transmit with security the fruits of their industry to their posterity; they are shut out from the acquirement of all honours and distinction in the state, and are forced to rest any consequence they may obtain in society upon the mere ground of accumulated wealth. It cannot, therefore, be supposed that the Jews will, to any extent, exert themselves for the general good, or that they will abandon, for the benefit of others, any individual advantages which they may possess.

That being said, it is curious to note that Blunt also believed the story about the Jews trying to buy St Paul's and the Bodleian, but this did not alter his favourable view of the Jews and the need to improve their legal position in England.[97] Likewise, the history of Anglo-Jewry by John Mills was a rather transparent attempt to present the Jews in a favourable light, and included lists of Jewish schools and charities as support for the argument that the Jews would make model citizens if all disabilities were removed.[98] The last fifty-odd pages of the book consisted on an essay by Professor Hyman Hurwitz of University College, London on the 'Sources of Modern Judaism'.[99]

It was also during this period that the Anglo-Jewish press was born. Jacob Franklin (1809–77) founded a newspaper called the *Voice of Jacob* in 1841 in the wake of the Damascus Affair, at a meeting which included Dr Abraham Benisch (1811–78) and Dr Morris J. Raphall (1798–1868), a Birmingham rabbi who between 1834 and 1836 edited a journal called the *Hebrew Review and Magazine of Rabbinical Literature*.[100] Moses Montefiore and Lionel Rothschild helped fund Franklin's newspaper, although not everyone thought that a specifically Jewish periodical was such a good idea. At the same time, Isaac Vallentine (1793–1868), a Belgian-born bookseller and almanac maker, was thinking about starting a Jewish newspaper with David Meldola (1797–1853), acting *haham* of the Spanish and Portuguese Synagogue, and Moses Angel (1819–98), a graduate of University College, London. Their paper was called

[97] John Elijah Blunt, *A History of the Establishment and Residence of the Jews in England: With an Enquiry into their Civil Disabilities* (London, 1830), esp. pp. iii, vi, x–xii, 68.

[98] John Mills, *The British Jews* (London, 1853), esp. 2–3, 8, 256, 259–60 (list of synagogues and seatholders), 275–86 (list of Jewish charities), 296–323 (list of Jewish schools), 324–6. [99] Ibid. 356–413.

[100] Other early Anglo-Jewish periodicals were the *Hebrew Intelligencer* (three numbers, 1823); and *Kos Yeshuoth; 'Cup of Salvation'*, published between 1845 and 1866 in Liverpool by D. M. Isaacs and Moses Samuels. See generally [C. Roth], *The Jewish Chronicle: A Century of Newspaper History* (London, 1949); *Magna Bibliotheca Anglo-Judaica*, ed. C. Roth (London, 1937), s. A14.

the *Jewish Chronicle* and began to appear on 12 November 1841, two months after the *Voice of Jacob* was issued on 18 September 1841. Both papers were also against the Reform Movement, and the *Jewish Chronicle* took the excommunication order of the Chief Rabbi so seriously that they were unable to send a reporter to cover the opening of the Reform synagogue and had to rely on a report in the *Morning Chronicle*. Both papers were soon losing money: Franklin proposed a merger; Vallentine refused. But when Meldola was ordered by his synagogue employers to leave journalism and Angel jumped ship to the other paper, the *Jewish Chronicle* was forced to close down in May 1842, leaving the *Voice of Jacob* as the only Anglo-Jewish newspaper until it too closed six years later.[101]

In October 1844 the *Jewish Chronicle* was revived by a mysterious man named Joseph Mitchell (d. 1854) and was renamed the *Jewish Chronicle and Working Man's Friend* to reflect a new working-class editorial line. Mitchell's partner and part-time enemy was Marcus Bresslau, a Jew of Hamburg who had been involved with the *Hebrew Review*. The first campaign of the new-style *Jewish Chronicle* was against elections for the post of Chief Rabbi under the current system which gave the franchise only to 'free members' of the synagogues (those who had purchased lifetime seats) and denied it to 'regular seatholders' (those who only rented their places). In the end, Chief Rabbi Solomon Hirschell was replaced by Nathan Marcus Adler (1803–90), who was given a difficult time by the *Jewish Chronicle* at first. At the same time, the newspaper was critical of the Reform Movement and enthusiastic about the fight for Jewish emancipation.[102]

In January 1853 an additional Jewish newspaper appeared on the scene, the *Hebrew Observer*, founded by Abraham Pierpoint Shaw, about whom almost nothing is known. It was edited by Abraham Benisch, who had been co-editor with Jacob Franklin on the old *Voice of Jacob*. Benisch bought the *Hebrew Observer* in 1854 and the following year merged it with the *Jewish Chronicle*, soon taking over the entire operation as owner and editor, and retaining both names until 1868. Benisch was from Bohemia, and had studied surgery in Prague and Vienna, where he met such Jewish luminaries as Steinschneider, and became part of the Zionist circle that included Albert Lowy, later minister of the Reform congregation in London. In 1841 Benisch came to London to work for

---

[101] The last few issues of the *Voice of Jacob* appeared as the *Anglo-Jewish Magazine*. For some interesting documents regarding its foundation, see University Library, Leeds, MS 250.

[102] [Roth], *The Jewish Chronicle*. See also J. L. Altholz, *The Religious Press in Britain, 1760–1900* (New York, 1989), 110–14.

the Zionist cause, and it was there that he became involved with Jewish journalism. Bresslau was soon ousted after Benisch's take-over, and the newspaper put on a more secure financial footing: it was discovered that although there were 1,000 subscribers, only about half of them actually paid for the copies they received. Under Benisch's editorship such important causes as the new Board of Guardians (founded March 1859) were promoted, as were emancipation and reconciliation with the Reform Jews.[103]

IV

These were some of the forces which helped present the Jews in a favourable light in the half-century before Emancipation, but there was one area which no amount of cosmetic reportage could beautify: the role of the Jews in Victorian crime. G. F. A. Wendeborn, the pastor of a German Lutheran church on Ludgate Hill and London reporter for the Hamburg press writing at the end of the eighteenth century, described a condition which would only grow worse. 'The praise which is due to the generality of the Portuguese, relative to their manners and morals, cannot be bestowed upon the majority of the German Jews', he asserted.

They are great sticklers for their old tenets and usages; but they allow themselves great liberties in regard to their morals. I believe few burglaries, robberies, and false coinages are committed, in which some of them are not, in one shape or other, concerned. They steal not only themselves, but assist Christian thieves by receiving their stolen goods, and buying them at a very reasonable price. In Duke's-place, where hardly any but Jews live, during the whole night furnaces are ready to melt the stolen silver and gold as soon as the thieves bring it, that it may be rendered indistinguishable before day-light.[104]

This may be something of an exaggeration, but not completely without truth.

We have already seen how significant the Jewish crime problem was in the eighteenth century, and certainly it continued to be a worry until at least the 1830s. In many ways the slip towards breaking the law was unavoidable for many Jews, given the professions in which they predominated. So many Jews were petty traders and pedlars, the old-clothes men of London, and when buying and selling commodities they

---

[103] S. W. Baron, 'Abraham Benisch's Project for Jewish Colonization in Palestine (1842)', in S. W. Baron and A. Marx (eds.), *Jewish Studies in Memory of George A. Kohut*, (New York, 1935), 72–85; J. M. Shaftesley, 'Dr Abraham Benisch as Newspaper Editor', *TJHSE* 21 (1968), 214–31.

[104] G. F. A. Wendeborn, *A View of England towards the Close of the Eighteenth Century* (London, 1791), ii. 471.

were not in the business of enquiring too closely about provenance. Many pedlars crossed the line between ignorance and intent and knowingly purchased stolen goods, which, according to popular belief, were often shipped abroad, especially to Holland. As one contemporary observer of the criminal scene put it,

Cheats of the Society of Jews are to be found in every part of the Metropolis, who, under the pretence of purchasing old clothes and metals of different sorts, prowl about the houses and stables of respectable persons for the purpose of holding out temptations to the servants to pilfer and steal small articles, which they purchase at about one-third of the real value.[105]

George Smeeton, another expert on London life, suggested that 'if, on occasions of robbery, a reward was offered for the receiver, instead of the thief, Petticoat Lane, and Houndsditch, and Whitechapel, and the Jew-streets and alleys in the neighbourhood of the Strand, would no longer be places of refuge and barter for the prosperous ruffian'. He was sure that few Jews ever refused to receive stolen goods, and indeed encouraged theft by their behaviour.[106] The most notorious Jewish criminal of those years was Ikey Solomons (*c.*1785–1850), the 'prince of fences', whose exploits became legendary.[107]

Apart from fencing, other particularly Jewish criminal areas in the first decades of the nineteenth century fell into the category of frauds and swindles. Among these might be included passing bad coins, itself (like fencing) an offshoot of legitimate activity. A Jewish pedlar spent much of his time making change and could easily move from unwittingly passing bad coins to taking part in the active market for counterfeit money. Jews were also notorious for staging mock auctions, where a partner would drive up the price, and for arranging fake bankruptcies. This latter swindle involved laying a claim to the Commissioners of Bankrupts, swearing that large sums of money were owed to false creditors, thereby reducing the amount of money that could be paid to the genuine ones. Jews were also active in legitimate areas of exploitation, such as 'crimping', whereby sailors were endebted virtually on debarking from one ship and thereby forced to enlist once again for the Royal Navy or the East India Company. In addition, Jews were prominent in running 'sponging houses', detention centres for debtors, such as the father of Charles Dickens, who was sent to such a place in

---

[105] [John Wade], *A Treatise on the Police and Crimes of the Metropolis* (London, 1829), 337; cf. 152 for the claim that the Jews were the chief brothel keepers of London.
[106] George Smeeton, *Doings in London or Day and Night Scenes of the Frauds, Frolics, Manners, and Depravities of the Metropolis* (London, [1828]), 104.
[107] See esp. J. J. Tobias, *Prince of Fences: The Life and Crimes of Ikey Solomons* (London, 1974).

1834, only a few years before Fagin was created. Interestingly, Jews were hardly involved at all in money-lending, except at the highest level to aristocratic debtors.[108]

Most of the crimes with which Jews were involved were non-violent, and those Jews who were sentenced to death or transportation were usually convicted of offences not normally associated with Jews, such as burglary, or stealing from shops, warehouses, and carts. The courts could be very heartless. In 1814 Henry Wolf, aged 12, was sentenced to death for stealing a three penny knife. In the same year Moses Solomon received the same death sentence, even though he was only 9 years old, for stealing a pair of shoes after breaking into a house, although the court did recommend mercy. Proper statistics on the Jewish involvement in crime, capital or otherwise, are notoriously difficult to determine, for the same reason that Jews cannot be isolated with precision from any other English resident in determining voting patterns. A further problem is that in this period it was the responsibility of the victim to prosecute, not the government, and many crimes went unreported. Most serious crimes in the London and Middlesex areas came before juries in the Old Bailey. Professor T. M. Endelman made a list of those criminals brought before that court between 1730 and 1829 who are either specifically referred to as Jews, or who have unquestionable Jewish names. The result is a rogue's gallery of 621 Jews, of whom ninety-two were sentenced to death, 352 to transportation, and a further 177 to other punishments, such as prison, whipping, or a fine.[109] According to another source, of the 145,000 people who were transported between 1788 and 1852, about 1,000 were Jews. Whether or not one chooses to regard these figures as indicating a high or a low crime rate among the Jews of London, what is certain is that in contemporary eyes, the Jewish connection with certain kinds of crime was axiomatic, and this had a great influence on the English conception of the Jew.[110]

Another area of Jewish prominence, bordering sometimes very closely on the criminal world, was boxing and prize-fighting, in which a number of well-known Jews made their name in late eighteenth- and early nineteenth-century England. Between the 1760s and the 1820s at least thirty Jews were active in this sport, by far the most famous of whom was Daniel Mendoza (1763–1836), who single-handedly dominated the entire field. Pierce Egan, one of the early historians of the sport and a

---

[108] For Jews and crime, see esp. T. M. Endelman, *The Jews of Georgian England 1714–1830* (Philadelphia, 1979), 192–219; and M. A. Shepherd, 'Popular Attitudes to Jews in France and England 1750–1870' (Oxford University D.Phil. thesis, 1983).

[109] Endelman, *Georgian England*, 192–219.

[110] J. S. Levi and G. F. J. Bergman, *Australian Genesis: Jewish Convicts and Settlers 1788–1850* (London, 1974); Endelman, *Georgian England*, 299.

contemporary of Mendoza, elegized him in most extravagant, but wholly typical, terms:

Mendoza was considered one of the most elegant and scientific Pugilists in the whole race of Boxers, and might be termed a complete artist . . . He rose up like a phenomenon in the pugilistic hemisphere, and was a star of the first brilliancy for a considerable period . . . The name of Mendoza has been resounded from one part of the kingdom to the other; and the fame of this once-celebrated pugilist was the theme of universal panegyric—and, though not

> 'The Jew
> That Shakespeare drew — — —'

yet he was that *Jew*, the acknowledged pride of his own particular persuasion, and who, so far interested the *Christian*, that, in spite of his prejudices, he was compelled to exclaim—*'Mendoza was a pugilist of no ordinary merit!'*

Mendoza remained a legend, and a popular hero, even after he left boxing for nearly seven years after being defeated in April 1795 by his chief rival. Mendoza went into business as a publican for a time, running the *Lord Nelson* in Whitechapel and supporting his wife and eleven children.[111] He also did a little mob work, as reported by Marianne Thornton, whose father, a member of the reforming Clapham Sect, campaigned for Parliament in Southwark. A mass of people demonstrated against him, partly because of his support for Roman Catholic emancipation, including 'Mendoza the Jew boxer', who shouted 'No Popery! No Popery!', having been hired to encourage the others.[112] None the less, Mendoza seems to have been personally popular, described by Egan as 'an intelligent and communicative man'. He became the symbol of the Jewish fighter, 'the *Hebrew* with points', whose opponents were 'as inferior to the Jewish hero as Dr. Priestley when opposed to the Rabbi, David Levi'.[113]

Other Jews were outstanding in boxing apart from Mendoza, especially Elias 'Dutch Sam' Samuel (1775–1816). 'Among his own persuasion (the Jews)', wrote Egan, 'he is an object of great notoriety, and no money is ever wanting to back him upon any pugilistic occasion, his INTEGRITY having been proved of the first quality.' Mendoza even served as Dutch Sam's attendant in 1806–7, linking the two in the public eye. 'Young Dutch Sam' (1801–43) his son was also a fighter, but

---

[111] On Mendoza, see Pierce Egan, *Boxiana; or, Sketches of Ancient and Modern Pugilism* (London, 1824–30), i. 253–80; Frank R. Dowling, *Fistiana* (London, 1852), 71, for list of major fights. Cf. L. Edwards, 'Daniel Mendoza', *TJHSE* 15 (1946), 73–92. On Jews and boxing, see generally Endelman, *Georgian England*, 219–23.

[112] E. M. Forster, *Marianne Thornton: A Domestic Biography, 1797–1887* (New York, 1956), 52: quoted in Endelman, *Georgian England*, 221.

[113] Egan, *Boxiana*, i. 280; iii. 118 n.; A. Rubens, *Anglo-Jewish Portraits* (London, 1935), 78: etching of fight between Mendoza and Humphries, published May 1789.

unfortunately linked up with a number of aristocratic rakes and fell into a rather dissolute life. Among the other famous Jewish pugilists were Abraham 'Aby' Belasco (1797–1824), who also owned a night-club, Barney 'The Star of the East' Aaron (1800–50), Ikey Pig, Gideon the Jew, Elisha Crabbe the Jew, Lazarus the Jew Boy, and Gadzee, otherwise Cat's-Meat, the 'little laughing *Israelite*'.[114]

The spectacle of muscled Jews defeating Christians in the ring, while not entirely inconceivable, was somewhat unexpected. The explanation for this natural phenomenon combined existing stereotypes of the Jew with the fact of their unquestioned victories. Discussing Mendoza's virtues, one of the observers of the boxing scene explained that as 'a teacher of the *science* it was Mendoza that immediately trod in the steps of Broughton. He made the art of self-defence, when quite a boy, his peculiar study,—his success, as a professor, was unrivalled'. Equally, in looking at the career of other boxers, the intellectual rather than the physical elements are stressed. 'The superior *science* of the Jew prevented the hitherto *slashing hitting*' of the Christian Englishman. This was the key to the success of men like '*Abraham Belasco*, the *scientific* Jew', who without his study of boxing could not have defeated stronger opponents. For Robert Southey, it was training that distinguished 'the academies of the two great professors Jackson and Mendoza, the Aristotle and Plato of pugilism'.[115] George Borrow (1803–81), linguist and traveller, whose fame would rest on his adventures with the Bible in Spain as an agent for the British and Foreign Bible Society, had even more unkind words to say about Jewish boxers. Amongst the English pugilists, he wrote,

there are fellows with dark sallow faces, and sharp shining eyes; and it is these that have planted rottenness in the core of pugilism, for they are Jews, and, true to their kind, have only base lucre in view. It was fierce old Cobbett, I think, who first said that the Jews first introduced bad faith amongst pugilists. He did not always speak the truth, but at any rate he spoke it when he made that observation. Strange people the Jews—endowed with every gift but one, and that the highest, genius divine—genius which can alone make of men demigods, and elevate them above earth and what is earthly and grovelling; without which a clever nation—and who more clever than the Jews?—may have Rambams in plenty, but never a Fielding nor a Shakespeare. A Rothschild and a Mendoza, yes—but never a Kean nor a Belcher.[116]

There was, then, something somewhat disreputable about Jewish victories in the ring, an unfair application of inappropriate organs in

---

[114] Egan, *Boxiana*, i. 78, 243–4, 320–34; ii. 61, 86–90, 454–8, 481–2, 485–6; iii. 396–401, 488–90.   [115] [Southey], *Letters from England*, 451.

[116] George Borrow, *Lavengro: The Scholar—the Gypsy—the Priest* (London, 1851), i. 329–30.

what was meant to be a test of strength.[117] Whether Jewish success in the boxing ring gave them increased self-esteem, or perhaps made them more valued in the Christian community, is something that is rather hard to judge. Egan tells a number of stories of Jewish boxers protecting weaker Jews when under attack.[118] Francis Place noted that

About the year 1787 Daniel Mendoza, a Jew, became a celebrated boxer and set up a school to teach the art of boxing as a science, the art soon spread among the young Jews and they became generally expert at it. The consequence was in a very few years seen and felt too. It was no longer safe to insult a Jew unless he was an old man and alone . . . But even if the Jews were unable to defend themselves, the few who would [now] be disposed to insult them merely because they are Jews, would be in danger of chastisement from the passers-by and of punishment from the police.[119]

Just as with crime, the link between Jews and boxing was a well-known image in early Victorian London.

V

One solution for the plight of the Jewish poor which might reduce the steady slide into crime was charity and education. Existing parish institutions were not equipped to deal with the Jews, by and large, although Jews certainly had recourse to them and often were accepted, depending on the time and the place. In one well-known early nineteenth-century case, however, it was made explicit that Jews would be able to exploit Christian charity only as a privilege rather than as a right. The unclear legal position of Anglo-Jewry during this period can be seen quite clearly from the conduct of both the Jews and the courts in the Bedford Charity Case of 1818–19. A fund established in the reign of Edward VI had provided a number of important social benefits for the inhabitants of the town, most especially in that it supported a free school, provided dowries for poor girls, enabled children to compete by lottery to have their apprenticeship fees paid for, and granted a sum of money to those who finished their apprenticeship. Joseph Lyon, a Jewish inhabitant of Bedford who had been living in the town for twenty-one years, brought his 14-year-old daughter Sheba as appointed after Michaelmas 1816 to receive a lot for drawing in the competition for an apprenticeship fee. To his surprise, he was told that she could not compete, 'alleging as a reason for such refusal that the petitioner *Joseph*

---

[117] Egan, *Boxiana*, ii. 11; iii. 396–7.   [118] Ibid. ii. 87–90.

[119] BL Add. MS 27287, fos. 145–6: quoted in M. D. George, *London Life in the Eighteenth Century* (New York, 1964 [1925]), 132.

Lyon was of the Jewish persuasion'. To his mind, this was an odd excuse, as the children of co-religionist Michael Joseph had not only competed in the apprenticeship draw, but had won, and others had been given places in the free school and marriage portions in the past. The few Jews in the town decided to lay the entire matter before the courts, and, consulting the Great Synagogue, also won the support of Isaac Lyon Goldsmid, who in this matter, as in many others before and after, saw an important question of principle at stake. Enquiring of the Lord Mayor of Bedford, John Wing, Goldsmid had a reply on 5 January 1818,

informing him, that although the children of the petitioner *Michael Joseph* had been allowed the benefit of the charity without objection, yet the trustees finding the number of Jews increasing in *Bedford*, entertained considerable doubts whether such persons were objects of the charity, and that they had been advised to refuse, and had refused, to admit Jews to participate in the benefit of the charity, leaving it to the persons so refused, if they should think proper, to bring the matter before the Lord Chancellor.

Considering that there were only four or five Jewish families in Bedford, such a claim was ludicrous.

The Great Synagogue and the New Synagogue were willing to fight the case and shoulder the legal expenses; the Hambro and Bevis Marks refused to get involved, saying that it was the province of the Board of Deputies to deal with such matters. Sir Samuel Romilly was engaged as their lawyer, and the case eventually came up to the Court of Chancery, under Lord Chancellor Eldon. The Solicitor-General argued against the Jews' petition, and it was quite clear from the outset that it was bound to raise issues that were better left undecided. He put the point that Jews may be allowed to live in England at this time, but 'though born in this country, yet professing Judaism, the law distinguished them as alien enemies'. Furthermore, if the founder's intentions were to be any guide, it was inconceivable, 'nor can it be supposed that *Edward* the Sixth, a most religious monarch, designed to found an establishment for the support of infidels, by letters patent'. Allowing Jews to benefit from the Bedford charity would be indirectly to encourage a particular mode of faith, and an undesirable one at that. Sir Samuel Romilly, speaking for the Jews, noted sarcastically that Edward VI had also founded a hospital: should Jews be excluded from being patients as well? and what about Quakers? Summing up, Romilly argued that 'On their re-admission to this country, after the virtual repeal of the flagrant act of injustice which had banished them, the Jews were restored to the privileges of other subjects, and became entitled to the benefit of all institutions not confined to members of the established church.' Making his decision, Lord Chancellor Eldon effectively rejected Romilly's major argument about Jewish equality before the law, and ruled against the ability of Jews to enjoy the Bedford charity. His understanding of the case made the entire issue not only unfortunate for the specific Jews concerned, but created a potentially ruinous legal precedent. 'I apprehend', he wrote, 'that it is the duty of every judge presiding in an *English* Court of Justice, when he is told that there is no difference between worshipping the Supreme Being in chapel, church, or synagogue, to recollect that Christianity is part of the law of England.' With that, Lord Chancellor Eldon excluded the Jews from a wide variety of privileges, if only others took their own grievances to court.[120]

Perhaps one reason why the Spanish and Portuguese Synagogue, the parent congregation of Anglo-Jewry, had declined to participate in this legal venture was that they perceived that defeat would raise more questions than could justify rectifying the injustice against a handful of Jews in a provincial town. Certainly the Bedford Charity Case was remembered and in some sense left a good number of issues unresolved. It was not until 1874 that Jews were formally allowed to enjoy the benefits of the charity, due to the campaign led by Moses (Morris) Lissack, a Hebrew teacher and jewel dealer in the town. Lissack was originally from Posen, and after coming to England in 1835 took on a number of issues, especially the status of Jewish converts to Christianity. By the time he won his victory, the question of dowries and apprentices' fees had largely become academic, as there seem to have been few other Jews in Bedford, but the point of principle was won, nearly twenty years after Emancipation.[121]

Even before the Bedford Charity Case had come to life, the Jews of London had taken certain steps to try and alleviate both the lot of the poor and to avoid having the mistakes of one generation pass over into the next. Clearly the key point was education, both as a value in itself and as a means of training young Jewish men and women for trade. Before the end of the eighteenth century the only provision whatsoever for education in the Anglo-Jewish community was the old Talmud Torah of the Ashkenazi Great Synagogue established in 1732, which in any case was no more than an elementary school on a very low level, and not open to Sephardim. A number of small charities for clothing

[120] Clement Tudway Swanston, *Reports of Cases Argued and Determined in the High Court of Chancery, during the Time of Lord Chancellor Eldon* (London, 1821–7), ii. 470–532. Cf. Picciotto, *Sketches*, 281, 474; Endelman, *Georgian England*, 112. Sir Samuel Romilly, the famous law reformer, was also in favour of Roman Catholic emancipation. He committed suicide on 2 Nov. 1818, four days after the death of his wife: *DNB*.

[121] M. Lissack, *Jewish Perseverance; or, The Jew, at Home and Abroad: An Autobiography* (London, 1851), 117–22. Lissack (p. 122) refers to 'my brother Jews at Bedford'. See also Endelman, *Radical Assimilation*, 151–2; and Picciotto, *Sketches*, 474.

orphans and apprenticing poor boys did exist, but their activity was minimal.[122] In 1788, partly as a result of the initiative of Dr Joseph Hart Myers, a plan was made to reorganize completely the Ashkenazi Talmud Torah and make it more like an English school. The men behind the plan included such distinguished figures as Abraham and George Goldsmid, the three Goldsmid brothers-in-law Daniel Eliason, Nathan Solomons, and Lyon de Symons, and the other worthies E. I. Keyser, E. P. Salomons, Levy Barent Cohen, and Samson Gompertz. The new school was designed to teach secular subjects, and the specifically Jewish part of the curriculum was drastically reduced. Six months after their bar mitzvah at age 13, the boys were sent as apprentices to masters of respectable character, mostly in the fields of tailoring, glass-cutting, watch-finishing, and pencil-making. The school met in a few rooms at Ebenezer Square, Houndsditch, between Stoney Lane and Gravel Lane, in a group of houses that would soon shelter other Jewish educational institutions.[123]

The entire enterprise was conducted on an absolutely minute scale, however, and had a minimal effect on the problem of poverty. In 1793 only eighteen boys were in attendance, and ten years later the number had increased to only twenty-one pupils. Still, it was a beginning, and from 1795 the two Goldsmids saw the Talmud Torah as the core of a major poor-relief plan which would include a school, a hospital, and an old-age home. They began collecting funds from both Jews and Christians: by 1797 they had raised £20,000; by 1806 they had £22,000, invested in imperial annuities of 3 per cent. In the end they had an endowment which yielded £900 per annum, administered by trustees. The new institution was called Jews' Hospital, 'Naveh Tzedek', and was officially launched on 17 February 1806. The governor was to be Asher Goldsmid, with his wealthy brother Abraham Goldsmid as patron.

---

[122] S. Stein, 'Some Ashkenazi Charities in London at the End of the Eighteenth and the Beginning of the Nineteenth Centuries', *TJHSE* 20 (1964), 63–81. Cf. the regulations of a society for assisting widows and orphans, London, Dec. 1788: University College, London, Mocatta Library, Mocatta Cupboard, Mocatta BA 27; and another discussed ibid. for infant orphans, 1795.

[123] On the revitalized Talmud Torah, see (in English!) *Rules Framed for the Management of the Orphan Charity School ... Belonging to the German Jews* (London, 1788): only copy in library of Jews' College, London; Stein, 'Charities', 68–71; Roth, *Great Synagogue*, 227–9; Endelman, *Georgian England*, 229–31. See also A. Cohen, 'Levi Barent Cohen and Some of his Descendants', *TJHSE* 16 (1952), 11–23; C. Roth, 'Educational Abuses and Reforms in Hanoverian England', in M. Davis (ed.), *Mordecai M. Kaplan Jubilee Volume* (New York, 1953), 469–80. The minute book of the Talmud Torah for the period 1791–1818 survives (250 foolscap pp.): cf. S. S. Levin, 'The Origins of the Jews' Free School', *TJHSE* 19 (1959), 97–114.

Freehold land was purchased on the Mile End Road for £2,300, and a further £2,000 was used to buy the adjoining land so that the hospital could expand when the term of the sitting tenant expired. Finally, on 28 June 1807 the house was opened for five old men, five old women, ten boys, and eight girls. Dr Myers offered to serve as physician without pay, and Joshua van Oven volunteered to be the surgeon.[124]

Standards for admission to a place in Jews' Hospital were quite exacting. Boys might be admitted as early as age 10, but they left after their bar mitzvah to be apprenticed. Girls came in between the ages of 7 and 10 and stayed until they were 15 years old, when 'they direct proper measures for finding a situation to place her in, either as a servant in a good family for a certain time, or to some employment'. The hospital was meant to serve the respectable and deserving Ashkenazi poor of London, so it was laid down that in order to be considered for a place, a child must have parents who had lived in London for at least ten years, and belonged to one of the three Ashkenazi synagogues. 'Those are preferred who shall prove that they have been reduced in life, from a respectable situation', it was ruled. In order to begin studying, boys were required to be already able to read the Hebrew prayers 'and those are preferred who add thereto a knowledge of English reading'. The old folk needed to be at least 55 years of age and widowed or unmarried. Highmore, the chronicler of London's charities, noted with admiration that the Jews' Hospital combines 'a code of such rules which are seldom found in houses of charity; and which, if they are punctually observed here, are well calculated to render this one of the best governed of any house of charity in the metropolis'.[125]

In many ways, Jews' Hospital was more a symbol than a solution. By 1821 the 'inmates', as they were called, had increased to only forty-seven boys and twenty-nine girls. Even by 1844 only 135 boys had been

---

[124] A. Highmore, *Pietas Londinensis: The History, Design, and Present State of the Various Public Charities in and near London* (London, 1810), 87–9; Endelman, *Georgian England*, 231.

[125] Highmore, *Pietas Londinensis*, 90–5. Cf. *Rules and Regulations for the Management of the Jews' Hospital, Mile End, called Neveh Tsedek* (London, 1808); 'A Daughter of Israel', *The Jewish Preceptress; or, Elementary Lessons Written Chiefly for the Use of the Female Children Educated at the Jews' Hospital* (London, 1818), with forewords by I. L. Goldsmid and I. I. Bing; Henry Faudel, *A Brief Investigation into the System of the Jews' Hospital* (London, 1844). See also Jews' Hospital, Governors' Reports of Visits (1811–63), General Committee Minute Book (1819–22, 1822–7), and Lady Visitors' Book (1811–61): Mocatta Library, University College, London, Anglo-Jewish Archives: Norwood Homes for Jewish Children Collection. Stein, 'Charities', 71, suggests where these indigent boys might have learned to say Hebrew prayers in order to qualify for admission.

apprenticed, mostly having learned to make shoes and mahogany chairs, and eighty-eight girls had been placed in domestic service.[126] Yet the Hospital's annual dinner at the City of London tavern was a great attraction, bringing together almost 400 subscribers, both Jews and Christians, for the support of the institution. One contemporary chronicler of London life noted that

It is to be observed that the Christian subscribers to this hospital differ very widely in opinion from those persons who enter into subscriptions for supporting sermons and lectures for the conversion of the Jews. The former are those, who, without wishing to impose any conditions upon the Jew as to his belief, and without the least interference with his religious opinions, wish to relieve him merely as a man and a brother.[127]

The philo-Semitic duke of Sussex became a patron of the Hospital, whose building was described as being a structure 'remarkably plain, but capacious, and well calculated by its internal arrangement for the purpose to which it is applied'.[128]

While great strides had been made, at least in providing a basis for further educational and charitable work, it was clear that much more had to be done. From about 1811, Joshua van Oven began discussing the idea of founding a school for the poor based on the so-called Lancastrian system, whereby a single master would instruct senior students who would in turn teach younger pupils. The result of this deliberation was the Jews' Free School, which opened on Ebenezer Square, Stoney Lane next to the Jews' Hospital in 1817 with about 200 boys, and expanded even further when girls were admitted as well the following year. According to Highmore, about half of the initial intake had no knowledge even of the Hebrew alphabet (and thus were ineligible for study at the Jews' Hospital). By 1822 about 150 boys had finished their studies, and there were then 262 boys enrolled in the school, studying Hebrew and secular subjects, and preparing themselves for apprenticeship. 'From experience in this method,' Highmore wrote, 'any boy of moderate capacity may be enabled to read both Hebrew and

---

[126] A. Highmore, *Philanthropia Metropolitana: A View of the Charitable Institutions Established in and near London, Chiefly during the Last Twelve Years* (London, 1822), 276–80.

[127] Edward Brayley, Joseph Nightingale, *et al.*, *London and Middlesex; or, An Historical, Commercial, & Descriptive Survey of the Metropolis of Great-Britain* (London, 1810–16), iii. 121.

[128] C. F. Partington, *National History and Views of London and its Environs* (London, 1834), ii. 153, with an engraving of Jews' Hospital (*c.*2″ × 2″), ii. 17 of plates; Highmore, *Philanthropia*, 277–8; Picciotto, *Sketches*, 277: Picciotto says that Sussex became a patron in 1813 when asked by van Oven.

English, write tolerably well, and know the first rules of Arithmetic in about 18 or 20 months.' A new building was inaugurated in 1822 in Bell Lane, Spitalfields, for 500–600 boys and 300 girls. The benefactions amounted to over £4,000, with substantial contributions from the Great Synagogue and from the Rothschild family. In fact, when N. M. Rothschild died in 1836, a special delegation of children from the Jews' Free School took part in the funeral procession. In recognition of the first reformers of Jewish education in the 1780s, there remained a special section of the Jews' Free School named after the Talmud Torah and including twenty-odd of the best pupils.[129]

None of these solutions, however, served the Sephardi community, which had to go it alone. Naturally enough, in terms of antiquity, their institution had pride of place; in 1664–5 had been founded the *Hebra de Bikur Holim e Guemilut Hasadim*, their first charitable institution, intended to serve the poor. Unfortunately, although it was active for several years, and seems to have been refounded several times, it soon collapsed, and despite sporadic protests and revivals, little was done until the *Beth Holim*, the Sephardi Jews' hospital, was founded in 1747. At a meeting on 18 October 1747 three doctors offered their services free of charge, Dr Jacob de Castro Sarmento, Dr Philip de la Cour (alias Abraham Gomes Ergas), and Dr Joseph Vaz de Silva, later joined by the surgeon Jacob de Castro. Although there was initial opposition for some reason to the hospital, by the following summer they opened their doors on Leman Street, Goodman's Fields, and managed to struggle on despite numerous quarrels and personal disputes. For many years it was the only hospital in England where the Jewish dietary laws were observed, apart from the London Hospital, founded in 1740, which had many Jewish patients due to its location. In 1756 Jewish patients in the London Hospital were allowed 2½ pence in lieu of meat and broth. Ashkenazi patients were admitted to the Sephardi *Beth Holim* on payment of fees from 1790, and two years later it moved out to Mile End. During a good part of this period, the physician there was the Italian-Jewish poet-doctor Ephraim Luzzatto, who came to London in 1763 and remained there until he left for Italy in 1792, dying *en route* in

---

[129] Highmore, *Philanthropia*, 269–75; Roth, *Great Synagogue*, 229; Picciotto, *Sketches*, 339; Endelman, *Georgian England*, 243–4. Generally, see Levin, 'Free School', and the Minute Books of the Jews' Free School, 28 May 1818–23 June 1831: Woburn House, London: London Board of Jewish Religious Education. The Jews' Free School also ran a nursery, the Jews' Infant School, which had 200 children in 1850: Lipman, *Social History of the Jews in England 1850–1950*, 46–8; S. Singer, 'Jewish Education in the Mid-nineteenth Century: A Study of the Early Victorian London Community', *JQR* 77 (1986–7), 163–78, esp. 164.

Lausanne.[130] By the nineteenth century, however, it had long been an old-age home alone.[131]

Of course, it was no secret that one of the chief reasons for this increased Jewish charitable activity was the very aggressive efforts by the Christian missionaries in this area. The London Missionary Society opened a free school for Jewish girls and boys in January 1807 which served a dozen children throughout the first year. Rabbi Solomon Hirschell delivered a sermon on 10 January 1807 warning Jews against sending their children there, and distributed an abstract of his talk in Yiddish and English for those who had missed it. Indeed, he ruled,

the whole purpose of this seeming kind exertion, is but an inviting snare, a decoying experiment to undermine the props of our religion: and the sole intent of this Institution is, at bottom, only to entice innocent Jewish Children, during their early and unsuspecting years, from the observance of the Law of Moses; and to eradicate the religion of their fathers and forefathers.[132]

The opening of the Jews' Hospital in June 1807 was thus much more than a coincidence. The London Society for Promoting Christianity amongst the Jews likewise continued the work in later years, admitting over 200 pupils by 1814. This important missionary organization was founded in 1809 and was represented for seven years by Joseph Frey, a Jewish convert to Christianity.[133] Other conversionist charity institutions included the National School Society charity schools of the Established Church, the Episcopal Jews' Chapel (1813), and the school at Palestine

---

[130] R. N. Salaman, 'Ephraim Luzzatto (1729–1792)', *TJHSE* 9 (1922), 85–102.

[131] For a photograph of the page of the minutes of 1747 when the elders appointed a committee to report on the possibility of founding a hospital, see *Bevis Marks Records*, i, ed. L. D. Barnett (Oxford, 1940), pl. xiii; and cf. p. 49. See also Hyamson, *Sephardim*, 39, 59, 83–4, 226, 302, 326; Picciotto, *Sketches*, 478; E. W. Morris, *A History of the London Hospital* (London, 1910), 126–35; L. D. Barnett, 'The First Record of the Hebra Guemilut Hasadim, London, 1678', *TJHSE* 10 (1924), 258–60.

[132] *Abstract of an Exhortation Delivered by the Rev. Solomon Hirschel* (London, 1807): see plate section here.

[133] Generally, see W. T. Gidney, *History of the London Society for Promoting Christianity amongst the Jews* (London, 1908); and S. Kochav, 'Britain and the Holy Land: Prophecy, the Evangelical Movement, and the Conversion and Restoration of the Jews, 1790–1845' (Oxford University D.Phil. thesis, 1989), which supersedes both R. M. Smith, 'The London Jews' Society and Patterns of Jewish Conversion in England, 1801–1859', *JSS* 43 (1981), 275–90; and H. W. Meirovich, 'Ashkenazic Reactions to the Conversionists, 1800–1850', *TJHSE* 26 (1979), 6–25. The Unitarians also tried their luck with the Jews. Richard Wright, one of their chief evangelists, boasted in 1815 that among his audience of 500 in the market square at Falmouth were 'two Jews, who are said to be men of considerable learning, especially one of them, who is from Morocco, and was in a Moorish dress': *Monthly Repository*, 119/10 (1815), 719.

Place, Bethnal Green. The British and Foreign School Society, a voluntary organization supported by Dissenters and evangelicals, ran a school in Ebenezer Square, Houndsditch, from 1817 which included some Jewish children. Clearly the Jews faced stiff competition from Christian charitable organizations which directed their efforts particularly at them.[134]

VI

At the same time that the Jews of London were attempting to improve their own education, the Gentiles of England with Hebraic leanings also hoped to enhance their opportunities for obtaining Jewish knowledge. Obviously the initial key was the purchase of Hebrew books and manuscripts. An important public source of such works already existed at the British Museum, which opened its collection to the public in 1759 at Montagu House. Parliament had six years earlier purchased the library of Sir Hans Sloane, and this formed the basis of the Museum's books and manuscripts. Only one Hebrew book was to be found there, a Talmud which had once belonged to George II. In order to rectify this deficiency from the very beginning, the British Museum was presented at its opening with a large collection of Hebrew books and manuscripts by Solomon da Costa, a Sephardi Jew from Holland who had been living in England for more than fifty years. Da Costa accompanied his gift with a letter in Hebrew complete with English translation, in which he explained, in lofty biblical tones, that, in addition to the valuable Hebrew manuscripts he was donating,

I have added to them 180 Volumes of printed Books, old Editions, which were collected, and richly bound, by Order of Charles the Second, late King of England, &c. and are marked with his Cypher, all in the Hebrew Language; which I purchased *in the Days of my Youth*; the Particulars whereof, *Behold they are written in the Book*, or Catalogue, that accompanieth this letter. *And I said unto myself*, let these be likewise deposited in the said Museum, *that they may stand as a Witness for me*, that I have the Love of this Nation always present in my Mind, and that I am not ungrateful *for the Favours I have received.*

---

[134] Thomas Witherby, *A Vindication of the Jews* (London, 1809), 101–4; Endelman, *Georgian England*, 241–7; Roth, *Great Synagogue*, 227. See the interesting list of Jewish charities in E. H. Lindo, *A Jewish Calendar* (London, 1838), 101–4. Cf. Thomas Witherby, *An Attempt to Remove Prejudices Concerning the Jewish Nation* (London, 1804). Slightly outside the Jewish centre, there was also the Western [Synagogue] Jews' Free School, with 115 pupils in 1850; and the West Metropolitan Jewish School of the Reform Movement with 279 children in 1853: Singer, 'Education', 164; C. Cassell, 'The West Metropolitan Jewish School 1845–97', *TJHSE* 19 (1960), 115–28.

So spoke Solomon da Costa, the self-described 'Minor of Minors'.[135]

According to Thomas Hollis, the radical editor and a friend of da Costa's, the collection of books was made during the Interregnum and became royal property after the Restoration. For some reason, possibly due to lack of interest, the books were sold and eventually bought by Solomon da Costa from a private bookseller. Hollis claimed that Charles II had sent the books to be rebound and failed to collect them, whereupon the bookseller sold them himself for £80. In any case, the books are stamped with the royal crown and an indication of their belonging to King Charles. When Solomon da Costa donated them to the British Museum in 1759, he was presenting the nation with three Hebrew manuscripts and far more than 180 books, since many of the volumes were made up of more than one book, bound together. Of the sum total of 220 books, all are in Hebrew apart from a lone work in Spanish. Da Costa also provided two manuscript catalogues, one in Hebrew and the other in Hebrew, Latin, and English, all in his own hand. According to Hollis, da Costa had during the course of his life honestly amassed a fortune of £100,000, with considerable sums distributed as charity. Certainly da Costa's generosity at the British Museum was important, providing the basis for the formidable collection of Hebrew books and manuscripts there.[136]

The Bodleian Library in Oxford, meanwhile, made its own purchase of Hebrew books and manuscripts which raised it to the same sort of level as the British Museum in Hebrew studies. The opportunity presented itself in 1829 to acquire the collection of materials put together by David Oppenheimer (1664–1736), chief rabbi of Moravia, and afterwards of Bohemia. Paradoxically, when he took the post in Prague, he was forced to leave his treasure behind, fearing its confiscation, and left it for safe-keeping in his father-in-law's house at Hanover, paying the occasional visit, and augmenting the unseen library from time to time. When he died in 1736 it was inherited by his son Joseph, who in turn passed it on to his son-in-law Hirschel Isaac Oppenheimer, who was rabbi of Hildesheim, and who transferred the

[135] Solomon da Costa, 'My Translation from the Hebrew of a Letter I Wrote in that Language the 31st Day of May, 1759, to the Trustees of the British Museum' (London, 1759): broadsheet: copy in Mocatta Library, University College, London, Mocatta Cupboard. The original Hebrew letter has not been found. For other (variant) copies of the letter, see also *Gents. Mag.* 30 (1760), 51; Moses Margoliouth, *The History of the Jews in Great Britain* (London, 1851), ii. 101 ff.; Thomas Hollis, *Memoirs* (London, 1780), app., pp. 613–15; *Annual Register* (1760); *Jewish Intelligencer* (Apr. 1844), 106–8.

[136] Da Costa's three Hebrew MSS are now BL Add. MSS 4707–9. The two MS catalogues are bound together as Add. MSS 4710–11. See generally *Catalogue of the Hebrew Books in the Library of the British Museum*, ed. J. Zedner (London, 1867).

treasure to that city. The library passed through various hands throughout the eighteenth century, a number of partial catalogues were issued, and valuations solicited and obtained by the famous Moses Mendelssohn and the great Christian Hebraist J. D. Michaelis. The library was even unsuccessfully offered to Napoleon's Sanhedrin. The question of ownership had become incredibly complicated, but despite these obstacles, the library was eventually purchased by the Bodleian for slightly over £2,000. Some Hebrew scholars thought that Oxford was the least likely place for such a collection, and argued that it had found its grave there and would have been better off had Napoleon carried it away to Paris. Nevertheless, it formed the basis of Oxford's Hebrew collection, and Jewish studies there today would be nearly inconceivable without it.[137]

Another important source of Hebrew books was the notable philo-Semite and bibliophile Augustus Frederick, duke of Sussex (1773–1843). Prince Augustus was the sixth son of George III, and until 1804 spent most of his early life abroad, being educated at the university of Göttingen. He married the daughter of an earl in 1793 without permission, and, despite the fact that two children were produced, George III declared the marriage invalid. Raised to the peerage as the duke of Sussex in 1801, this black sheep satisfied all of his father's worst fears by supporting every possible progressive cause, including the abolition of the slave-trade, the abolition of the corn laws, parliamentary reform, and the removal of civil disabilities for Roman Catholics, Dissenters, and Jews. Probably an early factor in his famous philo-Semitism was his visit to Duke's Place synagogue on Friday night, 14 April 1809, along with the royal dukes of Cumberland and Cambridge. Their path from the carriage was strewn with flowers, and a special order of service printed on silk was produced. The event itself was probably inspired by an earlier visit of their uncle the duke of Gloucester, the king's brother, to Duke's Place on another Friday evening eight years before. In any case, the duke of Sussex went on to greater things, including the presidency of the Royal Society, where he ruled from 1830 until 1838, while at the same time building an impressive collection of Hebrew books in his quarters at Kensington Palace. Sussex was taught Hebrew by Solomon Lyon from Cambridge, and on the duke's death he left behind over 50,000 books, including

---

[137] A. Marx, 'Some Notes on the History of David Oppenheimer's Library', *Revue des études juives*, 82 (1926), 451–60, repr. in his *Studies in Jewish History and Booklore* (New York, 1944), 238–55, itself repr. Westmead, 1969; C. Roth, 'An Episode in the History of the Oppenheimer Collection', *Bodleian Library Record*, 5 (1956), 104–8. Of course, see the great *Catalogus librorum Hebraeorum in Bibliotheca Bodleiana* (Berlin, 1852–60).

1,000 editions of the Bible, and many Hebrew manuscripts. His second marriage to the widow of the earl of Arran did not produce children, and he was buried by his own wishes in a public cemetery at Kensal Green. According to the Anglo-Jewish press, the duke of Sussex 'intended to urge the necessity of a collegiate training for our ministry, at the approaching anniversary of the Jews' Hospital, but it pleased God to spare him to preside once more at that festival'.[138] In any case, when a short-lived venture for providing a Jewish cultural centre came to fruition in 1845, it was christened Sussex Hall in his honour.[139]

Solomon Lyon, the Hebrew tutor of the duke of Sussex, was himself the author of a Hebrew grammar which presumably he produced with an eye towards providing the written material to go with the teaching that he did at Cambridge.[140] Numerous other Hebrew grammars and dictionaries were produced in England during the early part of the nineteenth century, written by Jews and Gentiles, including converts from Judaism. Moses Marcus, formerly a Jew and now curate of Brigstock cum Stanion in Northamptonshire, published his grammar in 1825, noting that the 'Hebrew Language, which for years had formed no part of a liberal education, now attracts very general attention. The conversion of the Jews to the Christian faith, to which the public mind had been called, and a laudable desire of reading the Old Testament in its original tongue, have probably been the chief causes of this revival of BIBLICAL LEARNING'.[141] W. Heinemann also wrote an introduction to the Hebrew language, deploring the 'deficiency of elementary works for the Hebrew Language', which he used while continuing 'to attend Ladies and Gentlemen, in giving Private Lectures in the *Hebrew* and *German Languages*'.[142] James Crocker, under-master at Felsted School in Essex, produced a Hebrew grammar for his boys, thanking 'his worthy friend, Mr. Oppenheim, Teacher of Languages in Cambridge' for his

---

[138] Picciotto, *Sketches*, 259, 277, 472, 474; *DNB*, s.v. 'Augustus Frederick, Duke of Sussex (1773–1843)'; *Gents. Mag.* NS 19 (1843), 645–52; L. Gluck-Rosenthal, *A Biographical Memoir of the Duke of Sussex* (London, 1846); *Bibliotheca Sussexiana: A Descriptive Catalogue*, ed. T. J. Pettigrew (London, 1827–39). A letter by Abraham Goldsmid describing the visit of the royal dukes was hanging on the wall of the committee room of the Great Synagogue 100 years later, but went missing before 1930: *Archives of the United Synagogue*, ed. C. Roth (London, 1930), 12.

[139] It survived until 1859: see A. Barnett, 'Sussex Hall: The First Anglo-Jewish Venture in Popular Education', *TJHSE* 19 (1960), 65–79.

[140] Solomon Lyon, *A Theological Hebrew Grammar and Lexicon* (Liverpool, 5575 [1815]).

[141] Moses Marcus, *A Grammar of the Hebrew Language, with Points* (London, 1825), p. v. Cf. 237–40 for the list of subscribers, including the dukes of York and Gloucester, the archbishop of York, the primate of Ireland, and many other nobles and high clergy, as well as Alexander Nicoll, the Regius professor of Hebrew at Oxford.

[142] W. Heinemann, *An Introduction to the Hebrew Language* (London, 1823), pp. v, vii.

advice.[143] George Offor, jun., one of these Hebrew grammaticians, complained about 'the exorbitant charge made for Hebrew elementary works, as if those who wrote on this subject were influenced by Jewish principles', and presented the inexpensive price of his book as being a chief reason for its production.[144]

From the 1820s Christian students of Hebrew had the advantage of having an English translation of Gesenius's celebrated Hebrew lexicon to the Old Testament. Christopher Leo, the translator of the work, taught Hebrew and German at both Cambridge and Sandhurst, and testified that this was 'a period when the utmost regard and attention are bestowed on the Hebrew Language by this nation, and the learned works of those celebrated men, Lightfoot, Castellus, Poole, and Lowth, are so eagerly sought after; when the desire of reading the Bible in the original tongue begins to increase'. It was not an easy task to acquire the Hebrew language, he warned:

To obtain a perfect knowledge of these characters and signs, so as to read a Hebrew book with facility and pleasure, is the result of no small application and perseverance. Indeed a fluency of reading is not to be obtained by the Orientals themselves without much labour; and no nations acquire it more slowly than the Hebrews and Arabs, although, to these, who learn it at a very early age, the difficulty is in a great degree lessened. To be convinced of the truth of this assertion, we need only attend the Jewish schools in this or any other country: and if such is the case with the Hebrews themselves, who learn from their very infancy a language, which they consider vernacular, the difficulty of acquiring it at a maturer age must increase.

Leo's greatest regret, he said, was that at least a reading knowledge of Hebrew was not yet considered a necessary part of study in the English grammar schools.[145]

Another interesting attempt to improve the teaching of Hebrew in the schools came in the form of a Hebrew and English dictionary produced by Abigail Lindo, the third daughter of David Abarbanel Lindo, a contentious and strictly orthodox member of the Sephardi community. This long work, published in 1846 and dedicated to Moses Montefiore and expressing thanks to David Meldola, the head of the Sephardi community, was especially interesting in her invention of new Hebrew

---

[143] James Crocker, *Essentials of Hebrew Grammar, Arranged Agreeably According to the Plan of Gesenius* (London, 1829).

[144] George Offor, jun., *An Easy Introduction to Reading the Hebrew Language* (London, 1814), pp. v–vi. Offor thanks 'my worthy friend Mr. Frey . . . for introducing me to a language which has afforded many delightful hours of profitable recreation'.

[145] D. Wilhelm Gesenius, *A Hebrew Lexicon to the Books of the Old Testament*, ed. and trans. Christopher Leo (Cambridge, 1825–8), 2nd numbering: i, iii.

words to express modern concepts and objects. She devised a word for steamship with a literal Hebrew meaning of 'the ship of vapour', and called a wheelbarrow 'a wagon with one wheel'. Instead of the single English word 'bankrupt', she proposed a Hebrew expression which translates literally as 'a man in debt has it not in his power to pay his debts', and, even if the modern Hebrew uses two words where English has one for the concept, her efforts must not be seen as entirely successful.[146] Nevertheless, it was a valiant attempt, and a rather rare accomplishment for an Anglo-Jewish lady, and was praised as such in at least one Anglo-Jewish review.[147] Meldola himself composed a verse obituary on her premature death, which he published in pamphlet form.[148]

From about 1830 until his death in 1857 the most prominent Hebrew teacher at Cambridge was Herman Hedwig Bernard (1785–1857). Born in the Ukraine as Hirsch Baer Hurwitz, this son of a wealthy timber merchant in Uman received a European education, and was sent to Leipzig frequently on business and thereby came into contact with the more progressive Jewish elements that made up the German *haskalah* movement. Hurwitz, as he was then, became convinced that the Jews should concentrate on the original biblical message and reject the Talmud as superstitious, possibly with the help of the secular state which could force the Jews to modernize. Towards this end, Hurwitz founded a school at Uman which would put his ideas into practice, but when it went bankrupt, he was forced to decamp to England in 1825. He originally settled in Lincoln, but by 1830 had established himself in Cambridge as a tutor of Hebrew, arriving there with a new name and a new Anglican religious identity. Bernard rapidly became a sought-after figure there, and was engaged by six Cambridge worthies to teach them Maimonides, a group which included the Regius professor of Hebrew and the professor of Arabic. From 1837 he had an official stipend of £30 per annum from the University as a preceptor in the Hebrew language. Hurwitz kept his Jewish past under wraps, if not entirely hidden, claiming that his father had been an Austrian Jew who had converted before his birth. Even his daughter now argued that her father had been brought up a Christian.[149] In any case, Bernard published a series of

---

[146] Abigail Lindo, *A Hebrew and English and English and Hebrew Dictionary with Roots and Abbreviations* (London, 1846), printed by Samuel Meldola, although, according to the title-page, 'not published'.

[147] Review in the Anglo-Jewish periodical of Liverpool, *Kos Yeshuoth*, 1 (1846–7), 185–8.

[148] D. Meldola, *Epitaph to the Memory of the Much Lamented Abigail* (n.p., 1848).

[149] Generally on Bernard, see the 'Life of Dr. Bernard', including his portrait, in Herman Hedwig Bernard, *The Book of Job*, ed. Frank Chance (2nd edn., London, 1884),

books which he used in his teaching, including editions and translations of the Book of Job and Maimonides's *Yad Hazakah*, and a guide for the student of Hebrew, based on the methods and texts used in Germany. Bernard died on 15 November 1857, after a very prominent Cambridge career.[150]

Another great Cambridge Hebrew scholar was Joseph Crooll (1760–1829), who was born in Hungary and emigrated to England sometime at the end of the eighteenth century. Crooll's first posts were in Manchester[151] and Nottingham, but by 1808 he was firmly entrenched in Cambridge as a Hebrew teacher. Unlike Bernard, Crooll remained a steadfastly orthodox Jew. According to a begging letter that he sent to the Revd J. W. Whittaker in March 1828, it was not always an easy life. 'It is now past twenty years since I am Hebrew Teacher in this University,' he complained, 'during that period I always obtained a living, but could never save any thing, but since the year 1826 the times are changed, for the Vice chancellor has given permission to converted Jews to teach the Hebrew.'[152] Perhaps he was already worried about competition from Bernard, but in any case he was obliged to ask Whittaker for some money to tide him over, and Crooll may have been lucky here, since, according to Christopher Leo, 'The Rev. J. W. Whittaker has several times, in the course of conversation, introduced the name of Mr. Crool as a profound Hebrew scholar.'[153] Other contemporaries at Cambridge were not so full of praise. Crooll was thought to be an eccentric, perhaps because he wore a parchment girdle

pp. lxxxix–ciii; *Gents. Mag.* 102 (1832), ii. 52–6; *DNB*; Endelman, *Radical Assimilation*, 49–50; I. Zinberg, *A History of Jewish Literature* (New York, 1978), xi. 18–20; S. Levy, 'English Students of Maimonides', *MJHSE* 4 (1942), 75–6. The article in the *DNB* does not mention his Jewish background.

[150] Apart from the Book of Job cited above, Bernard's other books were: *The Main Principles* (Cambridge, 1832); *The Guide of the Hebrew Student* (London, 1839); [with P. H. Mason, his student], *Gently Flowing Waters: An Easy, Practical Hebrew Grammar* (Cambridge, 1853); and *Cambridge Free Thoughts and Letters on Bibliolatry: Translated from the German of G. E. Lessing*, ed. Isaac Bernard (London, 1862). Isaac Bernard described himself as 'Commander, P. and O. Company's Service'.

[151] See the *Service Performed in the Synagogue of the Jews, Manchester . . . Delivered in Hebrew, by Rabbi Joseph Crool; and Translated by him, into English* (Manchester, 1803): sermon of 19 Oct. 1803: cited in Roth, *Magna Bibliotheca* 315. Generally on Crooll, see Endelman, *Georgian England*, 280; M. C. N. Salbstein, *The Emancipation of the Jews in Britain: The Question of the Admission of the Jews to Parliament, 1828–1860* (London, 1982), 59, 72, 78–85; I. Finestein, 'Anglo-Jewish Opinion during the Struggle for Emancipation', *TJHSE* 20 (1964), 116–17. On the beginnings of the Jewish community there, see Williams, *The Making of Manchester Jewry*.

[152] Joseph Crooll to Revd J. W. Whittaker, 24 Mar. 1828: Jewish Museum, London, MS 4 (1).

[153] Gesenius, *Hebrew Lexicon*, ed. Christopher Leo, p. iv (2nd numbering).

on which were inscribed passages from the Torah and the Talmud. While it was customary for university lecturers to give twenty lectures each year, Crooll never gave any lectures at all, nor did he offer to do so.[154]

Joseph Crooll is himself a very interesting figure who transcends his role as a Hebrew teacher in Cambridge, for he was the author of a number of millenarian works which were used by Gentile opponents of Jewish emancipation. His first such book on the restoration of Israel was published in 1812 and combines traditional Protestant scholarship with Jewish needs. Like the millenarians in the seventeenth century, Crooll thought that there was a special significance in the fact that Adam and Noah were separated by 1,656 years. Unlike those who therefore set the year 1656 as a possible date for the Second Coming, Crooll thought that 1840 would be a more likely candidate, since it would correspond to the Hebrew year 5600. 'By a particular calculation of my own,' he revealed, 'it appears to me that the following ten years will produce strange things in the world, and it further appears that all things will be accomplished by the year 5600 [1840] of the creation of the world.' Crooll was not alone among Jewish thinkers of the time in settling on 1840, but his work was in English and published in London or Cambridge and therefore was of more immediate significance. In another book on the fifth monarchy, Crooll identified the first four as Babylon, Persia-Media, Alexander the Great, and Rome, in an analysis once again more suited to earlier centuries. Finally, in 1829 Crooll argued for the separation of the Jews in a divinely ordained state until their miraculous restoration to the Holy Land, at which time

on the day of the restoration of the Jews to their own land, every one of them will be gathered in all four quarters of the world;—at that time the converted Jew will not be able to defend himself in saying I am a converted Jew now, I will not go with the Jews, but God will not look to what he will profess at that time, but as being born under the covenant of the law,—a Jew he was born, and a Jew he must be again,—for the very land wherein the converted Jew will be at that time, will afford him no shelter, but will cast him out, and he will wander like a Cain, from place to place, until he will join the rest of the Jews.

This was the reason that Crooll opposed emancipation so vigorously, in that it would lead to the assimilation of the Jews and the loss of their identity, so crucial for the fulfilment of their historical role. That being said, Crooll predicted that those European nations which treated the

---

[154] From Crooll's obituary in the *Jewish Chronicle*, 30 June 1848, 590, based on a letter from the Revd F. R. Hall published in the *Cambridge Independent Press*, 11 June 1848: quoted in Salbstein, *Emancipation*, 78.

Jews badly would be forced to pay for their crime at the End of Days.[155]

Crooll's stand on these matters made him the darling of the anti-emancipationists, especially Sir Robert Inglis, who in 1833 triumphantly quoted in the House of Commons a letter Crooll had actually sent to him, proclaiming that 'whether the Jews spend two days or two months or twenty years in a country, they are equally strangers and sojourners, they must look to another home and another country'. 'Birth does not make a Jew an Englishman,' Inglis announced, and had Crooll to back him up.[156] Samuel Wilberforce, the bishop of Oxford, also used Crooll's writings in a speech in the House of Lords in 1848.[157] Francis Henry Goldsmid, Isaac Lyon's son, published a number of pamphlets in which he hoped to combat Crooll's detrimental influence, but the damage had already been done.[158] Joseph Wolff, the flamboyant convert missionary to the Jews, argued that Crooll was writing against Christianity itself, and thought it surprising that he was answered 'with meekness and candour', but in anti-emancipationist circles the Cambridge rabbi was authority itself.[159]

A more famous Jewish convert to Christianity in the field of Hebrew studies was Moses Margoliouth (1820–81), a Polish Jew who began studying the New Testament in Liverpool in 1837 and converted to the Church of England the following year. He began preparing for ordination at Trinity College, Dublin, in 1840, and four years later was given a parish near Dublin, the second in a long list of church appointments. Margoliouth was a tireless missionary among the Jews, and even visited the Holy Land in 1847, writing an account of his

---

[155] See Joseph Crooll's works, *The Restoration of Israel* (London, 1812), with 2nd edn. in 1814 with answer by Thomas Scott; *The Fifth Empire* (London, 1829), esp. 4–8, 9–10, 47–8, 73–4, 74; *The Last Generation* (Cambridge, 17 July 1829), esp. 14–19, 22; *The Great Mystery Revealed* (1836): Jews' College, London, MS 49 [21 folio pp.]. For some contemporary Christian writings which express similar views, see William Craven, *The Jewish and Christian Dispensations* (3rd edn., Cambridge, 1813), 318–19, 346; Anon., *A Short Inquiry into the Import of the Prophecies Relative to the Restoration of Israel* (London, 1820), 4–6, 14; Anon., *Dialogues between a Pilgrim, Adam, Noah, & Simon Cleophas* (Manchester, 1816), 338.

[156] Speeches of Sir Robert Inglis in the House of Commons in Hansard, 3rd ser., viii. 50–1 (22 May 1833), xxxv (3 Aug. 1836), lvii (10 Mar. 1841), xcv (16 Dec. 1847), 1263–4.

[157] Speech of Wilberforce in the House of Lords, ibid., 3rd ser., xcviii (25 May 1848).

[158] D. W. Marks and A. Löwy, *Memoir of Sir Francis Henry Goldsmid* (2nd edn., London, 1882). For F. H. Goldsmid, see below, pp. 386, 388 n.

[159] Joseph Wolf[f], *Missionary Journal and Memoir*, rev. and ed. John Bayford (London, 1824), 266: I am grateful to Dr Sarah Kochav for this reference. For a millenarian poem in the same spirit, see *The Olive Branch; or, A Plea for Israel* (London, 1851).

travels. During the 1850s Margoliouth was a firm supporter of emancipation, and worked towards that end. Two of his nephews continued in the same field. George Margoliouth (1853–1952) was also a minister in the Church of England, and between 1891 and 1941 served as keeper of the Hebrew, Syriac, and Ethiopic manuscripts at the British Museum. David Samuel Margoliouth (1858–1940) became a Fellow of New College, Oxford, and was elected Laudian professor of Arabic in 1889, a post he held for nearly half a century.[160]

The pull of Jews, converts or otherwise, to Hebrew studies in early Victorian England is inherently understandable. What is interesting is to see the attitude that Christians had towards turning to this admittedly somewhat esoteric field of study.[161] In the eighteenth century a common view was that attributed to Moses Lowman, 'a thorough Master in Jewish Learning and Antiquities, which was indeed his favourite Study'. Lowman 'was fully persuaded there were perpetual Allusions in the Writings of the New Testament to the Rites, Facts, Sentiments and Forms of Expression that we find in the old, and that from hence very great Light might be thrown upon some of the principal Doctrines of Christianity'.[162] Gerald Fitz-Gerald, professor of Hebrew in the University of Dublin, mused that 'We feel a kind of instinctive reverence for the productions of antiquity, and for none more than the Hebrew, which clothes the Divine truths contained in it for the information of man, in the easiest and most familiar dress.' Like many before and since, Fitz-Gerald believed that 'the original and once universal language of mankind still exists in the unaltered and uncorrupted characters of our Biblical Hebrew'.[163] William Green, Fellow of Clare Hall, Cambridge, criticized those who complain about the dearth of Hebrew and Old Testament studies but do nothing about it. The fault is not with the Scriptures, he argued: 'If then we are desirous to have the Scriptures more generally read, we must make our Translation more intelligible.'[164]

---

[160] On Moses Margoliouth, see *DNB*, and his important works: *The History of the Jews in Great Britain* (London, 1851); *The Anglo-Hebrews: Their Past Wrongs, and Present Grievances* (London, 1856); and *Vestiges of the Historic Anglo-Hebrews in East Anglia* (London, 1870); and on David Samuel, see the article by Gilbert Murray in the *DNB*, *1931–1940*.

[161] See the interesting Hebrew literary pieces in I. Abrahams, 'Hebrew Loyalty under the First Four Georges', *TJHSE* 9 (1922), 103–30.

[162] Moses Lowman, *Three Tracts* (London, 1756), pp. iii–iv.

[163] Gerald Fitz-Gerald, *An Essay on the Originality and Permanency of the Biblical Hebrew* (Dublin, 1796), pp. xi–xii. See also D. S. Katz, 'The Language of Adam in Seventeenth-Century England', in H. Lloyd-Jones, V. Pearl, and B. Worden (eds.), *History & Imagination: Essays in Honour of H. R. Trevor-Roper* (London, 1981), 132–45.

[164] William Green, *The Song of Deborah, Reduced to Metre* (Cambridge, 1753), p. iii. Cf. his *A New Translation of the Prayer of Habakkuk* (Cambridge, 1755), esp. the preface.

Robert Young studied Hebrew with Alexander Meyrowitz in Edinburgh, and translated bits of Maimonides. The work, he wrote, 'was originally commenced simply as an amusement, for the sake of cultivating an acquaintance with Hebrew Literature, and with no intention of publication', but it soon took on an interest and a life of its own.[165] Sometimes the very arguments of the Jews seeped into the mental world of the Hebraists. Theodore Preston, a Fellow of Trinity College, Cambridge, in the 1840s, a former student of H. H. Bernard, explained that, although his work might at 'first sight . . . appear fanciful or chimerical; and the more so to some readers, because it is based on the most literal interpretation of the prophecies wherein the restoration of the Jews to the land of Palestine, and the eternity of the Divine favour to them as a nation, seems to be predicted', yet it was no more unreasonable than any other kind of theological speculation.[166] Even the Jews were taken up with this same argument, and during a debate in the vestry board of Bevis Marks Sephardi congregation, in which the Jewish texts were cited out of the translations of Christian writers, a number of members 'urged the necessity of being supplied with an English translation from persons of their own faith', whereupon David de Sola and Morris J. Raphall were called upon to translate the Mishnah into English.[167] Another work which was produced by the Jews themselves during this period was Moses Mocatta's translation of Isaac of Troki's classic 'Hizuk Emunah'. 'As we Israelites do not seek to impose our faith on others', explained Mocatta, 'the following work is intended exclusively for distribution among our Hebrew community.' To make the point even clearer, Mocatta noted on the title-page that the book was 'printed but not published'.[168]

Undoubtedly, much of the Christian interest in the Jews was conversionist in intent, but the Hebraic contact often produced very interesting results. Among these was a lithographically printed translation of the Book of Common Prayer into Hebrew, produced 'by Marianne Nevill in one Month for the use of the Christian Israelites in Smyrna' and published in 1829. Smyrna was at the time the second largest city in the Turkish Empire, and a report to the London Society in 1825 that a missionary there would have access to about 14,000 Jews

---

[165] Robert Young, *Book of the Precepts* (Edinburgh, n.d.), pp. ix–x.

[166] Theodore Preston, *The Hebrew Text, and a Latin Version of . . . Ecclesiastes* (London, 1845), pp. v–vi, ix.

[167] D. A. de Sola and M. J. Raphall, *Eighteen Treatises from the Mishna* (London, 1843), esp. p. iii. Cf. the periodical that Raphall published between Oct. 1834 and July 1836, *[Galed] Hebrew Review and Magazine of Rabbinical Literature*.

[168] Isaac of Troki, *[Hizuk Emunah] or Faith Strengthened* (London, 1851), iii.

prompted them to send a resident emissary who worked there between 1829 and 1838. Marianne Nevill of Dublin supplied this crucial Anglican text, careful to include a certificate

that during the time I was translating and transcribing this Prayer book for the use of the Christian Israelites that lest they should deem it an offence to use a book of prayer written by a Gentile, I abstained from eating any thing forbidden by the Law of Moses, nor did I use any Pens but new ones, that had not been used in any other writing.[169]

The text used by the industrious lady was the oldest translation of the Book of Common Prayer into Hebrew, a work which had been accomplished by Abraham Jacobs (1656–fl. 1725), a Polish Jew who settled in Dublin at the beginning of the eighteenth century, and was baptized in 1706. Jacobs's translation was apparently commissioned by William King, archbishop of Dublin, perhaps as an excuse for continuing to support him. The work was presented to the archbishop in 1717, and remained unpublished until Marianne Nevill supplied it to the Jews of Smyrna.[170] Also in 1817 the London Jews' Society completed the project of publishing a fresh translation of the New Testament into Hebrew, using only biblical words but translating the Old Testament quotations therein from the Greek. Further editions appeared in 1817, 1821, 1828, and later as well.

With Marianne Nevill we return almost full cycle to the earliest days of early modern Christian interest in the Jews during the Renaissance. Bible, Hebrew studies, converts—these were the issues which focused the attention of the Tudors no less than their early Victorian counterparts. The influx of Jewish immigrants after mid-century would change all that, and create a Jewish community significantly different from the one which prevailed before.

---

[169] Marianne Nevill, *The Book of Common Prayer* (Dublin, 25 Oct. 1829): the copy in the Bodleian Library [Heb. f. 45] itself had an interesting history, being from the library of George Margoliouth, who himself had obtained it from the books belonging to Moses Margoliouth. A book-plate on the endpaper also reveals it to have been once the possession of 'J. Wilson, Professor of Phrenology' in 1836. Cf. J. Bloch, 'An Early Hebrew Translation of the Book of Common Prayer', in A. Marx and H. Meyer (eds.), *Festschrift für Aron Freimann* (Berlin, 1935), 145–8.

[170] Abraham Jacobs, *Address to the Jews* (Dublin, 1716). There are three extant copies of Jacobs's MS: the original, with the archbishop's signature, is in the diocesan library of Cashel in County Tipperary; for the second (with faulty pointing) see *Catalogue of the Manuscripts in the Library of Trinity College, Dublin*, ed. T. K. Abbott (Dublin, 1900), 402: no. 1499; and the third has no vowels at all and seems to have been copied ten years later: Marsh's Library, Dublin, MS Z.4.4.1: L. Hyman, *The Jews of Ireland* (London, 1972), 27–9, 295.

EPILOGUE

IT is hardly surprising that people like Joseph Crool and Marianne Nevill seem today to be extraordinarily naïve and old-fashioned. What is interesting is that even in their own day they must have appeared to be rather eccentric theological dinosaurs who might have been more at home in Cromwell's England where devout Protestants followed the Mosaic law and the Quakers sent missionaries to Turkey to convert the Jews. Although conversionist and even millenarian attitudes to the Jews would remain potent religious forces, the reality of a Jewish people dwelling alone was becoming increasingly frayed at the edges. By the very end of our period, Jews were so successfully integrated into so many areas of English life that to speak of the autonomous history of Victorian Anglo-Jewry is meaningless unless we largely confine ourselves to the history of Anglo-Jewish institutions and businesses. Even the concentration of Jews in certain trades does not necessarily transform, say, the history of tailoring into a branch of Anglo-Jewish history. The demographic growth of the Anglo-Jewish community in the second half of the nineteenth century will give its history an entirely different orientation. We have already seen how a handful of Jews were influential in the making of the English Reformation and the Glorious Revolution. As representatives of an ancient biblical people whose Book had helped bring salvation to the Christian world, the Jews and their culture were far more important than their numbers would suggest. Their perceived abilities made even the Jewish presence in areas such as boxing or crime far more keenly felt than their absolute numbers would suggest. The middle of the nineteenth century, then, marked the end of the period, beginning with the Tudors, when it might be argued that the importance of the Jews greatly outweighed their actual numerical presence. Afterwards, it is possible to tell the story of Anglo-Jewry as more conventional social history.

It is therefore quite easy to understand how difficult it was for Jewish historians to avoid presenting the history of nineteenth-century Anglo-Jewry as anything else than a slow but steady progress to emancipation. The right to sit in Parliament was more than a symbol of assimilation; it was a legal and public recognition that in the most important of affairs the rights of Jews would not be less than those of native-born Englishmen. The crashing failure of the Jew Bill demonstrated that the path to the acquisition of further rights would probably be smoother if

Jews were to continue as they had done since the days of Cromwell, that is, to make progress of the sort that did not require noisy public confirmation. Jews had acquired numerous privileges in the seventeenth century, such as the right to trade as brokers, to testify in a court of law, to refuse to appear on a Sabbath, and so on, and this process continued even after the Jew Bill was repealed. A Jew was admitted as solicitor in 1770, and a little later a practising Jew was given an officer's commission in the king's army. Ironically, Parliament passed a statute in 1826 which abolished the need to take the Anglican sacrament before naturalization, thereby achieving the goal of the Jew Bill without any fuss at all.[1]

By that time the question of Jewish emancipation had already begun to be discussed in Parliament. The curious fact was that there was no actual law which forbade Jews to sit there. The case, rather, was that any Jew elected to a seat in Parliament would have to take the statutory three oaths, those of Allegiance, Supremacy, and a third one against the descendants of the Old Pretender, which concluded with the words 'on the true faith of a Christian'. Even the administration of these oaths on the New Testament was not critical, for this particular practice was not laid down by law. The oaths, however, were set by statute, and a further parliamentary statute would be required to change them. As early as 1820 the subject was raised in the House, and indeed, under the original terms of the repeal of the Test and Corporation Acts in 1828 (laws which restricted a number of civil positions to members of the Anglican Church), Jews would have been eligible to hold public office. At the eleventh hour, however, Edward Copleston the bishop of Llandaff, sitting in the House of Lords, managed to convince the others to insert the words 'on the true faith of a Christian' into the declaration to be required, thereby excluding the Jews and perhaps the Unitarians as well.[2] In a sense, the situation was now worse than before, since at least until 1828 the Jews could take solace in the fact that they were not being particularly excluded but shared the lot of all Nonconformists. Now, however, it was clear that they had been specifically discriminated against by a parliamentary statute. This situation was made even more

---

[1] Generally, on the Emancipation, see: A. Gilam, *The Emancipation of the Jews in England, 1830–1860* (New York, 1982); M. C. N. Salbstein, *The Emancipation of the Jews in Britain: The Question of the Admission of the Jews to Parliament, 1828–1860* (London, 1982); U. R. Q. Henriques, *Religious Toleration in England, 1787–1833* (London, 1961), 175–205; id., 'The Jewish Emancipation Controversy in Nineteenth-Century Britain', *Past & Present*, 40 (1968), 126–46; P. Pinsker, 'English Opinion and Jewish Emancipation (1830–1860)', *JSS* 14 (1952), 51–94; I. Finestein, 'Anglo-Jewish Opinion during the Struggle for Emancipation', *TJHSE* 20 (1964), 113–43; H. S. Q. Henriques, *The Jews and the English Law* (Oxford, 1908), 200–20, 248–305.

[2] He did, however, support the admission of Dissenters to the universities: *DNB*.

irksome when the Roman Catholics were emancipated in April 1829, a concession which was far more problematic in many ways, being tied in with traditional English fears and prejudices of a political and practical nature.

Among those prominent Anglo-Jews who felt particularly humiliated by the recent events in Parliament was Isaac Lyon Goldsmid (1778–1859), nephew of the famous Goldsmid brothers whose financial activities were legend in the eighteenth century.[3] He was aided by the Rothschild family, and by the Prime Minister himself, the duke of Wellington, but it was decided to wait until the following year when tensions and tempers over Catholic emancipation would have somewhat died down. On 5 April 1830 a bill 'for the Relief of His Majesty's Subjects professing the Jewish Religion' was introduced in the House of Commons by Sir Robert Grant, representing the Whig party. Surprisingly, opposition proved to be insurmountable, and the bill was defeated at the second reading, a failure which was followed by the collapse of Wellington's government itself. The Reform Bill of 1832 occupied most parliamentarians' minds during the following year, but in 1833 the Jewish question surfaced once again, propelled by Grant.[4] The bill actually passed the House of Commons this time, championed by Macaulay the great historian, whose defence of Jewish emancipation has become a classic text in itself.[5] In the Lords, however, despite vocal support of the philo-Semitic duke of Sussex, the opposition carried the day, led by Archbishop William Howley of Canterbury with the support of King William IV himself. Howley had organized the opposition to the Roman Catholic Relief Bill, had opposed the Reform Bill, and now refused to allow the Jews to slip through the net. Howley baptized Victoria and crowned her, and his implacable opposition until his death in 1848 was a serious problem. Two more failed attempts in 1834 and 1836 led to a general feeling that Jewish emancipation was not the sort

[3] Two volumes of his correspondence with MPs regarding emancipation were lent to the Mocatta Library by his descendant Sir Henry d'Avigdor-Goldsmid: see the latter's article, 'Lord George Bentinck and the Jews', *TJHSE* 23 (1971), 44–52. See also L. Abrahams, 'Sir I. L. Goldsmid and the Admission of the Jews of England to Parliament', *TJHSE* 4 (1903), 116–29; and the *DNB*.

[4] I. Abrahams, 'Text of Mr. Robert Grant's Bill, 1830', *TJHSE* 6 (1912), 249–53; Hansard, 3rd ser. xx (1833), 221–55.

[5] T. B. Macaulay, 'Civil Disabilities of the Jews', *Edinburgh Review* (Jan. 1831), repr. in his *Critical and Historical Essays, Contributed to the Edinburgh Review* (London, 1843), i. 295–310. Cf. I. Finestein, 'A Modern Examination of Macaulay's Case for the Civil Emancipation of the Jews', *TJHSE* 28 (1984), 39–59. Both Macaulay and Robert Grant were involved with the Philo-Judaean Society, a more elevated missionary group that saw the conversion of the Jews to be a natural consequence of the improvement of their political and social situation.

of issue which should be occupying the English Parliament at this particular time.

During these years and afterwards, English Jews were active in extending their rights and privileges. Isaac Lyon Goldsmid's son, Francis Henry Goldsmid (1808–78) was admitted to the Bar in 1833 as the first Jewish barrister, swearing on the Senior Bencher's insistence on an oversized rabbinical Bible.[6] Two years later, in 1835, Englishmen were relieved from taking any oaths before voting, and thus Jews were incidentally allowed to elect members to Parliament, although many already did so in areas where the administration of oaths was thought to be a tiresome preliminary.[7] The appointment of Coleridge's friend Hyman Hurwitz as professor of Hebrew at University College, London in 1828, while not in itself a great success, signified a change in attitude to the subject and its practitioners.[8] In 1837 the University of London was incorporated and, unlike Oxford and Cambridge, allowed students of any religious faith to study and to take their degrees there.[9] Here too Isaac Lyon Goldsmid was very active, and in 1841 he was rewarded for his diligence with the title of baronet, thus becoming the first Jew to be given a hereditary title. In 1845 David Salomons (1797–1873), a prominent member of London's financial community, after having repeatedly been elected to the Court of Aldermen, only to be sent down for his inability to swear 'on the true faith of a Christian', was allowed to take a seat by virtue of a Jewish Disabilities Removal Act passed in Parliament which opened municipal offices to Jews as well. Ten years before, upon being elected sheriff of the City of London, he had successfully pressured Parliament to enact a special Sheriffs Act to spare him the Christian oath. David Salomons's election as Lord Mayor of

[6] D. W. Marks and Albert Löwy, *Memoir of Sir Francis Henry Goldsmid* (2nd edn., London, 1882), 16–17. See P. S. Lachs, 'A Study of a Professional Elite: Anglo-Jewish Barristers in the Nineteenth Century', *JSS* 44 (1982), 125–34, who notes (p. 126) that Jewish solicitors had existed since about 1770, and that by the second half of the 19th century there were about fifty Jewish solicitors in London. Cf. E. R. Samuel, 'Anglo-Jewish Notaries and Scriveners', *TJHSE* 17 (1953), 113–59; and *DNB*. F. H. Goldsmid was also the first Jewish QC (1858): Marks and Löwy, *Memoir*, 72.

[7] For example, Rabbi Asher Ansell of Liverpool voted in the general election of Dec. 1832 and was so registered in the Liverpool Poll Book: G. Alderman, *The Jewish Community in British Politics* (Oxford, 1983), 10.

[8] L. Hyman, 'Hyman Hurwitz: The First Anglo-Jewish Professor', *TJHSE* 21 (1968), 232–42.

[9] Jews' College opened in 1855, and, although it did run a grammar school until 1879, it was really limited to training clergymen: A. M. Hyamson, *Jews' College, London 1855–1955* (London, 1955); I. Harris, *History of Jews' College* (London, 1906). The University College School opened in 1833: H. H. Bellot, *University College London 1826–1926* (London, 1929).

London in 1855 would later seem a natural consequence of his pioneering limited emancipation of the Jews, valid as yet only on the municipal level, despite Salomons having unsuccessfully offered himself as a parliamentary candidate on a number of occasions.[10] The last bastion was now clearly the House of Commons.

In 1847 Lionel Nathan de Rothschild (1808–79), English-born and Jewish, Disraeli's 'Sidonia', was elected for the City of London representing the Liberal party and supporting the Liberal Prime Minister Lord John Russell. When Parliament assembled in December, Rothschild was unable to take the required oaths, and the House of Commons resolved itself into a committee to discuss the possible removal of Jewish disabilities. The bill which was introduced the following year was the subject of heated debate, not the least because so many disabilities had already been removed that it was rightly felt that this was the thick end of the wedge. By now, not only Disraeli but Gladstone as well was in favour of the bill, yet even their support did not allow it to pass. Rothschild's further elections and subsequent ejections were followed by further bills in a campaign which continued until 1851, being centred not only on the form of the oath, but also on the use of the Old Testament for such a purpose. David Salomons, meanwhile, who had always believed in tougher tactics, was finally sent to the House at a by-election at Greenwich, and, unlike Rothschild, who would always withdraw politely, Salomons recited the required oath, omitting the offensive words, and actually took his seat, ignoring all orders to withdraw. In the ensuing debate, Salomons not only participated but actually voted three times, thus making him, rather than Rothschild, the first Jew to sit in the English Parliament, although he was fined £500 for each occasion he voted.[11]

The campaign for full political rights for Jews reached an interesting snag in September 1850 when Nicholas Wiseman was appointed cardinal and announced the reinstatement of English bishops, resulting in a violent anti-Roman Catholic backlash in England, led by Lord John Russell and *The Times*. The slogans stressed the ideas of 'Church in Danger' and 'England as a Protestant Country', so the Jews were bound to be affected. In February 1851 Russell introduced a bill to regulate ecclesiastical titles as a means of curbing the Roman Catholics, and the

[10] For an interesting Jewish account of a Guildhall banquet and reception for Queen Victoria in 1837 see Kaufman Meyers to M. H. Meyer, 17 Nov. 1837: Jewish Museum, London; Lazarus & Co. papers: repr. W. S. Samuel, ' "Lord Meyer's" Show Day 1837', *Jewish Monthly*, Nov. 1949, also repr. as pamphlet (London, 1950).

[11] Cf. A. Gilam, 'Anglo-Jewish Attitudes toward Benjamin Disraeli during the Era of Emancipation', *JSS* 42 (1980), 313–22. See also id., 'The Burial Grounds Controversy between Anglo-Jewry and the Victorian Board of Health, 1850', *JSS* 45 (1983), 147–56.

Jewish Chronicle joined with him in the hate campaign against them. In the 1852 general election the *Jewish Chronicle* urged their readers to lobby and work for the Liberals, although when Disraeli became Chancellor of the Exchequer in a minority Conservative government they took solace from the possibility that their former co-religionist might push emancipation.[12]

The attempt to pass a bill enabling Jews to sit in Parliament became somewhat of a public spectacle, repeated annually and always ending in failure. Eventually, even the Tories realized that they could not endlessly continue to oppose a measure which denied constituents the right to send whomever they chose to represent them in Parliament. It was decided to end the struggle by a draw: each House of Parliament would be permitted to decide what form of oath might be administered to Jewish victors in parliamentary elections. A bill to this effect was introduced, but it was still opposed by some die-hards, who added two precautionary clauses: the first, that Jews be excluded from certain rather ceremonial offices of state which had also been denied Roman Catholics; and the second, that Jews would not be permitted to present clergymen for benefices even if that right normally went with the particular office of state held, this privilege being exercised by the archbishop of Canterbury instead. These amendments were hardly worth discussing, and the Jewish Relief Act passed both houses, being the fourteenth attempt to achieve the right for a Jew to sit in Parliament. Accordingly, on 26 July 1858 Baron Lionel de Rothschild took his place in the House of Commons, and the battle for emancipation was declared won, despite the fact that he never made a speech.[13]

Lionel de Rothschild achieved far more than Menasseh ben Israel had ever hoped for. Menasseh merely wanted the right for Jews to live in England unmolested. Rothschild wanted them to enjoy all of the rights which accrued to native-born Englishmen. Certainly there was some inflation of expectation between 1657 and 1858, but, in at least one sense, both of these men wanted the same thing, that is, official recognition of Jewish status in such a way that justice would be seen to

[12] At the same time, the *Jewish Chronicle* tried to show that their people harboured civilized values by promoting the Jews' and General Literary and Scientific Institution at Sussex Hall, founded in 1845 but unfortunately ultimately unsuccessful. By this time too the *Jewish Chronicle* was trying to ameliorate the persecution of the Reform Jews by official Anglo-Jewish institutions.

[13] 21 & 22 Victoria, c.29. His son Nathaniel (Natty) Mayer Rothschild (1840–1915) would become the first Jewish peer in 1885. F. H. Goldsmid, the first Jewish barrister, was elected MP for Reading in 1860 as a Liberal. He was killed in 1878 while stepping out of a still-moving train at Waterloo Station: Marks and Löwy, *Memoir*, 3.

be done, and would not be a secret and unknown achievement. Menasseh left England in 1657 as a self-professed failure because he had never managed to acquire that elusive piece of paper which would have given the Jews a written guarantee of settlement. Nevertheless, as we have seen, the Jews were hardly the worse off without it, and indeed, it might be argued that the piecemeal, gradual acquisition of rights and privileges was more suited to the English temper and yielded greater benefits in the long run. Similarly, Rothschild's victory of 1858 should be seen as a convenient milestone rather than the End of Anglo-Jewish History. The right of Jews to sit in Parliament, misleadingly called 'Emancipation', despite the fact that Jews became legally able to vote more than two decades previously, was far more symbolic than anything else. Anglo-Jewry was still on the eve of its greatest challenge, that of mass immigration. No more than about 35,000 Jews lived in England on the day Rothschild took his seat, the vast majority in London.[14] Today ten times that number call themselves British Jews. 'Emancipation' was not the End of Anglo-Jewish History even in popular perspective, but rather the end of the first period of Jewish resettlement, when the right of Jews to live in England at all might still be questioned.[15]

[14] See an analysis of the information revealed by the religious census in V. D. Lipman, 'A Survey of Anglo-Jewry in 1851', *TJHSE* 17 (1953), 171–88. Cf. V. D. Lipman, 'The Structure of London Jewry in the Mid-nineteenth Century', in H. J. Zimmels, *et al.* (eds.), *Essays Presented to Chief Rabbi Israel Brodie* (London, 1967), 253–73; T. M. Endelman, 'Communal Solidarity among the Jewish Elite of Victorian London', *Victorian Studies*, 28 (1985), 491–526.

[15] For a survey of recent secondary sources, see L. P. Gartner, 'A Quarter Century of Anglo-Jewish Historiography', *JSS* 48 (1986), 105–26.

BIBLIOGRAPHY

1. MANUSCRIPT SOURCES

Amsterdam

Bibliotheca Rosenthaliana, University of Amsterdam Library
ROS. 1: regulations of *Saar Asamaim* (1693–1724).
ROS. PL. B-62: Portuguese riddle composed by Solomon Judah Leao Templo for Moses Mocatta in 1691.
ROS. 585: Jacob Abendanon's two Hebrew lamentations on the death of Queen Mary Stuart, 1694.

University Library
MS III E 9 (31):   Menasseh ben Israel to Isaac Vossius, 10 Jan. 1651.
MS III E 9 (37):   same to same, 10 Mar. 1651.
MS III E 9 (76):   same to same, 2 Feb. 1652.
MS III E 9 (193): same to same, 8 Feb. 1655.

Banbury

Broughton Castle
Royal grant: Sampson, son of Samson Gideon, raised to the peerage as Lord Eardley [on display in rear staircase].

Jerusalem

Jewish National and University Library
Yahuda MSS: Isaac Newton's theological papers.

Leeds

University Library
Roth MSS:

251: Foley to Richard Brothers, 25 Dec. 1801.
267: Minutes of the London Beth Din, 1805–35: 65 fos.
730: sermons delivered at the New Synagogue, 1794–1806.

Leiden

University Library
BPL 191: Menasseh ben Israel to J. van Beverwijk (Beverovicius), 25 Nov. 1639.
BPL 293a: Menasseh ben Israel to D. de Wilhem, 28 May 1642.
Pap. 2: Menasseh ben Israel to C. Saumaise, 14 July 1638.
Pap. 7: same to same, 15 Oct. 1638.

London

British Library
Additional MSS:

4106, fo. 253: memorandum of BL, MS Eger. 2542, fos. 240^v–241^r.

4292, ii, fos. 157–63: discovery of 'mysterious' Hebrew verses in Cromwell's time.

4377, fos. 34–5: 'A Scheme whereby any Person of the meanest Capacity may in a very short time perfect himself in the Hebrew Language without the assistance of a Master . . . Invented by Moses Marcus.'

4459, fos. 164^r–165^v: original MS of Dury's *Case of Conscience*; fos. 166^r–167^v: Dury's note on the Jews of Hesse.

4707–9: Solomon da Costa's three Hebrew MSS (India Office Library).

4710–11: Solomon da Costa's two MS catalogues (India Office Library).

5832: Revd. William Cole, commonplace book.

21599: bill of indictment against Lopez (drafts).

23650, fos. 5–8: Gen. Charles Rainsford, 11 Nov. 1777, from The Hague: correspondence (copies) re 'Baal Shem of London'.

23669, fos. 85–6: same re same, Oct. 1782.

23819, fos. 61–3^r: papers relating to the expulsion of the Jews from Bohemia in 1744, and the action taken by George II.

28542, fos. 90–2: Salvador to E. M. da Costa, 22 Jan. 1785.

29867, fos. 19^v–28^r: genealogy of da Costa family, compiled by Emanuel Mendes da Costa.

29868, fos. 15–16: da Costa lists of secret Jews in London, *c.*1660.

32876, fo. 35: William Villareal to Newcastle, 19 Nov. 1757: declines to serve as High Sheriff.

32883, fo. 98: same to same, 25 Aug. 1758: offers himself as candidate for Nottingham; fos. 141–3: Newcastle to Job Charlton, 28 Aug. 1758; fo. 170: Newcastle to Villareal, 29 Aug. 1758; fo. 308: Lady Howe to Newcastle, 5 Sept. 1758.

32886, fo. 243^{r-v}: Devonshire to Sampson Gideon, 13 June 1758: copy made by Gideon; enclosed in letter to 9 Dec. 1758; fo. 241: Gideon to Newcastle, 9 Dec. 1758; fo. 245: Gideon's certificate proving baptism of children, 8 Dec. 1758: enclosed in letter of 9 Dec. 1758.

32887, fos. 274–275^v: Gideon to Newcastle, 21 Jan. 1759, re scheme to raise supplies by annuities, enclosing: fo. 276: reminder to Newcastle re Gideon's son.

32890, fos. 162–3: J. West to Newcastle, 18 Apr. 1759; fos. 233–234^v: Gideon to Newcastle, 21 Apr. 1759.

33053, fo. 56^{r-v}: Joseph Salvador to the duke of Newcastle, 14 Jan. [1753], regarding Jewish naturalization; fos. 69–70: 'An Act to repeal . . .' [the Jew Bill, 1754].

33055, fo. 219: Sampson Gideon to Newcastle, *c.*1757, demonstrating that Jews have been ennobled in Roman Catholic countries, and noting that his own children had been baptized; fos. 221–3: Gideon's paper listing his services to England, 1742–57.

34015, fos. 25ᵛ, 43, 46, 73: Jewish aliens arriving in London, 1656–7, recorded in 'A Booke contayning the names aswell of all such persos as have come from beyond yᵉ Seas & made their psonall appearances at this Office'.

48029, fos. 147–84ᵛ: report of Lopez conspiracy, by Sir William Waad.

Arundel MSS:

151, fos. 190–1: Hebrew reply of Jacob Raphael Peglione (rabbi of Modena) to question regarding Henry VIII's divorce: 'I have been asked by a distinguished priest, whose name is Messer Francisco Curtiso, concerning a point in the law of the levirate'.

Egerton MSS:

1049, fo. 6ʳ⁻ᵛ: Dormido to Cromwell, 3 Nov. 1654 (autobiographical account).
fo. 7ʳ⁻ᵛ: Dormido to Cromwell, 3 Nov. 1654 (on behalf of the Jews).

2227: war diary (1758) of David Mendes da Costa, contractor for the supply of wagons for the commissariat service in the army in Germany under Prince Ferdinand of Brunswick, with copies of his letters (June 1757–Jan. 1759): written in English.

2542, fos. 238ʳ–239ʳ: Charles II to Middleton, 24 Sept. 1656.
fos. 240ᵛ–241ʳ: Charles II to Middleton, 24 Sept. 1656 (particularly on the Jews).

Harleian MSS:

871, fos. 7–64: report of Lopez conspiracy.
fos. 65–70ᵛ: 'The Declaration delivered (in March 1593–4) by Judazer Fatim, a Jew, sent from Constantinople to England by his master Salomon (whom Armurath III had made Duke of Metilli; and who settled the Jews at Tiberias) to know whether Qu. Elizabeth would assist the Emperor against the Turks, or not.' [French].
fos. 71–74ᵛ: 'Answers (in French) to many Questions, propounded to the same Judazer Fatim, by the Lords of the Council, as it seems'.

7013, fos. 91ᵛ–101ᵛ: nine 18th-century Yiddish letters, 'Given by Humfrey Wanley; who bought it of a Person that took it up in the street, having seen it drop from a Gentle woman as she passed along.'
fo. 102: 18th-century Hebrew letter.
fo. 103: 18th-century Ladino letter.

Lansdowne MSS:

33, fo. 76ʳ⁻ᵛ: Nuñez to Burghley, 28 June 1581.

67, fo. 252: Elizabeth I to the sultan, in Latin (copy), Mar. 1591–2.

69, fo. 70: Salomon Cormano to Elizabeth I, in Spanish (copy), Mar. 1591–2.

588: notes of cases at King's Bench, 13 Geo. I and 1 Geo. II, including legal opinions in Kitty/Philip Villareal case.

629 and 630: Philip Carteret Webb's notebooks, 1720–33, including about thirty Jewish cases.

982: Bishop White Kennett's collection of biographical notes.

988, fos. 174ᵛ–180: J. Greenhalgh to Thomas Crompton, 22 Apr. 1662 (copy) about the Jews of London.

fo. 374: Moses Marcus to Marcus Moses and wife, 2 May 1724 (copy).

Sloane MSS:

4055, fos. 162–163ᵛ: Moses Marcus to Sir Hans Sloane, 16 Aug. 1737.

Stowe MSS:

166, fo. 151ʳ⁻ᵛ: Robert Cecil to Sir Thomas Edmondes, 30 Oct. 1594.
    fo. 167: Burghley to Edmondes, 28 Nov. 1594.
    fo. 177: Cecil to Edmondes, 11 Dec. 1594.

Corporation of London Record Office
Assessment Box, no. 35.
Census Lists of 1695.
Remembrancia, ix.

Guildhall Library
1123/1/146: Vestry Minutes, St Katherine Coleman, London, 23 Apr. 1701.

Jewish Museum
First minute book, The Board of Deputies of British Jews.
4 (1): Joseph Crooll to Rev. J. W. Whittaker, 24 Mar. 1828.
8a: document testifying to transfer on 22 May 1712 of a £1,000 treasury loan
    by Moses Hart, signed by Walpole.
85: advertisement and cover letter regarding full payment by Jews on packet
    boats from Holland, 9 Sept. and 10 Oct. 1774.
98: 18th-century begging letters.
130: Ashkenazi cemetery deed, 2 Feb. 1696/7 (with plan).
190: certificate pasted on back of a portrait of a soldier, 1803.
647: Hambro Synagogue minute book, 1726–91.

Jews' College
4: MS copy of Solomon Bennett, *Temple of Ezekiel* (London, 1824): 40 pp.
116: six diplomas and certificates of Solomon Bennett.

Mocatta Library, University College [although note that much of this material will
    eventually be housed in the Parkes Library, University of Southampton]
Anglo-Jewish Archives:

Norwood Homes for Jewish Children Collection: Jews' Hospital, Governors'
    Reports of Visits (1811–63), General Committee Minute Book (1819–22,
    1822–7), and Lady Visitors' Book (1811–61).
AJ/96: Latin diary of Johann Schult, Nov. 1702–Jan. 1703.
AJ/144: Cortizos papers (50 items).
AJ/151/13/1: typescript of David Mendes da Costa war diary (BL MS.
    Egerton 2227).
AJ/151/13/3: photocopy of Schult's diary.
AJ/151/17: Sasportas to Pardo, n.d. (copy).
AJ/266/1–2: New Synagogue, burial register, *c.*1777–83; 1786–*c.*1795.

Collyer Ferguson Collection of ephemera:

Contemporary report of Jewish soldiers in fight against Napoleon, 1803.

Mocatta Cupboard:

BA 27: regulations for a society for assisting widows and orphans, London, Dec. 1788.
BA 27 GRE: Great Synagogue, adjustment of disputes book, 1835–58.
RN 20 MYE: lectures in English given at the Hambro Synagogue in 1840 by I. M. Myers.
   3304: Richard Beere to William Pitt, 10 Nov. 1790.

Myers Collection:

Mocatta Cupboard RP 6 Ale: Alexander's wrappers for the prayer books.

Public Record Office
SP. 18/*passim*: State Papers, Domestic, Interregnum.
SP. 25/*passim*: Council of State Order Book.
SP. 29/*passim*: State Papers, Domestic, Charles II.
SP. 44/*passim*: Council Entry Book, Charles II.

Spanish and Portuguese Jews' Congregation
Mahamad, records (incl. summaries in English by R. D. Barnett, kept with the original documents).
163: Enquiry of the Mahamad to Attorney-General Edward Northey, and his reply, 12 June 1705.
344/1a: Jews to Charles II, 1664.
344/1b: Jews to Charles II, 1673–4.
344/1c: James II, Privy Council Order, 13 Nov. 1685.
344/1d: James II, Privy Council Order, 4 Dec. 1685; note by Herbert, 9 Dec. 1685.
344/2–6: various land deeds and related material.
344/7: copy of part of will of Jos. Henriques de Sequeira made in Amsterdam, in English, 19 Aug. 1715.
344/8: will of Jacob Mazahod, in English, 8 Apr. 1718.
344/9: copy of petition to Lord Mayor and aldermen by group of Gentiles that more Jews be admitted as brokers; with petition of six Jews requesting same in view of suit against them for acting as brokers without being admitted, with other papers relating to issue of brokering, 1721–2, with P. C. Webb's bill.
344/10a: statement regarding Ishac Barmentos uttering unorthodox opinions about the Midrash, 1725.
344/10b: Barmentos's defence.
344/11: Lord Chancellor's view regarding Alvaranga case, with P. C. Webb's notes, 2 Jan. 1727.
344/12: abstract of synagogue deeds.
344/13: rough draft of above.
344/14: order of the Master of the Rolls regarding Jewish orphans, 12 Feb. 1732.
344/15: will of Abraham Gonsales, 28 Dec. 1739.
344/16: *responsa* of Italian rabbis declaring turbot kosher, 1740.

344/17: will of Hannah de Avila, 1741–3, with bill from P. C. Webb.

344/18–19: documents regarding estate of Abm. de Jos. Capadoce.

344/20: documents regarding Jac. Mendes da Costa, May 1743.

344/21: assignments of stocks, 17 Jan. 1744, to Benjamin Mendes da Costa.

344/22: privileges granted by king of Sweden to certain Portuguese Jews, 1745.

344/23: documents regarding a Jewish orphan, 17 Mar. 1753.

344/24: Samson Gideon to the community, 5 Sept. 1753.

344/25a: bill by P. C. Webb for acting during Jew Bill controversy, and before, 1742–54.

344/25b: order by Mahamad for payment.

344/25c: statement of case regarding Jewish poor acting as brokers without licence.

344/26: regarding glazier's work, 20 Aug. 1754.

344/27: regarding building work, 21 May 1754.

344/31: report of Board of Deputies to Mahamad, 3 Apr. 1761.

344/35: Joseph Salvador to the Mahamad, 24 Apr. 1761, objecting that his view that most of the oxen killed are *treif* was omitted from the minutes.

344/46: Bevis Marks to George III, Mar. 1789.

344/53g: Isaac Nieto to the Mahamad, 13 May 1757, asserting that of the 3,000 oxen killed in the previous twelve months by Rabbi Haim Albahaly, only 100 were kosher; and declaring that all cattle killed by Ashkenazim are *treif.*

344/53f: Isaac Nieto to Joseph Salvador, 28 Oct. 1760, thanking him for sympathy expressed on death of his daughter Esther, and criticizing Cohen d'Azevedo.

344/53h: Benjamin Mendes da Costa to the rabbinical court of Amsterdam, stating that he intends to nominate Cohen d'Azevedo as *haham,* 28 Heshvan 5521 [1761].

344/53h: Isaac Nieto, memo in objection of disciple [Cohen d'Azevedo] being preferred when his master is in the town, n.d. [?1761].

344/53i–j: questionnaire in Hebrew submitted by the London Mahamad to rabbinical court in Amsterdam concerning the authority of Isaac Nieto, with Portuguese summary, n.d. [?1761].

344/53k: Mahamad to Amsterdam acknowledging letter and saying that they would be referring the questions of their own rabbinical court, the office of *haham* being vacant, asking for a prompt reply, 10 Kislev 5521 [1761].

344/53l: 20 Kislev 5521 [1761], Amsterdam to Mahamad.

344/53m–o: Amsterdam rabbinical court to London Mahamad endorsing unanimous decision against Isaac Nieto, with Hebrew copy, n.d. [1761].

344/56a: written opinion of Lord Kenyon regarding Jews and Gordon Riots, 24 Jan. 1782.

344/57a–f: twelve lawyers' opinions on whether Jews could own land, 1724.

344/63: £500 fire insurance policy on Sephardi burial ground, 2 Jan. 1794.

344a: report of deputies to Mahamad, 20 Nov. 1761.

344b: duke of Manchester to Joseph Salvador, 23 Nov. 1761.

344c: Lord Boston to Salvador, 20 Nov. 1761.
641: Jews to James II, 1685.

Oxford

Bodleian Library
Ballard MSS:
13, fos. 116^r–117^v: Humphrey Wanley to Dr Arthur Charlett, 1 Aug. 1705, about Philip Levi.
    fo. 121^r: same to same about Isaac Bernard, a Jewish possible replacement for Levi, 15 Jan. 1710/11.

Carte MSS:
31, fo. 19^r: Thomas Violet to the duke of Ormonde, 17 Aug. 1660.
73, fo. 325: Pepys to Edward Montagu, 3 Dec. 1659.

Oppenheimer MSS:
Opp. add. 8° II. 63: MS supplement to Nieto's *Es Dath.*

Rawlinson MSS:
A 260, fo. 57: Cromwell to the king of Portugal, 26 Feb. 1654/5.
A 261, fo. 37^v: the same.
A 336, fos. 3 ff.: Samuel Weale, 'Remarks in Defence of the Exaction of Alien Duty from the Jews by the Commissioners of the Customs', *c.*1685.
C 206, fo. 107^{r-v}: Menasseh to Cromwell, English trans. of petition.
D 864, fos. 59–60^v: Lilly to Ashmole, 27 Oct. 1673.

Codrington Library, All Souls
239, fo. 423a: Anglesey to [Bennett], 6 Aug. 1680.

Sheffield

University Library
Hartlib Papers, *passim* (the entire collection is now computerized, and can be easily searched).

Zurich

Zentralbibliothek
RP 17: Lady Jane Grey to Bullinger, in Latin, 12 July 1551, regarding her desire to learn Hebrew.
RP 18: same to same, 7 July 1552.
RP 19: same to same, before June 1553.

2. SELECT PRINTED SOURCES

A. Primary works

ABENDANA, ISAAC, *Discourses of the Ecclesiastical and Civil Polity of the Jews* (London, 1706).
ABOAB, DAVID, *The Mercy and Truth* (London, 1748).

An Act to Oblige the Jews to Maintain and Provide for their Protestant Children (London, 24 June 1702).

An Act to Permit Persons Professing the Jewish Religion to be Naturalized by Parliament; and for Other Purposes therein Mentioned (London, 1 June 1753).

ADAMS, HANNAH, *The History of the Jews* (London, 1818).

ADDISON, L., *The Present State of the Jews* (2nd edn., London, 1676).

An Address to the Friends of Great-Britain (London, 1753).

ADLER, NATHAN MARCUS, *Laws and Regulations for All the Synagogues K. K. Ashkenazim in the British Empire* (London, 1847).

ALEXANDER, ALEXANDER, *The Evening and Morning Service of the Beginning of the Year* (London, 5331 [1771]).

ALEXANDER, A. [i.e. Levi], *The Form of Prayers, for the Day of Atonement* (London, 1807).

ALEXANDER, A., and MEYERS, B., *Tephilloth* (London, 5530 [1770]).

ALEXANDER, DANIEL [Tnangam], *A Call to the Jews* (London, n.d.).

—— [ben], *A Declaration of the Christian Faith* (2nd edn., London, 1703).

ALEXANDER, JOHN, *God's Covenant Displayed* (London, 1689).

ALEXANDER, LEVI, *Answer to Mr. Joshua van Oven's Letters on the Present State of the Jewish Poor in London* (London, 1802).

—— *The Axe Laid to the Root; or, Ignorance and Superstition Evident in the Character of the Rev. Solomon Hirschell, Major Rabbi* (London, 1808).

—— *Alexander's Hebrew Ritual, and Doctrinal Explanation of the Whole Ceremonial Law* (London, 1819).

—— [and Henry Lemoine], *Memoirs of the Life and Commercial Concerns of the Late Benj. Goldsmid* (London, 1808).

ALLEN, JOHN, *Modern Judaism; or A Brief Account of the Opinions, Traditions, Rites, and Ceremonies, of the Jews in Modern Times* (London, 1816).

ALLIX, PETER, *A Confutation of the Hope of the Jews* (London, 1707).

ALMANZA, ANTHONY [Aron], *The Case of Anthony d'Almanza* (London, 1704).

—— *A Declaration of the Conversion* (London, 1703).

The Amorous Convert (London, 1679).

ANLEY, CHARLOTTE, *Miriam* (London, 1829).

An Apology for the Naturalization of the Jews (London, 1753).

ARCHENHOLZ, JOHANN WILHELM VON, *A Picture of England* (Dublin, 1791).

[ARNALL, WILLIAM] 'Solomon Abrabanel', *The Complaint of the Children of Israel* (7th edn., London, 1736).

AUSTIN, WILLIAM, *Letters from London* (Boston, 1804).

B., B., *A Historical and Law Treatise Against the Jews and Judaism* (London, 1703).

BACON, FRANCIS, 'A True Report of the Detestable Treason, Intended by Dr. Roderigo Lopez', in *Works*, ed. J. Spedding, *et al.* (London, 1857–74), viii. 271–87.

[BADCOCK, JOHN] Jon Bee, *A Living Picture of London, for 1828* (London, [1828]).

—— *Slang: A Dictionary* (London, 1823).

BAILEY, THOMAS, *Annals of Nottinghamshire* (London, 1852–5).

BAKER, RICHARD, *The Marchants Humble Petition and Remonstrance, To his Late Highnesse* (London, 1659).

BALLARD, JOSEPH, *England in 1815* (Boston, 1913).

BARLOW, THOMAS, 'The Case of the Jews', in *Several Miscellaneous and Weighty Cases of Conscience* (London, 1692).

BARNET, JACOB, *Remarks upon Dr. Priestley's Letters* (London, 1792).

BASNAGE, JACQUES, *Histoire des Juifs* (The Hague, 1716).

—— *The History of the Jews* (London, 1708).

[BAYLY, ANSELM] 'Antisocinus', *Remarks on David Levi's Letters to Dr. Priestley* (London, 1787).

BEERE, RICHARD, *Dissertation on . . . Daniel* (London, [1790]).

—— *Epistle to the Chief Priests* (London, n.d. [?1789]).

BENNETT, SOLOMON, *The Constancy of Israel . . . Reply to . . . Lord Crawford* (London, 1812).

—— *A Discourse on Sacrifices* (London, 1815).

—— *The Present Reign of the Synagogue of Duke's Place* (London, n.d.): not seen; very rare.

—— *Specimen of a New Version of the Hebrew Bible* (London, 1836).

—— *The Temple of Ezekiel* (London, 1824).

—— *Tenneh Bikkurim* (Hebrew) (London, [1817?]).

—— *Theological and Critical Treatise on the . . . Holy Language* (London, 1835).

[BERLIN, SAUL] 'Obadiah b. Baruch', *Mitzpeh Yekutiel* (Berlin, 1789).

BERNARD, HERMAN HEDWIG, *The Book of Job*, ed. Frank Chance (2nd edn., London, 1884; 1st pub. 1864).

—— *The Guide of the Hebrew Student* (London, 1839).

—— *The Main Principles* (Cambridge, 1832).

—— *Cambridge Free Thoughts and Letters on Bibliolatry; Translated from the German of G. E. Lessing*, ed. Isaac Bernard (London, 1862).

—— [with P. H. Mason, his student], *Gently Flowing Waters: An Easy, Practical Hebrew Grammar* (Cambridge, 1853).

Bevis Marks Records, i, ed. L. D. Barnett (Oxford, 1940).

BICHENO, JAMES, *A Friendly Address to the Jews* (London, n.d.).

—— *The Restoration of the Jews* (London, 1800).

BIRCH, THOMAS, *Memoirs of the Reign of Queen Elizabeth . . . From the Original Papers of . . . Anthony Bacon* (London, 1754).

BLAND, JOHN, *The Majesty and Singular Copiousness of the Hebrew Language Asserted and Illustrated* (London, 1744).

BLUNT, JOHN ELIJAH, *A History of the Establishment and Residence of the Jews in England: With an Enquiry into their Civil Disabilities* (London, 1830).

BOADEN, JAMES, *Memoirs of the Life of John Philip Kemble, Esq.* (Philadelphia, 1825).

BOLAFFEY, H. V., *The Aleph-Beth; or, The First Step to the Hebrew Language* (London, n.d.).

—— *Prospectus . . . The Jewish Preceptor* (n.p., n.d.).

BORROW, GEORGE, *Lavengro: The Scholar—The Gypsy—The Priest* (London, 1851).

BOYER, ABEL, *Political State of Great-Britain* (London, 1717).

BRAYLEY, EDWARD, NIGHTINGALE, JOSEPH, et al., *London and Middlesex; or, An*

Historical, Commercial, & Descriptive Survey of the Metropolis of Great-Britain (London, 1810–16).

[?BRETON, NICHOLAS], 'The Plot of the Play, Called "England's Joy." To be Playd at the Swan this 6. of Nov. 1602', in W. Oldys (ed.), *Harleian Miscellany* (London, 1808–13), x. 199.

'BRISTOW, AMELIA' [pseud.], *Emma de Lissau* (London, 1828).

—— *The Orphans of Lissau* (London, 1830).

—— *Sophia de Lissau* (2nd edn., London, 1828).

BUDGELL, EUSTACE, *Memoirs of the Lives and Characters of the Illustrious Family of the Boyles* (London, 1737).

BURGESS, THOMAS, *The Hebrew Reader* (London, 1808).

BURKE, EDMUND, *Reflections on the Revolution in France* (London, 1790).

BURNET, GILBERT, *The Conversion & Persecutions of Eve Cohan* (London, 1680).

—— *History of his Own Time* (London, 1724–30).

—— *The History of the Reformation of the Church of England* (London, 1903).

[BYRON, GEORGE GORDON, Lord] I. Braham, I. Nathan, and Lord Byron, *A Selection of Hebrew Melodies Ancient and Modern*, ed. F. Burwick and P. Douglass (Tuscaloosa, Ala., 1988).

—— *Byron's Hebrew Melodies*, ed. T. L. Ashton (Austin, Tex., 1972).

—— *The Complete Poetical Works*, ed. J. J. McGann (Oxford, 1980–6), iii. 249–72, 465–72.

—— *Letters and Journals*, ed. L. A. Marchand, 12 vols. (Cambridge, Mass., 1973–82).

CALVERT, THOMAS, *The Blessed Jew of Marocco* (York, 1648).

CAMDEN, WILLIAM, *The Historie of . . . Elizabeth* (London, 1630).

CARTENWRIGHT, JOHANNA, and CARTWRIGHT, EBENEZER, *The Petition of the Jewes* (London, 1649).

Case of Many Hundreds of Poor English-Captives, in Algier (n.p., 1687).

Case of Mr. Francis Francia, the Reputed Jew (London, 1716).

The Case of the Jevves Stated (London, 1656).

The Case of the Jews Stated (n.p. = London, n.d. = 11 Nov. 1689).

CAVENDISH, GEORGE, *The Life and Death of Cardinal Wolsey*, ed. R. S. Sylvester (Early English Text Society, ccxliii, 1959).

CHILD, JOSIAH, *Brief Observations Concerning Trade, and Interest of Money* (London, 1668).

—— *A New Discourse of Trade* (London, 1693).

CHURCHILL, JOHN, 1st duke of Marlborough, *The Letters and Dispatches*, ed. G. Murray (London, 1845).

CIBBER, THEOPHILUS, *The Harlot's Progress* (London, 1733).

CLARKE, RICHARD, *Signs of Times* (London, 1773).

CLAYTON, ROBERT, *The Chronology of the Hebrew Bible Vindicated* (London, 1747).

—— *A Dissertation on Prophecy* (London, 1749).

—— *An Enquiry into the Time of the Coming of the Messiah* (London, 1751).

—— *An Impartial Enquiry into the Time of the Coming of the Messiah* (London, 1751).

—— *A Vindication of the Histories of the Old and New Testament, in Answer to . . . Bollingbroke* (Dublin, 1752).

CLOWES, WILLIAM, *A Proved Practice* (London, 1591).

COBBETT, WILLIAM, *The Parliamentary History of England* (London, 1806–20).

[COCHRANE, CHARLES] 'Juan de Vega', *Journal of a Tour* (London, 1830).

COHEN, L., *New System of Astronomy* (London, 1825).

—— *Sacred Truths, Addressed to the Children of Israel, Residing in the British Empire* (Exeter, [?1807]).

COHEN, S. I., *Elements of Faith, for the Use of Jewish Youth of Both Sexes* (London, 1815).

COHEN D'AZEVEDO, MOSES, *The Form of Prayer . . . 13th December, 1776* (London, 1777).

A Collection of the Best Pieces in Prose and Verse, Against the Naturalization of the Jews (London, 1753).

A Collection of State Papers . . . Reposited in the Library at Hatfield House, ed. William Murdin (London, 1759).

[COLLET, SAMUEL], *The Full and Final Restoration of the Jews and Israelites* (London, 1753).

—— *A Treatise of the Future Restoration of the Jews* (London, 1747).

[COLQUHOUN, PATRICK], *A Treatise on the Police of the Metropolis* (3rd edn., London, 1796).

A Confutation of the Reasons for Naturalizing the Jews (London, 1715).

[CONINGESBY, GEORGE], *The Jewish Naturalization Considered* (n.p., 1753).

COOPER, WILLIAM, *Christ the True Messiah* (2nd edn., London, 1796).

—— *The Promised Seed* (3rd edn., London, 1796).

COPLEY, JOSEPH, *The Case of the Jews is Altered* (London, 1656).

[CORRY, JOHN], *The Detector of Quackery* (2nd edn., London, 1802).

—— *A Satirical View of London at the Commencement of the Nineteenth Century* (London, 1801).

CRAVEN, WILLIAM, *The Jewish and Christian Dispensations* (3rd edn., Cambridge, 1813).

CROCKER, JAMES, *Essentials of Hebrew Grammar, Arranged Agreeably According to the Plan of Gesenius* (London, 1829).

CROMWELL, OLIVER, *The Writings and Speeches*, ed. W. C. Abbott (Cambridge, Mass., 1937–47).

CROOLL, JOSEPH, *The Fifth Empire* (London, 1829).

—— *The Last Generation* (Cambridge, 17 July 1829).

—— *The Restoration of Israel* (London, 1812), with 2nd edn. in 1814 with answer by Thomas Scott.

—— *Service Performed in the Synagogue of the Jews, Manchester . . . Delivered in Hebrew, by Rabbi Joseph Crool; and Translated by him, into English* (Manchester, 1803): sermon of 19 Oct. 1803.

CROSS, WALTER, *The Taghmical Art* (London, 1698).

[CROUCH, NATHANIEL], 'The Proceedings of the *Jews* in *England* in the Year 1655', in *Two Journeys to Jerusalem*, ed. R. B[urton=Crouch] (London, 1719), pp. 167–74. This book was published in several forms under different titles, including *Memorable Remarks* and *Judaeorum memorabilia*.

CUMBERLAND, RICHARD, *The Fashionable Lover* (London, 1772).
—— *The Jew* (London, 1794).
—— *The Jew of Mogadore* (London, 1808).
—— *Observer*, 38 (1785), repr. *The British Essayists*, ed. James Ferguson (London, 1819), xxxviii. 252–3.
[CUNINGHAME, WILLIAM] 'Talib', *Remarks Upon David Levi's Dissertations* (London, 1810).
DA COSTA, JACOB [PHILIP] MENDES, *Proceedings at Large in the Arches Court of Canterbury, between Mr. Jacob Mendes da Costa and Mrs. Catherine da Costa Villa Real, Both of the Jewish Religion, and Cousin Germans. Relating to a Marriage Contract* (n.p.=London, 1734).
DA COSTA, SOLOMON, 'My Translation from the Hebrew of a Letter I Wrote in that Language the 31st Day of May, 1759, to the Trustees of the British Museum' (London, 1759): broadsheet: copy in Mocatta Library, University College, London, Mocatta Cupboard.
D'ALMANZA, ANTHONY, *The Case of Anthony d'Almanza* (London, 1704).
'A Daughter of Israel', *The Jewish Preceptress; or, Elementary Lessons Written Chiefly for the Use of the Female Children Educated at the Jews' Hospital* (London, 1818).
[DEFOE, DANIEL], *Memoirs of Captain Carleton*, ed. C. H. Hartmann (London, 1929).
DEKKER, THOMAS, *A Strange Horse-Race* (London, 1613), including 'The Diuels Last Will and *TESTAMENT*', in *The Non-dramatic Works of Thomas Dekker*, ed. A. B. Grosart (New York, 1963), iii.
—— *The Whore of Babylon* (London, 1607), in *The Dramatic Works*, ed. F. Bowers (Cambridge, 1953–61), ii. 491–592.
DE LARREY, *Histoire d'Angleterre* (Amsterdam, 1707–13).
DE SOLA, D. A., and RAPHALL, M. J., *Eighteen Treatises from the Mishna* (London, 1843).
Dialogues between a Pilgrim, Adam, Noah, & Simon Cleophas (Manchester, 1816).
DIBDIN, THOMAS, *The Reminiscences* (London, 1827).
DICKENS, CHARLES, *Barnaby Rudge* (London, 1841).
[D'ISRAELI, ISAAC], *The Genius of Judaism* (London, 1833).
—— *Vaurien* (London, 1797).
The Divorce Tracts of Henry VIII, ed. E. Surtz, S. J., and V. Murphy (Angers, 1988).
[DOVE, JOHN], *The Importance of Rabbinical Learning* (London, 1746).
DOWLING, FRANK R., *Fistiana* (London, 1852).
DURY, JOHN, *A Case of Conscience, Whether it be Lawful to Admit Jews into a Christian Common-wealth?* (London, 1656), repr. W. Oldys (ed.), *Harleian Miscellany* (London, 1808–13), vii. 251–6.
DU VEIL, CHARLES-MARIE, *A Commentary on the Acts of the Apostles*, ed. F. A. Cox (Hanserd Knollys Soc., London, 1851; 1st pub. 1685).
An Earnest and Affectionate Address to the Jews (London, 1774).
An Earnest and Serious Address to the Freeholders (London, 1753).
An Earnest Persuasive and Exhortation to the Jews (London, 1753).

EDGEWORTH, MARIA, *Harrington*, in *Tales and Novels*, ed. R. L. Edgeworth, vol. ix (London, 1893; 1st pub. 1817).

EDREHI, MOSES, *An Historical Account of the Ten Tribes* (London, 1836).

—— *Sefer Ma'aseh Nissim* (Hebrew and Yiddish) (Amsterdam, 1818).

—— *Sefer Yad Mosheh* (Hebrew) (Amsterdam [1809]).

EGAN, PIERCE, *Boxiana; or, Sketches of Ancient and Modern Pugilism* (London, 1824–30).

ELTON, G. R., *The Tudor Constitution* (Cambridge, 1972).

ENTICK, JOHN, *A New and Accurate History and Survey of London* (London, 1766).

ERASMUS, *Opus epistolarum*, ed. P. S. Allen (Oxford, 1906–58).

The Eton College Register 1441–1698, ed. W. Sterry (Eton, 1943).

EVELYN, JOHN, *Diary*, ed. E. S. de Beer (Oxford, 1955).

—— *The History of the Three Late Famous Impostors, viz. Padre Ottomano, Mahomed Bei, and Sabatai Sevi* (London, 1669); also Augustan Reprint Soc., pub. no. 131, ed. C. W. Grose (Los Angeles, William Andrews Clark Memorial Library, 1968).

EYRE, JOSEPH, *Observations upon the Prophecies Relating to the Restoration of the Jews* (London, 1771).

FARIA, FRANCISCO DE, *The Narrative* (London, 1680).

—— *The Information* (London, 1680).

FAUDEL, HENRY, *A Brief Investigation into the System of the Jews' Hospital* (London, 1844).

[FELTHAM, JOHN], *The Picture of London, for 1818* (19th edn., London, 1818).

The First Table of the Celestiall Constellations, Expressed by Hebrew Characters (n.p., n.d.).

FITZGERALD, *Dukes and Princes of the Family of George III* (n.p., 1882).

FITZ-GERALD, GERALD, *An Essay on the Originality and Permanency of the Biblical Hebrew* (Dublin, 1796).

[FLETCHER, HENRY], *The Perfect Politician* (London, 1660).

FRANCIS, JOHN, *Chronicles and Characters of the Stock Exchange* (Boston, 1850; another edn. pub. London, 1849).

FRANCO, SOLOMON, *Truth Springing out of the Earth* (London, 1668).

The Full and Final Restoration of the Jews and Israelites, Evidently Set Forth to be Nigh at Hand (London, 1753).

GESENIUS, D. WILHELM, *A Hebrew Lexicon to the Books of the Old Testament*, ed. and trans. Christopher Leo (Cambridge, 1825–8).

GILL, JOHN, *A Dissertation Concerning the Antiquity of the Hebrew-Language* (London, 1767).

GLUCK-ROSENTHAL, L., *A Biographical Memoir of the Duke of Sussex* (London, 1846).

GOLDNEY, EDWARD, *Epistles to Deists and Jews* (London, 1759).

—— *A Friendly Epistle to the Deists* (London, 1760).

GONZALES, DON MANOEL, *The Voyage*, in *Travels*, ed. John Pinkerton (London, 1808–14).

GOOCH, ELIZABETH SARAH VILLA REAL, *The Life of Mrs. Gooch: Written by herself* (London, 1792).

GOODMAN, GODFREY, *The Court of King James the First*, ed. J. S. Brewer (London, 1839).

GORDON, GEORGE, *Copy of a Letter* (London, 1783).

—— *The Prisoners Petition* (London, 1786).

—— *To W. Smith, Esq. M.P.* (London, 2 Aug. 1792).

GRATZ, REBBECCA [*sic*], *Letters*, ed. D. Philipson (New York, 1929).

Great Synagogue, *Laws of the Congregation* (London, 1863).

GREEN, WILLIAM, *A New Translation of the Prayer of Habakkuk* (Cambridge, 1755).

—— *The Song of Deborah, Reduced to Metre* (Cambridge, 1753).

GREY, ANCHITELL, *Debates of the House of Commons, from the Year 1667 to the Year 1694* (London, 1763).

GRINDLEY, JOHN, *The Farmers Advice, to the Unbelieving Jews* (Shrewsbury, n.d. [?1720]).

—— *The Jews Generosity Explain'd* (London, n.d. [1722]).

GROSLEY, *Londres* (Lausanne, 1770).

—— *A Tour to London* (London, 1772).

HAKLUYT, RICHARD, *The Principal Navigations Voyages Traffiques & Discoveries of the English Nation* (London, 1927–8).

Hambro Synagogue, *Takkanot* (Hebrew) (London, 1788).

HARRINGTON, JAMES, *The Common-Wealth of Oceana* (London, 1656).

—— *The Political Works*, ed. J. G. A. Pocock (Cambridge, 1977).

[HART, AARON] Uri Phoebus Hamburger, *Urim v'Tumim* (Hebrew) (London, 1707).

HASTED, E., *History of Canterbury* (Canterbury, 1799).

HAYNE, SAMUEL, *An Abstract of All the Statutes Made Concerning Aliens Trading in England . . . Proving that the Jews . . . Break them All* (n.p., 1685).

HEARNE, THOMAS, *Remarks and Collections*, ed. H. E. Salter, xi (Oxford, 1921).

HEINEMANN, W., *An Introduction to the Hebrew Language* (London, 1823).

HENDERSON, WILLIAM, *Notes on the Folk Lore of the Northern Counties of England*, ed. S. Baring-Gould (London, 1866).

HERRERA, ABRAHAM COHEN, *Puerta del cielo*, ed. K. Krabbenhoft (Madrid, 1987).

HIGHMORE, A., *Philanthropia Metropolitana: A View of the Charitable Institutions Established in and near London, Chiefly during the Last Twelve Years* (London, 1822).

—— *Pietas Londinensis: The History, Design, and Present State of the Various Public Charities in and near London* (London, 1810).

HIRSCHEL, SOLOMON, *Address Delivered on Laying the Foundation-Stone of the Intended New Synagogue* (London, 1837).

Historical Manuscripts Commission, *3rd Report, Appendix* (1872).

—— *4th Report, Appendix* (1874).

—— *5th Report, Appendix* (1876).

—— *7th Report, Appendix* (1879).

—— *8th Report, Appendix* (1881).

—— *11th Report, Appendix* (1887).

—— *lii, Astley.*

—— *lxxv, Downshire I.*

—— *x, Eglington & c.*

—— lxiii, *Egmont Diary*.

—— lxxi, *Finch III*.

—— xxx, *Fortescue X*.

—— xvii, *House of Lords MSS*, n.s., *V*.

—— xxii, *Leeds MSS*.

—— lxxii, *Laing MSS*.

—— xxix, *Portland IV*.

—— xxix, *Portland V*.

—— xxix, *Portland VII*.

—— xxix, *Portland VIII*.

—— *Salisbury IV*.

—— *Salisbury V*.

—— lvi, *Stuart II–VII*.

HOLLESCHAU, JOCHANAN, *Ma'aseh Rav* (Hebrew) (Amsterdam, 1707).

HOLLIS, THOMAS, *Memoirs* (London, 1780).

HOLLOWAY, BENJAMIN, *The Primaevity and Preeminence of the Sacred Hebrew* (Oxford, 1754).

HOWELL, T. B., *State Trials* (London, 1809–28).

H[UGHES], W[ILLIAM], *Anglo-Judaeus; or, The History of the Jews, whilst here in England* (London, 1656).

HUNT, [JAMES HENRY] LEIGH, *The Autobiography* (London, 1850).

Illustrations of British History, ed. E. Lodge (London, 1791).

The Impartial Observer (London, 1753).

ISAAC, ISRAEL, *Christ Jesus the True Messiah* (London, 1682).

ISAAC OF TROKI, *Faith Strengthened* (London, 1851).

ISAACS, HYAM, *The Awakening of the Jews from their Slumbers* (London, 1842).

—— *Ceremonies, Customs, Rites, and Traditions of the Jews* (London, n.d. [?c. 1830]).

—— *A Solemn and Affectionate Address to Both Jews & Christians* (London, n.d. [?c. 1820]).

JACKSON, S. H., *The Jew* (New York, 1824).

JACKSON, WILLIAM, *The New and Complete Newgate Calendar* (London, [1795]).

JACOB, JOHN, *The Jew Turned Christian* (London, 1678–9).

JACOBS, ABRAHAM, *Address to the Jews* (Dublin, 1716).

[JESSEY, HENRY], *A Narrative of the Late Proceeds at White-Hall* (London, 1656).

The Jew Apologist (London, 1765).

The Jewish Ritual (London, 1753): separately issued introduction to [Abraham Mears], *The Book of Religion* (London, 1738).

The Jews Catechism (London, 1721).

JOHN, THEODORE, *An Account of the Conversion* (London, 1693).

JOSEPH HAKOHEN, *Emek ha-Baka*, ed. M. Letteris (Vienna, 1852): repr. *The Jew in the Medieval World*, ed. J. R. Marcus (Philadelphia, 1938), 251–5.

The Journals of All the Parliaments during the Reign of Queen Elizabeth, ed. Simonds d'Ewes (London, 1682).

KIELMANSEGGE, FREDERICK, *Diary of a Journey to England in the Years 1761–1762* (London, 1902).

KING, RICHARD, *The Complete Modern London Spy* (London, 1781).

KING, RICHARD, *The Frauds of London Detected* (London, [1770]).

KNAPP, ANDREW and BALDWIN, WILLIAM, *The New Newgate Calendar* (London, 1826).

KRAUTER, PHILIP DAVID, *New Succinct and Candid Examination of Mr. David Levi's Objections* (London, 1787).

[LACOMBE, FRANCOIS], *Observations sur Londres et ses environs* (Paris, 1777).

LA CREQUINIÈRE, *Agreement of the Customs of the East-Indians, with those of the Jews* (London, 1705).

Leicester's Commonwealth (London, 1584): repr. W. Oldys (ed.), *Harleian Miscellany* (London, 1808–13), iv. 576–83.

LEMOINE, HENRY, 'On the Present State of the *Jews*', *Gents. Mag.* 80 (1810), i. 15–18, 514–16.

LETI, G., *La Vie d'Olivier Cromwel* (Amsterdam, 1746).

LEVI, DAVID, *A Defence of the Old Testament . . . Addressed to Thomas Paine* (London, 1797).

—— *Dissertations on the Prophecies . . . Revised and Amended by J. King* (London, 1817).

—— *The Holy Bible* (London, 1822).

—— *Letters to Dr. Priestley . . . Part. II* (London, 1789), dated 14 Oct. 1788.

—— *Lingua sacra: In Three Parts* (London, 1785–7).

—— *A Succinct Account, of the Rites, and Ceremonies, of the Jews* (London, n.d.= 1783).

LEVI, PHILIP, *A Compendium of Hebrew Grammar* (Oxford, 1705).

LEVI DE BARRIOS, DANIEL, *Triumpho del govierno popular y de la antiguedad holandesa* (Amsterdam, 1683).

El libro de los acuerdos, ed. L. D. Barnett (Oxford, 1931).

LIGHTFOOT, JOHN, *The Whole Works*, ed. J. R. Pitman (London, 1822–5).

—— *The Works* (London, 1684).

LINDO, ABIGAIL, *A Hebrew and English and English and Hebrew Dictionary with Roots and Abbreviations* (London, 1846).

LINDO, E. H., *A Jewish Calendar for Sixty-Four Years* (London, 1838).

LISSACK, MOSES (Morris), *Jewish Perseverance; or, The Jew at Home and Abroad: An Autobiography* (London, 1851).

A List of Converts to Judaism in the City of London, 1809–1816, ed. B. A. Elzas (New York, 1911).

LOCKE, JOHN, *A Letter on Toleration*, ed. and trans. R. Klibansky and J. W. Gough (Oxford, 1968).

'London in 1689–90', ed. D. Maclean, *Transactions of the London and Middlesex Archaeological Society*, NS, (1933–7).

LOWMAN, MOSES, *Three Tracts* (London, 1756).

LURIA, J., *A Penitential Sermon* (London, 1803).

LUTTRELL, NARCISSUS, *A Brief Historical Relation of State Affairs* (Oxford, 1857).

LYON, ANGEL, *A Letter from Angel Lyon, to . . . Lord George Gordon, on Wearing Beards: with Lord George Gordon's Answer* ([London, June 1789]): very rare; repr. I. Solomons, 'Lord George Gordon's Conversion to Judaism', *TJHSE* 7 (1915), 251–5.

LYON, SOLOMON, *A Theological Hebrew Grammar and Lexicon* (Liverpool, 5575 [1815]).

MACAULAY, T. B., 'Civil Disabilities of the Jews', *Edinburgh Review* (Jan. 1831), repr. in his *Critical and Historical Essays, Contributed to the Edinburgh Review* (London, 1843), i. 295–310.

MACCAFFREY, W. T., *Elizabeth I: War and Politics, 1588–1603* (Princeton, NJ, 1992).

[MACHADO DE SEQUEIRA, DAVID], *An Account of the Cruelties Exercis'd by the Inquisition in Portugal* (London, 1708): reissued with new title-page as *The History of the Inquisition* (London, 1713).

MAITLAND, WILLIAM, *The History of London* (London, 1739).

MALCOLM, JAMES PELLER, *Anecdotes of the Manners and Customs of London during the Eighteenth Century* (2nd edn., London, 1810).

—— *Londinium redivivum; or, An Ancient History and Modern Description of London* (London, 1803–7).

MANGEY, THOMAS, *Remarks upon Nazarenus* (London, 1718).

MARCUS, MOSES, *An Answer to the Letter to Dr Walerstand in Relation to the Point of Circumcision* (London, 1731).

—— *A Defence of the Hebrew Bible, in Answer to . . . Whiston* (London, 1729).

—— *The Principal Motives and Circumstances that Induced Moses Marcus to Leave the Jewish, and Embrace the Christian Faith* (London, 1724).

MARCUS, MOSES, *A Grammar of the Hebrew Language, with Points* (London, 1825).

MARGOLIOUTH, MOSES, *The History of the Jews in Great Britain* (London, 1851).

—— *The Anglo-Hebrews: Their Past Wrongs, and Present Grievances* (London, 1856).

—— *Vestiges of the Historic Anglo-Hebrews in East Anglia* (London, 1870).

MARKS, D. W., and LÖWY, ALBERT, *Memoir of Sir Francis Henry Goldsmid* (2nd edn., London, 1882).

MARKS, HENRY JOHN, *Narrative of Henry John Marks, Formerly a Jew, now a Follower of the Lord Jesus Christ* (London, 1838).

MARLOWE, CHRISTOPHER, *Complete Works*, ed. F. Bowers (Cambridge, 1973).

MARSTON, JOHN, *Eastward-Hoe* (London, 1605), in *The Plays*, ed. H. H. Wood (Edinburgh, 1934–9), iii.

—— *The Malcontent* (London, 1604), ibid. i.

[MEARS, ABRAHAM] 'Gamaliel Ben Pedahzur, Gent.', *The Book of Religion, Ceremonies, and Prayers; of the Jews* (London, 1738).

MEISTER, HENRY, *Letters Written during a Residence in England* (London, 1799).

MELDOLA, D., *Epitaph to the Memory of the Much Lamented Abigail* (n.p., 1848).

MENASSEH BEN ISRAEL, *The Hope of Israel*, ed. Moses Wall (2nd edn., London, 1652); ALSO ED. H. MÉCHOULAN AND G. NAHON (OXFORD, 1987).

—— 'The Relation of Master Antonie Monterinos', in Thomas Thorowgood, *Ievves in America* (London, 1650), 129–38.

—— *To His Highnesse the Lord Protector . . . The Humble Addresses of Menasseh Ben Israel* (London, n.d. = 1655).

—— *Vindiciae Judaeorum* (n.p., 1656).

MILLS, JOHN, *The British Jews* (London, 1853).

[MILMAN, HENRY HART], *The History of the Jews* (London, 1829).

Miscellaneous Correspondence . . . Sent to the Author of the Gentleman's Magazine, 5 (1745).

MONSON, WILLIAM, *The Naval Tracts*, ed. M. Oppenheim (London, 1902–14).

MOREIRA, JACOB RODRIGUES, *Kehilath Jahacob: Being a Vocabulary of Words in the Hebrew Language* (London, 1773).

MORITZ, CARL PHILIP, *Journeys of a German in England in 1782*, ed. and trans. R. Nettel (London, 1965).

Motives to the Study of Hebrew (Carmarthen, 1809).

Mr Christopher Dodworth's Proceedings against the Exportation of Silver by the Jews and Others (London, [1690]): single sheet folio.

'Mr. David Levi, The Learned Jew', *European Magazine*, 35 (1799), 291–4.

MURPHY, ARTHUR, *The Works* (London, 1786).

NASHE, THOMAS, *The Works*, ed. R. B. McKerrow (Oxford, 1966).

NATHAN, ISAAC, *Fugitive Pieces and Reminiscences of Lord Byron* (London, 1829).

—— *Musurgia vocalis* (London, 1823).

NEVILL, MARIANNE, (Greek and Hebrew) *The Book of Common Prayer* (Dublin, 25 Oct. 1829).

NEWCOME, HENRY, *Autobiography*, ed. R. Parkinson (Chetham Soc., xxvi–xxvii, 1852).

The Nicholas Papers, ed. G. F. Warner (Camden Soc., NS xl, l, lvii; 3rd ser. xxxi; 1886–1920).

NICHOLS, J., *Illustrations of the Literary History of the Eighteenth Century* (London, 1817–58).

[NIETO, DAVID], *De la Divina Providencia* (London, 1704).

—— *Devota, y humilde suplicación* [London, 1701].

—— *Esh Dath* (Hebrew) (London, 1715).

NIETO, ISAAC, *Orden de las oraciones* (London, 1740–71).

—— *Sermao funebre* (London, 1728).

—— *Sermon . . . y problemático diálogo* (London, 1703).

The Northern Lord; or, The Cruel Jew's Garland (Hull, [c.1785]).

O., R., *Reasons why Jews, Turks, Infidels, and Hereticks Cannot be Saved* (Douai, 1720).

OFFOR, GEORGE, jun., *An Easy Introduction to Reading the Hebrew Language* (London, 1814).

OLDYS, WILLIAM (ed.), *Harleian Miscellany* (London, 1808–13).

The Olive Branch; or, A Plea for Israel (London, 1851).

Order of Service Performed at the Consecration of the New Synagogue (London, 1837).

Order of Service to be Performed at the Great Synagogue, Duke's Place, on the Occasion of the Presence of their Royal Highnesses the Dukes of Cumberland, Sussex, & Cambridge on Friday, April 14. A.M. 5569 (London, [1809]).

Original Letters Illustrative of English History, ed. H. Ellis (2nd ser. iv, London, 1827).

Original Letters Relative to the English Reformation, ed. H. Robinson (Parker Soc., Cambridge, 1846–7).

OUTRAM, WILLIAM, *Two Dissertations on Sacrifices*, trans. John Allen (2nd edn., London, 1828; 1st pub. 1677).

Pamphlets Relating to the Jews in England in the Seventeenth and Eighteenth Centuries, ed. P. Radin (San Francisco, 1939).

PARKER, G., *A View of Society and Manners in High and Low Life* (London, 1781).

Parliamentary History of England, ed. William Cobbett (London, 1806–20): when taken over by the printer T. C. Hansard in 1812 [=vol. xiii] the title was changed to *The Parliamentary History*.

PARTINGTON, C. F., *National [sic?] History and Views of London and its Environs* (London, 1834).

PASQUIN, P. P., *Jewish Conversion* (London, 1814).

PECKARD, PETER, *The Popular Clamour against the Jews Indefensible* (London, 1753).

A Peep into the Synagogue; or, A Letter to the Jews (London, n.d.).

PELLATT, APSLEY, *Brief Memoir of the Jews* (London, 1829).

PEPYS, SAMUEL, *Diary*, ed. R. Latham and W. Matthews (London, 1970).

The Pepys Ballads, ed. H. E. Rollins (Cambridge, Mass., 1929–32).

PEREZ, ANTONIO, *A Spaniard in Elizabethan England: The Correspondence of Antonio Perez's Exile*, ed. G. Ungerer (London, 1974–6).

PETERS, HUGH, *A Word for the Armie* (London, 1647).

PHILO-JUDAEIS, *A Letter to Abraham Goldsmid . . . on Mr. Joshua van Oven's Letters* (London, 1802).

PHILO-PATRIAE, *Considerations on the Bill to Permit Persons Professing the Jewish Religion to be Naturalized by Parliament* (London, 1753).

—— *Further Considerations on the Act to Permit Persons Professing the Jewish Religion, to be Naturalized by Parliament* (London, 1753).

Prayer Used at the Opening of the Great Synagogue ([London], 1766).

'The Present State of the Jewish Nation', *New Universal Magazine; or, Gentleman and Lady's Polite Instructor* (May 1752), 338–42.

PRESTON, THEODORE, *The Hebrew Text, and a Latin Version of . . . Ecclesiastes* (London, 1845).

PRIESTLEY, JOSEPH, *Life and Correspondence*, ed. J. T. Rutt (London, 1831–2).

—— *Theological and Miscellaneous Works*, ed. J. T. Rutt (London, 1817–31).

Proposals for Establishing a Charitable Fund (London, 1706).

PRYNNE, WILLIAM, *A Short Demurrer to the Jewes* (2nd edn., London, 1656).

RAGUENET, *Histoire d'Olivier Cromwel* (Utrecht, 1692).

Records of the Reformation: The Divorce, 1527–33, ed. N. Pocock (Oxford, 1870).

Remarks on the Reverend Mr. Tucker's Letter (London, 1753).

A Reply to the Famous Jew Question (London, [1754]).

Reports of Cases Argued and Determined in the Consistory Court of London, ed. John Haggard (London, 1822).

[RINTEL], MEIR HACOHEN, *Minkhat Kanaoth* (Hebrew) (London, 1817).

RODRIGUES MOREIRA, JACOB, *Kehilath Jahacob: Being a Vocabulary of Words in the Hebrew Language* (London, 5533 [1773]).

[ROMAINE, WILLIAM], *An Answer to a Pamphlet, Entitled, Considerations on the Bill* (2nd edn., London, 1753).

Rules and Regulations for the Management of the Jews' Hospital, Mile End, Called Neveh Tsedek (London, 1808).

Rules Framed for the Management of the Orphan Charity School, Known by the Name of H.K. Talmud Torah, Belonging to the German Jews (London, 1788).

RYCAUT, PAUL, *The Turkish History* (6th edn., London, 1687).

SASPORTAS, JACOB, *Ohel Ya'akov* (Hebrew *responsa*) (Amsterdam, 1737).

SAUSSURE, CÉSAR DE, *A Foreign View of England in the Reigns of George I & George II: The Letters of Monsieur César de Saussure to his Family*, trans. and ed. Madame van Muyden (London, 1902).

[SCHOMBERG, RALPH], *The Modern Quacks Detected* (London, 1752).

Seasonable Remarks on the Act Lately Pass'd in Favour of the Jews (London, 1753).

SHIFF, DAVID SOLOMON, *A Song and Praise . . . at the Dedication of the Great Jews Synagogue* (London, 1790).

A Short Answer to His Grace the D. Buckingham's Paper, Concerning Religion, Toleration, and Liberty of Conscience (London, 1685).

A Short Inquiry into the Import of the Prophecies Relative to the Restoration of Israel (London, 1820).

SILLIMAN, BENJAMIN, *A Journal of Travels in England, Holland and Scotland* (New York, 1810).

SMEETON, GEORGE, *Doings in London or Day and Night Scenes of the Frauds, Frolics, Manners, and Depravities of the Metropolis* (London, [1828]).

SMITH, HORACE, *Zillah, a Tale of the Holy City* (2nd edn., London, 1828).

SOLOMON DE A. R., *The Reply of the Jews to the Letters Addressed to them by Doctor Joseph Priestley* (Oxford, 1787).

—— *A Second Letter to Dr. Joseph Priestley* (Oxford, 1790).

[SOUTHEY, ROBERT] Don Manuel Alvarez Espriella, *Letters from England*, ed. J. Simmons (London, 1951; 1st pub. 1807).

—— *Selections from the Letters of Robert Southey*, ed. J. W. Warter (London, 1856).

SPENCE, JOSEPH, *Anecdotes, Observations, and Characters, of Books and Men* (2nd edn., London, 1858).

—— *Observations, Anecdotes, and Characters of Books and Men*, ed. J. M. Osborn (Oxford, 1966).

SPENCER-STANHOPE, ELIZABETH, *The Letter-Bag of Lady Elizabeth Spencer-Stanhope*, ed. A. M. W. Stirling (London, 1913).

SPINDLER, *The Jew* (London, 1832).

Statutes of the Realm, ed. T. E. Tomlins, *et al.* (London, 1810–28).

STEPHENS, LEWIS, *The Excellencies of the Kindness . . . Delivering Joseph Ottolenghe, a Poor Convert Jew* (Exeter, [1735]).

STOW, JOHN, *The Annals of England*, ed. J. Strype (London, 1755).

—— *Chronicles* (London, 1631).

—— *A Survey of the Cities of London and Westminster* (London, 1720).

Strange and Wonderful News from Borton: Near the City of Canterbury (London, 1686).

SWAIN, JOHN HADLEY, *Objections of Mr. David Levi* (London, 1787).

SWANSTON, CLEMENT TUDWAY, *Reports of Cases Argued and Determined in the High Court of Chancery, during the Time of Lord Chancellor Eldon* (London, 1821–7).

Swedish Diplomats at Cromwell's Court, 1655–1656, ed. M. Roberts (Camden Soc., 4th ser. xxxvi, 1988).

TANG, NAPHTALI, *Pirkei Avoth The Sentences and Proverbs* (London, 1772).

TAYLOR, THOMAS, *Ten Sermons on the Millennium* (Hull, 1789).

TEGG, THOMAS, *The Rise, Progress, and Termination of the O.P. War* (London, 1810).

THURLOE, JOHN, *A Collection of the State Papers*, ed. Thomas Birch (London, 1742).

'TIMOTHY TELLTRUTH', *A Proposal Humbly Offered to the Legislature of this Kingdom* (London, 1753).

TOLAND, JOHN, *Nazarenus; or, Jewish, Gentile, and Mahometan Christianity* (London, 1718), incl. 'Two Problems Concerning the Jewish Nation and Religion'.

—— *Reasons for Naturalizing the Jews in Great Britain and Ireland* (London, 1714).

TOVEY, D'BLOSSIERS, *Anglia Judaica; or, The History and Antiquities of the Jews in England* (Oxford, 1738).

TOWNLEY, JAMES, *The Reasons of the Laws of Moses: From ... Maimonides* (London, 1827).

TOWNSHEND, HENRY, *Diary*, ed. J. W. Willis (Worcestershire Hist. Soc., xxxi, 1915–20).

A True and Exact Account of a Famous New Prophet now Residing at Alkair a City in Ægypt (London, 1687).

A Trve Report of Sondry Horrible Conspiracies of Late Time Detected to Have (by Barbarous Murders) Taken away the Life of the Queen's Most Excellent Maiesty; whom Almighty God Hath Miraculously Conserved against the Treacheries of her Rebelles, & the Violences of her Most Puissant Enemies (London: Charles Yetsweirt, Nov. 1594).

Tryal of Francis Francia (London, 1717).

TUCKER, JOSIAH, *A Letter to a Friend Concerning Naturalization* (London, 1753).

—— *A Second Letter to a Friend Concerning Naturalizations* (London, 1753).

[TWYNE, THOMAS?], *The Schoolemaster; or, Teacher of Table Philosophie* (London, 1576).

USQUE, SAMUEL, *Consolation for the Tribulations of Israel*, ed. M. A. Cohen (Philadelphia, 1977).

[VAN HELMONT, FRANCIS], *A Cabbalistical Dialogue* (London, 1682).

—— *A Letter to a Gentleman* (London, 1690).

—— *Seder Olam; or, The Order of Ages* (London, 1694).

VAN OVEN, JOSHUA, *Letters on the Present State of the Jewish Poor in the Metropolis with Propositions for Ameliorating their Condition* (London, 1802).

Victoria County History, *Bucks*.

A Vindication of the Reverend Mr. John Gill (London, n.d. [1750?]).

VIOLET, THOMAS, *The Advancement of Merchandize* (London, 1651).

—— *A Petition against the Jewes* (London, 1661).

W., R., *Letter to the Jews* (London, 1787).

[WADE, JOHN], *A Treatise on the Police and Crimes of the Metropolis* (London, 1829).

WALPOLE, HORACE, *Correspondence*, ed. W. S. Lewis, *et al.* (London, 1937–83).
—— *Memoires of the Last Ten Years of the Reign of George the Second* (London, 1822).
WALSINGHAM, FRANCIS, *Journal*, ed. C. T. Martin (Camden Soc., civ, Misc., vi, 1871).
WATSON, ROBERT, *The Life of Lord George Gordon: With a Philosophical Review of his Political Conduct* (London, 1795).
[WEBB, PHILIP CARTERET], *The Question, Whether a Jew, Born within the British Dominions, Was, before the Making the Late Act of Parliament, a Person, Capable, by Law, to Purchase and Hold Lands to him, and his Heirs, Fairly Stated and Considered* (London, 1753).
WENDEBORN, [GEBHARDT] FRED. AUG., *A View of England towards the Close of the Eighteenth Century* (London, 1791).
[WESTMACOTT, C. M.], *The English Spy* (London, 1907; 1st pub. 1826).
WHITAKER, E. W., *A Dissertation on the Prophecies Relating to the Final Restoration of the Jews* (Canterbury, 1784).
—— *The Manual of Prophecy* (Egham, 1808).
Whole Proceedings on the Trials of . . . Lord George Gordon (London, 1787).
WILMOT, JOHN EARDLEY, 'A Memoir of the Life of Samson Gideon', in J. Nichols, *Illustrations of the Literary History of the Eighteenth Century* (London, 1817–58), vi. 277–84.
WILSON, THOMAS, *The Diaries*, ed. C. L. S. Linnell (London, 1964).
WINSTANLEY, T., *A Sermon Preached . . . on Occasion of the Clamours against the Act for Naturalizing the Jews* (London, 1753).
WITHERBY, THOMAS, *An Attempt to Remove Prejudices Concerning the Jewish Nation* (London, 1804).
—— *A Vindication of the Jews* (London, 1809).
WOLF[F], JOSEPH, *Missionary Journal and Memoir*, rev. and ed. John Bayford (London, 1824).
The Wonderful Discovery of the Murder of a Jew (Dublin, 1823).
WOOD, ANTHONY, *Athenae Oxonienses*, ed. Philip Bliss (London, 1813–20).
—— *Fasti Oxonienses*, ed. P. Bliss (3rd edn., London, 1815–20).
WOTTON, HENRY, *The State of Christendom* (London, 1657).
WRANGHAM, FRANCIS, *The Restoration of the Jews: A Poem* (Cambridge, 1795).
WRIOTHESLEY, CHARLES, *A Chronicle of England during the Reigne of the Tudors*, ed. W. D. Hamilton (Camden Soc., NS xi, xx, 1875, 1877).
WROE, JOHN, *An Abridgement of John Wroe's Life and Travels* (4th edn., Gravesend, 1851).
—— *Communications Given to John Wroe* (4th edn., Gravesend, 1852).
—— *Divine Communications and Prophecies* (Wakefield, 1834).
—— *A Guide to the People Surnamed Israelites* (Gravesend, 1852).
—— *The Laws and Commands of God* (Wakefield, 1835).
—— *The Vision of an Angel* (Bradford, 1820).
—— *The Word of God* (Wakefield, 1834).
XERES, JOHN, *An Address to the Jews* (London, 1710).
YOUNG, ROBERT, *Book of the Precepts* (Edinburgh, n.d.).
—— *The Ethics of the Fathers* (Edinburgh, [1849]).

ZAGACHE, ABRAHAM, 'Memoria de la gente que ay en la nación de Londres': Ets Haim Library, Amsterdam: repr. *Bevis Marks Records*, i, ed. L. D. Barnett (Oxford, 1940), 16–20.

ZVI ASHKENAZI, *Decisión del doctíssimo, y excelentíssimo Senōr H.H. . . . Zevi Asquenazi* (London, 1705).

B. *Secondary works*

ABRAHAMS, B. Z. L., 'Grace Aguilar', *TJHSE* 16 (1952), 137–48.

ABRAHAMS, D., 'Jew Brokers of the City of London', *MJHSE* 3 (1937), 80–94.

ABRAHAMS, I., 'Hebrew Loyalty under the First Four Georges', *TJHSE* 9 (1922), 103–30.

—— 'Isaac Abendana's Cambridge Mishnah and Oxford Calendars', *TJHSE* 8 (1918), 98–121.

—— 'Joachim Gaunse: A Mining Incident in the Reign of Queen Elizabeth', *TJHSE* 4 (1903), 83–101.

——'Note on Isaac Abendana', *TJHSE* 10 (1924), 221–4.

—— 'Text of Mr. Robert Grant's Bill, 1830', *TJHSE* 6 (1912), 249–53.

—— and SAYLE, C. E., 'The Purchase of Hebrew Books by the English Parliament in 1647', *TJHSE* 8 (1918), 63–77.

ABRAHAMS, L., 'Sir I. L. Goldsmid and the Admission of the Jews of England to Parliament', *TJHSE* 4 (1903), 116–29.

ABULAFIA CORCOS, D., 'Samuel Pallache and his London Trial' (Hebrew), *Zion*, 25 (1960), 122–33.

ADLER, E. N., *About Hebrew Manuscripts* (London, 1905).

—— *Jewish Travellers* (London, 1930).

ADLER, H., 'The Baal Shem of London', *TJHSE* 5 (1908), 148–73.

ADLER, M., *Jews of Medieval England* (London, 1939).

ÅKERMAN, S., *Queen Christina of Sweden and her Circle* (Leiden, 1991).

ALDAG, P., *Das Judentum in England* (Berlin, 1943).

ALDERMAN, G., *The Jewish Community in British Politics* (Oxford, 1983).

—— *Modern British Jewry* (Oxford, 1992).

ALLEN, W., *Translating for King James* (London, 1970).

ALTHOLZ, J. L., *The Religious Press in Britain, 1760–1900* (New York, 1989).

AMZALAK, M. B., *David Nieto* (Lisbon, 1923).

ANDERSON, S. P., *An English Consul in Turkey: Paul Rycaut at Smyrna, 1667–1678* (Oxford, 1989).

Anglo-Jewish Historical Exhibition, Royal Albert Hall, London, 1887, *Catalogue* (London, 1888).

—— *Papers Read at the Anglo–Jewish Historical Exhibition* (London, 1888).

Archives of the United Synagogue: Report and Catalogue, ed. C. Roth (London, 1930).

BARNETT, A., 'Solomon Bennett, 1761–1838: Artist, Hebraist and Controversialist', *TJHSE* 17 (1953), 91–111.

—— 'Sussex Hall: The First Anglo-Jewish Venture in Popular Education', *TJHSE* 19 (1960), 65–79.

BARNETT, A., *The Western Synagogue through Two Centuries (1761–1961)* (London, 1961).

BARNETT, L. D., 'The First Record of the Hebra Guemilut Hasadim, London, 1678', *TJHSE* 10 (1924), 258–60.

BARNETT, R. D., 'The Correspondence of the Mahamad of the Spanish and Portuguese Congregation of London during the Seventeenth and Eighteenth Centuries', *TJHSE* 20 (1964), 1–50.

—— 'Dr Jacob de Castro Sarmento and Sephardim in Medical Practice in 18th-Century London', *TJHSE* 27 (1982), 84–114.

—— 'Haham Meldola and Hazan de Sola', *TJHSE* 21 (1968), 1–38.

—— 'Isaac Leonini Azulay', *TJHSE* 19 (1960), 81–96.

—— 'More Letters of Hazan de Sola', *TJHSE* 24 (1975), 173–82.

BAROWAY, I., 'Toward Understanding Tudor-Jacobean Hebrew Studies', *JSS* 18 (1956), 3–24.

BARZILAY, I. E., 'John Toland's Borrowings from Simone Luzzatto', *JSS* 31 (1969), 75–81.

BATTEN, J. M., *John Dury: Advocate of Christian Reunion* (Chicago, 1944).

BAUMER, F. L., 'England, the Turk and the Common Corps of Christendom', *AHR* 50 (1944–5), 26–48.

BEDOUELLE, G., 'The Consultations of the Universities and Scholars Concerning the "Great Matter" of King Henry VIII', in D. C. Steinmetz (ed.), *The Bible in the Sixteenth Century* (Durham, 1990), 21–36.

—— and LE BAL, P., *Le 'Divorce' du roi Henry VIII: Études et documents* (Geneva, 1987).

BEINART, H., 'The Jews in the Canary Islands: A Re-evaluation', *TJHSE* 25 (1977), 48–86.

BELLOT, H. H., *University College London 1826–1926* (London, 1929).

BENTWICH, N., 'Anglo-Jewish Causes Célèbres', *TJHSE* 15 (1946), 93–120.

BERLIN, I., 'Benjamin Disraeli, Karl Marx and the Search for Identity', in his *Against the Current* (London, 1980), 252–86.

BERTIE, C. H., *Isaac Nathan: Australia's First Composer* (Sydney, 1922).

BEVAN, E. R., and SINGER, C. (eds.), *The Legacy of Israel* (2nd edn., Oxford, 1928).

Biblioteca española–portugueza–judaïca, ed. M. Kayserling (Strasburg, 1890).

Bibliotheca Sussexiana: A Descriptive Catalogue, ed. T. J. Pettigrew (London, 1827–39).

BLAKE, R., *Disraeli* (New York, 1967).

BLAU, J. L., *The Christian Interpretation of the Cabala in the Renaissance* (New York, 1944).

BLEACKLEY, H., *Some Distinguished Victims of the Scaffold* (London, 1905).

—— *Trial of Henry Fauntleroy* (London, 1924).

BLOCH, J., 'An Early Hebrew Translation of the Book of Common Prayer', in A. Marx and H. Meyer (eds.), *Festschrift für Aron Freimann* (Berlin, 1935).

BLOOM, H. I., *The Economic Activities of the Jews of Amsterdam in the Seventeenth and Eighteenth Centuries* (Port Washington, NY, 1969 [1937]).

BOSSY, J., *The English Catholic Community 1570–1850* (London, 1975).

BOXER, C. R., 'Antonio Vieira S. J. and the Institution of the Brazil Company in 1649', *Hispanic American History Review*, 29 (1949), 474–97.

BOYER, R. E., *English Declarations of Indulgence 1687 and 1688* (The Hague, 1968).

BROWN, C., *A History of Nottinghamshire* (London, 1891).

BROWN, M., 'Anglo-Jewish Country Houses from the Resettlement to 1800', *TJHSE* 28 (1984), 20–38.

BRUGMANS, H. K. and FRANK, A., *Geschiedenis der Joden in Nederland*, (Amsterdam, 1940).

BUENO DE MESQUITA, D., 'The Historical Association of the Ancient Burial-Ground of the Sephardi Jews', *TJHSE* 10 (1924), 225–54.

'The Burial Register of the Spanish and Portuguese Jews, London, 1657–1735', ed. R. D. Barnett, *MJHSE* 6 (1962), 1–72.

BURN, J. S., 'Protestant Refugees in 1563 and 1571', *Notes and Queries*, 2nd ser. 8 (3 Dec. 1859), 448.

BUSSE, G. W., 'The Herem of Rabenu Tam in Queen Anne's London', *TJHSE* 21 (1968), 138–47.

BUTLER, M. S., *Maria Edgeworth* (Oxford, 1972).

BUTTERFIELD, H., 'Toleration in Early Modern Times', *Journal of the History of Ideas*, 38 (1977), 573–84.

CALISCH, E. N., *The Jew in English Literature, as Author and as Subject* (Richmond, 1909).

CAPP, B. S., *The Fifth Monarchy Men* (London, 1972).

CARABELLI, G., *Tolandiana: Materiali bibliografici per lo studio dell'opera e della fortuna di John Toland (1670–1722)* (Florence, 1975).

CARLISLE, N., *A Concise Description of the Endowed Grammar Schools in England and Wales* (London, 1818).

CARMOLY, E., *Histoire des médecins juifs* (Brussels, 1844).

CARPI, D., 'On Rabbi Jacob Mantino's Stay in Padua (1531–1533)' (Hebrew), in his *Between Renaissance and Ghetto* (Tel Aviv, 1989), 85–95.

CASSELL, C., 'The West Metropolitan Jewish School 1845–97', *TJHSE* 19 (1960), 115–28.

CASSUTO, J., 'Aus dem ältesten Protokollbuch der Portugiesisch-Jüdischen Gemeinde in Hamburg', *Jrb. Jud.-Lit. Gft.* 6 (1909).

CASTRO, D. H. DE, *De Synagoge der Portugeesch-Israelietische Gemeente te Amsterdam* (The Hague, 1875).

CASTRO, J. DE, *The Gordon Riots* (London, 1926).

Catalogue of an Exhibition of Anglo-Jewish Art and History in Commemoration of the Tercentenary of the Resettlement of the Jews in the British Isles [Victoria and Albert Museum] (London, 1956).

Catalogue of Prints and Drawings in the British Museum: Division I: Political and Personal Satires, i (London, 1870).

CHANDAMAN, C. D., 'The Financial Settlement in the Parliament of 1685', in H. Hearder and H. R. Loyn (eds.), *British Government and Administration: Studies Presented to S. B. Chrimes* (Cardiff, 1974), 144–54.

CHRIMES, S. B., *Henry VII* (London, 1972).

CLAPHAM, J., *The Bank of England* (Cambridge, 1944).

COHEN, A., 'Levi Barent Cohen and Some of his Descendants', *TJHSE* 16 (1952), 11–23.

COHEN, N., 'Non-religious Factors in the Emergence of the Chief Rabbinate', *TJHSE* 21 (1968), 304–13.

COHEN, R. (ed.), *The Jewish Nation in Surinam* (Amsterdam, 1982).

COHN, N., *The Pursuit of the Millennium* (rev. edn., London, 1970).

COHN-SHERBOK, D., *The Jews of Canterbury 1760–1931* (Canterbury, 1984).

COLSON, P., *The Strange History of Lord George Gordon* (London, 1937).

CRANFIELD, G. A., 'The "London Evening-Post" and the Jew Bill of 1753', *History Journal*, 8 (1965), 16–30.

CROOK, R. E., *A Bibliography of Joseph Priestley* (London, 1966).

DAICHES, D., *The King James Version of the English Bible . . . with Special Reference to the Hebrew Tradition* (Chicago, 1941).

DAICHES-DUBIN, R., 'Eighteenth-Century Anglo-Jewry in and around Richmond, Surrey', *TJHSE* 18 (1958), 143–69.

DANN, U., 'Jews in 18th-Century Oxford: Further Observations', *Oxoniensia*, 54 (1989) [1991], 345–53.

D'AVIGDOR-GOLDSMID, H., 'Lord George Bentinck and the Jews', *TJHSE* 23 (1971), 44–52.

DAVIS, R., *The English Rothschilds* (Chapel Hill, NC, 1983).

DE MARLY, D., 'Sir Solomon de Medina's Textile Warehouse', *TJHSE* 27 (1982), 155.

DIAMOND, A. S., 'The Cemetery of the Resettlement', *TJHSE* 19 (1960), 163–90.

—— 'The Community of the Resettlement, 1656–1684: A Social Survey', *TJHSE* 24 (1975), 134–50.

—— 'Problems of the London Sephardi Community, 1720–1733: Philip Carteret Webb's Notebooks', *TJHSE* 21 (1968), 39–63.

DIBDIN, E. R., 'Isaac Nathan', *Music and Letters*, 22 (1941), 75–80.

DICKENS, A. G., *The English Reformation* (New York, 1964).

DIMOCK, A., 'The Conspiracy of Dr. Lopez', *EHR* 9 (1894), 440–72.

DONALD, M. B., *Elizabethan Copper* (London, 1955).

DOWELL, S., *A History of Taxation and Taxes in England* (London, 1884).

DRUMONT, E., *La France juive* (Paris, 1887).

DUKER, A. G., 'Swedenborg's Attitude towards the Jews', *Judaism*, 5 (1956), 272–6.

DUSCHINSKY, C., 'Jacob Kimchi and Shalom Buzaglo', *TJHSE* 7 (1915), 272–90.

—— 'The Rabbinate of the Great Synagogue, London, from 1786–1842', *JQR* NS 9 (1918–19), 103–37, 371–408; 10 (1919–20), 445–527; 11 (1920–1), 21–81, 201–36, 345–87: also repr. in book form (London, 1921; repr. 1971).

EDWARDS, L., 'Daniel Mendoza', *TJHSE* 15 (1946), 73–92.

ELLIOTT, J. H., *Imperial Spain* (London, 1963).

ELLIOTT, R. W., *The Story of King Edward VI School Bury St Edmunds* (Bury St Edmunds, 1963).

ELON, M., 'Levirate Marriage and Halizah', *EJ* xi. 122–31.

ELTON, G. R., *Reform and Reformation* (London, 1977).
—— *The Tudor Constitution* (Cambridge, 1972).
EMANUEL, C. H. L., *A Century and a Half of Jewish History: Extracted from the Minute Books of the London Committee of Deputies of the British Jews* (London, 1910).
EMDEN, P. H., 'The Brothers Goldsmid and the Financing of the Napoleonic Wars', *TJHSE* 14 (1935–9), 225–46.
Encyclopaedia Judaica (Jerusalem, 1972).
ENDELMAN, T. M., 'The Checkered Career of "Jew" King: A Study in Anglo-Jewish Social History', *AJSR* 7–8 (1982–3), 69–100.
—— 'Communal Solidarity among the Jewish Elite of Victorian London', *Victorian Studies*, 28 (1985), 491–526.
—— 'Disraeli's Jewishness Reconsidered', *Modern Judaism*, 5 (1985), 109–23.
—— 'The Englishness of Jewish Modernity in England', in J. Katz (ed.), *Towards Modernity: The European Jewish Model* (New Brunswick, 1987), 225–46.
—— *The Jews of Georgian England 1714–1830* (Philadelphia, 1979).
—— *Radical Assimilation in English Jewish History, 1656–1945* (Bloomington, Ind., 1990).
EPSTEIN, I., 'The Story of Ascama I of the Spanish and Portuguese Jewish Congregation of London with Special Reference to Responsa Material', in M. Ben-Horin (ed.), *Studies and Essays in Honour of Abraham A. Neuman* (Leiden, 1962), 170–214.
'Equity Proceedings in the Court of Chancery (1750–1800)', ed. G. Dworkin, *MJHSE* 6 (1962), 195–8.
ETTINGER, S., 'The Beginnings of the Change in the Attitude of European Society towards the Jews', *Scripta Hierosolymitana* 7 (1961), 193–219.
—— 'Jews and Judaism as Seen by the English Deists of the 18th Century' (Hebrew), *Zion*, 29 (1964), 182–207.
EVANS, R. J. W., *The Making of the Hapsburg Monarchy, 1550–1700* (Oxford, 1979).
FELSENSTEIN, F., 'Jews and Devils: Anti-Semitic Stereotypes of Late Medieval and Renaissance England', *Journal of Literature and Theology*, 4 (1990), 15–28.
FENN, P. J., 'Queen Elizabeth's Poisoner', *St. Bartholomew's Hospital Journal* (Feb. 1957), 49–55.
FERGUSON, J. P., *An Eighteenth Century Heretic: Dr. Samuel Clarke* (Kineton, 1976).
FINBERG, H. F., 'Jewish Residents in Eighteenth-Century Twickenham', *TJHSE* 16 (1952), 129–35.
FINES, J., ' "Judaising" in the Period of the English Reformation: The Case of Richard Bruern', *TJHSE* 21 (1968), 323–6.
FINESTEIN, I., 'Anglo-Jewish Opinion during the Struggle for Emancipation', *TJHSE* 20 (1964), 113–43.
—— 'An Aspect of the Jews and English Marriage Law during the Emancipation: The Prohibited Degrees', *JJ Soc.* 7 (1965), 3–21.

FINESTEIN, I., 'A Modern Examination of Macaulay's Case for the Civil Emancipation of the Jews', *TJHSE* 28 (1948), 39–59.

FIRTH, C. H., *Scotland and the Protectorate* (Scot. Hist. Soc., xxxi, 1899).

FISCH, H., *The Dual Image* (London, 1971).

—— *Jerusalem and Albion* (London, 1964).

FISHER, H. E. S., 'Jews in England and the 18th-Century English Economy', *TJHSE* 27 (1982), 156–65.

FLETCHER, H. F., *Milton's Rabbinical Readings* (Urbana, Ill., 1930).

—— *Milton's Semitic Studies* (Chicago, 1926).

FORSTER, E. M., *Marianne Thornton: A Domestic Biography, 1797–1887* (New York, 1956).

FRASER, A., *Royal Charles* (New York, 1979).

FRIEDENWALD, H., *The Jews and Medicine* (Baltimore, 1944).

FRIEDMAN, L. M., *Early American Jews* (Cambridge, Mass., 1934).

—— 'Francisco de Faria, an American Jew, and the Popish Plot', *PAJHS* 20 (1911), 115–32.

—— 'A Petition for the Readmission of the Jews', *TJHSE* 16 (1952), 222–3.

FROUDE, J. A., *The Divorce of Catherine of Aragon* (2nd edn., London, 1891).

FRUCHTMAN, J., jnr., *The Apocalyptic Politics of Richard Price and Joseph Priestley: A Study in Late Eighteenth-Century Republican Millenarianism* (Philadelphia, 1983).

FUKS, L. and R., 'Menasseh ben Israel as a Bookseller in the Light of New Data', *Quaerendo*, 11 (1981), 34–45.

FULLER, J. O., *The Comte de Saint-Germain: Last Scion of the House of Rakoczy* (London, 1988).

GARRETT, C., *Respectable Folly: Millenarians and the French Revolution in France and England* (Baltimore, 1975).

GARTNER, L. P., 'Emancipation, Social Change and Communal Reconstruction in Anglo-Jewry, 1789–1881', *PAAJR* 54 (1987), 73–116, esp. 90–1.

—— 'A Quarter Century of Anglo-Jewish Historiography', *JSS* 48 (1986), 105–26.

—— 'Urban History and the Pattern of Provincial Jewish Settlement in Victorian England', *JJ Soc.* 23 (1981), 37–56.

GASTER, M., *History of the Ancient Synagogue of the Spanish and Portuguese Jews* (London, 1901).

GEORGE, M. D., *London Life in the Eighteenth Century* (New York, 1964 [1925]).

GIBBS, F. W., *Joseph Priestley* (London, 1965).

GIDNEY, W. T., *History of the London Society for Promoting Christianity amongst the Jews* (London, 1908).

GILAM, A., 'Anglo-Jewish Attitudes toward Benjamin Disraeli during the Era of Emancipation', *JSS* 42 (1980), 313–22.

—— 'Benjamin Disraeli and Jewish Identity', *Wiener Library Bulletin* 32–3 (1980), 2–8.

—— 'The Burial Grounds Controversy between Anglo-Jewry and the Victorian Board of Health, 1850', *JSS* 45 (1983), 147–56.

—— 'Disraeli in Jewish Historiography', *Midstream* (Mar. 1980).

—— *The Emancipation of the Jews in England, 1830–1860* (New York, 1982).

GIMLETTE, T., *The History of the Huguenot Settlers in Ireland, and Other Literary Remains* (n.p., 1888).

GIUSEPPI, J. A., 'Early Jewish Holders of Bank of England Stock (1694–1725)' [lists], *MJHSE* 6 (1962), 143–74.

—— 'Sephardi Jews and the Early Years of the Bank of England', *TJHSE* 19 (1960), 53–63.

GLASSMAN, B., *Anti-Semitic Stereotypes Without Jews: Images of the Jews in England, 1290–1700* (Detroit, 1975).

GOLDSTEIN, D., 'Hebrew Printed Books in the Library of Westminster Abbey', *TJHSE* 27 (1982), 151–4.

GOLLANCZ, H., 'A Contribution to the History of the Readmission of the Jews', *TJHSE* 6 (1912), 189–204.

GOODMAN, P., *Bevis Marks in History* (London, 1934).

GORIS, J. A., *Étude sur les colonies marchandes méridionales à Anvers de 1488 à 1567* (Louvain, 1925).

GOULSTON, M., 'The Status of the Anglo-Jewish Rabbinate, 1840–1914', *JJ Soc.* 10 (1968), 55–82.

GREENSLADE, S. L. (ed.), *The Cambridge History of the Bible*, ii. (Cambridge, 1963).

GRIFFITH, A., 'Dr Roderigo Lopes', *St. Bartholomew's Hospital Journal* (Nov. 1964), 449–52.

GUTTENTAG, G. D., 'The Beginnings of the Newcastle Jewish Community', *TJHSE* 25 (1977), 1–24.

GUY, J., 'Scripture as Authority: Problems of Interpretation in the 1530s', in A. Fox and J. Guy (eds.), *Reassessing the Henrician Age* (Oxford, 1986).

GWYNN, R. D., 'James II in Light of his Treatment of Huguenot Refugees in England', *EHR* 92 (1977), 820–33.

HALPER, B., *Post-biblical Hebrew Literature* (Philadelphia, 1921).

HARRIS, I., 'A Dutch Burial-Ground and its English Connections', *TJHSE* 7 (1915), 113–46.

—— *History of Jews' College* (London, 1906).

HARRISON, J. F. C., *The Second Coming: Popular Millenarianism 1780–1850* (London, 1979).

HEERTJE, A., 'On David Ricardo (1772–1823)', *TJHSE* 24 (1975), 73–81.

HENRIQUES, H. S. Q., *Jewish Marriages and the English Law* (London, 1909).

—— *The Jews and the English Law* (Oxford, 1908).

—— 'Proposals for Special Taxation of the Jews after the Revolution', *TJHSE* 9 (1922), 39–66.

—— *The Return of the Jews to England* (London, 1905).

HENRIQUES, U. R. Q., 'The Jewish Emancipation Controversy in Nineteenth-Century Britain', *Past & Present*, 40 (1968), 126–46.

—— *Religious Toleration in England, 1787–1833* (London, 1961).

HERZOG, I., 'John Selden and Jewish Law', *Publications of the Society for Jewish Jurisprudence*, 3 (1931).

HEWETT, O. W., *Strawberry Fair: A Biography of Frances, Countess Waldegrave, 1821–1879* (London, 1956).

HIBBERT, C., *King Mob* (London, 1959).

HILL, C., 'John Mason and the End of the World', in his *Puritanism and Revolution* (London, 1958).

HILLS, G. P. G., 'Notes on Some Contemporary References to Dr. Falk, the Baal Shem of London, in the Rainsford MSS. at the British Museum', *TJHSE* 8 (1918), 122–8.

HILTON, C., 'St Bartholomew's Hospital, London, and its Jewish Connections', *TJHSE* 30 (1989), 21–50.

HIRSCHBERG, H. Z. (J. W.), 'Jews and Jewish Affairs in the Relations between Great Britain and Morocco in the 18th Century', in H. J. Zimmells, *et al.* (eds.), *Essays Presented to Chief Rabbi Israel Brodie* (London, 1967), 153–81.

The Historical Register of the University of Cambridge, ed. J. R. Tanner (Cambridge, 1917).

The Historical Register of the University of Oxford (Oxford, 1900).

HOPKINS, J. K., *A Woman to Deliver her People: Joanna Southcott and English Millenarianism in an Era of Revolution* (Austin, Tex., 1982).

HUME, M. A. S., 'Conspiración del Dr. Ruy López contra Isabel de Inglaterra y supuesta complicidad de Felipe II', in his *Españoles e ingleses en el siglo XVI* (Madrid, 1903), 205–33.

—— *Treason and Plot: Struggles for Catholic Supremacy in the Last Years of Queen Elizabeth* (London, 1901).

—— *The Year after the Armada* (London, 1896).

HUNTER, G. K., 'The Theology of Marlowe's *The Jew of Malta*', *Journal of the Warburg & Courtauld Institutes* 27 (1964), 211–40.

HYAMSON, A. M., *A History of the Jews in England* (London, 1908).

—— 'The Jew Bill of 1753', *TJHSE* 6 (1912), 156–88.

—— *Jews' College, London 1855–1955* (London, 1955).

—— 'The Lost Tribes and the Influence of the Search for them on the Return of the Jews to England', *JQR* 15 (1903), 640–76.

—— 'The Lost Tribes and the Return of the Jews to England', *TJHSE* 5 (1908), 115–47.

—— *The Sephardim of England* (London, 1951).

HYMAN, L., 'Hyman Hurwitz: The First Anglo-Jewish Professor', *TJHSE* 21 (1968), 232–42.

—— *The Jews of Ireland from Earliest Times to the Year 1910* (London, 1972).

ISRAEL, J. I., 'The Economic Contribution of Dutch Sephardi Jews to Holland's Golden Age, 1595–1713', *Tijdschrift voor Geschiedenis*, 96 (1983), 505–36.

—— *European Jewry in the Age of Mercantilism, 1550–1750* (Oxford, 1985).

—— 'Manuel Lopez Pereira of Amsterdam, Antwerp and Madrid: Jew, New Christian, and Adviser to the Conde-Duque de Olivares', *Studia Rosenthaliana*, 19 (1985).

JACOB, A. M., 'Aaron Levy Green, 1821–1883', *TJHSE* 25 (1977), 87–106.

JACOB, M. C., *The Radical Enlightenment* (London, 1981).

JACOBS, J., and WOLF, L., *Bibliotheca Anglo-Judaica* (London, 1888).

JAFFEE, B., 'A Reassessment of Benjamin Disraeli's Jewish Aspects', *TJHSE* 27 (1982), 115–23.

JONES, G. L., *The Discovery of Hebrew in Tudor England: A Third Language* (Manchester, 1983).

JONES, P. E., and JUDGES, A. V., 'London Population in the Late Seventeenth Century', *Econ. HR* 6 (1935), 45–63.

JORDAN, W. K., *The Development of Religious Toleration in England* (London, 1932–40).

JOSEPHS, Z. (ed.), *Birmingham Jewry 1749–1914* (Birmingham, 1980).

—— (ed.), *Birmingham Jewry, Volume II: More Aspects 1740–1930* (Birmingham, 1984).

KAPLAN, YOSEF, *et al.* (eds.), *Menasseh ben Israel and his World* (Leiden, 1989).

KATZ, D. S., 'The Abendana Brothers and the Christian Hebraists of Seventeenth-Century England', *Journal of Ecclesiastical History*, 40 (1989), 28–52.

—— 'Anonymous Advocates of the Readmission of the Jews to England', *Michael*, 10 (1986), 117–42.

—— 'The Chinese Jews and the Problem of Biblical Authority in Eighteenth- and Nineteenth-Century England', *EHR* 105 (1990), 893–919.

—— 'The Conundrum of the Bodleian Bowl', *Bodleian Library Record*, 44 (1990), 290–9.

—— 'English Charity and Jewish Qualms: The Rescue of the Ashkenazi Community of Seventeenth-Century Jerusalem', in A. Rapoport-Albert and S. J. Zipperstein (eds.), *Jewish History: Essays in Honour of Chimen Abramsky* (London, 1988), 245–66.

—— 'English Redemption and Jewish Readmission in 1656', *JJ Stud.* 34 (1983), 73–91.

—— 'Henry Jessey and Conservative Millenarianism in Seventeenth-Century England and Holland', *Dutch Jewish History*, 2 (1989), 75–93.

—— 'Henry More and the Jews', in S. Hutton (ed.), *Henry More (1614–1687): Tercentenary Studies* (Dordrecht, 1990), 173–88.

——. 'The Hutchinsonians and Hebraic Fundamentalism in Eighteenth-Century England', in D. S. Katz and J. I. Israel (eds.), *Sceptics, Millenarians and Jews* [Festschrift for R. H. Popkin] (Leiden, 1990), 237–55.

—— 'The Jews of England and 1688', in O. P. Grell, J. I. Israel, and N. Tyacke (eds.), *From Persecution to Toleration: The Glorious Revolution and Religion in England* (Oxford, 1991), 217–49.

—— 'The Language of Adam in Seventeenth-Century England', in Hugh Lloyd-Jones, Valerie Pearl, and Blair Worden (eds.), *History & Imagination: Essays in Honour of H. R. Trevor-Roper* (London, 1981), 132–45.

—— 'The Marginalization of Early Modern Anglo-Jewish History', in T. Kushner (ed.), *The Jewish Heritage in British History: Englishness and Jewishness* (London, 1992), 60–77.

—— 'Menasseh ben Israel's Christian Connection: Henry Jessey and the Jews', in Y. Kaplan, M. Mechoulan, and R. H. Popkin (eds.), *Menasseh ben Israel and his World* (Leiden, 1989), 117–38.

KATZ, D. S., 'Menasseh ben Israel's Mission to Queen Christina of Sweden', *JSS* 45 (1983–4), 57–72.

—— 'The Phenomenon of Philo-Semitism', *Studies in Church History*, 29 (1992), 327–61.

—— *Philo-Semitism and the Readmission of the Jews to England, 1603–1655* (Oxford, 1982).

—— *Sabbath and Sectarianism in Seventeenth-Century England* (Leiden, 1988).

KATZ, D. S., and ISRAEL, J. I. (eds.), *Sceptics, Millenarians and Jews* (Leiden, 1990).

KAUFMANN, D., 'Consultation de Jacob Rafael Peglione de Modene sur le divorce de Henri VIII', *Revue des études juives*, 30 (1895), 309–13.

—— 'Jacob Mantino', *Revue des études juives*, 27 (1893), 30–60, 207–38.

—— 'Rabbi Zevi Ashkenazi and his Family in London', *TJHSE* 3 (1899), 102–25.

KAYSERLING, M., *The Life and Labours of Menasseh Ben Israel* (London, 1877; 1st pub. Berlin, 1861).

KELLENBENZ, H., *Sephardim an der Unteren Elbe* (Wiesbaden, 1958).

KELLY, H. A., *The Matrimonial Trials of Henry VIII* (Stanford, Calif., 1976).

KENYON, J. P., *The Stuart Constitution* (Cambridge, 1986).

KOBLER, F., 'Sir Henry Finch (1558–1625) and the First English Advocates of the Restoration of the Jews to Palestine', *TJHSE* 16 (1952), 101–20.

KOCHAV, S., 'Britain and the Holy Land: Prophecy, the Evangelical Movement, and the Conversion and Restoration of the Jews, 1790–1845' (Oxford University D.Phil. thesis, 1989).

KOHLER, M. J., 'Dr. Rodrigo Lopez, Queen Elizabeth's Jewish Physician, and his Relations to America', *PAJHS* 17 (1909), 9–25.

KRENGEL, J., 'Die englische Intervention zu Gunsten der böhmischen Juden im Jahre 1744', *Monatsschrift für Geschichte und Wissenschaft des Judenthums*, 44 (1900), 259–81.

LACHS, P. S., 'A Study of a Professional Elite: Anglo-Jewish Barristers in the Nineteenth Century', *JSS* 44 (1982), 125–34.

LANDA, G. and M. J., *Kitty Villareal: An Historical Romance* (London, 1934).

LANDA, M. J., 'Kitty Villareal, the da Costas and Samson Gideon', *TJHSE* 13 (1936), 271–91.

LANE, L., 'Dickens' Archetypal Jew', *Proceedings of the Modern Language Association*, 73 (1958), 94–100.

LASKI, N., *The Laws and Charities of the Spanish and Portuguese Jews Congregation of London* (London, 1952).

LEE, S. L., 'Elizabethan England and the Jews', *Transactions of the New Shakspere Society*, 2 (1888), 143–66.

—— 'The Original of Shylock', *Gents. Mag.*, 246 (1880), 185–200.

—— 'The Topical Side of the Elizabethan Drama', *Transactions of the New Shakspere Society*, 1 (1887), 14–15.

LEHMANN, R. P., *Anglo-Jewish Bibliography 1937–1970* (London, 1973).

—— [-GOLDSCHMIDT], 'Nathan Marcus Adler: A Bibliography', in *Studies in Judaica, Karaitica and Islamica Presented to Leon Nemoy* (Ramat-Gan, 1982), 208–61.

LE NEVE [Peter Neve], *Pedigrees of Knights*, ed. G. W. Marshall (London, 1873).
LESLIE-MELVILLE, R., *The Life and Work of Sir John Fielding* (London, 1934).
LEVI, J. S. and BERGMAN, G. F. J., *Australian Genesis: Jewish Convicts and Settlers 1788–1850* (London, 1974).
LEVIEN, J. M., *The Singing of John Braham* (London, 1944).
LEVIN, S. S., 'The Origins of the Jews' Free School', *TJHSE* 19 (1959), 97–114.
LEVY, A., *History of the Sunderland Jewish Community* (London, 1956).
—— 'The Origins of Scottish Jewry', *TJHSE* 19 (1960), 129–62.
LEVY, M., *The Western Synagogue* (London, 1897).
LEVY, S., 'English Students of Maimonides', *MJHSE* 4 (1942), 61–84.
—— 'John Dury and the English Jewry', *TJHSE* 4 (1903), 76–82.
—— 'Menasseh ben Israel's Marriage Banns', *TJHSE* 10 (1924), 255–7.
—— 'A Supposed Jewish Conspiracy in 1753', *TJHSE* 6 (1912), 234–9.
LEWIS, D. M., *The Jews of Oxford* (Oxford, 1992).
LIBERLES, R., 'From *Toleration* to *Verbesserung*: German and English Debates on the Jews in the Eighteenth Century', *Central European History*, 22 (1989), 3–32.
—— 'The Jews and their Bill: Jewish Motivations in the Controversy of 1753', *Jewish History*, 2 (1987), 29–36.
—— 'The Origins of the Jewish Reform Movement in England', *AJSR* 1 (1976), 121–50.
LILJEGREN, S. B., *Harrington and the Jews* (Lund, 1932).
LINDO, E. H., *The History of the Jews of Spain and Portugal* (London, 1848).
LINGARD, JOHN, *A History of England* (London, 1819–30).
LIPMAN, V. D., 'The Rise of Jewish Suburbia', *TJHSE* 21 (1968), 78–102.
—— 'Sephardi and Other Jewish Immigrants in England in the Eighteenth Century', in A. Newman (ed.), *Migration and Settlement* (London, 1971), 37–62.
—— *Social History of the Jews in England 1850–1950* (London, 1954).
—— 'The Structure of London Jewry in the Mid-nineteenth Century', in H. J. Zimmels, *et al.* (eds.), *Essays Presented to Chief Rabbi Israel Brodie* (London, 1967), 253–73.
—— 'A Survey of Anglo-Jewry in 1851', *TJHSE* 17 (1953), 171–88.
—— 'Synagogal Organization in Anglo-Jewry', *JJ Soc.* 1 (1959) 80–93.
—— *Three Centuries of Anglo-Jewish History* (London, 1961).
LIPTON, M., 'Francis Francia—the Jacobite Jew', *TJHSE* 11 (1928), 190–205.
'A List of Jewish Persons Endenizened and Naturalised 1609–1799', ed. W. S. Samuel, R. D. Barnett, and A. S. Diamond, *MJHSE* 7 (1970), 111–44.
'A List of Jews and their Households in London Extracted from the Census Lists of 1695', ed. A. P. Arnold, *MJHSE* 6 (1962), 73–5, 78–141.
LOEWE, H., 'Solomon ben Joseph Buzaglo', *TJHSE* 16 (1952), 35–45.
LOEWE, R., 'Solomon Marcus Schiller-Szinessy, 1820–1890: First Reader in Talmudic and Rabbinic Literature at Cambridge', *TJHSE* 21 (1968), 148–89.

LOEWE, R., 'The Spanish Supplement to Nieto's *"Esh Dath"* ', *PAAJR* 48 (1981), 267–96.

LOGAN, F. D., 'The Origins of the So-Called Regius Professorships: An Aspect of the Renaissance in Oxford and Cambridge', *Studies in Church History*, 14 (1977).

MACAULAY, T. B., *The History of England* (Everyman edn., London, 1906).

MACKERRAS, C., *The Hebrew Melodist: A Life of Isaac Nathan* (Sydney, 1963).

MAILLARD, J.-F., 'Henry VIII et Georges de Venise: Documents sur l'affaire du divorce', *Rev. Hist. Rel.* 181 (1972), 157–86.

MAITLIS, J., 'London Yiddish Letters of the Early Eighteenth Century', *JJ Stud.* 6 (1955), 153–65, 237–52.

MANUEL, F. E., *The Broken Staff: Judaism through Christian Eyes* (Cambridge, Mass., 1992).

—— 'Israel and the Enlightenment', *Daedalus* (1982), 33–52, repr. in his *The Changing of the Gods* (London, 1983), 105–34.

—— *The Religion of Isaac Newton* (Oxford, 1974).

MARCHAND, L., *Byron: A Biography*, 3 vols. (New York, 1957).

MARCUS, J. R. (ed.), *The Jew in the Medieval World* (Philadelphia, 1938).

MARGOLIOUTH, M., *The History of the Jews in Great Britain* (London, 1851).

MARKS, D. W., and LÖWY, ALBERT, *Memoir of Sir Francis Henry Goldsmid* (2nd edn., London, 1882).

MARMUR, D. (ed.), *Reform Judaism: Essays on Reform Judaism in Britain* (London, 1973).

MARX, A., 'Some Notes on the History of David Oppenheimer's Library', *Revue des études juives*, 82 (1926), 451–60, repr. in his *Studies in Jewish History and Booklore* (New York, 1944), 238–55, itself repr. Westmead, 1969.

MATAR, N. I., 'The Controversy over the Restoration of the Jews in English Protestant Thought: 1701–1753', *Durham University Journal*, 80 (1988), 241–56.

—— 'The Controversy over the Restoration of the Jews: From 1754 until the London Society for Promoting Christianity among the Jews', *Durham University Journal*, 82 (1990), 29–44.

—— 'The Idea of the Restoration of the Jews in English Protestant Thought: Between the Reformation and 1660', *Durham University Journal*, 78 (1985), 23–35.

—— 'The Idea of the Restoration of the Jews in English Protestant Thought, 1661–1701', *Harvard Theological Review*, 78 (1985), 115–48.

MATTHEWS, R., *English Messiahs* (London, 1936).

MEIROVICH, H. W., 'Ashkenazic Reactions to the Conversionists, 1800–1850', *TJHSE* 26 (1979), 6–25.

'The Membership of the Great Synagogue, London, to 1791', ed. C. Roth, *MJHSE* 6 (1962), 175–85.

MEYERS, C., 'Dr Hector Nunez: Elizabethan Merchant', *TJHSE* 28 (1984), 129–31.

MICHELSON, H., *The Jew in Early English Literature* (Amsterdam, 1926).

MODDER, M. F., *The Jew in the Literature of England* (Philadelphia, 1939).

MONTMORENCY, J. E. G. DE, *State Intervention in English Education* (Cambridge, 1902).

MORRIS, E. W., *A History of the London Hospital* (London, 1910).

MORTON, F., *The Rothschilds* (London, 1961).

MUNK, W., *The Roll of the Royal College of Physicians of London* (2nd edn., London, 1878).

MURPHY, V. M., 'The Debate over Henry VIII's First Divorce: An Analysis of the Contemporary Treatises' (Cambridge University Ph.D. thesis, 1984).

NAMIER, L. B., *The Structure of Politics at the Accession of George III* (London, 1957).

NAUERT, C. G., *Agrippa and the Crisis of Renaissance Thought* (Urbana, Ill., 1965).

NECHELES, R. F., *The Abbé Grégoire 1787–1831* (Westport, Conn., 1971).

NEWMAN, A., *The Board of Deputies of British Jews 1760–1985* (London, 1987).

—— 'The Expulsion of the Jews from Prague in 1745 and British Foreign Policy', *TJHSE* 22 (1970), 30–41.

—— *Leicester Hebrew Congregation: A Centenary Record 1874-5634-1974-5734* (Leicester, 1974).

—— *Provincial Jewry in Victorian Britain* (London, 1975).

NEWMAN, L. I., *Richard Cumberland* (New York, 1919).

NUGENT, C., *Memoir of Robert, Earl Nugent* (London, 1898).

OGDEN, J., *Isaac d'Israeli* (Oxford, 1969).

—— 'Isaac d'Israeli and Judaism', *HUCA* 37 (1966), 211–22.

OLSOVER, L., *The Jewish Communities of North-East England 1755–1980* (Gateshead, 1980).

O'MALLEY, J., *Gilles de Viterbe on Church and Reform* (Leiden, 1968).

OPPENHEIM, M., *A History of the Administration of the Royal Navy and of Merchant Shipping in Relation to the Navy* (London, 1896).

OSTERMAN, N., 'The Controversy over the Proposed Readmission of the Jews to England (1655)', *JSS* 3 (1941), 301–28.

OSTERWEIS, R. G., *Rebecca Gratz: A Study in Charm* (New York, 1935).

PARMITER, G. DE C., *The King's Great Matter: A Study of Anglo-Papal Relations 1527–1530* (London, 1967).

PATINKIN, D., 'Mercantilism and the Readmission of the Jews to England', *JSS* 8 (1946), 161–78.

PEARS, E., 'The Spanish Armada and the Ottomon Porte', *EHR* 8 (1893), 439–66.

PERRY, N., 'Anglo-Jewry, the Law, Religious Conviction, and Self-Interest (1655–1753)', *Journal of European Studies* 14 (1984), 1–23.

—— 'La Chute d'une famille séfardie, les Mendes da Costa de Londres', *Dix-huitième siècle*, 13 (1981), 11–25.

PERRY, T. W., *Public Opinion, Propaganda, and Politics in Eighteenth-Century England: A Study of the Jew Bill of 1753* (Cambridge, Mass., 1962).

PETUCHOWSKI, J. J., *The Theology of Haham David Nieto* (New York, 1954).

PHILIPSON, D., *The Reform Movement in Judaism* (New York, 1907).

PHILLIPS, O. S., *Isaac Nathan: Friend of Byron* (London, 1940).

PICCIOTTO, J., *Sketches of Anglo-Jewish History* (new edn., London, 1956; 1st pub. 1875).

PIERCY, J. S., *The History of Retford* (Retford, 1828).

PINSKER, P., 'English Opinion and Jewish Emancipation (1830–1860)', *JSS* 14 (1952), 51–94.

PINTO, V. DE SOLA, *Peter Sterry* (Cambridge, 1934).

'The Plymouth Aliens List 1798 and 1803', ed. V. D. Lipman, *MJHSE* 6 (1962), 187–94.

POLLARD, A. F., *Henry VIII* (London, 1905).

POLLINS, H., *Economic History of the Jews in England* (London, 1982).

POPKIN, R. H., *Isaac La Peyrère (1596–1676*: His Life, Work and Influence (Leiden, 1987).

—— *The Third Force in Seventeenth-Century Thought* (Leiden, 1992).

PORTER, R., *English Society in the Eighteenth Century* (Penguin edn., Harmondsworth, 1982).

PRAWER, S. S., *Israel at Vanity Fair: Jews and Judaism in the Writings of W. M. Thackeray* (Leiden, 1991).

PRINS, J. H., 'Prince William of Orange and the Jews' (Hebrew), *Zion*, 15 (1950), 93–106.

PRIOR, R., 'Jewish Musicians at the Tudor Court', *Musical Quarterly*, 69 (1983), 253–65.

RABINOWICZ, O. K., *Sir Solomon de Medina* (London, 1974).

READ, C., *Lord Burghley and Queen Elizabeth* (London, 1959).

—— *Mr. Secretary Walsingham and the Policy of Queen Elizabeth* (Oxford, 1925).

—— 'Sir William Cecil and Elizabethan Public Relations', in *Elizabethan Government and Society: Essays Presented to Sir John Neale* (London, 1964).

Records of the Western Synagogue 1761–1932, ed. C. Roth (London, 1932).

A Register of the Members of St. Mary Magdalen College, Oxford, ed. W. D. Macray (London, 1894–1915).

A Report on the Records of the Board of Deputies of British Jews 1839–1966, ed. R. A. Routledge (Hist. MSS Comm., 1976).

REZNIKOFF, C., and ENGELMAN, U. Z., *The Jews of Charleston* (Philadelphia, 1950).

ROBBINS, C., 'Honest Heretic: Joseph Priestley in America', *Proceedings of the American Philosophical Society*, 106 (1962), 60–76.

—— 'A Note on General Naturalization under the Later Stuarts and a Speech in the House of Commons on the Subject in 1664', *Journal of Modern History*, 34 (1962), 168–77.

ROBSON, R. J., *The Oxfordshire Election of 1754: A Study in the Interplay of City, County and University Politics* (London, 1949).

ROSENBERG, E., *From Shylock to Svengali: Jewish Stereotypes in English Fiction* (London, 1960).

ROSENTHAL, E. I. J., 'Edward Lively: Cambridge Hebraist', in D. W. Thomas (ed.), *Essays and Studies Presented to S. A. Cook* (London, 1950), 95–112.

—— 'Rashi and the English Bible', *Bulletin of the John Rylands Library*, 24 (1940), 138–67.

—— *Studia Semitica* (Cambridge, 1971).

Ross, J. M., 'Naturalisation of Jews in England', *TJHSE* 24 (1974), 59–70.

Roth, C., 'The Amazing Clan of Buzaglo', *TJHSE* 23 (1971), 11–21.

—— *Anglo-Jewish Letters* (London, 1938).

—— 'An Attempt to Recall the Jews to England, 1648', *Jewish Monthly*, 1 (1948), 11–17.

—— *Archives of the United Synagogue: Report and Catalogue* (London, 1930).

—— *Benjamin Disraeli* (New York, 1952).

—— 'Edward Pococke and the First Hebrew Printing in Oxford', *Bodleian Library Record*, 2 (1948), 215–20.

—— 'Educational Abuses and Reforms in Hanoverian England', in M. Davis (ed.), *Mordecai M. Kaplan Jubilee Volume* (New York, 1953), 469–80.

—— 'An Episode in the History of the Oppenheimer Collection', *Bodleian Library Record*, 5 (1956), 104–8.

—— *Essays and Portraits in Anglo-Jewish History* (Philadelphia, 1962).

—— *The First Jew in Hampstead* (London, 1932): i.e. Eliezar Isaac Keyser (1746–1820).

—— 'Gamaliel Ben Pedahzur and his Prayer Book', *MJHSE* 2 (1935), 1–8.

—— *The Great Synagogue London 1690–1940* (London, 1950).

—— 'Haham David Nieto', in his *Essays and Portraits*, 113–29.

—— and C[ASSUTO], U., 'Halfan, Elijah Menahem', *EJ*.

—— 'The Haskalah in England', in H. J. Zimmels, *et al.* (eds.), *Essays Presented to Chief Rabbi Israel Brodie* (London, 1967), 365–76.

—— *A History of the Jews in England* (3rd edn., Oxford, 1964).

—— *A History of the Marranos* (Philadelphia, 1932).

—— *The House of Nasi* (Philadelphia, 1947–8).

[——] *The Jewish Chronicle 1841–1941: A Century of Newspaper History* (London, 1949).

—— 'The Jews in the English Universities', *MJHSE* 4 (1942), 102–15.

—— 'Jews in Oxford after 1290', *Oxoniensia*, 15 (1950), 63–80.

—— *The Jews in the Renaissance* (Philadelphia, 1959).

—— 'The Jews of Jerusalem in the Seventeenth Century: *An English Account*', *MJHSE* 2 (1935), 99–104: NB the text printed here is very inaccurate.

—— *The Jews of Medieval Oxford* (Oxford, 1951).

—— 'Leone da Modena and England', *TJHSE* 11 (1928), 206–27.

—— 'Leone da Modena and his English Correspondents', *TJHSE* 17 (1953), 39–43.

—— 'The Lesser London Synagogues of the Eighteenth Century', *MJHSE* 3 (1937), 1–7.

—— *A Life of Menasseh ben Israel* (Philadelphia, 1934).

—— 'The Lord Mayor's Salvers', *Connoisseur*, 95 (1935), 296–9.

—— *Magna Bibliotheca Anglo-Judaica* (London, 1937).

—— 'The Middle Period of Anglo–Jewish History (1290–1655) Reconsidered', *TJHSE* 19 (1960), 1–12.

—— 'New Light on the Resettlement', *TJHSE* 11 (1928), 112–42.

—— 'The Portsmouth Community and its Historical Background', *TJHSE* 13 (1936), 157–87.

ROTH, C., 'The Remarkable Career of Haham Abraham Gabay Yzidro', *TJHSE* 24 (1975), 211–13.

—— 'The Resettlement of the Jews in England in 1656', in V. D. Lipman (ed.), *Three Centuries of Anglo-Jewish History* (London, 1961), 1–25.

—— *The Rise of Provincial Jewry* (London, 1950).

—— 'Salomon Israel, Writing Master in Oxford, 1745—*alias* Ignatius Dumay', *Oxoniensia*, 28 (1963), 74–8.

—— 'Sir Thomas Bodley—Hebraist', *Bodleian Library Record*, 7 (1966), 242–51.

—— '1656: English Jewry's Annus Mirabilis: Was there a Formal Readmission?', *Commentary*, 21 (1956), 509–15: unreliable.

ROUTLEDGE, R. A., 'The Legal Status of the Jews in England 1190–1790', *Journal of Legal History*, 3 (1982), 91–124.

RUBENS, A., *Anglo-Jewish Portraits* (London, 1935).

—— 'Francis Town of Bond Street (1738–1826) and his Family', *TJHSE* 18 (1958), 89–111.

—— *A History of Jewish Costume* (2nd edn., London, 1973).

—— *A Jewish Iconography* (London, 1981).

RUBENS, C., 'Joseph Cortissos and the War of the Spanish Succession', *TJHSE* 24 (1975), 114–33.

RUDÉ, G., *Wilkes and Liberty* (Oxford, 1965).

RUMNEY, J., 'Anglo-Jewry as Seen through Foreign Eyes', *TJHSE* 13 (1936), 323–40.

RUSSELL, C., 'Arguments for Religious Unity in England, 1530–1650', *Journal of Ecclesiastical History*, 18 (1967), 201–26.

SALAMAN, R. N., 'Ephraim Luzzatto (1729–1792)', *TJHSE* 9 (1922), 85–102.

SALBSTEIN, M. C. N., *The Emancipation of the Jews in Britain: The Question of the Admission of the Jews to Parliament, 1828–1860* (London, 1982).

SAMUEL, E. R., 'Anglo-Jewish Notaries and Scriveners', *TJHSE* 17 (1953), 113–59.

—— 'Dr. Meyer Schomberg's Attack on the Jews of London, 1746', *TJHSE* 20 (1964), 83–111.

—— 'Dr Rodrigo Lopes' Last Speech from the Scaffold at Tyburn', *Jewish Historical Studies [TJHSE]*, 30 (1989), 51–3.

—— 'The Jews in English Foreign Trade: A Consideration of the "Philo Patriae" Pamphlets of 1753', in J. M. Shaftesley (ed.), *Remember the Days: Essays on Anglo-Jewish History Presented to Cecil Roth* (London, 1966), 123–43.

—— 'Manuel Levy Duarte (1631–1714): An Amsterdam Merchant Jeweller and his Trade with London', *TJHSE* 27 (1982), 11–31.

—— 'Portuguese Jews in Jacobean London', *TJHSE* 18 (1958), 171–230.

—— 'The Provenance of the Westminster Talmud', *TJHSE* 27 (1982), 148–50.

—— ' "Sir Thomas Shirley's Project for Jewes": The Earliest Known Proposal for the Resettlement', *TJHSE* 24 (1974), 195–7.

SAMUEL, W. S., 'Anglo-Jewish Ships' Names', *MJHSE* 3 (1937).

—— 'Carvajal and Pepys', *MJHSE* 2 (1935), 24–9.

—— 'The First London Synagogue of the Resettlement', *TJHSE* 10 (1924), 1–147.

—— 'The "Jewes Church" in Austin Friars', *Jewish Monthly*, 2 (1948–9), 360–5.

—— 'A Jewish Naval Officer under the Stuarts?', *MJHSE* 3 (1937), 105–7.

—— 'The Jewish Oratories of Cromwellian London', *MJHSE* 3 (1937), 46–56.

—— 'The Jews of London and the Great Plague (1665)', *MJHSE* 3 (1937), 7–15.

—— ' "Lord Meyor's" Show Day 1837', *Jewish Monthly* (Nov. 1949), also repr. as pamphlet (London, 1950).

—— 'A Review of the Jewish Colonists in Barbados in the Year 1680', *TJHSE* 13 (1936), 1–111.

—— 'Sir William Davidson, Royalist (1616–1689) and the Jews', *TJHSE* 14 (1940), 39–79.

—— 'The Strayings of Paul Isaiah in England, 1651–1656', *TJHSE* 16 (1952), 77–87.

SANDS, M., 'John Braham, Singer', *TJHSE* 20 (1964), 203–14.

SARAIVA, A. J., 'Antonio Vieira, Menasseh ben Israel et le cinquième empire', *Studia Rosenthaliana*, 6 (1972), 25–57.

SCARISBRICK, J. J., *Henry VIII* (London, 1968).

SCHAIBLE, K. H., *Die Juden in England* (Karlsruhe, 1890).

SCHECHTER, S., 'The "Baalshem"—Dr. Falk', *Jewish Chronicle*, 9 Mar. 1888, 15–16.

SCH[ERESCHEWSKY], B. Z., 'Bigamy and Polygamy', *EJ*.

SCHISCHA, A., 'Spanish Jews in London in 1494', *MJHSE* 9 (1975), 214–15.

SCHMIDT, H. D., 'Chief Rabbi Nathan Marcus Adler (1803–1890): Jewish Educator from Germany', *Leo Baeck Inst. Year Book*, 18 (1962), 289–311.

SCHOEPS, H. J., *Barocke Juden Christen Judenchristen* (Bern, 1965).

—— *Philosemitismus im Barock Religions—und geistesgeschichtliche Untersuchungen* (Tübingen, 1952).

—— 'Philosemitism in the Baroque Period', *JQR* NS 47 (1956–7), 139–44.

SCHOLEM, G., *Kabbalah* (Jerusalem, 1974).

—— *Sabbatai Sevi* (London, 1973).

SCHUCHARD, M. K., 'Swedenborg, Jacobitism, and Freemasonry', in E. J. Brock, *et al.* (eds.), *Swedenborg and his Influence* (London, 1988), 359–79.

SCOULOUDI, I., 'A immigration into London', *Proceedings of the Huguenot Society of London*, 16 (1937–8), 27–49.

SCULT, M., *Millennial Expectations and Jewish Liberties: A Study of the Efforts to Convert the Jews in Britain up to the Mid Nineteenth Century* (Leiden, 1978).

SECRET, F., *Les Kabbalistes Chrétiens de la Renaissance* (Paris, 1964).

SHAFTESLEY, J. M., 'Dr Abraham Benisch as Newspaper Editor', *TJHSE* 21 (1968), 214–31.

SHANE, A. L., 'Rabbi Jacob Judah Leon (Templo) of Amsterdam (1603–1675) and his Connections with England', *TJHSE* 25 (1977), 120–36.

SHAPIRO, I. (ed.), *Birmingham Jewry, 1749–1914* (Manchester, 1980).

—— and JOSEPHS, Z., *Birmingham Jewry 1749–1914* (Manchester, 1980).

SHAROT, S., 'Reform and Liberal Judaism in London, 1840–1940', *JSS* 41 (1979), 211–28.

SHAW, W. A., *Knights of England* (London, 1906).

SHEPHERD, M. A., 'Cheltenham Jews in the Nineteenth Century', *JJ Soc.* 21 (1979), 125–33.

—— 'Popular Attitudes to Jews in France and England 1750–1870' (Oxford University D.Phil. thesis, 1983).

SHILLMAN, B., *A Short History of the Jews in Ireland* (Dublin, 1945).

SIGSTEDT, C. O., *The Swedenborg Epic* (New York, 1952).

SIMONS, H. A., *Forty Years a Chief Rabbi: The Life and Times of Solomon Hirschell* (London, 1980).

SIMONSOHN, S., 'David Reubeni's Second Mission in Italy' (Hebrew), *Zion*, 26 (1961), 198–207.

SINGER, S., 'Early Translations and Translators of the Jewish Liturgy in England', *TJHSE* 3 (1899), 36–71.

—— 'Jews and Coronations', *TJHSE* 5 (1908), 79–114.

SINGER, S., 'The Anglo–Jewish Ministry in Early Victorian London', *Modern Judaism*, 5 (1985), 279–99.

—— 'Jewish Education in the Mid-nineteenth Century: A Study of the Early Victorian London Community', *JQR* 77 (1986–7), 163–78.

SKILLITER, S. A., *William Harborne and the Trade with Turkey, 1578–1582* (London, 1977).

SLATER, J., 'Byron's Hebrew Melodies', *Studies in Philology*, 49 (1952), 75–94.

SMITH, R. M., 'The London Jews' Society and Patterns of Jewish Conversion in England, 1801–1859', *JSS* 43 (1981), 275–90.

SOKOLOW, N., *History of Zionism 1600–1918* (London, 1918–19).

SOLOMONS, I., 'David Nieto and Some of his Contemporaries', *TJHSE* 12 (1931), 1–101.

—— 'Lord George Gordon's Conversion to Judaism', *TJHSE* 7 (1915), 222–71.

—— 'Satirical and Political Prints on the Jews Naturalisation Bill, 1753', *TJHSE* 6 (1912), 205–33.

SPECK, W. A., *Reluctant Revolutionaries: Englishmen and the Revolution of 1688* (Oxford, 1988).

SPECTOR, D., 'The Jews of Brighton, 1770–1900', *TJHSE* 22 (1970), 42–52.

STEIN, S., *The Beginnings of Hebrew Studies at University College* (London, 1952).

—— 'Phillipus Ferdinandus Polonus: A Sixteenth-Century Hebraist in England', in I. Epstein, *et al.* (eds.), *Essays in Honour of . . . J. H. Hertz* (London, 1944), 397–412.

—— 'Some Ashkenazi Charities in London at the End of the Eighteenth and the Beginning of the Nineteenth Centuries', *TJHSE* 20 (1964), 63–81.

STIRLING, B., 'Introduction', to *The Merchant of Venice*, in William Shakespeare, *The Complete Works*, ed. A. Harbage (Baltimore, 1969).

STOKES, H. P., *A Short History of the Jews in England* (London, 1921).

—— *Studies in Anglo-Jewish History* (Edinburgh, 1913).

STONE, H., 'Dickens and the Jews', *Victorian Studies*, 2 (1958–9).

STONE, L., *An Elizabethan: Sir Horatio Palavicino* (Oxford, 1956).

SUSSER, B., 'Social Acclimatization of Jews in Eighteenth and Nineteenth Century Devon', in R. Burt (ed.), *Industry and Society in the South-West* (Exeter, 1971).

SUTHERLAND, L. S., 'Samson Gideon and the Reduction of Interest, 1749–50', *Econ. HR* 16 (1946), 15–29.

—— 'Samson Gideon: Eighteenth Century Jewish Financier', *TJHSE* 17 (1953), 79–90.

SZAJKOWSKI, Z., 'French 17th–18th Century Sources for Anglo-Jewish History', *JJ Stud.* 12 (1961), 59–66.

TANNENBAUM, S. A. (ed.), *Shakespeare's The Merchant of Venice (A Concise Bibliography)* (New York, 1941).

TEICHER, J. L., 'Maimonides and England', *TJHSE* 16 (1952), 97–100.

TENISON, E. M., *Elizabethan England* (Leamington Spa, 1932–51).

—— *Error Versus Fact, A Study in Contrasts, 1880 and 1594* (Leamington Spa, 1953).

TOBIAS, J. J., *Prince of Fences: The Life and Crimes of Ikey Solomons* (London, 1974).

TOON, P. (ed.), *Puritans, the Millennium and the Future of Israel: Puritan Eschatology 1600 to 1660* (Cambridge, 1970).

TOVEY, D'BLOSSIERS, *Anglia Judaica; or, The History and Antiquities of the Jews in England* (Oxford, 1738).

TREVOR-ROPER, H. R., 'Three Foreigners: The Philosophers of the Puritan Revolution', in his *Religion, the Reformation, and Social Change* (London, 1967), 237–93.

Trinity College, Dublin, *Catalogue of the Manuscripts in the Library of Trinity College, Dublin*, ed. T. K. Abbott (Dublin, 1900).

TURNBULL, G. H., *Hartlib, Dury and Comenius* (London, 1947).

VAN DEN BERG, J., 'Priestley, the Jews and the Millennium', in D. S. Katz and J. I. Israel (eds.), *Sceptics, Millenarians, and Jews* (Leiden, 1990), 256–74.

VASOLI, C., *Profezia e ragione* (Naples, 1974).

VEGA, L. A., *The Beth Haim of Ouderkerk* (Assen, 1975).

VERETÉ, M., 'The Restoration of the Jews in English Protestant Thought, 1790–1840', *Middle Eastern Studies*, 8 (1972), 3–50: mostly a trans. of his Hebrew article in *Zion*, 33 (1968), 145–79.

WALKER, D. P., *Spiritual and Demonic Magic from Ficino to Campanella* (London, 1958).

WATTS, M., *The Dissenters* (Oxford, 1978).

WEBSTER, C., *The Great Instauration* (London, 1975).

WERNHAM, R. B., *After the Armada* (Oxford, 1984).

WHITLEY, W. T., 'Charles-Marie de Veil', *Baptist Quarterly*, 5 (1930–1), 74–85, 118–29, 177–89.

WIENER, M., 'John Toland and Judaism', *HUCA* 16 (1941), 215–42.

WILENSKY, M., 'Four English Pamphlets on the Sabbatain Movement, Published in 1665–1666' (Hebrew), *Zion*, 17 (1952), 157–72.

—— 'The Literary Controversy in 1656 Concerning the Return of the Jews to England', *PAAJR* 20 (1951), 357–93.

WILENSKY, M., *The Return of the Jews to England in the Seventeenth Century* (Hebrew) (Jerusalem, 1943): trans. into English in his articles.
—— 'The Royalist Position Concerning the Readmission of the Jews to England', *JQR* NS 41 (1950–1), 397–409.
—— 'Thomas Barlow's and John Dury's Attitude towards the Readmission of the Jews to England', *JQR* NS 50 (1959–60), 167–75, 256–68.
WILLIAMS, B., *The Making of Manchester Jewry, 1740–1875* (Manchester, 1976).
WILSON, H. B., *The History of Merchant-Taylors' School* (London, 1814).
WOLF, L., 'American Elements in the Re-Settlement', *TJHSE* 3 (1899), 76–100.
—— 'Crypto-Jews under the Commonwealth', *TJHSE* 1 (1895), 55–88.
—— 'The Disraeli Family', *TJHSE* 5 (1902–5), 202–18.
—— *Essays in Jewish History*, ed. C. Roth (London, 1934).
—— 'The First English Jew', *TJHSE* 2 (1896), 14–46.
—— 'The First Stage of Anglo-Jewish Emancipation', in his *Essays*, 115–43.
—— 'The Jewry of the Restoration, 1660–1664', *TJHSE* 5 (1908), 13–18.
—— 'Jews in Elizabethan England', *TJHSE* 11 (1928), 1–91.
—— 'Jews in Tudor England', in his *Essays*, 73–90.
—— *Menasseh ben Israel's Mission to Oliver Cromwell* (London, 1901).
—— *Notes on the Diplomatic History of the Jewish Question* (London, 1919).
—— 'Notes on the Early History of the Dublin Hebrew Congregation', *TJHSE* 11 (1928), 162–7.
—— 'Status of the Jews in England after the Re-Settlement', *TJHSE* 4 (1903), 177–93.
WOOLF, M., 'Eighteenth-Century London Jewish Shipowners', *TJHSE* 24 (1975), 198–204.
—— 'Foreign Trade of London Jews in the Seventeenth Century', *TJHSE* 24 (1974), 38–58.
—— 'Joseph Salvador, 1716–1786', *TJHSE* 21 (1968), 104–37.
—— 'Notes on the Census Lists of 1695', *MJHSE* 6 (1962), 75–7.
WRIGLEY, E. A., and SCHOFIELD, R., *The Population History of England, 1541–1871* (London, 1981).
YATES, F. A., *The French Academies of the Sixteenth Century* (London, 1947).
—— *Giordano Bruno and the Hermetic Tradition* (London, 1964).
—— *The Occult Philosophy in the Elizabethan Age* (London, 1979).
—— *The Rosicrucian Enlightenment* (London, 1972).
YOGEV, G., *Diamonds and Coral: Anglo-Dutch Jews and Eighteenth-Century Trade* (Leicester, 1978).
ZANGWILL, L., 'Richard Cumberland Centenary Memorial Paper', *TJHSE* 7 (1915), 147–79.
ZATLIN, L. G., *The Nineteenth-Century Anglo-Jewish Novel* (Boston, 1981).
ZEMAN, F. D., 'The Amazing Career of Doctor Rodrigo Lopez', *Bulletin of the History of Medicine*, 39 (1965), 295–308.
ZINBERG, I., *A History of Jewish Literature* (New York, 1978).

INDEX